Leabharlann na Mí EMPLOYMENT LAW

UNITED KINGDOM
Sweet & Maxwell Ltd
London

AUSTRALIA
LBC Information Services Ltd
Sydney

CANADA and USA
Carswell
Toronto

NEW ZEALAND
Brooker's
Wellington

SINGAPORE and MALAYSIA
Sweet & Maxwell
Singapore and Kuala Lumpur

Employment Law

SECOND EDITION

MICHAEL FORDE

B.A. (Mod.), LL.B. (Dublin), LL.M. (Brussels), Ph.D. (Cantab.)

of King's Inns and Middle Temple

Barrister-at-law

DUBLIN
ROUND HALL LTD
2001

Published in 2001 by
Round Hall Ltd.
43 Fitzwilliam Place
Dublin 2
Ireland

Typeset by
Devlin Editing, Dublin

Printed by
MPG Books, Cornwall

No natural forests were destroyed to make this product;
only farmed timber was used and replanted

A CIP catalogue record for this book is available from the British Library

First edition 1992

ISBN 1-85800-188-9 paperback
ISBN 1-85800-221-4 hardback

FOREWORD TO FIRST EDITION

It seems that the print is hardly dry on one work before Dr. Forde goes once more into the breach with another valuable legal treatise. His is a truly insatiable talent and dedication. A test of any general work is whether it provides an answer to a problem in a specialised area—one which might have a book to itself. I have found Dr. Forde's previous works did meet that test and I have said so. This is a book which will be used on many occasions by practitioners and judges. Dr. Forde's style, now well established, is to be economical and to the point.

This is a very thorough book—thorough in its background history, in its research, in its analysis of national law and, perhaps, most of all in putting our labour law in a European context. Once more we are reminded that it is an unjustifiable luxury to regard European law as a separate subject best left to the specialist; rather is it now part of every lawyer's essential baggage. Here in this very basic area of law the European dimension is to be found at every turn.

The book recounts the origin and development of the Employment Appeals Tribunal. The first chairman of its predecessor was my good friend and mentor, former Circuit Court judge, John Gleeson SC. He can be credited with establishing a modern administrative tribunal, combining a lack of formality with adherence to the rules of natural justice, John Gleeson had a remarkable career. He had a rich store of knowledge and experience, having been a senior counsel when I was first called to the bar, then a solicitor, first chairman of the Redundancy Appeals Tribunal and then (having returned to the bar) he was appointed a judge.

It is a sad matter to record that for many people in this country what they desire most is a job because a country can have the fairest employment laws in the world but if there is no employment to go with them they are of little moment to the jobless. This is a problem not solely in the political domain; it must be of concern to us all. The requirement of goodwill on the part of employers and employees is of the essence to give the many who are out of work hope. But it must also mean that the law is not to be stretched so as to frustrate the well-intentioned employer so that he does not feel it is worth his while to lend his strength and resources to the giving of employment.

I have already mentioned practitioners and judges and I add my recommendation to purchase this book to the students, the trade union officers and all who play a part in our estimable dispute-resolving machinery. Indeed, I urge all who are interested in employment—whether as givers or receivers—to support this enterprise. A story about another Michael, Michaelangelo, is worth recalling. As recounted in Vasari's Lives of the *Painters, Sculptors and Architects*, once in Florence, when snow lay on the ground, one of the Medici asked him to construct a snow statue in the palace garden which he did and which proves that a job may be minor and temporary and yet capable of producing a stunning result which, undoubtedly, Michaelangelo's snowman represented. This work is not minor and will not be of short duration but, yes, it too has been executed by a master crafts-man.

HUGH O'FLAHERTY

The Supreme Court,
Four Courts,
Dublin
March 26, 1992

PREFACE

In the eight years since the first edition was published, there have been very significant changes in employment legislation, many of these measures being prompted by E.C. initiatives. I have sought to incorporate in this edition all of those developments, as well as the ever expanding reported case law. The treatment of most topics is comparatively summary but, in order to give a fuller account of the law, a work of at least three times the size would be required. Fortunately, in the intervening years several excellent books on discrete aspects of employment law have been published (most notably, Dr. White's three-volume work on health and safety, Dr. Redmond's second edition on dismissals, Mr. Byrne's treatment of transfer of undertakings, Mr. Finucane and Mr. Buggy's exposition of pension law and practice, and Mr. Corrigan's two-volume treatise on taxation) that users of this edition may consult for a more complete analysis of those subjects. Conor Quigley of Brick Court Chambers kindly allowed to quote extracts from his masterly work on E.C. Contracts law, which summarise the Luxembourg Court's rulings on sex discrimination. What I have endeavoured to do here is to provide an over-view of the entire subject, with emphasis on the case law, assuming readers can check details of statutory requirements by consulting the Act in question.

I was surprised at how long it took to finish this edition; perhaps the extent of the changes is far greater than I had anticipated. As on previous occasions, Marie Armah-Kwantreng did an excellent job with the manuscript. Although Michael and Bart are no longer with Round Hall, Therese Carrick and Dave Ellis are worthy replacements and their and Terri McDonnell's efforts contributed enormously to a much-improved (I hope) new edition. I would like to give special thanks to the Honourable Mr. Justice Hugh O'Flaherty for his kind and imaginative foreword to the 1992 edition. His retirement from the Supreme Court in 1999 deprived that tribunal of a prodigious talent, which will be difficult if not impossible to replace. Peter, Patrick and Catherine once again were supportive and provided encouragement far beyond the normal call of duty.

Jimmy, to whom this book is dedicated, has passed on to a happy hunting ground where it is said, *inter alia,* that salmon and trout are plentiful all the year round. His partner and co-dedicatee Jane remains as ever robust and alert, although very rarely venturing the journey to Dublin.

The law as summarised here is based on what was available up to May 2001, with the late brief edition of Carers Leave Act passed in July of that year.

M.F.

Mountain View Road,
Dublin 6

Lucia Day, 2001

CONTENTS

TABLE OF CASES

TABLE OF STATUTES

TABLE OF STATUTORY INSTRUMENTS

EUROPEAN UNION LEGISLATION

CHAPTER 1

INTRODUCTORY

Employment law is concerned with the relations existing between employers and their employees. The employment relationship is governed principally by the contract of employment between the employer and employee;[1] the rights and responsibilities of employees derive from this contract and also from various Acts which lay down employment standards. Just as the relationships between members of families have generated their own body of law, based on an amalgam of contractual obligations, equitable principles and statutory provisions, the relations between employers and workers have given rise to their own distinctive set of legal rules. Indeed, in some continental European countries there is an entirely separate tier of courts for determining practically all labour law questions. The Employment Appeals Tribunal, which deals with many issues under the more important pieces of employment protection legislation, is a much diluted version of the continental labour courts.

Relations between employers, their representative organisations and trade unions and other workers' associations, which have a vital bearing on terms and conditions of employment, are considered separately in this author's *Industrial Relations Law*.[2]

HISTORICAL CONTEXT

On the eve of the industrial revolution and indeed for many decades later, employment law was regarded in much the same light as family law. In his masterly account of the "Laws of England",[3] which perhaps is the most important law book ever to be published in the English-speaking world, the jurist Blackstone, writing in the eighteenth century, placed his account of the law of "Master and Servant" in his first book, dealing with the "Law of Persons", in between sections on "Army and Navy" and on "Husband and Wife". According to Blackstone, the great relationships in private life are the family relationship and the employment relationship. Regarding the latter, he observed that it is "founded in convenience, whereby a man is directed to call in the assistance of others, where his own skill and labour will not be sufficient to answer the cares incumbent on him."[4]

---

1. See, generally, M. Freedland, *The Contract of Employment* (1976).
2. (1991).
3. W. Blackstone, *Commentaries on the Laws of England* (4 vols. 1765-69). *Cf.* M. Dutton, *The Law of Masters and Servants in Ireland* (1723), the significance of which is discussed in M. Redmond, *Dismissal Law in Ireland* (2nd ed., 1999) at 9-15.
4. Vol. 1, p. 422 (*ibid.*, 1825). Cf. Kahn Freund, "Blackstone's Neglected Child: The Contract of Employment", 93 L.Q.R. 508 (1977) and Cairns, "Blackstone, Kahn Freund and the Contract of Employment", 105 L.Q.R. 300 (1989).

He listed four principal categories of employees of his time: domestic or menial servants, apprentices, labourers hired by the day or by the week and "superior servants", like stewards, bailiffs, etc. The vast majority of employees or servants at that time were either domestics or farm labourers. Most persons carrying on a trade or a profession were self-employed. Outside of domestic service, women workers hardly featured in the labour market. Although he did not refer to them, even by Blackstone's time a significant number of persons worked in industry and commerce. The main feature of the labour market since that time has been the steady contraction in the number of domestic and agricultural workers, matched with an expansion of employment in trade, particularly in the service of limited companies, and also the emergence of the State, either at central or local government level, as a major employer.

By the middle of the last century it was generally recognised that the legal lynchpin of the employment relationship was the contract which the employee and employer entered into, to provide services in return for remuneration. Occasionally, there might be an actual written agreement spelling out in detail the rights and obligations of the parties. More often, the contract was oral, with the parties agreeing that the terms of employment should be the same as apply to others then employed at the same kind of work. Most of the labour legislation in the nineteenth century was concerned with industrial relations and trade unionism. As is explained elsewhere,[5] workers would band together in trade unions in order to seek for themselves improved terms and conditions of employment. Because the great majority of workers did not have the franchise, they did not possess the political influence to secure the enactment of legislation that would significantly improve their rights over those of their employers. However, some protective measures were enacted in the Victorian era.

An important measure, which remained on the statute book until July 1991, is of a slightly earlier vintage - the Truck Act 1831.[6] Among the main measures adopted in the last century affecting employees (other than trade union legislation) were the several Factories Acts,[7] which laid down minimum standards of safety in factories, and the Workmen's Compensation Act of 1897,[8] which established a no-fault compensation system for workers who were injured during the course of their employment. In 1909 the trade boards system was established which sought to set minimum wages for badly paid workers who were not unionised.[9] In the 1930s measures were enacted dealing with questions like employment conditions in industrial establishments, in shops and in bakeries, and with minimum wages for agricultural workers, most notably the Conditions of

---

[5.] See, n. 2 *supra*.

[6.] There was an earlier Truck Act of 1743 (17 Geo. II, c. 8).

[7.] Beginning with the Act of 1802 for the Preservation of the Health and Morals of Apprentices and Others in Cotton and Other Mills and Cotton and Other Factories, 3 Geo., 73, which was followed by Acts of 1821, 1825 and 1831, eventually resulting in the Act to Regulate the Labour of Children and Young Persons in Mills and Factories, 3 & 4 Will. 4, c. 103.

[8.] 60 & 61 Vict., c. 37. See, generally, B. Shillman, *Employers' Liability and Workmen's Compensation in Ireland* (2nd ed., 1942). In 1966 this system was replaced by social welfare occupational injuries benefits: Social Welfare (Occupational Injuries) Act 1966.

[9.] Trade Boards Act 1909 (9 Edw. 7, c. 22). In 1946 these were replaced by joint labour committees: Part IV of the Industrial Relations Act 1946, and see *Industrial Relations Law*, pp. 218-220.

Employment Act 1936 (amended in 1944), the Shops (Conditions of Employment) Act 1938, the Shops (Hours of Trading) Act 1938, and the Agricultural Wages Act 1936. This latter Act was repealed in 1976[10] by a more general measure and the other Acts of the 1930s were replaced principally by the Organisation of Working Time Act 1997.

In the 1960s the whole system of industrial training was reorganised, under the Industrial Training Act 1967, and in the same year the first of the Redundancy Payments Acts was passed, which was aimed at encouraging flexibility in the labour market by compensating persons who lost their jobs through major changes at their workplace.

The 1970s saw the enactment of two of perhaps the most important labour laws still on the statute book. One is the Minimum Notice and Terms of Employment Act 1973 (part of which was replaced in 1994), which sets down minimum periods of notice for terminating employment contracts and also requires certain information about their terms and conditions to be supplied to employees. The other is the Unfair Dismissals Act 1977 (which was considerably amended in 1993), which greatly circumscribed employers' freedom to dismiss their workers. The Anti-Discrimination (Pay) Act 1974, and the Employment Equality Act 1977, both of which proscribed sex discrimination in the workplace, were replaced by a more general employment equality measure in 1998.

With the exception principally of the Safety in Industry Act 1980, the Safety, Health and Welfare at Work Act 1989, much of the Pensions Act 1991, the Payment of Wages Act 1991, the Adoptive Leave Act 1995, Part IV of the Employment Equality Act 1998, the National Minimum Wage Act 2000 and the Carer's Leave Act 2001, the major labour laws enacted since 1980 have resulted from European Community initiatives in the form of Directives addressed to the E.C. Member States to harmonise their laws in several respects and also from decisions of the European Court of Justice.[11] These principal E.C. inspired measures enacted in the last 20 years are as follows:

- the European Communities (Safeguarding of Employees' Rights on Transfer of Undertakings) Regulations 1980,[12] which seek to preserve the jobs of persons whose workplace is the subject of a take-over by a new employer;

- the Protection of Employees (Employer's Insolvency) Act 1984,[13] which compensates employees, when their employer becomes bankrupt;

- the Terms of Employment (Information) Act 1994,[14] which requires employers to give their employees specified information about their terms and conditions of employment;

[10.] Industrial Relations Act 1976, s. 6.
[11.] See *post,* p. 7.
[12.] See *post,* p. 230 *et seq.*
[13.] See *post,* p. 248 *et seq.*
[14.] See *post,* p. 50 *et seq.*

- the Maternity Protection Act 1994,[15] which provides for maternity leave and other safeguards for pregnant women (replacing an Act of 1981);

- the Protection of Young Persons (Employment) Act 1996,[16] which contains safeguards for young persons who work;

- the Organisation of Working Time Act 1997,[17] which deals with maximum permitted working times, work-breaks and holidays;

- Part III of the Employment Equality Act 1998,[18] on equality between men and women in the workplace, which replaced two earlier Acts on this subject enacted in 1974 and 1977 respectively;

- the Parental Leave Act 1998,[19] which gives parents leave in order to look after young children who are ill; it also entitles persons to "force majeure" leave in order to look after a relative who becomes ill.

There are several E.C. Directives that remain to be implemented.[20]

By far the most significant judicial development since 1937 was the decision of the Supreme Court in May 1997, in *Re the Employment Equality Bill, 1997*,[21] which declared certain key provisions of that Bill to be unconstitutional. This was the first time that the Court struck down for unconstitutionality a law designed to protect employees, on the grounds that it encroached disproportionately on employers' property and related rights.

Perhaps the most notable political occurrence in the last half-century is that, since 1993, there no longer is a Minister for Labour whose exclusive function is to supervise labour issues. At present, that task is shared with the more general function of supervising most aspects of trade, commerce and industry, in the office of the Minister for Enterprise, Trade and Employment.

SOURCES OF RIGHTS AND DUTIES

As has been stated, the legal kernel of the employment relationship is the contract of employment agreed between employer and worker. Often this contract is little more than the worker agreeing to accept employment on the employer's usual terms; at times most or some of those terms will have been agreed between the employer, or an employers' organisation, and one or more trade unions representative of the worker. These contractual rights and duties are supplemented by obligations arising in the laws of tort and, in respect of what may be described as key executive personnel, certain fiduciary obligations are imposed by equity. Modern employment legislation places an extensive range of statutory duties especially on employers.

[15.] See *post*, p. 93 *et seq.*

[16.] See *post*, p. 87 *et seq.*

[17.] See *post*, p. 85 *et seq.*

[18.] See *post*, p. 124 *et seq.*

[19.] See *post*, p. 96 *et seq.*

[20.] *Inter alia*, on postal workers (see *post*, p. 253 n. 3) and on transfer of undertakings (see *post*, p. 230 n. 16.

[21.] [1997] 2 I.R. 321.

Contract

The contract of employment may be written or unwritten; its main terms may have been the subject of express agreement between the parties or they may be implied from the surrounding circumstances, such as collective agreements with trade unions, works or office rules, custom and practice at the workplace. Where either party contravenes any of the terms of their contract, the other party can seek redress by suing for breach of contract and will recover damages for any consequent loss suffered. Exceptionally, breach of the contract may be enjoined or it may be sanctioned by the employer refusing to pay wages for work that is not done. The general principles of the law of contract, therefore, have a very strong bearing on employment law.

Tort

The employment relationship is also affected by the law of tort.[22] Tort law is concerned with a variety of duties which the common law imposes on persons over and above whatever obligations they may have assumed under contracts. By far the most important of these obligations in the employment relationship is the duty of care that employers owe for their employees' safety while at work. Long before the famous "snail in the ginger ale bottle" case[23] and its Irish counterpart, the "maggot in the jam jar" case,[24] were decided, the courts laid down a variety of obligations in tort in respect of employees' safety at work and these duties were supplemented and expanded by statutory provisions. Exceptionally, there can be tort liability for purely financial loss as contrasted with personal injury and tangible damage to property.

Equity

Apart from the question of confidential information and the general principles governing injunctions, it is not clear what role equity[25] plays in the employment relationship. Certain senior employees, like executive directors of companies and holders of prominent public offices, owe fiduciary duties to their employers over and above such duties as may arise under their contracts.[26] Consequently, they are amenable to equitable remedies that are not available against more conventional employees, like the imposition of constructive trusts. Employees generally owe a duty of loyalty and fidelity to their employers, but it arises by virtue of contract, either expressly or by an implied term.

Statutes

Legislative provisions concerning employment-related matters, be they contained in Acts of the Oireachtas or of previous Parliaments, or in regulations made under Acts, affect employers and workers in several different ways. The standard of

---

[22.] See, generally, B. McMahon & W. Binchy, *Irish Law of Torts* (3rd ed., 2000).
[23.] *Donoghue v. Stevenson* [1932] A.C. 562.
[24.] *Kirby v. Burke* [1944] I.R. 207.
[25.] See, generally, H. Delany, *Equity and the Law of Trusts in Ireland* (2nd ed., 1999).
[26.] See, *post,* p. 67.

conduct prescribed in the Act in question may be deemed to be a term of the employment contract and thereby become enforceable like any other contractual term. Alternatively, the Act in question may establish or incorporate some special mode or process by which its requirements may be enforced, for instance by the Labour Court or by the Employment Appeals Tribunal. Or the Act may simply render certain conduct a criminal offence. The Act may even lay down some standard of conduct but not indicate when or in what manner its requirements may be enforced. Thus, there is the vexed question of when do statutory obligations give persons a civil right of action in the ordinary courts whenever the legislative requirements have been contravened. In other words, although perhaps over-simplifying the question, when are criminal or regulatory offences, or other statutory obligations, also actionable torts?[27] In the employment law field, this question arises most frequently in connection with prescribed safety standards, where the plaintiff suffered injury because those standards were not complied with.

Regulations

Nearly all of the statutes that regulate the employment relationship empower the executive, usually the Minister for Enterprise, Trade and Employment, to supplement the legislation, or indeed occasionally to adapt it, by way of regulations or orders, usually in the form of statutory instruments. Although many employment law requirements imposed by the E.C. are embodied in primary legislation, some are implemented in the form of statutory instruments, most notably the European Communities (Safeguarding of Employees' Rights on Transfer of Undertakings) Regulations 1980.

Codes of practice

There are what are known as codes of practice in respect of certain matters, which are not strictly legally binding norms but which nevertheless may be taken into account by courts and tribunals. The National Authority for Occupational Safety and Health is empowered, with the consent of the Minister, to issue codes of practice on aspects of safety and health at work "for the purpose of providing practical guidelines" on the requirements in the Safety, Health and Welfare at Work Act 1989.[28] Breach of these codes' requirements is not a criminal offence but, nonetheless, those requirements are admissible in evidence as indicae of what standards are expected.[29] Following consultation with the Minister or other appropriate body, the Equality Agency may issue codes of practice aimed at eliminating discrimination in and promoting equality of opportunity in employment.[30] Again, breach of these codes is not *per se* unlawful but the codes are admissible in evidence and account can be taken of their requirements.

Codes of practice may also be issued by the Labour Relations Commission, with the Minister's consent, to provide practical guidance on what is required by the Organisation of Working Time Act 1997.[31] Again, failure to observe stan-

---

[27.] See, generally, Buckley, "Liability in Tort for Breach of Statutory Duty", 100 L.Q.R. 204 (1984).
[28.] s. 30.
[29.] s. 31.
[30.] Employment Equality Act 1998, s. 56.
[31.] s. 35.

dards set out in such codes does not make a person liable criminally or civilly, but those standards may still be taken into account by courts or tribunals when deciding whether there has been a breach of the 1997 Act. Codes of practice on industrial relations questions may be issued by the Minister, having consulted the Labour Relations Commission, which similarly are not binding but which nonetheless a court or tribunal may take into account.[32]

E.C. Directives

There are Directives issued by the European Communities (E.C.) on employment questions.[33] Most of these have been translated into Irish law by statute, beginning with the since-replaced Anti-Discrimination (Pay) Act 1974. One major Directive in the field, generally described as the "Acquired Rights Directive", has been implemented into law by way of a statutory instrument made in 1980.[34] Sometimes, as with the Acquired Rights Directive, the very terms of the Directive in question are made part of domestic law without any reformulation whatsoever of those terms.

Directives that have not been implemented into domestic law do not create enforceable rights against private sector employers (*i.e.* "horizontal direct effect").[35] Where, however, a Directive imposes specific obligations but the State or other public authority fail to do what the Directive requires, they will not be permitted to hide behind the failure to implement the measure into Irish law. This is the "vertical direct effect" principle, by which unambiguous requirements set out in Directives are directly applicable in the courts and enforceable against all public authorities.[36] This principle holds that a Member State "which has not adopted the implementing measures required by the Directive within the prescribed period may not plead, as against individuals, its own failure to perform the obligations which the Directive entails".[37] Because the State and public agencies are very large employers, this principle has particular relevance in the employment field. Accordingly, although the State may decide to delay giving effect to E.C. Directives for some years, nevertheless, clear and unconditional requirements laid down in them can be enforced against it *qua* employer.[38]

Whether State-owned industrial and commercial employers such as Radio Telefís Éireann, Coras Iompair Éireann and Aer Lingus, fall within the vertical direct effect principle remains to be seen. It was held by the European Court of Justice in *Foster v. British Gas plc*,[39] that any body which performs a public

---

32. Industrial Relations Act 1990, s. 42.
33. See, generally, C. Barnard, *E.C. Employment Law* (2nd ed., 2000); B. Bercusson, *European Labour Law* (1996); C. Quigley, *European Community Contract Law* (1998), Chap. 3; A. Neal, *European Labour Law and Social Policy* (1999); P. Conlon ed., *E.C. Labour Legislation in Ireland* (1996); P. Rodiere, *Droit Social de l'Union European* (1998).
34. Directive 77/187, O.J. No. L61/26 (1977), implemented by S.I. No. 306 of 1980 see post p. 230.
35. *Faccini Dori v. Recreb* (Case C91/92) [1994] E.C.R. 3325 and *Mann v. Secretary of State for Employment* [1999] I.C.R. 898.
36. See, generally, T.C. Hartley, *Foundations of European Community Law* (4th ed., 1998), pp. 199 *et seq.*
37. *Marshall v. Southampton and South West Herts H.A.* (Case 152/84) [1986] E.C.R. 723 (para. 47).
38. *e.g.Gibson v. East Riding of Yorkshire Council* [1999] I.C.R. 622.
39. (Case C 188/89) [1990] E.C.R. 3313.

service and is controlled by the State is an emanation of the State for this purpose. That case concerned whether British Gas, which at the time was a State-owned public utility with a monopoly in the supply of gas, could be held bound by one of the Directives against sex discrimination. According to the Luxembourg Court:

> "A body, whatever its legal form, which has been made responsible, pursu-
> ant to a measure adopted by the State, for providing a public service under
> the control of the State and has for that purpose special powers beyond those
> which result from the normal rules applicable in relations between individu-
> als is included in any event among the bodies against which the provisions
> of a Directive capable of having direct effect may be relied upon."[40]

It was then left for the English courts to determine whether British Gas met this description.[41]

Although non-implemented Directives do not have horizontal direct effect, there are two ways in which they may nevertheless have a degree of applicability to private sector employment where they stipulate clear and unqualified require-ments for employers. Where the national law deals with a question that is also the subject of an unimplemented Directive, courts are required to interpret that law in a manner that makes it consistent with the Directive.[42] Secondly, the private sec-tor worker may have a right of action in damages against the State for its failure to implement, or to fully implement, the Directive in question.[43]

The Constitution

The Constitution affects employment law in several ways. Laws and regulations will be declared invalid where they contravene some provision of the Constitu-tion. For instance, Part III of the Trade Union Act 1941 was struck down because it infringed the guarantee of freedom of association;[44] section 34 of the Offences Against the State Act 1939 was declared invalid because it contravened the right to work;[45] the Employment Equality Bill 1996 was held repugnant on several grounds;[46] and in 1978 a minimum wage order for the hotels industry was con-demned because employers who would be adversely affected by that order had not been given adequate opportunity to air their objections to it.[47] The basis for constitutional challenge to measures can be that they contravene the separation of powers between the legislature and the executive and the courts, or that they impose unfair procedures, or that they discriminate unfairly, or that they infringe

---

[40] *ibid.* at para. 20.
[41] *Foster v. British Gas p.l.c.* [1991] 2 A.C. 306; see too *National Union of Teachers v. St. Mary's School* [1997] I.C.R. 334.
[42] *Marleasing S.A. v. La Commerciale Internacionale de Alimentacion S.A.* (Case 106/89) [1990] E.C.R. 4135 and see, generally, T.C. Hartley, *supra*, n.36, pp. 211 *et seq.*
[43] *Francovich v. Italian Republic* (Case C 6/90) [1991] E.C.R. 5357 and see generally, T.C. Hartley, *supra*, n.36, pp. 226 *et seq.*
[44] *National Union of Railwaymen v. Sullivan* [1947] I.R. 345.
[45] *Cox v. Ireland* [1992] 2 I.R. 503.
[46] *Re Employment Equality Bill, 1996* [1997] 2 I.R. 321.
[47] *Burke v. Minister for Labour* [1979] I.R. 354.

one of the other specified or unspecified right, such as the right to work. As is explained elsewhere,[48] industrial action by trade unions can be unlawful because it contravenes the constitutional right of persons affected by that action, such as women workers being prevented from getting jobs,[49] and primary school children being prevented from receiving education.[50] In determining questions of constitutionality, the courts have shown little enthusiasm for the European Convention on Human Rights, or cases decided under it by the Strasbourg court,[51] as providing relevant guidelines but that state of affairs is unlikely to last for much longer.

The extent to which the Constitution affects relations between employers and workers outside the industrial action and trade union sphere is largely unexplored territory. One reason perhaps for the dearth of authority on the question is that many of the issues which might give rise to constitutional rights have been made the subject of legislative provision. Thus, the extent to which the Constitution may guarantee non-discrimination between the sexes and others in the workplace is no longer of great practical importance because sex discrimination is regulated by Part III of the Employment Equality Act 1998, as well as by Article 141 of the E.E.C. Treaty and several E.C. Directives on equality between the sexes.

Non-governmental action

The State, in the guise of the legislature, the executive and other public authorities, is bound by the various obligations imposed by the Constitution. The principal purpose of having a Constitution which gives persons entrenched rights is to ensure that the State is properly run and to protect individuals from abuses of power by the State and its agencies. A matter which still requires some clarification, however, is to what extent private individuals and organisations, notably employers and employees, are bound by the Constitution in their dealings with each other.[52] Assuming that a certain practice would constitute unfair discrimination or unfair procedures or other unconstitutional action on the part of a public sector employer, does a private employer who engages in that practice violate the Constitution? In some countries constitutional guarantees apply only to governmental or public action and not to private activities and arrangements, for instance in the U.S.A. and in Canada.[53] The position is more nuanced in Germany, where the issue is known as the *dritt wirkung* question.[54] As for Ireland, a categorical answer has not yet been given to this question, although on several occasions it has been held that industrial action being taken by trade unions contravened others' constitutional rights.

[48.] *Industrial Relations Law*, pp. 179-181.
[49.] *Murtagh Properties Ltd. v. Cleary* [1972] I.R. 330.
[50.] *Crowley. v. Ireland* [1980] I.R. 102.
[51.] *cf.* Palmer, "Human Rights: Implications for Labour Law" 59 C.L.J. 168 (2000).
[52.] See, generally, M. Forde, *Constitutional Law* (1987), Chap. 26.
[53.] See, generally, L. Tribe, *American Constitutional Law* (2nd ed., 1988), Chap. 18, and P. Hogg, *Constitutional Law of Canada* (4th ed., 1997), pp. 841 *et seq.*
[54.] See, generally, B. Markesenis, *The German Law of Obligations* (3rd ed., 1977) Vol. 2, pp. 352 *et seq.* Following the Human Rights Act 1998, this question has generated considerable debate in Britain, summarised in Bamforth, "The True 'Horizontal Effect' of the Human Rights Act, 1998", 60 Cam. L.J. 34 (2001).

In the light of what was said in some of the trade union cases, it would seem that private sector employers are bound by the Constitution. According to Budd J. in a case concerning picketing to enforce a closed shop:

"If an established right in law exists a citizen has the right to assert it and it is the duty of the Courts to aid and assist him in the assertion of his right. The Court will therefore assist and uphold a citizen's constitutional rights, obedience to the law is required of every citizen, and it follows that if one citizen has a right under the Constitution there exists a correlative duty on the part of other citizens to respect that right and not to interfere with it. To say otherwise would be tantamount of saying that a citizen can set the Constitution at nought and that a right solemnly given by our fundamental law is valueless. It follows that the Courts will not so act as to permit any body of citizens to deprive another of his constitutional rights and will in any proceedings before them see that these rights are protected, whether they be assailed under the guise of a statutory right or otherwise."[55]

And according to Walsh J. in another closed shop case:

"If the Oireachtas cannot validly seek to compel a person to forego a constitutional right, can such a power be effectively exercised by some lesser body or by an individual employer? To exercise what may be loosely called a common law right of dismissal as a method of compelling a person to abandon a constitutional right, or as a penalty for him not doing so, must necessarily be regarded as an abuse of the common law right because it is an infringement, and an abuse, of the Constitution which is superior to the common law and which must prevail if there is a conflict between the two."[56]

However, what was decided in these cases is not authority for the proposition being canvassed here; one case involved picketing which was expressly authorised by the terms of the Trade Disputes Act 1906, and the employer in the second case was the State-owned public transport monopoly, Coras Iompair Éireann.

In the only reported case where the Supreme Court had to consider whether a private employer is bound by substantive guarantees in the Constitution, the Court found in favour of the employer. That was *McGrath v. Maynooth College*,[57] where the two plaintiffs were dismissed from their posts as professors in Maynooth College. This college was founded in 1795 as a seminary for training Catholic priests and, until 1966, it admitted only clerical students and all its teaching staff were clerics. It then became empowered to grant degrees from the National University of Ireland and it hired some non-clerical teachers. The plaintiffs had been priests and full-time teaching officers of the college until they were dismissed from their posts in 1976 for breaking several college regulations. It was contended, unsuccessfully, that their dismissal was unlawful because it contravened their freedom of religion, on the grounds that the regulations they had broken forbade them from publishing matter without the consent of the college

---

[55.] *Educational Co. of Ireland v. Fitzpatrick* [1961] I.R. 345 at p. 368.
[56.] *Meskell v. C.I.E.* [1973] I.R. 121 at 135.
[57.] [1979] I.L.R.M. 166.

authorities and forbade wearing non-clerical dress in the college. Their dismissal was upheld principally because the guarantee of freedom of religion entitled the college to take measures which would safeguard the institution's special religious ethos. Kenny J. took the view that, in any event, the guarantee of freedom of religion is confined to the State and does not even apply to bodies which obtain financial subventions from the State.[58] None of the other judges addressed this point.

Fair procedures are implied into employment contracts and that implication frequently is accompanied by reference to the Constitution's guarantee of fair procedures.[59] However, in countries which do not have constitutions guaranteeing fundamental rights, courts also imply fair procedures into those contracts. What has not been addressed is, assuming there are constitutionally guaranteed fair procedures in the employment relationship, in what circumstance may they not be bargained away by the parties or their representatives?

It, therefore, would seem that the courts will hold private sector employers to terms of the Constitution. However, the full rigours of constitutional obligation may not obtain in private sector employment because employers will invoke their own countervailing guaranteed rights of private property, the right to conduct their business affairs as they choose, subject to whatever duties are imposed on them by legislation and the common law and to any obligations they may assume under contract. The position may very well be that it is an implied term of the employment contract that employees' constitutional rights will be respected, except where the contrary is expressly stipulated by the parties.

The right to work

The expression "the right to work" means different things to different people. For the Paris revolutionaries of 1848, the *droit au travail* meant an obligation on the State to provide employment for everybody who needed a job. In the old Soviet Constitution that right was defined as the right to "guaranteed employment and pay in accordance with the quantity and quality of their work, and not below the state-established minimum".[60] The term also signifies a right to an income from the State when one is unemployed, *i.e.* social security during unemployment. It also means a right not to be unfairly excluded from a job, or at the least not to be unfairly deprived of a job one already holds.

The right to work as envisaged by Article 1 of the European Social Charter[61] is formulated as follows:

"With a view to ensuring the effective exercise of the right to work, the Contracting Parties undertake:

(1) to accept as one of their primary aims and responsibilities the achievement and maintenance of as high and stable a level of

---

[58.] *ibid.* at 214.
[59.] *e.g. Glover v. B.L.N. Ltd.* [1973] I.R. 388 and *post,* p. 175
[60.] Replaced by Constitution of 12 December 1993.
[61.] [1965] Ir.T.S. No. 3.

employment as possible, with a view to the attainment of full employment;

(2)   to protect effectively the right of the worker to earn his living in an occupation freely entered upon;

(3)   to establish or maintain free employment services for all workers;

(4)   to provide or promote appropriate vocational guidance, training and rehabilitation."

There is no express reference in the European Convention on Human Rights to employment as such (apart from trade union questions) and the only reference to employment in the Constitution is contained in the "directive principles" in Article 45, which cannot be invoked by the courts in order to strike down post-1937 legislation. These principles state, *inter alia*, that

"[t]he State shall . . . direct its policy towards securing: That the citizens (all of whom, men and women equally, have the right to an adequate means of livelihood) may through their occupations find the means of making reasonable provisions for their domestic needs."

But it has been held that the right to work is one of the unspecified rights under Article 40.3 of the Constitution.

Obtaining employment: In the first case in which the constitutional right to work obtained judicial recognition, that right was not founded on Article 40.3 but on the Article 45.2 directive principle quoted above; indeed, the outcome of that case could also have been justified under Article 40.1, the equality clause. That was *Murtagh Properties Ltd. v. Cleary,*[62] where trade union members picketed the plaintiff's property, a public house, in order to prevent non-union bar staff from being employed there. Since the union's membership was all male and it would not accept women into its membership, the picketers effectively sought to prevent women from being employed by the plaintiff. Kenny J. held that Article 45.2 clearly means that "in so far as the right to an adequate means of livelihood was involved, men and women were to be regarded as equal."[63] Accordingly, he concluded:

"Policy or general rule under which anyone seeks to prevent an employer from employing men or women on the ground of sex only is prohibited by the Constitution. [And] a demand backed by a threat of a picket that women should not be employed at all in any activity solely because they are women (and not because the work is unsuitable for them or too difficult for them or too dangerous) is a breach of this right (*i.e.* to an adequate means of livelihood)."[64]

Since this was precisely the defendants' policy and mode of action, it was unlawful and their picketing of the plaintiff's premises was enjoined. In subsequent

---

[62.]   [1972] I.R. 330.

[63.]   *ibid.* at 336.

[64.]   *ibid.*

cases, several of them concerning trade unions, it was accepted that the right to work also derives from Article 40.3.[65]

The existence of such a right does not prevent the State from employing only certain categories of persons or from prohibiting the employment of certain groups of individuals. But because earning a living is vital for most persons' contented existence, prohibitions against employment require substantial justification. Several legislative prohibitions against employing women, which were enacted with the declared object of protecting women from exploitation, have been repealed by modern anti-sex discrimination law. Employing young persons is extensively restricted by the Protection of Young Persons (Employment) Act 1996. In *Landers v. Attorney General*,[66] it was held that a statutory prohibition against young persons giving singing performances in public houses was not an unconstitutional interference with young persons' right to work and to earn a livelihood. And in *Greally v. Minister for Education*,[67] a scheme whereby applications for permanent teaching posts in Catholic schools were entertained only from persons who were on a panel, with previous teaching experience in those schools, was held to be justified in the circumstances.

Dismissal from employment: Persons cannot be dismissed from public employment for unconstitutional reasons, such as religion, sex or lawful political activities. Whether the Constitution proscribes dismissal from private sector employment on similar grounds has not been resolved. The Supreme Court has held that persons being removed from permanent posts in the public service have a constitutional right to a fair hearing before the decision to dismiss them is taken. In *The State (Gleeson) v. Minister Defence*,[68] where a permanent member of the defence forces was discharged in circumstances that would have damaged his reputation and would have adversely affected his future employment prospects, it was held that his dismissal was unlawful because he had not first been given a fair hearing. According to Henchy J.:

> "We are not concerned here with discharges for creditable or neutral reasons. Where . . . the discharge is for a reason that is discreditable, the fundamentals of justice require that the man shall have an opportunity of meeting the case for discharging him for that reason. That is the minimum that is needed to guard against injustice . . . . The requirements of natural justice imposed an inescapable duty on the army authorities, before discharging the prosecutor from the Army for the misconduct relied on, to give him due notice of the intention to discharge him, of the statutory reason for the proposed discharge, and of the essential facts and findings alleged to constitute that reason; and to give him a reasonable opportunity of presenting his response to that notice."[69]

[65.] *e.g. Murphy v. Stewart* [1973] I.R. 97.
[66.] (1975)109 I.L.T.R. 1.
[67.] [1999] 1 I.R. 1.
[68.] [1976] I.R. 280.
[69.] *ibid.* at 296.

A provision in the Offences Against the State Act 1939, barring from public service employment persons who had been convicted of what may be termed "subversive" offences, was struck down in *Cox v. Ireland*.[70] The plaintiff, a school-teacher, had been convicted in the Special Criminal Court of a scheduled offence under the 1939 Act and got a two-year sentence. On his release, he was informed that he no longer had his job, which had been forfeited under that Act; according to section 34 of that Act, persons employed in the public sector forfeited their jobs and also any accumulated pension entitlements on being so convicted. Because that section operated so drastically, without qualification, across the entire public sector, regardless of the gravity or comparative triviality of the offence in question, the Supreme Court held that it violated the implied right to work as well as property rights in respect of pensions. What made section 34 particularly objectionable was that it was entirely within the discretion of the Director of Public Promotions to prosecute the offence in question in the Special Criminal Court rather than before the ordinary courts, thereby introducing a peculiarly arbitrary dimension. That in any single instance the Government could waive application of section 34 did not save it from unconstitutionality.

Freedom to manage

By virtue of the Constitution's guarantees of private property, employers have a fundamental right to carry on and manage their businesses without excessive interference from the State. Under the banner "substantive due process", in the early part of this century the United States Supreme Court condemned several reforming labour laws as unconstitutional,[71] for instance, laws providing for minimum wages and for maximum working hours in certain kinds of employments. But, from 1937 onwards, that court has allowed the federal and the state legislatures a very wide discretion in the regulation of labour markets and employment conditions. It was not until 1997 that Ireland's Supreme Court had the opportunity to examine a major piece of labour (as distinct from trade union) legislation against the provisions of the 1937 Constitution.

As its title declared, *Re Employment Equality Bill, 1996*,[72] concerned a challenge to a Bill adopted in 1996 designed to update and significantly extend the existing laws on equality in the workplace. Legislative action against sex discrimination at work commenced in 1919 and, following Ireland's accession to European Communities, was expanded by a law of 1974 on equal pay and a law of 1977 on equal treatment of the sexes; these were supplemented in 1981 by a law on maternity leave, which has been replaced by a law of 1994. The "Rainbow Coalition" Government of 1996, which produced two Bills on equality in that year, professed a particular commitment to equality and indeed had established, for the first time, a Ministry of Equality (along with Law Reform). It would seem that the principal task that this Ministry set itself was a far more ambitious and comprehensive enactment on equality and, in due course, presented to the Oireachtas the Employment Equality Bill 1996, and the Equal Status Bill 1997.

[70.] [1992] 2 I.R. 503.
[71.] See, generally, L. Tribe, *American Constitutional Law* (3rd ed., 2000) at pp. 1343 *et seq.*
[72.] [1997] 2 I.R. 321.

These were passed by both Houses but were referred to the Supreme Court under Article 26 of the Constitution, which held that certain of their provisions were repugnant.

Much of the attack on the 1996 Bill was on the grounds that it unfairly discriminated, which is a somewhat odd proposition when the whole purpose of that Bill was to combat discrimination in the workplace. Those challenges did not succeed. Two of the successful attacks concerned points of criminal procedure; section 15 of the Bill was held to impose vicarious criminal responsibility on employers for infringements by their employees of various provisions of the Bill[73] and section 63 made a certified document setting out certain facts prima facie evidence of those facts in a criminal prosecution. Both of these were held to contravene the guarantee in Article 38.1 of a criminal trial in due course of law.

The successful attack on the 1996 Bill's substantive provisions concerned the prohibition against discrimination on grounds of disability. There was a broad proscription against this kind of discrimination; it was supplemented by a stipulation that a disabled person shall not be treated as not being fully competent and capable of doing the job if "the assistance of special treatment and facilities" would render him so able; these were then qualified by a proviso that the absence of such facilities would not constitute discrimination if their provision would cause the employer undue hardship, taking into account, *inter alia*, their cost to the employer, his financial circumstances, the amount of disruption that would be caused and the amount of benefit that would accrue to the employer. This, it was held, constituted an unjustifiable interference with employers' property rights because it sought to impose on them the cost of solving society's obligation to be fair to disabled persons. In other words, in much the same way as the Rent Restriction Act 1960 was condemned, because it sought to put on the shoulders of a limited number of property-owners the cost of providing low rent housing to persons in need,[74] these provisions of the 1996 Bill were a form of taxation on employers in favour of disabled persons when the financial burden should have been cast across the community generally. Employers, it was held, should not be required to spend money on facilities for disabled employees; if discrimination against these persons is to be outlawed, then the cost to employers of providing the requisite facilities should be defrayed from taxation.

A distinction was drawn with expenditure that employers may have to make in order to ensure that working conditions shall be safe:

"Society should bear the cost of doing it. It is important to distinguish between the proposed legislation and legislation to protect the health and safety of workers. It is entirely proper that the State should insist that those who profit from an industrial process should mange it as safely, and with as little danger to health, as possible. The cost of doing the job safely and in a healthy manner is properly regarded as part of the industrialist's costs of production. Likewise it is proper that he should pay if he pollutes the air, the

---

[73] *cf.* Decision of French *Conseil Constitutional* of December 2, 1976, Work Accidents.
[74] *Blake v. Attorney General* [1982] I.R. 117 and *Re Housing (Private Rented Dwellings) Bill 1981* [1983] I.R. 181.

land or the rivers. It would be unjust if he were allowed to take the profits and let society carry the cost. Likewise it is just that the State, through its planning agencies, should insist that the public buildings and private buildings to which the general public are intended to have access for work or play should be designed in such a way as to be accessible by the disabled as well as by the able-bodied."

The difficulty with the section now under discussion is that it attempts to transfer the cost of solving one of society's problems on to a particular group. The difficulty the Court finds with the section is, not that it requires an employer to employ disabled people, but that it requires him to bear the cost of all special treatment or facilities which the disabled person may require to carry out the work unless the cost of the provision of such treatment or facilities would give rise to "undue hardship" to the employer.[75]

ENFORCING LABOUR STANDARDS

Terms and conditions of employment that have been agreed between employers and workers, or between their representative associations and trade unions, are usually adhered to and the question of their enforcement will not normally arise; employers and employees ordinarily do what they have agreed to do. Disputes occur from time to time about what actually has been agreed; these generally are resolved through negotiation, which may be informal or, at the other extreme, may take place in a joint industrial council, which is a disputes-resolution committee established under the terms of a collective agreement. At times, disputes are referred to the Labour Court, which may make a recommendation on the matter. These do not have any legally binding force but parties usually accept the solution which is recommended. Exceptionally, parties resort to industrial action in order to resolve disputes, for instance, strikes, pickets, lockouts, boycotts and black-listing. The following are the principal techniques contained in employment legislation designed to ensure that their substantive requirements are effectively implemented.

Displaying information

Some of these Acts require employers to display prominently at the workplace information about the Act in question's requirements. Thus, sections 120-121 of the Factories Act 1955[76] require, *inter alia*, that there be posted at the principal entrance of every factory an abstract of that Act and a copy of every notice and document that the Act requires to be posted in the factory. There are comparable provisions in, *inter alia*, section 12 of the Protection of Young Persons (Employment) Act 1996. It is assumed that, by drawing attention to the relevant statutory requirements in this manner, workers and their representatives, and indeed

---

75. [1997] 2 I.R. at 367-368.
76. As amended by s. 46 of the Safety in Industry Act 1980.

employers too, will be more vigilant in ensuring that those requirements are adhered to.

Record keeping

Several of these Acts require employers to keep records of relevant information, which in particular facilitates labour inspectors monitoring the extent to which the Acts are being complied with. Thus, section 122 of the Factories Act 1955 requires that there be kept in every factory a general register which is to record several matters, for instance, particulars of every accident that has occurred and every industrial disease that has occurred in the factory. There are comparable provisions in *inter alia* section 15 of the Protection of Young Persons (Employment) Act 1996 (records to show that this Act's requirements are being satisfied), section 25 of the Organisation of Working Time Act 1997, and section 22 of the National Minimum Wage Act 2000.

Labour inspectorate

The appointment of officials whose task it was to visit workplaces, to conduct inspections there in order to monitor compliance with the legislation in question, has existed for many years. Provisions to this effect are contained in *inter alia* Part V (sections 32-41) of the Safety, Health and Welfare at Work Act 1989, sections 51-52 of the Industrial Relations Act 1946 (monitoring orders fixing minimum wages and employment conditions), section 22 of the Protection of Young Persons (Employment) Act 1996, section 8 of the Organisation of Working Time Act 1996, section 9 of the Payment of Wages Act 1991 (called "authorised officers"), section 94 of the Employment Equality Act 1998, section 18 of the Pensions Act 1990, as amended (called "authorised persons"), and section 33 of the National Minimum Wage Act 2000. Some of these inspectors are employed directly by, and are accountable to, the Minister; others are employed by the Agency that the Act in question has established.

Their powers are broadly similar. Thus, "designated officers", under the Employment Equality Act 1998, are empowered to peaceably enter premises at all reasonable times; to require persons to give access to and produce records, books, documents and other things relating to the workplace; to inspect and copy or take extracts from that material; and to inspect any work in progress. A dwelling may not be so entered unless the Minister has given a certificate in respect of it. A search warrant, if needed, can be obtained from a District Judge, which may authorise forcible entry to the premises.

Regulatory agencies

Three major agencies have been established to supervise application of the legislation on health and safety, on employment equality, and on pensions. Additionally, there is the Labour Relations Commission, established in 1990,[77] the main function of which is to provide a conciliation service and to give advice on industrial relations questions generally. It also prepares draft codes of practice, which

---

[77.] Industrial Relations Act 1990, s. 24 and Schedule 4; see *Industrial Relations Law,* pp. 37-38.

may be implemented by the Minister. The three specialised agencies are the National Authority for Occupational Safety and Health (NAOSA),[78] the Equality Authority,[79] and the Pensions Board,[80] which, as their names indicate, are concerned with health and safety at work, with equality in the workplace, and with pension entitlements, respectively.

Prosecuting offenders

While compliance with some of the employment legislation is secured principally through civil proceedings in the courts, breach of many of the statutes constitutes criminal offences in respect of which persons can be prosecuted and, if convicted, fined and, indeed, sent to prison. Extensive criminal sanctions are contained in the legislation on health and safety, in the Payment of Wages Act 1991, and in the Protection of Young Persons (Employment) Act 1996. Victimisation of persons who exercise their statutory rights or who facilitate others in exercising them is made an offence in some of the legislation, most notably section 98 of the Employment Equality Act 1998, and section 80 of the Pensions Act 1996, as amended, but oddly not in section 17 of the 1996 Act concerning young persons.

As well as prosecutions being instituted by the Director of Public Prosecutions, power to prosecute summarily is often conferred on the Minister and/or the agency that supervises the legislation in question, most notably the NAOSA. Trade unions can prosecute under section 24 of 1996 Act on young persons. It is debatable how effective criminalisation has been as a sanction; no research seems to have been carried out on the question.

Because many employers are registered companies, provision is usually made in the Act in question for responsible officers of the company being made criminally responsible. The formula generally used stipulates:

> "Where an offence under this Act is committed by a body corporate and is proved to have been committed with the consent or connivance of, or to be attributable to any neglect on the part of, a person being a director, manager, secretary or other officer of that body corporate, or a person who was purporting to act in that capacity, that person shall also be guilty of an offence and be liable to be proceeded against and punished as if he or she were guilty of the first-mentioned offence."[81]

One of the grounds on which the Employment Equality Bill 1996 was declared to be unconstitutional[82] was that one of its enforcement sections imposed criminal penalties and the following section went on to make employers vicariously responsible for the actions of their employees in the course of their employment. The Supreme Court construed these as meaning that vicarious liability was being imposed here for the purposes of criminal as well as civil liability, which is unprecedented in labour legislation. Of course, the main enforcement provision of the 1996 Bill against the various forms of outlawed dis-

---

78. Part III of the Safety, Health and Welfare at Work Act 1989.
79. Part V of the Employment Equality Act 1998.
80. Part II of the Pension Act 1990.
81. *e.g.* Protection of Young Persons (Employment) Act 1996, s. 23(1).
82. *Re Employment Equality Bill 1996* [1997] 2 I.R. 321.

crimination was a complaint to either the envisaged Director of Equality Investigations, the Labour Court or the Circuit Court, which were authorised to award the appropriate redress. What the 1996 Bill sought to criminalise in section 14 was a third party procuring or attempting to procure another to unlawfully discriminate. What section 15, headed "vicarious liability", stated was that, for the purpose of that Bill, anything done in the course of one's employment shall be treated as done by his employer, even if it has not the employer's knowledge or approval; although subsection (3) made it a defence where the employer took reasonably practical steps to prevent his employee doing that kind of act in the course of employment. The contention that section 15 should not be construed as imposing vicarious criminal liability (because it did not do so in terms) was rejected; it was held that there was insufficient ambiguity to come within the "double construction rule" in constitutional adjudication. The Court found the defence in subsection (3) to be far too narrow if injustice were to be avoided. Third-party procurement of discrimination on the enumerated grounds was held not to be a sufficiently pressing social problem to warrant imposing vicarious criminal responsibility on employers.

Punishing victimisation

Several of the Acts regulating employment practices seek to deter individuals being victimised because they assert rights under those Acts or assist others in asserting them. If for those reasons an employee is dismissed, the employer commits a criminal offence under the legislation on employment equality[83] and on pensions.[84] No such sanction is specified for victimisation in section 17 of the 1996 Act on young persons nor in section 26 of the Organisation of Working Time Act 1997, nor in section 36 of the Minimum Wages Act 2000. But, these provide that where an employee is dismissed in circumstances that constitute victimisation, that shall be deemed to be unfair for the purposes of the Unfair Dismissals Acts 1977-93.

Civil actions

Workers often sue their employers for breach of contract or in tort in the District Court, in the Circuit Court or in the High Court. At times, it is employers who are the plaintiffs, notably in actions for breach of confidence or for breach of a non-competition clause in the contract. Trade unions sometimes fund litigation being brought by their members and many small to medium-sized employers have litigation insurance to cover all or part of the costs they incur.

In addition to whatever terms and conditions are contained in the employment contract, modern labour legislation places employers and, to a lesser extent, employees under a variety of obligations, for instance, furnishing a written statement of the main terms and conditions of the job, maintaining a safe and healthy workplace, equal pay for men and women, non-discrimination on several grounds, maximum working hours, minimum wages and paid holidays, maternity, parental and adoptive leave. Enforcement of these statutory requirements is

---

[83.] Employment Equality Act 1998, s. 98.
[84.] Pensions Act 1990, s. 80.

left mainly to the parties, who can go to the courts or else to the Labour Court or to the Employment Appeals Tribunal (E.A.T.) or some other administrative agency, in the event of a dispute arising.

In the case of some of these statutory rights, *locus standi* is conferred on the employee in question's trade union, or on an administrative agency, or occasionally on the Minister, to institute the appropriate proceedings - for instance section 39 of the National Minimum Wages Act 2000.

CHAPTER 2

PERSONAL SCOPE – THE EMPLOYMENT RELATIONSHIP

The personal scope of a body of law is concerned with the question of "who are those directly affected by those laws; what persons are the subjects of the rights and duties thereby imposed". Company law is concerned mainly with registered companies, their shareholders, directors and creditors; family law regulates the rights and responsibilities of members of families; employment law applies principally to employers and employed persons.

EMPLOYEES AND THE CONTRACT OF EMPLOYMENT

Those who work for others fall into two main legal categories. They may be employees, that is persons who work under what is known as a contract of employment or of service. Alternatively, they may be self-employed, working for numerous persons under contracts for services. A typical employee works only for one employer, arrives at and departs from the job at pre-ordained times, is paid a fixed rate, which is usually based on the hours spent working, and takes instructions from the employer on how the work is to be done. Examples include regular factory workers, clerks and the like. However, there are significant numbers of what may be described as atypical workers, who are neither obviously employees nor plainly self-employed. It is probable that developments in the labour market in recent years, such as the greater use of employment agency personnel, the trend towards flexible service arrangements, and the increased integration of professional persons into large bureaucratic institutions, has considerably expanded the numbers of atypical workers. Much of the case law is concerned with which of the two categories those workers should be classified into.

So far as most contractual rights and obligations are concerned, it matters little whether the person who is engaged to perform work for another is classified as an employee or as self-employed. Because of its very nature, however, certain terms will be implied into a contract of employment, notably, the employer's extensive obligations regarding safety at work[1] and the employee's obligation of fidelity.[2] The employee/self-employed distinction is important in the law of tort because an employer is vicariously liable for the wrongs committed by his employees in the course of their work but not, generally, for the wrongs of those he engaged under a contract for services.[3] It is in respect of the many statutory rights and

---

[1.] See *post*, p. 65.
[2.] See *post*, p. 67.
[3.] See generally, B. McMahon & W. Binchy, *Irish Law of Torts* (3rd ed., 2000) Chap. 43.

duties that the distinction between the two categories is particularly significant, because most of the modern employment protection legislation applies only to employer/employee relationships and not to independent contractors. Thus, the Unfair Dismissals Acts 1977-93 apply only to employees (and certain apprentices), who are defined as any "individual who has entered into or works under . . . a contract of employment."[4]

When dealing with disputes concerning relations between persons who hire others to work and those who are hired, a vital preliminary question therefore is whether the hiring is under a contract of employment or under a contract for services; whether the person hired is an employee or is self-employed. If he is an employee, then, subject to exceptions, the full panoply of employment law should govern his circumstances. If he is self-employed, most employment laws do not directly affect him.

A few employment protection laws apply to some self-employed workers as well as to employees because of the way in which those Acts define the term "employed" and "employee". Thus the equal pay provisions of the Employment Equality Act 1998, which apply to "employed persons", define employed as including employed "under a contract personally to execute any work or labour."[5] This definition embraces the self-employed provided that, under their terms of engagement, they must perform the work themselves rather than have the option of hiring others to do whatever the job undertaken requires.[6] The Minimum Notice and Terms of Employment Act 1973 and the Redundancy Payments Acts 1967-1979 define the term "employee" for their purposes as any person working under a "contract with an employer . . ., whether it is a contract of service or of apprenticeship or otherwise. . . ."[7] The "or otherwise" here suggests that these Acts may apply to self-employed persons who are hired by an employer, especially when this definition is contrasted with a similar one in the Employment Equality Act 1998, except the later Act goes on to add that the term "employer" in relation to an employee means "the person with whom the employee has entered into a contract of employment. . . ."[8] While the literal meaning of the definition in the Minimum Notice and Terms of Employment Act and in the Redundancy Payment Acts includes some self-employed workers, it is probable that the courts would conclude that these Acts apply only to employees, on the grounds that if the Oireachtas really intended to extend them to the self-employed it would have said so in a more direct manner. Employees within the Payment of Wages Act 1991 include those who have agreed "to do or perform personally any work or service for a third person";[9] this does not include a professional person-client relationship or a business undertaking-customer relationship.

---

4.   s.1.
5.   s.19(2).
6.   *cf. Kelly v. Northern Ireland Housing Executive* [1998] N.I. 240 and *Mirror Group Newspapers Ltd. v. Gunning* [1986] 1 W.L.R. 546.
7.   s.1.
8.   s.1(1).
9.   s.1.

Purposes of classification

Disputes about whether someone is an employee or self-employed arise in a variety of contexts, principally in order to decide if employment protection legislation, such as the Unfair Dismissals Acts, is applicable. These disputes are not always between the employer and his alleged employee or self-employed helper. At times, the plaintiff is someone who never had any dealings with the alleged employer, such as someone injured in an accident and who claims that the defendant is the wrongdoer's employer and, accordingly, is vicariously liable for the loss suffered.[10] Many of the older cases concern claims under the since-repealed Workmen's Compensation Acts; if the plaintiff was indeed the defendant's employee, under those Acts he was entitled to be compensated for the injuries suffered in the course of his employment regardless of who was at fault.[11]

Many of the more recent cases arise under the social security laws and the tax laws. The Social Welfare (Consolidation) Act 1993 requires that social insurance contributions be paid in respect of persons employed "under any contract of service or apprenticeship".[12] Some of the employment protection legislation applies only to workers who are insured under the Social Welfare Acts, notably the Redundancy Payments Acts 1967-1979,[13] and the Protection of Employees (Employers' Insolvency) Act 1984.[14] The Taxes Consolidation Act 1997 imposes income tax under Schedule E on *inter alia* "emoluments" paid to employees, which are defined as "all salaries, fees wages, prerequisites or profits or gains whatsoever arising from an office or employment".[15] The earnings of self-employed persons are taxed under Schedule D, which, from the taxpayer's perspective, is a more favourable arrangement. Thus, in many of the cases, a person working is claiming that he is not an employee in order that he will not be taxed under Schedule E and be subject to P.A.Y.E., or his employer is claiming that he is not an employee so that P.R.S.I. contributions do not have to be paid in respect of him. Although it has never been so held,[16] it would seem that the purpose for which the classification is being determined, whether for vicarious liability, employment protection, social security or taxation in practice may have some bearing on how the person is categorised by a court.

The tests

Various tests are applied in order to determine whether in the circumstances an individual is an employee or is self-employed. There is no simple master test; at times, greater emphasis is placed on one test over the others. The proper approach to questions of classification was put by Kennedy C.J. in *Graham v. Minister for Industry and Commerce*[17] as follows:

---

[10] *e.g. Phelan v. Coillte Teo.* [1993] 1 I.R. 18 and *Maguire v. P.J. Langan (Contractors) Ltd.* [1976] N.I. 49.

[11] *e.g. Kelly v. Donegal C.C.* [1946] I.R. 228.

[12] s.6(1) and Schedule 1; *cf. FAS v. Minister for Social Welfare* (Sup. *Ct.*, May 23 1995).

[13] s.4.

[14] s.2(1).

[15] s.19. See, generally, K. Corrigan, *Revenue Law* (2000) Vol. 2, Chap. 14.

[16] Indeed, the contrary has been stated, *Lee Ting Sang v. Chung Chi Keung* [1990] 2 A.C. 374.

[17] [1933] I.R. 156.

"No exhaustive definition of either category has yet been settled and established either by statute or by judicial decision and there is a zone of uncertainty. A commonly accepted test is that of control. Is the alleged 'employed person' . . . subject to be controlled by the employer in executing the work, *e.g.* as to the order and manner in which he carries out the work in detail? As to the disposal of his time while engaged in it? This, the most usual test, is . . . far from sufficient as a single test . . . . [T]here are other and equally important tests, *e.g.* is the 'engaged person' engaged to execute the whole of a given piece of work? Can the engagement be terminated before completion of the piece of work without cause assigned, or only for misconduct or for malperformance of the work? Is the agreed remuneration on a wage basis or on a percentage or other commercial profit basis? Are the necessary materials to be procured by the engaged person on his own account and, if necessary, his own credit? Are such other workmen (if any) as have been taken into employment upon the work by the engaged person so employed by him as agent for the principal, or are they his own employees paid by and subject to him? Is the engaged person required to give all the time of his working day to the work until completed, or is he free to arrange his own time as he pleases? Is he a member of a trade union and are trade union rules and conditions applicable to the work."[18]

A similar approach has been adopted in Britain, in the *Market Investigations* case:

"The fundamental test to be applied is this: 'Is the person who has engaged himself to perform these services performing them as a person in business on his own account?' If the answer to that question is 'yes', then the contract is a contract of services. If the answer is 'no', then the contract is a contract for service. No exhaustive list has been compiled and perhaps no exhaustive list can be compiled of the considerations which are relevant in determining that question, nor can strict rules be laid down as to the relative weight which the various considerations should carry in particular cases. The most that can be said is that control will no doubt always have to be considered, although it can no longer be regarded as the sole determining factor; and factors which may be of importance are such matters as whether the man performing the services provides his own equipment, whether he hires his own helpers, what degree of financial risk he takes, what degree of responsibility for investment and management he has, and whether and how far he has an opportunity of profiting from sound management in the performance of his task."[19]

In applying the various tests, not alone are such documents as were exchanged at the outset of the relationship relevant, but so too are any subsequent documentation and the manner in which the parties actually conducted themselves. The documentation exchanged at the outset may be decisive where it appears from the

---

18. *ibid.* at 159-160.
19. *Market Investigations Ltd. v. Minister for Social Security* [1969] 2 Q.B. 173 at 184-185.

terms or from what the parties said or did at the time that what was stated then constitutes an exclusive memorial of their relationship.[20]

Control

The most commonly used test is that of control: whether, under the terms of the contract, express or implied, the employer has "the power of deciding the thing to be done, the way in which it shall be done, the means to be employed in doing it, the time when and the place where it shall be done."[21] In *Roche v. Kelly*,[22] a vicarious liability case, Walsh J. observed that "[w]hile many ingredients may be present in the relationship of master and servant, it is undoubtedly true that the one principal one, and almost invariably the determining one, is the fact of the master's right to direct the servant not merely as to what is to be done but as to how it is to be done. The fact that the master does not exercise the right, as distinct from possessing it, is of no weight if he has the right."[23] If the contract gives the employer extensive control over the work to be done or spells out in detail how it is to be done, the presumption is that it is a contract of employment, absent strong indications to the contrary from other features of the relationship. That the parties may have formally designated their relationship as one of independent contract is not conclusive.[24]

However, an employer-employee relationship can exist without there being any right of extensive control. In the case of highly skilled personnel, especially those doing work of a professional nature, the employer may exercise very little control. Carroll J. in *In re Sunday Tribune Ltd.* remarked that "[i]n the present day when senior staff with professional qualifications are employed, the nature of their employment cannot be determined in such a simplistic way" as the control test.[25] The issue there was whether several journalists who worked for a Sunday newspaper were employees; if they were, their unpaid wages would be preferred debts in the winding up of their employer.[26] Although the company exercised relatively little control over them, Carroll J., using a different test, concluded that two of them were indeed employees. There are numerous reported decisions in the same vein concerning doctors in hospitals,[27] dentists engaged by local authorities,[28] engineers,[29] architects,[30] lecturers,[31] authors,[32] pupil barristers.[33] There

---

[20.] *Carmichael v. National Power p.l.c.* [1999] 1 W.L.R. 2042.
[21.] *Ready Mixed Concrete (South East) Ltd. v. Minister for Pensions* [1968] 2 Q.B. 497 at 515.
[22.] [1969] I.R, 100.
[23.] *ibid.* at 108. Similarly, *Phelan v. Coillte Teo* [1993] 1 I.R. 18.
[24.] *infra,* p. 28
[25.] [1984] I.R. 505 at 508.
[26.] Companies Act 1963, s.285(2)(b).
[27.] *O'Friel v. St. Michael's Hospital* [1982] I.L.R.M. 260.
[28.] *Greater London Council v. Minister for Social Security* [1971] 1 W.L.R. 641.
[29.] *Morren v. Swinton & Pendlebury B.C.* [1965] 1 W.L.R. 576.
[30.] *WHPT Housing Ass'n Ltd. v. Secretary of State* [1981] 1.C.R. 737.
[31.] *Narich Pty. v. Commissioners of Pay Roll Tax* [1984] I.C.R. 286.
[32.] *Beloff v. Pressdram Ltd.* [1973] 1 All E.R. 241.
[33.] *Edmonds v. Lawson* [2000] 2 W.L.R. 1091.

may be certain other features of the job which explain why the employer has very little detailed control and yet the relationship will be classified as one of employment.[34]

On the other hand, there can be extensive control but the engaged person is nevertheless an independent contractor. For instance, in *D.P.P. v. McLoughlin*,[35] it was held that share fishermen who worked for the defendant were not his employees. The defendant, as skipper of the fishing boat, exercised extensive control over the men while at sea but that right "arose as much from the nature of the operations being carried on as from the contractual relationship which existed" between the parties.[36] A similar analysis was applied in *Hitchcock v. Post Office*,[37] which concerned the status of a postmaster engaged by the English Post Office. Although the terms of his engagement set out in great detail how the plaintiff should do the work, it was held that several other features of the relationship showed that it was not a contract of employment. Similarly, in *Tierney v. An Post*,[38] which concerned a postmaster employed at a sub-post office in Cavan, the terms of his agreement with An Post were held to constitute a contract for services.

Integration

Another commonly used test is that of integration: whether the engaged person is "employed as part of the business, and his work done as an integral part of the business", as opposed to being "not integrated into but only accessory to" the business.[39] The usefulness of this test is debatable; one judge has remarked that it "raises more questions than I know how to answer".[40] But it was applied in *In re Sunday Tribune Ltd.*[41] in order to determine which category several journalists fell into. One of the journalists wrote a column for the Sunday newspaper for 50 out of the 52 weeks in the year and took part in editorial conferences and received holiday pay. She was held to be an integral part of the business of the newspaper and, accordingly, one of its employees. Another of them wrote for the paper on a regular basis but her contributions were not published virtually every week; she visited the paper's offices, usually once a week, to suggest a topic for contribution or to be requested to make a contribution, although she would not work on a contribution until it was commissioned by the editor. She was paid not at a rate per word but on the basis of a collective agreement with the National Union of Journalists. Carroll J. concluded that she was "not an integral part of the business" of the newspaper and, therefore, was an independent contractor in respect of her dealings with the company.

[34.] *e.g. Market Investigations* case, *supra* n.19.

[35.] [1986] I.R. 355.

[36.] *ibid.* at 360. Similarly, *Duncan v. O'Driscoll* [1997] E.L.R. 38 and *Doherty v. Kinclassagh Trawlers* [1999] E.L.R. 251. *cf. Minister for Social Welfare v. Griffiths* [1992] 1 I.R. 103.

[37.] [1980] I.C.R. 100.

[38.] [2000] 1 I.R. 536.

[39.] *Stevenson, Jordan & Harrison Ltd. v. Macdonald & Evans* [1952] 1 T.L.R. 101 at 121.

[40.] *Ready Mixed Concrete case* [1968] 2 Q.B. at 524.

[41.] [1984] I.R. 505. Similarly, *Beloff v. Pressdram Ltd.* [1973] 1 All E.R. 241.

Significant integration in the employer's business operations may make up for a lack of detailed control by the employer. However, self-employed persons can be highly integrated in another's commercial operations, for instance, the second journalist in the *Sunday Tribune Ltd.* case, the share fishermen in the *McLoughlin* case, persons who deliver newspapers for a wholesaler,[42] and caddies at the Royal Hong Kong Yacht Club.[43] The very nature of the business activity may require a high degree of integration. The difficulty with this test for identifying employees is that the courts have not spelt out in general terms what is meant by integration. As is explained below, if the engaged person assumes some commercial risk in doing the job, he most likely will be classified as self-employed regardless of how integrated he is in the employer's business.

Enterprise

Another test that is used, and perhaps the most important test, is the entrepreneurial criterion: "is the person who has engaged himself to perform these services performing them as a person in business on his own account."[44] If the engaged person's performance of the task requires significant capital investment on his part and especially if he is on risk, in the sense of standing to make a sizeable profit or incur a substantial loss, depending on how efficiently he does the job, he will be regarded as an independent contractor. As the United States Supreme Court once put it, are the engaged persons "small business men"?[45] Where this enterpreneurial element is present, as a rule it points to a contract for services regardless of how much control is exercised over one party or how much integration there may be. In *McDermott v. Loy*,[46] which concerned classification for the purposes of income tax, the respondent's occupation was collecting premiums for a life insurance company. He had to buy the "collection book", he had no fixed hours, he could canvass business wherever and whenever he wished, he could employ somebody else to collect the premiums for him and he could sell the collection book; he was also a trade union member and a member of the company's pension fund. Barron J. upheld the Appeal Commissioners' decision that he was self-employed. Similarly, in *O'Coindealbhain v. Mooney*,[47] the respondent's job was as branch manager of the social welfare office in a country town; his remuneration comprised certain allowances and a fixed fee related to the volume of work performed; he was required to provide and furnish his own premises and to employ competent assistants. He was held to be self-employed, principally because "his profit is the amount by which his remuneration exceeds his expenses; the lower he can keep his expenses the greater the profit."[48] But a

---

[42.] *McAuliffe v. Minister for Social Welfare* [1995] 2 I.R. 238.
[43.] *Cheng Yuen v. Royal Hong Kong Golf Club* [1998] I.C.R. 131.
[44.] *Market Investigation Case* [1969] 2 Q.B. 173 at 184; see, too, *Lee Ting Sang v. Chung Chi Keung* [1990] 2 A.C. 374.
[45.] *United States v. Silk*, 331 U.S. 704 (1946).
[46.] Barron J., July 29, 1982.
[47.] [1990] 1 I.R. 422.
[48.] *ibid.* at 1432.

tradesman who supplies his own tools and equipment is not thereby rendered self-employed.[49]

Even when the engaged person has not undertaken investment in his function, he may be self-employed under this test, such as the share fishermen in *D.P.P. v. McLaughlin*.[50] When the defendant took his fishing boat to sea, he usually had a crew of five persons. They were engaged on a voyage basis, although the same persons went on most voyages. Their remuneration was based on a sharing arrangement dependent on the size of each catch; after deducting the expenses of the trip, about half of the gross proceeds of a catch would be divided among them and the skipper, the precise proportion to be determined by consultation with him. If there was a poor catch they would not be remunerated but they were not required to contribute towards any loss incurred in a voyage. Costello J. held that the relationship between them and the defendant was not one of employer and employee; they were partners in an enterprise and, accordingly, were self-employed.[51]

Parties' own characterisation

In an evenly balanced situation, where several features point to employee status but others just as convincingly point to self-employed status, account will be taken of how the parties themselves decided to characterise their relationship. Thus, in *Massey v. Crown Life Insurance Co. Ltd.*[52] the plaintiff had managed an insurance company's branch office for two years and, although he was then classified as an employee, he was paid partly on commission and he was permitted to do work for an outside insurance broker. On being advised by his accountant that there were tax advantages for him in changing his status, he and the company agreed that thenceforth he would be treated as self-employed. There was no other material change in the terms of his engagement. On the question of whether he still was an employee for the purposes of the Unfair Dismissals Acts, it was held that, in the circumstances, the parties' own classification of their relationship was determinative. According to Lord Denning M.R., provided that "their relationship is ambiguous and is capable of being one or the other, then the parties can remove that ambiguity, by the very agreement itself which they make with one another. The agreement then becomes the best material from which to gather the true legal relationship between them."[53]

But self-classification is only decisive in relatively evenly balanced situations. The law is that "if the true relationship of the parties is that of master and servant under a contract of service, the parties cannot alter the truth of that relationship by putting a different label upon it. . . ."[54] As Carroll J. put it in *In re Sunday Tribune Ltd.*, "[t]he Court must look at the realities of the situation in order to determine whether the relationship of employer and employee in fact exists, regardless

---

49. *Phelan v. Coillte Teo.* [1993] 1 I.R. 18.

50. [1986] I.R. 355.

51. *cf.* several cases concerning players in orchestras, *e.g. Winfield v. London Philharmonic Orchestra Ltd.* [1979] I.C.R. 726, *Addison v. London Philharmonic* [1981] I.C.R. 261 and *Midland Sinfonia Concert Soc. v. Secretary of State* [1981] I.C.R. 454; also *Hall v. Lorrimer* [1994] 1 W.L.R. 676.

52. [1978] 1 W.L.R. 676.

53. *ibid.* at 679. See too *Ready Mixed Concrete* case [1968] 2 Q.B. 497 and *Calder v. H. Kitson Vickers & Son (Engineers) Ltd.* [1988] I.C.R. 233.

54. *Massey* case [1978] 1 W.L.R. at 679.

of how the parties describe themselves."[55] It was held there that the fact that the journalists opted for self-employed status for the purposes of income tax was not determinative; that was merely a convenient arrangement agreed by the Revenue for journalists who would be contributing material to several newspapers at any one time. Similarly, in *Henry Denny & Sons (Ireland) Ltd. v. Minister for Social Welfare*,[56] where the individual had been hired as a shop demonstrator, initially as an employee but later under a contract which described her as self-employed and purported to make her responsible for her own tax affairs, the social welfare deciding officer's finding that, notwithstanding, she was an employee was upheld by the Supreme Court.

Special features of the relationship

In applying the above tests, the court or tribunal will consider several key aspects of the contractual terms, which, if not express, will be implied.

Provide own services

If the engaged person is permitted to get somebody else to do all or any of the work contracted for, the relationship is that of employer and independent contractor. Perhaps the key feature of the contract of employment is that the employee agrees to "provide his own work and skill in the performance of some service" for the employer.[57] That the agreement stipulates that the individual may sub-contract the work to others, with the employer's prior consent, will not take it out of the employment contract category.[58]

Engagement and dismissal

Where the worker is engaged by somebody other than the alleged employer or his agent, often indicates, if anything, that he is employed by the person who did the hiring.[59] Thus, workers in the building industry engaged by "labour only sub-contractors" have been held not to be employees of the construction firm which contracted the work out to the "subbie".[60] Yet circumstances can arise where the construction firm exercises such close control over the work being done and actually pays the engaged persons their remuneration and becomes entitled to dismiss them that they become its employees.[61] In appropriate circumstances, the "sub-

---

55. [1984] I.R. at 508. See too, *Narich Pty Ltd. v. Commissioner Pay Roll Tax* [1984] I.C.R. 286, *Ferguson v. John Dawson & Partners (Construction) Ltd.* [1976] 1 W.L.R. 1213, *Davis v. New England College of Arundel* [1977] I.C.R. 6, *Tyne & Clyde Warehouses Ltd. v. Hamerton* [1978] I.C.R. 661 and *Downish v. Radio Ireland Ltd.* [2001] E.L.R. 1.
56. [1998] 1 I.R. 34.
57. *Ready Mixed Concrete* case [1968] 2 Q.B. 497 at 515 and *Express & Echo Publications Ltd. v. Tanton* [1999] I.C.R. 693.
58. *Henry Denny & Son (Ireland) Ltd. v. Minister for Social Welfare* [1998] 1 I.R. 34.
59. cf. *Kelly v. Owner of the Ship "Miss Evans"* [1913] 2 I.R. 385.
60. *Re C.W. & L. Hughes Ltd.* [1966] 1 W.L.R. 1369.
61. Compare *Limerick C.C. v. Irish Insurance C'mrs* [1934] I.R. 364 with *Down C.C. v. Irish Insurance C'mrs* [1914] 2 I.R. 110; cf. *Graham v. Minister for Industry & Commerce* [1933] I.R. 156.

bie" who hired those workers and who works along with them may even be an employee of the construction firm which awarded him the contract.[62]

Where staff are supplied to an enterprise by an employment agency, who their employer is depends on the nature of the arrangements regarding performing the work, remuneration, discipline, dismissal and the like made between the agency and the enterprise.[63]

Remuneration

If the work is performed gratuitously, the relationship cannot be that of employer and employee;[64] one party must have agreed to work "in consideration of a wage or other remuneration."[65] Often significance will be attached to the method agreed for calculating the remuneration. If payment is based on the amount of time spent doing the job, such as a rate per day, per week, etc., the tendency is to regard the relationship as one of employment.[66] Of course, many employees are paid on the basis of piece rates or their remuneration is determined by reference to the profits made in the employing enterprise. Where the remuneration is paid in aggregate to those engaged as a group and they decide how it should be divided up between them, that is a strong indication that they are not employees,[67] but is far from being decisive on the question.[68]

Times of work

The greater the choice an engaged person has over when the work shall be done, the more likely it is that he will be an independent contractor.[69] Similarly, if the agreed duration of the work is short, the likelihood is that he is self-employed. But there are instances where the engaged person had considerable freedom when to work and so was held to be an employee.[70] Recently, so-called flexi-time has become a feature of many employments.[71]

Workplace

The typical employee attends the employer's factory, office, shop or whatever and performs the work there. But the very nature of certain jobs may require that the work is done away from the employer's establishment, such as interviewing for a market research agency,[72] collecting contributions to be paid into a fund,[73] or as guides taking parties on tours.[74] Where it is convenient for the employer to

---

62. *Limerick C.C. v. Irish Insurance C'mrs* [1934] I.R. 364.
63. See *infra,* p. 32.
64. *cf.* discussion of trainees and apprentices, *infra,* p. 39.
65. *Ready Mixed Concrete* case [1968] 2 Q.B. at 515; compare *Liscoe v. Henry* [1926] I.R. 137 with *Minister for Industry and Commerce v. Jones* [1927] I.R. 216.
66. *e.g. Logue v. Pentland* [1930] I.R. 6.
67. *e.g. O'Friel v. St. Michael's Hospital* [1982] I.L.R.M. 260.
68. *Louth v. Minister for Social Welfare* [1993] 1 I.R. 339.
69. *Minister for Industry and Commerce v. Hales* [1967] I.R. 50 at 69.
70. *e.g. Market Investigations* case [1969] 2 Q.B. 273.
71. *cf. Carmichael v. National Power p.l.c.* [1999] 1 W.L.R. 2042.
72. *Market Investigations* case [1969] 2 Q.B. 273.
73. *Hale's* case [1967] I.R. 50 and *McDermot v. Loy* (Barron J., July 29, 1982).
74. *Carmichael* case [1999] 1 W.L.R. 2042.

have the work done outside his establishment, such as in the worker's own home, the general tendency is to regard the arrangement as one for services, especially because, in those situations, the engaged person usually will have considerable freedom when to do the work, will be paid on the basis of the work actually done, and may even get assistance from others in doing the work.[75] But in appropriate circumstances "outworkers" can be employees, notably where they have undertaken to do a specified quantity of work in a period and that arrangement subsists over a long duration.[76]

Equipment for the work

Where the equipment necessary to do the work in question requires considerable capital investment, significance will be attached to who is to pay for the equipment. If it is the engaged person who must pay, that tends to indicate that he falls on the self-employed side of the line.[77]

Appeals

It is a matter of some debate whether the question about a worker's classification, whether he is an employee or is self-employed, is a question of fact or one of law, or is it what may be termed a mixed question of fact and law.[78] If it is a question of law, the principal practical consequence is that it is far easier for appellate tribunals to overrule decisions made by subordinate tribunals regarding this issue; for most subordinate tribunals' decisions are subject to an appeal on a point of law. But if the classification is a question of fact, then such determinations by subordinate tribunals can only be overturned on appeal in very limited circumstances. The vast majority of claims made under the employment legislation are determined initially by the Employment Appeals Tribunal (E.A.T.), so that the legal or factual nature of the decision concerning the worker's classification affects the extent to which the E.A.T.'s decisions in particular instances can be set aside on appeal.[79]

It was held by the Supreme Court in *Graham v. Minister for Industry and Commerce*,[80] which concerned appealing a determination made under social insurance legislation, that the classification question is one of fact. As Kennedy C.J. put it, "[t]he question whether a particular individual is an employed person . . . or is an independent contractor, is a question of fact often difficult of solution depending in each case on the particular facts of that case."[81] This view was reiterated by Barron J. in *McDermott v. Loy*,[82] which concerned a determination

---

[75.] *e.g. Minister for Industry & Commerce v. Healy* [1941] I.R. 545 and *Westall Richardson Ltd. v. Roulson* [1954] 2 All E.R. 448.

[76.] *e.g. Airfix Footwear Ltd. v. Cope* [1978] I.C.R. 1210 and *Nethermere (St. Neats) Ltd. v. Gardiner* [1984] I.C.R. 612.

[77.] *e.g. Readymix Concrete* case [1968] Q.B. 497, *McAuliffe v. Minister for Social Welfare* [1995] 2 I.R. 238 and *Hughes v. Quinn* [1917] 2 I.R. 442.

[78.] *cf.* Speech of Lord Hoffman in *Carmichael v. National Power p.l.c.* [1999] 1 W.L.R. 2042 and Pitt, "Law, Fact and Casual Workers", 101 L.Q.R. 217 (1985).

[79.] Appeals under the Unfair Dismissals Acts are complete re-hearings of the case.

[80.] [1933] I.R. 156.

[81.] *ibid.* at 159; see too Fitzgibbon J. at 162.

[82.] Barron J., July 29, 1982.

about a taxpayer's status, whether he was subject to schedule D or schedule E. There is no authority that deals with this matter exhaustively in the context of appeals from decisions of the E.A.T. A strong case could be made that the question is one of law and not of fact, on the grounds that determining what class other types of contracts fall into - for instance, whether a contract is one for the sale of goods or is one for work and materials, or is a contract for the sale of land, is regarded generally as a question of law.

Classification of a worker's legal status being regarded as a matter of fact does not render the E.A.T.'s or other decision-maker's (such as the Labour Court, the Social Welfare Appeals Tribunal or the Income Tax Special Commissioners) determination on this matter entirely unappealable. In the first place, appeals from the E.A.T.'s determinations under the Unfair Dismissals Acts to the Circuit Court are by way of a full re-hearing, and appeals from the Circuit Court to the High Court under those Acts are also by way of a re-hearing of the entire evidence.[83] Where, as is generally the case, the right of appeal is confined to points of law, a determination about a worker's classification will be set aside only if the subordinate tribunal applied the wrong legal test or if, on the evidence before that body, the appellate tribunal concludes that no reasonable decision-maker would have made the determination in question.[84]

Agency staff

Where staff are supplied to an enterprise by an employment agency, who their employer is depends on exactly what has been agreed regarding performing the work, remuneration, discipline, dismissal and the like made between the individual, the agency and the enterprise. In *O'Rourke v. Cauldwell*,[85] where the first defendant, a recruitment agency, hired the plaintiff under a one-year contract and he then was assigned to work for the second defendant, on the basis of the written agreement between them it was held that the agency was his employer insofar as liability to pay his salary was concerned. As was pointed out in *McMeechan v. Secretary of State*,[86] the contract or general engagement with an agency may not be a contract of employment but, when an agency worker is on a particular assignment, the relationship may then become an employment contract. There, the plaintiff had an agreement with an employment agency whereby he would furnish services to it as a self-employed worker; he would not be obliged to accept any assignment given to him by the agency but, if he did accept, he would carry out instructions. He was paid a weekly wage, calculated on an hourly rate, from which social welfare contributions and income tax were deducted. The agency could dismiss him summarily for improper conduct. Following the agency's insolvency, he sought payment in respect of wages due to him from the insolvency fund. It was held by the Court of Appeal that, at least when he was engaged on a specific assignment, he was an employee of the agency. The Court

---

83. *McCabe v. Lisney & Co.* [1981] I.L.R.M. 289.
84. *McAuliffe v. Minister for Social Welfare* [1995] 2 I.R. 238 and *Lee Ting Sang v. Chung Chi Keung* [1990] 2 A.C. 374.
85. [1998] E.L.R. 287.
86. [1997] I.C.R. 549.

left open the question whether his overriding contract with the agency was also one of employment.[87]

Beginning with section 13 of the Unfair Dismissals (Amendment) Act 1977, most of the employment protection statutes enacted since then define "employee" to include agency staff. Thus, in section 2(1) of the Organisation of Working Time Act 1977, a contract of employment is defined to include:

> "any other contract whereby an individual agrees with another person, who is carrying on the business of an employment agency within the meaning of the Employment Agency Act 1971, and is acting in the course of that business, to do or perform personally any work or service for a third person (whether or not the third person is a party to the contract)."

Office-holders

At times a distinction is drawn between employees and office-holders; on other occasions office-holders are regarded as a particular species of employee. An office has been described as "a position or place to which certain duties are attached, especially of a more or less public character; a position of trust, authority or service under constituted authority; a place in the administration of government, the public service, the direction of a corporation, company, society etc."[88] Most senior public sector appointees are office-holders;[89] numerous what may be termed intermediate public sector posts are classified by legislation as offices. Whether these office-holders are employees for the purposes of the general employment protection legislation rarely arises because several of those Acts do not apply to non-industrial public service workers.[90] On occasions, office-holders have been held not to be employees; for instance, the Commissioner of the Garda Síochána was held not to be a mere servant or employee of the State,[91] a rate collector was held not to be a "clerk or servant" of the corporation which appointed him,[92] and a district health nurse was held not to be a "workman" for the purposes of the Workmen's Compensation Acts.[93] Regardless of their employment law status, the remuneration of all public service office-holders is taxable under the Schedule E.[94]

As for private sector officers, the only modern legislation affecting them as such is Schedule E of the Taxes Consolidation Act 1997, which renders the emoluments deriving from any "office or employment" subject to tax under that schedule.[95] Among the principal private sector offices are directorships of companies and certain senior positions in trade unions and in various voluntary, social, sporting or philanthropic bodies. Whether a particular office-holder is an

---

87. Compare *Construction Industry Training Board v. Labour Force Ltd.* [1970] 3 All E.R. 220, *Costain Building & Civil Engineering Ltd. v. Smith* [2000] I.C.R. 215, *Montgomery v. Johnson Underwood Ltd.* Times L.R. March 16 2001 and *Saltire Press Ltd. v. AB* (1998) S.C. 718 (where workers were supplied by their union).

88. *Edwards v. Clinch* [1981] 1 Ch.1 at 5.

89. *Walker v. Dept. of Social, Community and Family Affairs* [1999] E.L.R. 260.

90. See *post,* p. 279 *et seq.*

91. *Garvey v. Ireland* [1981] I.R. 75.

92. *People v. Warren* [1945] I.R. 24.

93. *O'Brien v. Tipperary South Riding Board of Health* [1938] I.R. 761.

94. *Mitchell & Eldon v. Ross* [1960] Ch. 498.

95. See *post,* p. 323 *et seq.*

employee for the purposes of employment legislation will depend on all the incidents of the office; the tests for determining employee status, described above,
will be applied in the same way. In *In re Dairy Lee Ltd.*,[96] it was held that, for the
purposes of preferential debts in a company's liquidation, a salaried full-time
executive director was an employee. According to Kenny J., when a company
director other than a managing director is working whole-time for the company
"the inference that he was a . . . salaried employee seems . . . to be justified unless
there is evidence that he was a whole time director only and was paid as such."[97]
But that inference can be rebutted in various circumstances.[98] On occasion, even
managing directors have been held in the circumstances to be employees of their
company,[99] even where they also were the sole or controlling shareholders.[100]
Among the matters which suggest that a director may be an employee are his
being designated by the company as, for instance, managing director or technical
director, his hiring being the subject of a special contract or it being specially
minuted at a board meeting, his remuneration being by way of salary rather than
directors' fees, the main tasks contracted for being performed under the board's
directions. Regardless of their employment law status, all company directors'
remuneration is taxable under Schedule E.

Where the senior clerk to a set of barristers' chambers in England agreed to
provide, at his own expense, a full clerking service in return for a specified percentage of chambers' earnings, he was held not to hold an office that was taxable
under Schedule E.[101]

Workers

Occasionally, employment legislation uses the term "worker" instead of
employee, most notably some of the E.C. rules regarding employment[102] and the
definition of a "trade dispute" in the Industrial Relations Act 1990.[103] This term
was also used in the Workmen's Compensation Acts; for the purposes of those
Acts workers were employees or apprentices. The now repealed Truck Act 1831,
which required payment of wages in cash and not in kind, applied to "artificers",
who were defined as "workmen" engaged in manual labour. Workers for the purposes of that Act were held to include certain categories who would be regarded
as self-employed under modern legislation, such as "gangers" and their men
working on railways, the "butty" in coal mines, and "lumpers" in the building
industry.

---

[96]. [1976] I.R. 314.
[97]. *ibid.* at 316.
[98]. *e.g. Parsons v. Albert J. Parsons & Sons Ltd.* [1979] I.C.R. 271 and *Fleming v. Xaniar Ltd.* (1998)
S.C. 8.
[99]. *e.g. Folami v. Nigerline (U.K.) Ltd.* [1978] I.C.R. 272 and *Smith v. Secretary of State for Trade
and Industry* [2000] I.C.R. 69.
[100]. *Secretary of State for Trade and Industry v. Bottrill* [1999] I.C.R. 592 and *Connolly v. Sellers Arenascene Ltd.* Times L.R. 8 March 2001.
[101]. *McMenamin v. Diggles* [1991] 1 W.L.R. 1249.
[102]. See *post,* p. 153 and C. Barnard, *E.C. Employment Law* (2nd ed., 2000), pp.133-136.
[103]. s.8.

EXCLUDED AND OTHER EMPLOYMENTS

It has already been remarked that legislation which regulates various aspects of the employment relationship is very much a modern phenomenon. Most of these laws date from either the mid-1930s or from the 1970s and later. Some of these laws apply only to a particular type of workforce, such as those employed in factories or in offices or in shops; others purport to apply practically universally. A feature which runs through many of these laws is that certain categories of employees are excluded from their scope - some categories being excluded by only some of the laws, other categories being excluded by all or virtually all of the laws. Some of the laws empower the Minister by order, usually requiring the Oireachtas' approval, either to extend or to restrict the scope of these excluded categories.[104] Only one of these laws contains an exempting technique that features in labour legislation in some countries, *viz.* if a collective agreement applicable to a category of workers provides for matters in a manner at least equivalent to what the legislation provides for them, then the legislation will not apply to them for so long as that agreement is in force.[105] Additionally, there are several occupations in respect of which the employment Acts make special provision, either designating them as employees or as self-employed for particular purposes. Several of these occupations are difficult to classify as one or the other, so that the legislature intervened to avoid uncertainty regarding their position. The Social Welfare legislation classifies various groups as either employed or self-employed for the purpose of those Acts and enables the Minister to further classify persons.[106]

The public service

Civil servants and numerous other categories of non-industrial public service workers are excluded from the scope of many of the employment Acts.[107] There is considerable divergence between the Acts as to which public sector employees are excluded and even as to the legislative technique used for making the exclusion. Because the public sector is highly unionised and elaborate procedures exist for dealing with employment grievances that arise there,[108] perhaps there is not quite the same need for protective legislation as there is in the private sector.

Thus, the Unfair Dismissals Acts 1977-93 do not apply to, *inter alia*, the following categories:[109]

(a) A person employed by or under the State;[110]

(b) Members of the defence forces and of the Garda Síochána;

[104.] *cf. Minister for Industry & Commerce v. Hales* [1967] I.R. 50.
[105.] Organisation of Working Time Act 1997, s.4(5).
[106.] Social Welfare (Consolidation) Act 1993, Sched.1 and *Hales* case [1967] I.R. 50.
[107.] See *post,* p. 279 *et seq.*
[108.] See *Industrial Relations Law,* Chap.7.
[109.] 1977 Act, s.2(1).
[110.] See *post,* p. 281.

(c) Officers of a local authority or of a health board, vocational education committee or committee of agriculture;[111]

(d) A person being trained by or apprenticed to FAS.[112]

By contrast, for the purposes of the Employment Equality Act 1998, an employee is defined as including a person holding office or in the service of the State, including members of the Garda Síochána, the Defence Forces, the civil service and also officers and servants of any local authority, health board or vocational education committee.[113] Although the Redundancy Payments Acts are concerned with the consequences of various changes in business, the term business there is defined to include "any activity carried on . . . by a public or local authority or a Department of State, and the performance of its functions by a public or a local authority or a Department of State."[114]

However, since the redundancy legislation applies only to persons insured for all benefits under the Social Welfare legislation,[115] most public service officers are outside its scope. As has been explained, E.C. Directives which have not been appropriately implemented by the State, if they contain very specific requirements, can have "horizontal effect" against the State and State agencies.[116]

Temporary and part-timers

In order to obtain the protection of many statutory provisions, especially with regard to dismissal from employment, the employee must have worked continuously for the employer in question for a specified period — be it 13 weeks, 12 months or two years, as the case may be.[117] Therefore, those who have worked for the employer for less than the requisite period do not get the benefit of the relevant Act. Many of these Acts moreover, only apply if the employee works for a minimum period in each working day or week. Up to 1991 the commonest requirement was being expected to work for not less than 18 hours in a week; by the Workers Protection (Regular Part Time Employees) Act 1991, employees who worked for no less than eight hours a day and for more than 13 continuous weeks with an employer, were afforded protection under most of the modern Acts.[118]

These Acts also lay down or incorporate special rules for reckoning an employee's duration of continuous employment, such as what interruptions shall not be regarded as breaking continuity and whether time off work for certain purposes shall be deemed to be time spent in employment for those purposes.[119] There are no continuity requirements for the laws against discrimination.

[111.] Amended by 1993 Act, s.3(a); see *post,* p. 281.
[112.] *cf. FAS v. Minister for Social Welfare* (Sup. Ct., May 23, 1995), *Morey v. Rock Foundation* [1997] E.L.R. 236 and *Flood v. Athlone Bowl and Leisure Ltd.* [1997] E.L.R. 67.
[113.] s.2(1).
[114.] s.2(1).
[115.] s.4(1).
[116.] *Foster v. British Gas Corp* (Case C-188/89) [1990] E.C.R. 3313.
[117.] See *post,* pp. 188 *et seq.*
[118.] See *post,* p. 192.
[119.] See *post,* p. 193.

Beyond retiring age

Several of the employment Acts exclude employees who have reached the normal retiring age or pensionable age for similar employees, notably the Unfair Dismissals Acts 1977-93, and the Redundancy Payments Acts 1967-1979.[120] Sixty-six years of age is the maximum age for insurable employment under the Social Welfare Acts and employees over that age are in any event excluded from the scope of several employment Acts notably in respect of redundancy payments and maternity protection.

Under-aged

Employers are legally free to employ persons over the age of 18; the Protection of Young Persons (Employment) Act 1996 places various restrictions on the employment of children and young persons regarding the kinds of work they may do and the hours during which they may work.[121] The minimum age for being an insured worker under the Social Welfare legislation is 16 years, so that the requisite continuity of employment for the purposes of several employment Acts does not commence until that age, notably for redundancy compensation and maternity protection.

Employer a close relative

Several of the employment Acts exclude employees who are close family relations of their employers. The Protection of Young Persons (Employment) Act 1996,[122] and the three principal Acts dealing with dismissal from employment (the Minimum Notice and Terms of Employment Act 1973, the Unfair Dismissals Acts 1977-93, and the Redundancy Payments Acts 1967-1979) do not apply where the employer is a relative as defined in those Acts and, additionally, where both parties dwell in the employer's house or on his farm. The legislative formula used for this purpose is that these Acts shall not apply to a person who is employed by his spouse, father, mother, grandfather, grandmother, stepfather, stepmother, son, daughter, grandson, granddaughter, stepson, stepdaughter, brother, sister, half-brother or half-sister who is a member of the employer's household, and whose place of employment is a private dwelling-house or a farm in which both the employer and the employee reside.

Uninsured

Employees who are not insured for all benefits under the Social Welfare Acts do not fall within the Redundancy Payments Acts or the Protection of Employees (Employers' Insolvency) Act 1984.

---

[120] See *post,* p. 199.

[121] See *post,* pp. 87-88.

[122] s.9 and Protection of Young Persons (Employment of Close Relatives) Regulations 1997, S.I. No. 2.

Illegal employment

A person's employment may be illegal in whole or in part. For instance, he may be a non-E.C. alien working in a job which has not been duly authorised by the Minister for Justice;[123] he may be a child or young person employed in breach of the Protection of Young Persons (Employment) Act 1996, or of apprenticeship regulations laid down under section 27 of the Industrial Training Act 1967; or he may be a "disqualified person" under section 37 of the Stock Exchange Act 1995, or a person whose employment is prohibited by section 36 of the Investment Intermediaries Act 1995; or he may be working in the aviation industry without the requisite licence. Perhaps the commonest example of partial illegal employment is where the parties do not declare to the Revenue the full remuneration being paid; all or part of the agreed remuneration is "paid under the table". Apart from a "trade dispute" case in the 1950s,[124] the Superior Courts do not appear to have given careful consideration to the employment law rights and obligations of persons in what may loosely be described as in illegal employment. In that case, it was held that a dispute about the dismissal of an under-age barman, who had just joined a trade union, could not be a trade dispute under the Trade Disputes Act 1906.

Formerly, the practice in the Employment Appeals Tribunal was to dismiss claims brought by illegally employed workers, even where the element of unlawfulness was tax evasion in collusion with their employer. A similar practice was followed in Britain until recently.[125] In *Lewis v. Squash (Ireland) Ltd.*,[126] the plaintiff's claim for unfair dismissal was rejected by the E.A.T. because much of his remuneration had been dressed up as expenses. There the Tribunal followed several English tribunal decisions that the maxim *ex turpi causa non oritur actio* debars enforcing statutory rights arising from an employment relationship which is significantly tainted by illegality. The justice of this reasoning does not appear to have been questioned on appeal. In any event, for the purpose of unfair dismissals, the position was changed in 1993; contravention of the income tax or the social welfare legislation no longer precludes persons from obtaining redress under the Unfair Dismissals Acts 1977-93.[127] The position is similarly with the National Minimum Wage Act 2000[128] and also, it would appear, under the equality legislation.[129]

Trainees and apprentices

The definition of employee in many of the employment Acts includes apprentices; insured employments under the Social Welfare laws include apprenticeships. Special provision is made in sections 3 and 4 of the Unfair Dismissals Act 1977 regarding the requisite continuity of employment of probationers, trainees

---

[123.] *cf. Gleeson v. Chung* [1997] 1 I.R. 521.

[124.] *Corry v. National Union of Vintners* [1950] I.R. 315.

[125.] *Hall v. Woolston Hall Leisure Ltd.* [2001] 1 W.L.R. 225.

[126.] [1983] I.L.R.M. 363. Compare *Hewcastle Catering Ltd. v. Ahmed* [1982] I.C.R. 626.

[127.] s.7(d).

[128.] s.40.

[129.] *Supra,* n.125.

and apprentices for protection under that Act.[130] Where they are under 18 years of age, trainees and apprentices are covered by the Protection of Young Persons (Employment) Act 1996.[131] Persons undergoing training or receiving work experience are deemed to be employees for the purposes of the Safety, Health and Welfare at Work Act 1989.

Where special legislative provision has not been made for them, the question arises whether trainees and apprentices are employed under a contract of employment. The two major cases concern insurability of student nurses under the Social Welfare legislation.[132] In *Sister Dolores v. Minister for Social Welfare*,[133] the appellant was in charge of a children's hospital which trained young girls to nurse children by way of a two-year course, for which modest fees were charged. During the first year the girls were given a small monthly allowance, which was doubled in the second year. It was held that these trainees were not employed under a contract of service. According to Budd J., while it was clearly implied that they should do certain valuable work in the hospital, "the fact that a person does work of value to another does not of itself make that person an employee."[134] The work they did was "also part and parcel of their necessary training and part of the specialised training they receive."[135] Although they were paid remuneration that had some bearing on the work they did, what they got was more "properly described as pocket money."[136] Although they could be dismissed for neglecting their duties and for misconduct, it was held that the hospital's authority to dismiss them was not commensurate with an employer's ordinary dismissal powers. A very important consideration was that their training was a means to an end, it was to "fit them for a calling" and, when they are so fitted, they then "will become properly speaking, employed in that calling."[137] In *National Maternity Hospital v. Minister for Social Welfare*,[138] where the facts were very similar, Haugh J. concluded that student nurses at Holles Street Hospital were not employees, because "the preponderant feature of the relationship between the Hospital [and them] was almost entirely that of student and master."[139] In England, it has been held that police cadets are not employees for the purposes of the legislation on unfair dismissals[140] and that research fellows at Oxbridge Colleges are not employees for the purposes of laws against sex discrimination.[141] In New Zealand, paid student teachers were held not to be employees.[142]

[130.] See *post,* p. 200.

[131.] See *post,* post pp. 87-88.

[132.] A much earlier case is *The Case of Pupil Teachers and Monitors* [1913] 1 I.R. 219. *cf.* Reg. 7 of Schedule 1 to Social Welfare (Consolidation) Act 1993, that deems to be employments "employment as a trainee, student, pupil or probationary nurse or midwife".

[133.] [1962] I.R. 77.

[134.] *ibid.* at 83.

[135.] *ibid.*

[136.] *ibid.*

[137.] *ibid.*

[138.] [1960] I.R. 74.

[139.] *ibid.* at 81.

[140.] *Wilts Police Authority v. Wynn* [1981] 1 Q.B. 75.

[141.] *Hugh-Jones v. St. Johns College Cambridge* [1979] 1 C.R. 848.

[142.] *New Zealand Educational Inst. v. Director General* [1981] 1 N.Z.L.R. 538.

In the *Sister Dolores* case it was argued that, even if the student nurses were not employees, they were apprentices, but that view was rejected by the Supreme Court. According to the Court, "in order to establish the relation of apprentice and master there must be a binding agreement on the part of the apprentice to serve for a definite period and, on the part of the master, a reciprocal agreement to teach the apprentice his trade or calling."[143] The evidence there did not disclose a reciprocal contractual undertaking to serve and to teach for the entire two-year period; there was nothing to prevent student nurses from leaving at any time. No matter how practical the training is, there must be a "binding" of the student to his teacher for there to be an apprenticeship.

Out-workers

By "out-workers" is meant persons who perform their tasks on their own pre-mises, such as in their own homes. The numbers involved in this kind of work have increased considerably in recent years, mainly on account of developments in computer technology. Some employment Acts stipulate that they do not apply to out-workers, notably the Organisation of Working Time Act 1997.[144]

Whether an out-worker is employed under a contract of service or a contract for services depends on the entire nature of the arrangements with whoever he is working for. In *Minister for Industry and Commerce v. Healy*,[145] where the defen-dant worked in her own home making trousers in different styles for a tailoring firm which supplied her with the materials, it was held that she was an indepen-dent contractor. It was said that "a person does not cease to be an independent contractor because he is in a humble position."[146] That case involved a prosecu-tion under the Conditions of Employment Act 1936, and the Court emphasised that the Act's penal provisions should be construed strictly in favour of the defen-dant. In a 1984 English case,[147] the Court of Appeal accepted the conclusions of an industrial tribunal that a group of out-workers were employees. Their jobs involved sewing parts on to clothes, using machines provided by the company; they were paid in accordance with the amount of work they did, they had no fixed hours and they were not obliged to accept any particular quantity of work. It was held that "[t]he fact that the out-workers could fix their own hours of work, could take holidays and time off when they wished and could vary how many garments they were willing to take on any day or even to take none on a particular day . . . does not as a matter of law negative the existence of [an employment] con-tract."[148]

Religious activities

In what circumstances are priests, ministers, clergymen, nuns and the like, going about their ordinary activities, employed under a contract of employment? All

---

143. *Sister Dolores v. Minister for Social Welfare* [1960] I.R. 77.
144. See definition in s.2(1).
145. [1941] I.R. 545.
146. *ibid.* at 553.
147. *Nethermere (St. Neots) Ltd. v. Gardiner* [1984] I.C.R. 612.
148. *ibid.* at 634; similarly *Airfix Footwear Ltd. v. Cope* [1978] I.C.R. 1210.

depends on the entire circumstances surrounding the activity in question; the general practices of the different religious denominations vary considerably. The mere fact that an individual working is acting under the direction of religious superiors does not prevent him from being an employee. Thus, in *Dolan v. K.*,[149] which concerned a nun who was employed as a national teacher in a school managed by her order, it was held that her remuneration was taxable under Schedule E. That she handed her entire remuneration over to her religious superiors, as required by the rules of the Order, did not affect the taxable nature of those payments; she still was "exercising an office in respect of which she [was] paid a salary."[150]

In several English cases, which concerned religious officers being removed from their positions by their superior authorities, it was held that the relationship between them and their superiors could not be characterised as a contract either of service or for services. As Lord Templeman put it in a case involving the dismissal of a pastor in the Presbyterian Church of Wales, "the duties owed by the pastor to the church are not contractual or enforceable. A pastor is called and accepts the call. He does not devote his working life but his whole life to the church and his religion. His duties are defined and his activities are dictated not by contract but by conscience. He is a servant of God. If his manner of serving God is not acceptable to the church, then his pastorate can be brought to an end by the church in accordance with [its] rules."[151] On the other hand, it was accepted that "it is possible for a man to be employed as a servant or as an independent contractor to carry out duties which are exclusively spiritual."[152]

---

[149] [1944] I.R. 470.

[150] *ibid.* at 477. *cf. Wright v. Day* [1895] 2 I.R. 337 and *O'Dea v. O'Briain* [1992] I.L.R.M. 364.

[151] *Davies v. Presbyterian Church of Wales* [1986] 1 W.L.R. 323, at 329. Similarly, *President of the Methodist Conference v. Parfitt* [1984] 1 Q.B. 368, *Singh v. Gurdwara* [1990] I.C. 309, *Diocese of Southwark v. Coker* [1998] I.C.R. 140, *Mabon v. Conference of the Methodist Church* [1998] 3 N.Z.L.R. 513, *Greek Orthodox Community v. Ermogenous* [2000] S.A.S.C. 329 and *Millen v. Presbyterian Church in Ireland* [2000] E.L.R. 292.

[152] *Davies* case [1986] 1 W.L.R. at 329. *cf. Salvation Army v. Canterbury Hotel Employees Union* [1985] N.Z.L.R. 366.

CHAPTER 3

DETERMINING THE TERMS
OF EMPLOYMENT

Before discussing the actual rights and obligations of employers and workers, the mode of ascertaining what are the terms of employment calls for consideration of, in particular, the process of hiring workers and ascertaining what terms are incorporated in the contracts of employment.

HIRING WORKERS

Not long ago, the process by which workers were hired was not subject to any legal regulation. Employers were free to hire whosoever they chose and were entitled to refuse employment on any grounds, except of course where they were contractually bound under a collective agreement to do otherwise, for instance in "closed shop" clauses. Modern equality legislation has significantly reduced employers' freedom to hire, as has legislation aimed at protecting young persons at the workplace and restricting the employment of aliens. The Employment Equality Act 1998, which prohibits discrimination in employment, applies *inter alia* to "access to employment" and to "training or experience"[1] as well as to pay and conditions at work and other aspects of the relationship.

Fairness in hiring public service workers is secured principally by the Civil Service Commissioners Act 1956 and by the Local Appointments Commission for local government workers. Apart from statutory provisions to that effect, it would not seem that public service vacancies must be advertised and be the subject of a competition between applicants; an endeavour to establish the contrary did not succeed in the Supreme Court in July 2000.[2] The equality legislation applies in the public as well as in the private sector but the holding of a public service job can be conditional on the person being an Irish citizen and/or resident, and also on proficiency in the Irish language.[3] Decisions in the public sector not to hire an applicant for a post can be challenged by way of judicial review on substantive and also on procedural grounds but a rejected candidate has no legally enforceable right to be told why he was not hired.[4]

At times employees are recruited through agencies which are regulated by the Employment Agency Act 1971, which requires all such agencies to be licensed and prohibits them from charging any fee for agreeing to seek employment for another. Of course, the employer who takes on a person on an agency's books

---

[1] s.8(1)(a) and (c), (5) and (7).
[2] *Riordan v. An Taoiseach* S.C., July 21, 2000.
[3] Employment Equality Act 1998, s.36(2) and (3).
[4] *O'Dwyer v. McDonagh* [1997] E.L.R. 91.

will be charged a fee. Section 7(1) of the 1971 Act empowers the Minister to adopt a scale of approved fees for those agencies. Much of the employment legislation enacted since 1993 treats what may be described as agency staff as employees for the purpose of those Acts; generally as employees of the person legally obliged to pay the remuneration.

Obtaining references is an important aspect of getting a job. It probably is an implied term of most employment contracts that the employer will give a reference, if requested.[5] False statements in references can be the subject of defamation claims, although a practical difficulty is ascertaining what exactly the reference said to the prospective employer who refused to hire an applicant. It used to be thought no liability could arise in respect of erroneous references due to negligence, but that is no longer the case; employers providing references owe a duty of care to the employee who is the subject of the reference[6] and also to the addressee.[7]

There is no legislation that deals with the various testing practices, such as polygraphs, psychological and personality testing, intelligence and aptitude testing, physical ability testing, medical testing, general testing, drug and HIV testing, and fingerprinting. But some forms of testing may fall foul of the equality legislation and, possibly, the constitutionally guaranteed implied right of privacy.[8] This very controversial question of testing does not appear to have been addressed in the Irish case law to date. Nor is there any legislation regulating a prospective employers' access to job applicants' criminal records and credit records.

Whether a job applicant has indeed been hired depends on the contract law principles of capacity, offer and acceptance, although estoppel may play a role here too.

THE EMPLOYMENT CONTRACT

Apart from certain public service offices, the employment relationship is founded on contract. Rights and obligations, and the remedies for their breach arising from the employment relationship, therefore, are governed mainly by the law of contract.[9]

Formality

The great majority of employment contracts are oral in the sense that there is no actual written contract; the employee agrees to work on certain terms that are

---

5. *cf. Kidd v. Axa Equity Assur. Soc.* [2000] I.R.L.R. 301 and *Coote v. Granada Hospitality Ltd.* (Case C 185/97) [1998] E.C.R. 5199.
6. *Spring v. Guardian Assurance p.l.c.* [1995] 2 A.C. 296.
7. *e.g. Donlon v. Colonial Mutual Group Ltd.* [1998] S.C. 244
8. *Cf. Entroup v. Imperial Oil Ltd.* 189 D.L.R. (4th) 14 (2000).
9. See, generally, R. Friel, *The Law of Contract* (2nd ed., 2000), Chaps. 3-5, and M. Freedland, *The Contract of Employment* (1976), Chap. 1. *Cf.* Smith, "Is Employment Properly Analysed in Terms of a Contract?", 6 N.Z.L.Rev. 341 (1975) and Elias, "The Structure of the Employment Contract" [1982] C.L.P. 95.

explained verbally or which are set out in some written document drafted by the employer alone or with a trade union. Contracts for senior executive positions, which may impose certain elaborate duties and provide for complex remuneration arrangements, tend to take a written form; either the entire contract is a single document or it is a brief document which refers to terms and conditions that are set out in some other detailed document. The Appendix to this book contains model service contracts which may prove useful to the reader as precedents;[10] one is a standard terms and conditions of employment, the other an executive employment agreement for company directors.

There are two kinds of employment contract that the law requires to be written. Since 1797 the articles of agreement under which merchant seamen are hired must not only be in writing but must follow a prescribed form.[11] Although there is no equivalent absolute obligation in respect of apprentices, at common law, unless articles of apprenticeship are in writing and signed by both parties, the apprentice cannot enforce the employer's obligation to teach and the special restrictions against being dismissed. There are special statutory rules for apprentice solicitors[12] and for apprentice seamen.[13]

Express terms

The express terms of the employment contract are the terms actually agreed by the parties. Where the contract is written, these terms will appear on the document; where it is oral, practical difficulties can arise in proving what was agreed. Certain terms are forbidden by law, especially terms that purport to exclude application of protective legislation.[14] General contract law principles about illegal terms also apply, most notably the principle against unreasonable restraint of trade.

Where a difference arises between the parties concerning an issue which is covered by an express term, then it is a question of the true construction of that term as to what the outcome should be.[15] The law does not lay down any special rules for the interpretation of employment contracts as such. However, the courts tend to require good faith observance of specific terms[16] and to insist that terms which confer a wide discretion on one party (usually the employer) should not be exercised unreasonably in the circumstances.[17] On the other hand, it is not for the courts to re-write extravagant terms to which the parties actually have agreed.[18]

[10.] *post,* pp. 262-264.

[11.] Merchant Shipping Act 1894, s.114.

[12.] Solicitors Act 1954, ss.24-39.

[13.] Merchant Shipping Act 1894, ss.105-109.

[14.] *e.g.* Unfair Dismissals Act 1977, s.13; most of the modern employment legislation contains a similar provision.

[15.] See, generally, R. Friel, *Law of Contract* (2nd ed., 2000), Chap. 12.

[16.] See *infra,* pp. 48-49.

[17.] *Knox v. Down D.C.* [1981] I.R.L.R. 452 and *Johnstone v. Bloomsbury Health Authority* [1992] Q.B. 333.

[18.] There is no Irish equivalent of the U.K.'s Unfair Contract Terms Act 1997, other than regulations adopted in 1995 (S.I. No. 27) to deal with unfair terms in consumer contracts, involving selling goods or supplying services to "consumers".

In addition to the agreed terms, the Employment Equality Act 1998 inserts into employment contracts terms for equal remuneration and for equal terms and conditions of employment.[19] Orders made under Part IV of the Industrial Relations Act 1946 for minimum wages, terms and conditions operate similarly.[20]

Implied terms

Frequently, differences arise about a question on which the parties never reached actual agreement. When the contract was being made, they may never even have considered the matter or they may have done so briefly without reaching any firm conclusion. A frequent example is sick pay — should the employee be paid his basic wages while absent on account of illness?[21] The courts may be able to answer such questions by implying a term into the contract and thereby filling the legal void.[22] Whether particular terms should be implied into employment, commercial and other contracts is a matter that often comes before the courts. Judges will not readily imply terms; generally the parties themselves and not courts should decide what terms they are contracting under.

Implied from the facts

A common form of implied term is one which is implied by virtue of the particular facts of the case. In deciding whether to fill a gap in the contract by implying a term, the test usually adopted is, if the matter in question had been considered by the parties at the time they made their contract, would they almost certainly have agreed to the suggested term. The court attempts to guess what the parties would have decided had they faced up to the question at that time. As an English judge put it in one instance, "*prima facie* that which in any contract is left to be implied and need not be expressed is something that is so obvious that it goes without saying; so that, if while the parties were making their bargain, an officious bystander were to suggest some express provision for it in the agreement, they would testily suppress him with a common 'Oh, of course'."[23] Perhaps a more exhaustive formulation of the test is that of Lord Simon of Glaisdale:

> "For a term to be implied, the following conditions (which may overlap) must be satisfied: (1) it must be reasonable and equitable; (2) it must be necessary to give business efficacy to the contract, so no term will be implied if the contract is effective without it; (3) it must be so obvious that it 'goes without saying'; (4) it must be capable of clear expression; (5) it must not contradict any express term of the contract."[24]

Unless the existence of a term is practically compelled by these tests, it will not be implied by the courts. Merely because the term in question is a quite rea-

---

[19] ss.19, 21, 29 and 30.
[20] s.44.
[21] See *post*, p. 78.
[22] See, generally, R. Friel, *The Law of Contract* (2nd ed. 2000), Chap. 13.
[23] *Shirlaw v. Southern Foundries (1926) Ltd.* [1939] 2 K.B. 206 at 227.
[24] *B.P. Refinery (Westernport) Pty. Ltd. v. Shire of Hastings*, 52 A.L.J.L.R. 20 at 26. *cf. McLory v. Post Office* [1992] I.C.R. 758.

sonable one is not sufficient.[25] Thus, for instance, the courts have refused to imply into employment contracts a term that wages were not to be paid during absence on account of illness;[26] that the employer would take reasonable care to ensure that his employees' effects were not stolen;[27] that the employee would be appropriately insured in respect of injuries he suffered in the course of his work when he is working in some foreign country;[28] that the employee would be appropriately insured in respect of injuries suffered in an exceptionally dangerous occupation;[29] that the employer hospital would appoint a second permanent consultant to ease the burden on the plaintiff medical consultant.[30] Because employment contracts establish a somewhat unique continuing relationship, some courts tend to imply terms in circumstances where those terms might not be implied in ordinary commercial transactions.

When determining whether a particular term should be implied, the courts take account of various indicia. One of these is the subsequent conduct of the parties; what they did after the employment commenced is a very useful indication of what term they would have agreed upon when the contract was being made. As is explained below, where they are not directly incorporated into the contract, provisions in collective agreements applying to the workplace are often implied into the contract.[31] Very relevant also are works rules and appropriate customs and practices obtaining in the workplace.[32] Because the implication of terms into a contract is regarded as a question of law rather than of fact,[33] a decision by a lower tribunal or court on such a question can be fully reviewed on appeal to a higher court on a point of law.

Implied by law

Exceptionally, a term will be implied into the contract as a matter of law.[34] That is to say, because of the very nature of the legal relationship in question, the courts hold that the contract embodies certain common incidents. As Stephenson L.J. explained:

"There are contracts which establish a relationship, *e.g.* of master and servant, landlord and tenant, which demand by their nature and subject matter certain obligations, and those obligations the general law will impose and imply, not as satisfying the business efficacy or officious bystander tests applicable to commercial contracts where there is no such relationship, but as legal incidents of those other kinds of contractual relationship. In considering what obligations to imply into contracts of these kinds which are not complete, the actions of the parties may properly be considered. But the

[25] *e.g. Hughes v. Greenwich London B.C.* [1994] 1 A.C. 170.
[26] *Orman v. Savill Sportswear Ltd.* [1960] 1 W.L.R. 1055.
[27] *Deyong v. Shenburn* [1946] K.B. 227.
[28] *Reid v. Rush & Tompkins Group p.l.c.* [1990] 1 W.L.R. 212.
[29] *Sweeney v. Duggan* [1997] 2 I.R. 531.
[30] *Sullivan v. Southern Health Board* [1997] 3 I.R. 123.
[31] See *infra*, pp. 54-58.
[32] See *infra*, p. 53.
[33] *O'Brien v. Associated Fire Alarm Ltd.* [1969] 1 W.L.R. 1916.
[34] See, generally, G. Treitel, *The Law of Contract* (9th ed., 1995), pp.188 *et seq.*

obligation must be a necessary term; that is, required by their relationship. It is not enough that it would be a reasonable term."[35]

By implying a term as a matter of law, the court is laying down a general rule of law, that in contracts of this type a particular term almost invariably will exist unless the express terms of the contract or special circumstances of the case indicate otherwise.[36] These terms in employment contracts include the employer's duty of care for the safety of his employees and the employee's reciprocal duty to take reasonable care in how he performs his duties,[37] and also the employee's obligation of confidentiality.[38] Another way of describing this type of implied term is the common law of employment rights and obligations. Although the obligations arising from such an implied term often correspond with duties imposed on the basis of tort, it would seem that a duty of care in tort cannot exist in Irish law in certain circumstances where a contractual obligation to take care would not be implied.[39]

Good faith performance

A question that arises is whether the reciprocal obligations employers and employees assume are subject to an overriding good faith requirement. Traditionally, English and Irish law did not require parties to most types of contracts, including commercial and employment contracts, to exercise their express rights subject to some good faith constraint. In contrast, the laws of most civil law countries oblige contracting parties to act in good faith; provisions to that effect are contained in Article 1134(3) of the French Civil Code and in Article 242 of the German Civil Code and in the U.S.A., section 1-203 of the Uniform Commercial Code stipulates that every contract or duty imposed by that code "imposes an obligation of good faith in its performance or enforcement." Most modern text books on Contract Law do not contain any extended discussion of whether or in what circumstances a duty of good faith performance arises and what exactly is required by good faith in those instances where the principle applies; there are notable exceptions to this pattern.[40]

Apart perhaps from the odd dictum that the employment relationship is one of "mutual trust and confidence", the Irish Superior Courts do not appear to have addressed this question foursquare, either as a general proposition or in the context of employment contracts. For many years it has been accepted that, in certain discreet contexts, a particular obligation of good faith arises, such as, for instance, the obligation imposed on employees not to disclose confidential information where their employers would suffer loss in consequence[41] and the obligation on certain senior employees to disclose misconduct on the part of other

---

[35] *Mears v. Safecar Security Ltd.* [1983] 1 Q.B. 54 at 78.

[36] *cf. Siney v. Dublin Corp.* [1980] I.R. 400.

[37] *Lister v. Romford Ice and Cold Storage Co.* [1957] A.C. 555.

[38] *Thomas Marshall (Exports) Ltd. v. Guinle* [1979] 1 Ch.227.

[39] *Sweeney v. Duggan* [1997] 2 I.R. 531; see *infra*, p. 62.

[40] R. Friel, *The Law of Contract* (2nd ed., 2000), pp.183 *et seq.* and H. Collins, *The Law of Contract* (2nd ed., 1993). See, generally, J. Beatson and D. Friedman, *Good Faith and Fault in Contract Law* (1995).

[41] *Hivac Ltd. v. Park Royal Scientific Industries Ltd.* [1946] 1 Ch.169.

employees.[42] But an employment contract is not a contract *uberrimae fidei*, that requires disclosure by employees of their own past misconduct.[43]

In a case decided in 1990 concerning entitlements under an occupational pension scheme, Browne-Wilkinson V.C. observed that "[i]n every contract of employment there is an implied term – 'that the employers will not, without reasonable and proper cause, conduct themselves in a manner calculated or likely to destroy or seriously damage the relationship of confidence and trust between employer and employee' (referring to citations). I will call this implied term 'the implied obligation of good faith.'"[44] This view was subsequently endorsed by the House of Lords in *Malik v. Bank of Credit & Commerce Int'l S.A.*,[45] where employees of an insolvent bank claimed damages on the grounds that it had been managed in a spectacularly corrupt and dishonest manner. They contended that there was an implied term in their employment contracts that the employer would not conduct its business in that manner. In upholding this proposition, Lord Steyn observed that its origin lies in the general duty of co-operation between contracting parties and its development has been encouraged by "the changes which have taken place in the employer-employee relationship, with far greater duties imposed on the employer than in the past, whether by statute or by judicial decision, to care for the physical, financial and even psychological welfare of the employee."[46] It was "the change in legal culture which made possible the evolution of the implied term of trust and confidence."[47] The greater readiness on the part of courts to imply terms favourable to employees into employment contracts is an illustration of this cultural change.[48] In *Malik*, the somewhat novel term contended for was implied as a matter of law rather than of fact.

In contrast, in *Sweeney v. Duggan*,[49] where the injured employee sought to recover damages from the owner/director/manager of his former insolvent employer-company, the Supreme Court did not address the question of whether the defendant was under a duty to warn that there was no liability insurance coverage at the workplace, let alone whether it should be implied as a matter of law. Instead, the Court resorted to the classical nineteenth century criteria for implying terms as a matter of fact, ruling against the employee. The circumstances in which employers have an implied contractual duty to disclose relevant information to their employees has been the subject of litigation in Britain in recent years and the trend there is in the general direction of imposing a duty of disclosure.[50] Whether the courts there would have decided the issue in *Sweeney* in the same way as did the Supreme Court is debatable; the answer would appear to be no. It does seem extraordinarily harsh that an employer in a dangerous industry can get away with having no employers' liability insurance and not being required by the

---

42. *Sybron Corp. v. Rochem Ltd.* [1984] 1 Ch.112.
43. *Bell v. Lever Bros.* [1932] A.C. 161.
44. *Imperial Group Pension Trust Ltd. v. Imperial Tobacco Co.* [1991] 1 W.L.R. 589 at 597.
45. [1998] 2 A.C. 20.
46. *Spring v. Guardian Assurance p.l.c.* [1995] 2 A.C. 296 at 335.
47. *Malik v. Bank of Credit & Commerce International S.A.* [1998] A.C. 20 at 46.
48. *e.g. Scally v. Southern Area Health Board* [1992] 1 A.C. 294.
49. [1997] 2 I.R. 531.
50. See, generally, Collins, "Implied Duty to Give Information During Performance of Contracts", 55 Mod. L.R. 556 (1992); also cases concerning requirements of pension schemes, post pp. 352-354

implied terms of the contract to at least disclose to those working there that they
have no insurance cover, especially where it can be shown that the employees
would likely have then purchased their own cover. One would think that the good
faith nature of the relationship requires that the absence of such cover be disclosed. Not so in Irish law, it would seem, unless *Sweeney* is distinguished on the
grounds that the court there never addressed this particular question.[51]

Written statement of particulars

Ever since 1973,[52] employers have been required to furnish their employees with
a written record of the principal terms and conditions of their relationship. In the
event of any dispute, that record is very strong evidence of what had been agreed
or of what should be deemed to have been agreed. Following an E.E.C. Council
Directive of 1991,[53] this part of the 1973 Act was replaced by the Terms of
Employment (Information) Act 1994, which applies to apprentices and employment agency personnel, and to public sector employments as well, including the
civil service, Garda Síochána and the Defence Forces. It does not apply to part-
time or to short-term employment.[54]

Requisite particulars

Within two months of being hired, the employee must be given a statement in
writing, dated and signed by the employer, containing the following particulars of
the employment:[55]

(a) the employer's and employee's full names;

(b) the employer's address in the State;

(c) the workplace; where there is no single or main workplace, a statement
that the employee is required or is permitted to work in several places;

(d) the job title or nature of the work involved;

(e) the date the employment commenced;

(f) in the case of temporary and fixed term contracts, the expected duration
or the termination date;

(g) the rate of remuneration of its mode of calculation, and the "pay reference
period" for determining if the national minimum wage is being paid;

---

51. Plaintiff's skeleton submissions in *Sweeney* are reproduced in M. Forde, *Cases and Materials on Irish Company Law* (2nd ed. 1998), pp. 92-98.
52. Minimum Notice and Terms of Employment Act 1973, s.9.
53. Directive 91/533 on an employer's obligation to inform employees of the conditions applicable to the contract of employment relationships, O.J. No. L 288/32; see, generally C. Barnard, *E.C. Employment Law* (2nd ed., 2000), pp. 436-440.
54. s.2.
55. s.3, amended by s.44 of the National Minimum Wage Act 2000, and by the Terms of Employment (Additional Information) Order 1998, S.I. No. 49.

(ga) that the employee may request a statement of his average hourly rate of pay for that period;

(h) when the remuneration is to be paid, *e.g.* weekly, monthly or at some other intervals;

(i) hours of work including overtime;

(j) paid leave (other than sick leave), if any;

(k) terms and conditions, if any, regarding incapacity for work due to sickness or injury, including paid sick leave;

(k-ii) any terms and conditions relating to pensions and pension schemes;

(l) notice required to dismiss or to resign; if these cannot be ascertained, then the method of determining the notice periods;

(m) where a collective agreement "directly affect[s]" the employment terms and conditions, a reference to that agreement.

(*) times and duration of rest periods and breaks envisaged by the Organisation of Working Time Act 1997.

In the case of topics (g)-(l) above, if the relevant particulars are contained in some law or statutory instrument, or other administrative provision, or in a collective agreement, the statement of particulars may simply refer to these, provided however that they are reasonably accessible to the employee.[56]

Where there has been a change in the terms and conditions relating to any of the above matters, written particulars of that change must be furnished not later than one month from when it occurred.[57]

It was not clear under the 1973 Act how the obligation to supply particulars was to be enforced, other than by way of a criminal sanction.[58] That penalty was repealed in the 1994 Act and the process for enforcing entitlement to the above particulars is the making of a complaint to a rights commissioner,[59] with an appeal on to the Employment Appeals Tribunal and a further appeal to the High Court on a point of law.[60]

Contractual effects

Where the particulars furnished have not elicited protest from the employee, the courts tend to accept the employer's statement of them as the agreed terms of the employment contract. The precise relevance of these statements in determining the terms of the contract remains to be determined.[61] There have been differences of opinion on the matter in England, where it has been held that, in general, the statement "provides very strong *prima facie* evidence of what were the terms of

---

[56]. s.3(3).
[57]. s.5.
[58]. s.10; *cf. Scally v. Southern Area Health Board* [1992] 1 A.C. 294.
[59]. s.7.
[60]. s.8.
[61]. *cf. Kampelmann v. Landshaftsverband Westfalen – Lippe* (Case C 253/96) [1997] E.C.R. 6907.

the contract between the parties, but does not constitute a written contract between the parties. Nor are the statements of the terms finally conclusive; at most, they place a heavy burden on the employer to show that the actual terms of contract are different from those which he has set out in the statutory statement."[62]

The questions that remain to be resolved include the following: Does a signed acknowledgement that the document is a contract give it contractual status? Is the employee estopped from denying the particulars as stated merely because he did not raise a protest shortly after those particulars were furnished? Does estoppel operate only where the employee's very actions indicated his acceptance of the particulars in question? Dealing with the extent to which these statements give rise to an estoppel against the employee, Browne-Wilkinson J. has observed that the courts should be hesitant in this regard. In one instance, concerning the extent to which the employer was authorised to vary the workplace, under a term to that effect in the statement of particulars, it was said that to

> ". . . imply an agreement to vary or to raise an estoppel against the employee on the grounds that he has not objected to a false record by the employer of the terms actually agreed is a course which should be adopted with great caution. If the variation related to a matter which has immediate practical application (*e.g.*, the rate of pay) and the employee continues to work without objection after effect has been given to the variation (*e.g.* his pay packet has been reduced) then obviously he may well be taken to have impliedly agreed. But where, as in the present case, the variation has no immediate practical affect the position is not the same. It is . . . asking too much of the ordinary employee to require him either to object to an erroneous statement of his terms of employment having no immediate practical impact on him or be taken to have assented to the variation. So to hold would involve an unrealistic view of the inclination and ability of the ordinary employee to read and fully understand such statements.
>
> Even if he does read the statement and can understand it, it would be unrealistic of the law to require him to risk a confrontation with his employer on a matter which has no immediate practical impact on the employee."[63]

Another unresolved question is how relevant is the statement as furnished when some of the contract is written or the terms of a collective agreement are incorporated into the contract, either expressly or by implication?

Works rules

The employment contract may incorporate, either expressly or by implication, certain rules that are supposed to obtain at the workplace. At times these rules may have been drafted with the agreement of the employees' trade union. Many employers furnish employees with a book of rules regarding numerous aspects of the job. On other occasions rules may be displayed in notices at the workplace. These rules may relate only to disciplinary matters or they may cover a whole

---

62. *System Floors (U.K.) Ltd. v. Daniel* [1982] I.C.R. 54 at 58.
63. *Jones v. Associated Tunnelling Ltd.* [1981] I.R.L.R. 477 at 481.

range of subjects, like times of work, meal breaks, calculation of remuneration, holidays, sick pay; grievance and disciplinary procedures may also be set out.

Works rules become express terms of the contract where the parties so agree. Agreement to this effect may be express, such as by a written acknowledgement that the employment terms shall include those laid down in the rules. Or the consent may be tacit, like working for some period when the rules purported to be in operation. But in this case, it must be shown that the employee was furnished with reasonable notice of the rules. What notice is reasonable for these purposes will depend on the circumstances, for instance, the nature of the document in question and what steps were taken to bring it to the employee's attention. Where rules obtaining at the time of the hiring are changed later, the employee may very well be bound by the new rules if his conduct indicates that he consented to the change, such as by working in accordance with these new rules.[64] Doing that may be regarded either as a consensual variation of the terms or as an estoppel from denying that the terms had been varied. Even where works rules do not become express terms of the contract, they may be considered by the court as containing certain implied terms.

Custom and practice

Some customs and practices prevailing at the workplace may be implied as terms of the employment contract. In order to attain contractual status in this manner, the alleged custom must satisfy four requirements: it must be notorious, certain, reasonable and must be a custom that is regarded as obligatory. If the custom is not notorious, then it is impossible to say that the employee in question could have not been unaware of it on being hired. As in the case of works rules, it is essential to demonstrate that employees should have been fully aware of the custom or rule. In *Devonald v. Rosser & Sons*, it was said that "a custom cannot be read into a written contract unless . . . it is so universal that no workman could be supposed to have entered into the service without looking to it as part of the contract."[65] But it has been held that it is not essential that the employee in question was actually aware of the custom; that it "is immaterial whether he knew of it or not".[66] Secondly, the custom must be sufficiently certain. Thus, in the *Devonald* case, where it was contended that a custom existed whereby employers could temporarily close the workplace without paying their employees any remuneration, it was held that "there was no element of certainty about the alleged custom."[67] Thirdly, before it will be implied into the contract, the custom must be a reasonable one. Thus in the *Devonald* case, the alleged custom just referred to was rejected for being "eminently unreasonable".[68] Indeed, if a mode of acting is most unreasonable, it is difficult to understand how it can be an established custom.

The custom also must be one that was regarded as imposing an obligation. In *Meek v. Port of London Authority*,[69] the court refused to imply into the contract an

---

[64]. *Petrie v. MacFisheries Ltd.* [1940] 1 K.B. 258.
[65]. [1906] 2 K.B. 728 at 741.
[66]. *Sagar v. Ridehalgh Ltd.* [1931] 1 Ch.310 at 336.
[67]. [1906] 2 K.B. 728 at 741.
[68]. *ibid.* at 743.
[69]. [1918] 1 Ch. 415.

alleged custom whereby the employer paid the employee's income tax. Even if this practice had satisfied the requirement of notoriety, the court characterised it as a windfall, observing that "[i]t would require a very strong case indeed to turn a practice apparently of bounty into a usage of obligation."[70]

Collective agreements

Collective agreements are agreements made between trade unions and employers or employers' associations. As is explained elsewhere,[71] these agreements have several functions and, although undoubtedly they are contracts, often the parties cannot enforce the agreements against each other because they were not intended to be legally enforceable.[72] Provision is made in the Industrial Relations Acts 1946-1969, for registering collective agreements with the Labour Court and there is a mechanism for enforcing their terms through Labour Court procedures. But there are comparatively few agreements of this type.

Most collective agreements have a "normative" function, in the sense that they purport to lay down certain terms and conditions under which specified employees shall be employed - for instance, hours of work, rates of pay, arrangements for overtime and holidays. The subject matter of these provisions varies considerably from industry to industry; some agreements are confined to the bare minimum rates of remuneration, while other agreements deal with a wide range of topics. Generally, it is the implicit threat of retaliatory action against breach that deters employers and unions from contravening obligations they undertook in collective agreements. But where the term of an agreement is incorporated into a contract of employment, breach of the term constitutes an actionable breach of the employment contract. In this way the employer has a legal right to hold the employee to the collective agreement's terms; the employee has a similar right.

Provisions of collective agreements become terms of employment contracts in three ways: by the union in question making the agreement as agent of its employees, by express incorporation of the agreement and by way of an implied term. Even though a collective agreement purports to apply to a particular category of employee, those employees and their employer are legally free to agree between themselves on terms of employment that are inconsistent with those provided for in the collective agreement. Unlike the position in many countries, the normative terms in collective agreements normally, as a matter of law, do not override inconsistent terms in employment contracts.[73]

Agency

Generally, trade unions do not conclude collective agreements as agents of their members. Thus, in *Goulding Chemicals Ltd. v. Bolger*,[74] where the defendants' trade union agreed with their employer regarding the terms on which they should be made redundant, it was held that those terms were not legally binding on the

---

70. *ibid.* at 422.
71. *Industrial Relations Law,* Chap. 4.
72. *Ford Motor Co. v. Amalg. Union of Engineering Workers* [1969] 2 QB 303.
73. See, generally, O. Kahn Freund, *Labour and the Law* (2nd ed., 1977) pp. 140-149.
74. [1977] I.R. 211.

defendants. O'Higgins C.J. observed that he found it "very difficult to accept that membership of an association like a union could bind all members individually in respect of union contracts merely because such had been made by the union".[75] Unions in Ireland usually bargain for non-members as well as for their own members.

Occasionally a union will be deemed to have contracted as its members' agent, endowed with authority to legally bind them. It depends entirely on the circumstances whether the members gave their union that authority. An excellent example is *O'Rourke v. Talbot Motors Ltd.*[76] When the defendant company was contemplating extensive redundancies at its Santry plant, a group of its foremen-employees elected a small committee to negotiate with the company. At these negotiations, in return for assurances that the foremen would co-operate with management's re-organisation of production, the company guaranteed that they would not be made redundant and, at the committee's insistence, gave that guarantee in writing. When the company violated the guarantee, the foremen and not their trade union or their negotiating committee individually sued the company for breach of a term in their employment contracts, that term being that they would not be made redundant. It was held that the term of the agreement which had been reached with the committee had become a part of the plaintiffs' contracts because it was clear and unambiguous, and had been negotiated by their agents, who throughout had been adamant that the agreement should be legally effective.[77]

Express incorporation

Often employment contracts expressly stipulate that they shall incorporate the terms of collective agreements. In unionised establishments it is not uncommon for new employees to be informed that their rates of remuneration and several other terms shall be those set down in designated collective agreements. Instead of providing a list of the various particulars that the Terms of Employment (Information) Act 1994 requires to be given to new employees, the employer may refer them to some "document" containing the requisite particulars; frequently, that document is a collective agreement. The fact that the agreement was referred to in this way does not mean that its contents form express terms of employment contracts but such reference may lead to those terms being incorporated by implication.

In *National Coal Board v. Galley*,[78] where the defendant's written contract stated that its terms shall be subject to national collective agreements in the coal mining industry, it was contended that those agreements' terms regarding overtime were not part of the employment contract because they were too vague. What the agreement provided was that employees "shall work such days or part days in each week as may reasonably be required by the management." It was held that the "parties have expressly provided that reasonableness shall be the test" and that the "fact that it is difficult to decide in a given case should not deter

---

[75] *ibid.* at 231.
[76] [1984] I.L.R.M. 587.
[77] Similarly, *Edwards v. Skyways* [1964] 1 W.L.R. 349.
[78] [1958] 1 W.L.R. 16.

the court from deciding what is a reasonable requirement by the master in the light of the surrounding circumstances."[79] A somewhat similar case is *Knox v. Down District Council*,[80] which concerned the incorporation and application of what had been agreed at a national joint negotiating council. Those councils are among the commonest "constitutive" features of collective agreements; they are permanent joint negotiating bodies, comprised of employers' and employees' representatives, which continually revise various terms and conditions. The clause in question here concerned loans to employees: it provided that "[t]he employing authority may on receipt of an application for financial assistance . . . authorise the grant of a loan", subject to certain conditions being satisfied. The issue before the court was, where an employee indeed satisfied these conditions, had he a legal right to obtain a loan. It was held by the Northern Ireland Court of Appeal that this clause formed part of the plaintiff's employment contract and, while use of the term "may" gave the employer some discretion regarding loan applications, that was far from being an unfettered discretion. Referring to the negotiations that preceded adoption of this clause, Lord Lowry L.C.J. commented that "[i]t would be unrealistic and contrary to legal principle to overlook the background to the conditions of service and merely treat them as if they were agreed between a single employer and a single employee. Every contract has to be construed in the light of the surrounding circumstances. Once this is done here the absurdity is recognised of confiding to the unfettered discretion of the employer the decision on what terms to make a loan or whether to make a loan at all."[81] Consequently, the mere fact that the employer never put money by in order to provide for some loans was no lawful reason for refusing the plaintiff's application.

Implied incorporation

Where persons commence working in an establishment in which a collective agreement deals with conditions for employees in their category, the courts will readily imply that agreement's terms into their employment contracts, on the grounds that this almost certainly is what the parties intended. In the case of a collective agreement being introduced in an establishment where previously there were none, it will depend on all the circumstances whether its terms will be implied into the employment contracts.[82] In appropriate circumstances, a collective agreement's terms can even be implied where the employer in question was not even a party to nor was directly represented in the negotiation of the agreement.

Problem cases

There are a number of problems that often arise in connection with impliedly incorporating the provisions of collective agreements into individual employment

---

[79]   *ibid.* at 24.
[80]   [1981] I.R.L.R. 452.
[81]   *ibid.* at 455.
[82]   *cf. Young v. Canadian Northern Rly. Co.* [1931] A.C. 83 and *Re Andrew M. Patterson Ltd.* [1981] 2 N.Z.L.R. 89.

contracts. These issues are not the subject of any reported Irish authorities. Although there are numerous English cases where similar questions were considered, the analysis in at least some of those cases is faulty and may possibly not be followed here.

Where, as usually is the case, the collective agreement is not legally enforceable *inter partes*, being described as binding in honour only, does this prevent some of its provisions from becoming legally binding terms of an employment contract? The answer is no, unless there are special circumstances which suggest that those terms were not intended to be so incorporated in a binding manner.[83]

Not all terms of collective agreements can be incorporated into employment contracts; only terms which are appropriate for incorporation can be rendered enforceable in this manner. A distinction is drawn between provisions regarding, for example, wages, hours of work, sick pay and holidays, which are readily incorporated and, on the other hand, provisions regarding trade union responsibilities and facilities, which have no direct bearing on individual employees.[84] For instance in *National Coal Board v. National Union of Mineworkers*,[85] one question which arose was whether the conciliation procedures in a collective agreement between the parties were capable of incorporation into the Coal Board's employment contracts with the N.U.M. members. It was held that they were not in the least apt for contractual enforcement by individual employees. Because the machinery was designed to be operated either by the union or by the Coal Board, and no employee had any direct part to play in it, it "simply [did] not lend itself at all to enforceability at the suit of an individual mineworker".[86] So far the cases have not set out a comprehensive test for determining which terms are and are not apt for incorporation. In one instance, it was held that employees, union members, were individually bound by a no-strike clause in a collective agreement, whereby their union undertook not to institute any strike action.[87]

The fact that the employee in question is not a member of a union party to a collective agreement does not ordinarily prevent its terms from being incorporated into his employment contract.[88] Ordinarily, the employee either having left his union or being expelled from it does not prevent the provisions of a collective agreement with that union from being incorporated into his employment contract. However, the term in question may be one which is not appropriate to apply to non-union members, for instance a clause expressly providing for wage increases or certain benefits for union members only. The same applies where the employer ceases to be a member of an employers' federation which was a party to the relevant collective agreement.[89] That the agreement was subsequently terminated may not prevent its incorporation into the individual contract.[90]

---

83. *e.g. Robertson v. British Gas Corp.* [1983] I.C.R. 351 and *Marley v. Forward Trust Group Ltd.* [1986] I.C.R. 891.
84. *e.g. Griffiths v. Buckinghamshire C.C.* [1994] I.C.R. 265; compare *Burke v. Royal Liverpool University Hospital* [1997] I.C.R. 73 and *Ali v. Christian Salveser Food Services Ltd.* [1997] I.C.R. 25.
85. [1986] I.C.R. 736.
86. *ibid.;* similarly, *Tadd v. Eastwood* [1983] I.R.L.R. 320.
87. *Camden Exhibition and Display Ltd. v. Lynott* [1966] 1 Q.B. 343.
88. *Singh v. British Steel Corp.* [1974] I.R.L.R. 131.
89. *Burroughs Machinery Ltd. v. Timmoney* [1976] I.R.L.R. 343.
90. *Morris v. C.H. Bailey Ltd.* [1969] 2 Ll.L.R. 215.

Employees may be affected by several collective agreements, which contain inconsistent provisions. For instance, there may be a national industry-wide agreement, a plant agreement and also a craft agreement. There are no hard and fast rules for determining which agreement's provisions take precedence for the purpose of incorporation into the individual contracts.[91] Some assistance may be obtained from the statement of particulars given in accordance with the 1994 Act.

ALTERING THE CONTRACT

Since the employment relationship often is one which lasts for a prolonged period, some of its terms and conditions will be changed from time to time.[92] Usually, those changes will be made by agreement between the employer and the employee or their representatives; for instance, salary increases will often be negotiated so that at least employees' real earnings are not eroded by inflation. Neither party may change the contract unilaterally, except where the very terms of the contract authorise unilateral alteration.[93] In such a case, the power to change the terms without the other party's agreement cannot be used unreasonably.

Where an alteration has been agreed to by a "representative" of the employer, that representative must be someone who was duly authorised to agree to the change. In one instance where post office sorters claimed they had been given a 15-minute break during their overtime shift, O'Hanlon J. rejected their claim on the grounds that those who agreed to that break did not have authority to do so.[94] Nor does the willingness of an employee to give an alteration in the terms a trial constitute his acceptance of that change. In *McCarroll v. Hickling Pentecost & Co.*,[95] a foreman in a textile factory was ordered to revert to his original job as a machine operator, at which his employment conditions were less favourable. He obeyed the order, although he was clearly dissatisfied with it, but after ten days working as an operative he resigned. His claim that the employer had repudiated the employment contract, by unilaterally altering its terms, was upheld. The fact that he gave the changed terms a trial could not be taken as his having consented to the alteration.

It depends on the circumstances what kinds of changes amount to altering the very terms of the contract. Clearly, changes in agreed rates of pay, hours and place of work, and intrinsic nature of the job fall into that category. But changes in the way the work is done may not usually be so classified. Generally, an employee is expected to adapt to new methods and techniques in performing his duties, provided the employer arranged for him to receive the necessary training

---

91. *cf. Gascol Conversions Ltd. v. Merier* [1974] I.C.R. 420 and *Alexander v. Standard Telephones & Cables p.l.c.* [1990] I.C.R. 291.
92. See, generally, M. Freedland, *The Contract of Employment* (1976), Chap. 2.
93. *Bainbridge v. Circuit Foil (U.K.) Ltd.* [1997] I.C.R. 541 and *Brennan v. Religious of the Sacred Heart* [2000] E.L.R. 297.
94. *Keany v. An Post* [1988] I.R. 285.
95. [1971] N.I. 250.

in the new skills and the nature of the work did not alter so radically that it was outside the contractual obligations of the employee.

For instance, in *Cresswell v. Inland Revenue*,[96] the employer introduced computers to facilitate recording information at the workplace. A contention that this amounted to a unilateral change of the plaintiff's employment terms was rejected. The approach adopted there was followed by Kelly J. in *Raftery v. Bus Éireann*,[97] where under a viability plan adopted by the defendant bus company, a new method of rostering drivers was introduced, under which thenceforth they would have to spent 85 per cent of their working hours actually driving buses. In order to determine whether such a unilateral change was permissible, the test is, "is the effect of the changes ... such as to result in the bus driver doing a different job or is it merely to bring about a situation where they will be doing recognisably the same job in a different way?" It was held that the changes there constituted alterations to work practices rather than to conditions of service; they did not affect rates of pay, hours of work, length of holidays, sick leave or pension rights, nor did they alter the basic core of a driver's job.

In *Scally v. Southern Health and Social Services Board*,[98] it was held that there can be an implied term in the contract of employment to bring to the notice of employees certain changes in the terms of service. There a new system of contributions to a pension scheme was introduced by the employer but the plaintiffs were not notified of that change and, in consequence, they lost valuable pension entitlements.[99] It was also argued that the employer should be held liable for breach of statutory duty — for not disclosing the altered terms as required by the U.K. equivalent of the Terms of Employment (Information) Act 1994. But it was held the Parliament did not intend that those who suffered loss by virtue of a breach of that Act's requirements should have a civil remedy for damages.

Where the change in question involves any of the matters in respect of which particulars should be given under section 3 of that Act, written notice of the nature and date of the change must be given to the employee within one month of when it is to take effect.[100] The remedy for not furnishing that notice is to complain to a rights commissioner, with an appeal to the Employment Appeals Tribunal.

TORT LIABILITY

An aspect of employment law that, from an analytical perspective, is relatively unexplored is the obligations that the law of tort imposes on employers and employees, outside of the area of health and safety. As is explained in Chapter 5, for over a hundred years, employees have had a right of action in damages, either for negligence or for breach of statutory duty, in respect of injuries incurred or

---

[96.] [1984] 2 All E.R. 713.

[97.] [1997] 2 I.R. 424.

[98.] [1992] 1 A.C. 294.

[99.] Compare *University of Nottingham v. Eyett* [1999] I.C.R. 721 and *Petch v. Customs and Excise C'mrs* [1993] I.C.R. 789.

[100.] s.5.

diseases caused in the course of their employment. Section 28 of the Safety, Health and Welfare at Work Act 1989 permits regulations to be made that extend the scope of such liability. But it is principally in respect of exclusively financial or economic loss that difficult questions of legal analysis arise.

Ordinarily, it will not matter if a claim for breach of the duty in question is framed in contract or in tort; at one time, the distinction was vital but the old system of formal pleading was abolished in the 1850s. Occasionally, however, how the action is framed it can be decisive; most notably, where the defendant is in some non-E.C. Member State and notice of the proceedings must be served on him. In one such case, Keane J. held that a claim for damages for "breach of duty", where the plaintiff was fatally injured in the course of his work, was a claim in tort and not one for breach of contract.[101] Accordingly, the rules for service outside the jurisdiction in tort cases applied. The contract/tort distinction can also be relevant for the purposes of statutes of limitation. But where the claim is in respect of personal injuries there is the one limitation period regardless of how the claim is framed, that is whether the action is one for breach of contract, tort or breach of statutory duty.

Economic loss

There are certain kinds of intentional or premeditated acts that give rise to tort liability, most notably, in the present context, deceit, invasion of privacy, and defamation,[102] but these do not cause any special problems where the acts in question are done in the employment context. It is, predominantly, negligently caused financial loss that engenders the problems. It used to be thought that, except where he was in breach of contract, an employer could not be held liable for purely financial loss he negligently caused his employee. Given the obvious proximity that exists between the parties, it is hard to understand why that was taken for granted.

It, however, was shattered in *Spring v. Guardian Assurance p.l.c.*[103] The plaintiff, who previously had worked for the defendant insurers, could not get a new job because of what the defendant had said in the references it wrote on his behalf. Their contents were false and defamatory, but if the plaintiff had sued for libel, he would have been met by the defence of qualified privilege. Because the defendant had been negligent in writing the references but there was no suggestion of malice towards the plaintiff, that defence would have defeated the libel claim. Instead, he sued for negligence, lost at first instance and on appeal but succeeded before the House of Lords. It was held that "in cases such as the present the duty of care arises by reason of an assumption of responsibility by the employer to the employee in respect of the relevant reference."[104] In other words, the circumstances satisfied the criteriae in the famous *Hedley Byrne* case[105] and there were no special policy reasons why liability in damages should not arise.

[101.] *Campbell v. Holland Dredging Ltd.* (March 3, 1989).
[102.] See, generally, B. McMahon and W. Binchy, *Irish Law of Torts* (3rd ed., 2000).
[103.] [1995] 2 A.C. 296.
[104.] *ibid.* at 317-322.
[105.] *Hedley Byrne & Co. v. Heller & Partners Ltd.* [1964] A.C. 465.

In his concurring speech, Lord Woolf there demonstrated that the very same outcome would arise if the claim had been framed as one for breach of contract rather than for tortious negligence. He pointed to the following circumstances that would warrant implying a term in the contract, *viz.*:

> "(i) the existence of the contract of employment or services; (ii) the fact that the contract relates to an engagement of a claim where it is the normal practice to require a reference from a previous employer before employment is offered; (iii) the fact that the employee cannot be expected to enter into that claim of employment except on the basis that his employer will, on the request of another prospective employer made not later than a reasonable time after the termination of a former employment, provide a full and frank reference as to the employee."[106]

On the basis of this, Lord Woolf would imply a term into the contract that "the employer would during the continuance of the engagement or within a reasonable time thereafter, provide a reference at the request of a prospective employer which was based on facts revealed after making those reasonably careful enquiries which, in the circumstances, a reasonable employer would make."[107] More recently, in *Malik v. Bank of Credit & Commerce Int'l S.A.*,[108] the Law Lords held that employees could be entitled to compensation for the financial loss they suffered because their employer had been running its business in a consistently fraudulent manner. Liability there was founded on an implied term, rather than on the tort of negligence, but it would require little ingenuity to rationalise it on tort grounds.[109]

Non cumul

Under the doctrine of *non cumul*, French Civil law seeks to segregate contractual and tortious liability but concurrent remedies in tort and contract are permitted in other civil law countries, such as Germany.[110] With the remarkable expansion of negligence liability following the *Hedley Byrne* case, but with the traditional criteriae for implying terms from the facts into contracts, the question arises whether there can be liability in negligence between contracting parties where a commensurate term would not be implied into the contract. The English Court of Appeal in *Holt v. Payne Skillington*[111] answered this question in the affirmative. In a tort claim by a client against his solicitors, it was held that there is no reason in principle why a *Hedley Byrne*-type duty of care could not arise in an overall set of circumstances where, by reference to certain limited aspects of those circumstances, the same parties entered into a contractual relationship involving more limited obligations than those imposed by the duty of care in tort. In such

---

[106]. [1995] 2 A.C. at 353-354.

[107]. *ibid.* at 354.

[108]. [1998] 2 A.C. 20; followed by *Bank of Credit & Commerce Int'l v. Ali* [2001] 2 W.L.R. 735.

[109]. *cf. Briscoe v. Lubrizol Ltd.* [2000] I.C.R. 694, rejecting employee's claim against insurers of his employer's health scheme.

[110]. See, generally, C Van Bar, *The Common European Law of Torts* (1998), Vol. 1, pp.412 *et seq. cf. Henderson v. Merrett Syndicates Ltd.* [1995] 2 A.C. 145 at 184-186.

[111]. *Times L.R.,* December 22, 1995.

circumstances, the duty of care in tort and the duties imposed by the contract would be concurrent but not coextensive. The difference in scope between them would reflect the more limited factual basis which gave rise to the contract, which precluded or restricted the wider duty of care in tort.

However, in decisions made nine and twelve months after the *Holt* case was reported, the Supreme Court held that the express and implied terms of the parties' contracts define the outer limits of any liability in negligence as may arise between them. The earlier of those cases involved a claim by borrowers against their bank for withdrawing lending facilities allegedly promised.[112] The other was *Sweeney v. Duggan*,[113] where a former employee of a one-person company, that was insolvent, sued the 99 per cent shareholder of that company, who also (along with his wife) was its director and was the designated manager of its business, which was a quarry. The plaintiff was injured in the course of his employment and got an undefended judgment against the company, but received nothing because by then the company went into a creditors' voluntary liquidation and was insolvent. If the company had employers' liability insurance, the plaintiff would have been able to get his compensation but there is no statutory obligation to take out such insurance. It was contended by the plaintiff that the defendant there was under alternative duties of care, being either (i) to ensure that there was appropriate insurance cover, or (ii) to warn the employees, including the plaintiff, that there was no such cover; by inference, advise them that they should contemplate taking out their own insurance. Proposition (i) here was rejected but the Court declined to consider proposition (ii) even though the plaintiff had purchased a comparatively small insurance policy that covered *inter alia* injuries at work.

The basis of the plaintiff's argument was that: (i) the company's business, quarrying, was an exceptionally dangerous occupation; (ii) at the time of the accident the company's finances were precarious and it was in a "section 40" situation; (iii) the plaintiff had himself insured to a small extent; (iv) the plaintiff was advised by a co-employee that the company had employers' liability insurance. For those reasons, it was contended that the company's owner-cum-manager should have either arranged to get adequate insurance or else warned employees that they were working without any insurance cover other than what they might purchase themselves. Giving judgment for the Court, Murphy J. held that the defendant could not be subject to a duty to arrange insurance unless the company itself was under a similar duty. Further, unless such a duty could be implied into the employment contract, it could not arise extra-contractually.[114]

---

[112] *Kennedy v. Allied Irish Banks p.l.c.* [1998] 2 I.R. 48.

[113] [1997] 2 I.R. 531.

[114] *Shinkwin* v. *Quin-Can Ltd.*, Sup. C't, November 21, 2000, where *Sweeney* was distinguished.

CHAPTER 4

INCIDENTS OF THE EMPLOYMENT RELATIONSHIP

This chapter is concerned with the principal incidents of the employment relationship, *i.e.* the main rights and duties of the employer and employee *vis-à-vis* each other. The requirements for health and safety at work and regarding discrimination at work are considered separately in the following chapters. A "job" is defined in the three Acts that deal with parental and related leave as "the nature of the work that the employee is employed to do in accordance with his or her contract of employment and the capacity and place in which he or she is employed".[1]

For employees who come within the scope of the Unfair Dismissals Acts 1977-93, there are in a sense two entirely separate sets of employment rights and duties. One is the obligations described here arising either from the contract or from employment statutes. The other is standards of conduct which either justify or do not justify dismissal under the 1977-93 Acts. Sometimes breach of the contractual and statutory obligations will be held to justify a dismissal; on other occasions, a breach will not be so treated. For instance, in *Flynn v. Power*,[2] a young teacher in a convent school was dismissed because she was openly living with a married man, had a child by him and refused to change this aspect of her private life, and challenged her dismissal under the 1977 Act. In deciding the case, it was not necessary to determine what rights she had under her employment contract. The only question was whether, in all the circumstances, her dismissal was unfair.[3]

THE WORK OBLIGATION

A central feature of the employment relationship is the reciprocal provision and performance of work; during the agreed working hours and for the agreed remuneration, the employee should carry out the tasks assigned by the employer. If the employee refuses to perform those tasks, then, provided the job definition encompasses them, the employer is not obliged to pay the agreed remuneration. The position is more complex where the employee renders defective performance, *i.e.* he does the job but performs it badly.

Employer providing work

Generally, while the employee is contractually obliged to attend at the workplace during the agreed times for working, the employer is not obliged to furnish actual

---

[1]   *e.g.* Parental Leave Act 1998, s.2(1).

[2]   [1985] I.R. 648.

[3]   See *post,* p. 202 *et seq.*

work to be done.[4] All that usually is required of the employer is to pay the agreed remuneration for the period during which the employee is to be at work. As a judge put it, "[i]t is true that a contract of employment does not necessarily, or perhaps normally, oblige the master to provide the servant with work. Provided I pay my cook her wages regularly she cannot complain if I choose to take any or all of my meals out."[5] Although having no actual work to do may deprive the employee of job satisfaction, generally "a loss of job satisfaction is always regrettable but by itself provides no cause of action."[6] Thus, in *Turner v. Sawdon & Co.*,[7] the plaintiff was hired for four years as a salesman at a fixed salary. Before the contract expired, his employer refused to provide him with any more work to do, although the employer was content to continue paying his salary. It was held that the employer was not thereby in breach of his obligations.

This general principle does not apply where the employee's remuneration depends entirely on being provided with tasks to perform, for instance, where remuneration is based on piece rates or on commission. In those circumstances, absent express stipulation to the contrary, it is an implied term that the employee will be supplied with sufficient work to earn such remuneration as could reasonably be anticipated.[8] Where part of the agreed earnings are to be reckoned on a piece rate or a commission basis, the circumstances may warrant implying a similar term. Such a term was held to exist in *In Re Rubel Bronze & Metal Co.*,[9] where the plaintiff was the company's general manager for three years at a fixed salary together with a commission based on the company's net profits. Because he could have earned a very large commission on the profits, if made, it was held that he "had therefore the right to ask that he should have a full opportunity to be earning such commission."[10] There are also certain types of jobs where it will be implied that the parties intended that the employee should be provided with actual work to do. On several occasions, actors who were hired on a fixed salary have been held entitled to be given parts in performances in which they can show their talents.[11] This was because the employers were deemed, in one of these cases, to have contracted, "not only to pay . . . a salary, but to give an opportunity of appearing before the public in a part which answered to the stipulated description."[12] Where a person becomes employed, especially for a long period and at a low remuneration, in order to earn a skill or to gain business experience, the employer is obliged to furnish such work as is required to achieve those objectives.[13]

There can be other exceptional situations where an obligation to furnish work will be implied. Thus, in *Collier v. Sunday Referee Publishing Co.*,[14] where the

---

4. See, generally, M. Freedland, *The Contract of Employment* (1976) pp. 23-27.
5. *Collier v. Sunday Referee Publishing Co.* [1940] 2 K.B. 647 at 650.
6. *Cresswell v. Inland Revenue* [1984] 2 All E.R. 713 at 720.
7. [1901] 2 K.B. 653.
8. *R. v. Welch* (1853) 2 E. & B. 357.
9. [1918] 1 K.B. 315.
10. *ibid.* at 324. See, too, *Turner v. Goldsmith* [1891] 1 Q.B. 544.
11. e.g. *Marbe v. George Edwards (Day's Theatre) Ltd.* [1928] 1 K.B. 269.
12. *Clayton & Waller Ltd. v. Oliver* [1930] A.C. 209 at 221.
13. *Turner v. Sawdon & Co.* [1901] 2 K.B. 653.
14. [1940] 2 K.B. 647.

plaintiff was appointed as chief sub-editor of the defendants' newspaper and they then sold the paper, it was held that they were in breach of contract by paying him a salary but not providing him with any work to do. And in *William Hill Organisation Ltd. v. Tucker*,[15] it was held that a senior dealer in a very large spread-betting business, who was required to work such hours as were necessary to carry out his duties in a proper and professional manner, and where the employer had agreed to invest in staff to ensure that they had every opportunity to develop their skills, was similarly entitled to be given work until such time as his contract of employment was lawfully terminated.

Employee performing work

The employee's principal duty under the employment contract is to perform those tasks within the job description as are assigned to him during working hours and to obey all reasonable orders incidental to the performance of those tasks. Several features of these reciprocal duties are dealt with later in this chapter, such as identifying the workplace, determining the agreed times of work and calculating how much remuneration must be paid; the question of job description, of defining what exactly the employee can be required to do, has been considered to an extent in the previous chapter. The express terms of the contract may set out in detail what the job in question entails; they may also indicate the extent to which the employer is free unilaterally to alter various incidents of the job. Over and above any express terms, employees are obliged to obey all reasonable instructions incidental to performing their job, they must co-operate with the employer in doing their work and they must exercise reasonable care in the performance of the work. They also have an obligation of fidelity to their employer.

Competence and care

An employee must be reasonably competent to perform the job for which he was hired. Extreme incompetence will warrant instant dismissal; it has been held to be "very unreasonable that an employer should be compelled to go on employing a man who, having represented himself competent, turns out to be incompetent."[16] Many employments have elaborate disciplinary procedures aimed at ensuring that the work is done with a reasonable degree of competence. It is an implied term of the employment contract that employees will exercise a reasonable degree of care and skill in the performance of their work. Consequently, it was held in *Lister v. Romford Ice & Cold Storage Co. Ltd.*,[17] that where an employer suffered financial loss as a result of his employee's breach of this duty, that employee is under an obligation to indemnify the loss. In that case, an employee who negligently drove a van in the course of his work injured a fellow employee (who was his father). On the basis of vicarious liability, the employer had to compensate that fellow employee for his injuries. In consequence, it was held that the van driver was under an implied contractual duty to indemnify the employer in respect of that sum.[18]

---

15. [1999] I.C.R. 291.
16. *Harmer v. Cornelius* (1858) 5 C.B. (N.S.) 236.
17. [1957] A.C. 555.
18. Contrast *Harvey v. R. G. O'Dell Ltd.* [1958] 2 Q.B. 78.

Employers are subject to an extensive duty of care which is based on an implied term of the employment contract,[19] which also is founded in tort and was the subject of extensive statutory regulation, notably, the Safety in Industry Acts 1955-1980, the Mines and Quarries Act 1955, the Office Premises Act 1958, the Safety, Health and Welfare (Offshore Installations) Act 1987, and other comparable measures. Many provisions of these Acts have now been replaced by a comprehensive measure, the Safety, Health and Welfare at Work Act 1989.[20] The employer's common law duty of care is owed to each individual employee and employers must take due account of the different physiques and other attributes of their various employees. For instance, an employer owes a greater duty to take care of a one-eyed man than a normal man in respect of risk of injuries to the eyes.[21]

Obey reasonable orders

It depends on the circumstance of the case whether an employer's lawful orders are reasonable and, accordingly, must be obeyed by the employee. Generally, employers are not entitled to give orders regarding what employees do outside of their working hours, but there are some jobs which warrant giving certain instructions about what an employee should or should not do while not actually at work. The extent to which, under the Constitution, contractual stipulations may authorise employers to interfere with their employees' private lives has yet to be resolved by the courts. Indeed, there is no modern judicial exposition of when orders will be deemed to be unreasonable. Orders that concern what happens outside the employee's times of work would usually be regarded as unreasonable, unless the contract clearly envisaged giving those orders. But the courts would be most reluctant to strike down instructions given about how a particular task should be performed since, by the nature of the employment relationship, it is for the employer to determine how the work is to be done. An order would have to be wholly unconnected with the employee's job or be manifestly unreasonable before it would be rejected by the courts. Even where the contract expressly authorises the employer to give certain directions, ordinarily those must still take due account of the employee's health and safety.[22]

An example of orders which were held to be unreasonable is *Ottoman Bank v. Chakarin*,[23] involving a bank employee who had been based in London. Under his contract, he could be posted abroad to any branch in Turkey. He was ordered to work at a branch there where, to the employer's knowledge, his personal safety would be at risk. He disobeyed that order. It was held that, on account of the risk to which he would be exposed, the order was unlawful.

Co-operation

Because the employment contract envisages a continuing relationship between employer and employee, being what may be described as a "relational contract",

---

[19.] *Matthews v. Kuwait Bechtel Corp.* [1959] 2 Q.B. 57.
[20.] See Chap. 5.
[21.] *Paris v. Stepney Borough Council* [1951] A.C. 367.
[22.] *Johnstone v. Bloomsbury Health Authority* [1992] Q.B. 333.
[23.] [1930] A.C. 277.

the parties must perform their various contractual obligations with a degree of good faith.[24] It would appear that employers also must co-operate to an extent with their employees, *inter alia*, by disclosing certain vital information that would significantly bear on decisions employees may take.[25] As with the duty of obedience, the full extent of this obligation has not been articulated by the courts in recent times.

It has been held that "working to rule" in the course of industrial action, meaning observing the strict letter of the contract to such extent as frustrates the very enterprise which the employer is embarked upon, can contravene the employee's duty of co-operation. In *Secretary of State for Employment v. A.S.L.E.F. (No. 2)*,[26] which concerned a work to rule by train drivers and which was held to be in breach of those drivers' employment contracts, the judges spoke of an implied term to perform the contract in such a way as not to undermine its commercial objective. Roskill L.J. observed that it is an implied term that "each employee will not, in obeying his lawful instructions, seek to obey them in a wholly unreasonable way which has the effect of disrupting the system, the efficient running of which he is employed to ensure."[27]

Fidelity

Employees must serve their employer with fidelity and it would appear that employers also have a comparable obligation to their employees. As was observed in *Hivac Ltd. v. Park Royal Scientific Instruments Ltd.*, which concerned spare time working for a competing employer, "[i]t has been said on many occasions that an employee owes a duty of fidelity to his employer. As a general proposition that is indisputable. The practical difficulty in any given case is to find how far that rather vague duty of fidelity extends. . . . [I]t must be a question on the facts of each particular case. . . . [T]he obligation . . . may extend very much further in the case of one class of employee than it does in others."[28] The relationship is frequently described as one of "mutual trust and confidence".[29]

The whole question of employees competing with their former employer is dealt with separately below, as is the closely related question of disclosing and using confidential information obtained about the employer's business. Many of the leading authorities on the duty of fidelity concern using confidential information to compete with former employers. Save in exceptional circumstances, however, the duty of fidelity does not render employees fiduciaries for their employers. One such exceptional case is executive directors of their employing company;[30] another is senior public officials who hold special positions of trust,

---

24. See *ante,* pp. 48-49.
25. *e.g. Scally v. Southern Area Health Board* [1992] 1 A.C. 294.
26. [1972] 2 Q.B. 455.
27. *ibid.* at 508-509. See, too, *British Telecom p.l.c. v. Ticehurst* [1992] I.C.R. 383.
28. [1946] 1 Ch. 169 at 174.
29. See comments, "Mutual Trust and Confidence" in 25 Ind. L. J. 121 (1996) and in 28 Ind. L.J. 348 (1999).
30. *e.g. Thomas Marshall (Exports) Ltd. v. Guinle* [1979] Ch. 227. An excellent analysis of senior employees' fiduciary obligations is Elias J.'s judgment in *University of Nottingham v. Fishel* [2000] I.C.R. 1462.

such as a corrupt public prosecutor who had been accepting bribes for many years.[31] Although at times the courts may resort to remedies against employees, based on constructive trusts, that does not render them fiduciaries, let alone trustees[32] for their employers.

Enforcing of the wage/work obligation

There are various categories of breach of contract; principally, breach of warranty, breach of a condition and, perhaps, fundamental breach. The legal sanctions that can be used in response to a breach of contract often depend on what category that breach falls into; this also is the case with breaches of employment contracts. Where the breach is so serious that it amounts to a repudiation of the entire agreement, then the other party is entitled, in legal jargon, to accept that repudiation and to terminate the contract there and then.[33] Thus, where the employer does something that amounts to repudiation, like going into liquidation, the employee is entitled to resign immediately and claim damages for wrongful termination.[34] Similarly, in *Re Rubel Bronze & Metal Co.*,[35] which concerned a general manager whose remuneration was to include a commission on the company's profits, it was held that, by preventing him from managing the business, the company had repudiated the contract although it continued to pay him the agreed fixed salary. It depends on all the circumstances of the case whether a breach of the contract has such drastic ramifications. As was observed in that case, "[i]n every case the question of repudiation must depend on the character of the contract, the number and weight of the wrongful acts or assertions, the intention indicated by such acts or words, the deliberation or otherwise with which they are committed or uttered, and in the general circumstances of the case."[36]

Resignation/dismissal

Where the breach of contract is sufficiently serious as to amount to repudiation, the employee can forthwith resign or, in the case of repudiation by the employee, the employer is entitled to dismiss him summarily, without giving any notice or money in lieu of notice. Many of the reported cases on breach of employment contracts are concerned with whether the employee had repudiated the contract and, consequently, whether his summary dismissal was lawful[37] or, alternatively, whether the employer's conduct constituted a repudiation that was tantamount to dismissing the employee, *i.e.* "constructive dismissal".[38]

Suspension from work

There is little guidance in the case law on what circumstances may entitle employees, in response to their employers' breach of contract, to temporarily

---

[31.]   *e.g. Attorney General of Hong Kong v. Reid* [1994] 1 A.C. 324.
[32.]   *Attorney General's Reference* [1986] Q.B. 491.
[33.]   See, generally, R. Friel, *The Law of Contract* (2nd ed., 2000), Chap. 23.
[34.]   See *post*, pp. 160-162.
[35.]   [1918] 3 K.B. 315.
[36.]   *ibid.* at 322.
[37.]   See *post*, pp. 168-171.
[38.]   See *post*, pp. 160-162.

absent themselves from work. A sanction which may be open to the employer is to suspend the employee, who was in breach of contract, from work for a day, a week, a month or whatever.[39] The contract may expressly authorise suspension and even set out a disciplinary procedure. An express contractual power to suspend normally implies suspension without payment of remuneration for the relevant period; it usually means that "the contracting party, if he be an employer, never contracts to pay wages during the period referred to, any more than the other party, if he be a workman, contracts to work during that period."[40] A power to suspend without pay must be exercised reasonably.[41] Statutory provisions governing a variety of employments in the public service often authorise suspension, without pay, in prescribed circumstances and in accordance with set procedures.[42]

Absent an express power along these lines, disciplinary suspension is governed by two main principles. Apart from the exceptional situation described above where the employer must provide the employee with actual tasks to perform, the employee may be suspended from work at any time provided the employer continues to pay the agreed salary. Unless clearly authorised by the contract to do so, however, the employer is not entitled to suspend an employee without paying his agreed remuneration; if the employee has contracted to work in exchange for remuneration from, say, Mondays to Fridays, he is entitled to be paid for those days even if the employer chooses to suspend him from work. Thus in *Hanley v. Pease and Partners Ltd.,*[43] in breach of contract, the plaintiff did not turn up for work on one day and, on the following days when he arrived for work, he was suspended without pay because of the previous absence. It was held that, while the employers in the circumstances may have been entitled to dismiss the plaintiff, they had no implied right to suspend him without pay. This was because "[h]aving elected to treat the contract as continuing it was continuing. They might have had a right to claim damages against the servant, but they could not justify their act in suspending the workman for the one day and refusing to let him work and earn wages."[44] Exceptional circumstances however may warrant implying into the contract a power of suspension without remuneration, although the courts have been markedly reluctant to imply such a term.[45]

An employee who is wrongfully suspended from work can claim against the employer for the remuneration he would have earned during the period of suspension and, generally, that suspension would constitute a repudiation of the contract, thereby entitling the employee to treat it as a dismissal.

Unilateral reduction of earnings

Where the employee is in breach of the work obligation, the employer may, in the circumstances, be entitled to respond to that breach by reducing the employee's

---

[39.] See, generally, M. Freedland, *The Contract of Employment* (1976) pp. 80-86.
[40.] *Bird v. British Celanese Ltd.* [1945] 1 K.B. 336 at 342.
[41.] *McLory v. Post Office* [1992] I.C.R. 758 and *Gogay v. Hertfordshire C.C.* [2000] I.R.L.R. 703.
[42.] *e.g. Deegan v. Minister for Finance* [2000] E.L.R. 190.
[43.] [1915] 1 K.B. 698.
[44.] *ibid.* at 705.
[45.] *e.g. Bond v. CAV Ltd.* [1983] I.R.L.R. 360 and *Lawe v. Irish Country Meats (Pig Meats) Ltd.* [1998] E.L.R. 266.

earnings. In the first place, the employment contract may expressly authorise deduction from earnings; in that event, the grounds and procedures stipulated for making the deductions must be scrupulously followed. It has been held that where, in breach of contract, employees resort to forms of industrial action which would entitle their employer to claim damages against them, the employer may deduct the equivalent amount of damages from remuneration which is due, by way of a set off.[46] As is explained below, however, the Payment of Wages Act 1991 greatly circumscribes the power to make deductions from earnings. Where the employer deliberately and wrongly refuses to pay the agreed remuneration, the employee is entitled to treat such conduct as a repudiation of their agreement and the equivalent of a summary dismissal.[47]

Injunction

Generally, the courts will not compel an employer to continue employing an employee who was wrongfully suspended or dismissed, nor will the courts compel an employee who has wrongfully absented himself to perform his work. Because employment contracts involve the provision and acceptance of personal services, as a rule the courts did not use their equity jurisdiction to compel performance of such contracts.[48] However, the courts may grant interlocutory injunctions restraining persons' prima facie unlawful dismissal pending the trial of the action and, indeed, restraining their suspension from work; in the circumstances of those cases, damages would not be an adequate remedy if at the trial it transpired that the employer was not entitled to dismiss.[49] So far, however, it seems that a permanent injunction would not be granted where, at the trial, it is shown that the employer acted in breach of contract, other than in respect of those somewhat exceptional employments referred to earlier.

Damages

The employer or employee, as the case may be, may choose to bring an action for damages for the other's breach of the contract. Where the breach does not amount to a repudiation of their agreement, then both parties' primary legal remedy is a claim for damages. Because the amount of damages resulting from breach of the employment contract usually is relatively meagre (other than in cases of personal injury), damages actions between employers and employees are comparatively rare,[50] especially claims brought against employees. The employer's usual response to an employee's serious breach of contract is to suspend or to dismiss the employee; if the breach was not an extremely grievous one, the employer most likely would give the employee some weeks, notice of the dismissal or, more often than not, dismiss the employee and pay him a salary in lieu of notice,

---

46. *Sim v. Rotherham Metropolitan B.C.* 1 Chap. 216; also *Miles v. Wakefield Council* [1987] A.C. 539 and *Wiluszynske v. Tower Hamlet B.C.* [1989] I.C.R. 493. See *Industrial Relations Law*, pp. 112-115.
47. *Cantor Fitzgerald Int'l v. Callaghan* [1999] I.C.R. 639.
48. See, generally, I. Spry, *Equitable Remedies* (4th ed., 1997), pp. 119 *et seq.*
49. See *post*, p. 179.
50. *e.g. Sullivan v. Southern Health Board* [1997] 3 I.R. 123.

i.e. the equivalent of what would have been earned if the employee had remained at work during the notice period. Where, however, the employee has profited significantly from his breach of contract, for instance accepted bribes or gains from disclosing confidential information, substantial damages may be awarded against him, including an account of his profits.[51]

APPRENTICES AND TRAINEES

The status and position of apprentices has been the subject of statutory regulation for centuries. By an Act passed in 1814,[52] the old system of compulsory apprenticeships to guilds which enjoyed some monopolies of trades was abolished. Thereafter, the rights and duties of apprentices became principally a matter of contract. Frequently, that contract would be a sealed indenture of apprenticeship, although neither a seal nor writing are essential to create the master-apprentice relationship. Sometimes the provisions of trade union rules contain guidelines on apprentices and, formerly, controlling the number of apprentices in a trade was one means by which trade unions regulated their members' earnings.[53]

A contract of apprenticeship has been described as follows:

> "[it] secures three things for an apprentice; it secures him first a money payment during the period of apprenticeship, secondly that he shall be instructed and trained and thus acquire skills which would be of value to him for the rest of his life and, thirdly, it gives him status because 'once a young man . . . completes his apprenticeship and can show by certificate that he has completed his time with a well known employer, that gets him off to a good start in the labour market.'"[54]

Where the apprentice is a minor, that is under 18 years of age, then the general principles regarding contracts with minors apply to him. At common law, there is no implied term to pay wages to the apprentice, so that it is usual for the contract to expressly provide for remuneration.

The employment of persons under 18 years of age is regulated by the Protection of Young Persons (Employment) Act 1996, which restricts the times and hours during which children and young persons may work, and provides for rest periods while they are working.[55] Apprentices, as well as other employees, come within these restrictions

The determination of whether an apprentice is an employee for the purposes of employment protection legislation or otherwise depends entirely on the terms of the contract. In the *Sister Dolores* case[56] and the *National Maternity Hospital* case,[57] it was held that trainee nurses there were not employees for the purposes

---

[51.] *e.g. Attorney General of Hong Kong v. Reid* [1994] 1 A.C. 324 and *Attorney General v. Blake* [2000] 3 W.L.R. 625. *cf. University of Nottingham v. Fishel* [2000] I.C.R. 1462.

[52.] Act to Amend an Act of 5 Elizabeth, 54 Geo. 3, c. 96.

[53.] See *Industrial Relations Law,* pp. 213-214.

[54.] *Dunk v. George Waller & Sons Ltd.* [1970] 2 Q.B. 163 at 169.

[55.] See *infra,* pp. 87-88.

[56.] [1962] I.R. 77; see *ante,* p. 40.

[57.] [1960] I.R. 74; see *ante,* p. 39.

of the social welfare legislation. Most of the employment protection Acts apply as much to apprentices as to employees, the contract of employment generally being defined to include a contract of apprenticeship.[58] However, many apprentices are excluded from the National Minimum Wage Act 2000,[59] and certain categories of trainees and probationers are excluded from the Unfair Dismissal Acts 1977-93.[60] For apprentices who come within the 1977-93 Acts, it would seem that their dismissal at the expiry of their contract would not ordinarily be regarded as an unfair dismissal. Most likely, the dismissal would be justified as being for some other substantial reason which warrants dismissal. It has been held in England that a dismissal of an apprentice when his contract expires ordinarily would not be treated as a dismissal by reason of his redundancy.[61]

Persons being employed for the first time on reaching 18 years of age or, where already employed, who continue working at that age are not entitled to the full guaranteed minimum wage. Instead, they are entitled to 80 per cent of the national rate in the first of those years and 90 per cent in the second.[62] Where employees undergo prescribed study or training courses during their normal working hours, they too are not entitled to the full guaranteed minimum wage but to 75, 80 and 90 per cent of that rate over the period.[63]

Sections 27-40 of the Industrial Training Act 1967 give An Foras (before 1987, An Chomhairle) extensive authority to regulate the position of apprentices.[64] This power is contingent on the employer being involved in a "designated industrial activity" as classified by an industrial training order. The main objective of the 1967 Act is to foster training; to that end, levies are imposed on employers in designated activities and An Foras makes grants to encourage training from the proceeds of those levies. Regulations adopted by An Foras in respect of apprenticeship in a designated activity may deal with matters like minimum age for commencing employment, educational or other qualifications or suitability for employment, the circumstances in which trainees may be dismissed or suspended, the period of training to be undergone, the form of contract to be used, and prohibiting the taking of any premium or other consideration for employing an apprentice. Employers in designated activities must first obtain the consent of An Foras before they may hire an apprentice. An Foras is authorised to declare that every person employed in a particular manner shall be deemed to be an apprentice for the purposes of the 1967 Act. An Foras may also require apprentices to attend training courses provided by a vocational education committee, but the employer of an apprentice who attends a course of that nature is not obliged to pay remuneration in respect of the period attending the course.

---

58.   *e.g.* Parental Leave Act 1998, s.2(1).
59.   s.5(b); apprentices within the meaning of the Industrial Training Act 1967 or the Labour Services Act 1987.
60.   ss.3 and 4; see *post,* p. 200.
61.   *North East Coast Ship Repairers Ltd. v. Secretary of State* [1978] I.C.R. 755.
62.   National Minimum Wage Act 2000, s.15.
63.   *ibid.* s.16.
64.   Labour Services Act 1987, and Apprentices Rules 1997, S.I. No. 168.

THE WORKPLACE

Most work is performed at a particular workplace, such as at the employer's factory, shop, office or some other premises. But there are employments that are carried on in several locations and some jobs entail considerable travel from place to place. Indeed, much of a person's work may have to be done abroad.[65] It is for the employer and the employee to agree where the work is to be performed. For the purpose of locating the workplace, ordinarily "mobility clauses" in the employment contract will be disregarded and the enquiry is predominantly a factual one, *viz.* where has the employee been working for the purpose of the employer's business. Where there have been changes in the actual workplace, due account will be taken of them. Usually it will be quite obvious from the circumstances where that place is located.

Changing the workplace

Often employers seek to move their employees from one location to another. An employer cannot require an employee to work somewhere that is not envisaged by their agreement; any unilateral attempt to impose on the employee another workplace would be in breach of the employment contract. One of the circumstances that constitutes redundancy for the purposes of the Redundancy Payments Acts 1967-79, is that the employer "has ceased or intends to cease, to carry on that business in the place where the employee was employed".[66] Thus, a unilaterally imposed change of the workplace can render an employee redundant, thereby entitling him to a lump sum compensation as provided for by those Acts.[67] A forced change in the workplace may also render a dismissal unfair under the Unfair Dismissals Acts 1977-93.[68]

Employers may stipulate in the employment contract for considerable discretion regarding the locus of the workplace, by providing that the employee shall work anywhere in a specified region to which he is posted. Whether such a power must always be exercised reasonably in the circumstances remains to be determined.[69] In appropriate circumstances the courts may imply a mobility clause into the employment contract.[70] Any implied clause of that nature can only be exercised reasonably;[71] what changes in a workplace location are reasonable depends on all the circumstances of the case.

REMUNERATION

The employer's principal obligation under the contract of employment is to pay the agreed remuneration. If he does not do so, the employee can sue him for that

---

[65.] See *post,* Chap.11 on "transnational employment".

[66.] 1967 Act, s.7(2)(a).

[67.] See *post,* p. 216 *et seq.*

[68.] See *post,* p. 202 *et seq.*

[69.] *cf. Rank Xerox v. Churchill* [1988] I.R.L.R. 280, *White v. Reflecting Roadstuds Ltd.* [1991] I.C.R. 733 and *High Table Ltd. v. Horst* [1998] I.C.R. 409.

[70.] *e.g. O'Brien v. Associated Fire Alarm Ltd.* [1968] 1 W.L.R. 1916 and *Jones v. Associated Tunnelling Ltd.* [1981] I.R.L.R. 477.

[71.] *ibid.* and *Courtaulds Northern Spinning Ltd. v. Sibson* [1988] I.C.R. 451.

sum and, generally, is entitled to treat the non-payment as a repudiation of the contract. How much those wages should be is determined by agreement between the employer and employee, often represented by a trade union. Since 1909 there has been a mechanism for fixing minimum wages in particular sectors of the economy, which in 2000 was supplemented by an all-embracing guaranteed minimum wage, presently £4.70 per hour.

Subject to the Payment of Wages Act 1991, remuneration is to be paid in the manner agreed between the employer and the employee. In the past, payment in cash was the norm but today most "white collar" workers are paid either by cheque or by a credit transfer to their bank accounts. There are some employees who are partly remunerated in kind, like agricultural workers who may receive produce from the farm, employees of financial institutions who get low interest loans, and employees of various transport companies who benefit from cheap travel. Some employers provide their employees with luncheon vouchers and some have remuneration arrangements that involve issuing to employees shares in their employing company or in its holding company. The treatment of "benefits in kind" is a major concern of income tax law.[72]

The personal scope of the National Minimum Wage Act 2000 and of the Payment of Wages Act 1991, is very extensive. Both cover employees, apprentices and persons holding office in the public sector but, unlike the 1991 Act, the 2000 Act does not apply to certain apprentices, nor to members of the Garda Síochána nor of the Defence Forces. Both Acts also apply to persons who have made any other contract "to do or perform personally any work or service" for a third person (1991 Act) or for the other party or a third person (2000 Act). Subject to this, neither Act makes express reference to employment agency personnel. Neither Act addresses the question of their extraterritorial application, if any.

Defining "remuneration"

Remuneration in this context means what the employer has agreed to give an employee in exchange for the latter's work. There are various statutory provisions that deal with pay or remuneration and the question frequently arises of what exactly constitutes pay or remuneration for the statutory purposes. For instance, are pensions or employers' pension contributions "pay" for those purposes? Article 141 (formerly 119) of the EEC Treaty, which establishes the principle of equal pay for equal work, defines pay for its purpose as "the ordinary basic or minimum wage or salary and any other consideration, whether in cash or in kind, which the worker receives directly or indirectly, in respect of his employment from his employer."[73] The Unfair Dismissals Act 1977 contains a slightly different definition; under it, "remuneration", for the purpose of calculating the compensation to be paid to an employee who was unfairly dismissed, "includes allowances in the nature of pay and benefits in lieu of or in addition to pay."[74]

Special concepts of remuneration exist under tax law, social welfare law and family law, and what amounts to remuneration for these purposes is not always wages, pay or remuneration for the purposes of the employment legislation. The term used in Part V of the Taxes Consolidation Act 1997, which deals with

---

[72.] See *post*, p. 333-334.
[73.] See *post*, pp. 128-129.
[74.] Section 7(3); see *post*, p. 211.

Schedule E income taxation, is "emoluments", which mean, *inter alia*, "all salaries, fees, wages, prerequisites or profits or gains whatsoever arising from an
office or employment, or the amount of any annuity, pension or stipend as the
case may be."[75] The term used in section 2(i) of the Social Welfare (Consolidation) Act 1993, for the purpose of determining remuneration on which social welfare contributions are to be calculated, is "reckonable earnings", which is defined
as "earnings derived from insurable employment".[76]

For the purposes of the National Minimum Wage Act 2000, which sets a minimum wage for virtually all sectors of the economy, "pay" is defined as all
"amounts of payment ... made or allowed by an employer to an employee in
respect of [his] employment",[77] including any benefit in kind referred to in Part I
of that Act's schedule.

For the purposes of the Payment of Wages Act 1991, which provides for the
modes of paying wages and imposes restrictions on deductions from them,
"wages" are defined as follows:[78]

> "any sums payable to the employee by the employer in connection with his
> employment including
>
> (a) any fee, bonus or commission, or any holiday, sick or maternity pay,
>   or any other emolument, referable to his employment,[79] whether
>   payable under his contract of employment or *v.* otherwise, and
>
> (b) any sum payable to the employee upon the termination by the
>   employer of his contract of employment without his having given to
>   the employee the appropriate prior notice of the termination, being a
>   sum paid in lieu of the giving of such notice:[80]
>
> Provided however that the following payments shall not be regarded as
> wages for the purposes of this definition:
>
> (i)   any payment in respect of expenses incurred by the employee in car-
>   rying out his employment,
>
> (ii)   any payment by way of a pension, allowance or gratuity in connec-
>   tion with the death, or the retirement or resignation from his employ-
>   ment, of the employee or as compensation for loss of office,
>
> (iii) any payment referable to the employee's redundancy,
>
> (iv)   any payment to the employee otherwise than in his capacity as an
>   employee,
>
> (v)   any payment in kind or benefit in kind."

Fixing the remuneration - Minimum Wage

In most cases the parties to the contract of employment will determine, either
expressly or by implication, what remuneration is to be paid and when it shall

---

75. Taxes Consolidation Act 1997, s.113(1); see *post,* pp. 325-332.
76. See *post,* p. 346.
77. s.2(1).
78. s.1(1).
79. *cf. Nerva v. R.L. & F. Ltd.* [1997] I.C.R. 11 on waiters' "tips".
80. *cf. Delaney v. Staples* [1992] 1 A.C. 687.

become payable. Frequently, this is settled through collective bargaining, the outcome of which may be incorporated into the employment contract. Among the matters that must be notified to employees in the written statement of particulars, given under the Terms of Employment (Information) Act 1994, are the "rate or method of calculation of [the] remuneration" and the "length of the intervals between the times at which remuneration is paid, whether weekly, monthly or any other period";[81] changes in these terms must also be notified in writing.

Subject to three principal qualifications, the parties are legally free to determine the remuneration to be paid. Unlike the position in some countries, generally the employer and employee are legally free to agree on terms of remuneration that differ from those set down in a collective agreement that purports to apply to that very employment.

Equal pay

Employers are prohibited by Article 141 (formerly 119) of the EEC Treaty and also by the Employment Equality Act 1998, from paying women less than men who do similar work, and vice versa. Section 29 of this Act gives other designated minorities a right to equal pay. The whole question of "equal pay" is considered in Chapter 6.

Sector minimum wages

Under Part IV of the Industrial Relations Act 1946, compulsory minimum wages (and other terms and conditions) can be set by the Labour Court for specified economic sectors, and all employers affected by those orders in the relevant sector are obliged to pay at least the statutory minimum. Part IV of the 1946 Act is the successor to the old trade boards, which were first established in 1909 in order to combat what were known as "sweat shops". Not alone can payments due under a minimum wages order be recovered in a civil action for breach of contract but the employer can be prosecuted for not paying the prescribed rates of pay.[82] An employer who is convicted of that offence may be ordered to pay the difference between the statutory minimum and the actual wages paid for the preceding three years.[83] In April 2001 minimum wages and conditions orders were in force for the industries and occupations set out below.[84]

[81.]   s.3(1)(g) and (h), and s.5.

[82.]   Industrial Relations Act 1946, s.44.

[83.]   *ibid.* s.45 and *Minister for Labour v. Costello* [1988] I.R. 235.

[84.]   Aerated Waters and Wholesale Bottling Joint Labour Committee (no. 10 of 2001); Agricultural Workers Joint Labour Committee (no. 123 of 2001); Brush and Broom Joint Labour Committee (no. 207 of 1994); Catering Joint Labour Committee (Other than Dublin) (no. 285 of 2000); Contract Cleaning Joint Labour Committee (Dublin) (no. 84 of 2000); Hairdressing Joint Labour Committee (Cork) (no. 40 of 1994); Hairdressing Joint Labour Committee (Dublin) (no. 96 of 2001); Handkerchief and Household Piece Goods Joint Labour Committee (no. 277 of 2000); Hotels Joint Labour Committee (Other than Dublin) (no. 400 of 2000); Law Clerks Joint Labour Committee (no. 122 of 2001); Provender Milling Joint Labour Committee (no. 259 of 2001); Retail Grocery and Allied Trades Joint Labour Committee (no. 51 of 2000); Security Industry Joint Labour Committee (no. 35 of 2001); Shirtmaking Joint Labour Committee (no. 275 of 2000); Tailoring Joint Labour Committee (no. 276 of 2000); Women's Clothing and Millinery Joint Labour Committee (no. 274 of 2000).

National minimum wage

In many countries the law specifies a minimum wage that must be paid to all employees, regardless of what sector they work in, for instance the "SMIG" and the "SMIC" in France. For the last 80 years it was considered preferable in Ireland and also in Britain not to have a single all-embracing compulsory minimum wage and that the State should not directly involve itself in wage-fixing, except in sectors which were not unionised, which is the system as just described under Part IV of the Industrial Relations Act 1946. Then, in 1998, to implement an election promise made the previous year by the British Labour Party, a national minimum wage was established in the United Kingdom.[85] Two years later, a similar system was adopted in Ireland in the National Minimum Wage Act 2000, and that minimum is presently £4.70 per hour.[86]

Under the 2000 Act the Minister is empowered by order to determine the amount of the minimum wage and, on a recommendation from the Labour Court, may vary that figure.[87] Thereupon, all employees over 18 years of age must be paid an hourly rate that, on average over the relevant period, is not less than this minimum. Employees under 18 years are entitled to be paid 70 per cent of the national minimum[88] and there are graduations for employees between the ages of 18 and 20 years of age,[89] and for employees undergoing training or a course of study during their normal working hours.[90] Employers in financial difficulty can be exempted by the Labour Court for up to one year from having to pay the required minimum[91] but such exemption can be obtained only once.

In order to determine whether an employer is complying with its obligations, one divides the gross pay received for the relevant period by the total hours worked then.[92] Among the information that must be given to employees on being hired is the "pay reference period" for making this calculation.[93] "Pay" is defined to include shift premiae, productivity-related incentives and commissions, the value of board and lodgings, service charges and other items set out in Part I of the 2000 Act's schedule; Part II of that schedule then excludes several items, such as overtime and unsociable hours premiae, tips, employers' pension contributions, travelling and similar expenses. "Working hours" for these purposes[94] include overtime, time spent travelling on official business and time spent training during normal working hours, but not time travelling to and from home to work, on standby or on leave. Compliance is facilitated by employers being

---

[85.] National Minimum Wage Act 1998 (c.39); see generally, Simpson, "A Milestone in the Legal Regulations of Pay", (1999) 28 Ind. L.J. 1 and "Implementing the National Minimum Wage", (1999) 28 Ind. L. J. 171.

[86.] National Minimum Wage (National Minimum Hourly Rate of Pay) (No. 2) Order, 2000, S.I. No. 201.

[87.] ss.11-13.

[88.] s.14(a).

[89.] s.14(b).

[90.] ss.15 and 16. See National Minimum Wage Act 2000 (Prescribed Courses of Study or Training) Regulations 2000, S.I. No. 99.

[91.] s.41.

[92.] s.20.

[93.] s.44.

[94.] s.8.

required to keep records,[95] which may be examined by inspectors appointed by the Minister. On request, an employee is entitled to be given a written statement of his average hourly rate in the immediately previous 12-month period.[96]

Employees may sue their employers in the courts for breach of the implied term to pay the minimum wage which the 2000 Act puts into all contracts covered by that Act.[97] In certain circumstances, those proceedings may be brought by the Minister on behalf of and in the name of the employee,[98] that is where it is not reasonable to expect him or his trade union to bring the proceedings. Instead of going to court, a claim may be made to a rights commissioner,[99] from whose decision there is a right of appeal to the Labour Court, with a further appeal on a point of law to the High Court. Additionally, an employer's breach of this Act is a criminal offence[100] and, on top of the penalty when convicted, the court may order him to pay such sum as is due to the employee.[101] Provision is made giving employees protection against being victimised for asserting their rights under this Act.[102]

Sick pay

One of the particulars that the Terms of Employment (Information) Act 1994 requires to be provided to new employees within that Act are "any term or conditions relating to incapacity for work due to sickness or injury and sick pay."[103] Where these particulars are supplied, then generally, there is no great difficulty in determining whether or not the employee is to be paid when absent due to illness or incapacity. Where the parties have not agreed on this matter or where no particulars were supplied and have been accepted by the employee, the legal position is not entirely clear. There is a division of opinion in the cases decided in Britain and the only reported Irish authority[104] does not take sides on the point of principle.

One view is that, unless there is a term to the contrary in the contract, employees are entitled to receive remuneration while absent by reason of illness. As was observed in *Marrison v. Bell*,[105] "under a contract of service, irrespective of the question of the length of notice provided by that contract, wages continue through sickness and incapacity from sickness to do the work contracted for until the contract is terminated by [due] notice. . . ."[106] The reason for implying such a term was that "the great majority of employed persons in this country are employed on terms of a week's or, at any rate, a month's notice . . . ; and consequently there is no social need for protecting the employer from the liability of

---

[95.] s.22.
[96.] s.23.
[97.] ss.7(2) and 50(1).
[98.] s.39.
[99.] ss.24-30.
[100.] ss.35, 37 and 38.
[101.] s.50(2).
[102.] s.36.
[103.] s.3(k)(i).
[104.] *Flynn v. Great Northern Rly. (Ir.) Ltd.* (1955) 89 I.L.T.R. 46 at 60-61.
[105.] [1939] 2 K.B. 187.
[106.] *ibid.* at 198.

having to go on paying wages which he is always able to terminate after a short time".[107] It was held there that this implied term stood even where the employee was in receipt of sickness benefit under the National Insurance Acts.[108]

The other view does not quite go to the opposite extreme, that the presumption is "no work, no pay" and it is for the employee to rebut that presumption. Instead, there is no presumption one way or another; account should be taken of all the circumstances of the case and those should indicate what the parties would have decided about sick pay had they addressed the question.[109] Among the relevant matters is how the parties acted with reference to sick pay after they made their contract. In *Mears v. Safecar Security Ltd.,*[110] where this approach was endorsed, it was found that practically every relevant circumstance in that case indicated that there was to be no sick pay. The company's practice was not to pay sick pay and that was well known to the employees; the plaintiff had been sick for 7 out of 14 months and, at that time, never asked for sick pay; on leaving the job he only asked for holiday pay and it was some time later that he decided to claim sick pay. In *Flynn v. Great Northern Rly. (Irl.) Ltd.,*[111] under the collective agreement which applied to the plaintiff, *ex gratia* payments were to be made to employees during temporary illnesses. Budd J. held that this was inconsistent with there being any legal right to sick pay; the *ex gratia* payment was a substitute for whatever right to wages as might exist.[112]

Statement of wages and deductions

Section 4 of the Payment of Wages Act 1991 requires that all employees within that Act be given a written statement of what their gross wages are and of the nature and amounts of any deductions made from them. Employers are required to take reasonable steps to ensure that those statements are confidential. Ordinarily, this statement must be given at the time the wages are being paid. Where the wages are being paid by credit transfer, this statement must be given very shortly afterwards.

Payment by cheque or otherwise

The 250-year-old requirement in the Truck Acts 1743 *et seq.* that wages must always be paid in full in cash was replaced by section 2 of the Payment of Wages Act 1991. This authorises payment of the money due either in cash or by cheque, bill of exchange or several similar forms of payment. Other modes of payment may be laid down by the Minister and there is a *force majeure* provision for where there is a bank strike or lock-out. However, where before July 23, 1991, an employee was paid in cash, he must continue to be paid in cash unless he or his union agreed that he should be paid by one of the other permissible modes.[113]

---

107. *ibid.* at 204.
108. Similarly, *Orman v. Saville Sportswear Ltd.* [1960] 1 W.L.R. 1055.
109. *O'Grady v. Saper* [1940] 2 K.B. 469.
110. [1983] 1 Q.B. 54.
111. (1955) 89 I.L.T.R. 46.
112. Similarly, *Petrie v. MacFisheries Ltd.* [1940] 1 K.B. 258.
113. s.3(2).

This also applies where, by agreement, the employee was paid otherwise than in cash; if that agreement or arrangement is terminated, he again becomes entitled to be paid in cash unless he or his union agrees otherwise.

Deductions from remuneration

Subject principally to the provisions of the Payment of Wages Act 1991, employers and employees can agree to make deductions from the latter's remuneration, for instance, for trade union subscriptions, pension fund contributions and also in respect of defective work or for other disciplinary purposes. The contractual duty to pay the full amount of wages earned is qualified by any agreement regarding deductions. Furthermore, it has been held that the employer is not obliged to pay any remuneration in respect of periods during which the employee was deliberately absent from work.[114] There are certain deductions that are specifically forbidden by statute; in particular, to cover the employer's redundancy contribution under the Redundancy Payment Acts[115] or his contribution under the Social Welfare Acts.[116] On the other hand, there are deductions that employers are legally obliged to make without getting their employee's consent, notably P.A.Y.E. and P.R.S.I. contributions.[117] At one time a judgment creditor of an employee could obtain from a court a garnishee order attaching his salary, in which event the employer had to pay over to the judgment creditor whatever sum had been attached. That form of redress was stopped by the Wages Attachment Abolition Act 1870.[118] However, Part III of the Family Law (Maintenance of Spouses and Children) Act 1976 contains an elaborate mechanism for attaching the earnings of an employee against whom a maintenance order has been made. Section 1002 of the Taxes Consolidation Act 1997 confers extensive authority on the Revenue to attach debts and other sums that are owing to taxpayers who owe tax to the Revenue; but this power does not apply to taxable remuneration payable to an employee or an office-holder.

A major theme of the Truck Acts was regulating the circumstances in which employers could make deductions from wages; that is now dealt with by section 5 of the Payment of Wages Act 1991. As is explained above, the categories of workers covered by this Act and what constitutes wages for its purposes are defined very extensively. What is a deduction for these purposes is also defined very widely as any difference between the total amount of wages properly payable to the employee and the amount he receives.[119] In other words, wages which are properly payable but are not paid are to be treated to the extent of the non-payment as within the scope of the expression "deduction". Accordingly, transfer payments as well as sums retained by the employer are in principle deductions.

But what may appear at first sight to be a deduction may not be so because it is really the consequence of how the amount of wages payable is calculated. For example, in *Deane v. Wilson*,[120] the plaintiff was employed in a shirt factory and

---

114. *e.g. Sim v. Rotherham Metropolitan B.C.* [1987] 1 Ch.216.
115. 1967 Act, s.28(4), as amended.
116. Social Welfare Consolidation Act 1993, s.10(5).
117. See *post,* p. 341 *et seq.*
118. 33 & 34 Vict. c. 30.
119. s.5(6). *cf. Sullivan v. Dept. of Education* [1998] E.L.R. 217.
120. [1906] 2 I.R. 405.

was to be paid eight shillings a week; there was also "an attendance bonus" of two shillings which would be paid if there was full attendance at work throughout the week. One week when she was absent for a quarter of a day, she was not paid this two shillings. It was held that there was no breach of the Truck Acts because that sum had not been deducted from her wages; it was money that was never earned and never even became payable to her. Therefore, "a mode of calculating the wages to be paid in which deductions are made may take the case outside the [1991] Act altogether".[121] Where a worker is lawfully suspended from employment for a period without pay, the Truck Acts were not contravened because the employee "ceases to be under any present duty to work, and the employer ceases to be under any consequent duty to pay."[122]

Transfer payments

Transfer payments made by an employer to a third party fell outside the Truck Acts provided the employee agreed that part of his remuneration should be paid over to some third party.[123] Payments of that nature are allowed by the 1991 Act provided the employee gave his prior consent to them in writing and the third party notified the employer that the sum or sums in question are owed by the employee.[124] Transfer payments can be made without the employee's consent where, by virtue of any statutory provision, the employer is obliged to deduct a sum from wages and pay it over to a "public authority".[125]

Court orders

Subject to some exceptions, described below, an employer cannot set-off against wages payable by him a sum he is owed by the employee; this was so even where the employee's debt to the employer had been upheld by a court or tribunal.[126] But if the employee agreed in writing in advance to a deduction of that nature, it is permitted by the 1991 Act.[127] Deductions may also be made on foot of a court order in respect of debts owed by an employee to a third party or an amount payable into court or the tribunal.[128] In this case, the 1991 Act does not require the employee's prior consent.

Rectifying over-payments

Another permitted deduction is in order to rectify an over-payment made to the employee in respect of his wages or of expenses incurred by him in carrying out his work.[129] That deduction must not exceed the amount of the over-payment.

[121.] *Sagar v. Ridehalgh* [1931] 1 Ch.310 at 327.
[122.] *ibid.* and *Bird v. British Celanese Ltd.* [1945] 1 K.B. 336.
[123.] *Hewlett v. Allen* [1894] A.C. 383.
[124.] s.5(5)(d).
[125.] s.5(5)(c).
[126.] *Williams v. North's Navigation Collieries* (1889) A.C. 136.
[127.] s.5(5)(f); contrast *Penman v. Fife Coal Co.* [1936] A.C. 45.
[128.] s.5(5)(g).
[129.] s.5(5)(a).

Goods or services necessary to do the work

Deductions are also permitted by the 1991 Act where the employer has provided the employee with goods or services which are "necessary to the employment", for instance, tools of the trade and the provision of training. Of course, equipment to do the work and training are often supplied by employers free of charge. Before any deduction can be made in respect of these items, requirements similar to those described next for disciplinary measures must have been satisfied.[130]

Disciplinary measures

Deductions may be made for any "act or omission of" an employee provided that the stringent requirements of section 5(2) of the 1991 Act have been met. An exception is where the disciplinary deduction is made in consequence of disciplinary proceedings provided for by statute,[131] for instance, the Garda Síochána Discipline Regulations. The general requirements for deductions are sixfold:

1. They must have been authorised by a term of the employment contract; that term may be implied as well as express.

2. The amount deducted must be "fair and reasonable", having regard to all the circumstances, including the employee's earnings.

3. Before the act or omission being penalised ever occurred, the employee must have been given a written copy of the contractual term allowing deductions or he must have been given written notice of the existence and effect of that term.

4. At least one week before the deduction was made, the employee must have been given written particulars of the act or omission which caused the deduction.

5. If the deduction was to compensate the employer for loss he suffered as a result of the employee's acts or inaction, the amount withheld must not exceed the amount of the loss or damage suffered.

6. The deduction or, if more than one is being made, the first deduction must be made within six months of the employer discovering the employee's act or omission in question.

Employee taking industrial action

Certain deductions can be made from the wages of employees who have gone on strike or who have taken part in other industrial action. This gives legislative recognition to recent case law developments in Britain but the 1991 Act does not specify exactly what sums may be deducted from employees resorting to industrial action; all it says is that the deductions may be made "on account of having taken part in" that action.[132]

[130.] s.5(2).

[131.] s.5(5)(b).

[132.] s.5(5)(e).

Where an employee refuses to perform duties required by the contract, it has been held that, even if the contract does not expressly authorise deductions from remuneration, his employer may in effect make such deductions. By "in effect" here is meant, where the employer is entitled to damages in respect of the breach but the employee sues for wages for the period during which that breach was committed, the employer would be entitled to set-off those damages against whatever wages the employee would be entitled to. By virtue of the right of set-off, the employer is in effect authorised to make the deductions. Thus, in *Sim v. Rotherham Council*,[133] as a form of industrial action and in breach of their contracts, secondary school teachers refused to provide "cover" during school hours for absent colleagues. Instead of dismissing them, their employer deducted a sum from their monthly earnings; it was accepted that the amount of those deductions was at least equivalent to any damages the teachers would have been required to pay if they had been sued for breach of contract. It was contended that, as a matter of legal principle, no deduction could be made in those circumstances. But it was held that the employer is entitled to set-off the damages that could be recovered against the employees' weekly or monthly wages, as the case may be. As Scott J. put it, "if an employee, in breach of contract, fails or refuses to perform his contractual services, his right or title to recover his salary for the period during which the failure or refusal occurred is impeached by the employer's cross-claim for damages. It would be manifestly unjust in such a case to allow the employee to recover his salary in full without taking into account the loss to the employer of those services."[134]

Where the employee refuses to perform a particular task or tasks and, in response, the employer informs him that he is not needed at work during the period when those tasks call to be performed, it has been held that the employer's right to make deductions from remuneration is based on fundamental principles, and not merely on the law regarding set-off. That was in *Miles v. Wakefield Council*[135] where, in pursuance of industrial action and in breach of his obligations, the plaintiff refused to carry out his principal duties on Saturdays. Although he was willing to attend at the workplace on Saturdays, his employer told him that he should not do so for so long as he persisted in his refusal. His employer then deducted from his monthly salary a sum equivalent to what his earnings would have been had he actually worked on Saturdays. On the basis of the principle "no work, no pay", it was held that the employer was entitled to make those deductions. According to Lord Templeman:

"wages are remuneration which must be earned; in a claim for wages under a contract of employment, the worker must assert that he worked or was willing to work. . . . When a worker in breach of contract declines to work in accordance with the contract, but claims payment for his wages, it is unnecessary to consider the law relating to damages and unnecessary for the employer to rely on the defence of an abatement or equitable set-off. The employer may or may not sustain or be able to prove and recover damages

---

[133.] [1987] 1 Ch.216.
[134.] *ibid.* at 261-262.
[135.] [1987] A.C. 540.

by reason of the breach of contract for each worker. But so far as wages are concerned, the worker can only claim them if he is willing to work."[136]

The full implications of the "no work no pay" principle have yet to be determined by the courts. But there is no inherent or implied right to withhold wages for bad work or as a disciplinary measure.

Assignment and attachment of remuneration

Most forms of property, including future property, can be assigned to someone else by their owner or the owner-to-be. On account of the uniquely personal nature of the contract of employment, contracts of that nature cannot be assigned. But wages or remuneration received by employees are assignable. In *Picton v. Cullen*,[137] where the court appointed a receiver over the salary of a teacher which was due and payable, all of the judges accepted that his future earnings could not be assigned or attached. Whether this principle applies equally to private sector employees has not been determined but there does not appear to be any compelling reason why it should not be so extended.

As has been explained, subject to certain exceptions, wages cannot be attached in favour of an employee's creditor; in other words, future wages cannot be the subject of a garnishee order.[138] An exception to this is maintenance orders in family law proceedings.[139] That other creditors' remedy, the appointment of a receiver by way of equitable execution, cannot be applied to the future earnings of public officials nor of private sector employees. In *McCreery v. Bennett*,[140] a clerk to the petty sessions had assigned his official salary to the plaintiff to secure an annuity. When the annuity fell into arrears, the plaintiff sought to have a receiver appointed over the clerk's future salary. That application was rejected by Kenny J. on the grounds that public policy protects the remuneration of judicial officers from such process. But Barton J. would extend this principle much wider, observing that "[i]t makes no difference whether the judgment debtor is a public officer or a person earning a salary in private employment. Future earnings or salary could not have been attached by a writ of sequestration before the Judicature Act . . . and cannot be reached by the appointment of a receiver by way of equitable execution in any division of the High Court".[141] He further observed that the court was not concerned at that stage about the legality of the deed of assignment which the clerk had executed; that could be raised in the action to enforce the deed.[142] But once remuneration has fallen due it then can be subject to the appointment of a receiver.

Normal remuneration

Like the concept of normal working hours, an employee's normal pay can be central to measuring the exact extent of his entitlements under several legislative provisions. Statutory holiday pay is calculated on the basis of the employee's

---

[136.] *ibid.* at 564-565.
[137.] [1900] 2 I.R. 612.
[138.] Wages Attachment (Abolition) Act 1870, 33 & 34 Vict. c. 30.
[139.] See, generally, A. Shatter, *Family Law* (4th ed., 1997), Chap. 14.
[140.] [1904] 2 I.R. 69.
[141.] *ibid.* at 74.
[142.] ibid.

"normal weekly rate" as defined in the Organisation of Working Time Act 1997;[143] the lump sum statutory redundancy payment is based on the "normal weekly remuneration" as defined in the Redundancy Payments Act 1967;[144] compensation for employees who are unfairly dismissed is based on the "week's remuneration" as defined in regulations issued under the Unfair Dismissals Act 1977.[145]

TIMES OF WORK

It is for the employer and employee to agree when the work shall be done. In unionised establishments, working times, along with overtime and lay-off provisions, are usually the subject of collective agreements. Occasionally, employees may be given a degree of discretion as regards the precise working times. One of the particulars that the Terms of Employment (Information) Act 1994 requires to be provided to new employees is "any terms or conditions relating to hours of work or overtime";[146] changes in those times must also be notified in writing.

Since early in the last century there have been special provisions regarding the times when young persons and women were permitted to work. The reduction of hours of work and, in particular, the eight-hour day was one of the most constant demands of organised labour during the nineteenth century. Working times was also one of the major areas of concern of the International Labour Organisation (I.L.O.) in its early years, and the I.L.O. has promulgated Conventions on the standard eight-hour day, the standard 40-hour week, weekly rest periods, paid holidays and paid educational leave. State parties to the European Social Charter undertake "to provide for reasonable daily and weekly working hours, the working week to be progressively reduced to the extent that the increase of productivity and other relevant factors permit".[147] Employees in certain non-unionised sectors have their working times determined by employment regulation orders made under Part IV of the Industrial Relations Act 1946.[148]

Organisation of Working Time Act 1997

Many important aspects of working times are now regulated by the Organisation of Working Time Act 1997, which gives effect to an EC Council Directive of 1993[149] and repeals several Acts on the question that had been in force since the late 1930s and early 1940s. The 1997 Act applies to not only apprentices and agency personnel but also to the public sector, including the civil service and local government officials; but not to members of the Garda Síochána nor the

---

[143.] s.20(2) and (4).

[144.] See *post,* p. 221.

[145.] See *post,* p. 211.

[146.] ss.3(1)(i) and 5.

[147.] Art.2(1).

[148.] Industrial Relations Act 1946, Part IV; see *supra* p. 76 on "sector minimum wages".

[149.] Directive 93/104 concerning certain aspects of the organisation of working time, O.J. No. L307/18. See, generally, C. Barnard, *E.C. Employment Law* (2nd ed., 2000), pp. 402-420. It was upheld in *United Kingdom v. E.C. Council* (Case C84/94) [1986] E.C.R. 5755. It has been held not to have "direct effect": *Gibson v. East Riding of Yorkshire Council* [2000] I.C.R. 891.

Defence Forces, nor to several other categories of employment enumerated in sections 3 and 4 of that Act, *inter alia*, those fishing and working at sea, doctors in training, civil protection services and transport workers.[150] Several of this Act's statutory requirements can be derogated from in a sense by way of collective agreements which have been approved by the Labour Court under section 24 of the Act. Provision is made for the Labour Relations Commission issuing a Code of Practice, providing guidance on how the Act's requirements should be implemented.[151]

Compliance with this Act's requirements is policed by an inspectorate and employers are required to keep relevant records at the workplace.[152] Further, compliance with the Act's requirements is secured, *inter alia*, by the employee in question or his trade union making a complaint to a rights commissioner,[153] from whose decision there is an appeal to the Labour Court. An employee who was dismissed for opposing contravention of the Act may instead claim for unfair dismissal in the Employment Appeals Tribunal (E.A.T).[154]

48-hour week

Perhaps the 1997 Act's most significant feature is section 15, which stipulates that the average working week shall not exceed forty eight hours a week over a four or a six months period. When calculating this period, absences on annual or sick leave, or on what may be described as "statutory leave", are not counted. In the case of seasonal work and comparable work, where things are very busy for some months and then become slack, the relevant reference period may be determined by a collective agreement approved by the Labour Court.[155] There are additional restrictions on working hours for children and for young persons.[156]

8-hour night

Under section 16 of the 1997 Act in any 24-hour period a "night worker" shall not be required to work more than an average of eight hours a day in any two months or otherwise stipulated period in an approved collective agreement. When calculating this period, absences on annual or sick leave, or on what may be described as "statutory leave" and also "rest periods" under section 13 of the Act are not counted. Where the work involves special hazards or a heavy physical or mental strain, the employee may not be required to work more than eight hours in any 24-hour period. Employers must carry out risk assessments in order to determine whether night work involves special hazards or heavy physical or mental

---

[150.] *cf.* Organisation of Working Time (General Exemption) Regulations 1998 (S.I. No. 21), Organisation of Working Time (Exemption of Transport Activities) Regulations 1998 (S.I. No. 20), and *Coastal Line Container Ltd. v. S.I.P.T.U.* [2000] E.L.R. 1 and Organisation of Working Time (Exemption of Civil Protection Services) Regulations, 1998, S.I. no. 21.

[151.] s.35; see *infra*, n.159.

[152.] ss.25 and 36.

[153.] ss.27 and 28.

[154.] s.26.

[155.] s.15(5).

[156.] See *infra*, pp. 87-88.

strain.[157] There are additional restrictions on children and young persons being employed at night.

Rest periods

Sections 11-13 of the 1997 Act prescribe minimum rest periods and intervals for those employments subject to the Act and the details of these must be notified in writing to those employees.[158] A code of practice has been published regarding compensatory rest and related matters.[159] In every 24 hours, employees are entitled to a rest period of not less than 11 consecutive hours.[160] In every four and a half hours of actual working time, employees are entitled to a break of at least 15 minutes; in every six hours working time, that break must be at least 30 minutes.[161]

In every seven days, employees are entitled to a rest period of at least 24 consecutive hours;[162] that period shall be on or include a Sunday, unless the contract of employment provides otherwise. In lieu of this rest period, an employer may grant two rest periods each of not less than 24 consecutive hours, which also must include a Sunday. Generally, weekly rest periods must commence at the end of a daily rest period provided for in section 11 of the Act.

Zero hours

Section 18 of the 1997 Act applies to what are described as "zero hours" practices, under which employees are required to be available for work over a stipulated period or as and when so required by the employer,[163] except where the work is casual or where the employee is on call in the case of an emergency. The object here is to ensure that the employee is paid at least a minimum when he does not have to work for less than 25 per cent of that period. If he is not required to do any work in the week, he must be paid at least either for 14 hours work or for 25 per cent of the contract hours; if he worked for less than that percentage hours (and they are less than 15 hours) then his pay must be increased accordingly. Where the contract entitles him to be paid for all of the time he holds himself available, this section does not apply.

Young persons

Ever since the factories legislation in 1802,[164] the employment of children and young persons has been regulated and today is the subject of comprehensive international standards. Persons may not be employed on any full-time basis

---

[157.] Safety, Health and Welfare at Work (Night Work and Shift Work) Regulations 2000, S.I. No. 1.

[158.] Terms of Employment (Additional Information) Order 1998, S.I. No. 49.

[159.] Organisation of Working Time (Code of Practice on Compensatory Rest) Order 1998, S.I. No. 44.

[160.] s.11.

[161.] s.12.

[162.] s.13.

[163.] *cf. Johnstone v. Bloomsbury Health Authority* [1992] Q.B. 333, concerning doctors who had a standard 40-hour working week but had to be on call for an additional 48 hours a week on average; also *Sindicato de Medicos v. Conselleria Valenciana* (Case C 303/98) [2000] I.R.L.R. 845.

[164.] Cotton Mills and Factories Act 1802.

unless they have reached the minimum school leaving age. The employment of young persons between that age and 18 years of age is regulated by the Protection of Young Persons (Employment) Act 1996 giving effect to an EEC Council Directive of 1984[165] and repealing an Act of same name enacted in 1977. The 1996 Act applies not only to apprentices and agency personnel but also to the public sector, including the civil service, local government, the Garda Síochána and the Defence Forces. Breach of many of this Act's requirements is a criminal offence, which may be prosecuted summarily by the Minister or the employee's trade union.[166] Any sum due to the employee under this Act may be recovered in proceedings brought by his parent or guardian, or trade union.[167] Claims that the employee was victimised[168] or that his employment terms were improperly reduced may be made to the rights commissioner,[169] from whose decision there is an appeal to the E.A.T. An abstract of the 1996 Act must be given to all children and young persons employed.[170]

It is an offence to employ children aged under 16 years of age, unless the circumstances are covered by section 3 of the 1996 Act. A child over 14 years may be employed out of school term in light work, subject to certain conditions and also on work experience;[171] a child over 15 years of age may be employed in school term in light work for a maximum of eight hours a day and also on work experience;[172] the Minister, by license or regulation, may permit certain other forms of child employment, notably in cultural, artistic, sports or advertising activities.[173] A child under 16 years of age may not be employed between 8 p.m. and 8 a.m. on the following day and section 4 of the 1996 Act lays down maximum durations of employment and rest periods. A young person between 16 and 18 years of age may not be employed between 10 p.m. and 6 a.m. on the following day and section 6 of the 1996 Act lays down maximum durations of employment and rest periods for them. Double employment, *i.e.* working for two or more employers, is prohibited where the aggregate hours worked exceed the prescribed maxima.[174]

Any regulations the Minister makes or licence he grants in derogation of the above requirements can only be effective following consultation with representatives of trade unions and employers' organisations.[175] Employers are given a defence where the person's employment was necessitated by an emergency, such

---

[165.] Directive 94/33 on the protection of young persons at work, O.J. No. L216/12 (1994). See, generally, C. Barnard, *E.C. Employment Law, op. cit.*, pp. 421-426.

[166.] s.24.

[167.] s.16.

[168.] s.17.

[169.] ss.18 and 19.

[170.] Terms of Employment (Information) Act 1994 (Section 3(6)) Order 1997, S.I. No. 4. This abstract is contained in the Protection of Young Persons (Employment) (Prescribed Abstract) Regulations 1997, S.I. No. 3.

[171.] s.3(4) and (6).

[172.] s.3(5) and (8).

[173.] s.3(2) and (3).

[174.] s.10.

[175.] ss.7 and 8. See Protection of Young Persons (Employment of Close Relatives) Regulations 1997, S.I. No. 2, and Protection of Young Persons (Employment – Exclusion of Workers in the Fishing or Shipping Sectors) Regulations 1997, S.I. No. 1.

as a fire, flood, storm, or breakdown of plant or machinery.[176] Employers of persons under 18 years of age are required to get satisfactory evidence of the individual's age[177] and also to maintain satisfactory records.[178] In the case of employing a child under 16 years of age, there must be written permission of a parent or guardian.[179]

Drivers

In 1969 the EEC introduced regulations governing a wide category of drivers of heavy vehicles, like bus drivers and lorry drivers, which were replaced in 1985.[180] These contain rules regarding manning requirements, driving periods, daily rest periods and weekly rest periods; the tachograph, which is a special recording equipment, was made compulsory in order to ensure compliance with many of these requirements.[181] Ordinarily, the vehicle should not be driven for longer than nine hours, which is the "daily driving period", which may be extended twice in any week to ten hours. And after six daily driving periods, the driver must take a weekly rest, which is normally 45 hours but may in certain circumstances be reduced to 36 hours or indeed to 24 hours. Additionally, the driver must take a break after four and a half hours driving, which must last at least 45 minutes.

Normal working hours and overtime

The distinction between normal working hours and overtime is relevant for several purposes. Often the agreed remuneration payable for overtime will be proportionately greater than that for normal working hours; overtime may be paid at time and a quarter or time and a half, or whatever. Overtime does not count for certain statutory requirements. Usually, it is his normal working hours that determine if an employee is protected by particular Acts; for instance, under the Unfair Dismissals Acts and the Redundancy Payments Acts, it is only weeks during which the employee is "normally expected to work" at least eight hours a day which count for the purposes of continuity of employment.[182] But where overtime is not entirely optional, then the employee is normally expected to work for those extra periods. Overtime pay is not included for the purpose of determining the "normal weekly rate" of pay under the regulations made in respect of paid holidays.[183] In determining the amount to be paid to an employee being made redundant, the basis of measurement is his "normal weekly remuneration" as defined in the legislation; where he is "normally expect to work overtime", the relevant figure is his average weekly earnings.[184] When calculating the ceiling on compen-

---

[176.] s.14.

[177.] s.5.

[178.] s.15.

[179.] s.5(1)(b).

[180.] Regulation 3820/85 concerning harmonisation of certain social legislation relating to road transport, O.J. No. L 370/1 (1995).

[181.] See, generally, J. Canny, *The Law of Road Transport and Haulage* (1999), Ch.8.

[182.] See *post*, p. 192.

[183.] Organisation of Working Time (Determination of Pay for Holidays) Regulations 1997, S.I. No. 475.

[184.] Redundancy Payments Act 1967 and Sched. 3, paras 13 and 14.

sation payable under the Unfair Dismissals Acts which is 104 weeks' remuneration, the relevant figure is the remuneration for "normal hours"; where the employee is "normally required to work overtime", then his average weekly overtime earnings are included.[185]

Overtime may be compulsory or voluntary. Ordinarily employees are not obliged to work overtime. But their contracts may stipulate that they must work a certain amount of overtime when called on to do so[186] or, alternatively, they may be entitled to work a specified period of overtime should they choose to do so. Several of the reported cases concern provisions of this nature in collective agreements and the question to be considered was whether the overtime clause in those agreements was incorporated into the workers' employment contracts, either expressly or by implication. For instance, in *Gascol Conversions Ltd. v. Mercer*,[187] the issue was what were the employee's normal working hours for the purpose of calculating the amount of redundancy compensation which should be paid to him. When he commenced working in 1969, he agreed to work a 54 1/2 hour week, with overtime when required, and was remunerated on a 40-hour week basis, all extra hours being paid at overtime rates. This arrangement was confirmed the following year in a national collective agreement applicable to him. But in the year after that, a local collective agreement was concluded for his area, which provided that "working hours . . . will revert to 54 per week." It was held that his normal working hours were not 54 but 40 hours per week because the statement of particulars furnished to him referred only to the national agreement and, additionally, the receipt he signed when he got those particulars described them as "the contract". Perhaps the main principle to be derived from this case is the very strong emphasis the courts tend to put on memoranda and writing when seeking to ascertain the true terms and conditions of employment. The Irish Acts do not contain anything comparable to the provisions of the United Kingdom Acts which define when overtime is to be regarded as part of the normal working hours. The precise meaning of the expression "normally expected work" has not been settled by the Superior Courts.

Temporary absences and lay offs

Apart entirely from paid holidays, and also maternity and comparable leave, circumstances can arise where either the employee is not in a position to work or where the employer does not have sufficient work for him. The employee may have became ill or been injured in an accident; unless the contract of employment otherwise states or where the absence is of such long duration as to amount to frustration of the contract, the employment relationships will continue to subsist during the absence. It also depends on the terms of the contract whether the employee will be entitled to payment of remuneration while absent.

[185.] S.I. No. 287 of 1977, reg.4.
[186.] *cf. Johnstone v. Bloomsbury Health Authority* [1992] Q.B. 333 and *McLory v. Post Office* [1992] I.C.R. 758.
[187.] [1974] I.C.R. 420.

Jury service

An employee called up for jury service has no choice but to absent himself from work. Under section 29 of the Juries Act 1976, a person must be treated as employed or apprenticed when absent on jury service.

Political activities

The courts have not so far ruled on the question whether, and, if so, to what extent, an employee elected to public office is entitled to time off in order to perform his public duties. Special provision is made in almost all of the statutes constituting various public agencies on this point. For instance, section 19(2) of the Pensions Act 1990 provides that any employee of the Pensions Board who becomes a member of either House of the Oireachtas or of the European Parliament shall stand seconded from the Board's employment and shall not be paid any remuneration or allowances during that period. Similar rules apply to the National Authority for Occupational Health and Safety and most equivalent bodies.

Lay offs

Occasionally an employer may not have sufficient work to keep his employees busy and, accordingly, may want to lay them off for a comparatively short period. Whether, or to what extent, employers can do this depends on the terms of the employment contract. In the building industry, short time and lay offs on account of bad weather were so frequent that special "wet time" provisions for that industry were adopted in 1942 until they were phased out in 1985.

Absent a term in the contract to the contrary, the employer's fundamental obligation is to pay the agreed remuneration for the times of work during which the employee is prepared to work.[188] Ordinarily an employer is free to lay off workers for any reason provided he continues paying them.[189] A lay off without paying the normal agreed remuneration can be treated by the employee as a dismissal.

Where remuneration is based on piece work and in similar employments, it is an implied term of the contract that reasonable amounts of work will be provided. An employer therefore is not free to lay off workers employed on those terms, leading to a significant reduction in their earnings. Thus in *Devonald v. Rosser*,[190] which concerned piece rate workers in the tin-plate trade, it was held that their employer could not lay off those workers merely because business had drastically fallen off and there was a serious shortage of orders. The contention that there was a custom which entitled employers to lay off in those circumstances was rejected on the grounds of unreasonableness; such a custom would introduce undue uncertainty into the contract.

Where the workplace must be closed down for a period in order to do necessary repairs, an employer may have an implied contractual right to lay off workers. So it was held in *Browning v. Crumlin Valley Collieries Ltd.*,[191] concerning

---

188. *Hanley v. Pease & Partners* [1915] 1 K.B. 698; see *ante*, p. 69.
189. *Lawe v. Irish Country Meats (Pig Meats) Ltd.* [1998] E.L.R. 266.
190. [1906] 2 K.B. 728.
191. [1926] 1 K.B. 522.

piece workers, where the employers felt compelled to close their coal mines for some weeks in order to repair mine shafts. Because, in the circumstances, the dangerous state of the mines there was not the employers' fault, it was held that both parties to the contract should share the burden of the temporary closure. Since the employers lost "the advantages of continuing to have their coal gotten and being compelled to undertake expensive repairs", it was found reasonable to imply a term that the employees should "los[e] their wages for such time as was reasonably necessary to put the mine into a safe condition".[192] Whether this temporary *force majeure* principle applies to employees who are not paid on piece rates has not been determined. But this principle can never apply where the dangerous state of the workplace is due to the employer's fault.

As is explained later,[193] under sections 11-13 of the Redundancy Payments Act 1967 an employee who is laid off without pay or who is put on "short time" for four or more consecutive weeks, or for six or more weeks in a 13-week period, may be entitled to claim a lump sum redundancy payment as if he had been made redundant.

HOLIDAYS AND LEAVE

Usually the contract of employment will contain or will incorporate terms relating to holidays and perhaps other leave, and one of the particulars that employers are required to furnish new employees are any terms or conditions about paid leave.[194] Minimum requirements for holidays and other leave are contained principally in Part III of the Organisation of Working Time Act 1997, and the holidays of certain non-unionised employees are fixed by employment regulation orders made under Part IV of the Industrial Relations Act 1946.

Paid holiday

Every employee subject to the 1997 Act is entitled to at least four working weeks paid annual leave, if at least 1365 hours have been worked in that year.[195] There are two variations to this requirement. The paid leave shall be one-third of a working week for every month worked in the leave year, provided 117 hours have been worked in that month; or that leave shall be 8 per cent of the hours worked, subject to the four weeks maximum. Employees who have worked for at least eight months are entitled to take part of their leave in an unbroken period of two weeks.

Subject to that, the times at which annual leave shall be granted can be determined by the employer, who must take account of the employee's family responsibilities and the opportunities available for rest and recreation.[196] Employers should consult their employers' trade union, if any, on this question.

[192.] *ibid.* at 29.
[193.] See *post*, pp. 221-222.
[194.] Terms of Employment (Information) Act 1994, s.3(1)(j).
[195.] s.19.
[196.] s.20(1).

Holiday pay must be paid in advance of the employee taking leave and must be at the normal weekly rate.[197] Those whose employments cease but who have not availed of their full annual leave must be compensated by a sum calculated at their normal weekly rate.

Compliance with the 1977 Act's requirements in this regard is secured, *inter alia*, by the employee in question or his trade union making a complaint to a rights commissioner,[198] from whose decision there is an appeal to the Labour Court.

Public holidays

Public holidays for the purpose of the 1997 Act are Christmas Day, St. Stephen's Day, New Year's Day, St. Patrick's Day and the following Mondays, *viz*. Easter Monday, the first Monday in May, the first Monday in June, the first Monday in August and the last Monday in October. However, employers are permitted to treat as public holidays, in lieu of these, certain Church holidays. In the case of these public holidays, section 21 of the 1997 Act entitles employees to either a paid day off on these days, a paid day off within a month of these days, or either an additional day of annual leave or a day's pay. The rates of pay for these days to be prescribed in regulations.[199]

Maternity, paternity, adoptive, parental, health and safety, force majeure, and carer's leave

In 1981 legislation was enacted which entitled expecting mothers to take unpaid leave for the purpose of their confinement.[200] Following an EC Pregnancy Directive of 1985 designed to improve pregnant workers' health and safety,[201] that Act was replaced by the Maternity Protection Act 1994. In the following year, a similar measure was enacted to facilitate adopting parents and, in 1998, in response to another EC Directive of 1996,[202] provision was made for parental leave and also for paid "*force majeure*" leave of several days when a close family member is injured or becomes ill. Carer's leave was introduced in July 2001. There are considerable similarities in the structures of these four Acts. They apply not only to apprentices and employment agency personnel but also to the public sector, including the civil service, the Garda Síochána and the Defence Forces. Contractual provisions that purport to exclude or diminish rights given by these Acts are declared null and void. Disputes arising under them must first be referred to a rights commissioner, from whom there is a right of appeal to the Employment Appeals Tribunal.

[197.] s.20(2) and the Organisation of Working Time (Determination of Pay for Holidays) Regulations 1997, S.I. No. 475; *cf. Ocean Manpower Ltd. v. Marine Porteli Union* [1998] E.L.R. 299.

[198.] ss.27 and 28.

[199.] *Supra* n. 197.

[200.] Maternity Protection Act 1981.

[201.] Directive 92/85 on measures to encourage improvements in the safety and health at work of pregnant workers and workers who have recently given birth or who are breast feeding, O.J. No. L. 348/1. See, generally, C. Barnard, *E.C. Employment Law*, pp. 272-276.

[202.] Directive 96/34 on the framework agreement on parental leave, O.J. No. L. 145/4 (1996). See, generally, C. Barnard, *E.C. Employment Law*, pp. 276-278.

Maternity and paternity leave

As is explained in Chapter 5, the European Court of Justice has interpreted Article 141 (formerly Art. 119) of the EEC Treaty on equal pay and also what is referred to as the Equal Treatment Directive of 1976[203] generously in favour of pregnant workers. That trend was considerably reinforced by what is known as the Pregnancy Directive of 1985, which eventually was implemented in Ireland by the Maternity Protection Act 1994.[204] Four principal kinds of leave are provided for.

Under section 15 of the 1994 Act a woman is entitled to time off from work, without loss of pay, in order to get ante-natal or post-natal care and the content of this right is amplified by regulations.[205]

Under section 8 of this Act a pregnant employee is entitled to at least 18 consecutive weeks off work without pay.[206] In order to get this leave or any extended leave, she has to notify her employer as soon as is reasonably practical that she will be taking leave and must furnish an appropriate certificate confirming her pregnancy. She decides when this leave shall commence and shall end, provided that there are at least four weeks prior to the anticipated confinement and another four weeks after the confinement. Provision is made for a medical certificate for the leave to commence at a particular time. Leave will be extended where the confinement occurs a week or more later than was anticipated.[207] If the mother chooses, she is entitled to at least a further eight weeks leave on giving prior notice.[208] Although not obliged by the EC Directive nor by the 1994 Act to do so, many employers pay their employees who take maternity leave, either in full or in full for a specified duration, or in part. In such cases, it is permissible for the employer to condition payment of that salary on the employee undertaking to refund it in the event that she decides not to return to work.[209] Women earning more than £25 per week and who satisfy the Social Welfare Acts' contribution conditions are entitled to a maternity allowance of 70 per cent of weekly earnings, subject to a minimum payment of £86.70 per week and a maximum of £232.60 per week.[210]

Where the mother of the child dies within 14 weeks of her confinement, the child's father is entitled under section 16 of the 1994 Act to unpaid leave; he too may qualify for the social welfare maternity benefit. Leave must commence within seven days of the death and may extend either up to the tenth or the fourteenth week following the date of confinement; these periods can be extended for a further four weeks.

[203.] Directive 76/207 on equal treatment of the sexes in employment, O.J. No. L. 39/40 (1976); see *post*, pp. 138-140.

[204.] See, generally, M. Bolger & C. Kimber, *Sex Discrimination Law* (2000), pp. 327 *et seq.*

[205.] Maternity Protection (Time Off for Ante-Natal and Post-Natal Care) Regulations 1995, S.I. No. 18.

[206.] Maternity Protection Act (Extension of Periods of Leave) Order, 2001, S.I. no. 29.

[207.] s.12.

[208.] s.14 and *supra* n. 205.

[209.] *Boyle v. Equal Opportunities Comm.* (Case 411/96) [1998] E.C.R. 6401.

[210.] Social Welfare Act 1997, s.10, amending ss.37-41 of the Social Welfare (Consolidation) Act 1993, and regulations made thereunder.

Provision is then made for "employment protection" in order to ensure that persons who take time off on leave under any of the above headings are not disadvantaged in their employment rights. The principal categories of leave are deemed not to be absences from work which might affect any right arising under contract or any statute or otherwise,[211] except that relating to remuneration;[212] the additional four weeks maternity leave and leave for fathers do not break continuity of employment for any purpose. Any notice that has been given of suspension from work or of terminating the relationship is extended for the period of absence from work and periods of probation, training and apprenticeships are suspended.[213] At the expiry of the leave period, the employee is entitled to return to work, but if it is not reasonably practical to give her back her old job, then suitable alternative work must be provided, if needs be with an associated employer.[214]

A rights commissioner or the E.A.T. may award compensation under this Act, which may not exceed 20 weeks' remuneration.[215]

Adoptive Leave

The contention that the previous equality legislation (of 1977) entitled a man, who was about to adopt a child, to leave of absence from work to care for that child was rejected by the Supreme Court.[216] That question is now regulated by the Adoptive Leave Act 1995, which provides for four principal categories of unpaid leave.[217]

Under section 6 of the Act an adopting mother or a sole male adopter is entitled to not less than 14 consecutive weeks' leave beginning from the date of placement.[218] Prior written notice of the intention to take such leave must be given to the employer, along with a certificate of placement, and there are additional formalities where it is a foreign adoption. Although unpaid, she may be entitled to a social welfare allowance for that period.[219] There is an entitlement under section 8 to at least a further eight weeks leave on giving proper notice.[220]

Where the adopting mother dies, the adopting father is entitled to leave, generally for up to ten weeks, and in certain circumstances he is entitled to additional leave, generally for four more weeks.[221]

If a placement is for less than fourteen weeks, the employer must be so informed promptly in writing, who then may require the employee to return to work at a convenient date.[222]

[211.] s.22.

[212.] *cf.* the *Gillespie* (1996), *Boyle* (1998), *Lewen* (2000) and *Thibault* (1998) cases considered *post,* pp. 147-150.

[213.] ss.24 and 25.

[214.] ss.26 and 27. Cf. *Halfpenny* v. *IGE Medical Systems Ltd.* [2000] I.R.L.R. 96.

[215.] s.32(3); Maternity Protection (Disputes and Appeals) Regulations 1995, S.I. no.17 and Maternity Protection (Maximum Compensation) Regulations 1999, S.I. No. 134.

[216.] *Telecom Éireann v. O'Grady* [1998] 3 I.R. 432.

[217.] Adoptive Leave Act 1995, (Extension of Periods of Leave) Order 2001, S.I. no. 30.

[218.] See, generally, Bolger & Kimber, *supra* n.204 at pp. 345 *et seq.*

[219.] Social Welfare Act 1997, s.11 and regulations made thereunder.

[220.] *Supra* n. 217.

[221.] ss.9-11, *supra,* n. 217.

As in the case of maternity leave, the 1995 Act contains provisions on employment protection, to ensure that adopters will not be in any way disadvantaged at
work because they take the leave to which they are entitled, and that disputes
(other than relating to dismissals) shall be referred to a rights commissioner, with
an appeal to the E.A.T. Any compensation awarded cannot exceed 20 weeks'
remuneration.[223]

Parental leave

The contention that the Equality Directive entitled the father of a child to take
leave to look after it, when its mother had decided against taking any additional
maternity leave, was rejected by the European Court of Justice.[224] However, In
1996 the E.C. Council adopted a Directive on Parental Leave,[225] following a
"framework agreement" that had been reached between organisations representing employers' and workers' interests. It was implemented by the Parental Leave
Act 1998,[226] section 6 of which entitles all employees within that Act who are
natural or adoptive parents of a child under five years of age born since December 1993[227] to 14 weeks unpaid leave in order to take care of the child. Unlike the
Acts of 1994 and 1995 concerning comparable leave, the employee must have
had at least one year's continuous employment with the employer or his predecessor or associated employer. However, employees with between three months'
and 12 months' continuity are entitled to shorter periods of leave. The normal
leave is 14 continuous weeks but, with the employer's consent, leave can be for a
longer period if it is broken up, with a maximum duration of 14 weeks.[228] Where
an employee has several young children, such parental leave as is taken for any or
all of them shall not exceed 14, 18 or 22 continuous weeks, without the
employer's consent.

Where taking parental leave would have a "substantially adverse effect" on the
employer's business, the employer is entitled to require that the leave be post-
poned for up to six months.[229] However, the employer must have first consulted
the employee on the question of a postponement and must then provide a written
statement summarising the grounds for wanting to postpone the leave.

An employee intending to take parental leave must furnish the employer with
at least six weeks' written notice of intention, to include the commencement date,
proposed commencement date and duration. Even if such notice is not given, the
employer may treat leave granted as paternal leave. Not less than four weeks
before the commencement date, the employer must give written confirmation of
the leave. Thereafter, the employee will not be entitled to work during the stipulated period unless the parties agree to postpone the leave. If the leave is not

---

[222.] s.12, *supra*, n. 217.
[223.] s.33(3) and Adoptive Leave (Calculation of Weekly Remuneration) Regulations 1995, S.I. No.
196.
[224.] *Hofmann v. Barmer Ersatzkasse* (Case 184/83) [1984] E.C.R 3047.
[225.] *supra* n.202.
[226.] See, generally, Bolger & Kimber, *supra* n.224 at pp. 353 *et seq.*
[227.] European Communities (Parental Leave) Regulations, 2000, S.I. no. 231.
[228.] s.7. *cf. O'Neill v. Dunnes Stores* [2000] E.L.R. 306.
[229.] s.11.

being actually used in order to look after the child, the employer, may, by written notice cancel the leave, whereupon the employee is obliged to return to work;[230] similarly, where the employer has reason to believe that the leave will not be used for this purpose. But where leave is being either refused or terminated on grounds of the employee's "abuse", the employer must furnish a written summary of the reasons for so proposing and the employee is entitled to seven days within which to make representations on the question.

As in the case of the other two Acts on child related leave, there are provisions on employment protection, to ensure that parents will not be in any way disadvantaged at work because they take leave to which they are entitled, and also provisions for disputes (other than concerning dismissals) to be referred to a rights commissioner, with an appeal to the E.A.T. Any compensation awarded cannot exceed 20 weeks' remuneration.[231]

Health and safety leave

Part III (ss.17-20) of the Maternity Protection Act 1994 provides for paid leave for employees who are pregnant, or who have recently given birth or are breast feeding, where by virtue of E.C. Directives on health and safety, they cannot for the time being continue in their job.[232] If, in those circumstances it is not feasible to move that employee to another job, or her move to another job cannot reasonably be required, or there is no other work suitable for her, she is entitled to leave. For the first 21 days, she is entitled to be paid while on such leave; thereafter she may be entitled to a social welfare allowance known as the Health and Safety Benefit Scheme. Where that employee is pregnant, her leave under this part of the 1994 Act ends immediately before her maternity leave begins. In other cases, that leave ends when she ceases breast feeding, or when her condition renders her no longer vulnerable to the risk in question, or the employer has taken measures to ensure that she will no longer be exposed to that risk.

Force majeure leave

Employees are entitled by section 13 of the Parental Leave Act 1998 to paid leave for a very short period where, following an injury to or illness of a close family member, for urgent family reasons it is indispensable that that employee be with the injured or sick person.[233] The maximum periods are three days in any 12 months or five days in any 36 months. As soon as is reasonably practical, the employee must notify his employer that he has taken such leave, specifying the times.

[230.] s.12.

[231.] s.21(3) and Parental Leave (Maximum Compensation) Regulations 1999, S.I. No. 34.

[232.] See, generally, Bolger & Kimber, *supra* n.224 at pp. 337 *et seq.*

[233.] See, generally, Bolger & Kimber, *supra* n. 224 at pp. 356 *et seq. cf.* Parental Leave (Notice of Force Majeure Leave) Regulations 1998, S.I. No. 454, *Quinn v. J. Higgins Engineering (Galway) Ltd.* [2000] E.L.R. 102 and *Carey v. Penn Racquet Sports Ltd.* [2000] E.L.R. 27.

Carer's leave

The Carer's Leave Act 2001, which applies to employees with at least 12 months' continous employment, entitles employees to take up to 65 weeks unpaid leave in order to take full time care of a person with a certified disability. In the previous year a carer's benefit was introduced for such persons.

INTELLECTUAL PROPERTY

The principal forms of intellectual property are copyright, patents and confidential information; trade marks, merchandise marks and performers protection rights are not directly relevant to the discussion here. An author of any literary, dramatic or musical work is entitled to the copyright in it for the rest of his life and copyright remains in his estate for 70 years after his death.[234] Copyright also vests in the original maker of a sound recording, the maker of a film, the broadcaster of any material and the direct publisher of any published edition of a literary, dramatic or musical work. A person who invents an invention is entitled to take out a patent in respect of that, which will entitle him to the exclusive exploitation of the invention for 20 years, which period can be renewed.[235]

A question that often arises is, where an employee creates material which is protected by copyright or he invents something, is he entitled to the copyright or the patent, as the case may be, or does it belong to the employer. Frequently, this very matter will be determined by an express clause in the employment contract. A common practice among employers is to require their employees to give over rights in all inventions made during their employment. However, in one instance a clause of that nature was struck down for being an unreasonable restraint of trade.[236] That clause applied to all inventions made while the defendant was being employed, not just those devised during the course of his employment. Accordingly, a vacuum cleaning company could not require a senior storekeeper to surrender rights in an invention which he made at home in his spare time, even though it was an adapter for vacuum cleaner bags.

Copyright

Except where by agreement the parties have stipulated otherwise, the position regarding copyright is governed by section 23(1)(a) of the Copyright and Related Rights Act 2000. The general rule is that copyright material made "in the course of [the author's] employment" belongs to his employer and not to the author. Sometimes it can be difficult to determine the precise scope of an employment for these purposes, especially regarding teachers who may spend considerable parts of their spare time on work-related activities. For instance, the teacher may write a play to be performed by his students, which turns out to be a great commercial success. The outcome in this kind of case will usually turn on a careful consideration of the facts. The *Stevenson, Jordan and Harrison* case,[237] where the

---

[234.] Copyright and Related Rights Act 2000, s.24.
[235.] Patents Act 1992, s.36.
[236.] *Electrolux Ltd. v. Hudson* [1977] F.S.R. 312.
[237.] *Stevenson, Jordan and Harrison v. Macdonald & Evans* [1952] T.L.R. 101.

"integration test" for ascertaining whether the relationship was one of employer-employee was popularised,[238] concerned lectures written by an accountant, dealing with the business in which he was employed, to be given at universities and learned societies. His employer encouraged this activity by paying the expenses he incurred in it. Nevertheless, it was held that those lectures were not prepared in the course of his employment.[239]

Patents

Where the employment contract does not directly deal with the issue, the position regarding the ownership of patents is somewhat unsettled. Formerly, there were two kinds of case where the employee/inventor was obliged to hold the invention for his employer. One was where he was employed to use his skill and inventive ingenuity to solve a technical problem; where in effect he was "employed to invent". Thus, an engineering draftsman who was instructed to design an unlubricated cranebrake was obliged to hold the resultant patent on trust for his employer.[240] The other was where the employee occupied a senior managerial position; his extensive duty of fidelity included an obligation to give the employer the rights in whatever he may invent in connection with his employment. In one instance,[241] an American pump manufacturing company put a man in charge of its English business at a high salary and commission, making him vice-president of the company. He was held liable, under an obligation of good faith, to account for patents relating to developments in pumps.[242]

In a case in 1955, Lord Simonds purported to extend the rights of employers regarding their employees' inventions when he declared that "it is an implied term in the contract of service of any workman that what he produces by the strength of his arm or the skill of his hand or the exercise of his inventive faculty shall become the property of his employer".[243] It remains to be seen whether this statement of the law would be followed in Ireland.

Unlike the position with copyright, the Patents Act 1992 does not attempt to determine when employees' inventions should belong to their employers. All that section 16(1) of this Act states is that the question is governed by the law of the State where the employee is wholly or mainly employed. In the case of a dispute between an employer and his employee concerning ownership of a European patent, section 123 of that Act places some restriction on the jurisdiction of the Irish courts.

Confidential information

The law protects persons, including employers and employees, against confidential information about their affairs being used or disclosed against their wishes.[244]

[238.] *cf. Beloff v. Pressdram Ltd.* [1973] 1 All E.R. 241.

[239.] Compare *Danowski v. Henry Moore Foundation*, Times L.R. 19 Mar. 1996.

[240.] *British Reinforced Concrete Ltd. v. Lind* (1917) 34 R.P.C. 101.

[241.] *Worthington v. Moore* (1903) 20 R.P.C. 158.

[242.] Contrast *Selz's Application* (1954) 71 R.P.C. 158.

[243.] *Patchett v. Sterling* (1955) 72 R.P.C. 50 at 57.

[244.] See, generally, P. Lavery, *Commercial Secrets* (1996), especially Chap.7.

An employment contract may expressly stipulate what information belonging to them is confidential and may not be disclosed. Even where there is no such express provision, by virtue of an employee's general duty of fidelity, it is an implied term of almost all employment contracts that employees will not disclose or use their employer's confidential information without the latter's consent. That duty is broken, for instance, where the employee makes or copies a list of his employer's customers for use by him or by others when the employment ends or, indeed, where he memorises that very list for that purpose.[245] The extent to which an employer's confidential information is protected varies depending on whether the employee's activities in question are taking place during his employment or afterwards.

Confidentiality

What kinds of information are confidential for this purpose was summarised as follows:

> "First ... the information must be information the release of which the owner believes would be injurious to him or of advantage to his rivals or others. Second ... the owner must believe that the information is confidential or secret, *i.e.* that it is not already in the public domain. Third ... the owner's belief under the two previous headings must be reasonable. Fourth ... the information must be judged in the light of the usage and practices of the particular industry or trade concerned. It may be that information that does not satisfy all these requirements may be entitled to protection ...; but ... any information which does satisfy them must be of a type which is entitled to protection."[246]

In *Faccenda Chicken Ltd. v. Fowler*,[247] where an employee left his employment and went into the same business on his own account, taking other employees with him, the following considerations were stated to govern the question of improper use of confidential information:

> "In order to determine whether any particular item of information falls within the implied term so as to prevent its use or disclosure by an employee after his employment has ceased, it is necessary to consider all the circumstances of the case. . . . [T]he following matters are among those to which attention must be paid:
>
> (a) The nature of the employment. Thus, employment in a capacity where 'confidential' material is habitually handled may impose a high obligation of confidentiality because the employee can be expected to realise its sensitive nature to a greater extent than if he were employed in a capacity where such material reaches him only occasionally or incidentally.

[245.] *Robb v. Greene* [1895] 2 Q.B. 315.
[246.] *House of Spring Garden Ltd. v. Point Blank Ltd.* [1984] I.R. 611 at 663.
[247.] [1987] Ch.117.

(b)   The nature of the information itself. . . . [T]he information will only be protected if it can properly be classed as a trade secret, or as material which while not properly to be described as a trade secret, is in all the circumstances of such a highly confidential nature as to require the same protection as a trade secret. . . . It is clearly impossible to provide a list of matters which will qualify as trade secrets or their equivalent. Secret processes of manufacture provide obvious examples, but innumerable other pieces of information are capable of being trade secrets, though the secrecy of some information may only be short lived. In addition, the fact that the circulation of certain information is restricted to a limited number of individuals may throw light on the status of the information and its degree of confidentiality. . . .

(c)   Whether the employer impressed on the employee the confidentiality of the information. Thus, though an employer cannot prevent the use or disclosure merely by telling the employee that certain information is confidential, the attitude of the employer towards the information provides evidence which may assist in determining whether or not the information can properly be regarded as a trade secret. . . .

(d)   Whether the relevant information can be easily isolated from other information which the employee is free to use or disclose. . . . [T]he seperability of the information [is not] conclusive, but the fact that the alleged 'confidential' information is part of a package and the remainder of the package is not confidential is likely to throw light on whether the information in question is really a trade secret."[248]

An extensive range of confidential information in the public sector is protected by the Official Secrets Act 1963.[249]

Permitted Disclosure

Although the Constitution guarantees freedom of expression, there is hardly a general constitutional right to disclose confidential information about an employer's or a former employer's affairs. Leaving aside any constitutional rights as may exist, disclosure may be permitted in the public interest, for instance where the information relates to fraud committed by the employer. But the public interest is not confined to fraud. In *Initial Services Ltd. v. Putterill*,[250] it was held that disclosure applies to "any misconduct of such a nature that it ought in the public interest to be disclosed to others"; this extends to "crimes, frauds and misdeeds, both those actually committed and those in contemplation".[251] It was held there that the public interest defence could very well, in the circumstances, apply to information about a price ring to which the employer was a party.

[248.]   *ibid.* at 129-130. *cf. A.T. Poeton (Gloucester Plating) Ltd. v. Horton* [2000] I.C.R. 1208 and *S.J.B. Stephenson Ltd. v. Mandy* [2000] I.R.L.R. 233.

[249.]   *cf. Attorney General v. Blake* [2000] 3 W.L.R. 625.

[250.]   [1968] 1 Q.B. 396.

[251.]   *ibid.* at 405. *cf. Universal Thermosensors Ltd. v. Hibben* [1992] 1 W.L.R. 840.

Injunctions

Disclosure or use of confidential information can give rise to liability in damages; frequently the more appropriate measure of damages is the defendant's gain from the breach rather than the employer's loss.[252] Courts will not readily grant permanent injunctions in such cases as doing so may prohibit or discourage what in the course of time would become legitimate competition.[253] Where interlocutory injunctions pending the trial are sought, the usual *American Cyanamid* criteriae are applied. A question which has confronted the courts on several occasions in recent years is whether to award an interlocutory injunction restraining disclosure of confidential information where it is being claimed that disclosure is warranted in the public interest.[254]

Where confidential information has been given to the press, the question arises of whether the employer can get an order compelling disclosure to him of who gave that information to the press. The European Court of Human Rights has recognised a right in the press not to be compelled to reveal their sources,[255] but it is not an unqualified right and may be displaced depending on the surrounding circumstances.[256]

POST-EMPLOYMENT RESTRAINTS

Employees are often subject to restrictions regarding what they may work at when they cease being employed with a particular employer. As has been explained, it is an implied term of their contract that they will not use or disclose confidential information in a way that damages their former employer's business.[257] Additionally, the contract may contain express restrictions on their freedom to work. Exactly how extensive any such restriction is depends on the true meaning of the contract. But if the employer repudiates the contract by a wrongful dismissal, which the employee accepts, the entire contract including the restraint comes to an end, regardless of what the contract may say.[258]

Where the ex-employee's activities are caught by the terms of a contractual restriction, that clause may be void and unenforceable by virtue of the doctrine of unreasonable restraint of trade.[259] Restraints on persons working or being engaged in one or more lines of business by definition are restraints of trade. In the famous *Ballymacelligot Co-Op* case,[260] the test of whether such a restriction would be enforced by the courts was expounded as being two-fold, *viz.* "A contract which is in restraint of trade cannot be enforced unless (a) it is reasonable as between the parties; (b) it is consistent with the interests of the public".[261]

[252.] *Blake* case, *supra* n. 249 and *Universal* case, *supra* n. 251.
[253.] *Roger Bullivant Ltd. v. Ellis* [1987] I.C.R. 464.
[254.] *e.g. Lion Laboratories Ltd. v. Evans* [1985] 1 Q.B. 526.
[255.] *Goodwin v. United Kingdom*, 22 E.H.R.R. 123 (1996).
[256.] *Camelot Group p.l.c. v. Centaur Communications Ltd.* [1999] Q.B. 124.
[257.] *Hivac Ltd. v. Park Royal Scientific Industries Ltd.* [1946] 1 Chap. 169.
[258.] *Rock Refrigeration Ltd. v. Jones* [1997] I.C.R. 938.
[259.] See, generally, M. Forde, *Commercial Law* (2nd ed., 1997), pp.421 *et seq.*
[260.] *McEllistrim v. Ballymacelligot Co-Op. Agr. & Dairy Soc. Ltd.* [1919] A.C. 548.
[261.] *ibid.* at 562.

Whether or to what extent restraints in employment contracts are governed by the Competition Act 1991 is debatable and remains to be authoritatively resolved. In 1991 the Competition Authority published guidelines as to when, in its opinion, restrictions in employment contracts would contravene the 1991 Act,[262] being where the relationship has ended and the ex-employee then sets up his own business.

Public interest

The public interest is that the community should not unnecessarily be deprived of talents and services which are valuable. As has been observed, "the public interest . . . might be gravely endangered or contravened by a restriction or impairment of the liberty of the subject to enter the ranks of business or of labour and work for and earn his living."[263] However, very few of the restraint of trade cases focus mainly on the public interest being adversely affected.

Reasonableness inter partes

Regarding reasonableness between the parties, there is a presumption that all restrictions on work activities are unlawful unless the former employer can point to some very strong justification for the restraint in question, and also show that the range and extent of that restraint does not go beyond the proper demands of that justification. An employer is not entitled to prevent his former employee from competing against him, either directly or as an employee of some third party. Thus in *Bull v. Pitney-Bowes Ltd.*[264] the court refused to enforce a clause in a pension scheme whereby pensions would be forfeited if ex-employees should work for any firm which competed against their former employer. This is one of the few restraint of employment cases where the public interest was discussed by the court.

According to Lord Wilberforce in the leading authoritative case, *Stenhouse (Australia) Ltd. v. Phillips*,

> "the proposition that an employer is not entitled to protection from mere competition by a former employee means that the employee is entitled to use to the full any personal skill or experience, even if this has been acquired in the service of his employer: it is this freedom to use to the full a man's improving ability and talents which lies at the root of the policy of the law regarding this type of restraint. Leaving aside the case of misuse of trade secrets or confidential information . . . , the employer's claim for protection must be based upon the identification of some advantage or asset inherent in the business which can properly be regarded as, in a general sense, his property, and which it would be unjust to allow the employee to appropriate for his own purposes, even though he, the employee, may have contributed to its creation."[265]

---

262. Iris Oifigiúil, September 18, 1992.
263. *Mason v. Provident Clothing & Supply Co.* [1913] A.C. 724 at 738.
264. [1967] 1 W.L.R. 273.
265. [1974] A.C. 391 at 400.

An employer is entitled by contract to restrict a former employee from can-vassing the employer's former clients, provided there is some element of good-will attaching to that clientele and the extent of the canvassing restriction is not excessive. Thus, in the *Stenhouse (Australia) Ltd.* case, a clause was upheld which prohibited a formerly employed insurance broker, for a period of five years, from canvassing the employer's clients within a radius of 25 miles of the employer's headquarters in Sydney. And in *Home Counties Dairies Ltd. v. Skilton*[266] a clause was upheld which prevented a milk roundsman from selling milk to his ex-employer's customers during the 12 months after his job came to an end. Occasionally, a restriction which does not expressively refer to former cus-tomers being part of the employer's goodwill will be construed as applying to them. Thus in *Marian White Ltd. v. Francis*,[267] the court upheld a clause whereby an employee of a hairdresser had agreed not to work as a hairdresser within a half a mile of her former employer's establishment in a provincial town. An express prohibition against working for a competitor may even be upheld where the employee is in a senior managerial position and there is a strong likelihood that he possesses trade secrets which will be put to use in that competitor's busi-ness.[268] It depends on the circumstances whether such a danger exists.

Both the duration and the geographical scope of any restriction on working must not be excessive. What is excessive depends very much on the nature of the work in question and the structure of the business. A canvassing restriction over a 25-mile radius of the centre of Sydney was upheld with regard to a senior execu-tive insurance broker.[269] So too was a clause in the contract of an experienced Eurobonds broker preventing him for 12 months being engaged in any competing Eurobond business and from canvassing or soliciting former clients of the employer.[270] But a clause seeking to prevent a person who sold credit facilities for buying clothes from doing so within a 25-mile radius of the centre of London was declared to be unreasonable and void.[271] So too was a clause purporting to stop a senior executive insurance broker from acting in any town in Australia where a company within his former employer's group of companies had an establish-ment.[272] Similarly, in *Mulligan v. Carr*,[273] the Supreme Court refused to enforce a restraint clause in a contract between a solicitor and his former apprentice, who later qualified, under which the latter was not to practice within 30 miles of Ballina or Charlestown, or within 20 miles of Ballaghadereen.

Where the clause in question is capable of several interpretations, some of which render it unreasonable but one or more of which render it reasonable, the courts tend to give it the reasonable interpretation and thereby uphold the restraint. However, if in order to prevent the clause from being too wide it is nec-essary virtually to rewrite it and give it a different meaning from that of its proper construction, the courts will not so construe the clause.[274] Where an employment

---

[266.] [1970] 1 W.L.R. 526.

[267.] [1972] 1 W.L.R. 1423.

[268.] *Littlewood's Organisation Ltd. v. Harris* [1977] 1 W.L.R. 1472.

[269.] *Stenhouse* case [1974] A.C. 391.

[270.] *Dawny Doy & Co. Ltd. v. D'Alphen* [1998] I.C.R. 1088.

[271.] *Mason v. Provident Clothing & Supply Co.* [1913] A.C. 724.

[272.] *Stenhouse* case [1974] A.C. 391.

[273.] [1925] 1 I.R. 169.

[274.] *Home Counties Dairies Ltd. v. Skilton* [1970] 1 W.L.R. 526.

contract contains several restrictions on what an employee may do after his job ends, and one or more of them is an unreasonable restraint, it may be possible to "sever" the offending parts and enforce the remainder.[275] However, where an attempted severance would give the remaining clause a meaning significantly different from what it was intended to possess, the clause cannot be saved in that manner.[276]

Restraints contained in an employer's pension scheme may be regarded as being part of the employment contract. Although the forfeiture of pension benefits for working for a competitor may not be as drastic as being enjoined by the court from engaging in that work, the loss of a pension in those circumstances falls within the restraint of trade principle.[277]

On several occasions, persons engaged in professional sport have challenged restrictions on their activities, imposed both by their employers and the governing sporting organisations. In determining the effectiveness of these restrictions, special consideration tends to be given to the public interest claims of the governing organisations. These considerations did not save the old "retention and transfer" rules in English soccer[278] but were held to justify some restrictions placed by the New Zealand rugby league on the employment of players with overseas clubs.[279]

Injunctions

Breach of a valid restraint can give rise to liability in damages, although it can be difficult in cases of this nature to quantify the damages recoverable; at times, an easier measure is the defendant's gain rather than the employer's loss. Breach of the restraint can also be prevented by an injunction, which ordinarily will be granted subject to one major proviso. If enforcing the injunction has the practical effect of compelling the employee to continue working for his former employer, the injunction is almost an order for specific performance of an employment contract, which will not be granted.[280] But there is no comparable objection ordinarily to an injunction restraining an ex-employee from working for some third party. [281] It depends on all the circumstances of the case whether what is being sought is equivalent to specific performance.

In an application for an interlocutory injunction, pending a full trial of the action, account will be taken of the general *American Cyanamid* considerations and other relevant circumstances, for instance, the likelihood of trade secrets being disclosed to others.[282] Where the duration of the restraint most likely would have expired before the trial took place, account will be taken of the likelihood of the plaintiff succeeding at the trial.

[275.] *e.g. Stenhouse* case [1974] A.C. 391 and *Marshall v. N.M. Financial M'gt Ltd.* [1997] I.C.R. 1065.

[276.] *e.g. Mulligan v. Carr* [1925] 1 I.R. 169 and *T. Lucas & Co. Ltd. v. Mitchell* [1972] 1 W.L.R. 938.

[277.] *e.g. Bull v. Pitney Bowes Ltd.* [1967] 1 W.L.R. 273 and *Wyatt v. Kreglinger & Ferman* [1933] 1 K.B. 793.

[278.] *Eastham v. Newcastle Utd. F.C.* [1964] 1 Chap. 413.

[279.] *Kemp v. New Zealand R.F. League Inc.* [1989] 3 N.Z.L.R. 463; *cf. Johnston v. Cliftonville F.C. Ltd.* [1984] N.I. 9 striking down minimum wage and bonus agreements.

[280.] *Whitwood Chemical Co. v. Hardman* [1891] 2 Ch.416.

[281.] *cf. Warren v. Mendy* [1989] 1 W.L.R. 853.

[282.] *Lawrence David Ltd. v. Ashton* [1989] I.C.R. 123.

CHAPTER 5

HEALTH AND SAFETY AT WORK

Every year a substantial number of persons suffer injuries in the course of their work or contract some disease at work. Over the last two years, an average of 62 persons have been killed at work every year; about a quarter of these fatalities were on farms and in 2000 there were 26 fatalities in the construction industry. In the past the workplace was often a very dangerous location but the enactment of health and safety legislation and greater awareness of the risks existing at work have led to a significant decline in injuries and fatalities. The entire question of safety and health at work was the subject of an enquiry chaired by Mr. Justice Barrington, which reported in 1983.[1] This report led to the enactment of the Safety, Health and Welfare at Work Act 1989, which replaced much of the existing safety legislation. It is in connection with health and safety that the E.C. so far has adopted the most initiatives in the area of employment law.[2]

THE REGULATORY SYSTEM

Legislation designed to protect employees' health and safety at work can be traced back to the passing of the first factories statute in 1802, which was a response to the appalling conditions in which children worked in the Lancashire cotton mills.[3] Even before the establishment of the International Labour Organisation (I.L.O.), questions of industrial hygiene and safety were being dealt with at the international level. For technological reasons and also because of simple economic and commercial reasons, adoption of measures to protect workers' health and safety is a particularly apt subject for international investigation and co-ordination; hence the recent E.C. initiatives in this area. A large part of the I.L.O.'s standards relate directly or indirectly to health and safety, and deal with matters such as specific risks (*e.g.* white phosphorous, white lead, anthrax, benzene poisoning, occupational cancer, radiation protection, guarding machinery, maximum weight, pollution and noise in the work environment), special branches of activity (*e.g.* industrial establishments, building and construction sites, bakeries, dock work, merchant seamen), and preventative measures (*e.g.* preventing industrial accidents, protecting workers' health, occupational health services).[4] Many of these provisions have been incorporated into various regulations, and presumably

---

[1]   Report of Committee of Enquiry on Safety, Health and Welfare at Work (1983).
[2]   See, generally, C. Barnard, *E.C. Employment Law* (2nd ed., 2000), Chap. 6, B. Bercusson, *European Labour Law* (1996), Chaps. 21-24, and J. Hendy *et al.*, *Redgrave's Health and Safety* (2nd ed., 1993), Part I.
[3]   See *ante,* p. 2, n.7.
[4]   See, generally, N. Valticos, *International Labour Law* (1979), pp.147-157.

particular account will be taken of the I.L.O. guidelines by the National Authority for Occupational Health and Safety when it is issuing its codes of conduct.

The pre-1989 Acts

A whole mass of regulatory legislation going back for more than 60 years was replaced and consolidated by the Factories Act 1955. By 1989 there were numerous Acts in force for different types of work environments,[5] notably the Factories Act 1955, as supplemented by the Safety in Industry Act 1980, the Mines and Quarries Act 1965, the Office Premises Act 1958, and the Safety, Health and Welfare (Offshore Installations) Act 1987, as well as provisions of the Shops (Conditions of Employment) Act 1938 and of the Merchant Shipping Act 1894. Mention should also be made of the E.C. (Major Accident Hazards of Certain Industrial Activities) Regulations 1986, which are not aimed exclusively or even predominantly at protecting employees. Some sectors, notably agriculture, were virtually unregulated in this regard. The Factories Act and the Mines and Quarries Act are very bulky affairs, laying down an elaborate set of detailed prescriptions, which were supplemented by a body of statutory instruments that expanded on those prescriptions. However, many of the main provisions of these Acts were replaced by the Safety, Health and Welfare at Work Act 1989, which adopts a radically different approach to the entire question.

There is a vast body of case law dealing with the interpretation of the Factories Acts and the other legislation now being revoked. The extreme technicality and even the artificiality of some of the distinctions made in these cases were referred to by Hailsham L.C., in an action for damages for an accident where it was alleged that the moving parts of a machine had not been properly fenced as required by the regulations:

> "While the policy of the [Factories] Act is well established, some of the protection to the workmen which at first sight may be thought to be available turns out on closer scrutiny to be illusory. Thus (1) since it is only parts of the machinery which have to be fenced, there is no obligation to fence a machine . . . if it is dangerous as a whole but without having dangerous parts; (2) it is now established that . . . what is referred to as part of the machine does not include a work-piece moving under power and held in the machinery by a chuck; nor does it include other material in the machine as distinct from parts of the machinery; (3) the dangers against which the fencing is required do not include dangers to be apprehended from the ejection of flying material from the machine whether this is part of the material used in the machine or whether it is part of the machine itself; (4) the workman is not ordinarily protected if what comes into contact with the dangerous part of a machine is a hand tool operated by the workman as distinct from the workman's body or his clothes, nor if the danger created arises because of the proximity of moving machinery to some stationary object extraneous to the machine."[6]

[5.] See, generally, J. White, *Civil Liability for Industrial Accidents* (1993), 3 vols.
[6.] *F.E. Callow (Engineering) Ltd. v. Johnson* [1971] A.C. 335 at 342-343.

As with the body of case law on the Workmens' Compensation Acts built up between 1897 and 1977, much of the vast *ratio decidendi* and *obiter dicta* on the Factories Acts and comparable legislation will become a dead letter when what remains of those Acts is repealed in accordance with section 4(3) of the 1989 Act. A great deal of the 1955 Act and Regulations made under it, as well as the entire Office Premises Act 1958, and provisions of the Mines and Quarries Act 1965 and of the Safety, Health and Welfare (Offshore Installations) Act 1987, were repealed in 1995 by the Safety, Health and Welfare at Work Act 1989 (Repeals and Revocations) Order.[7]

The 1989 Act and 1993 Regulations

Instead of laying down numerous detailed rules for various categories of employment, the 1989 Act's requirements bind every employer and apply to every employee. It therefore is no longer decisive whether the employee in question works in a factory or in a mine or in an office, which often involved consideration of whether the workplace fell within the complex definitions of a "factory", a "building operation", a "work of engineering construction" and the like.[8] Regardless of the nature of the workplace, the 1989 Act's requirements apply. They apply throughout the public service as well as the private sector, even to prisons and places of detention except where their application is not compatible with "safe custody, good order and security". The other major difference between the 1989 legislation and its predecessors is the intrinsic nature of the 1989 requirements. Instead of being very detailed rules of conduct, these lay down broad standards of behaviour. For instance, the Factories Act 1955 contains elaborate requirements concerning matters such as prime movers, transmission machinery, unfenced machinery, self-acting machines, hoists and lifts, cranes and other lifting machines, steam boilers and receivers, air receivers, gasholders, humid factories, underground rooms, laundries, lifting excessive weights, etc. There is nothing comparable in the 1989 Act, which in sections 6-11 lays down several broadly formulated duties; the remainder of the Act deals with the different modes of enforcing and securing compliance with those duties.

In 1993 those duties were amplified and extended by regulations made under this Act giving effect to several E.C. Directives, in particular the Safety, Health and Welfare at Work (General Applications) Regulations.[9]

The main employers' duties

An overriding duty of care is imposed on employers by section 6(1) of the 1989 Act: "It shall be the duty of every employer to ensure, so far as is reasonably practicable, the safety, health and welfare at work of all his employees". The remainder of that section sets out several ways in which this duty may arise, being:

---

7. S.I. No. 357 of 1995.
8. Factories Act 1955, s.3.
9. S.I. No. 44 of 1993 amended by S.I. no. 188 of 2001.

"(a) as regards any place or work under the employer's control, the design, the provision and the maintenance of it in a condition that is, so far as is reasonably practicable, safe and without risk to health;

(b) so far as is reasonably practicable, as regards any place of work under the employer's control, the design, the provision and the maintenance of safe means of access to and egress from it;

(c) the design, the provision and the maintenance of plant and machinery that are, so far as is reasonably practicable, safe and without risk to health;

(d) the provision of systems of work that are planned, organised, performed and maintained so as to be, so far as is reasonably practicable, safe and without risk to health;

(e) the provision of such information, instruction, training and supervision as is necessary to ensure, so far as is reasonably practicable, the safety and health at work of his employees;

(f) in circumstances in which it is not reasonably practicable for an employer to control or eliminate hazards in a place of work under his control, or in such circumstances as may be prescribed, the provision and maintenance of such suitable protective clothing or equipment, as appropriate, that are necessary to ensure the safety and health at work of his employees;

(g) the preparation and revision as necessary of adequate plans to be followed in emergencies;

(h) to ensure, so far as is reasonably practicable, safety and the prevention of risk to health at work in connection with the use of any article or substance;

(i) the provision and the maintenance of facilities and arrangements for the welfare of his employees at work; and

(j) the obtaining, where necessary, of the services of a competent person (whether under a contract of employment or otherwise) for the purpose of ensuring, so far as is reasonably practicable, the safety and health at work of his employees."

Under the 1993 General Application Regulations, detailed provision is made for, *inter alia*, the physical lay out of the workplace (Part III), machinery and other equipment being used (Part IV), personal protective equipment (Part V), manual handling of loads (Part VI), display screen equipment (Part VII), the safe use of electricity (Part VIII), first aid (Part IX), and reporting accidents and dangerous occurrences (Part X).

Duties to persons who are not employees

The statutory duty of care is not confined to safeguarding employees. Section 7 of the 1989 Act places an obligation of reasonable care on employers in respect of persons who are not their employees but who are exposed to risks to their safety or health as a result of how the employer's undertaking is being conducted.

A similar obligation is placed on self-employed persons in respect of unsafe or unhealthy activities they may be engaged in. Section 8 of the Act imposes a form of occupier's liability on every person in control of a workplace, in respect of self-employed persons and employees of third parties who approach or come on to their premises, where that control is exercised for carrying on some trade or business or other undertaking.

Defective equipment or premises

Section 10 imposes duties regarding defective equipment for use at work.[10] These duties apply to any person who designs, manufactures, imports or supplies any article for use at work; to any person who erects or installs any article for use at a workplace; and to any manufacturer, importer or supplier of any substance which may be used at or in connection with work. Designers, manufacturers and others involved in supplying defective equipment or substances have a defence where the fault lay beyond their control or did not occur in the course of their trade or business. Section 11 imposes a duty of care on the designer and on the builder of any workplace.

Duties on employees

Finally, section 9 of the Act subjects employees to a duty of care. They must, *inter alia*, take reasonable care of their own safety, health and welfare and that of others who may be affected by what they do at work.

Elaborating the duties

It is necessary to give more precise content to the 1989 Act's well-meaning but vague standards of conduct. To that end, the Minister is empowered to introduce regulations. In addition to the 1993 General Application Regulations already referred to, among the more important regulations to be adopted in the last ten years are the following:

Safety, Health and Welfare at Work (Carcinogens) Regulations 2001 (S.I. No. 78),

European Communities (Protection of Workers) (Exposure to Asbestos) Regulations 1989 (S.I. No. 34), 1993 (S.I. No. 276) and 2000 (S.I. No. 74);

Safety, Health and Welfare at Work (Biological Agents) Regulations 1994 (S.I. No. 146) and 1998 (S.I. No. 248);

Safety, Health and Welfare at Work (Chemical Agents) Regulations 1994 (S.I. No. 445);

European Communities (Protection of Outside Workers from Ionising Radiation) Regulations 1994 (S.I. No. 144);

Safety, Health and Welfare at Work (Construction) Regulations 1995 (S.I. No. 138);

[10.] Modelled on the U.K.'s Employers Liability (Defective Equipment) Act 1969. Section 10 is amplified by Part IV of the 1993 General Application Regulations (S.I. No. 44).

Safety, Health and Welfare at Work (Signs) Regulations 1995 (S.I. No. 132);

Safety, Health and Welfare at Work (Extractive Industries) Regulations 1997 (S.I. No. 467);

Safety, Health and Welfare at Work (Children and Young Persons) Regulations 1998 (S.I. No. 504);

Safety, Health and Welfare at Work (Night Work and Shift Work) Regulations 1998 (S.I. No. 485) and 2000 (S.I. No. 11).

Provision is made by the 1989 Act for issuing "codes of practice", which are intended to "provid[e] practical guidance with respect to the requirements or prohibitions" in that Act.[11]

Provision is made for pregnancy and motherhood in section 18 of the Maternity Protection Act 1994, and in regulations adopted in 2000.[12] Under this Act, such persons are entitled to paid leave for up to 21 days and to unpaid leave thereafter where, by virtue of her pregnancy, she was prevented by regulations from doing her job and the employer has no other suitable alternative work for her. Under the Safety, Health and Welfare at Work (Pregnant Employees) Regulations 2000,[13] employers are required to assess any risk to the safety or health of their employees by virtue of their pregnancy or breast feeding and are required to take appropriate steps in order to eliminate any such risk. Where a doctor certifies that such an employee should not work at night, on account of her condition, the employer must transfer her to day work or, where that is not feasible, grant her leave or extend the period of her maternity leave.

Implementation

As is the case with other walks of life which are the subject of extensive regulation, the modes of securing compliance with and of enforcing the prescribed standards are at least as important as the very content of those standards. For without adequate techniques for implementation, the standards would tend to be honoured more in their breach than in their observance. A distinctive feature of the 1989 Act is the extent to which it concentrates on ensuring that the standards laid down are being met in the great majority of workplaces. Additionally, breach of the 1989 Act's requirements often will also constitute the tort of negligence, for which the person injured can recover damages to cover his loss; in the case of serious injury those damages will be substantial.

The Authority

An autonomous executive agency is set up by Part III of the 1989 Act to oversee implementation of its requirements, the National Authority for Occupational Health and Safety.[14] Among its principal functions, as defined, are "to make adequate arrangements for the enforcement of the relevant statutory provisions" and

---

[11] s.30; see *infra*, p. 113.
[12] See *ante*, pp. 93-95. and Maternity Protection (Health and Safety Leave Remuneration) Regulations 1995, S.I. No. 20, and *ibid.* (Certification) Regulations 1995, S.I. No. 19.
[13] S.I. No. 218 of 2000. *cf. Coffey v. Byrne* [1997] E.L.R. 230.
[14] 1989 Act, ss.14-26.

to "promote, encourage and foster the prevention of accidents and injury to health at work . . . ."[15] The Authority is tripartite in the sense that some that its members must be nominees of a representative employers' organisation and of a representative workers' organisation; for practical purpose, this means nominees of the Federation of Irish Employers and of the Irish Congress of Trade Unions. Among the tasks entrusted to the Authority are issuing codes of practice, advising the Minister on draft regulations, applying to the High Court for prohibition orders, obtaining information about aspects of the workplace, appointing inspectors who visit workplaces and investigate accidents and working conditions, and conducting special investigations into workplace incidents and related matters.

Inspectors

A factory inspectorate has been in existence since around 1830. The National Authority and any other "enforcing agency" is empowered to appoint inspectors, who are given wide-ranging powers by section 34 of the 1989 Act. For instance, at any time they may enter and inspect any premises which they believe is a workplace, carry out an inquiry there as to compliance with the legal safety and health requirements, demand the production of relevant books, registers, records and the like. Inspectors can issue "improvement notices" directing that measures be taken to remedy alleged breaches of the 1989 Act,[16] and also issue "prohibition notices" directing that specified dangerous activities shall cease.[17]

Codes of practice

The adoption of codes of practice on various aspects of health and safety is a central feature of the 1989 Act.[18] Codes will be issued by the Authority, after consulting any appropriate Government Minister and other person or body, like employers' associations and trade unions. Presumably, codes will be issued for various categories of activity and for numerous operations and processes. These codes are intended not to lay down hard and fast rules but to "provid[e] practical guidance" on the Act's requirements.[19] Breach of the standards laid down in a code does not automatically mean that the statutory requirements have been contravened, for the purpose of criminal proceedings.[20] However, in determining whether the Act was broken, the codes are admissible in evidence and the courts can take account of what they require.[21] Employers and others who do not comply with the codes of practice, therefore, run the distinct risk of being convicted. The Act does not state what weight, if any, the codes should have in civil proceedings.

---

15. s.16(1)(a) and (b).
16. s.36.
17. s.37.
18. s.30.
19. s.30(3).
20. s.31(1).
21. s.31(2).

Prosecution

The principal enforcement technique under the 1989 Act and under the Safety in Industry Acts and the other legislation, is prosecuting employers and others for breach of the statutory requirements. How effective prosecutions are depends to an extent on the success rate of detecting breaches, the ratio of prosecutions which end in convictions and the sanctions imposed by the courts. No empirical research seems to have been done on the success of criminalisation in this regard. Efficient detection will require that the National Authority and its inspectors be given sufficient resources to carry out their task. Summary offences under the 1989 Act will be prosecuted by the Authority or by the relevant enforcing agency appointed for that purpose.[22] For many of these offences, the maximum fine is £1,000[23] for summary convictions.[24]

In order to secure a conviction, it must be proved beyond reasonable doubt that the employer or other defendant committed the offence in question.[25] Section 50 of the 1989 Act will assist prosecutors, however. This reverses the burden of proof where the issue is whether the defendant did whatever was practicable in the circumstances, or whether he acted so far as was reasonably practicable or he used the best practicable means to do something. It is for the defendant to show that he took all such steps as were practicable in the circumstances.

Prohibition orders

Where the use of any workplace or part of it constitutes a very serious risk to health and safety, the National Authority or other enforcing agency may make an *ex parte* application to the High Court for an injunction. Section 39 of the 1989 Act empowers the Court to make an interim or an interlocutory order restricting or prohibiting the use in question. Resort to this procedure will be exceptional and probably will be confined to urgent situations. The more usual procedure will be that under section 37 of the Act whereby any of the Authority's inspectors can issue a "prohibition notice" against an activity which he believes involves or may involve a risk of serious personal injury to persons at any workplace. An appeal can be made to the District Court against such a notice. Where activities are carried on in breach of a prohibition notice, an order of the High Court can be obtained enjoining continuance of those activities.

Licensing

Certain kinds of activity can be prescribed by the Minister which cannot be carried on without possessing an appropriate licence.[26] Presumably, it is particularly dangerous kinds of work which will be regulated in this manner. The National Authority is the licensing agency and it may attach such conditions as it thinks proper to any license. Carrying on an activity without possessing the appropriate

---

[22]   *cf. National Authority for Occupational Safety & Health v. Fingal C.C.* [1997] 2 I.R. 547.
[23]   s.49(10).
[24]   *cf. National Authority for Occupational Safety and Health v. O'Brien Hire Ltd.* [1997] 1 I.R. 543.
[25]   Except for prosecution for breach of a license condition: s.49(3).
[26]   s.59.

license or breach of the terms of a license is a very serious offence; where the offender is prosecuted on indictment, he may be imprisoned for up to two years.[27]

Investigations and reports

In addition to the extensive powers inspectors enjoy to enter any premises they believe to be a workplace and to carry out enquiries there into compliance with the 1989 Act's requirements, sections 46 and 47 of the Act provide for what may be termed special reports and inquiries. Under the former, the National Authority may appoint someone to investigate "the circumstances surrounding any accident, disease, occurrence, situation or any other matter related to the general purposes of" the Act and to report thereon. Under section 47, the Minister may appoint a judicial tribunal to hold an inquiry into "any accident, disease, occurrence, situation or any other matter related to the general purposes" of the Act and to report thereon. The reports made following either of these inquiries may be published by the Authority. Provision is made in section 56 for the conduct of a coroner's inquest where what killed the deceased may have been an accident at the workplace or a disease contracted there. Witnesses at the inquest may be questioned by *inter alia* a representative of the majority of the persons employed at that workplace or by someone appointed by a trade union to which the deceased belonged or which has one or more members in that workplace.

Safety representatives

The complex system of safety representatives, safety committees and safety delegates, introduced in 1980 for factories, is simplified by section 13 of the 1989 Act and extended to all workplaces. Employees are given a right to "make representations to and consult their employer on matters of safety, health and welfare in their place of work".[28] Employers are required to consult their employees in this regard and to take account of any representations made by them. For these purposes, employees may appoint a safety representative from among their number. Their representative is entitled to such information from the employer as is necessary to safeguard health and safety at the workplace; he must get time off from his normal duties, without loss of remuneration, in connection with his task; and he is given a range of powers to investigate accidents and dangerous occurrences, to carry out inspections and to investigate potential hazards and complaints, and to have various dealings with the safety inspector. His independence and freedom of action are protected by the stipulation that "[a]rising from the discharge of his functions [he] shall not be placed at any disadvantage in relation to his employment".[29] The Minister may adopt regulations in order to give effect to the general thrust of these provisions.

Safety statements

Section 12 of the 1989 Act requires all employers to have prepared a safety statement. The terms of this statement must be notified to employees and to any other persons at the workplace who may be affected by it. This statement must set out

---

27. s.49(3).
28. s.13(2).
29. s.13(9).

the manner in which employees' health and welfare will be secured, being based on an identification of the hazards and an assessment of the risks at work, and specifying the arrangements made and resources available for safeguarding employees, the co-operation required for that purpose, and identifying who are responsible for the tasks being assigned. If the inspector decides that a safety statement is inadequate in any material particular, he can direct that it be revised. In the case of registered companies, their annual report of the directors must contain an evaluation of the extent to which the policy set out in the safety statement was realised during the relevant period. It is anticipated that, by getting employers to focus on possible dangers and modes of avoiding them in this manner, accidents will be greatly reduced.

EMPLOYERS' LIABILITY

An employee who is injured in the course of his work as a result of his employer's negligence can recover compensation for the losses he suffered in consequence of that injury.[30] Where the employer's negligence brought about the employee's death, his dependents and also his estate may be entitled to recover damages.[31] This exposure to potential claims for damages is a powerful incentive for employers to ensure that their workplaces are safe and healthy. Although these risks can be covered by insurance, where several successful claims are made against an employer his insurance premium is bound to rise steeply. It is sometimes claimed that the high cost of employers' liability insurance cover renders segments of Irish industry uncompetitive. There is no statutory obligation on employers to take out liability insurance in the same way as the owners of motor vehicles must have their vehicles insured.

Negligence

For employers' common law liability in damages to arise, the following must be shown.

Duty of care

The employer should have owed a duty of care to the plaintiff in the circumstances which arose. Almost always the duty question will be answered in the affirmative where the accident or damage occurred in the workplace. The classic formulation of the employer's duty of care is that he is required to provide competent staff, a safe place of work, proper plant and appliances, and a safe system of work.[32] But these are far from being rigid sub-divisions; they are particular manifestations of the general duty not to subject employees to unreasonable and unnecessary risk.

---

[30] See, generally, J. White, *Civil Liability for Industrial Accidents*, (1993), 2 Vols., and B. McMahon and W. Binchy, *Irish Law of Torts* (3rd ed., 2000), Chap. 18.

[31] Civil Liability Act 1961, Parts II and IV.

[32] *Wilsons and Clyde Coal Co. v. English* [1938] A.C. 57 and *Johnstone v. Bloomsbury Health Authority* [1992] 1 Q.B. 333.

Liability is not confined to personal injury in the narrow sense but, in appropriate circumstances, can apply to psychiatric injury[33] and to what is known as "repetitive strain"[34]

Standard of care

Secondly, it must be shown that the employer did not live up to the standard of care to be expected of a reasonable employer. This is mainly a pragmatic question and one of fact; whether in all the circumstances the danger to the plaintiff was reasonably foreseeable and whether the employer took adequate precautions to prevent the risk of damage or to control that risk. A classic instance is failure to provide clothing or other equipment which would have protected the employee. The standard of care imposed is high and has become increasingly stringent over the years, to the extent that there is almost a presumption of employer liability where one of his employees was injured in the course of his work. In principle, however, the burden of proof resides with the plaintiff to show that, in all the circumstances, his employer did not exercise reasonable care. As Henchy J. put it, "[t]he law does not require the employer to ensure in all circumstances the safety of his workmen. He will have discharged his duty of care if he does what a reasonable and prudent employer would have done in the circumstances".[35] As is explained below, workplace regulations are often treated by the courts as laying down what is the appropriate standard of care. Where the accident occurs at some place other than the employer's premises, which is not under his constant supervision, the standard of care is not as exacting as for what occurs on his premises.[36]

A great number of reported and unreported cases exist on the standard of care required in different circumstances. While these cases lay down a variety of general propositions about what kinds of action should be expected of employers in various situations, there is always the danger of exalting, into the status of propositions of law, statements made with reference to the facts of particular cases. As an English judge once remarked, a judge "naturally gives reasons for the conclusions formerly arrived at by a jury without reasons. It may sometimes be difficult to draw the line, but if the reasons given by a judge for arriving at the conclusions previously reached by a jury are to be treated as law and citable, the precedent system will die from a surfeit of authorities".[37]

Causation

Thirdly, it must be shown that what caused the employee's injury was the negligent act of the employer or his agents. Occasionally, the real cause of the loss may have been some extraneous matter. For instance, in the case of defective

---

[33] *Frost v. Chief Constable of South Yorkshire* [1999] 2 A.C. 455 and *Walker v. Northumberland C.C.* [1995] I.C.R. 702 and *Waters v. Commissioner of Police* [2000] I.R.L.R. 720.

[34] *Pickford v. Imperial Chemical Industries p.l.c.* [1998] 1 W.L.R. 1189 and *Alexander v. Midland Bank p.l.c.* [2000] I.C.R. 464.

[35] *Bradley v. C.I.E.* [1976] I.R. 217 at 223.

[36] e.g. *Maclure v. Southern Health Board* [1988] I.L.R.M. 689.

[37] *Qualcast (Wolverhampton) Ltd. v. Haynes* [1959] A.C. 743.

equipment which the employee was using at work, which injures him, often the employer will not be held liable at common law for that loss.[38] But he would be liable where the defect was one which could easily have been discovered on any reasonable inspection of that equipment.[39] Causation can give rise to difficult questions of proof, especially where the injury is some form of disease which progressed slowly over time.[40]

Defences

Exceptionally, the employer can raise the defence of *volenti non fit injuria*, that is that the damage was caused entirely by the employee's own actions.[41] The scope of this defence has been radically diminished by section 34(1)(c) of the Civil Liability Act 1961 to situations where the plaintiff actually waived his legal rights before the event in question occurred. However, the actual extent of the employer's liability can be reduced, perhaps significantly, where it is shown that the damage was partly caused by the plaintiff's contributory negligence.

It is no defence for an employer that he delegated to a subordinate, no matter how expert, the responsibility of ensuring that adequate precautions were taken in the circumstances.[42] Even if the person who was the immediate cause of the injuries was some third party and not a fellow-employee, the employer may still be held liable for not maintaining a safe workplace.[43]

Tort or contract

Although the employer's duty of care is an implied term of the employment contract as well as one arising in tort, generally actions for damages arising out of injuries suffered at work are framed in tort. The extent to which employers' liability can be excluded by contract provisions has not been considered by the courts.

Breach of statutory duty

On top of the common law duties, the parts still in force of the Factories Acts and equivalent legislation for mines and quarries and for several other workplaces are regarded as imposing absolute duties. If injury results from an employer's breach of any of the statutory or regulatory requirements, he could be made liable for the tort of breach of statutory duty; non-observance of most of the statutory requirements constitutes *per se* negligence. As described by the late Professor Fleming:

> "Dominating the industrial field nowadays is a vast volume of statutory regulation imposing detailed duties upon employers for the protection of their workers, such as Factory Acts requiring the fencing of dangerous machinery. These statutes have been construed to confer a claim for damages on

---

38. Liability could arise under Part IV of the General Application Regulations, S.I. No. 44 of 1993.
39. *Keenan v. Bergin* [1971] I.R. 192.
40. *e.g. O'Mahony v. Henry Ford & Son Ltd.* [1962] I.R. 146.
41. *Imperial Chemical Industries Ltd. v. Shatwell* [1965] A.C. 656.
42. *Connolly v. Dundalk U.D.C.* [1990] 2 I.R. 1.
43. *McDermid v. Nash Dredging & Reclamation Co.* [1987] A.C. 906.

any employee injured as the result of his employer's failure to comply even if, as is usual, the statute provides only a penal sanction for its enforcement. Not infrequently these statutory duties are couched in absolute terms demanding compliance even if it would render the work in question commercially inpracticable or mechanically impossible. Failure to conform to the legislative safety standard is negligence per se, and if the statutory command is peremptory rather than demanding merely all reasonable care, liability is in effect strict and independent of fault in the conventional sense.

Most commonly such regulations prescribe specific precautions to be taken for particular industrial operations, like the use of specified scaffolding for work above minimum heights, of guards around moving machinery or duck boards for work on glass roofs. Regulations of this type in effect merely spell out precisely and beyond argument what the general duty of reasonable care would in any event require. More drastic by far in promoting strict liability are regulations, increasingly common, which prescribe that certain equipment be of sound construction, suitable material and adequate strength. These in effect import a warranty of fitness, covering even latent defects, and thereby far transcend the common law duty of employers. Although this has in other areas . . . militated conclusively against attaching civil sanctions, no similar scruples have prevailed in the industrial context. This striking difference in judicial attitude, which has indeed for all practical purposes at least in Britain made the whole doctrine of statutory negligence an almost exclusive preserve of industrial accident law, is of course in no small measure due to a desire to make up for the lower level of workers' compensation."[44]

Until section 4(3) of the Safety, Health and Welfare at Work Act 1989 is implemented entirely, some of the requirements in the pre-1989 legislation and statutory instruments remain in force.

The principal source of statutory duties on employers today are the regulations that have been adopted under that subsection, in particular, the 1993 General Application Regulations and the several others previously mentioned,[45] which give effect to numerous E.C. Directives relating to workers' health and safety. Practically all of the duties contained in the 1993 Regulations are strict and some of them are even absolute duties.[46] Unlike many of the provisions which were repealed by order in 1995, those in the 1993 Regulations do not contain limitations such as "so far as is [reasonably] practical", "as far as possible", "if necessary" and the like.

Occupational diseases

Diseases contracted in the course of work can be radically different from accidental injuries. Accidents are dramatic and discrete events where a very clear relationship exists between what happened and the injury suffered. By contrast,

---

[44.] *The Law of Torts* (7th ed., 1987) at p. 487.

[45.] *supra*, pp. 111-112.

[46.] *Stark v. Post Office* [2000] I.C.R. 1013 and *Everitt v. Thorsman Ireland Ltd.* [2000] 1 I.R. 256.

diseases develop and manifest themselves over time and their origins often are far less obvious. On account of the very nature of disease, it is more difficult for an employee, who is suffering from a debilitating malady he probably acquired by working in a certain environment for a long period, to succeed in an employers' liability claim.[47] Where, however, it is demonstrated that the employer's negligence or breach of statutory duty caused the employee's disease, that employee or, if dead, his dependants should succeed in an action for damages.[48]

Employees have succeeded in obtaining damages for deafness they contracted due to excessive noise in the workplace. The leading case perhaps is the thoughtful judgment of Mustill J. in *Thompson v. Smiths Ship Repairers (North Shields) Ltd.,*[49] where the plaintiffs were several labourers and skilled workers who had worked in the defendant's shipyard for many years. They claimed damages for the loss of hearing they suffered due to working in that yard. Extensive scientific evidence was given regarding the causes of deafness, especially at work, which is set out in detail in the judgment. The plaintiffs succeeded but were not compensated completely for the loss they had suffered. It was held that, although there had been actual knowledge for many years that employees in ship-building and ship-repair yards suffered from deafness as a result of excessive noise, the risk had been considered as an inescapable feature of the industry. Accordingly, any liability of the defendants in negligence for failing to protect their employees against the risk of deafness had to be considered against the general practice in the industry of inaction and acceptance of the situation. The defendants could only rely on the general practice while there was a lack of social awareness of the need to protect employees generally against industrial noise, and there was not readily available information and the means of protecting employees against noise. But once information could be obtained and ear protection devices were available on the market, the defendants came under a duty of care because either they should have sought the knowledge or they should have known that effective precautions could be taken in their yards to protect their employees against the risk of deafness.

Damage claims by many members of the defence forces, arising from deafness caused while in the service, led to the enactment of the Civil Liability (Assessment of Hearing Injury) Act 1998, which incorporates what is described as the "Green Book", containing a formula for assessing the extent of disability.[50]

A particularly vexed question is disability caused by exposure to asbestos many years ago, which poses the additional problem of limitation of actions. Among the matters covered by E.C. Directives, which have been implemented in Ireland, are exposure to noise[51] and exposure to asbestos,[52] to lead[53] and to other unsafe agents.[54] For the purposes of the Safety, Health and Welfare at Work Act

---

[47.]   *supra*, pp. 111-112.

[48.]   *e.g. McGhee v. National Coal Board* [1973] 1 W.L.R. 1 (dermatitis) and *Holby v. Brightman & Cowan (Hull) Ltd.* [2000] I.C.R. 1086 (asbestos).

[49.]   [1984] Q.B. 405. *cf. Hatby v. Brigham & Cowan (Hull) Ltd.* [2000] I.C.R. 1086.

[50.]   *cf. Greene v. Minister for Defence* [1998] 4 I.R. 464 and *Hanley v. Minister for Defence* [1998] 4 I.R. 496.

[51.]   S.I. No. 157 of 1990.

[52.]   S.I. No. 34 of 1989, No. 276 of 1993 and No. 74 of 2000.

[53.]   S.I. No. 219 of 1988.

[54.]   See regulation listed *ante,* p. 111.

1989, the term personal injury is defined to include "any disease and any impairment of a person's physical or mental condition".[55] Moreover, section 6(3)(h) of that Act obliges employers to take appropriate measures to prevent risk to health at work.

Civil liability and the 1989 Act

The obligations laid down in the 1989 Act to ensure that the workplace is a safe and a healthy place are enforced by criminal sanctions. Many of these obligations also arise at common law; however, there are obligations under this Act which in particular circumstances would not arise at common law, for instance, in relation to defective equipment. Thus, the question arises of when does breach of the 1989 Act also provide a civil remedy to persons who suffer damage in consequence of that breach. The Act takes an almost entirely neutral stance on this issue. Section 60(1) provides that nothing in the Act confers any right of action in civil proceedings in respect of breach of any duty imposed by sections 6-11 of the Act (summarised above). Against that, the Act does not in any way cut back on the existing scope of tort liability, nor indeed does the Act cut back on any civil liability for breach of statutory duty under the pre-1989 safety legislation. Accordingly, the entire civil liability position as of mid-1989 is preserved by the Act.

Section 28 of the 1989 Act empowers the Minister to adopt regulations to deal with a very wide range of matters or otherwise to give effect to the Act. Breach of these regulations is deemed to be an actionable wrong unless the regulation provides otherwise.[56] What constitutes damage which can be recovered under any such breach is defined to include death or personal injury; it remains to be seen whether a work-related disease will be regarded as damage for these purposes. Liability for damages for breach of any of these regulations cannot be contracted out of. As has been observed, codes of conduct may be issued under the 1989 Act but the express provision for the court taking account of them applies only to criminal proceedings. It is possible, nevertheless, that some account may be taken of the codes in claims for damages, as indicating what would constitute taking reasonable care.

Liability insurance

Most employers provide for potential liability in claims for damages arising out of workplace injuries and diseases by taking out insurance.[57] Since 1969 in Britain there has been a statutory duty on employers to have appropriate liability insurance;[58] that requirement was extensively revised in 1998.[59] There is no comparable duty under Irish law and it has been held by the Supreme Court that it is not an implied term of an employment contract that employers should be so

---

55. s.2(1).

56. See, *supra*, p. 60.

57. *Cf. Buckley Stores Ltd. v. National Employees etc. Ass'n Ltd.* [1978] I.R. 351.

58. Employers Liability (Compulsory Insurance) Act 1969.

59. Employers Liability (Compulsory Insurance) Regulations 1998, S.I. No. 2573; *cf.* Parsons, 'Employers' Liability Insurance - How Secure is the System', 29 Ind. L. J. 109 (1999).

insured, even where the work in question is particularly dangerous and the employer is not financially sound.[60] Nor, the Court held by inference, were employers required to warn their employees that there is no liability insurance in the workplace. Perhaps having a dangerous workplace without any insurance may constitute "reckless trading" under the Companies Acts.[61]

SOCIAL WELFARE BENEFITS

Duly insured employees may be entitled to be paid social welfare occupational injury benefit or disablement benefit when they are put out of work or are incapacitated due to an injury they incurred at work.[62] If the accident occurred in the course of the person's employment, it is deemed to have arisen out of that employment unless the contrary is established. There is a substantial body of case law, which is supplemented by legislation, regarding when does an accident arise out of work for these purposes. The fact that the employee's contract of employment is unlawful or that he was acting unlawfully when the accident occurred does not prevent it from being the basis for a claim for benefit.

Benefit is payable in respect of personal injury caused at work to the claimant; it is payable where the claimant "suffers as a result of the accident from loss of physical or mental faculty" or from disablement to the prescribed extent. There is also compensation for any "prescribed disease" which was contracted at work but cannot be attributed to a direct accident, for instance occupational deafness and pneumoconiosis. Perhaps the most notorious of those diseases, although it rarely occurs in Ireland because of the absence of any substantial mining industry, is the "black lung" disease from which many coal miners suffer. Several Conventions and Recommendations have been issued by the International Labour Organisation dealing with what ailments and maladies should be deemed to be occupational diseases for the purpose of receiving social security benefits.

[60.] *Sweeney v. Duggan* [1997] 2 I.R. 531; see *ante,* p. 62.
[61.] See, generally, M. Forde, *Company Law* (3rd ed., 1999), pp.729-731. *cf. Brittles v. Walls Timber Contractors Ltd.* [1996] E.L.R. 191, where the company notified the plaintiff that it could not afford insurance cover.
[62.] Social Welfare (Consolidation) Act 1993, ss.48 *et seq.*

CHAPTER 6

DISCRIMINATION IN EMPLOYMENT

Discrimination of many kinds occurs at the workplace. Choices must frequently be made between employees, and the very process of choosing involves discrimination. Employers prefer to hire certain types of people rather than others. Some attributes are vital when it comes to allocating particular jobs or promotion. Other characteristics or conduct influence the decision to dismiss a worker. At common law, employers are entirely free to discriminate between members of the workforce on whatever basis they choose. As Lord Davey once observed, "[a]n employer may refuse to employ a [worker] from the most capricious, malicious or morally reprehensive motives that can be conceived but the workman has no right of action against him, and a man has no right to be employed by any particular employer and has no right to any particular employment if it depends on the will of another".[1]

This freedom is now circumscribed by legislation and by E.C. rules; for the last 30 years sex discrimination and discrimination against nationals of E.C. Member States and their dependants has been the subject of extensive prohibitions. Article 141(1) of the EEC Treaty on equal pay for men and women has "direct effect" in all categories of employment, private as well as public,[2] and provisions of unimplemented E.C. Directives on equality that are sufficiently precise and unconditional can be invoked against all public sector employers[3] but not against employers in the private sector.[4] Ambiguities in national legislation will be construed in a manner consistent with the E.C.'s requirements.[5] What is meant in E.C. law by discrimination (on prohibited grounds) is treating people in similar circumstances differently or treating people in different circumstances similarly. As stated by the European Court of Justice ("the E.C.J.") in numerous decisions, "it is settled case law that discrimination involves the application of different rules to comparable situations or the application of the same rule to different situations."[6]

In 1998 the E.C. proscriptions were augmented by legislation outlawing discrimination on grounds of family status, sexual orientation, religion, age, disability, race, and belonging to the traveller community. Additionally, there are the Unfair Dismissals Acts 1977-93, which outlaw dismissals for unfair reasons; among the grounds which are presumptively unfair under those Acts, are the employee's religious or political opinions, the employee's pregnancy or the fact

---

[1.] *Allen v. Flood* [1898] A.C. 1 at 172-173.
[2.] *Defrenne v. SABENA* (Case 43/75) [1976] E.C.R. 455.
[3.] *Marshall v. Southampton and South West Herts. H.A.* (Case 152/84) [1976] E.C.R. 723.
[4.] *Faccini Dori v. Recreb* (Case C 91/92) [1994] E.C.R. 3325.
[5.] *Marleasing S.A. v. L.A. Commercial Int'l de Alimentacion S.A.* (Case C 106/89) [1990] E.C.R. 4135.
[6.] *Boyle v. Equal Opportunities Comm.* (Case 411/96) [1998] E.C.R. 6401, para 39.

that she exercised her rights to maternity leave, and other discriminatory grounds.[7]

The question of discrimination must also be considered in the light of the Constitution, which forbids discrimination on religious[8] and on political grounds, and unfair discrimination on the basis of a person's membership of a family. Article 40.1 of the Constitution goes further, in that it contains a broad affirmation of equality:

> "All citizens shall, as human persons, be held equal before the law. This shall not be held to mean that the State shall not in its enactments have due regard to differences of capacity, physical and moral, and of social function."

Most of the cases arising under this guarantee have concerned claims that legislative provisions were unfairly discriminatory.[9] The extent to which this guarantee applies to employment practices in the public sector has not been considered by the courts, but it can hardly be doubted that discrimination by public service employers on the grounds of a worker's sex or status at birth would be unconstitutional. Nevertheless, until comparatively recently most women who were employed in the public service were obliged to resign when they got married.[10] Whether private sector employers and trade unions are bound by this guarantee remains to be resolved; for instance, a question remains as to whether refusing to employ persons because of their political views would be unconstitutional.

Many of these questions no longer arise for consideration because statute law now proscribes discrimination in respect of work for numerous reasons. The Employment Equality Act 1998 replaced the Acts of 1974 and of 1977 that outlawed sex discrimination, and added several additional bases for unlawful discrimination. An earlier version of this Act was declared invalid by the Supreme Court in *Re Employment Equality Bill, 1996*,[11] which contained several features that conflicted with the Constitution. The 1998 Act is divided into two main substantive parts, Parts III (sections 18-27) and IV (sections 28-37); the former, headed "equality between men and women", deals exclusively with sex discrimination, and Part IV then addresses discrimination on the other grounds outlined above.

Compliance with the 1998 Act's requirements is supervised by the Equality Authority, which is given extensive powers of investigation, can prosecute summarily for breaches of the Act, and can apply for injunctions restraining certain forms of discrimination. Individuals aggrieved by what they regard as prohibited discrimination may complain to the Director of Equality Investigation (Part VII), who will endeavour to resolve the issue by mediation and may, if unsuccessful, determine the complaint. Persons claiming they were dismissed in contravention

---

7.   See *post*, pp.204-205.
8.   *cf. Greally v. Minister for Education* [1999] 1 I.R. 1.
9.   *e.g. Re Employment Equality Bill* [1997] 2 I.R. 321.
10. Prior to the Civil Service (Employment of Married Woman) Act 1973; several major public and private sector employers had a similar requirement, *e.g.* Aer Lingus air hostesses and banks, as illustrated in *Bank of Ireland v. Kavanagh* [1990] 1 C.M.L.R. 86 and *post*, p. 134.
11. [1997] 2 I.R. 321; see *ante*, pp. 14-16.

of the 1998 Act may seek redress from the Labour Court;[12] but if the alleged discrimination is based on sex, as proscribed by Part III of the Act, they may instead seek redress from the Circuit Court.[13] Provision is made to ensure that claims for redress under the 1998 Act and claims for common law damages in respect of the same events cannot both be prosecuted; aggrieved individuals are required to elect between these remedies.[14]

Since the rules against sex discrimination have been in force for many years and practically all the relevant Irish and E.C. case law is on that topic, that question will be considered first under the headings, *viz.* equal pay, equal treatment apart from pay, and maternity protection.[15]

EQUAL PAY (MEN AND WOMEN)

Although the earliest anti-discrimination law was the Sex Disqualification (Removal) Act 1919,[16] which was followed in the 1970s by the removal of the marriage bar in the public service, perhaps the most legally significant of these laws is the requirement that men and women should be paid the same rates for doing the same kind of work. Such a requirement was incorporated into the EEC Treaty in 1956,[17] principally at the instigation of France, which had its own equal pay laws but was concerned that the absence of similar laws in the other Member States would place French industry at a competitive disadvantage. Notwithstanding that rationale, the equal pay principle is presently regarded as having a predominantly social objective, being that of vindicating the fundamental human right of equality as between the sexes.[18] As the cases involving part-time work and also pregnant women demonstrate particularly, not only must there be formal equality in the way in which men and women are paid but there must be equality in substance, meaning, *inter alia*, that pregnancy and its incidents cannot be a justification for paying a woman less than a man or of having other work arrangements that result in pregnant women being remunerated less than their male counterparts. However, where women take maternity leave, they are not for the time being entitled to receive the full pay they would get if they were working.[19]

On joining the Communities in 1972, Ireland became bound by, *inter alia*, this requirement, which eventually was implemented by the Anti-Discrimination (Pay) Act 1974, which along with the Employment Equality Act 1977, was replaced by Part III of the Employment Equality Act 1998. There is a very extensive E.C.J. case law on what the equal pay principle demands of Member States and also of employers and trade unions, and that Court has given the principle a very broad interpretation, extending it to indirect (or by impact) discrimination

---

[12.] ss.77(1) and (2) and 78-79.
[13.] ss.77(3) and 80.
[14.] s.101.
[15.] See, generally, C. Barnard, *E.C. Employment Law* (2nd ed., 2000), Chap. 4 and M. Bolger and C. Kimber, *Sex Discrimination Law* (2000).
[16.] *cf. Frost v. The King* [1919] I.R. 81 and [2000] I.L.R.M. 479.
[17.] Article 119 (now Art. 141).
[18.] *Deutsche Telecom A.G. v. Vick* (Case C 234/96) [2000] E.C.R. Times L.R., March 28, 2000.
[19.] *Gillespie v. Northern Health and Social Services Board* (Case C 342/93) [1996] E.C.R. 475.

and rejecting historical and social reasons as justification for disparities between men's and women's wages and other remuneration.

"Equal pay" in this context means that persons doing the same or similar work for the same or an associated employer shall not be paid different remuneration because they are of different sexes. If men and women are doing similar work but are being paid differently, the burden is on their employer to demonstrate some reason other than their sex why they are not receiving the same pay. This principle in former Article 119 of the EEC Treaty, which, following amendments made by the Amsterdam Treaty of 1997, was revised and has become Article 141(1), states that "[e]ach Member State shall ensure that the principle of equal pay for male and female workers for equal work of equal value is applied." In order to confer rights and to impose duties on individuals, Article 141 does not need to be embodied in an E.C. Regulation nor in national legislation nor regulations. In the second *Defrenne* case,[20] where an air hostess with the Belgian carrier Sabena sued it for damages, it was held that "since (former) Article 119 is mandatory in nature, the prohibition on discrimination between men and women applies not only to the action of public authorities but also extends to all agreements which are intended to regulate paid labour collectively, as well as contracts between individuals".[21]

Former Article 119's (now Article 141's) requirements are amplified in several respects by Directive No. 75/117 on equal pay.[22] Both former Article 119 and this Directive are given legislative form in sections 18-20 and related provisions of the Employment Equality Act 1998. The core stipulation is section 19, according to which it is a term of every employed person's contract that he or she is "entitled to the same rate of remuneration for work [when an employee of the other sex] is employed to do like work by the same or an associated employer." Much of the 1998 Act is devoted to the procedures and other techniques for implementing this principle.

Principle of equal pay

The E.C. case law on this fundamental principle has been summarised by Conor Quigley as follows:[23] this principle means, for the same work or for work to which equal value is attributed, the elimination of all discrimination on grounds of sex with regard to all aspects and conditions of remuneration. Discrimination involves the application of different rules to comparable situations or the application of the same rule to different situations. Accordingly, Article 141 also prohibits a difference in pay where the lower-paid category of workers is engaged in work of higher value. In order to ensure genuine transparency, the principle of equal pay applies to each of the elements of remuneration granted. Indirect discrimination arises where separate categories of employees are treated differently and where that difference affects considerably more women than men and is not objectively justifiable. In this context, any criterion for establishing a

---

[20.]   (Case 43/75) [1976] E.C.R. 455.
[21.]   *ibid.* at 476 (para. 39). *cf. Brides v. Minister for Agriculture* [1998] 4 I.R. 250.
[22.]   O.J. No. L 45/19 (1975).
[23.]   *European Community Contract Law* (1998), pp. 159-160. See, generally, Barnard, *supra* n.15, pp. 227-237 and Bolger & Kimber, *supra* n.15, Chap. 4.

rate of pay which is based on values appropriate only to workers of one sex carries with it a risk of discrimination.

Actual discrimination in relation to pay may only be inferred from comparisons made on the basis of concrete appraisals of the work actually performed by employees of different sex within the same establishment or service. While the principle of equal pay is not confined to situations in which men and women are contemporaneously employed, an employee cannot rely on Article 141 in order to claim pay to which he could be entitled if he belonged to the other sex in the absence, now or in the past, in the undertaking concerned of employees of the other sex who performed or performed comparable work (*i.e.* "comparators"), since the essential criterion for ascertaining equal pay for equal work cannot be applied. Generally, the principle of equal pay presupposes that the men and women to whom it applies are in identical situations. Thus, for instance, it is contrary to Article 141 to impose an age condition which differs according to sex in order to determine entitlement to an occupational pension. However, where a special pension, payable to both men and women taking early retirement on grounds of ill health, is intended to provide an income equivalent to previous earnings, it is not contrary to Article 141 to reduce the special pension by the amount of the State pension even though only women and not men receive that State pension between the age of 60 and 65. Also, where a person who works part-time is in receipt of a retirement pension and is thereby treated under the applicable arrangements as being in the same position as a person pursuing a main occupation, the grant of a lower rate of pay for the part-time work compared to full-time work is not contrary to Article 141 merely because the pension has been reduced as a result of time spent off work bringing up a child.

It follows from the principle of equal pay that work actually carried out must be remunerated in accordance with its nature. Thus, there is nothing to prevent the use in determining wage rates of a criterion based on the degree of muscular effort objectively required by a specific job or the objective degree of heaviness of the job. Indeed, a criterion based on values corresponding to the average performance of workers of the weaker sex would result in another form of pay discrimination, in that work objectively requiring greater strength would be paid at the same rate as work requiring less strength.

Personal scope

The right to equal pay under the 1998 Act applies not alone to apprentices and employment agency personnel but extends to persons who are technically self-employed, provided they act under a contract "personally to execute any work or labour" for another.[24] Unlike some of the modern employment legislation, this part of the 1998 Act does not expressly exclude from its scope categories of public service employment and certain other jobs. No form of employment is exempted from its or from Article 141's requirements.

[24.] s.19(2)(a); *cf. Mirror Group Newspapers Ltd. v. Gunning* [1985] 1 W.L.R. 394.

"Pay"

In order to succeed in an equal pay claim, the complainant must show that he or she is earning less than a comparable man or woman. Pay or remuneration, for this purpose, is defined by section 2(1) of the 1998 Act (and Article 141(2) of the EEC Treaty) as including "any consideration, whether in cash or in kind, which an employee receives, directly or indirectly, in respect of his employment from his employer in respect of the employment". An extensive concept of what constitutes pay has been adopted as including, for instance, sick pay, bonus payments, overtime payments, skills allowances, marriage gratuities, free accommodation, redundancy payments, commissions to sales assistants, and house purchase loans. Pensions under occupational pension schemes have been held to be remuneration for this purpose, but were excluded from the above definition because special provisions for equality in occupational pensions exist under the Pensions Act 1990.[25]

The E.C. case law on what is pay for these purposes is summarised by Conor Quigley as follows:[26] Pay means the ordinary basic or minimum wage or salary and any other consideration, whether in cash or in kind which the employee receives, directly or indirectly, in respect of his employment from his employer. The assumption underlying Article 141 is that the employer commits himself to pay his employees defined benefits or to grant them specific advantages and that the employees in turn expect the employer to pay them those benefits or provide them with those advantages. Anything that is not a consequence of that commitment and does not therefore come within the corresponding expectations of the employees falls outside the concept of pay. This concept covers all payments made whether immediately or in the future, and includes compensation for attending training courses, maternity pay, continued payment of wages to an employee in the event of illness, benefits paid after the termination of the employment relationship, and compensation granted in connection with redundancy. It follows that it applies in certain cases to consideration paid even where the employee is not performing any work provided for under the contract of employment. Article 141 also applies to consideration received indirectly from the employer. Thus, it applies to benefits paid under a pension scheme set up in the form of a trust and administered by trustees who are technically independent of the employer. Moreover, a survivor's pension payable under a private occupational pension scheme also falls within the scope of Article 141 since it derives from the employee's membership of the scheme.

The legal nature of the payment is immaterial provided that it is granted in respect of the employment by the employer, so that Article 141 applies irrespective of whether the worker receives it under a contract of employment, by virtue of legislative provisions, or on a voluntary basis. Thus, for example, a redundancy payment made by the employer does not cease to constitute a form of pay on the sole ground that, rather than deriving from the contract of employment, it is a statutory or *ex gratia* payment. Furthermore, statutory benefits paid by the employer come within the concept of pay, even though such benefits also reflect

---

[25.] See *post*, pp. 369-371 and Bolger & Kimber, *supra* n.15, Chap.6.
[26.] *supra* n.23, pp.157-159.

considerations of social policy. Pay does not, however, include payments under national social security schemes. Nor does it include benefits directly governed by legislation, without any element of agreement within the undertaking or the occupational branch concerned, which are obligatorily applicable to general categories of workers and which the worker will normally receive not by reason of the employer's contribution but solely because he fulfils the legal conditions requiring them to be granted.

Sums, such as employees' contributions to retirement benefit schemes, which are included in the calculation of the gross salary payable to the employee and which directly determine the calculation of other advantages linked to the salary, such as redundancy payments, unemployment benefits, family allowances and credit facilities are considered as pay even if they are immediately deducted by the employer and paid to a pension fund on behalf of the employee. Consequently, the amounts which a public authority is obliged to pay in respect of contributions owed to a social security scheme in respect of its public service employees and which are included in the calculation of the gross salary are included in the notion of pay in so far as these affect the calculation of other benefits dependent on salary. It also follows that if men and women receive the same gross salary but a deduction is made solely from the men's salary as a contribution to a widows' pension scheme (whether occupational or statutory), the disparity in net pay is not the result of either a benefit paid to employees or a contribution paid by the employer and as such does not infringe Article 141.

Like work

The work of the persons being compared does not have to be entirely identical for the 1998 Act to apply; it suffices that they are engaged in "like work".[27] That term is defined by section 7(1) of that Act as follows:

"in relation to work which one person is employed to do, another shall be regarded as employed to do like work if:

(a) both perform the same work under the same or similar conditions, or each is interchangeable with the other in relation to the work, or

(b) the work performed by one is of a similar nature to that performed by the other and any differences between the work performed or the conditions under which it is performed by each either are of small importance in relation to the work as a whole or occur with such irregularity as not to be significant to the work as a whole, or

(c) the work performed by one is equal in value to that performed by the other having regard to such matters as skill, physical or mental requirements, responsibility and working conditions."

In other words, the jobs being compared may be either the same, similar or of "equal value". Most equal pay claims now are brought on the basis that the jobs in question are of equal value, which often involves using professional job evalu-

---

[27] s.19(1) and E.E.C. Treaty Art. 141(1).

ation techniques as evidence. The question is one of fact and not of law[28] and, while in rulings Article 235 (formerly Article 177) references preliminary the E.C.J. may give guidance, ultimately the question is to be decided by the national court.

A most curious case on the subject was *Murphy v. Telecom Éireann*,[29] where Keane J. held that a woman's job, which demonstrably was more exacting and rewarding than a job held by a comparable man, but he was earning more than she, was not work of equal value to the man's job for this purpose. That interpretation was rejected by the E.C.J.,[30] as being inconsistent with the very objective of former Article 119, which is to outlaw unfair discrimination on the grounds of sex with regard to remuneration. In the light of the ruling, Keane J. then held that the (then in force) 1974 Act should be given a "teleological interpretation", meaning that whenever possible it should be construed in accordance with the requirements of former Article 119.[31] The British courts were reluctant to take account of Community requirements when interpreting their legislation on equality until eventually that approach was abandoned in the *Pickstone* case.[32] Section 7(3) of the 1998 Act precludes adopting the original Keane J. approach and the Amsterdam amendment to Article 119 expressly refers to work being of equal value.

Perhaps the leading E.C.J. case on the question[33] is the Austrian psychotherapist case[34] where predominantly female psychotherapists, with degrees in psychology, employed by the Vienna Area Health Fund sought parity with doctors employed as psychotherapists. It was contended that because both groups' training was similar and they performed similar tasks, there was sufficient equivalence in their work. However, their training was not the same, nor were their formal qualifications. Further, although the task both groups performed appeared to be identical, in treating their patients they drew on knowledge and skills acquired in different disciplines. Further, the doctors were also qualified to perform tasks other than psychotherapy. That patients were charged the same sum whether they were treated by a doctor or by a psychotherapist was not relevant.[35]

The question that arose in the Swedish midwives' case[36] was how are pay comparisons to be made where, assuming there is like work, insofar as equivalent tasks are being performed, there are very considerable differences in the manner in which those tasks are being executed. Two midwives working at a hospital in Orebro sought parity with a clinical technician there. Their basic monthly salary was 17,000 Skr, whereas his was 19,650 Skr. However, whereas he worked the

---

[28]   *C. & D. Foods Ltd. v. Cunnion* [1997] 1 I.R. 147; however, to say that the question is invariably one of fact and not of law may be an over-simplification.

[29]   [1986] I.L.R.M. 483.

[30]   Case 157/86 [1988] E.C.R. 673.

[31]   [1989] I.L.R.M. 58.

[32]   *Pickstone v. Freemans p.l.c.* [1989] A.C. 66.

[33]   In *Enderby v. Frenchay Health Authority* (Case C 127/92) [1993] E.C.R. 5535, it was assumed for the purpose of the questions posed there (see *infra*, p. 133) that there was like work.

[34]   *Angesteleitenbetriebsrat der Wiener v. Wiener Gebietskrankenkasse* (Case C 309/97) [1999] ECR 2865.

[35]   *cf. British Coal Corp. v. Smith* [1996] I.C.R. 515.

[36]   *Jamstalldletsombudsmannen v. Orebo Lans Landsting* (Case C 236/98) [2000] I.R.L.R. 421.

standard 40-hour week and never worked shifts, the midwives worked a three-shift system over a 34-hour week, for which they were paid an "inconvenient hours" supplement. Because this supplement appeared to be intended to compensate for inconvenience and disruption to family and social life, and for interrupted sleep patterns, it was held that there was a prima facie case of discrimination. And although the midwives worked a shorter week, they should be regarded as working a full-time week just as much as the technician did. Accordingly, it was held, if it were shown that a considerably higher percentage of women than men worked as midwives, there was a prima facie case of unlawful discrimination unless the employer could put forward an explanation for the wage differential unrelated to the employees' sex.

For the equal pay principle to apply there must be an actual identifiable man doing a job who is to be compared with a woman worker, or *vice versa*; a comparison with some hypothetical worker does not suffice. The woman claiming equal pay is entitled to select who that comparator shall be.[37] But it is no longer necessary that the two or more employees being compared work in the same workplace, nor is it necessary that the employees being compared are simultaneously doing like work; it suffices that the comparators were engaged in like work within three years prior to or subsequent to the alleged discrimination.[38] Where it is sought to establish a prima facie case of discrimination by comparing a group of predominantly female workers with a group of predominantly male workers, there must be a sufficient statistical basis for the alleged gender imbalance.[39]

The relevant man and woman or groups being compared must be working for the one employer, or for an "associated employer", in the latter case provided that either all the employees or the particular category of employees of both employers had similar terms and conditions of employment.[40] An associated employer is a corporation or company which controls the other, directly or indirectly, or where both are under common control.[41] It was contended unsuccessfully in *Brides v. Minister for Agriculture*[42] that, in the light of E.C. law, this definition should be extended somewhat, to enable women poultry officers employed by the Minister to be compared with male agricultural development officers employed by Teagasc, a distinct statutory body that is closely linked with the Department of Agriculture.

Where job classification systems are being used to determine pay, the E.C. case law has been summarised by Conor Quigley as follows:[43] Any such system must be based on the same criteria for both men and women and be so drawn up as to exclude any discrimination on grounds of sex. The nature of the work to be carried out must be considered objectively. Where duties by their nature require particular physical effort or are physically heavy, in differentiating rates of pay, it

---

37. *Wilton v. Steel Co. of Ireland Ltd.* [1999] E.L.R. 1.
38. s.19(2)(b).
39. *IMPACT v. Irish Aviation Authority* [2000] E.L.R. 29.
40. s.19(3).
41. s.2(2).
42. [1998] 4 I.R. 250.
43. *supra* n.23, at p. 161.

is consistent with the principle of non-discrimination to use a criterion based on the objectively measurable expenditure of effort necessary in carrying out the work or the degree to which, viewed objectively, the work is physically heavy. Even where a particular criterion, such as that of demand on the muscles, may in fact tend to favour male workers, since it may be assumed that in general they are physically stronger than female workers, it must, in order to determine whether or not it is discriminatory, be considered in the context of the whole job classification system, having regard to other criteria influencing rates of pay. Although a system is not necessarily discriminatory simply because one of its criteria makes reference to attributes more characteristic of men, in order for a job classification system as a whole to be non-discriminatory, it must be established in such a manner that it includes, if the nature of the tasks in question so permits, jobs to which equal value is attributed and for which regard is had to other criteria in relation to which women workers may have a particular aptitude.

Justification

An employer who is paying different remuneration to men and women for like work being performed by them has a defence under section 19(5) if he or she can establish that the reason for the differential treatment is "grounds other than … gender". For the purposes of former Article 119 of the EEC Treaty, it was held that, in order to defend an equal pay claim on these grounds, the employer must demonstrate objectively justifiable grounds for the pay differential and not merely that he or she had no intention to discriminate on the basis of sex. For this defence to succeed, the differential treatment must "correspond to a real need on the part of the undertaking" and be "appropriate with a view to achieving the objective being pursued and necessary to that end".[44] Relevant factors include length of service in all cases; training, if such training is of importance for performing the particular tasks assigned; and mobility, in the sense of adaptability to varying hours and varying workplaces.

As with the concepts of "pay" and "like work", there are a great number of E.C.J. decisions on what considerations warrant paying different remuneration to men and women who do essentially the same job, which have been summarised by Conor Quigley as follows:[45] Where employees in one job are paid less than employees in a comparable job and the former are almost exclusively women whereas the latter are predominantly men, there is a prima facie case of discrimination. In this regard, however, a differential pay practice may be objectively justified if the measures chosen are unrelated to any discrimination based on sex and correspond to a real need on the part of the employer and are appropriate and necessary. Furthermore, if a particular measure reflects a legitimate aim of a Member State's social policy, is appropriate to achieve that aim and is necessary in order to do so, the mere fact that it affects more women workers than men is not to be regarded as a breach of Article 141. Factors which may be taken into account in justifying a differential pay practice include the level of training and adaptability to variable hours and varying places of work,

---

[44] *Rinner Kuhn v. FWW Spezial GebaUdereinigung GmBH* (Case 171/89) [1989] E.C.R. 2743.
[45] *supra* n.23, at 163-164.

where these are of importance for the performance of specific tasks entrusted to the employee, and length of service. This is so even though, in the cases of training and length of service, this may involve less advantageous treatment of women in so far as they have entered the labour market more recently than men or more frequently suffer an interruption of their career. Although experience goes hand in hand with length of service and enables the worker to improve performance of the tasks allotted to him, the objectivity of such a criterion depends on all the circumstances in a particular case and, in particular, on the relationship between the nature of the work performed and the experience gained from the performance of that work upon completion of a certain number of working hours. Another factor which may be taken into account is the state of the employment market, which may lead an employer to increase the pay of a particular job in order to attract candidates. However, it is never objectively justifiable simply to determine that the quality of work done by women is generally less good than work done by men.

In what perhaps is the leading E.C.J. case on the question, *Enderby v. Frenchay Health Authority*,[46] predominately women speech therapists were being paid less than predominantly male pharmacists and psychologists. It was assumed there that there was like work and, because of the statistical disparity, the onus fell on the employer to justify the difference. His explanation, that the two groups had different non-discriminatory collective bargaining histories, was held to be insufficient because both belonged to the same trade union. According to Advocate General Lenz:

> "It cannot be sufficient to explain the causes leading to the discrimination. In particular, references to historical and social reasons cannot, in a case such as [this] be recognised as factors which are objectively justified and unconnected with discrimination on the basis of sex .... The historical and social context of a "purely female profession" is most probably sex-related. If an explanatory approach were accepted as sufficient justification, that would lead to perpetuation of sexual rules in working life. [That] would be ... a legal argument for maintaining the status quo."[47]

By contrast, in *Flynn v. Primark*,[48] where female sales assistants sought equality with male storemen employed in a Penny's store in Dublin, it was held that their pay difference was justified because in the past the storemen had exceptional industrial relations strength, which they used to negotiate five productivity agreements and, it was concluded, that differential had to be maintained down to present times in order to maintain flexibility and productivity. Similarly, the pay difference between communications assistants and radio officers employed in Dublin Airport was upheld because, under international conventions, radio officers were required to have higher qualifications.[49]

---

46. Case C 127/92 [1993] E.C.R. 5535.
47. *ibid.,* para. 49. *cf. Enderby v. Frenchhay Health Authority (No. 2)* [2000] I.C.R. 612 and *Glasgow City Council v. Marshall* [2000] 1 W.L.R. 333.
48. [1999] E.L.R. 89.
49. *O'Leary v. Minister for Transport* [1998] E.L.R. 113. Also *Grogan v. Cadbury (Ireland) Ltd.* [2000] E.L.R. 214.

Whether *Bank of Ireland v. Kavanagh*,[50] concerning bank employees' marriage gratuities, was correctly decided is debatable. In the past women bank employees who got married had to retire and, in that event, were paid a lump sum gratuity in lieu of a pension which could not be obtained because of early retirement. In 1974 the banks' "marriage bar" to women being employed was abolished but the gratuity was retained for all female employees working at that date. The claimant in the case, a man who worked for the defendant bank from 1969 to 1980, contended that he had been denied equal pay because no gratuity was paid to him when he got married. One would have thought that, since only women qualified for the gratuity, he had a clear case. Although the equality officer and the Labour Court upheld his claim, that was rejected on appeal. According to Costello J., female employees got the gratuity not because they were women but because they were also employed prior to 1974; the pre-1974 aspect means that the higher "pay" was not based on sex but on other grounds. This, it was held, was "convincingly demonstrated" by the fact that women employed since 1974 did not get the gratuity. However, since men employed prior to that date did not qualify for it, that would suggest that the distinction was indeed based on sex. The unconvincing reasoning there[51] resembles the now discredited logic that regarded discrimination on the grounds of pregnancy not to be sex discrimination, entirely disregarding the fact that only women can get pregnant.

In the *Danish Clerical Union* case,[52] the question arose of how to evaluate a remuneration system in which all employees were paid the same basic rates, regardless of sex, but when account was taken of various mobility, training and seniority allowances, men on average were paid significantly more than women or *vice versa*. It was held that in these circumstances the E.C. Directive transferred the burden of proof on to the employer. Where an employer operates an opaque pay system, such that workers are unable to compare their wages because no reasons are given for pay differentials, and where there is a substantial difference between the average men's and women's wages, it is presumed that the Directive is being contravened. Accordingly, it is up to the employer in those circumstances to demonstrate that his remuneration arrangements are non-discriminatory.

Part-time work

The appropriate treatment of part-time workers, who tend to be overwhelmingly female, has been the subject of extensive litigation. On whether there is unequal treatment for these purposes, the test is whether the total remuneration paid to full time workers is higher, hour for hour, than that paid to part-timers.

Conor Quigley has summarised the E.C. case law as follows:[53] Although there is unequal treatment wherever the overall pay of full-time employees is higher than that of part-time employees for the same number of hours worked, the fact

---

50.   [1990] 1 C.M.L.R. 86.
51.   D. Curtin, *Irish Employment Equality Law* (1989), p. 157, demonstrates the fallacy, as do Bolger & Kimber, *supra*, n.15, p. 127.
52.   *Handels-Og Kontorfunktionaererernes Forbund i Danmark v. Danik Arbejdsigiverforforening* (Case 109/88) [1988] E.C.R. 3199.
53.   *supra*, n.23, pp. 162-163.

that part-time work is paid at a rate lower than pay for full-time work does not amount *per se* to discrimination contrary to Article 141, provided that the hourly rates are applied to employees belonging to either category without distinction based on sex and that the difference in rates is objectively justified. Such may be the case when, by giving rates of pay which are lower for part-time work than for full-time work, the employer is endeavouring, on economic grounds which may be objectively justified, to encourage full-time work irrespective of the sex of the employee. However, a difference in pay between part-time and full-time workers is contrary to Article 141 if it is in reality merely an indirect way of reducing the level of pay of part-time workers on the ground that that group of workers is composed exclusively or predominantly of women. Thus, if it is established that a considerably lower percentage of women than of men perform the minimum number of weekly working hours required in order to be able to claim the full-time rate of pay, the inequality in pay will be contrary to Article 141 where, regard being had to the difficulties encountered by women in arranging to work that minimum number of hours per week, the pay policy of the undertaking in question cannot be explained by factors other than discrimination based on sex. Similarly, Article 141 will be infringed where an employer excludes part-time employees from its occupational pension scheme or from the right to receive continued payment of wages in the event of illness or redundancy payments, or where a part-time employee is entitled to lesser compensation for attending training courses or is required to complete a longer period of service in order to qualify for a higher salary grade, where this affects a far greater number of women than men, unless the employer shows that the exclusion is based on objectively justified factors unrelated to any discrimination on grounds of sex. On the other hand, it is not contrary to Article 141 to restrict payment of overtime supplements to cases where the normal working hours of full-time employees are exceeded.

In one of the more recent cases, *Hill v. Revenue Commissioners*,[54] the E.C.J. had to consider the system for determining wage increases in the Irish civil service and whether it unlawfully discriminated against former part-time job-sharers who converted back to full-time employment. Under a points system, full-time officials were credited with one point for every satisfactory year of service. There was a parallel scale for those who worked part-time and they got a half point for every satisfactory year worked. When part-timers reverted back to full-time service, they carried over the accumulated half points on the latter scale, thereby getting full credit for the actual time worked throughout their careers. However, 98 per cent of such employees were women and they contended that the system unlawfully discriminated. It was held that, unless the State could justify this system with objective criteria, it would so discriminate, but it is for the national court ultimately to decide whether in fact justification has been established.

Several justifications suggested by the State were given short shrift by the Court. Those were that:

> "the rules are in keeping with the standard practice of the civil service whereby incremental progression is related to service and only actual paid service is credited;

[54.] (Case C 243/95) [1998] E.C.R. 3739.

that practice is valuable to the employer in that it gives incentives to improve the quality of work performed;

to make an exception of job-sharing service would lead to arbitrary and inequitable situations;

to make such an exception because the majority of job-sharers are women would amount to discrimination in favour of women, and

the present practice ensures that the incremental cost of job-sharing staff is the same as that of full-time staff, thus making the cost of work done by job-sharers the same as the cost of work done by full-time staff.)"[55]

The E.C.J.'s response was that

"[N]either the justification ... to the effect that there is an established practice within the Civil Service of "crediting" only actual service, nor that stating that this practice establishes a reward system which maintains staff motivation, commitment and morale, is relevant. The first justification is no more than a general assertion unsupported by objective criteria. With regard to the second, the system of remuneration for employees working on a full-time basis cannot be influenced by the job-sharing scheme.

So far as concerns the justification that, if an exception were to be made in favour of job-sharing, that would result in arbitrary or inequitable situations or would amount to impermissible discrimination in favour of women, it should be pointed out, as is clear from paragraph 29 of the present judgment, that to grant to workers who convert to full-time employment the same point as that which they had under their job-sharing contract does not constitute discrimination in favour of female workers.

So far as the justification based on economic grounds is concerned, it should be noted that an employer cannot justify discrimination arising from a job-sharing scheme solely on the ground that avoidance of such discrimination would involve increased costs.

It must be borne in mind that all the parties to the main proceedings, and the national tribunal, agree that almost all job-sharing workers in the Irish public sector are women. It is apparent from the case file that approximately 83 per cent of those who chose that option did so in order to be able to combine work and family responsibilities, which invariably involve caring for children.

Community policy in this area is to encourage and, if possible, adapt working conditions to family responsibilities. Protection of women within family life and in the course of their professional activities is, in the same way as for men, a principle which is widely regarded in the legal systems of the member states as being the natural corollary of the equality between men and women, and which is recognised by Community law.

[55.]   Para. 39 of Advocate General la Pergola's opinion.

The onus is therefore on the [State] to establish before the Labour Court that the reference to the criterion of service, defined as the length of time actually worked, in the assessment of the incremental credit to be granted to workers who convert from job-sharing to full-time work is justified by objective factors unrelated to any discrimination on grounds of sex. If such evidence is adduced by those authorities, the mere fact that the national legislation affects far more women than men cannot be regarded as constituting a breach of article 119 of the Treaty and, consequently, a breach of the Directive."[56]

Piece work

Another issue of some general controversy is the appropriate treatment of piece workers, where the entire or at least a very substantial component of their earnings is based on individual effort, being the number of units produced (work rate) and the absence of flaws in those units (quality of work). The mere fact that the average pay of workers of predominantly one sex exceeds that of a group comprising predominantly those of the opposite sex is not sufficient to demonstrate discrimination, let alone to move on to the question of justification.

Conor Quigley has summarised the E.C. case law as follows:[57] Equal pay without discrimination based on sex means that pay for the same work at piece rates must be calculated on the basis of the same unit of measurement, and that pay for work at time rates must be the same for the same job. It follows that, where the unit of measurement is the same for two groups of workers, one predominantly men and the other predominantly women, carrying out the same work or work of equal value, the principle of equal pay does not prohibit workers belonging to one or other group from receiving different total pay that is due to their different individual outputs. The mere finding that there is a difference in the average pay of two groups of workers, calculated on the basis of the total individual pay of all the workers belonging to one or other group, does not suffice to establish that there has been discrimination. In order to establish the correct basis for comparing pay as between two groups of workers paid by the piece, each group must comprise all the workers who, taking account of a set of factors such as the nature of the work, the training requirements and the working conditions, can be considered to be in a comparable situation. The comparison must cover a relatively large number of workers in order to ensure that the differences found are not due to purely fortuitous or short-term factors or to differences in the individual output of the workers concerned.

Procedures for redress

Where a worker seeks redress for breach of the employer's equal pay obligation, or indeed for the other obligations laid down by the 1998 Act regarding equal treatment or non-discrimination on the several grounds other than sex, procedures are provided for in Part VII of that Act as an alternative to a damages claim for breach of contract.[58] These put emphasis on mediation.

[56.] *cf. Barry v. Midland Bank p.l.c.* [1999] 1 W.L.R. 1465.

[57.] *supra*, n.23, pp. 161-162.

[58.] See, generally Bolger & Kimber, *supra*, n.15, Chap.12.

A complaint regarding equal pay may be made to the Director of Equality Investigations.[59] Complaints may be made within six months of the most recent failure to provide equal pay but, in exceptional circumstances, that period can be extended to twelve months.[60] The Director then will endeavour to resolve the issue through the offices of an employment mediation officer, unless either party objects to mediation.[61] If there is such objection or its efforts towards resolution in that manner prove futile, the Director will have the complaint investigated, which will be done in private.[62] If the complaint is upheld the Director may direct that the worker be compensated, in the form of back-pay, which award cannot be for a period exceeding three years prior to the complaint having been made.[63]

Decisions of the Director may be appealed to the Labour Court within the next 42 days.[64] Appeals are heard in private, unless one party wants a public hearing and the Labour Court agrees to dealing with the appeal in public. Any award made on appeal is subject to the same financial constraints as bind the Director. Both the Director and the Labour Court are required, on request, to furnish their decision or determination in writing, stating the reasons.[65] The Labour Court's decision is subject to a further appeal to the High Court but on a "point of law" only.[66]

Instead of following this procedure, the employee may commence proceedings in the Circuit Court for damages for breach of the equal pay clause in her employment contract.[67] There is a six-month limitation period that may be extended to twelve months.[68] Where this route is chosen, the Equality Authority is empowered to furnish the plaintiff with assistance if the case raises an important issue of principle or where, in the circumstances, it would not be reasonable to expect the plaintiff to present the case without help from the Authority.[69] As well as ordering that equal remuneration shall be paid from the date the claim was made, the court may award compensation in the form of back-pay for as far back as six years prior to the complaint having been made.[70]

EQUAL TREATMENT (MEN AND WOMEN)

For many years a major area of concern of international employment law has been to protect women from excessively arduous conditions at work, especially in case of maternity, and to ensure equality of rights and treatment for men and women workers. Numerous conventions and recommendations have been

---

[59]. s.77(1).
[60]. s.77(5) and (6).
[61]. s.78.
[62]. s.79.
[63]. s.82(1)(a) and (b).
[64]. s.83.
[65]. s.88.
[66]. s.90(3).
[67]. s.77(3).
[68]. s.77(5) and (6).
[69]. s.67.
[70]. s.82(3).

adopted by the International Labour Organisation on topics such as maternity protection, night work, employment of women in unhealthy and dangerous occupations, equal remuneration, equality of treatment generally, and the employment of women with family responsibilities. Article 8 of the European Social Charter gives employed women protection in several respects. However, none of these instruments have any direct legal effect in domestic law, and one scans in vain the Irish law reports to see any reference to them as guidelines for interpreting the Constitution or related statutory provisions.

Prohibitions against discrimination on the grounds of sex feature in the employment laws of most industrial states today. These measures were often adopted in order to encourage female participation in the workforce at a time of labour shortages. Some anti-discrimination laws were enacted for philosophical or ideological reasons: that it is wrong to handicap women who may wish to earn their living by obtaining employment. One such measure is the Sex Disqualification (Removal) Act 1919, which put an end to many disqualifications based on sex and on marital status in the public sector and in the professions.[71] According to section 1 of this very short Act, which is still in force:

"A person shall not be disqualified by sex or marriage from the exercise of any public function, or from being appointed to or holding any civil or judicial office or post, or from entering or assuming or carrying on any civil profession or vocation."

But this Act permitted exceptions to its requirements for civil service employments and married women could not work in the Irish civil service until the "marriage bar" was removed in 1973.[72] In 1958 the law permitted women to join the Garda Síochána[73] and in 1979 women were permitted to become members of the armed forces.[74]

Employment equality in this context means that, in matters other than pay or remuneration, persons should not be discriminated against at work on account of their sex. Although former Article 119 of the EEC Treaty did not refer to employment equality in this sense, in 1976 the E.C. Council adopted Directive No. 76/207 on equal treatment of the sexes in employment.[75] In the following year the Employment Equality Act 1977 was enacted, which gave effect to this Directive; that Act was replaced by Part III of the Employment Equality Act 1998. When former Article 119 was revised in the Amsterdam amendments of 1997 and became Article 141 of the EEC Treaty, it made express reference to "measures to ensure the application of the principle of equal opportunities and equal treatment of men and women in matters of employment and occupation". Neither this part of Article 141 nor the "Equal Treatment" Directive are "directly applicable" in Irish courts. However, to the extent, if any, that the 1998 Act does not implement this Directive's clear and specific requirements, they can be invoked against the State and other public agencies *qua* employer.[76]

---

71.   *cf. Nagle v. Fielden* [1966] 2 Q.B. 633; *Frost v. The King* [1919] I.R. 81 and [2000] I.L.R.M. 479.
72.   Civil Service (Employment of Married Women) Act 1973.
73.   Garda Síochána Act 1958.
74.   Defence (Amendment) Act 1979.
75.   O.J. No. L 39/40 (1976). See, generally, Barnard, *supra*, n.75, pp. 238-252.
76.   *i.e.* "vertical direct effect", *e.g. Marshall* case, *supra* n.3.

The key provisions of the 1998 Act in this regard are section 6(1), (2)(a), section 8 and section 21. The former of these is a general definition of "discrimination", being "where, on any of the grounds (*inter alia*, that one is a woman and the other is a man...) one person is treated less favourably than another is, has been or would be treated". Section 8 then contains a prohibition against discrimination by employers (or agencies) in relation to hiring, conditions at work, training or work experience, promotion, or regarding and classification of posts. The remainder of this section elaborates on the prohibition and sections 9-13 forbid sex discrimination in collective agreements and in advertisements relating to employment. Discrimination by trade unions, by employers' organisations and by employment agencies is also proscribed.

Section 21 stipulates that, where a male and a female are in the "same employment" and doing work that is not "materially different", the terms of their contracts are deemed to contain a "gender equality clause", meaning that they shall be treated "not less favourabl[y]" than the other or shall contain "a similar term benefiting" the other.

Principle of equal treatment

The E.C. case law on the fundamental principle of equal treatment has been summarised by Conor Quigley as follows:[77] This principle means that there may be no discrimination whatsoever on grounds of sex either directly or indirectly by reference, in particular, to marital or family status. If a person has been refused employment on grounds constituting discrimination on grounds of sex, there is no need to prove that a person of the opposite sex applied for or was offered the post. Indirect discrimination arises where the application of a provision is more advantageous to one sex than the other, unless that difference in treatment is justified by objective factors unrelated to any discrimination on grounds of sex. An example is the exclusion of small businesses from the application of legislation which provides for compensation if it were established that small businesses employ a considerably higher percentage of women than men. Even if such a disproportion were established, the exclusion might be justified by a policy of alleviating the constraints burdening small businesses which plays an essential role in economic development and the creation of employment.

Any laws, regulations and administrative provisions contrary to the principle of equal treatment are prohibited. Apart from those cases where one of the exceptions laid down by Council Directive 76/207/EEC itself applies, any breach of the principle of equal treatment is sufficient to make the employer liable. It is unnecessary for the person discriminated against to prove fault. Furthermore, no regard may be had to any other grounds of exemption envisaged by national law.

Directive 76/207/EEC is without prejudice to provisions concerning the protection of women. Member States enjoy a discretion as regards the nature of these protective measures and the detailed arrangements for their implementation. However, as far as the aims of protecting female workers are concerned, these protective measures are valid only if, having regard to the principle of equal treatment, there is a justified need for a difference of treatment as between men and

---

[77.] *supra*, n.23, pp. 176-178.

women. Thus, for instance, although it is permissible for national law to prohibit nightwork by women when they are pregnant, since the risks to which women are exposed when working at night are not, in general, inherently different from those to which men are exposed, it is discriminatory to prohibit nightwork by women where nightwork by men is not prohibited. Measures which go beyond protection of women, such as the granting of special rights to women, do not come within the scope of this exception.

Directive 76/207/EEC also is without prejudice to the right of Member States to exclude from its field of application those occupational activities and, where appropriate, the training leading thereto, for which, by reason of their nature or the context in which they are carried out, the sex of the worker constitutes a determining factor. This provision, which is to be interpreted strictly, must be applied only to specific activities, and reliance on it must be capable of being adapted to social developments. It may not be used to exclude from the scope of application of the directive whole classes of occupational activity, such as employment in private households or in small undertakings with no more than five employees, where the reason for discrimination is too general such that it goes beyond the objectives allowed by the directive. An example of where gender does constitute a determining factor is the occupation of midwife where a limitation on access by men to the occupation may be permissible if it is justified on the ground that personal sensitivities play an important role in the relations between midwife and patient. Similarly, the carrying on of certain policing activities may be such that the sex of police officers constitutes a determining factor.

Personal scope

The equal treatment provisions in Part III of the 1998 Act have much the same personal scope as the equal pay requirement, applying to employees, apprentices, employment agency personnel and virtually the entire public sector. But they do not apply to self-employed persons, notwithstanding that under their contracts they must personally perform work; such persons however are subject to another E.C. Directive on equal treatment.[78] Nor do they apply to jobs of a personal nature where the sex is a determining factor, most notably caring for elderly and incapacitated people in their homes.[79] There are also exceptions to the requirements with regard to members of the Garda Síochána and of the prison service.[80]

Proscribed discrimination

Part III of the 1998 Act has a somewhat complex structure and may be summarised as follows. There are three core concepts in anti-discrimination laws. One is direct discrimination, *i.e.* where an act, provision or requirement is overtly discriminatory; for instance a stipulation that "no women need apply" or "only men will be promoted or given full pensions" or whatever. Section 21 of the Act

---

[78] Directive 86/613, O.J. No. L 359/56 (1986). See, generally, Barnard, *supra*, n.75, pp. 252-253.

[79] s.26(2). *cf. E.C. Commission v. U.K.* (Case 165/82) [1983] E.C.R. 3431, concerning restrictions on men becoming midwives.

[80] s.27; *cf. Johnson v. Chief Constable of the RUC* (Case 222/84) [1986] E.C.R. 1651 and *E.C. Commission v. France* (Case 318/86) [1988] E.C.R. 3559, concerning police duties.

provides that, where a man and a woman are doing work that is "not materially different", a "gender equality clause" is incorporated into one or other of their contracts to ensure that he or she is not treated less favourably on account of sex. Unlike the concept "like work" in the equal pay provisions, there is no statutory definition for the phrase "not materially different" work.

Secondly, there is indirect discrimination or discrimination by impact; that is where a requirement that is not in terms discriminatory nonetheless does discriminate in the way it operates. Perhaps the best example of the latter, taken from equal pay litigation, is special rules for part-time workers; since the great majority of part-timers happen to be women, rules that disadvantage part-timers often discriminate against women. Indirect discrimination is proscribed by section 22, meaning that in the application of any provision affecting men and women, if a "substantially higher proportion" of one or the other, as the case may be, are disadvantaged and such detriment cannot be justified on objective factors unrelated to sex, there is unlawful discrimination. This prohibition also applies where those disadvantaged by impact comprise a "substantially higher proportion" with regard to their marital status or family status *i.e.* are single, married, separated, divorced or widowed, or have parental responsibilities as defined in section 2(1) of the 1998 Act. A major area of contention is going to be the appropriate use of statistics and how substantial this proportion must be for it to constitute discrimination by impact.[81] Indirect discrimination was held to exist, for example, where a Health Board set an age limit of 27 years for applicants for permanent clerical posts;[82] there the claimant had worked for the Board for several years before she got married and subsequently worked part-time for the Board but was disqualified from obtaining a permanent post because of that limit.

Thirdly, there are certain circumstances where, even though there is discrimination on sex grounds, it can be objectively justified. What constitutes such justification may give rise to considerable controversy (*infra*).

The way in which discrimination is attacked by the 1998 Act is both negative and positive. It contains several prohibitions against discrimination of various kinds, whether direct or indirect. Additionally, as stated, it incorporates into every employment contract a "gender equality clause" (section 21) (as well as a "same remuneration" clause). There is a prohibition against employers discriminating (section 8) in respect of access to employment, conditions of employment, training or experience, promotion or re-grading and re-classification of posts. Regarding each of these, discrimination means treating persons less favourably than another because one has to be a man or a woman, as the case may be. Any provision in a collective agreement that gives rise to such discrimination is decreed null and void (section 9). There is no express reference here to dismissal from employment on grounds of sex but it is clear from section 77 that a dismissal can constitute a breach of the 1998 Act.

---

81. *cf. R. v. Secretary of State, ex p. Seymour Smith* (Case C 167/97) [1999] E.C.R. 623, paras. 114-133 of Advocate General Cosmas's opinion and paras. 53-65 of the judgment; also *London Underground Ltd. v. Edwards (No. 2)* [1999] I.C.R. 494.

82. *North Western Health Board v. Martyn* [1987] I.R. 505. Similarly, *Gleeson v. Rotunda Hospital* [2000] E.L.R. 206.

There are specific prohibitions against discrimination in job advertisements (section 10), by employment agencies (section 11), by persons offering vocational training courses (section 12), and by trade unions and comparable professional or trade organisations (section 13). Regarding vocational training, exceptions are made so that the particular religious ethos of certain hospitals or schools may be maintained.

Sexual harassment at work is defined and proscribed (section 23), meaning sexual overtures of various kinds that are unwelcome and could reasonably be regarded as offensive, humiliating or intimidating on gender grounds.[83]

Discrimination on grounds of sex or gender for these purposes would appear to cover discrimination against transsexuals,[84] who had or are contemplating a sex change. Part III of the 1998 Act does not apply to discrimination on grounds of sexual orientation, *i.e.* against homosexuals;[85] that comes under Part IV of the Act. Circumstances can arise however where discrimination against homosexuals of one sex is covered by Part III.[86]

Justification

There are circumstances in which discrimination on the grounds of sex or gender is nonetheless permissible under Part III. In particular, section 25 of the 1998 Act identifies limited circumstances where a person's sex is an acceptable "occupational qualification", envisaging types of case. These are where the very nature of the job requires a man or a women, on grounds of physiology, other than physical strength or stamina; where, for reasons of authenticity, the role in an entertainment ought to be played by a man or a woman, as the case may be; where the job involves providing "personal services"; where the job involves using communal sleeping and sanitary accommodation and where it would be unreasonable or impractical to provide separate accommodations for men and for women; lastly, where the job involves working abroad where the laws or conditions discriminate on the basis of sex. As stated above, Part III does not apply to certain aspects of employment in the Garda Síochána and in the prison service.

A gender equality clause will not be implied into an employment contract where disparate treatment is "genuinely based on grounds other than the gender ground".[87] And there is no indirect discrimination where, even though the measure in question has a substantially more proportionate impact on one sex than another, it can be justified by "objective factors unrelated to … sex".[88] Under the previous legislation, it was assumed that, in order to establish indirect discrimination, there must be some "causal connection" between the person's sex and how he or she is being treated, but in 1996 that interpretation was rejected by the Supreme Court.[89] Where cases are referred to the E.C.J. under Article 235

---

[83]. *cf.* Code of Practice, E.C. Recommendation 92/131, O.J. No. L 49/1 (1992) and *A Female Employee v. A Company* [2000] E.L.R. 147; see generally, Bolger & Kimber, *supra*, n.15, Chap. 8.

[84]. *cf. P. v. S.* (Case C 13/94) [1996] E.C.R. 2143.

[85]. *cf. Grant v. South-West Trains Ltd.* (Case C 249/96) [1998] E.C.R. 621.

[86]. *Smith v. Gardner Merchant Ltd.* [1999] I.C.R. 134.

[87]. s.21(3).

[88]. s.22(1)(c).

[89]. *Nathan v. Baily Gibson Ltd.* [1998] 2 I.R. 162.

(formerly Art. 177) of the EEC Treaty, that Court will furnish guidelines about what may be justification but leaves it to the national court to determine whether, on the facts of the particular case, what is prima facie discriminatory can be justified.

Thus, in *Seymour-Smith*,[90] where the two years' continuous employment requirement for bringing unfair dismissals claims in Britain was challenged, all that the Advocate General said about justification was that the Directive requires the measure to be necessary, appropriate and proportionate to the aim pursued and, further, that reliance on generalisations and abstract considerations of social policy cannot justify such a measure, adding that it is for the national court to evaluate whether the requirement was indeed justified.[91] Examples of disparate treatment that were held to be objectively justifiable include *Conlon v. University of Limerick*,[92] where the applicant challenged her failure to get promoted to a senior academic post in the University. The manner in which the Labour Court addressed the case was criticised by McCracken J., but he held that, notwithstanding, the decision taken was justified. This was because the criteria adopted for selection were entirely appropriate, being possession of a higher law degree, several years experience at a senior academic level, and having published research in a specialised field of law. In view of this, it could not be said that the selection procedure lacked transparency.

Part-timers

Part-time workers tend to be predominantly female and, as in respect of equal pay, their appropriate treatment for the purposes of employment equality generally has also been the subject of litigation. In what perhaps is the leading case, *Gerster v. Freistaat Bayern*,[93] at issue were the rules of a State civil service system regarding promotion; for the purpose of calculating the length of a worker's service, periods of employment at less than half of normal working hours were treated as equivalent to two thirds of the relevant period. A woman who had worked full-time for 18 years and then, following leave of absence, returned to work part-time for six years, contended that this regime constituted unlawful indirect discrimination. The eventual issue was whether this plainly disparate treatment between a large proportion of female civil servants and their male counterparts was objectively justifiable. It was argued by, *inter alia*, the Irish Government that the same general test as that used in equal pay cases should apply, namely pro rata equality. But that view was rejected by the E.C.J. Although length of service is a factor in determining eligibility for promotion, it ought not be a predominant factor save in special circumstances. As the Court put it:

> "although experience goes hand in hand with length of service, and experience enables the worker in principle to improve performance of the tasks allotted to him, the objectivity of such a criterion depends on all the circum-

---

90.   *supra*, n.81.
91.   *cf. R. v. Secretary of State, ex p. Seymour-Smith (No. 2)* [2000] 1 W.L.R. 435.
92.   [1999] 2 I.L.R.M. 131.
93.   (Case C 1/95) [1997] E.C.R. 5253.

stances in each individual case, and in particular on the relationship between the nature of the work performed and the experience gained from the performance of that work on completion of a certain number of working hours."[94]

The Advocate General pointed out that, if the criterion for access to employment and to promotion were to be pro rata seniority, existing disadvantages for women would be perpetuated. The matter was remitted to the national court to ascertain whether, in the circumstances there, the rule did indeed unlawfully discriminate.

Positive discrimination

Discrimination in favour of women is permitted on two grounds. One is where it is in connection with pregnancy and maternity, including breastfeeding or adoption (section 28(1)). The other is much broader (section 24(1)), comprising measures to "promote equal opportunity", in particular by removing existing inequalities that affect women regarding work. In *Badeck*,[95] the E.C.J. upheld a Hesse law that gave women in the public service certain advantages when seeking promotion to posts where women were under-represented. There the Court noted that even where candidates were equally qualified, males tended to do better in promotions, particularly because of prejudices and stereotypes concerning women's roles and capacities. Accordingly, just because a man and a woman were equally qualified did not ensure that they had the same chance in competition for promotion. Positive discrimination, therefore, was permissible but provided that (i) it did not automatically and unconditionally give priority to women when they and men were equally qualified and (ii) the candidatures were the subject of an objective assessment which took account of the specific personal circumstances of all candidates. Previously, the Court condemned a quota system operated by the state of Bremen designated to give women priority in parts of the public service where they were under-represented.[96]

Procedures for redress

Part VII of the 1998 Act contains procedures through which aggrieved workers may obtain redress for breach of the several anti-discrimination rules, as an alternative to a civil claim for breach of the equality clause incorporated into their employment contracts, where applicable.[97] These put emphasis on mediation. Where a person is aggrieved by decisions in a recruitment or selection process in respect of the Defence Forces, the Gardaí, the civil service or local authorities, the dispute must first be referred to the Minister, the Commissioner or the relevant Commission before it can be processed in the manner set out in Part VII of the Act.[98] Special provision is made for complaints being made by members of the Defence Forces.[99]

[94.] Para. 39.
[95.] *Application by Badeck* (Case C 158/97) [2000] ECR 1875.
[96.] *Kalanke v. Freie Hansestadt Bremen* (Case C 450/93) [1995] E.C.R. 3051.
[97.] See, generally, Bolger & Kimber, *supra*, n.15, Chap.12.
[98.] s.77(7)-(9).
[99.] s.104.

A complaint of unlawful discrimination or victimisation may be made to the Director of Equality Investigations. But where the complaint is one of dismissal, redress may instead be sought from the Labour Court.[100] The limitation period is six months but it can be extended to 12 months. In either case, an attempt will first be made to have the issue resolved through mediation, unless one of the parties does not want that.[101] If mediation either is not attempted or it fails, the Director or the Labour Court as the case may be will investigate the complaint[102] and then issue a decision or make a determination, which on request must be in writing and set out the reasons.[103] If the complaint is upheld, the respondent may be ordered to pay money, or to treat equally the complainant in a relevant manner or to take some other specified course of action;[104] the Labour Court is empowered to order reinstatement or re-engagement, with or without compensation. There are limits to the amount of compensation the Director or the Labour Court may order to be paid, being 104 times the applicant's weekly remuneration, with an overall maximum of £10,000.[105] A complaint made to the Director may be appealed to the Labour Court; its determination or decision on appeal may be appealed to the High Court on a point of law.[106]

Where the allegation being made is sex discrimination, contrary to Part III of the Act, or where the Equal Treatment Directive has some bearing on the claim, the complainant may bring proceedings in the Circuit Court regardless of how large the damages or compensation being sought.[107] The limitation period is six months but it can be extended to 12 months.[108] If an important matter of principle arises in the claim or it would not be reasonable in the circumstances to expect the plaintiff to prosecute the case without help, the Authority has power to furnish assistance in running the case.[109] Those remedies available to the Circuit Court on upholding complaints, other than for equal pay claims, are as follows:[110]

1. Directing payment of compensation for the effects of discrimination or victimisation that occurred within six years of the claim having been made; the £30,000 ceiling for Circuit Court damages does not appear to apply here.

2. Directing that there shall be equal treatment in the relevant respects.

3. Ordering a person or persons to take a specified course of conduct.

4. Ordering reinstatement in the job or re-engagement in employment, with or without compensation.

[100.] s.77(2).
[101.] s.78.
[102.] s.79.
[103.] s.88.
[104.] s.82.
[105.] s.82(4).
[106.] ss.83 and 90.
[107.] s.77(3).
[108.] s.77(5) and (6).
[109.] s. 67.
[110.] s.82(3).

Employees dismissed on account of their sex or pregnancy can also claim unfair dismissal under the Unfair Dismissals Acts 1977-93. Curiously, sex is not a presumptively unfair ground for dismissal under those Acts whereas, *inter alia*, sexual orientation, pregnancy and related grounds are so presumed

MATERNITY

A major concern of anti-discrimination law is the proper treatment of women who become pregnant, particularly when a confinement and its aftermath may cause some degree of disruption in the workforce.[111] At the E.C. level, these questions are dealt with on three separate bases. Most of the cases on the topic were decided under the Equal Pay Directive or the Equal Treatment Directive, neither of which directly addresses maternity as such, although the latter permits Member States to make special provisions to facilitate mothers. These two Directives have since been supplemented by Directive 92/85 on the introduction of measures to encourage improvements in the safety and health at work of pregnant workers and workers who have recently given birth or are breastfeeding,[112] which for short may be called the Pregnancy Directive; its provisions have been implemented by the Maternity Protection Act 1994. It has since been supplemented by Directive 96/34, which gives effect to a framework agreement on parental leave,[113] which was implemented by the Parental Leave Act 1998.

Equal pay

Pregnancy and confinement are not in themselves a reason for diminishing a worker's remuneration. It does not follow, however, that women must continue to receive their full pay when they take maternity leave. A man who is at work and a woman who is absent on maternity leave are not in comparable positions; nor can a man absent on sick leave be compared with a woman who is absent on maternity leave. Pregnant women get their leave not because they are ill but in order to safeguard their biological state during and after their confinement and to protect the special relationship between the mother and child during the ensuing period.

Thus, in *Gillespie v. Northern Health etc. Board*,[114] the plaintiffs took maternity leave but, under their employment terms, were to be paid only a proportion of what their normal pay would be if they remained at work. It was held by the E.C.J. that the equal pay principle had not thereby been contravened; how much women in those circumstances should be paid, either directly by their employer or else though the social security system, was a matter for the Member States, provided however the amount was not so low as to deter women from availing of their minimum maternity leave. And it was held permissible in the *Boyle* case,[115] where the employer paid full pay for three months of its employees' maternity

---

[111.] See, generally, M. Bolger & C. Kimber, *Sex Discrimination Law* (2000) Chaps. 9 and 10.

[112.] O.J. No. L 348/1 (1985). See, generally, C. Barnard, *EC Employment Law* (2nd ed., 2000), pp. 272-276.

[113.] O.J. No. L 145/4 (1996). See, generally, Barnard, *supra*, n.13, pp. 276-278.

[114.] (Case C 342/93) [1996] E.C.R. 475.

[115.] *Boyle v. Equal Opportunities Comm.* (Case C 411/96) [1998] E.C.R. 6401.

leave, to require that those employees undertook to repay the difference between the State maternity benefit and their pay in the event of them not returning to work.

But a woman absent on maternity leave may not be otherwise financially disadvantaged by her employer. Thus, in *Gillespie*, the Court held that certain wage increases granted while the plaintiffs were on leave, but not back-dated in their case for that very reason, were being improperly withheld from them. The non-discrimination principle "requires that a women who is still linked to her employer by a contract of employment … during maternity leave must, like any other worker, benefit from any pay rise, even if back-dated, which is awarded between the beginning of the period covered by reference pay and the end of maternity leave".[116] Similarly, in *Boyle*, it was held that absence on paid maternity leave could not be a ground for interrupting the accrual of pension rights under the employer's scheme, even if she is not receiving full pay or is being paid otherwise than by her employer, meaning under a State maternity pay scheme. The issue that arose in *Lewen v. Denda*[117] was whether the employer could refuse to pay what he characterised as an *ex gratia* Christmas bonus to an employee who at the time was absent on maternity leave; the plaintiff there had completed her eight weeks' leave and was taking voluntary parenting leave. The answer depended on whether the bonus was a retroactive reward for work already done or was in the nature of an incentive to work in the future or otherwise; if the former, then it was not permissible to withhold the bonus.[118] While an employer may reduce the amount of the bonus pro rata to reflect absence on parenting leave, that cannot be done for absence on maternity leave.

That distinction between maternity leave as such and other forms of leave connected with childbirth was not decisive in *Hay Pedersen*[119] where, prior to her maternity leave commencing, the employee became ill and was unable to work for reasons connected with her pregnancy. She was paid only half her salary, whereas under the employment contract the normal rate of sick pay was the full salary. That, it was held, unfairly discriminated against her, unless the difference could be made up by the State sick pay system.

Equal treatment

There have been differences of view about whether distinctions made on the grounds of pregnancy and its immediate aftermath constitute discrimination based on sex. The United States Supreme Court divided on this question,[120] with the majority holding that pregnancy was not a classification founded on sex, even though it is an attribute that only women can possess. But in the *Dekker* case,[121] the E.C.J. came to the opposite conclusion; it held that when the most important

---

[116.] *supra*, n.15, para. 22. *cf. Ormond v. Dept. of Finance* [1999] E.L.R. 25.

[117.] (Case C 333/97) [2000] I.C.R. 649.

[118.] *cf. Gallaher (Dublin) Ltd. v. SIPTU* [1998] E.L.R. 98.

[119.] *Handels-Og Kontorfunktionaerernes Forbund i Denmark v. Faellesforeningen for Danmarks* (Case C 66/96) [1998] E.C.R. 7327.

[120.] *General Electric Co. v. Gilbert*, 429 U.S. 125 (1976).

[121.] *Dekker v. Stichting Vormingscentrum Voor Jong Volwassenen (VJV-Centrum) Plus* (Case 177/88) [1990] E.C.R. 3941.

reason for taking certain action is one which applies exclusively to persons of one sex, then they are the subject of discrimination based on sex. Although she was the best of the applicants for a vacancy, the plaintiff there was refused the job because at the time she was pregnant. This was because, if she were hired, her employer would suffer some adverse financial consequences in that its sickness insurance cover did not provide for confinement or any illness attributable to pregnancy. Because the refusal to hire her was direct discrimination, in breach of the Equal Treatment Directive, that additional potential cost could not be a legal justification for the decision. In his conclusions to the Court, Advocate General Darmon remarked that: "the principles involved . . . ask the Court to decide on the place which we must give to maternity in a European society. For a long time economic life has been reserved to men and physiological differences between sexes did not have to be taken into account. This is no longer the case today. Now we must reconcile with difficulty the requirements of professional life with those of motherhood."[122] Accordingly, to reject a job applicant on the grounds of her pregnancy would contravene the Employment Equality Act 1998, unless the job is one of the very few where pregnant women are not allowed to work on account of health risks.

Four years later in the *Webb* case,[123] the E.C.J. held that it contravened the Directive to dismiss an employee on account of her becoming pregnant. The plaintiff there was hired to fill in for an employee absent on maternity leave. On discovering that she was pregnant she immediately informed the employer, which caused her to be dismissed two weeks after she had commenced a three-months probationary period, because her condition would have prevented her from doing the job for which she had been hired. Advocate General Tesauro emphasised that, at the time she was being hired, she did not know she was pregnant; that it was far from certain that she would not have been retained once the woman she was replacing returned to work. She was hired for an indefinite period and, even if her pregnancy made it impossible to do the job for which she was hired, that disability would last for a comparatively short time and would not justify dismissing her entirely. That her employer may in consequence have to incur financial and organisational burdens was no justification and, in any event, her employer in this instance would not have been obliged to pay her if she had to absent herself on account of her condition. Under the Unfair Dismissals Acts 1977-93, an employee's dismissal is deemed to be unfair where done on the grounds of her "pregnancy, giving birth, breast feeding or any matter connected therewith" unless there were "substantial grounds justifying" that dismissal.[124] Where a woman is dismissed not on the grounds of pregnancy or taking maternity leave but because she contracted some illness connected with her pregnancy, that too contravenes the Directive[125] and would be deemed to be unfair. If, however, the illness that prevents her from working continued after the full statutory maternity leave has expired, she is no longer protected by that Directive.[126]

[122.] Para. 3960.

[123.] *Webb v. EMO Air Cargo (U.K.) Ltd.* (Case C 32/93) [1994] E.C.R. 3567.

[124.] See *post*, p. 205.

[125.] *Brown v. Rentokil Ltd.* (Case C 394/96) [1998] E.C.R. 185.

[126.] *Handels-Og Kontorfunktionaerernes Forbund i Denmark v. Dansk Arbjdsgiverforening* (Case C 177/88) [1990] E.C.R. 3979.

The above reasoning was applied in the *Thibault* case,[127] where, on account of, *inter alia*, being on maternity leave, the plaintiff did not qualify to be assessed for a wage rise or for promotion. To so qualify in any one year, she was required to have worked for at least six months. But in the year in question she had been on sick leave for 52 days and later took 16 weeks' maternity leave and then six weeks' childcare leave; under her employment terms, she was entitled to leave on the those terms and to be paid in full. Although on its face the employer's six months working prerequisite for making assessments may seen reasonable, in reality it was obvious that the rule was liable to operate consistently to the disadvantage of women, since it allowed the employer to refuse to assess them when a substantial cause of their absence from work in a year was their maternity leave. If a woman took her contractual maximum maternity leave within the one year, she is very likely not to qualify for assessment, especially if she also was off sick for a short period. Employers must devise a method of assessment which does not so obviously discriminate against women.

Although the Equal Treatment Directive does not entitle men in somewhat comparable circumstances to the equivalent of maternity leave,[128] both men and women are so entitled under section 16 of the Maternity Protection Act 1994,[129] the Adoptive Leave Act 1995[130] and the Parental Leave Act 1998.[131]

OTHER PROSCRIBED DISCRIMINATION

Part IV of the Employment Equality Act 1998 (sections 28-37) prohibits employment discrimination on eight additional grounds, namely, "marital status", "family status", "sexual orientation", "religious belief", "age", "disability", membership of the "Traveller community" and, finally, "race, colour, nationality or ethnic or national origins or any combination of those factors". Additionally, E.C. law proscribes employment discrimination against nationals of other E.C. Member States and their dependants and, indeed, against a Member State's own nationals where that would impair free movement within the EEC. Unlike the position in Northern Ireland,[132] there is no prohibition against discrimination on the grounds of political opinion, although in exceptional cases such a requirement may arise under Article 40.1 of the Constitution.

Part IV of the 1998 Act

Section 2(1) of the 1998 Act defines most of the these eight grounds of discrimination, namely:

    i. Marital status means "single, married, separated, divorced or widowed".

[127.] *Thibault v. Caisse Nationale d'Assurance Vieillesse des Travailleurs Salaries (CNAVTS)* (Case C 136/95) [1998] E.C.R. 2011.
[128.] *Telecom Éireann v. O'Grady* [1998] 3 I.R. 432.
[129.] Summarised *ante*, p. 95.
[130.] Summarised *ante*, p. 95.
[131.] Summarised *ante*, p. 96.
[132.] Fair Employment (Northern Ireland) Act 1989.

ii. Family status means "responsibility

    (a) as a parent or as a person in *loco parentis* in relation to a person who has not attained the age of 18 years, or

    (b) as the parent or the resident primary carer in relation to a person of or over that age with a disability which is of such a nature as to give rise to the need for care or support on a continuing, regular or frequent basis".

iii. Sexual orientation means "heterosexual, homosexual or bisexual orientation".

iv. Religious belief "includes religious background or outlook".

v. Age is not defined but the protection against age discrimination does not apply in respect of persons under 18 and over 65 years of age.

vi. Traveller community is defined in a 2000 amendment as "the community of people commonly so called who are identifiable (both by travellers and others) as people with a shared history, culture and tradition including, historically, a nomadic way of life on the island of Ireland".

No definition is provided for the other protected categories, namely disability, race, colour, nationality or ethnic or national origins.

The structure of Part IV of the 1998 Act closely resembles that of Part III, which is summarised above. Briefly,

i. Discrimination by employers with regard to access to work, employment conditions, training and work experience, promotion, re-grading or classification of posts is proscribed (section 8).

ii. Indirect discrimination on those same grounds is then proscribed (section 31).

iii. Into every employment contract there is imported a "same remuneration" clause, entitling the employee to the same pay as his or her comparator doing "like work", unless there are non-discriminatory grounds for the pay differential (section 29).

iv. Similarly, there is imported into every employment contract a "non-discriminatory equality" clause, entitling the employee to terms and conditions no less favourable than those of his or her comparator, again unless the difference is genuinely based on non-discriminatory grounds (section 30).

v. Harassment at work on discriminatory grounds is outlawed (section 32).

vi. There are specific prohibitions against discrimination in job advertisements (section 10), by employment agencies (section 11), by persons offering vocational training courses (section 12), and by trade unions and comparable professional or trade organisations (section 13).

vii. A degree of positive discrimination in favour of persons over 50 years of age, persons with a disability and members of the travelling community is permitted (section 33). Additionally, certain special provisions can be made for workers with a disability (section 35).

Certain exceptions to the non-discrimination requirements are permitted, most notably:

i. Members of the Defence Forces, the Garda Síochána and the prison service are excluded from the age and disability discrimination rules (section 37(6)).

ii. Members of the Defence Forces, the Garda Síochána and also civil servants and most local government officers and employees may have their jobs conditioned on requirements about Irish citizenship and residence, and proficiency in the Irish language (section 36(1)-(3)).

iii. Where services are provided by a religious, educational or medical institution, controlled by some religious body, they may give preference to employees or prospective employees of that religion (section 37(1)).

iv. There are circumstances where age, disability, race and religion can be treated as bona fide occupational qualifications (section 37(3)).

v. Different treatment based on a worker's disability or age may be justified where there is clear actuarial or other evidence that, otherwise, the employer would incur significantly increased costs (section 34(3)).[133]

vi. Pay and other differentials are not unlawful age discrimination where they are based on relative seniority in a post or employment (section 34(7)).

vii. There can be different retirement ages for employees, or any class or description of them; also maximum retirement ages are permissible where justifiable (section 34(2) and (3)).[134]

Redress for breaches of Part IV of the 1998 Act can be obtained by making a complaint to the Director of Equality Investigations or, where the grievance is a dismissal, to the Labour Court. Provision is not made under this Part for suing in the Circuit Court. Ordinarily, mediation will be attempted but if that is not tried or it fails, then the Director or the Labour Court, as the case may be, will make a decision or determination, which must be in writing and give the reasons. There is an appeal from the Director's decision to the Labour Court and a further appeal from it to the High Court on a point of law.

Employees who are covered by the Unfair Dismissals Acts 1977-93, will get compensation under those Acts if they can show that their dismissal in the circumstances was unfair. For the purpose of such claims, dismissals "wholly or mainly" on the grounds of the employee's race, colour, sexual orientation, age, membership of the travelling community, and also religious or political opinions,

---

[133.] *cf. Clarke v. TGD Ltd.* (Times L.R., April 1,1999).
[134.] *cf. Taylor v. Secretary of State for Scotland* [2000] I.C.R. 595.

are deemed to be unfair unless the employer can show some other "substantial reason justifying" the dismissal.

E.C. Article 39 and Regulation 1612/68

The employment of foreign workers, meaning persons who do not possess Irish nationality, is regulated by the Aliens Act 1935 and the many statutory instruments made under that Act. An alien may be employed only where his employment is duly authorised by the Minister for Justice.[135] However, these restrictions never applied to British subjects and, since Ireland joined the European Communities, do not apply to nationals of the E.C. Member States or their dependants. Until quite recently, the treatment of foreign and migrant workers in Ireland has not been a topic of great practical legal significance. What little immigration there was into the State in the past tended to be from Northern Ireland and many of those persons either possess or are eligible to have Irish citizenship.

Discrimination against nationals of E.C. Member States is proscribed by Article 12 (formerly Article 7) of the EEC Treaty, within the general framework of that Treaty. One of the main policies in that Treaty is to promote the free movement of workers between E.C. Member States which, according to Article 39(2) (formerly Article 48(2)) of the Treaty, "shall entail the abolition of any discrimination based on nationality between workers of the Member States as regards employment, remuneration and other conditions of work and employment".

Article 39 of the Treaty is supplemented by Regulation 1612/68,[136] which, along with Regulations on social security,[137] are the principal legislative measures giving effect to the principle of the free movement of workers. It has been held that Article 39(2) and the prohibition against discrimination contained in the 1968 Regulation are directly applicable in the courts of the Member States.[138] Accordingly, any worker who suffers treatment which is banned by these provisions is entitled to legal redress, even against employers in the private sector, the Regulation being equivalent to national legislation.

"Worker"

In order to obtain the benefit of these provisions, the person must be a national of an E.C. Member State and also be a "worker", whether he actually has a job or is seeking work. The concept of a worker for these purposes is similar to that of an employee for the purpose of employment legislation. But the concept is still a Community one; if the person falls within the category of worker under E.C. law, he obtains the protection regardless of whether he may be regarded as self-employed or otherwise under national law.[139]

---

[135] Aliens Order, 1946, S.I. No. 395, as amended; *cf. Gleeson v. Chi Ho Chung* [1997] 1 I.R. 521.

[136] O.J. No. L 254/2 (1968 sp. ed.,), as amended. See, generally, C. Barnard, E.C. *Employment Law, op. cit.*, Chap.3 and C. Quigley, *European Community Contract Law* (1998), pp. 117-155.

[137] Regulation 1408/71, O.J. No. L 149/2 (1971), as amended; see, generally, C. Barnard, *supra,* n.136, pp. 299-328.

[138] *Van Duyn v. Home Office* (Case 41/74) [1974] E.C.R. 1337.

[139] *Levin v. Secretary of State* (Case 53/81) [1982] E.C.R. 1035.

According to the European Court of Justice in one of the "Spanish Fishermen" cases:

> "the Community concept of 'worker' must be defined in accordance with objective criteria which distinguish the employment relationship by reference to the rights and duties of the persons concerned. The essential feature of an employment relationship, however, is that for a certain period of time a person performs services for and under the direction of another person in return for which he receives remuneration."[140]

It was held there that "share fishermen" working on trawlers, who might be regarded as self-employed for the purposes of national law,[141] are "workers" within E.C. law. Similarly, trainee teachers were regarded as workers for these purposes,[142] as were foreign language assistants employed in universities[143] and persons who were prepared to work only part time.[144] But persons employed in a special rehabilitation scheme for the physically and mentally handicapped, in order to facilitate their social integration, were held not to be workers.[145]

The prohibitions

Regulation 1612/68 seeks to guarantee equal treatment for E.C. nationals and their dependants in obtaining employment and in the exercise of their employment. Article 1 of the Regulation provides that:

> "1. Any national of a Member State, shall, irrespective of his place of residence, have the right to take up an activity as an employed person, and to pursue such activity, within the territory of another Member State in accordance with the provisions laid down by law, regulation or administrative action governing the employment of nationals of that State.
>
> 2. He shall in particular have the right to take up available employment in the territory of another Member State with the same priority as nationals of that State."

And according to Article 7 of the Regulation,

> "1. A worker who is a national of a Member State may not, in the territory of another Member State, be treated differently from national workers by reason of his nationality in respect of any conditions of employment and work, in particular as regards remuneration, dismissal, and should he become unemployed, re-instatement or reemployment. . . .
>
> 4. Any clause of a collective or individual agreement or of any other collective regulation concerning eligibility for employment, employment remuneration and other conditions of work or dismissal shall be null and void

---

[140.] *R. v. Minister for Agriculture, ex p. Agegate Ltd.* (Case C 3/87) [1989] E.C.R. 4459 at para. 35.
[141.] *D.P.P. v. McLaughlin* [1986] I.R. 355; see *ante*, p. 26.
[142.] *Lawrie Blum v. Land Baden Wurtemberg* (Case 66/85) [1986] E.C.R. 2121.
[143.] *Allue and Coonan v. Universita Degli Studi di Venezia* (Case 33/88) [1989] E.C.R. 1591.
[144.] *Kempf v. Staatsecretaris van Justitie* (Case 139/85) [1974] E.C.R. 359.
[145.] *Bettray v. Staatsecretaris van Justitie* (Case 344/87) [1989] E.C.R. 1621.

insofar as it lays down or authorises discriminatory conditions in respect of workers who are nationals of the other Member States."

Several successful cases have been brought by the E.C. Commission against Member States in connection with provisions in their legislation stipulating a national requirement in order to obtain certain jobs, most notably a case dealing with a requirement that only French nationals could become seamen in the merchant navy there.[146] In the *Trinity House London Pilotage Committee* case,[147] the body with statutory responsibility for allocating river pilots' licences formerly granted those licences only to U.K. nationals. On joining the E.C., that practice had to change but, as an interim measure designed to prevent unemployment among British pilots, this body adjusted the practice of refusing licences to foreign applicants. It was held that rejecting applications from fully qualified Danish and German nationals contravened the E.C. rules.

Indirect as well as direct discrimination comes within the prohibitions. In the *Allue* and *Coonan* case,[148] it was held that all covert forms of discrimination which, by applying other distinguishing criteria, obtain the same result as if a nationality criterion was used, are proscribed. There, the regulations allowed assistants in universities, who taught foreign languages, to be employed for no longer than five years; there was no comparable restriction on other university staff. Because the great majority of those assistants would be other E.C. nationals, it was held that those rules contravened Article 48(2). A common form of indirect discrimination against aliens is the imposition of a residency requirement; that the person must either reside in the State or have resided there for a prescribed period. In the *Spanish Fishermen* case,[149] such a practice was condemned by the European Court. As a condition of obtaining a licence to fish inside U.K. waters, the U.K. regulations required that 75 per cent of the crew of the applicant's vessel be U.K. residents. The justification given was that they would be fishing against the quotas allocated to the U.K. under the E.C.'s Common Fisheries policy. But it was held that this requirement contravened Community law.

Another common method of practising indirect discrimination is by refusing to give due weight to qualifications for the job which have been obtained abroad. For instance, qualified engineers are required for a job but the employer refuses to accept applicants with foreign engineering qualifications. Or the law may prevent employers from accepting persons with foreign qualifications. In the latter situation the law may contravene the EEC Treaty. In *Union Nationale des Entraineurs etc. v. Heylens*,[150] the defendant was a Belgian football trainer who was hired by the Lille football club, which was in the French first division. He was prosecuted for breach of the Criminal Code on the grounds that he did not possess the requisite qualifications for the job. If the French regulations simply provided that only persons duly qualified in France could do the job, that clearly would contravene former Article 48 of the Treaty because its substantial effect

---

[146.] *E.C. Commission v. France* (Case 167/73) [1974] E.C.R. 359.
[147.] [1985] 2 C.M.L.R. 413.
[148.] *supra*, n. 143.
[149.] *supra*, n. 142.
[150.] (Case 22/86) [1987] E.C.R. 4097.

would be to discriminate against nationals of other E.C. States.[151] According to Advocate General Mancini: "the existence of a straight-forward power to negate the validity of certificates obtained outside the national territory but within the Community must be ruled out. . . . [M]ember States must recognise that such certificates are valid, at least in as much as they certify that the holders are in possession of qualifications equivalent to the competence certified by the corresponding national documents."[152] In this instance, France had a procedure for recognising foreign qualifications which were based on standards equivalent to those obtaining in France. The defendant sought to have his Belgian trainers' diploma accepted under this process but he was refused, without any reason being given. The European Court held that this refusal to assign reasons contravened the Treaty because it facilitated covert discrimination against other E.C. nationals. If reasons were given, which were untenable, the defendant could challenge them in the courts. Regarding how foreign qualifications should be treated, the Court held that the: "procedure for the recognition of equivalence must enable the national authorities to assure themselves, on an objective basis, that the foreign diploma certifies that its holder has knowledge and qualifications which are, if not identical, at least equivalent to those certified by the national diploma."[153]

Measures have been taken by the E.C. authorities to ensure that certain qualifications are duly recognised in all Member States but this process is far from complete.[154] In cases concerning applicants for a job with qualifications which have been the subject of an E.C. Directive, a public authority employer might be estopped from refusing to recognise the qualification obtained in another Member State;[155] but Directives which have not been implemented in national law do not "horizontally" bind private sector employers.

Requiring a candidate for a job to have a knowledge of the Irish language, even if the job does not actually involve using Irish, may be permissible.[156] In *Groener v. Minister for Education*[157] it was held that requiring teachers in a V.E.C.-managed art school to demonstrate a knowledge of Irish was permissible. Although a degree of indirect discrimination may result, the status of the Irish language in the Constitution and the need to preserve cultural and linguistic diversity in the Community warranted upholding the language requirement. However, requiring persons to have an extremely advanced knowledge of Irish would not ordinarily be acceptable under the Treaty. Measures to encourage the language "must not in any circumstances be disproportionate in relation to the aim pursued and the manner in which they are applied must not bring about discrimination against nationals of other Member States."[158]

[151.] In any event it would contravene Art. 8 of Reg. 1612/68.
[152.] *supra*, n. 136.
[153.] *ibid.*, para. 4108.
[154.] See, generally, C. Barnard, *supra*, n.37, pp.160-165.
[155.] *Foster v. British Gas p.l.c.* (Case 188/89) [1990] E.C.R. 3313.
[156.] *cf.* Employment Equality Act 1998, s.36.
[157.] (Case 379/87) [1989] E.C.R. 3967.
[158.] *ibid.*, para. 19.

Exceptions

Workers' rights to freedom of movement within the European Community are subject to two principal exceptions or qualifications. The first is that Article 39 of the EEC Treaty, by its very terms, does "not apply to employment in the public service". Accordingly, it is permissible to exclude other E.C. nationals from public service employment. On several occasions, the European Court has explained that this exception will be construed narrowly. The mere fact that the State in question regards a job as a public service occupation is not sufficient to place it outside the freedom of movement principle. Successful actions have been brought by the E.C. Commission against Member States which sought to confine to their own nationals jobs such as railway workers,[159] manual workers employed by local authorities,[160] nurses in public hospitals[161] and researchers in national research institutions.[162]

In the *Lawrie Blum* case,[163] it was held that Germany could not exclude other E.C. nationals from becoming trainee teachers merely because those positions were classified as civil service jobs there. According to the Court:

> "access to certain posts may not be limited by reason of the fact that in a given Member State persons appointed to such posts have the status of civil servants. . . . [E]mployment in the public service [in this context] must be understood as meaning those posts which involve direct or indirect participation in the exercise of powers conferred by public law and in the discharge of functions whose purpose is to safeguard the general interests of the State or other public authorities and which therefore require a special relationship of allegiance to the State on the part of persons occupying them and reciprocity of rights and duties which form the foundation of the bond of nationality. The posts excluded are confined to those which, having regard to the tasks and responsibilities involved, are apt to display the characteristics of the public service in the spheres described above."[164]

Accordingly, it would seem, where the exercise of public law powers is entirely marginal and ancillary to the post's principal functions, it is not excepted from the fundamental principle of non-discrimination. In 1988 the Commission published a list of public sector jobs which, in its view, are not excepted from that principle,[165] and, in a different context, that list has been accepted by the European Court of Human Rights at Strasbourg as a guide to what are excepted public sector jobs.[166]

---

[159] *E.C. Commission v. Belgium* (Case 149/79) [1980] E.C.R. 3881.

[160] *ibid.*

[161] *E.C. Commission v. France* (Case 307/89) [1987] E.C.R. 2625.

[162] *E.C. Commission v. Italy* (Case 225/85) [1987] E.C.R. 2725.

[163] *Lawrie Blum v. Land Baden-Wurttemberg* (Case 66/85) [1986] E.C.R. 2121.

[164] *ibid.* paras 26 and 27.

[165] Communication of March 18, 1988, O.J. C 72/2 (1988). This was followed by several enforcement proceedings, *e.g. E.C. Commission v. Luxembourg* (Case 473/93) [1996] E.C.R. 3263, *E.C. Commission v. Belgium* (Case 173/94) [1996] E.C.R. 3265 and *E.C. Commission v. Greece* (Case 290/94) [1996] E.C.R. 3285.

[166] *Pellegrin v. France*, Judgment of December 8, 1999.

In 1996 and in 1999 these criteria were relied on by the Northern Ireland courts to justify not hiring citizens of the Republic for certain posts in the public sector. In *Re Colgan*,[167] where the plaintiff had applied to become a management trainee in the Northern Ireland civil service, she contended that she should not be excluded because the ban on citizens of the Republic being hired was not absolute, that there was no ban on hiring citizens of any Commonwealth country and, further, there was no equivalent ban in the rest of the United Kingdom. Similar arguments were made in *Re O'Boyle*,[168] where the plaintiffs had applied for the posts of deputy chief fire officer and of recurring temporary revenue officer, respectively, but were rejected by the Court of Appeal.

The other exception to the principle of the free movement of workers within the Community is that this freedom is subject to "limitations justified on grounds of public policy, public security or public health". Most of the major cases on this exception have concerned aspects of immigration and deportation regulations and practices.[169]

[167.] [1996] N.I. 124.
[168.] [1999] N.1. 126.
[169.] *e.g. R. v. Secretary of State, ex p. Adams* [1995] All E.R. (EC) 177.

CHAPTER 7

TERMINATION OF EMPLOYMENT – CONTRACTUAL RIGHTS

The termination of employment, especially termination at the employer's insistence (dismissal from employment), causes far more litigation than any other aspect of the employment relationship. Although disputes will arise when the relationship is subsisting, often those differences are resolved by negotiation, either between the parties directly or with the assistance of one or more trade unions. But when an employee resigns or an employer purports to dismiss an employee, the parties may have reached confrontation point. Where a dismissed employee may suffer a significant loss of earnings and indeed be faced with a prolonged period of unemployment, he will be inclined to challenge his dismissal, either in court or through industrial action. This chapter considers the various common law rules regarding termination of a job, especially by dismissal.[1] The next chapter then looks at the elaborate set of statutory restrictions and rights, established mainly in the last 30 years, affecting dismissal. There are special statutory regimes for many who work in the public sector and those are considered separately in Chapter 13.

MODES OF TERMINATION

The employment relationship can be brought to an end either by the agreement of the parties, the unilateral act of one of them, in the form of a dismissal or a resignation, or by operation of law, which can take several forms.

Agreement

The employment contract can come to an end through the agreement of the parties. If the contract is for a particular task, once that task has been done the contract will have been performed. Similarly, if the contract is for a specified period, the contract comes to an end when that time has elapsed. Although termination following performance of a specific task or on the expiry of a fixed term is not a dismissal, those terminations are often characterised by legislation as dismissals, thereby attracting certain statutory protection.

With regard to contracts which are terminable on giving notice, either by the employer or the employee, the parties may agree the circumstances in which the contract shall be terminated. Sometimes that agreement is made subject to a period elapsing before termination occurs. Alternatively, the employee may be

---

[1.] See, generally, M. Redmond, *Dismissal Law in Ireland* (2nd ed., 1990), Chaps. 2-11, and M. Freedland, *The Contract of Employment* (1976), Chaps. 5-9.

paid a sum in lieu of notice on the understanding that the relationship shall come to an end forthwith, or the parties may agree to immediate termination without any payment being made.

At times, disputes arise regarding whether the employee indeed resigned or was forced to resign, because forcible resignation is in law and in fact a dismissal. The answer will depend on the entire circumstances of the case — whether the employee's action was truly voluntary or whether he was virtually compelled to resign. In *O'Reilly v. Minister for Industry and Commerce*,[2] a civil servant with over 45 years' service resigned under a misapprehension that he had been left with no choice but to retire voluntarily or else he would be dismissed. Carroll J. held that, in the circumstances, the Minister should have corrected the very obvious error the plaintiff had made, that he thereby had been forced to resign and, accordingly, his purported voluntary resignation was ineffective.

Dismissal

A dismissal is a unilateral termination of the contract by the employer; by word or by deed, the employer tells the employee that their relationship has or shall come to an end. Where the employer did not give the agreed notice of dismissal, he repudiates his most fundamental obligation under the contract, which is to pay wages in return for work done. Usually, the employee will accept that repudiation, in the sense of accepting that the relationship has come to an end, although he may well bring an action for damages for wrongful dismissal. Generally, an unequivocal dismissal puts an end to the legal relationship there and then. Exceptionally, a dismissed employee may take the view that the legal relationship has not ended; in that event, unless full remuneration in lieu of notice is paid, the contract will still subsist until the proper period of notice expires,[3] although this state of affairs affords few practical benefits to the employee.

Repudiation

As well as in cases of outright dismissals and forced resignations, an employer repudiates the contract, for example, by not paying any remuneration for a period when the employee was at work, by unilaterally reducing the remuneration it was agreed would be payable,[4] by unilaterally changing the entire nature of the job[5] or the place where,[6] or times during when,[7] it was agreed the work was to be performed. The question is whether the employer has broken or has threatened to break one of the main terms of the contract. It has been held, for instance, that there was repudiation where, when there was a severe breakdown of personal relationships between employees, their employer insisted that one of them, a con-

---

[2]   [1997] E.L.R. 48.
[3]   *Gunton v. Richmond upon Thames L.B.C.* [1981] Ch.448 and *Skilton v. T. & K. Home Improvements Ltd.* [2000] I.C.R. 1162.
[4]   *Cantor Fitzgerald Int'l v. Callaghan* [1999] I.C.R. 639.
[5]   *Woods v. W.M. Car Services (Peterborough) Ltd.* [1982] I.C.R. 693, *Norwest Holst Group Adm. Ltd. v. Harrison* [1985] I.C.R. 668 and *Lewis v. Motorworld Garages Ltd.* [1986] I.C.R. 158.
[6]   *Courtaulds Northern Spinning Ltd. v. Sibson* [1988] I.C.R. 451, *Jones v. Associated Tunnelling Ltd.* [1981] I.R.C.R. 477 and *O'Brien v. Associated Fire Alarms Ltd.* [1986] 1 W.L.R. 1916.
[7]   *cf. Hogg v. Doner College* [1990] I.C.R. 39.

sultant surgeon, underwent a psychiatric examination and then suspended him for refusing to do so .[8] In the circumstances, the employer had no reasonable cause to insist on that examination and, by doing so, the employer had acted "in a manner calculated or likely to destroy or seriously damage the relationship of confidence or trust between [them]".[9] The question of employer repudiation has become particularly significant in legislation regarding dismissal, through the concept of "constructive dismissal"; that is if an employee leaves a job in response to a repudiation by the employer, the employee is deemed for the purposes of the Act in question to have been dismissed.

However, except where there has been an unequivocal dismissal or a forced resignation, the employer's repudiation as such does not put an end to the contract. Thus, in *Rigby v. Ferodo Ltd.,*[10] when the plaintiff's employer was in serious financial difficulties, it unilaterally imposed wage reductions on the workforce. The plaintiff sued for damages, while remaining in the job. According to Lord Oliver, the basic principle is that:

> "the unilateral imposition by an employer of a reduction in the agreed remuneration of an employee constitutes a fundamental and repudiatory breach of the contract of employment which, if accepted by the employee, would terminate the contract forthwith. . . . [But], as a general rule, an unaccepted repudiation leaves the contractual obligations of the parties unaffected. . .
>
> Whatever may be the position under a contract of service where the repudiation takes the form either of a walk out by the employee or of a refusal by the employer any longer to regard the employee as his servant, [there is] no principle of law that any breach which the innocent party is entitled to treat as repudiatory of the other party's obligations brings the contract to an end automatically."[11]

The repudiatory conduct may be on the part of the employee and not the employer. In that case the same principles as just explained apply. If the employee unambiguously leaves the job, generally, that operates to terminate the contract there and then. But his other breaches of the contract, no matter how fundamental they are, do not bring it to an end. The employer always has the option of either accepting the repudiation, thereby treating the contract as ended or, alternatively, choosing to continue that relationship. According to Templeman L.J. in *London Transport Executive v. Clarke,*[12] a case where the employee deliberately absented himself from work for seven weeks:

> "If a worker walks out of his job or commits any other breach of contract, repudiatory or otherwise, but at any time claims that he is entitled to resume or to continue his work, then his contract of employment is only determined if the employer expressly or impliedly asserts and accepts repudiation on the part of the worker. Acceptance can take the form of formal writing or can

---

[8.] *Bliss v. South East Thames Regional H.A.* [1987] I.C.R. 700.
[9.] *ibid.* at 715.
[10.] [1988] I.C.R. 29.
[11.] *ibid.* at 33 and 34.
[12.] [1981] I.C.R. 355.

take the form of refusing to allow the worker to resume or continue his work. . . . [T]he acceptance by an employer of repudiation by a worker who wishes to continue his employment notwithstanding his repudiatory conduct constitutes the determination of the contract of employment by the employer."[13]

An employee who does not perform his work because he is serving a prison sentence has not repudiated his contract — except were the very terms of the contract require that he not put himself in jeopardy of being imprisoned or otherwise similarly detained.[14] However, prolonged imprisonment may in the circumstances bring the contract to an end by way of frustration.[15]

Frustration

One of the fundamental rules of the law of contract is that a contract will be discharged by frustration; if circumstances arise that amount to frustration, the contract automatically comes to an end. Frustration arises where performance of the contract becomes impossible, such as by the death of either of the parties, or where performance becomes illegal. The underlying principle was formulated as follows:

> "[F]rustration occurs whenever the law recognises that without default of either party a contractual obligation has become incapable of being performed because the circumstances in which performance is called for would render it a thing radically different from that which was undertaken by the contract. *Non haec in foedera veni*. It was not this that I promised to do. . . . [I]t is not hardship or inconvenience or material loss itself which calls the principle of frustration into play. There must be as well such a change in the significance of the obligation that the thing undertaken would, if performed, be a different thing from that contracted for."[16]

Thus, if either of the parties become physically or legally incapable of performing their obligations under the contract, it is frustrated and they no longer have any rights or liabilities under it.

In determining whether an employment contract has been frustrated,[17] it is often necessary to construe its terms — to ascertain precisely what obligations were assumed and in what circumstances the parties had undertaken them. That exercise in construction may demonstrate that the parties either did or did not intend that their obligations should continue in the light of the event in question. According to Hanna J. in *Herman v. Owners of the S.S. Vica*, "[f]rustration depends on the terms of the contract and the surrounding circumstances of each case, as some kinds of impossibility may not discharge the contract at all".[18] That case concerned seamen who had been hired to serve on a Finnish registered ship

---

13. *ibid.* at 368.
14. *F. Shepherd & Co. Ltd. v. Jerrom* [1987] 1 Q.B. 301.
15. *infra.*
16. *Davis Contractors Ltd. v. Farnham U.D.C.* [1956] A.C. 696 at 729.
17. See, generally, M. Freedland, *The Contract of Employment* (1976), Chap. 8.
18. [1942] I.R. 305 at 321.

during World War II. For about six months the ship had the protection of a British ship's warrant, and when that was not renewed, the owners were assured by British shipping agents that its ship would not be seized by the British authorities. The ship arrived in Dublin three months after diplomatic relations between Britain and Finland were broken off. Some weeks later the master paid off the crew, claiming that the imminence of war between Britain and Finland rendered further performance of their contracts practically impossible. Two weeks later, war was declared between the two countries. The plaintiffs sued for breach of the express term in their contracts that they would be repatriated at their employers' expense at the end of their service. It was held that their contracts had not been frustrated in the circumstances obtaining when the crew were discharged; at that time it was not obvious that the ship would probably be seized by the British on leaving port. In any event, even if there were frustration then, that could not affect the "accrued right [to be repatriated], vested in the seamen under their contracts before the alleged frustration".[19]

In another war-time seamen's case, *Byrne v. Limerick S.S. Co. Ltd.,*[20] the plaintiff was discharged by the master in Dublin because the British shipping authorities did not give him clearance when the crew list was submitted to them. Overend J. accepted that it was "impossible, from a practical point of view, to undertake this voyage save under the aegis and with the facilities afforded by the British".[21] Nevertheless, the contract was not frustrated because, "where an essential licence or permission is refused, the defendants must prove that they have taken all reasonable steps to have such refusal withdrawn".[22] In the circumstances here, it was probable that the refusal to give clearance for the plaintiff would have been revoked had the owners seriously questioned the British authorities' decision.[23]

That the event which is claimed frustrates the contract must be unexpected and entirely beyond the parties' contemplation, even as a possibility, and must amount to more than unanticipated hardship and material loss, was emphasised by Murphy J. in *Zuphen v. Kelly Technical Services (Irl.) Ltd.*[24] There technicians were recruited from South Africa to work in Ireland for a year and it was contemplated that they would work on a contract to be obtained by their employers from Eircom p.l.c. Over two months after they arrived in the State, Eircom notified their employers that it no longer required them to work under that contract. The employers advised the technicians that they should return to South Africa, as there was no further work available to be done. The contention that their contracts of employment had thereby been frustrated was rejected as the employees had not been hired specifically to work on an Eircom contract and, under that contract, work would be "allocated as the need arises". Moreover, the employees had been hired before that contract had been finalised and,

---

19. *ibid.* at 325.
20. [1946] I.R. 138.
21. *ibid.* at 149.
22. *ibid.*
23. Compare *Harlock v. Beale* [1916] 1 A.C. 486.
24. [2000] E.L.R. 277.

additionally, it had proved possible to find alternative work for some of those hired in mid-September to come to Ireland.

Destruction of the workplace

One of the earliest cases to recognise the doctrine of frustration in the law of contract concerned the destruction of the very subject matter of the contract; in that instance a music hall which the defendant had agreed to make available for four days for concerts.[25] Whether destruction, through fire or whatever, of the workplace automatically puts an end to the contracts of those employed there depends on the nature of the employer's business, the resources available to him and the terms of the contracts. There are no leading modern authorities that deal with the application of the principle in this situation.

Employee's illness

An employee's illness can result in his employment contract being terminated by frustration, but whether illness has that effect depends on the nature of the job and the terms of the contract. If an employee is hired for a task to be performed at a particular time but then falls ill at that very time, the contract will be automatically terminated.[26] By contrast, if the job is permanent and the employee falls ill for a few days or indeed for several weeks, the contract will subsist. Terms of employment for permanent posts usually contain express provisions regarding illness. In the case of the vast majority of employment contracts, which are terminable at comparatively short notice, there is a view that the doctrine of frustration, at least in the context of the employee's disability, has no application. It has been observed that "[i]n the employment field the concept of discharge by operation of law, that is frustration, is normally only in play where the contract of employment is for a long term which cannot be determined by notice."[27] But this view has also been rejected in England, where it has been held that "the mere fact that the contract can be terminated by the employer by relatively short notice cannot of itself render the doctrine of frustration inevitably inapplicable".[28]

In many of the instances where an employer is contending that a contract was terminated by frustration, the employer would be seeking to dismiss an employee who became ill and wants to avoid statutory obligations that arise in dismissal situations (*e.g.* compensation for unfair dismissal or a redundancy award) by claiming that the contract was terminated by way of frustration and not by way of dismissal. Because of this, generally the illness would need to be serious and lengthy before it would be characterised as bringing about frustration. In Britain the Employment Appeals Tribunal has formulated criteria for determining when an employment contract is frustrated on account of illness.[29] The central consideration is whether, looked at before the purported dismissal, the employee's inca-

---

[25]   *Taylor v. Caldwell* [1863] 3 B.BS. 826.
[26]   *e.g. Pousiard v. Spiers* (1876) 1 Q.B.D. 410.
[27]   *Harmon v. Flexible Lamps Ltd.* [1980] I.R.L.R. 418 at 419.
[28]   *Notcutt v. Universal Equipment Co. (Ireland) Ltd.* [1986] 1 W.L.R. 641 at 646.
[29]   *Marshall v. Harland & Wolff Ltd.* [1972] 1 W.L.R. 899, *Egg Stores (Stamford Hill) Ltd. v. Leibov- ichi* [1977] I.C.R. 260 and *Hart v. A.R. Marshall & Sons (Bolwell) Ltd.* [1977] 1 W.L.R. 1067.

pacity was of such a nature, or whether the illness appeared likely to continue for such a period, that further performance of his obligations in the future would either be impossible or would be a thing radically different from that undertaken by him and accepted by the employer under the agreed terms of his employment.[30]

Employee's imprisonment

An employee's imprisonment or other form of compulsory detention can also cause his employment contract to be frustrated.[31] It would be very rare for one week's imprisonment to have this effect but commencement of a long sentence almost always would bring the contract to an end.[32] Occasionally, employers treat the event of imprisonment as putting an end to the relationship without having to follow contractual dismissal procedures or complying with statutory rules applicable to dismissals.[33] In determining whether there was indeed frustration, all depends on the anticipated duration of the detention, the nature of the job and the terms of the contract.[34]

Dissolution of partnership

Generally, the dissolution of a partnership will put an end to employment contracts with the partnership. As stated in Lindley, the principle is that:

> "If the contract is of a personal character, to be performed by the individuals who have entered into it, or is dependent on the personal skill or honesty of the individual partners, a change in the firm will determine the contract by rendering its performance impossible. If on the other hand, upon a true construction of the particular contract, it is determined that the party contracting with the partnership was intending that the contract should be performed by the partnership as from time to time constituted, then a change in the firm would not per se automatically determine the contract or constitute a breach of it. This is a pure question of the construction of each particular contract and no general principles can be laid down in relation thereto."[35]

Receivership and liquidation

Undoubtedly the actual dissolution of a company when the winding up procedure has been completed will cause the employment contracts of any of its remaining employees to come to an end. But the actual commencement of a receivership or a liquidation does not automatically terminate the enterprise's employment contracts. The position, briefly,[36] is that the appointment by the court of a receiver operates as a dismissal of the employees but the appointment of a receiver by the

---

30. See *Flynn v. Great Northern Rly. Co. (Ir.) Ltd.* 89 I.L.T.R. 46 (1955) at 59-60.
31. *e.g. Morgan v. Manser* [1948] 1 K.B. 184.
32. *e.g. F.C. Shepherd & Co. v. Jerram* [1987] 1 Q.B. 301.
33. *ibid.* and *Hare v. Murphy Bros. Ltd.* [1974] 3 All E.R. 940.
34. *ibid.* and *Chakki v. United Yeast Co. Ltd.* [1982] I.C.R. 140.
35. *Lindley on Partnership* (15th ed., 1984), p. 50. See *Briggs v. Oates* [1990] I.C.R. 473.
36. For details, see *post*, pp. 241-244.

debenture-holders does not usually have this effect. Similarly, a compulsory liquidation operates as a dismissal of the employees but commencement of a voluntary liquidation usually does not have that effect.

NOTICE OF TERMINATION

At common law, provided the requisite notice of termination was given or the salary in lieu of that notice was paid, the employer can dismiss and the employee also can resign for any reason.[37] It was primarily to reduce abuses of the employer's common law prerogative to dismiss for any reason whatsoever, on giving due notice, that the Unfair Dismissals Act 1977 was enacted.[38] Statutory protection aside, dismissal from employment in certain circumstances can constitute breach of the employee's constitutional rights, although the application of the Constitution to dismissals by private sector employers is largely unexplored terrain.

Notifying resignation

The employment contract may stipulate, expressly or by implication, how much notice an employee must give of his intention to resign from his job. Absent such stipulation, reasonable notice must be provided; it depends on all the circumstances how long is reasonable notice in any particular case. An employee who is in a job for longer than thirteen weeks has a statutory obligation to give at least one week's notice of his resignation.[39]

Dismissal notice

One of the terms of every employment contract will concern how much notice the employer must give in order lawfully to terminate the contract, be it an hour's notice, a day, a week, a month or whatever. Where the contract is written, almost invariably one of its express terms will deal with notice of termination. Where there is no express term, if called upon, the court will have to imply a term. One of the particulars that section 9 of the Terms of Employment (Information) Act 1994 requires to be furnished to new employees is "the period of notice which the employee is required to give and entitled to receive ... to determine the employment contract. . . ."[40] Notice periods may be dealt with in a collective agreement applicable to the job.

Where the contract does not state or indicate how much notice an employer must give to terminate it, the courts hold that the employee must be given reasonable notice. If the employee is being dismissed for a very serious breach of contract on his part, he is not entitled to any notice. Otherwise, the duration of the requisite notice will depend on the nature of the job and other terms of the contract. Persons in well paid and prestigious jobs are entitled to relatively lengthy

---

[37]   See, generally, *Freedland, supra*, n.18, Chap. 5.
[38]   Discussed *post*, pp. 197-198.
[39]   Minimum Notice and Terms and Conditions of Employment Act 1973, s.6.
[40]   s.9(1)(f).

notices. In an instance in 1996, a senior accountant employed by a large construction company, who spent much of his time on foreign assignments, was held entitled to one year's notice;[41] similarly in 1966, the managing director of a small bank was held entitled to one year's notice;[42] in a case in 1940 a teacher was held to be entitled to six months' notice.[43]

Under section 4 of the Minimum Notice and Terms of Employment Act 1973, there is a statutory minimum notice period, ranging from one week to eight weeks, depending on the employee's length of service. Unlike "equal pay", these notice periods are not deemed to be a term of the employment contract and the remedy for failure to give the required notice is an application to the Employment Appeals Tribunal, which may award compensation.

Permanent employment

The fact that a job is described as permanent or as permanent and pensionable does not mean that it cannot be terminated by reasonable notice. According to Budd J. in *Walsh v. Dublin Health Authority*:

> "The word 'permanent' has various shades of meaning. Generally, it means something lasting, as distinct from temporary. In the case of a contract of service, a person may be said in one sense of the word to be 'permanently' employed when he is employed for an indefinite period on the regular staff of the employer, as distinct from persons taken on casually or for a temporary or defined period. That does not necessarily mean that such a person has a contract of employment for life. On the other hand a person may be given 'permanent' and pensionable employment in the sense that under his contract he holds his employment for life or for life subject to the right of his employer to dismiss him for misconduct, neglect of duty or unfitness or again it may mean that his employment is to last until he reaches full pensionable age, subject to the rights of the employer just mentioned. As to what is meant, and should be implied as being in the contemplation of the parties, depends upon the true construction of the whole contract viewed in the light of the surrounding circumstances and all relevant matters."[44]

In that case it was held that a carpenter, employed by a hospital on a permanent and pensionable basis, could be dismissed from his job on being given reasonable notice. In the circumstances, the description of the job did not mean that he could not be dismissed, before retirement age, other than for misconduct.

But there are cases where it was held that the employer's freedom to dismiss was so restricted by the terms of the contract. In *McLoughlin v. Great Southern Railways Co.*,[45] the employer gave the Minister for Transport an undertaking not to dismiss specified staff, except for misconduct, and then only after following a grievance procedure. That undertaking was assented to by the plaintiff's trade union. Since he fell within the category of staff specified, the company was held

---

41. *Lyons v. M.F. Kent & Co. (International) Ltd.* [1996] E.L.R. 103.
42. *Carvill v. Irish Industrial Bank Ltd.* [1968] I.R. 325.
43. *McDonald v. Minister for Education* [1940] I.R. 316.
44. 98 I.L.T.R. 82 (1964) at 86-87. *cf. Carr v. City of Limerick V.E.C.* [2000] E.L.R. 57.
45. [1944] I.R. 479.

to be precluded from dismissing him before retirement age other than for misconduct.[46] Similarly, in *Grehan v. North Eastern Health Board*,[47] the plaintiff was a
medical practitioner employed on terms which had been negotiated by the
Department of Health and the Irish Medical Organisation. The contract's terms
contained detailed provisions on dismissal, but did not say that the plaintiff could
be dismissed on reasonable notice. Costello J. refused to imply into the contract a
term to that effect, principally because its terms relating to termination were very
detailed and their comprehensive nature would strongly suggest that an implication of a further term, relating to the parties' right of termination, would not be
justified. A narrowly divided House of Lords came to the same conclusion in
McClelland v. Northern Ireland General Health Service Board,[48] where the
plaintiff, a clerk employed by a Health Board, was given six months' notice of
dismissal because she got married. As in the *Grehan* case, the contract contained
detailed terms regarding termination. It was held that these provisions: "all contain express powers of termination and . . . there is no ground for suggesting that
it is necessary to imply a further power to terminate the contract in order to give
[it] the efficacy which the parties must have intended it to have.[49] Accordingly,
'so long as she did not render herself liable to dismissal on one or other of the
grounds expressly stated in her contract and was willing and able to serve the
Board, [she] was entitled to continue in her employment for her life.'"[50]

Generally, therefore, where the contract sets out in some detail the circumstances in which it may be terminated by either party but does not state that the
employer may dismiss on giving a specified period of notice or reasonable notice,
the tendency is against implying a term to that effect. One of the decisive considerations in the *McClelland* case was that both parties regarded the job as in fact as
secure as the civil service. And in the *Grehan* case, Costello J. referred to the fact
that the terms of the relevant collective agreement must have been the subject of
protracted negotiations and, therefore, the reasonable inference was that the parties did not intend to confer a right to dismiss on giving reasonable notice.

SUMMARY DISMISSAL

Employers possess a common law right of summary dismissal, in the sense of
dismissing an employee without giving him the requisite notice.[51] This power is
exercisable in circumstances where the contract expressly authorises summary
dismissal. It can also be exercised where the employee is guilty of serious
misconduct, unless the contract precludes its exercise in the circumstances in
question.

---

46. Contrast *Flynn v. Great Northern Rly. Co. (Irl.) Ltd.*, 89 I.L.T.R. 46 (1955).
47. [1989] I.R. 422.
48. [1957] 1 W.L.R. 594.
49. *ibid.* at 599.
50. *ibid.* at 613. Similarly, *Wells v. Newfoundland*, 177 D.L.R. 3rd 73 (1999).
51. See, generally, *Freedland, supra*, n.18, Chap. 6.

Serious misconduct

Where the employment contract does not specify the grounds for summary dismissal, what constitutes serious misconduct for these purposes depends on the nature of the job in question and the terms of the contract. Certain actions almost invariably would be regarded as serious misconduct, like deliberately destroying the employer's valuable property, stealing from the employer, and gross insubordination.[52] Often the line is difficult to draw between what misconduct justifies summary dismissal and what calls at most for temporary suspension or a severe warning or reprimand. According to Kenny J. in *Glover v. B.L.N. Ltd*:

> "It is impossible to define the misconduct which justifies immediate dismissal. . . . There is no fixed rule of law defining the degree of misconduct which will justify dismissal. . . . What is or is not misconduct must be decided in each case without the assistance of a definition or a general rule. Similarly, all that one can say about serious misconduct is that it is misconduct which the court regards as being grave and deliberate. And the standards to be applied in deciding the matter are those of men and not of angels."[53]

Some general propositions can be stated concerning misconduct in this context. It was held in *Carvill v. Irish Industrial Bank*,[54] that the misconduct in question usually must have been known to the employer at the time he decided on the dismissal. That is to say, the employer "cannot, as a defence to an action for wrongful dismissal, rely on an act of misconduct on the part of his servant which was unknown to him at the time of the dismissal, unless the act is of so fundamental a character as to show a repudiation of the contract of employment by the servant".[55] In that case, the managing director of a bank arranged for a carpet in his house to be fitted in his office and he bought a new carpet for his house. He then charged the company about 60 per cent of the price of that new carpet. The Supreme Court overruled Kenny J.'s decision that this act constituted misconduct as would justify his summary dismissal.

A single isolated act can constitute sufficient cause to justify instant dismissal, like fraudulent conduct or wilful disobedience of an order which was lawful and reasonable. The *Glover* case, which also concerned a company director, provides several examples of the kinds of small scale profiting at the employer's expense which do and which do not amount to serious misconduct. Disobeying an order does not invariably warrant instant dismissal; rather, "one act of disobedience or misconduct can justify dismissal only if it is of a nature which goes to show (in effect) that the servant is repudiating the contract, or one of its essential conditions".[56] Moreover, the order must be within the scope of the employment. A worker hired to perform one kind of task cannot be compelled to do something entirely different; for instance a person hired in an executive capacity cannot ordinarily be expected to spend his working hours performing manual labour.[57] It

---

[52.] *e.g. Pepper v. Webb* [1969] 1 W.L.R. 514 and *Blyth v. Scottish Liberal Club* [1982] S.C. 140.
[53.] [1973] I.R. 388 at 405.
[54.] [1968] I.R. 325.
[55.] *ibid.* at 346.
[56.] *Laws v. London Chronicle Ltd.* [1959] 1 W.L.R. 698 at 701.
[57.] *Price v. Movat* (1862) C.B. (N.S.) 236.

depends very much on the circumstances of each case whether instructions given are reasonable.

There are no reported modern authorities on dismissal on the grounds of incompetence. If the employee represented to the employer that he possessed a certain skill or qualification, which was not in fact the case, his misrepresentation would be regarded as a form of serious misconduct, warranting his immediate dismissal.[58] However, mere inability of a worker to adapt to technical change ordinarily would not warrant summary dismissal. Inability to do a job may even be due to the employer's inadequate training methods or to inefficient techniques for selecting employees.

Grounds stipulated in contract

At times the contract of employment will set out in detail the circumstances in which it can be terminated forthwith by one or by both parties. Where the contract sets out the grounds for immediate dismissal, a court may conclude that those grounds supercede and displace the common law right of summary dismissal. In *Glover v. B.L.N. Ltd.,*[59] the plaintiff's contract enumerated the grounds and circumstances in which he could be instantly dismissed. Accordingly, it was held, "because of the express provisions of this clause, no implied term is to be read into the contract that the plaintiff might be *summarily* dismissed for misconduct. On the contrary, the clause expressly provides that the plaintiff could not be validly dismissed for misconduct unless it was serious misconduct and was of a kind which, in the unanimous opinion of the board of directors . . . injuriously affected the reputation, business or property of the [companies]".[60]

The plaintiff in *Glover* had been employed as the technical director of a group of car assembly companies, which later merged with another car assembly group. One of the terms of the contract was that:

> "[his] appointment may be terminated without giving rise to any claim for compensation or damages upon the happening of any events following, namely: . . . (c) if Mr. Glover shall be guilty of any serious misconduct or serious neglect in the performance of his duties or wilfully disobeys the reasonable orders directions or restrictions or regulations of the board of directors of any of the said companies which in the unanimous opinion of the board of directors for the time being of the holding company present and voting at the meeting injuriously affects the reputation business or property or management of either the holding company or the operating company or the sales company or the factors company."

At a board meeting of the holding company, a report was presented by the chairman accusing the plaintiff of a long catalogue of improprieties, such as being a shareholder in a company that supplied automotive goods to the group, getting company employees to do work on cars he owned without charging himself for

---

58. *Harmer v. Cornelius* (1858) 5 C.B. (N.S.) 236.
59. [1973] I.R. 388.
60. *ibid.* at 424.

their services, and getting company employees to work for several weeks on his own house without ever charging himself for their work. The board resolved that he should be instantly dismissed. It was held that the test of whether his dismissal was lawful was not whether he had been guilty of serious misconduct but whether he committed acts of misconduct as characterised by the above clause in his contract. If, in the circumstances, the directors could reasonably conclude that he had so misconducted himself, he could have been dismissed forthwith.

It was found that the conflict of interests arising by virtue of his involvement in a supplier to the group was not even misconduct, since its existence had been disclosed to the employer. It was held that, although getting work done on his cars without charge was misconduct, it was not serious misconduct as defined in the contract. While getting the work done on his house without charge amounted to such serious misconduct, his dismissal was held to be unlawful because he had been given no opportunity whatsoever to defend himself against the allegations made against him.

DISMISSAL PROCEDURES

Frequently the employment contract will specify or will incorporate dismissal procedures, that is procedures to be adopted before an employee can be dismissed. These procedures may be set out in relevant collective agreements or in works rules. Indeed, employers are obliged by statute to give all new employees, within a month of their commencing work, a notice setting out what the dismissal procedures are; where those procedures are changed, 28 days' notice must be given of the alterations made.[61] But this obligation to notify does not apply where no procedure was ever agreed with the employee or with his trade union or excepted body, or where no such procedure is based on custom and practice.

Where there are no agreed procedural arrangements for dealing with dismissals, at least for certain categories of employees the courts imply minimum standards of fair procedures; what are often referred to as the principles of natural justice or of constitutional justice.[62] By far the most important of these is summed up in the maxim *audi alteram partem*, that the decision-maker (that is the employer) must hear the employee's side of the argument before deciding to dismiss. The extent to which the maxim *nemo iudex in sua causa*, that nobody should be judge in his own cause, applies in this context is unclear. Nor is it clear whether, for employments where these principles apply, they can be waived in the employment contract. To the extent that the principles are based on the common law, undoubtedly they can be waived. But in *Glover v. B.L.N. Ltd.*,[63] the Supreme Court said that these principles also have constitutional underpinnings. Walsh J. there observed that "public policy and the dictates of constitutional justice require that . . . agreements setting up machinery for taking decisions which may affect rights or impose liabilities should be construed as providing for fair proce-

---

[61.] Unfair Dismissals Act 1977, s.14.
[62.] See, generally, G. Hogan and D. Morgan, *Administrative Law in Ireland* (3rd ed., 1998), Chaps. 10 and 11, and Freedland, *supra*, n.18, pp. 219-227.
[63.] [1973] I.R. 388.

dures".[64] Walsh J. then remarked that, in the circumstances there, it was "not necessary to decide to what extent the contrary can be provided for by agreement
between the parties".[65]

Public and private sector employment

Most of the leading reported cases on the application of the maxim *audi alteram
partem* to dismissals from employment concern jobs in the public service.[66] In
Garvey v. Ireland,[67] it was held that the decision to remove the plaintiff, the Commissioner of the Garda Síochána, abruptly and without giving him any reason
whatsoever, contravened natural justice and constitutional justice. Earlier in *State
(Gleeson) v. Minister for Defence*,[68] it was held that the decision to discharge the
plaintiff from the army was invalid because he "should have been given an opportunity of being heard before being discharged".[69] Constitutional law
considerations aside, the requirement to give a fair hearing to persons facing
some significant deprivation has been a principle of administrative law for
centuries. As summarised by McCarthy J. in a case that did not concern dismissal
procedures:

> "In all judicial or quasi-judicial proceedings, it is a fundamental requirement
> of justice that persons or property should not be at risk without the party
> charged being given an adequate opportunity of meeting the claim as identi-
> fied or pursued. If the proceedings derived from statute then in the absence
> of any set fixed procedures, the relevant authority must create and carry out
> the necessary procedures; if the set or fixed procedure is not comprehensive,
> the authority must supplement it in such a fashion as to ensure compliance
> with constitutional justice."[70]

Many of the reported cases on applying fair procedures when dismissing public service workers have concerned office-holders and persons with high-ranking
or middle-ranking jobs. It remains to be determined if these maxims apply to
public sector workers who could not be regarded as officers, such as dustmen
employed by the Corporation, road sweepers employed by the County Council,
hospital attendants in Health Authority hospitals, and bus drivers and conductors
who work for Bus Éireann. Practically all employees in the categories just
described are unionised and work under collective agreements which provide for
dismissal procedures. In a public sector case, Walsh J. observed, *obiter*, that the
application of the rules of natural justice "does not depend upon whether the person concerned is an office-holder as distinct from being an employee of some
other kind. . . . The quality of justice does not depend on such distinctions.'[71] Any
doubts on this question were resolved in *Mooney v. An Post*,[72] where it was held

[64] *ibid.* at 425.
[65] *ibid.*
[66] See *post*, pp. 285-289.
[67] [1981] I.R. 75.
[68] [1976] I.R. 280.
[69] *ibid.* at 295.
[70] *State (Irish Pharmaceutical Union) v. Employment Appeals Tribunal* [1987] I.L.R.M. 36 at 40.
[71] *Gunn v. Bord Cholaiste Naisiunta Eolaine* [1990] 2 I.R. 168 at 181.
[72] [1998] 4 I.R. 288.

that fair procedures must be followed before a postman could be dismissed for alleged serious misconduct. The above quotation from Walsh J. was described as saying that:

> "society is not divided into two classes, one of whom — office holders — is entitled to the protection of the principles of natural justice and the other of whom — employers — is not. Dismissal from one's job for alleged misconduct with possible loss of pension rights and damage to one's good name may, in modern society, be dangerous for any citizen. These are circumstances in which any citizen, however humble, may be entitled to the protection of natural and constitutional justice."[73]

Shortly afterwards in *Maher v. Irish Permanent p.l.c.*,[74] Laffoy J. held that the principles of fair procedures were just as applicable to dismissals of persons in the private sector. Additionally, most private sector employees are protected by the Unfair Dismissals Acts 1977-93, and, in determining whether a particular decision was unfair, the Employment Appeals Tribunal or the Circuit Court will usually insist on the employer having given the employee in question a fair hearing prior to deciding to dismiss.[75]

Fair hearing

The common law imposed no requirement on an employer, outside of the public service, that he should issue a warning before treating certain conduct as warranting dismissal or that the employee be given an opportunity to defend himself against any allegations made against him. As explained by Budd J. in 1953, "while a fair minded employer could undoubtedly give an employee an opportunity to answer a charge and state his case, an employer may if he sees fit to make up his mind from what he has learnt from other sources and observed himself".[76] However, in the *Carvill* case[77] and the *Glover* case[78] some of the traditional views about wrongful dismissal law were rejected by the Supreme Court, and the *Mooney*[79] case effectively overruled the above statement made 50 years ago. The question then arises of what exactly is required by fair procedures and the maxims *audi alteram* and *nemo iudex*.

Procedures stipulated in contract

Where the express terms of the employment contract, be they in the document itself or incorporated from some other document, lay down procedures to be followed when persons are being dismissed on specified grounds, then those procedures must be carried out in such cases. In *McLoughlin v. Great Southern*

[73.] *ibid.* at pp. 297-298.
[74.] [1998] 4 I.R. 302.
[75.] See *post*, p. 202.
[76.] *Flynn v. Great Northern Rly. Co. (Irl.) Ltd.*, (1955) 89 I.L.T.R. 46 at 54.
[77.] [1968] I.R. 325.
[78.] [1973] I.R. 388.
[79.] [1998] 4 I.R. 288.

Railways Co.,[80] where the plaintiff had been summarily dismissed on suspicion of having stolen goods, it was held that the combined effect of relevant collective agreements was that "while he could be dismissed for misconduct, neglect of duty or breach of discipline, he was entitled to demand that the procedure laid down" in the agreements for dismissal should be followed.[81] Accordingly, the employer was in breach of contract for dismissing him for alleged theft without affording him the stipulated hearing. In *Flynn v. Great Northern Railways Co.*,[82] which concerned substantially the same dismissals procedures, it was found that all of the prescribed steps had been followed by the employer. It has been held that where a public service employee's contract provides for a disciplinary procedure, the fact that he was given full notice before being dismissed for misconduct does not cure the failure to afford the agreed procedures.[83] Due notice is not a proper substitute for the procedures laid down.

Where the contract does not state what shall happen in certain circumstances, the decision-making body is the master of its own procedure, provided it acts fairly and reasonably. For instance, except where provided for expressly, the disciplinary tribunal need not follow the ordinary rules of evidence.[84]

It remains to be seen whether the contract can waive entirely even the very rudiments of fair procedure. As was stated by Barrington J. in the *Mooney* case, "[i]f ... the contract ... provides that the employee may be dismissed for misconduct without specifying any procedure to be followed ... the minimum he is entitled to is to be informed of the charge against him and to be given an opportunity to answer it and make submissions".[85]

Implying fair procedures

Where the employment contract makes no express or oblique reference to dismissal procedures, it depends on all the circumstances exactly what fairness will require over and above notice of the allegations and some opportunity to refute them. In the *Mooney* case, Barrington J. observed that:

> "The terms natural and constitutional justice are broad terms and what the justice of a particular case will require will vary with the circumstances of the case. Indeed two of the best known precepts of natural and constitutional justice may not be applicable at all in certain cases .... [T]he principle of *nemo iudex in sua causa* seldom applies in relation to a contract of employment where the employer judges the issue and is an interested party. Likewise it is difficult to apply, to a contract of employment, the principle of *audi alteram partem*, which implies the existence of an independent judge who listens first to one side and then to the other."[86]

---

80. [1944] I.R. 479.
81. *ibid.* at 484.
82. 89 I.L.T.R. 46 (1955).
83. *Marlborough Harbour Board v. Goulden* [1985] 2 N.Z.L.R. 378.
84. *ibid.*
85. [1998] 4 I.R. 288 at 298.
86. *ibid.* at 298.

But the point made there about *audi alteram* seems scarcely tenable because what it requires is principally notice of the charges and an opportunity to answer them.

An example of the *nemo iudex* principle being applied, albeit to an office-holder in the private sector, is *Connolly v. McConnell*,[87] which was an action by the dismissed financial secretary of a trade union against the union's trustees. The governing principles in dismissals cases were stated by Griffin J. as follows:

> "The law is quite clear. When a person holds a full-time pensionable office from which he may be removed, and thus be deprived of his means of liveli-hood and of his pension rights, the domestic tribunal or body having the power to remove him are exercising quasi-judicial functions. Therefore, they may not remove him without first according to him natural justice. He must be given the reasons for his proposed dismissal, and an adequate opportunity of making his defence to the allegations made against him — *audi alteram partem*. The members of the tribunal must be impartial and not be judges in their own cause — *nemo iudex in causa sua*. They must ensure that the pro-ceedings are conducted fairly. In determining whether the tribunal is impar-tial, a member is not to be regarded as impartial if his own interest might be affected by the decision; and this interest is not necessarily to be confined to pecuniary interest."[88]

In that case, the plaintiff had been given an adequate opportunity to defend him-self. But his accusers and others with an interest in upholding those charges par-ticipated in the decision to dismiss him, one of them even presiding at the meeting and voting on the proposal to dismiss. That action was a flagrant breach of the *nemo iudex* principle, which invalidated the decision taken. Whether the same principle applies to jobs which are not pensionable offices remains to be determined.

Perhaps the earliest example of the *audi alteram* principle being applied, albeit again to an office-holder, in the private sector, is *Glover v. B.L.N. Ltd.*[89] With regard to senior executive level employees who are being dismissed on spe-cific allegations of misconduct, this case established that they are entitled to a fair hearing into the accusation. Because of the very formulation of the dismissal power in the plaintiff's contract there, it was held that there was "necessarily an implied term of the contract that this inquiry and determination" by the directors into the allegations "should be fairly conducted".[90] And as the plaintiff was not told of the charges against him nor given any opportunity to defend himself, there was a breach of that implied term, since "failure to allow a person to meet the charges against him and to afford him an adequate opportunity of answering them is a violation of an obligation to proceed fairly".[91] Moreover, even if it could be shown that the employer would have come to the same conclusion if fair pro-cedures had been followed, that does not validate a dismissal made in breach of those procedures. As Walsh J. put it, "[t]he obligation to give a fair hearing to the

---

[87]. [1983] I.R. 172.
[88]. *ibid.* at 178-179.
[89]. [1973] I.R. 388.
[90]. *ibid.* at 425.
[91]. *ibid.* at 425-426.

guilty is just as great as the obligation to give a fair hearing to the innocent".[92] The reasoning here should apply as much to dismissal for serious misconduct where the contract does not expressly deal with the dismissal powers.

It would seem that ordinarily employees should be entitled to make oral representation to the person who decides on their dismissal. But where that decision requires approval within the employer's hierarchy, generally there is no implied obligation to provide a hearing at the apex of that hierarchy, for example a company's board of directors.[93] While generally employees are entitled to be represented by others, such as a trade union official, it has not been established whether they can insist on having legal representation; it would depend on the nature of the job and on the grounds the employer is relying on. The normal rules of evidence in court would not apply. The onus of proof is the usual onus in civil cases, the balance of probabilities, not the criminal "beyond reasonable doubt" standard.[94] That the employee was acquitted in a prosecution does not operate as a bar against disciplinary procedures taken against him in respect of the same facts.[95]

Consequences of not affording a hearing

Where the requisite procedures have not been followed, it depends on the employee's reaction whether his purported dismissal is legally ineffective or whether that dismissal took effect, leaving him with a right of action in damages. If he treats his dismissal as an effective albeit unlawful dismissal, he is left to a remedy in damages. In the jargon of the law of contract, the employee accepted the employer's repudiation of their agreement.[96] But the employee may choose to treat his contract as still subsisting, since it was not terminated in accordance with its terms. This is because, generally, a contractual breach or "repudiation" by one party standing alone does not terminate the contract. It takes two to end it — by repudiation, on one side, and acceptance of the repudiation on the other.[97] In was held in *Dietman v. Brent L.B.C.*[98] that, accordingly, in an appropriate case the court will enjoin the employer from dismissing an employee until the procedures laid down in the contract have been followed.

Whether the court should give an injunction in such cases depends on the entire circumstances. If the employee accepted the employer's repudiation, the question of an injunction does not even arise. For that reason, Hodgson J. counselled in the *Dietman* case, the employee "should make the position plain at once and at once bring proceedings and seek interlocutory relief. The [employer] can then decide whether, in cases of alleged procedural impropriety, to correct the impropriety or fight its corner with the consequences which may follow".[99] Since the plaintiff there commenced injunction proceedings far too late in the day, her

---

92. *ibid.* at 429.
93. *Mooney v. An Post* [1998] 4 IR 288.
94. *Georgopoulus v. Beaumont Hospital Board* [1998] 3 I.R. 132.
95. *Mooney v. An Post* [1998] 4 I.R. 288.
96. *e.g. Gunton v. Richmond upon Thames L.B.S.* [1981] Ch. 448.
97. *Heyman v. Darwins Ltd.* [1942] A.C. 356 at 361.
98. [1987] I.C.R. 737.
99. *ibid.* at 756.

only redress for breach of the procedure was damages. Moreover, if in the circumstances it is plain that the employer has lost all confidence and trust in the employee, an injunction will not issue to keep him in employment pending exhaustion of grievance procedures.[100] If, however, it can be shown that a claimed loss of confidence by the employer is based on some irrational ground, an injunction may issue. And it may be possible to obtain an interlocutory injunction despite the loss of confidence.[101]

In the case of office-holders whose positions were terminated without the requisite procedures having been followed, the decision to remove them is void and they continue in their offices. In *Garvey v. Ireland*,[102] the Government dismissed the Commissioner of the Garda Síochána without giving him any notice or indication of why he was being discharged. Under the legislation governing the Gardaí, his status was that of a statutory office-holder and not merely an employee of the State. Accordingly, it was held that his purported removal from office, without following fair procedures, was *ultra vires* and, therefore, a nullity, so that he had never been validly removed from the office. In the event, the plaintiff did not seek an injunction restraining attempts to prevent him from exercising the powers of that office; instead he settled for damages. Although company directors are office-holders, where they are executive directors holding employment contracts with the company, their rights then are primarily based on the contract. Accordingly, the principles stated in the *Dietman* case regarding injunctions apply to them. The plaintiff in *Glover v. B.L.N. Ltd.* only sought a declaration and damages.

REMEDIES FOR WRONGFUL DISMISSAL/RESIGNATION

The principal legal remedy open to a person who is wrongfully dismissed is damages for breach of the employment contract. Alternatively, the employee may have a claim for unfair dismissal under the 1977-93 Acts; if he pursues that claim, he is precluded from seeking damages for breach of the contract.[103] Exceptionally, the employee may obtain a declaration that the dismissal was unlawful or may even obtain an injunction restraining the dismissal. Employees in many parts of the public sector are entitled to seek judicial review of the decision to dismiss them[104] and, if that was unlawful, obtain orders that the decision is invalid, and damages. Extra-legal modes of redress may also be open to the employee, notably resort to industrial action. A dispute about a dismissal, even if that dismissal in the event is perfectly lawful, is a trade dispute for the purpose of the Industrial Relations Act 1990. However, the immunities under that Act from liability in tort for taking industrial action do not apply where the subject matter of the dispute is covered by individual grievance procedures which have not been exhausted.[105]

[100.] *e.g. Ali v. Southwark L.B.C.* [1988] I.C.R. 567.

[101.] See *infra*, p. 179.

[102.] [1981] I.R. 75. Similarly, *Marlborough Harbour Board v. Goulden* [1985] 2 N.Z.L.R. 378.

[103.] 1977 Act, s.15.

[104.] See *post*, pp. 283-285.

[105.] Industrial Relations Act 1990, s.9(2).

Declaration

In the case of many public sector jobs, decisions regarding dismissal can be challenged in court through the procedure known as judicial review. Alternatively, the employee may seek the declaration in ordinary plenary proceedings.[106] An office-holder or public service employee who sought to challenge the legality of his dismissal would seek a declaration that the dismissal or the decision to dismiss was unlawful. Strictly there is no particular benefit in having a mere declaration, in that the employer is not thereby obliged to reinstate the employee or to pay compensation. All that a declaration does is to state that the plaintiff was wrongfully dismissed. However, public sector employers are inclined to adjust their circumstances so as to bring them in line with the legal position as pronounced in a judicial declaration.[107]

Even in the private sector, circumstances can arise where a declaration can be a useful remedy and the courts will grant a declaration in such cases. *Kingston v. Irish Dunlop Co. Ltd.*[108] was not a dismissal case but concerned the correct interpretation of the terms on which an earlier action between the plaintiff and the defendant had been settled. The plaintiff sought a declaration to the effect that, under the settlement, he was entitled to be employed on light work in one section of the defendant's factory; he also sought damages but no loss was proved. It was argued that the Court could not make a bare declaration of his rights but that contention was rejected on the grounds that Order 19, rule 29, of the Rules of the Superior Courts gives an extensive jurisdiction to make declarations in appropriate cases. Ó Dalaigh C.J., giving judgment for the Supreme Court, pointed out that the declaration being sought there was not entirely valueless because it would establish what the parties' rights and duties were under the settlement. A court would not make the declaration if it was sought only to prove some hypothetical point. One of the reasons given for not granting a declaration that an employee was unlawfully dismissed is the principle that specific performance of an employment contract will not be ordered. But in *Glover v. B.L.N. Ltd.* Walsh J. "expressly reserved [his] opinion on the correctness of this statement if it is intended to convey that a court cannot make a declaration which would have the effect of reinstating a person wrongfully dismissed".[109]

A declaration that the plaintiff, a former employee who worked in the restaurant on the Cork-Dublin train, had been dismissed in defiance of fair procedures was refused by the Supreme Court in *Parsons v. Iarnrod Éireann*[110] where the plaintiff had already taken unfair dismissal proceedings in respect of the matter. Section 15 of the Unfair Dismissals Act 1997 requires employees to opt between their claim under that Act. Because he had exercised that option, he had lost his right to sue for damages. Any declaratory order would be in aid of that remedy and would have no independent existence apart from it; with the contractual

---

[106.] See *Freedland, supra*, n.18, pp. 278-291.
[107.] *e.g. Maunsell v. Minister for Education* [1940] I.R. 213 and *Cox v. Electricity Supply Board (No. 2)* [1943] I.R. 231.
[108.] [1969] I.R. 233.
[109.] [1973] I.R. at l427.
[110.] [1997] 2 I.R. 523.

claim gone, there was no free standing relief that he could claim either in law or in equity.

Injunction

It has been a fundamental principle of employment law for many years that, ordinarily, the courts will not order specific performance of an employment contract[111] or, what is the same thing, grant a mandatory injunction compelling an employer to continue employing somebody he does not wish to employ. Because employment is a personal relationship involving a degree of mutual confidence, the view was, and indeed still is, that there is little point in seeking to compel an employer to continue employing someone he does not really want. Also, the courts are reluctant to issue orders that might require continual supervision by them. But this principle is not a hard and fast rule. The complete position is as follows:

> "The court will not by injunction require an employer to let a servant continue in his employment, when the employer has sought to terminate that employment and to prevent the servant carrying out his work under the contract, unless it is clear on the evidence not only that it is otherwise just to make such a requirement but also that there exists sufficient confidence on the part of the employer in the servant's ability and other necessary attributes for it to be reasonable to make the order.
>
> Sufficiency of confidence must be judged by reference to the circumstances of the case, including the nature of the work, the people with whom the work must be done and the likely effect upon the employer and the employer's operations if the employer is required by injunction to suffer the plaintiff to continue in the work."[112]

If an employee wants to have his dismissal enjoined, he must move swiftly to seek relief of that nature.[113] Injunctions are discretionary remedies and there are several circumstances where the courts will refuse to make those orders. For instance, if the award of damages would be an adequate remedy, the tendency would be against granting an injunction in this type of case. The more senior the job is in the employer's hierarchy, the greater the likelihood that damages are not an adequate form of redress. If the employer demonstrates that he has lost all trust and confidence in the employee, ordinarily he will not be obliged to keep him in his employment.[114]

In the past it was extremely difficult to get an interlocutory injunction restraining a person's dismissal from an ordinary private sector job, pending the trial of the action; it was almost taken for granted that damages would be an adequate remedy in the event of the employee ultimately winning his claim for breach of contract.[115] More recently, the courts have shown less reluctance to grant interloc-

---

[111] I. Spry, *Equitable Remedies* (5th ed., 1997), pp.119-125; Freedland, *supra*, n.18, pp. 272-278.
[112] *Powell v. Brent L.B.C.* [1988] I.C.R. 176 at 194.
[113] *Dietman v. Brent L.B.C.* [1987] I.C.R. 737.
[114] *Ali v. Southwark L.B.C.* [1988] I.C.R. 567 and *Alexander v. Standard Telephones and Cables Ltd.* [1990] I.C.R. 291.
[115] *Marsh v. National Autistic Soc.* [1993] I.C.R. 453.

utory orders of this nature. Several of the recent cases have involved employees who also were or had been directors of the defendant companies.[116] In *Courtney v. Radio 2000 Ltd.*,[117] where the defendant had purported to dismiss a radio presenter because allegedly he had broken guidelines on what could be broadcast during an election, Laffoy J. refused to order his reinstatement pending the trial, because his employer no longer had trust and confidence in him. Subject to that, however, it was ordered that until the trial, the decision to dismiss him should not be put into effect and that he should continue to be paid the salary and other sums due to him under the contract. Exactly what will be enjoined depends on the nature of the job in question and other circumstances. In one instance,[118] O'Donovan J. ordered the employer to continue paying the salary, provided however the employee undertook to continue supplying his services as a safety officer, but refused to enjoin hiring a replacement, on the grounds that if he won his case, the plaintiff's most likely remedy would be damages. In another instance,[119] Macken J. directed that the employee's salary be paid up to the date of the trial and also enjoined appointing a replacement chief executive of the organisation. In another instance[120] where a building society manager had been suspended, pending disciplinary proceedings, Macken J. ordered that the suspension should end and he should be given back his job, pending the trial of the action, because he had been suspended for an unconscionably long time.[121]

Damages

In the private sector, and probably for jobs in the public sector that could not be characterised as offices, the principal legal (non-statutory) remedy for the wrongfully dismissed employee is damages. Since the essence of the claim is for damages for breach of contract, the measurement of those damages is determined by the general principles of the law of contract.[122] The normal measure of the damages is what the employee would have earned had he been allowed to remain working during the period for which notice should have been given. Thus, if under the contract he should have got two months' notice, his damages ordinarily would be two months' salary. In the leading case *Addis v. Gramophone Co. Ltd.*,[123] the plaintiff was employed by the defendant as a manager, under a contract entitling him to six months' notice of dismissal, his remuneration being £60 per month together with commission. He brought an action for wrongful dismissal and the central issue was how much damages he was entitled to in the circumstances. This amount was held to be the equivalent of six months' normal salary together with the commission he would have earned during that period.[124]

[116.] *e.g. Phelan v. BIC (Ireland) Ltd.* [1997] E.L.R. 208, *Harte v. Kelly* [1997] E.L.R. 125 and *Boland v. Phoenix Shannon* [1997] E.L.R. 113.

[117.] [1997] E.L.R. 198.

[118.] *Doyle v. Grangeford Precast Concrete Ltd.* [1998] E.L.R. 260.

[119.] *Lonergan v. Salter Townsend* [2000] E.L.R. 15.

[120.] *Martin v. Irish Permanent Bldg. Soc.* [1999] E.L.R. 241.

[121.] Most recently, *Howard v. University College Cork* [2001] E.L.R. 8.

[122.] See, generally, H. McGregor, *Damages* (16th ed., 1997), Chap. 27, and Freedland, *ante*, n.18 pp. 244-272.

[123.] [1909] A.C. 488.

[124.] *Cerberw Software Ltd.* v. *Rawly* [2001] I.C.R. 377.

Remuneration in lieu of notice

It is for these reasons that employers frequently pay an employee who is being dismissed salary in lieu of notice. Generally, if the employee is given the equivalent of what he would have earned during the due notice period, he has no action for breach of contract even though he was dismissed without any proper notice.

Additional damages

Are there special circumstances where an employee is entitled to damages in excess of what he would have earned during the remaining part of his notice period? Where the dismissal takes place in a particularly unfair manner or in notably unjust circumstances, which causes the employee great distress and perhaps lowers him in the estimation of others, is he entitled to additional damages for the loss he suffered? A categorical answer cannot be given about the position in Ireland because the superior courts have not ruled in the question in recent years; although the general belief is that additional damages may be awarded in appropriate circumstances.

In *Addis v. Gramophone Co. Ltd.,* the House of Lords held that additional damages cannot be awarded in such cases. Lord Loreburn L.C. could not:

> "agree that the manner of dismissal affects those damages. Such considerations have never been allowed to influence damages in this kind of case
> .... If there be a dismissal without notice the employer must pay an indemnity; but that indemnity cannot include compensation either for the injured feelings of the servant, or for the loss he may maintain from the fact that his having been dismissed of itself makes it more difficult for him to obtain fresh employment".[125]

It was held that the employee may have a separate action in tort for defamation or for deliberately causing nervous shock, but that the damages for breach of the employment contract are limited to what would have been earned during the notice period. In 1976 the English High Court departed from this principle[126] but in 1985 the Court of Appeal endorsed the position as stated in the Lords in the *Addis* case,[127] which view was reiterated by the House of Lords in 2001.[128] Other common law jurisdictions have rejected *Addis*, most notably New Zealand and Canada.[129] Thus in *Stuart v. Armourguard Security*,[130] the New Zealand High Court held that it was an implied term in employment contracts for which damages were recoverable, that the employee should not be dismissed in a manner likely to cause distress or loss of reputation, without proper cause. There a regional manager, who was summarily dismissed immediately after he refused

---

125. [1909] A.C. 488 at 491.

126. *Cox v. Phillips Industries Ltd.* [1976] 1 W.L.R. 638.

127. *Bliss v. South East Thames Regional H.A.* [1987] I.C.R. 700.

128. *Johnson v. Unisys Ltd.* [2001] 2 W.L.R. 1077.

129. *Vorvis v. Insurance Corp. of British Columbia*, 58 D.L.R. (4th) 193 (1989), but *Worster v. Universal Environmental Services Ltd.*, 167 D.L.R. (4th) 166 (1998).

130. [1996] 1 N.Z.L.R. 484; also *Ogilvy & Mather (N.Z.) Ltd. v. Turner* [1996] 1 N.Z.L.R. 641.

to give his "non-negotiable resignation," was awarded general damages not limited by the *Addis* cap.[131]

It remains to be seen what position the Irish courts will take, but most likely they will decline to follow *Addis* on the grounds that it was only concerned with compensation for injury to employees' feelings on account of the contumelious manner of their dismissal. Where, on the other hand, the way in which they were dismissed causes them foreseeable financial loss, they would appear to be entitled to be compensated fully. Often, that loss will result from the manner of their dismissal prejudicing their reputation in the labour market. The compensation payable to them is not for injury to reputation as such; that is the domain of the tort of defamation. But the fact that the circumstances might give rise to a claim for defamation does not prevent recovering damages in contract for the financial loss deriving from the injury to reputation.[132]

Of course, additional damages have always been recoverable under what is known as the "second rule" in *Hadley v. Baxendale*.[133] In the *Addis* case it was emphasised that the plaintiff's claim for additional damages was not being advanced under this rule. According to the "second rule", one measure of damages in an action for breach of contract is the sum "as may reasonably be supposed to have been in the contemplation of both parties, at the time they made the contract, as the probable result of the breach of it."[134] Accordingly, if, at the time they made the contract, the parties were aware of exceptional losses which would result from a wrongful dismissal, then if those losses did indeed take place, the employee must be compensated for them. This term may be implied as well as express, for instance where the employee would have been eligible for a discretionary bonus, circumstances may warrant that it should not have been unreasonably withheld.[135]

Mitigation

As with other successful plaintiffs in breach of contract actions, the wrongfully dismissed employee must mitigate his loss; he must take all reasonable steps to reduce the loss he stands to suffer. In this context, the employee must do what is reasonably necessary in order to find another job. If the employee got another job during the notice period, what he earned in that job for the remainder of that period will be deducted from the damages he otherwise would have obtained. An employer may contend that the dismissed employee can get or should have got other work during the notice period; it depends on the entire circumstances of the case whether that contention will succeed, thereby reducing the amount of damages to be paid.[136]

[131.] *cf. Johnson v. Gore Wood & Co.* [2001] 2 W.L.R. 72, at p. 109 and *Gogay v. Hertfordshire C.C.* [2000] I.R.L.R. 703.

[132.] *Spring v. Guardian Assurance p.l.c.* [1995] 2 A.C. 296.

[133.] (1854) 9 Exch. 341.

[134.] *ibid.* at 355.

[135.] *Clark v. Normura Int'l p.l.c.* [2000] I.R.L.R. 766.

[136.] *e.g. Hermon v. Owners of S.S. Vica* [1942] I.R. 305.

Collateral benefits

Collateral benefits which employees receive during the notice period may be deducted from the damages otherwise payable for the breach of contract. Those benefits include unemployment benefit payable under the Social Welfare Acts.[137] But the Irish courts have not considered in detail which particular benefits are so deductible.

Taxation

Is the measure of amount of damages recoverable by employees in respect of lost remuneration the pre-tax or post-tax earnings? It was held in *Glover v. B.L.N. Ltd. (No. 2)*[138] that damages recovered for wrongful dismissal, albeit measured by reference to lost earnings, are not intrinsically earnings or "emoluments"; accordingly, those damages cannot be taxed as the employee's income under Schedule E. But that still leaves the question, in measuring the damages payable, whether account be taken of what tax would have been deducted if the employee had continued earning remuneration in his job and whether only the net amount after tax be paid in damages. This is a matter which has divided courts in many common law jurisdictions. In the *Glover (No. 2)* case, Kenny J. followed the English precedents[139] on this point and held that the amount of tax which would have been paid must be deducted from the gross earnings which the plaintiff lost. This was because:

> "[a]n award of damages by a court is intended to compensate the plaintiff for the loss which he has suffered. . . . Therefore, it is irrelevant that the defendant will profit by an allowance being made for tax against the loss. If the damages . . . are not chargeable to tax while the lost remuneration would have been, the plaintiff would be getting an award which would exceed the loss which he had suffered by being deprived of the remuneration. Income tax enters into the lives of so many of our citizens that the law cannot ignore it when assessing damages."[140]

However, in Canada[141] and New Zealand[142] the courts have rejected this reasoning, so that it is conceivable that, if this issue went on to the Supreme Court, the rule as stated here would be overturned.[143] Among the arguments against the present rule is that the income tax legislation provides a comprehensive code for the tax consequences of loss of office and it is unsatisfactory that serious tax questions be dealt with by the employer and employee in the complete absence of the Revenue authorities. Indeed, in a case involving compensation for dismissal without giving adequate notice, as required by the Minimum Notice and Terms of

---

137. *Parsons v. B.N.M. Laboratories Ltd.* [1964] 1 Q.B. 95.
138. [1973] I.R. 432.
139. *British Transport Comm. v. Garley* [1956] A.C. 185.
140. [1973] I.R. at 441. See *Shove v. Downs Surgical p.l.c.* [1984] I.C.R. 532.
141. *R. (in right of the Province of Ontario) v. Jennings* (1966) 57 D.L.R. 2d 644.
142. *North Island Wholesale Groceries Ltd. v. Hewin* [1982] 2 N.Z.L.R. 176.
143. *cf. Sullivan v. Southern Health Board* [1997] 3 I.R. 123 at 137-138, accepting the rule as stated in *Glover (No. 2)*.

Employment Act 1973, Barrington J.[144] refused to follow a recent House of Lords decision on a similar question under English law. It was held that the employer was not entitled to deduct from the sum stipulated in that Act the unemployment benefit which the plaintiff had been receiving during the relevant period.

Employee's wrongful termination

Actions by employers against their former employees who have left their jobs, in breach of their employment contracts, are comparatively rare. Presumably in an appropriate case an employer might obtain a declaration that the employee broke his contract. The usual measure of damages is the cost of obtaining another person to do the work, less what would have been paid to the ex-employee under the contract.[145] Where a substitute for him cannot easily be obtained, the measure of damages is the value of work lost by reason of the defection, less what remuneration the ex-employee would have earned.[146] Exceptionally, the employer may be able to recover expenditure which was rendered futile by the employee's breach of contract.[147]

Ordinarily, an employee will not be enjoined from leaving or from working for others, because that would be tantamount to ordering specific performance of the contract. But where the employee possesses confidential information which he is likely to disclose to a rival, or where a valid restraint of employment clause exists, an injunction can be obtained against the employee working for a named or for designated third parties.[148] There may be an exception where, practically speaking, there is only one other person for whom that employee can work using his own special skills and expertise.[149]

In recent years an exception to the general principle about enjoining a breach of employment contract has been recognised. This is where the employee left without giving proper notice. If the employer undertakes to continue paying him during the remainder of the notice period, a court may enjoin him from working for rival employers during that period.[150] Interlocutory relief can also be given in those circumstances.

[144.] *Irish Leathers Ltd. v. Minister for Labour* [1986] I.R. 177.

[145.] *Richards v. Hayward* (1841) 2 M.C.G. 574.

[146.] *Ebbw Vale Steel Co. v. Tew* (1935) 79 Sol. J. 593.

[147.] *Anglia Television v. Reed* [1972] 1 Q.B. 60.

[148.] See *ante*, pp. 99-101 and 102-105.

[149.] *cf. Warren v. Mendy* [1989] 1 W.L.R. 853.

[150.] *e.g. Evening Standard Co. v. Henderson* [1987] I.C.R. 588 and *Provident Financial Group p.l.c. v. Hayward* [1989] I.C.R. 160.

CHAPTER 8

DISMISSAL – STATUTORY RIGHTS

If employers and employees always had equal bargaining power, perhaps the substantial body of legislation regulating dismissals would never have been enacted. The position might then be as it is in the United States; such protection as employees have against being dismissed lies in their employment contracts and in provisions contained in collective agreements applicable to them, an exception to this pattern being made for race, sex and some other forms of discrimination. By contrast, the labour laws of Continental European counties for many years have regulated extensively the employer's general prerogative to dismiss. In 1963 the International Labour Organisation adopted a Recommendation concerning Termination of Employment at the Initiative of the Employer (No. 119), which has proved extremely influential in this regard.[1] It partly contributed to the enactment in Britain of legislation on redundancy (1965), on minimum notice and on unfair dismissals (1971).[2] Similar measures were enacted in Ireland not too long afterwards — the Redundancy Payments Acts 1967-79, the Minimum Notice and Terms of Employment Act 1973, and the Unfair Dismissals Acts 1977-93, which are the subject of this chapter.[3]

DISMISSAL

Before the merits of a claim for any of the statutory remedies relating to dismissal will be considered, the claimant or plaintiff must have been dismissed. The ordinary meaning of dismissal connotes an employer unequivocally telling his employee that he is no longer being employed; this message may be conveyed either with or without giving due notice or tendering money in lieu of notice. Whether the expiry of a fixed term contract or a contract to perform a specified task amounts to a dismissal is debatable. In order to avoid any confusion and to ensure that the statutory protections apply to all forms of dismissals in a very wide sense of the term, the various Acts contain an extended definition of what is a dismissal for their own purposes.

The term is defined in section 1 of the Unfair Dismissals Act 1977 as meaning being sacked in the commonly accepted sense and also "constructive dismissal" (*i.e.* forced resignation) and the expiry of certain fixed term or task contracts, as follows:

---

[1] See, generally, Napier, "Dismissals – the New I.L.O. Standards", 12 Ind. L.J. 17 (1983).

[2] *cf.* H. Collins, *Justice in Dismissal* (1992) and R. Upex, *The Law of Termination of Employment* (5th ed., 1997).

[3] See, generally, M. Redmond, *Dismissal Law in Ireland* (2nd ed., 1999), Chaps 12-24 on unfair dismissals.

"(a) the termination by his employer of the employee's contract of employ-
     ment with the employer, whether prior notice of the termination was or
     was not given to the employee,

(b) the termination by the employee of his contract of employment with his
    employer, whether prior notice of the termination was or was not given to
    the employer, in circumstances in which, because of the conduct of the
    employer, the employee was or would have been entitled, or it was or
    would have been reasonable for the employee, to terminate the contract of
    employment without giving prior notice of the termination to the
    employer, or

(c) the expiration of a contract of employment for a fixed term without its
    being renewed under the same contract or, in the case of a contract for a
    specified purpose (being a purpose of such a kind that the duration of the
    contract was limited but was, at the time of its making, incapable of pre-
    cise ascertainment), the cesser of the purpose."

There is a similar tri-partite definition in section 9(1) of the Redundancy Payments Act 1967. In contrast, section 4 of the Minimum Notice and Terms of
Employment Act 1973 merely speaks of the employer terminating the contract of
employment. An employee who has taken maternity or related leave under the
Maternity Protection Act 1994, or leave under the Adoptive Leave Act 1995, the
Parental Leave Act 1998, or the Carer's Leave Act 2001, but then is not permitted
to return to work in accordance with those Acts,[4] is deemed to have been
dismissed for the purpose of statutory minimum notice, unfair dismissals and
statutory redundancy. Accordingly, the word "dismissal" in this context has
largely become a term of art, covering four main types of situation.

Unilateral termination by employer

The first is the commonest case where the contract is terminated by the employer,
that is where the employer unilaterally makes it quite clear that the relationship
has or shall come to an end. It is not essential that the employee has been furnished with due notice of dismissal. The principal problem which arises in this
kind of case is where the employee has been virtually compelled to resign; has he
resigned or was he dismissed? What matters is the substance and not the form of
the transaction.[5]

Where the dismissal is in breach of the notice requirements in the contract of
employment, the question arises as to when the contract came to an end. If notice
is given and the employee is not required to work the notice period, the contract
ends when the notice will have expired.[6] If, instead, a full payment in lieu of
notice is made and he does not work thereafter, the contract ends once the notice
and payment are received.[7]

---

4.   See *ante*, pp. 93-97.
5.   *Birch v. University of Liverpool* [1985] I.C.R. 470; *cf. O'Reilly v. Minister for Industry & Com-
     merce* [1997] E.L.R. 48.
6.   *Redmond v. British Building and Engineering Appliances Ltd.* [1974] 1 W.L.R. 171.
7.   *H.Q. Service Children's Education v. Davitt* [1999] I.C.R. 978.

Fixed term or specified purpose contracts

Secondly, some employment contracts are not for an indefinite duration but are entered into for a fixed term or for a specified purpose. A dismissal is deemed by the Unfair Dismissals and the Redundancy Payments Acts to have taken place where the agreed term of the contract has expired and the contract has not been renewed. For the purposes of unfair dismissal, that non-renewal must be "under the same contract", meaning with terms identical or substantially similar to those of the contract (except for the actual dates), which becomes extended. In other words, not giving the employee a new contract on similar terms, other than expiry date, to the previous contract; the argument that "under the same contract" means an extension pursuant to some right or power in the expiring contract has been rejected.[8] For the purposes of redundancy, there is a dismissal unless the fixed term contract was replaced by an identical or a similar contract.[9] Accordingly, giving a person whose fixed term contract expired a new contract, of indefinite duration and terminable by notice, constitutes a dismissal, even if many other terms of the new contract are more advantageous to the employee than the old contract. Of course if the new terms are on balance more advantageous, the dismissal is most unlikely to be regarded as unfair but it might, in circumstances, be regarded as redundancy.[10] Although the non-renewal of a fixed term contract is not defined as a dismissal for the purposes of the laws against discrimination, since many kinds of discriminatory dismissals are prohibited by the Unfair Dismissals Acts they come within the above tri-partite definition of the term.

Under the Unfair Dismissals Acts there is also a dismissal where a contract made for a specific purpose comes to an end. This is a contract where the employee was to achieve a defined objective but, at the time the contract was being entered into, it was not possible to tell how long it would take to realise that purpose. Non-renewal of a contract of this nature is not deemed to be a dismissal under the other two Acts.

Parties to these kinds of contracts, however, can waive application to them of the unfair dismissals regime if they stipulate in writing at the outset, signed by them, that the 1977-93 Acts shall not apply to their relationship.[11]

Constructive dismissal

Thirdly, by constructive dismissal is meant where an employee leaves his job in circumstances where the employer's improper conduct drove him to resigning. In the Acts on unfair dismissals, on redundancy and on discrimination,[12] a constructive dismissal occurs where, by reason of the employer's conduct, the employee is "entitled to terminate" the contract. In other words, the employer's conduct must have been so serious a breach of the agreement as to constitute a repudiation of it, thereby entitling the employee, should he choose, to rescind the agreement there and then. The test of what constitutes repudiation is based on ordinary con-

---

8. *British Broadcasting Corp. v. Kelly-Phillips* [1998] I.C.R. 587 at 593E.
9. 1967 Act, s.9(1)(b).
10. *cf. Loscher v. Mount Temple School* [1996] E.L.R. 98.
11. 1973 Act, s.2(2)(b); see *infra*, p. 201.
12. Employment Equality Act 1998, s.2(1).

tract law concepts and the express and implied terms of the contract in question.[13] Repudiation occurs where there has been any breach of the implied term that the employer will not, without reasonable and probable cause, act in a manner calculated or likely to destroy or seriously damage the relationship of confidence and trust with the employee. Examples include where, unilaterally, the employer reduced the employee's remuneration,[14] changed the very nature of the task for which he was employed,[15] or required him to work somewhere distant from the place it was agreed he should work.[16] Of course, alterations of this nature do not constitute repudiation where the contract's very terms enable the employer to change those terms in this manner.[17]

For the purpose of the law regarding unfair dismissals and discrimination, the scope of constructive dismissal is even more extensive. The concept extends to where the employer's actions were such as rendered it "reasonable" for the employee to terminate the contract without giving any prior notice. In other words, even if in the circumstances the employer's actions did not amount to so serious a breach as would entitle the employee to rescind the contract, nevertheless those actions were sufficiently grave, as a reasonable employee in that same position would easily have been driven to leave the job there and then. Whether an employee was constructively dismissed in this sense depends entirely on the particular facts of the case.

Excluded after taking statutory leave

The fourth type of situation is where an employee has taken leave under the Maternity Protection Act 1994, the Adoptive Leave Act 1995, the Parental Leave Act 1998,[18] or the Carer's Leave Act 2001 but is then not permitted to return to work by the relevant employer. Not alone are such exclusions deemed to be dismissals for the three main Acts that regulate dismissals,[19] but they shall also be deemed to be unfair dismissals unless in the circumstances there were substantial grounds justifying them.[20]

CONTINUITY OF EMPLOYMENT

In order to benefit from many of the statutory rights regarding dismissal,[21] the employee must have been continuously employed on a full-time basis by his employer for a specified period, for instance, for one year under the Unfair Dismissals Acts,[22] and for two years under the Redundancy Payments

---

13. See *ante*, pp. 160-162.
14. *Cantor Fitzgerald Int'l v. Callaghan* [1999] I.C.R. 639.
15. *Lewis v. Motor World Garage Ltd.* [1986] I.C.R. 158.
16. *Courtaulds Northern Spinning Ltd. v. Sibson* [1988] I.C.R. 451.
17. See *ante*, pp. 58-59.
18. See *ante*, pp. 93-97.
19. *e.g.* Maternity Protection Act 1994, s.40.
20. *ibid.*, s.40(4)(b).
21. And to parental leave under the Parental Leave Act 1998, s. 6(4), (8).
22. 1973 Act, s.2(1)(a).

Acts.[23] Continuity is not required under the 1977-93 Acts for dismissals on certain grounds,[24] nor for dismissals under the legislation against discrimination. Special rules are laid down for determining if the requisite continuity exists. There are two main sets of rules which differ in detail. Continuity for the purpose of claims for redundancy payments is dealt with in Schedule 3 of the Redundancy Payments Act 1967;[25] for the purpose of unfair dismissals and other rights, continuity is dealt with principally in the First Schedule of the Minimum Notice and Terms of Employment Act 1973. Legislation regarding some categories of employees in the public sector have their own unique rules regarding measuring continuity of service.

In the account of continuity here, the emphasis is placed on the rules under the 1973 Minimum Notice and Terms of Employment Act. There are very few decisions of the Superior Courts on these questions and many important issues of principle have not been considered by the tribunals. Because there are significant differences between the formulation of continuity rules here and those in the British legislation, care should be taken in seeking solutions to problems here in the substantial body of reported case law in Britain.

Date of commencement

The first matter to be ascertained is exactly when did the employee commence employment with that employer. This is principally a question of fact. The relevant time is not when the employee actually began working but when did the employment relationship commence. [26]

Date of dismissal

In determining when the employment ended, the focus is not on when the employee actually ceased working but when did the employment relationship come to an end. The answer does not turn entirely on contract law concepts because the legislation on unfair dismissals and on redundancy contains definitions of the "date of dismissal", which focus on two questions, *viz.* the requisite notice for dismissal and the position of fixed term contracts.[27]

Dismissal notice

Even though, as a matter of contract law, a summary dismissal may take effect immediately,[28] the employment relationship is not deemed to have ended at that time for the purposes of these Acts. Under the 1967 Act and the 1977-93 Acts where due notice was given, the contract ends when that notice expires, even if the employee departed earlier.[29] Where the due notice was not given, the dis-

---

[23.] 1967 Act, s.7(5), as amended by 1971 Act's Schedule. The applicant must also have been an employed contributor for all social welfare benefits for the four years immediately preceding the dismissal: 1967 Act, s.7(1)(b), as amended by 1971 Act's Schedule.

[24.] See *post*, p. 199.

[25.] Paras. 4-12, as amended by schedule to the 1991 Act.

[26.] *e.g. Brennan v. Religious of the Sacred Heart* [2000] E.L.R. 297.

[27.] 1967 Act, s.2(1) and 1977 Act, s.1.

[28.] See *ante*, pp. 168-171.

[29.] ss.2(1)(a) and 1(a), respectively.

missal is deemed to have occurred at the time such notice, if given, would have expired.[30] By due notice here is meant the notice required by the contract; for unfair dismissals it also means the statutory minimum notice under the Minimum Notice and Terms of Employment Act 1973, where this minimum is longer than what the contract provides for. A specified period of notice has been held to be a period clear of the time the notice was given; for instance, seven days' notice means seven days after the day the employee was notified.[31] In England the courts are of the view that, once the decision to dismiss has been communicated, the parties can agree that the termination date should be earlier than that specified in the statutory definition.[32]

Fixed term or purpose contract

In the case of a fixed term contract which was not renewed or a contract for a specified purpose and that purpose has ceased, the dismissal date is the day on which the contract term expired or its purpose ceased, as the case may be.[33] Where, however, within three months of the contract so terminating, the employee is re-engaged for a fixed period under a similar contract, which later expires, if it is shown that the original contract was not immediately extended in order to avoid liability under the 1977-93 Acts, then the date of termination is the time the new contract came to an end.[34] Otherwise, those Acts could easily be evaded by hiring under a series of fixed term contracts for short periods but with breaks between each of them.

Presumption of continuous employment

Having ascertained when the employment commenced and when it ceased, there is a statutory presumption that the employee was continuously employed between those dates. The employee's service is "deemed to be continuous unless that service is terminated by [his] dismissal. . . ."[35] The full effect of this provision does not appear to have been authoritatively decided. Its apparent meaning is that, unless it is shown that the employee was either dismissed or voluntarily left the job at an earlier stage, he shall be regarded as having been continuously employed between the dates of commencement and of dismissal.

Continuity not broken

Several circumstances are specified which are deemed not to break continuity of service, even if the actual contractual relationship has been disrupted by them.

[30.]   ss.2(1)(b) and 1(b), respectively.

[31.]   *West v. Kneels Ltd.* [1987] I.C.R. 486.

[32.]   *Cronk v. Her Majesty's Stationery Office* [1985] I.C.R. 1.

[33.]   1967 Act, s.2(1)(c), and 1977 Act, s.1(c).

[34.]   1993 Act, s.3(b).

[35.]   1967 Act, Schedule 3, para. 4, as amended by 1971 Act, s.10, and Minimum Notice and Terms of Employment Act 1973, Schedule, para. 1.

"Umbrella" contract

These special provisions do not even arise where the employee was employed under what may be termed an "umbrella" contract, meaning a contract which envisaged that the employee would occasionally cease working for short periods and would later re-commence work. For instance, a ship's captain who sailed on voyages, interspersed with periods ashore during which he drew unemployment benefit, was held to be subject to such a contract.[36] The contention that each voyage was a separate contract and no contractual relationship existed between voyages was rejected. But in another instance, concerning trawlermen in similar circumstances, it was held that each voyage they sailed was under a separate contract[37] — the parties there were not subject to any mutual obligations at the times when there was no subsisting crew agreement.

Immediate re-employment

There is no break in continuity where the employee's dismissal was "followed by [his] immediate re-employment".[38] How short a time must elapse between these two events has not been determined.

Avoidance technique

One of the amendments to the unfair dismissals regime introduced in 1993 was to strike at dismissals of employees followed by their re-employment where the purpose was simply to break continuity and thereby "avoid ... liability under" the 1977-93 Acts. If a dismissed employee is re-employed by the same employer within 26 weeks of his dismissal, his continuity of service is not regarded as broken if it is shown that the employer's objective was wholly or indeed partly to avoid such liability.[39] The same principle applies to employees under fixed term or specific purpose contracts which have expired but who, within three months, are re-hired under similar terms.

Lay-off

An employee who has been laid off for a period is deemed not to have been dismissed.[40] It depends on the circumstances whether there was a "lay-off" as contrasted with a dismissal or a voluntary leaving. That term connotes a temporary severing of relations in the anticipation that the worker will be re-employed in the not too distant future.[41] There is a definition of the term for redundancy payments purposes.[42] In the British legislation, instead of "lay off", the phrase "temporary cessation of work" is used, which has generated substantial litigation in the superior courts there.[43]

---

[36] *Boyd Line Ltd. v. Pitts* [1986] I.C.R. 244.

[37] *Hellyer Bros. Ltd. v. McLeod* [1987] 1 W.L.R. 726; it was not argued here that the employees had been laid off during the intervals.

[38] 1973 Act Schedule 1, para. 6; for redundancy claims, see 1967 Act, Schedule 3, para. 5A (inserted by 1971 Act).

[39] 1993 Act, s.3(c).

[40] 1973 Act, Schedule 1, para. 3, and 1967 Act, Schedule 3, para. 5(1)(b)(i).

[41] *e.g. Devonald v. Rosser & Sons* [1906] 2 K.B. 728.

[42] 1967 Act, s.11(1); *cf. Irish Leather Ltd. v. Minister for Labour* [1986] I.R. 177.

[43] *e.g. Fitzgerald v. Hall Russell & Co.* [1970] A.C. 984 and *Ford v. Warwickshire C.C.* [1983] 2 A.C. 71.

Transfer of business

An employer may decide to sell or otherwise dispose of all or part of his business and, at the same time, arrange that one or more employees working in that business be employed by the transferee or successor company. In that event, the actual dismissal and commencement of the new job are deemed not to have broken the employees' continuity; whatever continuity they had accrued with their former employer is carried over to their new employer. This question and related issues are the subject of an E.C. directive[44] and a statutory instrument,[45] which are considered in detail in Chapter 9.

Part-time employment

Formerly, many part-time workers were not protected by the dismissals legislation because they did not work for at least 18 hours a week for the one employer. That period has now been reduced to eight hours a week by the Worker Protection (Regular Part-Time Employees) Act 1991. The Redundancy Payment Acts do not apply to a person who is "normally expected to work" for his employer for less than eight hours in a week.[46] There is not quite the same exclusion of part-time workers from the Unfair Dismissals Acts and other legislation. Instead, working weeks will not be counted as weeks of continuous employment where the worker "is not normally expected to work for at least" eight hours in the relevant week.[47] What exactly is meant by "normally expected to work" in this context has not been authoritatively decided; the comparable phrase in the British legislation is being under a contract "which normally involves employment" for a specified period. Where the position is not clear from the very terms of the contract, account can be taken of the average hours the employee worked, although the average will not always be taken as conclusive.

It has been held that the times during which part-time firemen were on call constituted working hours for these purposes.[48] In *Limerick Health Authority v. Ryan*,[49] where a midwife sought redundancy compensation, Kenny J. observed that the then 18 hours minimum "does not apply when the employer does not or cannot specify the hours during which the employee is to do the work and when its nature requires that the person employed has to be available to do it at all times."[50] It has been held that teachers are entitled to add to the actual hours they teach, a period for preparation for classes and for dealing with homework.[51]

---

[44]. Directive 77/187, O.J. No. L 61/126 (1977).
[45]. European Communities (Safeguarding Employees' Rights on the Transfer of Undertakings) Regulations 1980, S.I. No. 306.
[46]. 1967 Act, s.4(2), as amended by 1991 Act.
[47]. 1977 Act, s.2(4), and 1973 Act, Schedule 1, para. 8, as amended by 1991 Act.
[48]. *Bartlett v. Kerry C.C.* (U.D. 178/78); compare *Suffolk C.C. v. Secretary of State* [1984] I.C.R. 882.
[49]. [1969] I.R. 194.
[50]. *ibid.* at 198.
[51]. *Sinclair v. Dublin City V.E.C.* (UD 349/86); compare *Girls Public Day School Trust v. Khanna* [1987] I.C.R. 339.

Absences which are deemed weeks of service

Unless special provision was made, an employee who was temporarily absent on account of illness or on holidays, or for some other reason, might not be entitled to credit for those periods, although he would not suffer a complete break in his continuity of service. Accordingly, it is provided that a period of absence due to a lay off, to sickness or injury, or otherwise "by agreement with his employers", shall count as a period of service for these purposes.[52] But not more than 26 weeks absence on these grounds, between consecutive periods of employment, can be so counted.[53] Any period of absence to serve in the Reserve Defence Force is counted.

Whether the absence was due to a lay off or to sickness or injury is a question of fact.[54] What exactly is meant by "agreement with" or "arrangement with" the employer is another key concept calling for authoritative exposition. It has been held in England that employees who worked on alternate weeks could have their "off weeks" counted for the purpose of continuity, because there was an arrangement with their employer that they could be absent on those weeks.[55] It was also held in England that where an employee was dismissed but was later re-employed, on the basis that he should be regarded as continuously employed from when he was first hired, the period during which he was dismissed was an absence from work by arrangement with his employer.[56] Holidays should fall within this term; they are expressly mentioned in the redundancy payments legislation.[57]

Special provisions for continuity are contained in the legislation on maternity, adoptive, parental and carer's leave. A mother absent for ante-natal care, on maternity leave and on leave for special health and safety considerations is deemed to have been in employment during these periods,[58] but not for the purpose of making social welfare contributions. Additional maternity leave does not break continuity.[59] An employee absent on adoptive leave, or on parental or carer's leave, is deemed to be in employment, except for social welfare contributions; carer's leave also affects superannuation benefits.[60]

Industrial action

There are special rules for continuity of employment when the employees are on strike or have been locked out, or the parties are engaged in some other forms of industrial action.[61]

[52.] 1973 Act, Schedule 1, para. 10, and 1967 Act, Schedule 1, para.8.

[53.] *cf.* 1967 Act, Schedule 1, para. 8, where the maximum periods for the different kinds of absences vary.

[54.] *e.g. Harte v. Telecord Holdings Co.* (McWilliam J., May 18, 1979).

[55.] *Lloyds Bank v. Secretary of State* [1979] 1 W.L.R. 498.

[56.] *Ingram v. Foxan* [1984] I.C.R. 685.

[57.] 1967 Act, Schedule 3, paras. 5(1)(b)(ii) and 7.

[58.] Maternity Protection Act 1994, s.22(1).

[59.] *ibid.* at s.22(2).

[60.] Adoptive Leave Act 1995, s.15, and Parental Leave Act 1998, s.14 and Carer's Leave Act 2001, s.13(1)(b).

[61.] See, *infra*, p. 226.

NOTICE AND REASONS

In addition to such rights as employees possess under their employment contracts or at common law to advance notice of dismissal and to be informed of the reasons why it is intended to dismiss them, since 1973 and 1977, respectively, they have a statutory right to minimum notice of dismissal and also to a statement of reasons in writing.

Minimum notice

As is explained in the previous chapter, under their employment contracts most employees are entitled to a period of notice before they can be lawfully dismissed, except in cases of summary dismissal for good cause. This right is supplemented by section 4 of the Minimum Notice and Terms of Employment Act 1973 which gives employees covered by that Act a right to a minimum period of paid notice of dismissal, which cannot be contracted out of. The 1973 Act does not deal with the actual form of a dismissal notice. As Henchy J. observed the Act: "is concerned only with the period referred to in the notice, and it matters not what form the notice takes so long as it conveys to the employee that it is proposed that he will lose his employment at the end of a period which is expressed or necessarily implied in the notice. There is nothing in the Act to suggest that the notice given should be stringently or technically construed as if it were analogous to a notice to quit."[62] All that the Act does is require that notice be given which is of at least a specified duration.

Workers covered

On account of how section 1 of the 1973 Act defines the term "employee" for the purposes of that Act, it would seem that some persons providing personal services who might strictly be self-employed fall within that Act. For the Act applies to a person working under a "contract with an employer . . . whether it be a contract of service, of apprenticeship or otherwise . . . ." The Act does not contain the stipulation that has become common since 1993 of applying to employment agency personnel. It does not apply to established civil servants, members of the permanent Defence Forces and of the Garda Síochána, merchant seamen and what may be described as close family/domestic employments. Also excluded from the Act are employees who are "normally expected to work" for that employer for less than eight hours a week.[63]

Notice periods

Depending on the circumstances, a notice that an employee is being laid off can be a dismissal notice. In *Industrial Yarns Ltd. v. Greene*,[64] as part of a settlement of an industrial dispute, a group of employees were laid off and could later apply to be made redundant. It was held that, in the circumstances there, their lay off

---

[62]   *Boland Ltd. v. Ward* [1988] I.L.R.M. 382 at 389, followed in *Waterford Multiport Ltd. v. Fagan* [1999] E.L.R. 185.

[63]   s.3(1)(a), as amended by Workers Protection (Regular Part-Time Employees) Act 1991.

[64]   [1984] I.L.R.M. 15.

constituted a dismissal because it was not really a lay off; the employer knew that there was no real prospect of them being re-employed in the foreseeable future. Since their employment contracts did not empower the employer to suspend employees without pay, by ceasing to employ them and pay them wages, the employer repudiated their contracts, thereby entitling them to treat his action as a dismissal. On the other hand, if an employee was indeed laid off by agreement, he was not dismissed. If subsequently a dismissal notice is served on him, the effect is that "the contract of employment, the operation of which had been suspended, had been reinstated for the purpose of terminating it".[65]

The length of notice to which an employee is entitled under the 1973 Act depends on how long he has worked for that employer. The initial qualifying period for the very minimum notice, of one week, is thirteen weeks continuous employment.[66] A week for these purposes is defined as seven consecutive days.[67] The maximum notice period under the Act of eight weeks, is for employees with fifteen years or more continuous service. The lengths of notice for relevant service are as follows:

Period of service	Length of notice
13 weeks — 2 years:	1 week
2 years — 5 years:	2 weeks
5 years — 10 years:	4 weeks
10 years — 15 years:	6 weeks
15 years upwards:	8 weeks

These periods can be varied by ministerial order.

An employee who is guilty of such misconduct as would warrant his summary dismissal is not entitled to notice of dismissal under the 1973 Act.[68]

Where an employer gave notice but then finds that there is work for an additional period, he may extend the notice week by week or perhaps longer. Ordinarily, the fact that he did not terminate the employment on foot of the original notice does not mean that an entirely new notice must be given when the relationship is eventually terminated. Thus, in *Bolands Ltd. v. Ward*,[69] a receiver appointed over the business gave bakery employees notices that complied with the Act. He then extended those notices for several weeks until the plant closed. It was held that the 1973 Act had been complied with. This would not be the case, however, where "an employer was improperly or fraudulently manipulating contracts of employment and, consequently, the Act itself, so as to evade the requirements of the Act by a series of such postponements".[70]

---

65. *Irish Leathers Ltd. v. Minister for Labour* [1986] I.R. 177 at 181.
66. *ibid.* at s.4(1).
67. s.1.
68. s.8.
69. [1988] I.L.R.M. 382.
70. *ibid.* at 391.

Payment

During the notice period required by the 1973 Act the employee is entitled to be paid the remuneration provided for in his contract.[71] This is so even if he does not do any work. If the job has normal working hours, the employee is entitled to be paid in respect of all times, during those hours, when he is ready and willing to work;[72] if there are no normal working hours, the remuneration payable is at least the average of what the employee earned during the 13 weeks before the notice was given.[73]

In *Irish Leathers Ltd. v. Minister for Labour*,[74] it was held that the full remuneration as prescribed in the Act must be paid and that an employer is not entitled in effect to set off, against that remuneration, any unemployment benefit the employee may have been receiving during the notice period. According to Barrington J., the employee's entitlement is to "receive from his employer a fixed sum of money determined in a manner set out by statute"; to hold otherwise "would be to hold that the State in effect would be obliged to subsidise employers who fail to fulfil their statutory duties".[75] If, on the other hand, the employee is re-employed on a temporary basis during the notice period, the employer can in effect set off the remuneration earned in that period against the sum prescribed by the Act. In *Irish Shipping Ltd. v. Byrne*,[76] where workers were dismissed on their employer being wound up, but they continued to work for the liquidator on a temporary basis, it was held that the remuneration they got from the liquidator could be deducted from the sums payable to them under the 1973 Act.

Peremptory nature

The minimum notice requirements are translated into a legal obligation by rendering them a term of the employment contract, should the contract provide for a shorter period for notice of dismissal.[77] The obligation to pay remuneration during the requisite period is rendered peremptory by stipulating that any provision in a contract which purports to exclude or limit this right shall be void.[78] However, an employee may accept payment of the remuneration he would have earned during the notice period in lieu of the prescribed notice.[79]

Additionally, "on any occasion" the employee may waive his right to notice. In the *Industrial Yarns Ltd.* case, it was held that any such waiver "must be clear and unambiguous".[80] There, applications sent in by workers, who believed they were laid off, for redundancy compensation were found not to be waivers of their right to be paid during the minimum notice period. It remains to be determined

---

71. Schedule 2, para. 1.
72. *ibid*., para. 2.
73. *ibid*., para. 3.
74. [1986] I.R. 177.
75. Compare *Westwood v. Secretary of State* [1985] A.C. 20.
76. [1987] I.R. 468.
77. s.4(5).
78. s.5(3).
79. s.7.
80. [1984] I.L.R.M. at 23.

how the prohibition against contracting out of the right to the stipulated payments is to be reconciled with permitting a waiver of the right to notice.

Reasons

Either arising from the terms of their employment contracts or from the common law and constitutional principle of *audi alteram partem*, many employees are entitled to be informed of the reasons why it is a proposed to dismiss them.

This is supplemented by section 14(4) of the Unfair Dismissals Act 1977, which entitles an employee (covered by the 1977-93 Acts) who has been dismissed to be given written particulars of the principal grounds for dismissing him. That information must be furnished within 14 days of the employee requesting it. No particular sanction is laid down for where such a request has not been complied with.

UNFAIR DISMISSAL

A most unsatisfactory feature in the 1970s common law and contractual rules concerning dismissal was that, provided an employer paid the salary in lieu of notice due, he could dismiss an employee for any reason whatsoever, no matter how arbitrary it might be, without paying any compensation. So far as the general law was concerned, a person's security of employment depended entirely on the employer's whim. If for any reason at all the employer took objection to an employee, the latter had no legal protection against being sacked. Perhaps dismissal on the grounds of the worker's sex, race or religion might be unconstitutional; that issue does not appear to have been canvassed in the Superior Courts in the context of private sector employment. A frequent cause of industrial disputes was dismissals; lacking any legal protection against what they saw as arbitrary dismissals, employees would often resort to strike action in order to protect their jobs. Disputes about dismissals are "trade disputes" for the purpose of the law regarding strikes, lock-outs and picketing,[81] but the usual immunity from liability in tort is conditioned on all individual grievance procedures being exhausted.[82] At times trade unions and employers negotiate dismissals procedure agreements, which contain a mechanism for dealing with employees' grievances in this area. Depending on the nature of the agreed procedure, it might become an implied term of the employment contract. When most categories of public sector employees are faced with dismissals, they can have their grievances aired in the appropriate conciliation and arbitration scheme.

The Unfair Dismissals Acts 1977-93

In response to the inadequacies in the general law, the Unfair Dismissals Act 1977 was passed. As well as providing protection for employees against arbitrary dismissal decisions, this Act was also aimed at cutting down the number of industrial disputes, leading to strikes, lock-outs and picketing. This Act, amended in 1993, is modelled on similar legislation introduced in Britain in 1971. However,

---

[81.] Industrial Relations Act 1990, s.8; see *Industrial Relations Law*, pp.125-126.

[82.] *ibid.*, s.9; see *Industrial Relations Law*, pp. 143-146.

the two measures are far from being identical and, accordingly, British cases on unfair dismissals should be treated with caution as guides to what the position under the 1977-93 Acts might be. Another source of inspiration for the 1977 Act was the International Labour Organisation's (I.L.O.) Recommendation No.119 on the Termination of Employment; that document was since reviewed by the I.L.O., eventually resulting in the Termination of Employment Convention of 1982.[83]

The 1977-93 Acts do not displace the common law claim for damages for breach of contract; that is an alternative mode of redress and at times it may be more advantageous to claim under the contract rather than pursue the statutory remedy before a rights commissioner or the Employment Appeals Tribunal. Formerly, the mere notification of a claim under the common law precluded making any claim for unfair dismissal and vice versa. Since 1993, however, the statutory redress is precluded once the hearing of a common law claim for damages has commenced. And no common law claim may be brought once a rights commissioner has made a recommendation or a hearing before the Tribunal has commenced.[84]

Although the 1977 Act has been in force for nearly 25 years, its requirements have been the subject of comparatively few reported Supreme Court and High Court cases. There has been a vast quantity of Employment Appeal Tribunal (hereinafter referred to as the E.A.T.) and Circuit Court decisions. An excellent selection of cases on these Acts have been published by the Federation of Irish Employers,[85] which readers seeking enlightenment on the present practice should consult. Unlike the position in Britain, the Superior Courts here have not yet laid down general guidelines for applying several of the 1977 Act's central requirements. Accordingly, there is the inevitable degree of inconsistency between the approaches taken by different divisions of the E.A.T. and the several Circuit Court judges.

Employees not covered

The Unfair Dismissals Acts apply to employees and apprentices, and have been extended to cover employment agency personnel.[86] But not all employees or apprentices are entitled to redress under these Acts. Generally, *locus standi* to bring claims requires one year's continuous employment and certain categories of worker are excluded from the Acts' scope.

Insufficient continuity of employment

To begin with, the employee must possess the requisite continuity of employment,[87] which is one year's service, meaning 52 weeks' continuous service in full-time or regular part-time employment.[88] It would seem that a week for these

---

[83] See *Napier, supra*, p. 185.
[84] s.15 of 1977 Act, as amended by s.10 of 1993 Act.
[85] D. Madden & T. Kerr, *Unfair Dismissal* (2nd ed., 1996).
[86] 1993 Act, s.13.
[87] See, *supra*, pp. 188-193.
[88] s.2(1)(a); *cf. McGavan v. McLaughlin* [2000] E.L.R. 106.

purposes means seven days. Special rules are contained in the First schedule to the Minimum Notice and Terms of Employment Act 1973, for calculating continuity of employment. Further, where it can be shown that an employee was dismissed but, within a short period, has been re-employed and the employer's purpose was wholly or partly to avoid liability under the 1997-93 Acts, continuity does not break.

The requisite one year's continuity is not required where the employee was dismissed for any of the following reasons: trade union membership or activities, as defined in section 6(2)(a) of the 1977 Act;[89] his actions in upholding the national minimum wage;[90] pregnancy, in circumstances set out in 1977 Act;[91] exercising any of the statutory rights to leave, under the legislation on maternity, adoptive, carer's and parental leave.[92]

Public service

Those public sector workers who are excluded are members of the Defence Forces and of the Garda Síochána,[93] persons employed "by or under the State"[94] and "officers" of any local authority, health board (other than temporary), vocational education committee or committee of agriculture.[95]

Part-time workers

Except for dismissals for protected trade union membership or activities,[96] part-time workers, meaning those who "are not normally expected to work for at least" eight hours a week, are excluded from these Acts.[97]

Over retirement age

Except for dismissals for protected trade union membership or activities,[98] these Acts do not apply to employees who have reached the pensionable age for social welfare purposes, which is 66 years of age, nor to employees who, on or before the date they were dismissed, had reached "the normal retiring age for employees of the same employer in similar employment. . . ."[99] For instance, a "lad porter" with Iarnrod Éireann, who lost his job on reaching 20 years of age, was held to fall outside the 1977 Act because that age was the normal retiring age for that category of employee.[100]

Where the employment contract does not stipulate any retirement age, what is the normal retiring age depends on the circumstances if there was a general prac-

---

89. 1993 Act, s.14, and 1977 Act, s.6(7).
90. National Minimum Wage Act 2000, s.36(2).
91. Maternity Protection Act 1994, s.38(5).
92. *ibid.*, Adoptive Leave Act 1995, s.25, and Parental Leave Act 1998, s.25(2)(b).
93. s.2(1)(d) and (e).
94. s.2(1)(h); see *post*, p. 281.
95. s.2(1)(i) and (j), as amended by 1993 Act, s.3(a).
96. 1977 Act, s.6(7), and 1993 Act, s.14.
97. s.2(4), as amended by Worker Protection (Regular Part-Time Employees) Act 1991.
98. 1993 Act, s.14.
99. s.2(1)(b).
100. *Humphries v. Iarnrod Éireann* (U.D. 1099/88).

tice that employees in the claimant's position would retire before the State pension age.[101] Even if there is a contractual provision, its requirements may be negated by the actual practice at the workplace of those employees' usually retiring at a later age.[102] The usual age here does not mean the statistical average age but the age at which those employees usually would expect to retire.[103] It remains to be seen whether an assurance given to an employee, that he would be retired at a date after the normal age, will operate as an estoppel against the employer, regarding when the normal retirement age is for the purpose of the 1977-93 Acts.[104]

Close family/domestics

Employees who are employed by a close member of the family in a domestic situation fall outside the Acts,[105] except where they are dismissed for protected trade union membership or activities,[106] for their pregnancy or related grounds,[107] or for seeking to avail of leave under the legislation on maternity, adoptive or parental leave.[108]

Trainees and probationers

Although the 1977-93 Acts apply to apprentices, excluded from their scope are several categories of trainees, apprentices and probationers. But these are not excluded where the dismissal was for protected trade union membership or activities,[109] for their pregnancy or related grounds,[110] or for seeking to avail of leave under the legislation on maternity, adoptive, carer's and parental leave.[111]

Those otherwise excluded from the 1977-93 Acts are employees who are undergoing training for any of the following purposes:[112] to become qualified or registered, as the case may be, as a nurse, pharmacist, health inspector, medical laboratory technician, occupational therapist, physiotherapist, speech therapist, radiographer or social worker. A statutory apprentice, within the terms of the Industrial Training Act 1977, is not protected by these Acts if he was dismissed either within six months after his apprenticeship commenced or within one month after the apprenticeship was completed.[113] In the case of any employee who is undergoing training or who is on probation, these Acts do not apply where the contract is in writing and it stipulates that its duration shall not be longer than one year.[114] Apprentices employed by FÁS and also persons receiving a training allowance from or undergoing training or instruction by FÁS are excluded.[115]

[101.] *Waite v. Government Communications Headquarters* [1983] 2 A.C. 714.
[102.] *ibid.*
[103.] *Muldoon v. British Telecommunications p.l.c.* [1987] I.C.R. 450.
[104.] *cf. Hughes v. Dept. of Social Security* [1985] 1 A.C. 776.
[105.] s.2(1)(c).
[106.] *supra*, n. 82.
[107.] *supra*, n. 83.
[108.] *supra*, n. 84.
[109.] *supra*, n. 82.
[110.] *supra*, n. 84.
[111.] *supra*, n. 92
[112.] s.3(2).
[113.] s.4.
[114.] s.3(1).

Fixed term or specific purpose contracts

Where the contract in question is for a fixed term or for a specific purpose, it is possible for an employee to waive in writing the protection of the 1977-93 Acts. The Acts do not define what exactly is envisaged as an employment contract for a fixed term; it is the opposite of a contract for an indeterminate duration. It has been held that not alone does a contract for a specified or ascertainable duration fall into this category but there is a fixed term contract even where it contains a provision enabling its lawful termination prior to the specified expiry date. In *Dixon v. B.B.C.*,[116] a contract due to expire on May 1, 1976, unless previously determined by one week's notice in writing by either side, was held to be a fixed term contract.[117] That is because, otherwise, the protective legislation could easily be evaded by the manipulation of contracts for specified terms, which could be extended but which also could be terminated at short notice. If contracts like that in *Dixon* were not fixed term contracts, their expiry on their specified due date and non-renewal would never constitute a dismissal as defined in the unfair dismissals legislation. The mere expiry of a term is only a dismissal in the case of fixed term contracts.

Where a fixed term contract expires and is not renewed, or where a specified purpose contract ceases, the 1977-93 Acts do not apply where the contract itself is in writing, it is signed by or for the employer and by the employee, and it expressly states that these Acts are not to apply to the contract on it expiring or ceasing.[118] But the termination of such contracts, other than by their normal expiry or cesser, remains a dismissal within the terms of these Acts. It was contended in *B.B.C. v. Kelly-Phillips*[119] that waivers of this nature are not effective where the term of a fixed term contract has expired but the employee is retained on broadly similar terms for another specified period, on the grounds that the extended period is subject to a new contract rather than being a prolongation of the original contract. That view was rejected by the Court of Appeal. The incentive for making that argument does not exist under the 1977-94 Acts; they do not require that the contract has a duration of at least a year for a waiver to operate.

An amendment was introduced in section 3(b) of the 1993 Act in order to ensure that employers would not abuse the exclusion of fixed term and specific purpose contracts.

Replacement for employees away on maternity, adoptive or carer's leave

The 1977-93 Acts do not apply to a person who is replacing an employee who has taken maternity or additional maternity leave or time off for ante or post-natal care, or statutory adoptive or carer's leave, in the following circumstances:[120]

[115.] s.2(1)(f).

[116.] [1979] 1 Q.B. 546.

[117.] Followed in *O'Mahony v. Trinity College* [1998] E.L.R. 159.

[118.] s.2(2)(b).

[119.] [1998] I.C.R. 587.

[120.] Maternity Protection Act 1994, s.38(2), Adoptive Leave Act 1995, s.23, and Carer's Leave Act 2001, s.27(1).

Those are where, at the commencement of the job, that employee is informed in writing by the employer that the job will be terminated when the absent employee returns and, secondly, where the actual dismissal was to enable the latter employee to return to work. The maternity-related exclusion here would not seem to fall foul of the E.C.J.'s decision in *Webb v. Emo Air Cargo (U.K.) Ltd.*,[121] where a replacement for a woman who had taken maternity leave was herself dismissed because she became pregnant. There, however, it had earlier been decided that the replacement would remain employed when the women she had stood in for returned.

Transnationals

Special provision is made by section 2(3) of the 1977 Act and by section 25 of the Redundancy Payments Act 1967, for employees who ordinarily work outside the State.[122]

Alternative remedies

Where an employee resorts to certain alternative remedies available to him in connection with his dismissal, he cannot then claim under the 1977-93 Acts.[123] Those remedies are seeking damages for wrongful dismissal, in breach of contract, and making a claim under Part VII of the Employment Equality Act. In the former case, commencement of the hearing of the damages claim operates as a bar to the statutory redress. In the latter case, the bar operates where a claim was made to the Labour Court which either has been settled by mediation or that court has commenced an investigation.

Dismissal

In order to claim under the Unfair Dismissals Acts the employee must have been "dismissed" from his work. What constitutes a dismissal, actual and constructive, for these purposes is defined in section 1 of the Act and has been considered above.[124]

Unfair or justifiable?

Section 6 of the 1977 Act sets out when a dismissal shall be regarded as contravening these Acts. Its general scheme is as follows. The burden of proof is not on the employee but falls on the employer; unless the employer can show that there were "substantial grounds for justifying" the dismissal, it will be deemed to be unfair. What grounds justify a dismissal depends on all the circumstances of the case. Section 6 provides some help in this regard because it enumerates certain grounds which ordinarily would justify a dismissal — misconduct, inability to do the job and redundancy. It also lists grounds of dismissal which will be deemed unfair — union membership or activities, religious or political opinions, race or

---

[121.] (Case C 32/93) [1994] E.C.R. 3567; *ante*, pp. 148-150.

[122.] See *post*, pp. 258-259.

[123.] 1977 Act, s.15, as amended by 1993 Act, s.10.

[124.] *supra*, pp. 185-188.

colour, pregnancy or taking maternity or comparable leave, and what is termed unfair redundancy. Special rules exist for dismissals of employees who are on strike or who have been locked out of their jobs.[125]

When considering claims against employers, the E.A.T.'s and Circuit Court's approach is not so much determine if in all the circumstances the employee deserved to be dismissed; instead, the focus is on whether a reasonable employer would have dismissed him in those circumstances. As stated in *Bunyan v. United Dominions Trust (Ireland) Ltd.*,[126] one of the few reported cases on the key "fairness" question:

> "[T]he fairness or unfairness of dismissal is to be judged by the objective standard of the way in which a reasonable employer in those circumstances in that line of business would have behaved. The Tribunal therefore does not decide the question whether or not, on evidence before it, the employee should be dismissed. The decision to dismiss has been taken and our function is to test such decision against what we consider the reasonable employer would have done and/or concluded."[127]

In another instance, concerning dismissal for alleged dishonesty, it was said that:

> "It is not for the Tribunal to seek to establish the guilt or innocence of the claimant, nor is it for the Tribunal to indicate or consider whether we, in the employer's position, would have acted as [he] did in his investigation, or concluded as [he] did or decided as he did, as to do so would substitute our own mind and decision for that of the employer. Our responsibility is to consider against the facts what a reasonable employer in [the same] position and circumstances at that time would have done and decided and to set this up as a standard against which [the employer's] action and decision can be judged."[128]

Considerable emphasis is placed on the employer following fair procedures, be they the actual grievance procedures obtaining at the workplace or the more general principles of fair play. Following fair procedures will ensure that the employer is more fully informed before he takes a serious decision; the employee also has the opportunity to defend himself against any allegations made against him. Thus, in the *Bunyan* case, where the claimant was dismissed for allegedly having attempted to undermine his managing director's authority, the dismissal was held to have been unfair because the employee had been denied natural justice.[129] The Tribunal's view there was that "compliance with the requirements of natural justice could have resulted in the decision to dismiss the claimant not being taken".[130] Exceptionally, however, a dismissal will be sustained even though the agreed or the customary procedures were not followed. According to Barron J. in *Loftus and Healy v. An Bord Telecom*,[131] the question to be

---

125. See *infra*, pp. 224-225.
126. [1982] I.L.R.M. 404.
127. *ibid.* at 413.
128. *Looney & Co. Ltd. v. Looney* (UD 843/1984).
129. Similarly, *McCarthy v. Coras Iompair Éireann* (Circ. Ct., May 10, 1985).
130. [1982] I.L.R.M. at 413.

determined is: "not whether the plaintiffs were deprived of procedures to which they were entitled, but whether the denial to them of such procedures is such that the (employer) must be deemed to have failed to establish [the stated basis of that dismissal] as the whole or the main reason for and justifying their dismissal."[132]

It was held in England that, in cases where agreed or fair procedures were not followed, the issue should not then be whether the employer would have decided differently if he had adopted the proper procedures. According to the Law Lords, in such cases "[i]t is what the employer did that wants to be judged, not what he might have done".[133]

Determining the reason

It must first be determined why the employee was dismissed. Employees have an express statutory right to be given a written statement of the reasons for their dismissal.[134] A request for this document must be made within 14 days of the dismissal. Where a claim is made under these Acts the employer is not confined to advancing the grounds contained in this statement; the Tribunal or court may take account of any other grounds which would justify the dismissal.[135]

Deemed unfair reasons

If it is demonstrated that the dismissal was wholly or mainly for any of the following reasons, it is deemed by section 6(2) of the Act to have been unfair. Except for trade union related dismissals, however, the catalogue of deemed unfair grounds in section 6(2) is stated to be "[w]ithout prejudice to the generality of" section 6(1) of the 1977 Act. It therefore would seem that this deeming is not an iron inflexible rule where these are the reasons; in other words, very exceptional circumstances may exist which may justify a dismissal on these grounds. The burden of proving that the dismissal was for one of these reasons is on the employee.

Trade union membership or activities Section 6(2)(a) of the 1977 Act deems it to be automatically unfair, regardless of whether there may be "substantial grounds justifying" it,[136] to dismiss an employee "wholly or mainly" on account of his:

> "Membership, or proposal that he or another person become a member of, or his engaging in activities on behalf of a trade union or excepted body ... where the times at which he engages in such activities are outside his hours of work or are times during his hours of work in which he is permitted [by contract] to so engage."

Most employees who normally are not protected by the 1977-93 Acts can avail of this prohibition, namely those with less than one's year's continuous service, part-time workers, those over the normal retirement age, close family/domestics,

---

131. Barron J., O.J.I.S. Lab.L. 135.
132. *ibid.* at 138.
133. *Polkey v. A.E. Dayton Services Ltd.* [1988] 1 A.C. 344 at 355.
134. s.14(4).
135. *ibid.*
136. s.6(7), which, *inter alia*, disapplies subs.(1) and (6).

and apprentices, trainees and probationers referred to in sections 3 and 4 of the 1977 Act.[137]

Upholding minimum wage Section 36(1) of the National Minimum Wage Act 2000 prohibits employers from taking action against employees because they might or will qualify for the statutory minimum wage, or for seeking to exercise a right under that Act or lawfully opposing breaches of that Act. A dismissal on any of those grounds is deemed to be an unfair dismissal in the absence of very substantial justifying grounds. This applies even where the employee has less than one year's continuous service, provided however he works for at least 18 hours per week.

Pregnancy and other leave It is presumed to be unfair, unless there are very substantial justifying grounds, to dismiss employees on account of pregnancy or availing of certain statutory leave connected therewith, including adoptive, parental and *force majeure* leave, and also carer's leave. Certain employees who normally are not protected by the 1977-93 Acts can claim unfair dismissal on these grounds, namely those with less than one year's continuous service, close relatives, and trainees, apprentices and probationers referred to in sections 2(1)(f), (g), 3 and 4 of the 1997 Act. Following the E.C.J.'s *Webb* case,[138] the pregnancy ground was amended to read dismissal on account of the employee's "pregnancy, giving birth or breastfeeding or any matters connected therewith".[139] Those categories of leave, entitlement to which is reinforced by the 1977-93 Acts, are the "exercise or proposed exercise" of any form of protective leave or natal care absence under the Maternity Protection Act 1994, adoptive leave or additional adoptive leave under the Adoptive Leave Act 1995, and parental and *force majeure* leave under the Parental Leave Act 1998, and leave under the Carer's Leave Act 2001.

Dismissal on the pregnancy grounds would also be remediable in the Circuit Court under Part VII of the Employment Equality Act 1998, as would dismissals for availing of the above leaves where that would amount to proscribed sex discrimination.

Sex, race, religion, politics, etc. Dismissal on the following grounds is deemed to be unfair for the purposes of the 1977-93 Acts unless there is a very substantial justifying ground, *viz.* the employee's "religious or political opinions", "race, colour or sexual orientation", "age" and "membership of the travelling community".[140] Unlike those dismissed for the three categories of reasons summarised above, employees with less than one year's continuous service cannot claim on these grounds and are left to a remedy under the Employment Equality Act 1998. Alternatively, persons dismissed for any of the above grounds, other than political opinion, may seek redress by applying to the Equality Authority or the Labour Court under Part VII of the Employment Equality Act 1998, even if they have less than one year's service.

[137.] *supra*, pp. 198-202.
[138.] (Case C 32/93) [1994] E.C.R. 3567; *ante*, p. 148-150.
[139.] Maternity Protection Act 1994, s.38(4), amending the 1977 Act. See, generally, M. Bolger & C. Kimber, *Sex Discrimination Law* (2000), pp. 309-313 and 329-331.
[140.] 1993 Act, s.6, amending the 1977 Act.

Victimisation A dismissal is deemed to be unfair, unless there is a very substantial justifying ground, where the reason was that the employee is either a party to or is a likely witness to civil or criminal proceedings which have been brought against the employer or which are proposed or threatened to be brought against the employer.[141]

Safety representative There is a general prohibition in the health and safety legislation against placing a safety representative at any disadvantage in relation to his employment[142] but it is not tied in with the 1977-93 Acts.

Transfer of undertaking Where all or part of the business or undertaking in which the worker was employed is transferred to another enterprise and the employee is dismissed on account of the transfer, such dismissals are prohibited and, in consequence, would be deemed to be unfair.[143] But that is not the case where the dismissal was for "economic, technical or organisational reasons entailing changes in the workforce".[144]

Justifying dismissals

Section 6(4) of the 1977 Act then sets out several grounds on which dismissals can be justified by the employer. In other words, if the dismissal was "wholly or mainly" for any of these reasons, there is a strong likelihood that it will not be unfair, *viz.* misconduct, inability for several reasons to do the job and redundancy. But these are not the exclusive reasons for upholding a dismissal; it will also be upheld where the employer can demonstrate "other substantial grounds" which would justify the dismissal. Except for dismissals for trade union related reasons set out in section 6(2)(a),[145] the other deemed unfair dismissals (section 6(2)(b)-(h)) can nonetheless be justified on other substantial grounds but it would seem that those grounds must be most compelling to warrant dismissing employees who, *inter alia*, uphold the minimum wage, are pregnant or take the various statutory leaves, or on account of their sex, race etc. An additional consideration is the reasonableness or otherwise of the employer in all the circumstances and whether, in particular, he complied with existing grievance procedures or other relevant procedures.

Misconduct If an employee commits one or more acts of misconduct, which would cause an average employer in the circumstances to dismiss him, his dismissal would usually be upheld, especially where fair or agreed disciplinary procedures were followed. The actual term used in section 6(4)(b) is "conduct" and not misconduct; the full significance of this remains to be determined. Among the questions which arise under this heading are whether the act or acts in the circumstances are sufficiently serious in general terms to warrant dismissal; whether they warrant summary dismissal or only dismissal with full notice; whether the

---

[141] s.6(2)(c) and (4).
[142] Safety, Health and Welfare at Work Act 1989, s.13(9).
[143] European Communities (Safeguarding of Employees' Rights on Transfer of Undertakings Regulations, 1980, S.I. No. 306; see *post*, p. 230 *et seq.*
[144] *ibid.*, reg. 5(1), e.g. *Whitehouse v. Charles Blatchford & Sons Ltd.* [2000] I.C.R. 542.
[145] *supra*, p. 204.

employee should have been warned in advance of the likely consequences of his acts; whether the requisite procedures were followed. The Tribunal has described its general approach to misconduct in these terms:

"In deciding whether or not the dismissal . . . was unfair we apply a test of reasonableness to misconduct in these terms

(1) the nature and extent of the enquiry carried out by the [employer] prior to the decision to dismiss . . . and

(2) the conclusion arrived at by the [employer] that on the basis of the information resulting from such enquiry, the [employee] should be dismissed."[146]

The overriding test is reasonableness: did the employer have reasonable grounds for believing that the employee had misconducted himself and was the sanction of dismissal proportionate to that conduct?

Incapacity for the job Another justification for upholding a dismissal is that the employee is not capable, qualified or competent to do his work or it would be unlawful for the employer to continue employing him. The catch-all heading "incapacity" used here perhaps puts the position too strongly; in the words of the Act the dismissal may be justifiable if it was due to:

"(a) the capability, competence or qualifications of the employee for perform-ing work of the kind which he was employed by the employer to do. . . . (or)

(d) the employee being unable to work or continue to work in the position which he held without contravention (by him or by his employer) of a duty or restriction imposed by or under any statute or instrument made under statute."[147]

Allegations of incapability to do the work usually concern absences from work, such as on account of illness, or irregular or persistent late attendance at work. When considering allegations of incompetence, account must always be taken of the employer's apparent failure to detect that defect when hiring the employee and not remedying it by appropriate training. The Tribunal does not yet appear to have dealt with a dismissal caused by the employee not having the requisite "qualification" for his job. Examples of where it would be illegal to continue employing a worker include where the requisite consents have not been obtained under the Aliens Act 1935. As is the case with dismissals for misconduct, the overriding test is that of reasonableness; had the employer reasonable grounds for believing that the worker was incapable as described here and, in all the circum-stances, was dismissal a reasonable and fair response to the situation.

Redundancy Another justification for upholding a dismissal is that the employee was made redundant.[148] Redundancy for these purposes has the same meaning as

---

[146.] *Hennessy v. Read and Write Shop Ltd.* (UD 192/28).

[147.] s.6(4)(a) and (d).

[148.] s.6(4)(c).

in the Redundancy Payments Acts 1967-1979.[149] However, even if there was a redundancy, the employee may succeed in a claim under the Unfair Dismissals Acts on the grounds that he was unfairly selected to be made redundant.[150] Many claims are made for compensation for so-called "unfair redundancy" because employees often stand to recover a larger sum under the 1977-93 Acts than the lump sum redundancy payment they would be entitled to under the 1967-1979 Acts. In order to succeed in a claim under this head, the employee must first demonstrate that "the circumstances constituting the redundancy applied equally to one or more other employees in similar employment" with the employer and who were not dismissed. In other words, there were other employees doing that type of work and who could have been made redundant but were not dismissed. It is not always essential that the employees being compared here all work in the very same location or unit, provided they are in "similar employment".

Where this is established, the claimant will succeed if he shows that the actual reason why he, and not one of his comparable employees, was selected is a ground which would not justify his dismissal. These grounds may be any of the deemed unfair reasons referred to above or some other reason which, in all the circumstances, was unfair to the employee. If the employee's selection was in breach of an agreed or customary arrangement for dealing with redundancies it will be deemed to have been unfair unless there were "special reasons" for departing from that procedure.

Other substantial grounds In an appropriate case, a dismissal will be upheld where it was caused by grounds other than redundancy, incapacity or misconduct, as described above. What these grounds are and whether in any particular instance they would justify a dismissal depends on the entire circumstances of the case. Thus, there are Tribunal cases where third-party pressure to have the employee dismissed was held to justify[151] and not to justify[152] dismissal. Another ground which may justify dismissal is inability to obtain employer's liability insurance for the employee.[153] In *Flynn v. Power*,[154] the plaintiff was a school teacher employed by nuns at a convent school in a country town. She was openly living with a married man and had a child by him. Her employers asked her to terminate her relationship with that man on account of the example she was giving the school children. Costello J. held that, in those circumstances, her employers were entitled to "regard her conduct as a rejection of the norms of behaviour and the ideals which the school was endeavouring to instil in and to set for" the children.[155] They, accordingly, were entitled "to foster in their pupils norms of behaviour and religious tenets which the school had been established to promote".[156] Therefore, it was found, there were substantial grounds for dismissing

---

[149] See *infra*, p. 212 *et seq.*
[150] s.6(3).
[151] *e.g. Jackson v. John McCarthy & Co.* (UD 297/78).
[152] *e.g. Merrigan v. Home Counties Cleaning (Ireland) Ltd.* (UD 904/84).
[153] *Browne v. Aga Khan* (UD 332/87).
[154] [1985] I.R. 648.
[155] *ibid.* at 657.
[156] *ibid.* Similarly, *Berrisford v. Woodward Schools (Midland Division) Ltd.* [1991] I.C.R. 564.

her. As with the other grounds discussed above, the overriding test of the employer's actions is that of reasonableness and proportionality.

Employer's reasonableness

Two additional considerations were introduced in the 1994 amendments,[157] namely whether in all the circumstances the employer acted reasonably and, if there was some procedure governing dismissals, whether or to what extent the employer complied with it. Accordingly, compliance with any dismissal procedure is a factor considerably in the employer's favour; if such procedures as existed were disregarded, that strongly indicates unfairness unless there were special circumstances warranting departure from them. The broad employer's "reasonableness" criterion extends the enquiry considerably and confers on the tribunals and courts an extremely broad discretion in determining whether indeed a dismissal was unfair.

Redress

Where a qualified employee has been unfairly dismissed, his redress may take the form of getting his job back or obtaining a different job, or else the payment of compensation.[158] A claim for redress under the 1977-93 Acts may be made to a rights commissioner or to the Employment Appeals Tribunal.[159] There is an appeal from a recommendation of the commissioner to the E.A.T.[160] and there is an appeal from a decision of the E.A.T. to the Circuit Court,[161] by way of a full re-hearing of the case; there is a further appeal to the High Court, also by way of a full re-hearing of the dispute.[162] Regulations have been adopted that set out in detail the procedure for bringing these claims.

Notice of the claim must be given within six months of the date of dismissal,[163] which can make the precise timing of when the dismissal took place extremely important. In exceptional circumstances this period can be extended for a further six months.[164] Ordinarily, the date of dismissal is when the contract has ended,[165] which may depend on whether or not notice was given and/or payment in lieu was made. Certain events are deemed to constitute dismissals, for instance not permitting persons who took maternity or related leave, adoptive leave or parental leave, to return to work when their leave has expired.

Subject to some exceptions summarised above, the claimant must have been continuously employed by that employer at least 52 weeks prior to the dismissal date.[166] Where the hearing of any court proceedings for wrongful dismissal has commenced, no claim for unfair dismissal may be brought in respect of the same

---

[157.] 1993 Act, s.5(b), amending the 1977 Act.
[158.] 1963 Act, s.7.
[159.] *ibid.*, s.8 and Unfair Dismissals (Claims and Appeals) Regulations 1977, S.I. No.286.
[160.] *ibid.*, s.9 and S.I. No. 286 of 1977, *supra*.
[161.] 1993 Act, s.11.
[162.] *McCabe v. Lisney & Son* [1981] I.L.R.M. 289.
[163.] s.8(2)(a).
[164.] s.8(2)(b), added by s.7 of the 1993 Act.
[165.] s.1 (defining "date of dismissal") and, *supra*, pp. 189-190.
[166.] s.2(1)(a) and *supra* p. 188 *et seq*.

circumstances.[167] If since the date of the dismissal, ownership of the employer's business has changed, then the new owner becomes obliged to comply with whatever order for redress is made in the proceedings.[168]

There is no indication in the 1977-93 Acts of when any one of the modes of redress discussed below should be preferred over others, apart from what seems "appropriate having regard to all the circumstances."[169] Before opting for any one or more remedies, the rights commissioner, E.A.T. or court should seek to ascertain the views of the parties on the matter,[170] although they are not obliged always to follow the parties' preference or the employee's preference. But they are obliged to furnish reasons why one or other of the remedies were not ordered,[171] which frequently entails explaining why only compensation was awarded and not re-instatement or re-engagement.

Re-instatement

By re-instatement is meant the claimant getting his old job back as if he had never been dismissed. It is defined in the 1977 Act as re-instatement "in the position which he held immediately before his dismissal. . . ."[172] But if in the meantime the terms and conditions of workers in comparable positions improve or if those of the workforce there generally have improved, then the re-instatement will be on those improved terms.

Reinstatement is the employee's preferred remedy usually and, where it is ordered, will operate as from the date the employee was dismissed, thereby entitling him to remuneration for the entire intervening period. However, circumstances regarding the job itself, the employer or the claimant may dictate that some other redress should be awarded. Where the employee's actions substantially contributed to his dismissal, full re-instatement tends not to be ordered; instead the Tribunal directs re-engagement or, at times, re-instatement but as from some time after the dismissal, or compensation. If the job no longer exists then re-instatement can not be ordered.

Re-engagement

By re-engagement is meant being re-employed by the employer either in the same job or in a suitable different job. It is defined in the 1977 Act as re-engagement "either in the position which he held immediately before his dismissal or in a different position which would be reasonably suitable for him on such terms and conditions as are reasonable having regard to all the circumstances".[173] Among the reasons for not directing re-engagement are that relationships between the parties had deteriorated badly or that, due to changes which have been made, no suitable job is available. There is a tendency not to require that

---

[167] s.15(3), amended by s.10 of the 1993 Act.

[168] s.7(1)(c), added by s.6 of the 1993 Act.

[169] s.7(1).

[170] *State (Irish Pharmaceutical Union) v. Employment Appeals Tribunal* [1987] I.L.R.M. 386.

[171] s.8(1A), added by s.7 of the 1993 Act.

[172] s.7(1)(a).

[173] s.7(1)(b).

senior executives be re-engaged, because their dismissal almost always would have ruptured the essential degree of confidence the parties should have in each other.

Compensation

Where neither of these two modes are appropriate, compensation will be awarded, up to a maximum of two years' normal remuneration.[174] But an award of compensation will not be made simply because that is what the claimant prefers; his views are not decisive where it appears that the employer would be prepared to take him back. Where the employee suffered no financial loss, nonetheless compensation up to the equivalent of four weeks remuneration may be awarded in an appropriate case.[175]

Measuring the loss: The criteria laid down in the 1977 Act for ascertaining the amount to be paid in compensation is in respect of any financial loss incurred by the claimant and attributable to the dismissal "as is just and equitable having regard to all the circumstances,"[176] and is calculated in accordance with regulations that have been made. When making this "just and equitable" evaluation, the tribunal has a very wide discretion and may take account of, *inter alia,* both parties' conduct prior to the dismissal.[177]

Financial loss for these purposes is defined as "includ[ing] any actual loss and any estimated prospective loss of income and the value of any loss or diminution, attributable to the dismissal, of the rights of the employee under the Redundancy Payments Acts . . . or in relation to superannuation".[178] And remuneration is defined there as "includ[ing] allowances in the nature of pay and benefits in lieu of or in addition to pay".[179] Thus, not only loss of wages but all forms of financial loss reasonably resulting from the dismissal will be compensated. For this purpose, payments received under the Social Welfare Acts since the dismissal and under the Income Tax Acts by reason of the dismissal shall be disregarded.[180]

Adding to or subtracting from that sum: Once the amount of the financial loss has been determined, an additional amount may be awarded because of how badly the employer acted in the circumstances, because agreed dismissal procedures or a code of practice for handling dismissals had not been complied with or failure to have any such procedures.[181] Conversely, a deduction may be made from that sum reflecting the fact that the employee had been substantially or partly at fault in causing the loss and or contributed to his own dismissal.[182] A deduction may also be made where the employee failed to mitigate his losses.[183]

---

[174]. s.7(1)(c), amended by s.6 of the 1993 Act.
[175]. s.7(1)(c)(ii), added by s.6(a) of the 1993 Act.
[176]. s.7(1)(c)(i).
[177]. *Carney v. Balkan Tours Ltd.* [1997] 1 I.R. 153.
[178]. s.7(3).
[179]. *Ibid.*
[180]. s.7(2A), added by s.6(c) of the 1993 Act.
[181]. s.7(2)(a), (d) and (e) added by s.6(b) of the 1993 Act.
[182]. s.7(2)(b).
[183]. s.7(2)(c).

Ceiling on compensation: There is an overall ceiling on the amount of compensation which can be awarded, being 104 weeks of "normal remuneration",[184] as defined in the Unfair Dismissals (Calculation of Weekly Remuneration) Regulation, 1977.[185]

REDUNDANCY

In order for their business to survive, employers must compete in the market place, domestic and international. Successful competition will often require changes in the employer's establishment in response to new commercial pressures and technological innovation. At times, changes of that nature will involve a reduction of the workforce — be it an all-over reduction or the replacement of some existing employees by others who are more suitable for the changed nature of the job. In order to overcome the inevitable resistance by employees to their being put out of work through no fault of their own, it was found necessary at least to guarantee them compensation for losing their jobs. Often trade unions negotiate the amount of compensation to be paid to employees being made redundant and, if the union is in a strong bargaining position, substantial sums can be secured on their members' behalf, the amounts usually being based on a multiplier of each employee's present salary and his seniority. Disputes about redundancy are "trade disputes" for the purpose of the law regarding strikes, lock-outs and picketing,[186] but immunity from tort liability is conditional on individual grievance procedures being exhausted.

For many years there were provisions for paying redundancy compensation to several categories of employees in the public sector. Perhaps the best known of these, which gave rise to a very substantial body of litigation, was Article 10 of the 1922 Treaty between Ireland and Great Britain, whereby civil servants who retired in consequence of the change of regime and government were to be compensated.[187] Legislation governing local authorities often provided for compensating persons who lost their offices when the structures of local government were changed.[188] The first schedule to the Electricity (Supply) Act 1927 is a scheme for compensating employees who were made redundant as a result of nationalising the electricity supply industry and there are numerous provisions in the many Transport Acts providing for redundancy compensation when *C.I.E.* employees lost their jobs in the many re-organisations of that business.[189]

The Redundancy Payments Acts

The Redundancy Payments Acts 1967-79, were enacted principally to make it easier for employers to reorganise their businesses, by guaranteeing substantial

---

[184.] s.7(1)(c)(i).
[185.] S.I. No. 287 of 1977.
[186.] *Goulding Chemicals Ltd. v. Bolger* [1977] I.R. 211.
[187.] *cf. Wigg v. Attorney General* [1927] I.R. 285.
[188.] *cf. O'Neill v. Tipperary C.C. (Sough Riding)* [1926] I.R. 397.
[189.] *cf. Stedman v. Coras Iompair Éireann* [1967] I.R. 409 and s.48 of the Redundancy Payments Act 1967.

lump sum payments to workers who stood to lose their jobs in the course of re-organisation. These Acts apply to public as well as private sector employees, except for those who are not insured for all social welfare benefits. The 1967 Act is modelled on its British predecessor of the previous year and many of the British cases are helpful for interpretation.[190] But there are significant differences between parts of the Irish and British legislation, most notably, regarding what exactly constitutes becoming "redundant". As in the case with minimum notice and unfair dismissals, therefore, great care should be taken when relying on the British cases for guidance.

The 1967 Act was amended extensively in 1971 and again in 1979. What the Redundancy Payments Acts 1967-1979 principally do is require that an eligible employee who is made redundant be paid a lump sum, the amount being determined with reference to his salary and seniority. In order to finance these payments, a special Redundancy Fund was established, into which all employers made contributions. In 1991 that Fund, which in 1984 became the Redundancy and Employers' Insolvency Fund, amalgamated with the general Social Insurance Fund;[191] it is now financed by the normal social insurance contributions. When any employer has to make a redundancy payment, he is entitled to be reimbursed 60 per cent of the amount from the Fund.[192] In addition to any lump sum, eligible employees who are about to be made redundant are entitled to notice of that fact and to time off to find a new job.[193] As well as the 1967-1979 Acts, there is the Protection of Employment Act 1977, dealing with "collective redundancies", which requires employers to consult with trade unions when they are considering making groups of employees redundant.[194] In 1994 and again in 2000 special legislation was enacted to provide compensation for two particular categories of employee who had been made redundant much earlier, the Irish Shipping Ltd. (Payments to Former Employees) Act 1994, and the Hospital Trust (1940) Ltd (Payments to Former Employees) Act 2000.

Employees not covered

The Redundancy Payments Acts 1967-1979 apply to employees and apprentices.[195] But not all employees are entitled to obtain compensation under these Acts. In addition to the groups set out hereunder, section 14(1) of the 1967 Act disentitles employees who were lawfully dismissed for misconduct.

Continuity of employment

To begin with, they must have the requisite continuity of employment, which is 104 weeks' (or two years') full-time or regular part-time employment.[196] A week in this context means a working week as contrasted with seven days.[197]

---

190. See generally, C. Grunfeld, *Law of Redundancy* (3 ed. 1989).
191. 1967 Act, s.27, as amended by Social Welfare Act 1991, s.39.
192. *ibid.*, s.29, as amended by s.13 of the 1971 Act, and Redundancy (Rebates) Regulations 1990, S.I. No.122. *cf. Secretary of State v. Cheltenham Computer Bureau* [1985] I.C.R. 381.
193. 1979 Act, s.7.
194. See *Industrial Relations Law*, pp. 83-84.
195. See definition of "employee" in 1967 Act, s.2(1).
196. 1967 Act, s.4(2), as amended by Worker Protection (Regular Part Time Employees) Act 1991.
197. *Gormley v. McCartin Bros. (Engineering) Ltd.* [1982] I.L.R.M. 215.

Continuous employment is presumed unless the contrary is proved.[198] Special rules are contained in the 1967 Act's Third Schedule for calculating continuity of employment.[199] In addition to having been continuously employed for the requisite period, the employee must have been employed at a job which is insurable for all benefits under the Social Welfare Acts for a period of four years before he was dismissed.[200]

The continuity requirement applies only to the lump sum payment; it does not affect otherwise eligible employees' entitlements to notice under section 17 of the 1967 Act and to time off under section 7 of the 1979 Act.

Public service

Public sector employment falls within the general scope of these Acts because a business, for their purposes, is defined as including "any activity carried on . . . by a public or a local authority or a Department of State, and the performance of its functions by a public or local authority or a Department of State".[201] However, the requirement of the employee being insurable for all benefits under the Social Welfare Acts excludes a substantial number of public service workers from entitlement to redundancy compensation.[202]

Part-time workers

These Acts do not apply to part-time workers, meaning those "normally expected to work" for the same employer for less than eight hours in a week.[203]

Pensioners

These Acts do not apply to employees who have reached the pensionable age under the Social Welfare Acts, which is 66 years of age.[204]

Close family/domestics

Employees who are employed by a close member of their family in a domestic situation are not covered by these Acts.[205]

Transnationals

Special provision is made by section 25 of the 1967 Act for employees who ordinarily work outside the State.[206]

[198.] 1971 Act, s.10(a).
[199.] As amended extensively by the 1971 Act; see, *supra*, p. 188 *et seq.*
[200.] 1967 Act, ss.4(1) and 7(1)(b), as amended by the 1971 Act.
[201.] *ibid.*, s.2(1).
[202.] The (non-industrial) civil service and other public officers are class B and class D contributors, respectively.
[203.] *supra*, p. 192.
[204.] 1967 Act, s.4(1), as amended by 1979 Act, s.5.
[205.] *ibid.*, s.4(3), as amended by 1971 Act's Schedule.
[206.] See *post*, pp. 259-259.

Dismissal and its date

In order to claim compensation under the Redundancy Payments Acts the qualified employee must have been "dismissed by reason of redundancy" or else was "laid off or kept on short time".[207] As has been explained, under section 9 of the 1967 Act a dismissal for these purposes means a unilateral termination of the employment contract by the employer, the non-renewal of a fixed term contract which has expired or "constructive dismissal", where the employee leaves as a result of action by the employer amounting to a repudiation of the contract.[208] Unlike for unfair dismissals, the expiry of a "specific purpose" contract and also constructive dismissal where the employee merely has acted reasonably in leaving his job do not constitute dismissals for redundancy purposes. Where an employer dies or some other event occurs which by law operates to terminate the employment contract, the employee is deemed to have been dismissed if his contract was not renewed or he was not re-engaged on the same terms and conditions.[209]

An employee is deemed not to have been dismissed where his contract has been renewed or where he is re-engaged by the same or by another employer in certain circumstances. In the case of renewal or re-engagement by his former employer,[210] the terms of the new contract must not differ from the corresponding terms in the previous contract; the re-employment must have commenced not later then four weeks after his dismissal; and his employer must have made a written offer of re-employment before the dismissal. In the case of re-engagement by another employer,[211] that must have happened with the agreement of the employee and of both the previous and the new employer; it must have commenced immediately after the previous job ended; and, before that, the employee must have been given a written statement of the terms and conditions of the new job and the period of continuous service with the former employer which will be carried forward in the new job.

For the purposes of these Acts the date of the dismissal is defined by section 2(1) of the 1967 Act as either the date on which dismissal notice given expires; where notice of dismissal was not given, the dismissal date is when the termination actually took place or the date when a fixed term contract expired. But where no or very little notice is given, the contract cannot terminate until the requisite minimum notice period under the 1973 Minimum Notice and Terms of Employment Act has expired. Unlike for unfair dismissals, no special provision is made for when less than the contractual notice is given. Where an employee receives notice of dismissal but he then notifies his employer that he will leave on a date before that notice is to expire, the date of the dismissal is deemed to be the time when the employee's notice expired.[212] But the employer may require him to withdraw that notice and ask that he continue in employment until the notice given by the employer expires.[213]

---

[207] 1967 Act, s.7(1).
[208] *ibid.*, s.9(1), and *supra*, pp. 187-188.
[209] *ibid.*, s.21; *cf.* Schedule 2 on effect of death on the parties.
[210] *ibid.*, s. 9(2).
[211] *ibid.*, s. 9(3).
[212] *ibid.*, s.10.
[213] *ibid.*, s.10(3).

Making employees redundant

The concept of redundancy for the purposes of the Redundancy Payments Acts is a term of art, defined by section 7(2) of the 1967 Act. The original definition was extended in 1971.[214] An employee who has been dismissed is presumed to have been dismissed by reason of redundancy.[215]

"Redundant"

According to section 7(2) of the 1967 Act as amended:

"an employee who is dismissed shall be taken to be dismissed by reason of redundancy if the dismissal is attributable wholly or mainly to:

(a)   the fact that his employer has ceased, or intends to cease, to carry on the business for the purposes of which the employee was employed by him, or has ceased or intends to cease, to carry on that business in the place where the employee was so employed, or

(b)   the fact that the requirements of that business for employees to carry out work of a particular kind in the place where he was so employed have ceased or diminished or are expected to cease or diminish, or

(c)   the fact that his employer has decided to carry on the business with fewer or no employees, whether by requiring the work for which the employee had been employed (or had been doing before his dismissal) to be done by other employees or otherwise, or

(d)   the fact that his employer has decided that the work for which the employee has been employed (or had been doing before his dismissal) should henceforward be done in a different manner for which the employee is not sufficiently qualified or trained, or

(e)   the fact that his employer has decided that the work for which the employee had been employed (or had been doing before his dismissal) should henceforward be done by a person who is also capable of doing other work for which the employee is not sufficiently qualified or trained."

   This definition is very extensive; it sweeps far wider than the comparable definition in Britain. Although redundancy often connotes cut-backs as a result of contracting orders for the employer's output, or relocation of the business and the necessary re-organisation in order to deal with harsher times, the concept under section 7(2) is not confined to that. Sub-sections (a) and (b), which are similar to those in the British Act, deal with contractions of that nature — the type of business for which the employee was hired ceasing or relocating, or economic or technical changes diminishing the need for employees with particular skills or other attributes. But sub-sections (c)-(e) could be satisfied without the employer

---

[214.]   1971 Act, s.4; this amendment was prompted by *Limerick Health Authority v. Ryan* [1969] I.R. 194.
[215.]   1971 Act, s.10(b).

being under any economic pressure to shed some of the workforce. These cover situations where, for one reason or another, the employer decides to reduce the workforce or, without any reduction, to replace an employee with another who has different training, or by replacing an employee with someone who will do both that job and other work as well, for which the departing employee is not adequately trained. Virtually all forms of rational re-organisation of a workforce fall within section 7(2). For instance, employees have been held to have been made redundant where the employer wanted them to change from day work to doing the same job at nights for part of the working week;[216] where the employer replaced full-time staff with part-time employees doing the same job;[217] where a long-standing employee was replaced by a member of the employer's family who had just finished secondary school.[218] Section 7(2)'s provisions have not yet been the subject of any exhaustive analysis in the Superior Courts and, indeed, do not seem to have caused much difficulty in the E.A.T. or the Circuit Court, on account of its extensive sweep.[219]

Because the 1967-79 Acts presume a redundancy situation until the contrary is shown, the burden of proof is on the employer-defendant/ respondent to show that the employee was not dismissed on account of redundancy. It would seem that these Acts apply even where there were several reasons for the dismissal, including redundancy, provided that redundancy was a significant reason. Section 7(1) of the 1967 Act states that a right to a lump sum arises once the plaintiff was dismissed "by reason of redundancy". Where redundancy is being invoked as a defence to an action for unfair dismissal, the burden of proof also falls on the employer, who must show that the dismissal resulted "wholly or mainly from redundancy".[220] The burden is also on the employer to show that the dismissal was not unfair in any of the ways described in section 6(3) of the 1977 Act.[221]

Redundancy notices and certificates

At least two weeks' written notice of the proposed redundancy must be given to all eligible employees affected by the employer's decision.[222] Eligibility here requires two years' continuous service. Two weeks' notice must also be given to the Minister for Labour.[223] In the case of employees being made redundant but who do not have the requisite two years' continuous employment to obtain a lump sum, they must be furnished with redundancy certificates before they are dismissed.[224] In the case of "collective redundancies" as defined in the Protection of Employment Act 1977, the Minister for Labour must be given at least 30 days'

---

216. *Dimworth v. Southern Health Board* (284/77).
217. *Kelleher v. St. James Hospital Board* (59/77).
218. *Hallinan v. Gilligan* (UD 564/810).
219. See D. Madden & A. Kerr, *Unfair Dismissals: Cases and Commentary* (1990) Chap.10 for a selection of instances.
220. See *supra*, pp. 207-208; e.g. *Daly v. Hanson Industrial Ltd.* (UD 719.86).
221. *Caladom Ltd. v. Hoare & Kelly* (Cir. Ct. 1985 nos. 48 and 49).
222. 1967 Act, s.17, and Redundancy (Notice of Dismissal) Regulations 1991, S.I. No. 348.
223. *ibid.* and Redundancy Certificate Regulations 1991, S.I. No.347.
224. *ibid.*, s.18, as amended by 1971 Act.

written notice of the employer's proposals[225] and there should be consultations with employees' representatives and with the Minister.[226]

Paid time off

Section 7 of the 1979 Act gives every eligible employee being made redundant a right to "reasonable time off . . . in order to look for new employment or make arrangements for training for future employment". Eligibility here requires two years' continuous service. Before granting time off for this purpose, the employer can require evidence to show that the time will be spent on searching for work or making arrangements about retraining. The time during which this right arises is in the last two weeks of the redundancy notice period. During the employee's absence, he is entitled to be paid the appropriate hourly rate obtaining on the day he received his redundancy notice.

Lay off and short time

A "lay off" involves an employee being suspended from work without pay for some specified or indefinite period. Unless the employment contract gives a right to lay off in this manner, normally such action is a repudiation of the agreement by the employer, entitling the employee to treat it as a dismissal.[227] "Short time" involves working for significantly less than the normal hours and, depending on the contract's terms, may also amount to a repudiation by the employer of the agreement. Where an employee is put on temporary lay off or short time work, he is not there and then entitled to claim compensation for having been made redundant. But if that lay off or short time exceeds a specified period, he then is entitled to be compensated, provided of course the other qualifying conditions have been satisfied.

A lay off for these purposes is defined by section 11(1) of the 1967 Act as where the employer is unable to provide work of the kind which the employee was hired to do but it is reasonable in the circumstances for the employer to believe that he will be re-hiring the employee. Notice to that effect must have been given to the employee before being laid off. Short time, for these purposes, is defined by section 11(2) of the 1967 Act[228] as where, because of a fall in the kind of work the employee was hired to do, his weekly pay is reduced to less than half his "normal weekly remuneration", or his working hours are correspondingly reduced, but it is reasonable in the circumstances for the employer to believe that this state of affairs will not be permanent. Again, notice to this effect must have been given to the employee before his earnings or working hours were cut. It depends on all the circumstances whether an employer was reasonable in believing that a lay off or short time would not be permanent.[229]

---

225. s.12 and *infra*, pp.222-224.
226. *Industrial Relations Law*, pp. 83-84.
227. *Devonald v. Rosser & Sons* [1906] 2 K.B. 728; compare *Browning v. Crumlin Valley Colleries Ltd.* [1926] 1 K.B. 522.
228. As amended by 1979 Act, s.10.
229. *cf. Industrial Yarns Ltd. v. Greene* [1984] I.L.R.M. 15 and *Irish Leathers Ltd. v. Minister for Labour* [1986] I.R. 177.

Entitlement to be paid the lump sum will arise when the lay off or short time exceeds the following periods:[230] One is where they last for four or more consecutive weeks; alternatively, where, within a period of 13 weeks, the employee was laid off or put on short time for six or more weeks and more than three of those weeks were consecutive. In either of these events, the employee may notify the employer of his intention to claim a redundancy payment.[231] Such an intention is deemed to have been notified where the employee gives his employer notice that he is terminating the employment contract.[232] However, if at the time the employee notifies his claim, it was reasonable to expect that, within the next four weeks, the employee would be resuming full-time employment for at least another 13 weeks, the employee is not entitled to the payment.[233] For practical purposes, therefore, a lay off or short time can last for up to eight weeks before a right to a lump sum can arise. The additional four weeks referred to here apply only if the employer had notified the employee of his intention to contest any claim being made for a redundancy payment.

Offer of new employment

Generally, the fact that an employee obtained another job immediately or shortly after being made redundant does not disentitle him to a lump sum payment otherwise due to him under the Redundancy Payments Acts. There is no rule whereby the amount payable to him is subject to mitigation in those circumstances or can be reduced because of his bad behaviour. This principle is subject to one major set of exceptions. An employee who was dismissed for redundancy is not entitled to compensation where he was offered suitable new employment, in accordance with sections 15, 16 or 20 of the 1967 Act and he "unreasonably refused" that offer. Additionally, an employee who has been re-engaged by or with the agreement of his old employer in accordance with section 9(2) and (3) of the 1967 Act is not even deemed to have been dismissed for the purposes of the Redundancy Payments Acts.[234]

In order for a dismissed redundant employee to become disentitled to a payment, the following must have taken place: the employer must have offered to renew the employment or have offered the employee a new contract.[235] The terms and conditions of employment offered may either be the same as those under the old contract or may differ from those terms. If the same terms are being offered, the employment must be one which commences on or before the date the old job was due to end. If different terms are being offered, the employer's offer must be made in writing, and the employment must be one which commences within four weeks of the old job ending. Moreover, the job offered must be "suitable employment in relation to the employee". It is only when an employee "unreasonably refuses" an offer in these terms that he becomes disentitled to a payment. Consid-

---

[230.] 1967 Act, s.12(1)(a), as amended by the 1971 Act, s.11.

[231.] *ibid.*, s.12(1)(b), as amended by the 1971 Act, s.11.

[232.] *ibid.*, s.12(2), as amended by the 1971 Act, s.11; *cf. Industrial Yarns Ltd. v. Greene* [1984] I.L.R.M. 15.

[233.] 1967 Act, s.13(1).

[234.] See *supra*, p. 216.

[235.] 1967 Act, s.15(1) and (2).

erable discretion is left to the tribunals and courts to determine what types of employment are "suitable" for these purposes and when a refusal of an offer is "unreasonable". Special provision is made for where the offer comes from an associated company of the present employer[236] and also for where the employee continued working for a purchaser of the old employer's business.[237]

"Suitable" alternative employment

Where the terms and conditions offered are different from those of the existing job, the offer must be of "suitable employment" for that employee. In determining suitability, presumably the focus is on determining whether, in the light of the employee's skills and experience, the job is one which he is well capable of performing and which also does not involve any significant element of demotion. According to Grunfeld,[238] the British courts and tribunals consider the following matters: *inter alia*, pay, greater distance from existing home, need to change place of residence, the employee's health, his skill and status, retraining, domestic circumstances and any collective offer.

"Unreasonable" refusal

Even where the job being offered is suitable, the employee may refuse it on reasonable grounds and thereby does not prejudice his entitlement to the lump sum. In determining what is reasonable and unreasonable, in practice account tends to be taken of the extent to which the old and the new terms and conditions diverge and also the suitability of the job for the employee, although the conflating of these has been criticised by judges in Britain. According to Grunfeld,[239] the most important consideration is personal domestic circumstances; others include pay, retraining, travelling time and expenses.

Offer by associated employer

Where the employer is a company, the alternative employment may be offered, for these purposes, by one of its associated companies.[240] An associated company for these purposes is a subsidiary company or, where the employer itself is a subsidiary, another subsidiary of the same parent company.

Offer by transferee of business

As is explained in detail in Chapter 9, a transfer of business for the purposes of employment law involves the transfer of all or part of a business as a going concern. It is to be contrasted with a sale or other disposal of the assets and no more. Whether what was transferred was ownership of all or some of the business or was merely assets depends on the circumstances of the case.[241] Where an employee was made redundant "immediately before" such a transfer and "in

---

[236.] *ibid.*, s.16.
[237.] *ibid.*, s.20.
[238.] The Law of Redundancy (*3* ed., *1989*) pp. 182-189.
[239.] *ibid.*
[240.] 1967 Act, s.16.

connection with" that transfer, the following applies: if immediately after the change of ownership, the employee accepts employment with the transferee, he is deemed not to have been dismissed; if instead he is offered re-employment with the transferee which would be "suitable" for him and he "unreasonably" refuses that offer, he is not entitled to the lump sum payment.

Lump sum payments

A qualified employee who was dismissed by reason of redundancy, or was laid off or placed on short time for the specified period, becomes entitled to a lump sum redundancy payment from the employer. A claim for a payment must be made to the employer within thirty weeks of the date the employee was dismissed or the contract was otherwise terminated.[242] Disputed claims are first referred to "deciding officers", who are appointed for that purpose by the Minister;[243] there is an appeal from them, in the form of a full re-hearing to the Employment Appeals Tribunal.[244] Instead of determining the dispute, the deciding officer at the very outset may refer it to the Tribunal.[245] The E.A.T.'s decision is final and conclusive but there is an appeal from it to the High Court on a point of law.[246]

The rules for ascertaining the amount of the sum due are contained in the Third Schedule to the 1967 Act as amended. That amount is determined by reference to the length of the employee's "continuous employment" and his "normal weekly remuneration". For these purposes, there is a different multiplier for service before and after the employee reached 41 years of age. Earnings in excess of £13,000 per annum are disregarded.[247] Because of the inflation in the last ten years, for practical purposes the normal earnings for which redundancy payments for most employees will be determined is £250 per week (*i.e.* £13,000).

Continuous employment

As has been explained above, the 1967 Act's Third Schedule lays down rules for ascertaining the length of a worker's continuous employment and reckonable service for these purposes,[248] dealing with what does and does not break continuity of service and when absences from work should be counted as periods of service.

Normal weekly remuneration

What an employee's "normal weekly remuneration" is for these purposes is also dealt with in the Third Schedule.[249] In the case of the average worker, whose

---

[241.] *cf. Nova Colour Graphic Supplies Ltd. v. Employment Appeals Tribunal* [1987] I.R. 426, *Marks v. Wellman* [1970] N.I. 236 and *Melon v. Hector Powe Ltd.* [1981] 1 All E.R. 313. For instances of transfers or "hire downs" by receivers, see *Dedway Trading Ltd. v. Calverly* [1973] 3 All E.R. 776 and *Pambankian v. Brentford Nylons Ltd.* [1978] I.C.R. 665.

[242.] 1967 Act, s.24.

[243.] *ibid.*, ss.37 and 38.

[244.] *ibid.*, s.39 and Redundancy (Redundancy Appeal Tribunal) Regulations, 1968, S.I. No. 24, amended by S.I. No. 114 of 1979.

[245.] *ibid.*, s.39(16).

[246.] *ibid.*, s.39(14).

[247.] S.I. No. 18 of 1990.

[248.] Paras. 4-12; *supra*, p. 188 *et seq.*

[249.] Paras 13-23.

remuneration does not vary with the actual amount of work done, his normal remuneration is as follows:

> "his earnings (including any regular bonus or allowance which does not vary in relation to the amount of work done and any payment in kind) for his normal weekly working hours as at the date on which he was declared redundant, together with, in the case of an employee who is normally expected to work overtime, his average weekly overtime earnings. . . ."[250]

Computation

The amount of the payment due is then determined as follows.[251] The number of weeks continuous service is divided by 52 to get the yearly figure. The normal weekly remuneration is calculated as just described. Then, for years of service with the employer between the ages of 16 and 41 years, the number of those years is multiplied by half the normal weekly remuneration. For years of service after 41 years of age (up to the State pension age), the number of those years is multiplied by the normal weekly remuneration. The employee is entitled in addition to one week's normal remuneration.

Collective redundancies

What are referred to as collective redundancies are regulated by the Protection of Employment Act 1977, which is based on E.C. Directive 75/129.[252] A "collective redundancy" for these purposes is the making redundant, over a period of 30 consecutive days, of a minimum number of employees, that minimum varying with the size of the establishment's workforce. For these purposes, "redundant" has the same meaning as under the 1967-79 Acts [253] and, as in those Acts a business is deemed to include any profession or undertaking or activity, including all public sector activities.[254] The 1977 Act's requirements do not apply to redundancies where the establishment in which the workers were employed was closed down following bankruptcy or winding-up proceedings;[255] also where that closure was the result of any other decision of a competent court, for instance, where an examiner into the company's affairs had recommended the closure and the court then shut down the establishment.

Certain categories of employee are excluded from the 1977 Act, notably those employed by or under the State, with the exception of "industrial" civil servants, officers of a local authority, and merchant seamen employed under a prescribed agreement.[256] The due expiry of a fixed term contract or the completion of an

---

[250.] Para. 13, as amended. See also paras. 14-15 and 17-23. Where employees are paid wholly or partly by piece rates, bonuses or commissions which are related directly to output, see para. 16 and elaborations in paras. 17-23.

[251.] Paras. 1-3.

[252.] O.J. No.L 48/29 (1975). See, generally, C. Barnard, E.C. *Employment Law* (2nd ed., 2000), pp. 488-498.

[253.] s.6(2); see *supra*, p. 216.

[254.] s.6(4).

[255.] s.7(2)(e).

[256.] s.7(2).

employment contract made for a specified purpose is not treated as a dismissal in this context.[257]

In order to trigger the 1977 Act's requirements, the minimum number of redundancies in a 30-days period for the employing "establishment" is as follows:[258] in establishments "normally employing" between 20 and 49 employees, at least five redundancies; in establishments normally employing between 50 and 99 employees, at least ten redundancies; in establishments normally employing between 100 and 299 employees, at least 10 per cent of the workforce being made redundant; in establishments normally employing more than 300 employees, at least 30 redundancies. For these purposes, an establishment is the particular location or locations where the employer carries on a business or comparable activity.[259] For determining the average size of the workforce, the measure is the average over the 12 months preceding the date of the dismissal.[260]

Consultations with workers' representatives

The extent of the employer's obligation to consult with workers' representatives about the proposed redundancies has been described elsewhere.[261]

Notifying and consulting with the Minister

A common feature of employment law in Continental Europe is that, before they may take various types of decisions, employers are often required to notify the Ministry for Labour and enter into negotiations with officials of the Minister. Provisions along these lines are contained in the 1977 Act. Where the employer proposes to create collective redundancies, he must notify the Minister at the earliest opportunity; at the very least, notice must be given 30 days before the first dismissals are to occur.[262] A copy of that notice must be supplied promptly to the employees' representatives, who may submit to the Minister written observations on the question. There is no obligation on employers to foresee or anticipate collective redundancies, for instance, when they are in financial difficulties, nor does the Act affect their freedom to decide whether and with whom they should draw up plans for collective dismissals.[263]

Employers are required to supply certain "relevant information" about the proposals to the employees' representatives; as soon as possible, a copy of that information must also be sent to the Minister.[264] That principally consists of details of the reasons for the proposed redundancies; the number, description and categories of employees to be affected; the number of employees normally employed and the period during which the proposed redundancies are to take place.

---

[257] s.7(2)(a).
[258] s.6(1).
[259] s.6(3).
[260] s.8.
[261] ss.9 and 10; see *Industrial Relations Law*, pp. 83-84.
[262] s.12.
[263] *Dansk Metalarbejderforbund Danmark v. Nielsen & Son* (Case 284/83) [1985] E.C.R. 553.
[264] s.10.

At the Minister's request, the employer must enter into consultations with him or his chosen representative, with the objective of seeking solutions to the problem caused by the proposed redundancies.[265] Any information about the proposals as he may reasonably require must be supplied to the Minister.

Timing

Regardless of what notice the employees may be entitled to under their employment contracts or under the Minimum Notice and Terms of Employment Act 1973, there is a 30 days' moratorium placed on collective redundancies.[266] Before the dismissals can take effect, at least 30 days must have expired after the Minister was notified by the employer about the proposed redundancies.

THE STATUTORY DISMISSALS REGIME AND INDUSTRIAL RELATIONS

The principal form of industrial action taken by employers is the lock-out, which involves dismissing all or part of the existing workforce. Employers, moreover, often react to strikes or other worker industrial action by dismissing those either organising or involved in that action. Whatever freedom to discharge the employer possesses at common law is now circumscribed by the Unfair Dismissals Acts in respect of employees who fall within the protection of those Acts. There is also legislation which protects workers' continuity of employment when industrial action is being taken. The extent to which those Acts restrict employers' freedom to dismiss in the context of industrial action was the subject of some confusion, which resulted in amendments being made in 1993. Consideration should also be given to the effect of industrial action on redundancy claims and on continuity of employment required in order to qualify for numerous statutory rights.

Unfair dismissals

A distinction must be drawn between lock-outs, on the one hand, and strikes and other forms of workers' industrial action on the other.

In very general terms, although it may not be unfair for the employer to dismiss all of his employees who are on strike, he may not victimise one or some of them when the strike is over by re-hiring some but not others. What is a "strike" is defined in section 18 of the 1977 Act. It involves more than one employee who, acting in concert, cease working or refuse to continue working for an employer. That must have happened in consequence of a dispute and the objective must be to compel their employer, or any employee or body of employees, to accept or not to accept terms or conditions of or affecting employment; alternatively, in order to aid other employees to compel their employer, or an employee or body of employees, to accept or not to accept such terms or conditions. Accordingly, a strike for those purposes need not be a lawful "trade dispute" within the Industrial Relations Act 1990.

[265.] s.15.
[266.] s.14.

Dismissal of an employee who has resorted to strike action is deemed to be unfair in two circumstances.[267] One is where one or more of his co-employees who had taken that action were not dismissed for so doing. The other is where one or more employees who had been so dismissed were later allowed to return to work on terms and conditions at least as favourable as they had prior to their dismissal. Where an employee succeeds in an unfair dismissal claim for victimisation in this manner and his re-instatement or re-engagement is directed, that becomes effective from the time when the majority of those who had been given back their jobs returned to work, but the applicant can agree another date with his employer. Even where a dismissal is not discriminatory as here described, in a very exceptional case it may nonetheless be unfair under section 6(1) of the 1977 Act.

The same principle as applies to strikes governs those dismissed "for taking part in" industrial action other than strikes:[268] selective dismissals are automatically unfair. Industrial action here is identical to that for strikes except that the action protected by section 5(2) must be "lawful". A major question that requires authoritative resolution is whether industrial action that is in breach of the employment contract is "lawful" for the purposes of this provision. Especially in the light of legitimation of strike notices by the *Becton Dickinson* case,[269] the answer most probably is that industrial action which was preceded by adequate notice is not unlawful.

At least two other problems arise under section 5(2) of the 1977 Act as amended. One concerns the *auto-réduction*, as described elsewhere:[270] is it a strike or is it other industrial action? It is a "cessation or work" but not a complete cessation. The other relates to picketing. Where only those who picket are sacked and not each and every striker, were the picketers dismissed "for taking part in" the strike or for participating in other industrial action? And if the picketers had been served with an interlocutory injunction to cease picketing, was their action "lawful"?

Finally, there is the situation where the initiative in industrial action is taken by the employer, the lockout, which is defined by reference to a "trade dispute" under the Industrial Relations Act 1946, involving excluding employees from or suspending their work, or terminating or suspending their employment. A similar no-victimisation principle applies.[271] If one or more of his co-employees are taken back to work on terms no less favourable than those they enjoyed before being locked out, but the aggrieved employer has not been similarly treated, dismissal is deemed to be unfair. In all other circumstances the matter is to be judged under the section 6(1) "substantial grounds" for dismissal criterion. That is to say, if the locked-out employee is not offered re-engagement at the end of the dispute, it depends on the entire circumstances of his situation whether his dismissal was unfair, with the burden falling on the employer of establishing that he acted fairly.

---

[267]. s.5(2), amended by 1993 Act s.4.
[268]. *ibid.*
[269]. *Beckton Dickinson Ltd.* v. *Lee* [1973] IR 1.
[270]. *Industrial Relations Law* p. 108.
[271]. s.5(1), amended by 1993 Act s.4.

Redundancy payments

Depending on the nature of the dispute and how it arose, a worker, by striking, may jeopardise his entitlements to redundancy pay. The Redundancy Payments Act 1967 in section 14(1) disentitles that a person lawfully dismissed for misconduct shall not be entitled to redundancy pay and, classically, taking part in a strike was treated as misconduct. This rule is subject to the following qualifications, however. It does not to apply where a strike takes place following receipt of notices of dismissal for redundancy, or of lay-off or short time.[272] There is no express provision in the Act for workers' industrial action short of striking - not even such action when taken in response to anticipated or proposed redundancies. Following the *Becton Dickinson.*[273] case, it may well be that a strike preceded by proper notice is not "misconduct" for these purposes. Moreover, some strikes that involve breaches of employment contracts may nevertheless be legally or morally justifiable so as not to constitute misconduct, such as where the action is taken in support of a Labour Court recommendation.

Continuity of employment

The period during which a worker has been continuously employed by an employer is very important. Seniority, and entitlement to and the amount of pensions, usually turn on the length of continuous employment, as does entitlements to the rights conferred by many of the individual protective labour statutes such as the Redundancy Payments Acts and the Unfair Dismissals Act. At common law a worker does not break continuity or employment merely by striking or by being locked out; this principle is now incorporated into the Minimum Notice etc. Act, 1973.[274] This Act then goes on to provide that any week during which an employee is absent from work by reason of taking part in a strike or being locked out shall not count as a period of service.[275] Accordingly, although absence from work due to a strike or a lock-out does not break continuity of employment, the period of that absence does not count for reckoning the length of the worker's continuous service.

By striking or engaging in other industrial action, workers run the risk of dismissal, with its consequent break in continuity. It is for this reason that one of the terms on which strikes and lock-outs are usually settled is that continuity shall be deemed not to have been broken. Arrangements of that nature, however, do not always bind third parties, such as pension fund trustees and the Minister as administrator of redundancy, maternity and insolvency funds. Persons re-instated or re-engaged following a successful claim, under the Unfair Dismissals Act 1977, are by that Act deemed to have been continuously employed since the date of their dismissal.[276]

---

[272] s. 14(2), (3); see definitions of "strike" and "lockout" in s.6.
[273] *Becton Dickenson v. Lee* [1973] I.R. 1.
[274] Schedule, paras 4 and 2; also Redundancy Payments Act 1967, 3rd Schedule.
[275] *ibid.* paras 11 and 12; also para 13.
[276] s. 71(1)(a), (b).

CHAPTER 9

TRANSFER OF EMPLOYER'S BUSINESS

An employee may not always have the same employer throughout his working life. He may resign from his job or be dismissed and either move to another job or become unemployed. Or his present employer may dispose of the business or part of the business to a new owner and the employee may then become employed by that successor. Business transfers are a comparatively frequent occurrence and take place for a variety of reasons. For instance, the present owner may want to retire entirely from business or he may see little future for the enterprise he is disposing of or, indeed, that concern may be insolvent and he is being compelled to liquidate it. The rights and duties of employees in business transfers[1] may be the subject of special contractual arrangements or special statutory provisions. In this regard the position of most employees is regulated by the E.C.-inspired Transfer of Undertakings Regulations of 1980.[2] Before dealing with these 1980 Regulations, the position at common law and some of the special arrangements made for protecting employees of a business or undertaking which is being transferred call for consideration.

IMPACT ON THE EMPLOYMENT CONTRACT

Where a business is transferred to another employer, at common law the transferor's employees are deemed to have thereby been dismissed. Where part of the employer's business has been transferred, it depends on the entire circumstances which employees, if any, were thereby dismissed; a source of difficulty has been where there was a "hive down" by a receiver of the viable part of the business.[3]

As regards the employee's position *vis-à-vis* the transferee or successor enterprise, the fundamental principle is that of privity of contract; the employee's contract is with the transferor of the business and cannot give rise to enforceable rights against and duties to a third party, such as the transferee of the business. Statutory provisions aside, in order to acquire rights against and assume obligations to the transferee, the employee must have entered into an enforceable contract with him. At times such a contract may exist, most notably where the employee's trade union made an agreement with the transferee on behalf of the employee governing the terms of the business transfer. Or the transferor of the business, as agent for his employees, may have extracted terms from the transferee affecting them. In both cases, the employee will not have enforceable rights

---

[1]. See, generally, G. Byrne, *Transfer of Undertakings* (1999) and M. Freedland, *The Contract of Employment* (1976) Chap. 9.

[2]. S.I. No. 306 of 1980, considered, *infra*, p. 230 *et seq.*

[3]. *e.g. Pambankian v. Brentford Nylons Ltd.* [1988] I.C.R. 665.

against the transferee unless the union or transferor, as the case may be, negotiated terms as his agent; whether they acted as agent depends on the circumstances of the case.[4]

Generally, employment contracts cannot be unilaterally assigned. While a party to various types of contracts, for instance, a creditor who is owed money, can assign his rights under the contract to a third party, who then can enforce that contract against the debtor, the obligations under a contract of employment cannot be transferred in that manner. This principle is illustrated in *Nokes v. Doncaster Amalgamated Collieries Ltd.,*[5] a company law case which involved a scheme of arrangement to reorganise the affairs of a company under the equivalent of sections 201-203 of the Companies Act 1963. In order to become effective, these schemes must be approved by the High Court which is empowered to make various directions to facilitate implementation of the agreed scheme. The Court may direct that one company's property shall be transferred to another company involved in the scheme; property for this purpose is defined as including "rights and powers of every description". Mr Nokes had been employed by one company as a coal miner and it was contended that, when the Court directed that all his employer's property and liabilities shall be transferred to the respondent colliery company, he thereby became an employee of that colliery. This view was rejected on the grounds that the section of the Companies Act did not expressly provide for the assignment of employment contracts. It was held to be a "fundamental principle . . . that a free citizen, in the exercise of his freedom, is entitled to choose the employer whom he proposes to serve, so that the right to his services cannot be transferred from one employer to another without his assent".[6]

SPECIAL ARRANGEMENTS FOR EMPLOYMENT PROTECTION

Express provision may be made by statute for transferring employees' rights and obligations from one employer to another. For the purpose of the major Acts that confer redress when workers are being dismissed, continuity of service can be vital; it determines the minimum length of notice to be given, and, for making claims under the legislation on unfair dismissals and on redundancy payments, ordinarily one year and two years' respectively continuous service is a prequisite. Frequently, when all or part of a business is being transferred, it will be stipulated in the transfer agreement that the acquiring or successor enterprise will recognise the seniority and continuity of employees it takes over from the transferror.

A general provision to that effect is contained in the schedule to the Minimum Notice and Terms of Employment Act 1973.[7] Where all or part of a trade, business or undertaking is transferred to another and employees of the transferor go to work for the successor, their continuity of service is deemed not to have been broken and their service with the transferor is deemed to be part of their service

---

4. See *ante,* p. 54.
5. [1940] A.C. 1014.
6. *ibid.* at 1200.
7. Schedule, reg. 7, amended by s.15 of the Unfair Dismissals Act 1993.

with the successor. Although it is not expressly stated, this seems to apply only to persons employed by the transferor in and around the time the transfer occurred. But it does not apply to its employees who got and kept a redundancy payment arising from the transfer.[8]

On the transfer of an undertaking, as conceived under the above 1980 Regulations, the transferee assumes all liabilities with regard to statutory minimum wages as the transferor had immediately prior to the transfer.[9] Where, under the legislation on maternity, adoption and parental leave, an employee is entitled to return to work at the end of the leave period but, in the meantime, the ownership of the undertaking where she or he was employed has changed, then the successor who acquired the undertaking must hire that employee on terms identical to those with the transferor employer.[10]

Provision is also made in the Redundancy Payments Act 1967 for business transfers. One of these,[11] which has since been extended to all contexts,[12] was that the transfer of all or part of a business or undertaking does not break an employee's continuous service and that continuous service with the transferor enterprise is carried over to the transferee. But this rule does not apply where all that has been transferred was assets, like plant and stock in trade, as opposed to the on-going business or part of it.[13] Section 20 of the 1967 Act deals with where an employee, who is being made redundant by the transferor, loses his right to lump sum compensation where the successor business offers to re-employ him.[14] That right is lost where, by prior agreement between the employee and the successor, the new owner renews his contract or re-engages him. Unreasonable refusal by the employee of an offer of similar and suitable employment by the successor can also deny the employee the lump sum payment.

More detailed provisions are often encountered in legislation which reorganises some part of the public service and where one public body is being replaced by another. Frequently in these measures, it is stipulated that the employees of the existing body shall be transferred to the new body, generally on the same terms as those on which they are presently employed. For instance, under the Postal and Telecommunications Services Act 1983, where An Post and (the former) Bord Telecom Éireann took over the activities of the former Department of Posts and Telegraphs, section 45 of that Act stipulated that each of these companies "shall accept into its employment" existing members of the Department's staff on terms and conditions of employment that are no "less favourable" than those they presently enjoyed. It was also provided there that a transferred employee's previous service with the civil service shall be reckonable service for the purpose of legislation governing employees' rights on being dismissed from their jobs. Those employees' tenure and their pay and terms and conditions of employment could only be made "less favourable" or "worsened" from those at the time of transfer

---

8. *ibid.; cf. Lassman v. Secretary of State* [2000] I.C.R. 1109.
9. National Minimum Wage Act 2000, s.46.
10. Maternity Protection Act 1994, s.26, Adoptive Leave Act 1995, s.18, Parental Leave Act 1998, s.15, and Carer's Leave Act 2001, s.14.
11. Schedule 3, para.6, as amended.
12. *supra,* n.7.
13. *cf. Nova Graphic Supplies Ltd. v. Employment Appeals Tribunal* [1987] I.R. 426.
14. See *ante,* pp. 219-220.

in accordance with a collective agreement negotiated with a recognised trade union or staff association. In determining whether this and identical provisions were complied with, the courts have distinguished mere changes in "working practices" from changes in terms and conditions.[15]

Examples of similar provisions include section 14 of the Transport (Reorganisation of Córas Iompair Éireann) Act 1986, section 37 of the Health Act 1970 (establishing the Health Boards), section 7(4)-(8) of the Labour Services Act 1987 (establishing An FAS), section 6 of the Agriculture (Research, Training and Advice) Act 1988 (establishing An Teagasc), section 20 of the Safety, Health and Welfare at Work Act 1989 (establishing the National Authority for Occupational Safety and Health), and section 6 of the Insurance Act 1990 (pre-privatisation of Irish Life); more recently, section 52 of the Qualifications (Education and Training) Act 1999, section 22 of the Irish Sports Council Act 1999, section 38 of the Food Safety Authority of Ireland Act 1998, section 51 of the Turf Development Act 1998, section 25 of the Courts Service Act 1998, section 20 of the Health (Eastern Regional Health Authority) Act 1999, section 9 of the Regional Technical College (Amendment) Act 1999, section 1(3)(d), (4) of the Harbours (Amendment) Act 2000, and section 40 of the Education (Welfare) Act 2000.

Cox v. Electricity Supply Board[16] concerned a former officer of Dublin Corporation who became an employee of the defendant under section 39(2) of the Electricity (Supply) Act 1927, when the defendant acquired the Corporation's electricity undertaking. Section 39(2) provided that the plaintiff was transferred to the Board's service "on the same terms" as those he enjoyed when serving the Corporation. It was held that, accordingly, for him to be lawfully dismissed, the Board had to follow precisely the same procedures as the Corporation would have been bound to follow — including, at that time, obtaining the consent of the Minister for Local Government.

TRANSFER OF UNDERTAKINGS REGULATIONS

In 1977 the E.C. Council adopted Directive 77/187 on the approximation of laws relating to the safeguarding of employees' rights in the event of transfers of undertakings, businesses or parts of businesses;[17] it was replaced by a measure taking effect by July 2001.[18] This Directive provides for the transfer of employees from the transferor to the transferee business, subject to certain exceptions, and for consultation with employees' representatives about aspects of the transfer. Its purpose, as described by the European Court, is "to ensure, so far as possible, that the rights of employees are safeguarded in the event of a change of employer by allowing them to remain in employment with the new employer on the terms and conditions agreed with the transferor".[19] It also aims to ensure, so far as possible,

---

15. *Rafferty v. Bus Éireann* [1997] 2 I.R. 424 and *O'Cearbhall v. Bord Telecom Éireann* (S.C., December 20, 1993).
16. [1943] I.R. 94.
17. O.J. No. L 61/126 (1977). See, generally, C. Barnard, *E.C. Employment Law* (2000), pp. 466-488 and C. Quigley, *European Community Contract Law* (1998), pp. 224-237.
18. Directive 98/50, O.J. No. L 201/88 (1998), which was to be implemented by July 17, 2001.

that the employment relationship continues unchanged with the transferee, particularly by compelling him to retain the terms and conditions of employment stipulated by a collective agreement and by protecting employees against dismissal solely on the ground of transfer.[20]

This Directive was made effective in Ireland by the European Communities (Safeguarding of Employees' Rights on Transfer of Undertakings) Regulations 1980.[21] These Regulations can have a very significant impact on calculations made when considering the sale or other disposition of a business or part of a business. They are not, however, confined to the private sector or to industrial and commercial activities; transfers of non-profit activities within the public sector are also capable of being within the Regulations, but not transfers of administrative functions. No express provision is made regarding their extra-territorial application.[22] Before examining the substantive rights conferred by the Regulations, their interpretation and scope call for comment.

Interpretation

Many cases have been referred from other jurisdictions to the European Court of Justice concerning the meaning of the 1977 Directive and a substantial body of case law now exists regarding its meaning, although there remain matters which require clarification. The terminology of the 1980 Regulations reproduces practically verbatim that of the Directive which, apart from other considerations, would suggest that the analysis adopted by the European Court would always be followed by Irish tribunals and courts. This matter is put beyond doubt by reg. 2(1) of the Regulations, which states that any word or expression used in the Regulations "shall . . . have the same meaning" as those in the Directive. An exception to this principle is made for where "the context otherwise requires. . . ."

Because the Directive is couched in very general terms and hardly goes into any detail, thereby often leaving it unclear whether it applies to particular circumstances, or how it is to apply, courts have emphasised the need to give it a "purposive" construction, which is to protect workers being disadvantaged in several ways on account of the undertaking where they were employed being transferred to another owner. In particular, the concept of a "relevant transfer" and whether a worker was dismissed "in connection with" such a transfer will be widely construed.

Relevant "business transfers"

The kind of transaction which affects employees' entitlements under these Regulations is defined in Article 1 of the Directive as "the transfer of an undertaking, business or part of a business to another employer as a result of a legal transfer or merger". What is an undertaking or a business here is not defined, which raises the question as to when a transfer of a part of some public service agency or

---

[19.] *Foreningen AF Arbejdsledeve i Danmark v. Daddy's Dance Hall A/S* (Case 324/86) [1985] E.C.R. 2639.

[20.] *Mikkelsen v. Danmols Inventar A/S* (Case 105/84) [1985] E.C.R. 2639.

[21.] S.I. No. 306 of 1980.

[22.] *Cf. Addison v. Denholm Management (U.K.) Ltd.* [1997] I.C.R. 770.

department, which is not engaged in business in the ordinary meaning of the term, is a relevant transfer for these purposes. As has been pointed out, transfers within the public service are often the subject of special legislative provisions, in order to ensure that all employees of the old service are re-employed in the new service on terms and conditions no less favourable than they hitherto enjoyed. The term "undertaking" has been given an expansive interpretation as applying to most parts of the public service, for instance, a State-funded non-profit association for treating drug addicts in Holland[23] and an institution for treating young offenders owned by the Home Office in England.[24] But the Directive does not apply to "the reorganisation of structures of the public administration or the transfer of administrative functions between public administrative authorities ...".[25] This interpretation is based on the very terms of the Directive which, for example, in its French version describes the subject of the transfer as the *"enterprise"* and its beneficiary as the *"chef d'enterprise"*.

Transfers of undertakings often take the form of legal transfers, notably sales of the business or mergers. But other forms of transfer can be affected by these Regulations. For instance, in the *Daddy's Dance Hall* case,[26] the employer leased premises to carry on a restaurant business. Because he was in breach of covenant, his lease was forfeited and another company took over the premises to run a restaurant there. It was held that the Directive applied. The triangular nature of the transaction did not matter, "provided that the economic unit in question retains its identity". According to Advocate General Mancini in a later case, also involving the forfeiture of a lease: "no significance is to be attached to the nature of the transaction, be it a contract or a deed taking effect on death, an administrative measure or a judicial decision, as a result of which one business man succeeds another. . . . The sole requirement [is] the capacity of the business transferred to retain its 'identity', that is to say, to remain in operation as a going concern . . . only a part of the business is transferred."[27]

These Regulations can apply to transfers within a group of companies, where the same work is being performed under the same management, especially where it is being done on the same premises. That two wholly owned subsidiaries, one of which transferred a business activity to another, would be regarded as the one undertaking for the purposes of Competition Law does not preclude them being regarded as distinct undertakings in the context of these Regulations.[28]

In cases of partial transfers, the criterion is "whether or not a transfer takes place of the department to which [those employees] were assigned and which formed the organisational framework within which their employment relationship took effect".[29] That the business was temporarily suspended prior to the

23. *Redmond Stichting v. Bartol* (Case C 29/91) [1992] E.C.R. 3189.
24. *Kenny v. South Manchester College* [1993] I.C.R. 934.
25. *Henke v. Gemeinde Schierke* (Case C 298/94) [1996] E.C.R. 4989, compare *Mayeur* v. *APIM* (Case 175/99) [2000] I.R.L.R. 783 and *Collins v. Telecom Italia SpA* (Case 343/98) [2000] I.R.L.R. 788.
26. *supra*, n.19.
27. *Landsorganisationen i Danmark v. My Moll Kro* (Case 287/86) [1987] E.C.R. 5465.
28. *Allen v. Amalgamated Construction Co.* (Case C 234/98) [2000] I.C.R. 436.
29. *Botzen v. Rotterdamsche Droogdok Maatschappij B.V.* (Case 186/83) [1985] E.C.R. 519, para. 14.

transfer, such as a restaurant business which was closed down during the winter season, does not prevent the Regulations from applying.

But if all that has happened is a mere sale of the transferor's assets and no more, the Regulations do not apply. It depends on the entire circumstances of the case whether the transaction is only a sale of assets, and, in this regard, the courts are vigilant lest the employees' protections are evaded by sales of businesses being dressed up to look like mere disposals of assets. According to the European Court in the *Spijkers* case,[30] involving the sale of a slaughterhouse which had ceased to trade:

> "It is necessary to determine whether what has been sold is an economic entity which is still in existence, and this will be apparent from the fact that its operation is actually being continued or has been taken over by the new employer, with the same economic or similar activities.

> To decide whether these conditions are fulfilled, it is necessary to take account of all the factual circumstances of the transaction in question, including the type of undertaking or business in question, the transfer or otherwise of tangible assets such as buildings and stocks, the value of intangible assets at the date of transfer, whether the majority of the staff are taken over by the new employer, the transfer or otherwise of the circle of customers, and the degree of similarity between activities before and after the transfer and the duration of any interruption in those activities. . . . [E]ach of these factors is only part of the overall assessment which is required and therefore they cannot be examined independently of each other."[31]

Where an enterprise providing services under a contract is replaced by a different firm, that does not constitute a relevant transfer for these purposes,[32] in the absence of additional special factors. Where a building contractor took over a sub-contract, together with workers and material that had been assigned to completing the contract, that too was held to be outside the Directive.[33] What must change hands is a stable economic entity whose activity is not limited to performing one specific works contract.[34] Thus in *Suzen*,[35] where an employee of a cleaning firm that had a contract to clean a school lost her job when the school awarded the contract to another cleaning company, it was held that there hadn't been a relevant transfer; the mere loss of a service contract to a competitor cannot, without more, come within the Directive. It is a different matter if the new contractor hired a substantial number of those employed at the task by the previous contractor.

However, where an individual has been employed to perform some ancillary service (*e.g.* cleaning, security) but his employer then engages a firm to provide

30. *Spijkers v. Gebroeders Benedik Abattoir B.V.* (Case 24/85) [1986] E.C.R. 1119.
31. *ibid.*, paras. 12 and 13.
32. *Suzen v. Zehnacker Gebaudereinigung G.m.b.H.* (Case C 13/95) [1997] E.C.R. 1259 (transfer of a cleaning a contract) and *Betts v. Brintel Helicopters Ltd.* [1997] I.C.R. 793.
33. *Ledernes Hovedorganisation (for Rygaard) v. Dansk Arbejdsgiverforening* (Case C48/94) [1995] E.C.R. 2754.
34. *ibid.*, para. 20.
35. *supra*, n.32.

that service on a contract basis, that can constitute a relevant transfer for the purpose of the 1980 Regulations.[36] Whether *Bannon v. Employment Appeals Tribunal*[37] would be decided today in the same way, in the light of the above decisions, is debatable. The plaintiff was employed as a security guard at the Drogheda Town Centre. The Centre decided to contract out its security requirements to an independent security firm, which employed five men for the purpose, including one ex-employee of the Centre who had been a security guard there. Blaney J. held that there had been a transfer of undertaking for these purposes.

In *Merckx v. Ford Motor Co.*,[38] where the defendant motor company's dealership for an area of Brussels was transferred to a different company but there was no transfer of assets of any kind, it was concluded that, in the circumstances, there had been a relevant transfer. That was because the motor company was the principal shareholder in the transferor, the dealership covered the very same area and was subject to the same conditions as previously, there was no temporary interruption in sales, some of the previous dealer's staff were taken over, and its customers were recommended to the successor. Although there was no formal transfer of any kind between the previous dealer and its successor, in practical terms the latter acquired the former's business and goodwill.

That the transferor immediately thereafter ceased trading and/or was put into liquidation is of no particular relevance.[39] That the transferor is insolvent does not as such take the transaction outside the Regulations, although the position of disposals by the liquidator of an insolvent company is still to be clarified.[40] In the *Abels* case,[41] it was held that the Directive applied to a disposal by a Dutch company which was in the process of *surseance van betaling*, which is similar to a scheme of arrangement under sections 201-203 of the Companies Act 1963 and to the Court-supervised examination under the Companies (Amendment) Act 1990. In *Mythen v. Employment Appeals Tribunal*,[42] Barrington J. held that the Regulations applied to a disposal of part of the undertaking by a receiver who had been appointed by a debenture-holder. Of course, where all that the liquidator or receiver disposes of is the bare assets of the company, the Regulations cannot apply. The position of disposals by examiners and liquidators is considered in the next chapter, dealing with employers' insolvency.

Workers covered

Unlike many of the modern employment protection measures, the Transfer of Undertakings Regulations do not set out the categories of workers who fall within or outside its terms. These deal with a contract of employment or an employment relationship, so that self-employed persons obtain no rights under them. Regard-

---

36. *Schmidt v. Spar-und Leihkasse der Fruheren Amter Bordesholm* (Case C 392/92) [1994] E.C.R. 1311.
37. [1993] 1 I.R. 500.
38. (Case C 172/94) [1996] E.C.R. 1253.
39. *ibid.*
40. See *post*, p. 244.
41. *Abels v. Administrative Board of the Bedrijsvereniging Voor de Metaal Industrie* (Case 135/83) [1985] E.C.R. 469.
42. [1989] I.L.R.M. 844.

ing who is an employee for the purpose of the Directive, it was held in another instance that there is no special European concept of employee for this purpose. Rather, these provisions can "be invoked by persons who in one way or another are protected as employees under rules or law of the member-State concerned", that is "any person who, in the Member State concerned, is protected as an employee under the national legislation relating to labour law".[43] Many categories of employee who fall outside the scope of measures like the Unfair Dismissals Acts and the Redundancy Payments Acts are protected by these Regulations, since they do not purport to exclude any categories of employee from their scope. They apply to public service employees and office-holders. Even if various categories of employees were excluded in the Regulations, as a matter of E.C. law, the State would be in breach of its obligations under the Directive if it sought to exclude any group who, under Irish law, enjoyed protection in connection with dismissal from employment. Thus, where Belgium sought to exclude from its implementing measure temporary employees and employees over the pensionable age, it was held that the obligation to implement the Directive had not been fully met, because those categories of employee enjoyed some protection against dismissal under Belgian law. According to the European Court, the Directive "applies to any situation in which employees affected by a transfer enjoy some, albeit limited, protection against dismissal under national law, with the result that, under the Directive, that protection may not be taken away from them or curtailed solely because of the transfer".[44]

A strategy which has been adopted in an attempt to avoid application of the Regulations is to dismiss the employees in question before the actual transfer of the undertaking occurs. Devices of this nature are not accepted by the courts. Although the Directive applies only to those employed by the transferor at the time of the transfer,[45] persons can be so employed even though not performing work for the transferor or not being paid by it.[46] Additionally, it was held by the European Court in the *Bork* case[47] that workers who are dismissed by the transferor prior to and in order to facilitate the transfer are protected by the Directive. According to the Court, "workers employed by the undertaking whose contract of employment or employment relationship has been terminated with effect on a date before that of the transfer, in breach of Article 4(1), must be considered as still employed by the undertaking on the date of transfer. . . ."[48]

Thus, in the *Litster* case[49] a blatant attempt to avoid application of the Regulations did not succeed because that would subvert their very object. In order to facilitate the transfer of part of a company which was in receivership, the receiver agreed to dismiss several employees one hour before the transfer was to occur. The transfer also took the form of the purchase of the company's tangible assets and the purchase of the lease on the property on which it had traded; there was no

---

43. *Mikkelsen* case [1985] E.C.R. 2639, paras. 27 and 28.

44. *E.C. Commission v. Belgium* (Case 237/84) [1986] E.C.R. 1247, para. 13.

45. *Wendbloe v. L. J. Music Aps* (Case 19/83) [1985] E.C.R. 457.

46. cf. *Governing Body of Clifton Middle School v. Askew* [2000] I.C.R. 186.

47. *P. Bork International AS v. Foreningen AF Arbejdsledere i Danmark* (Case 101/87) [1988] E.C.R. 3057.

48. *ibid.*, para. 18.

49. *Litster v. Forth Dry Dock & Engineering Co.* [1990] 1 A.C. 546.

disposal of goodwill. All of this was with the express design that the Regulations would not apply. But they were held to govern the case on account of that very objective.

Even where there is no question of attempted evasion, in an appropriate case a transfer will be treated as taking place over a period of time rather than at a particular moment. Thus, even though a person may not have an enforceable contract at the deemed transfer date, this does not mean that, for the purpose of the 1980 Regulations, he was not employed then.[50]

Continuing rights and duties

The first fundamental principle of the Directive is that, where an employer's business is transferred, its then employees become employees of the person or the company which acquired the business. What was not achieved in the *Doncaster Colleries* case[51] by the Companies Act (the assignment of the entire employment relationship to the successor or transferee company) is now the outcome of the Directive. According to Article 3(i) of the Directive (regulation 3 of the Regulations), "the transferor's rights and obligations arising from a contract of employment or from an employment relationship existing on the date of a transfer . . . shall . . . be transferred to the transferee". Accordingly, as from the date of the transfer, the transferor's employees at that time are entitled to be employed on the very same terms and conditions by the transferee, save where they were dismissed for "economic" etc. reasons, as described below.[52] Continuity of employment which was built up while working for the transferor is carried over to the transferee. Any money owing by the transferor to the employee arising from his job can be recovered from the transferee. All of the transferor's duties as employer become vested in the transferee, including liability in damages for injuries caused negligently in the course of employment. And if the transferor had insurance cover in respect of those injuries, his right of indemnity from those insurers also passes over to the transferee.[53] It remains to be seen whether rights to shares under an employees' share option scheme can be transferred in this manner.

Not alone are obligations and rights automatically vested in the transferee but, at the same time, the transferor is completely divested of those rights and duties; he no longer has any legal redress against the ex-employee nor does that employee any longer have redress against him in respect of matters which arose prior to the date of the transfer, provided however the employee accepted his transfer.[54]

The automatic vesting of rights and obligations in the successor has been held to be peremptory in two respects. The release of the transferor's obligations on the occurrence of the transfer is not conditional on the employee consenting to that release; it occurs automatically, regardless of the employee's wishes.[55] To an

---

50. *Clarke & Takeley Ltd. v. Oakes* [1999] I.C.R. 276.
51. [1940] A.C. 1014; see *supra*, p. 228.
52. *infra*, p. 239.
53. *Martin v. Lancashire C.C.*, [2001] I.C.R. 197.
54. *Katsakas v. Konstantinidis* (Case 132/91) [1992] E.C.R. 1 and *Humphreys v. Oxford University* [2000] I.C.R. 405.
55. *Berg v. Ivo Marent Besselsen* (Case 144/87) [1988] E.C.R. 2559 para. 11.

extent, therefore, the employee has become a chattel of his employing enterprise, capable of being assigned to a successor employer in the face of the most ardent objections. Of course, he cannot be compelled actually to work for his new employer. As has been stressed on several occasions, the Directive cannot be interpreted as obliging the employee to continue his employment relationship with the transferee because such an obligation would jeopardise the employee's fundamental right to choose for whom he shall work.[56]

Secondly, rights acquired by the employee under these Regulations cannot be waived in advance by him. The protection afforded to employees by the Directive has been described as "a matter of public policy (*ordre public*) and, therefore, independent of the will of the parties to the contract of employment".[57] Even if they are offered commensurate or even greater benefits for doing so, employees cannot contract out of their rights in this regard. However, this does not preclude them, following the transfer, from agreeing to a change in terms and conditions with their new employer.[58] In *Credit Suisse First Boston (Europe) Ltd. v. Lister*,[59] which concerned the purchase by the plaintiff bank of a small bank in London, employees of the latter signed "retention letters" shortly before the take-over took place. Under these, they agreed not to work for a competing bank within three months of their employment ever being terminated; in return, they were paid £2,000 each. Following the take-over, the purchasing bank sued some of them who had gone to work for a rival, for breach of these clauses. Its claim was dismissed on the grounds that these clauses were waivers of their rights under the Directive; those undertakings were obtained from them in the context of the take-over negotiations and, thus, must be regarded as purported waivers of their right that all the terms of their existing contracts and only those terms be transferred over to the successor enterprise. It is irrelevant that what they received in return may have been worth far more to them than the value of what they surrendered to their employer. On the basis of dicta in European Court cases, the court would not engage in a balancing exercise to ascertain whether, overall, the waiver and its quid-pro-quo put the employees in a better or worse position.

Express provision is made for carrying over any collective agreements affecting the employees, to which the transferor was a party. The transferee is required to continue observing those agreements' terms until they expire or are replaced.[60] Of course, if the collective agreement is not legally enforceable *inter partes*, it is not rendered so enforceable by these Regulations.

An exception to this "carry over" principle is made in respect of supplementary company and inter-company pension schemes.[61] However, the transferee is placed under a more general obligation to ensure that acquired rights under such schemes to old age, invalidity or survivors benefits are protected.

[56.] *Katsakas* case and *Humphreys* case, *supra* n.54.
[57.] *Daddy's Dance Hall* case [1985] E.C.R. 2639, paras. 14 and 15.
[58.] *ibid.*, paras. 17 and 18.
[59.] [1999] I.C.R. 794. See too *Credit Suisse First Boston (Europe) Ltd. v. Padiachy* [1999] I.C.R. 569.
[60.] Reg. 4(1).
[61.] Reg. 4(2) and *Adams v. Lanchashire C.C.* [1997] I.C.R. 834.

Dismissal

The other fundamental principle of the Directive is that, in general, the transfer of an undertaking should not cause its employees to be dismissed. Where an employee has been dismissed prior to the transfer taking place, such redress as he may have had against the former employer can be obtained against the successor.[62] Unless the dismissal was for "economic, technical or organisational reasons", as described below, Article 4(1) of the Directive (regulation 5(1) of the Regulations) provides that "the transfer . . . shall not in itself constitute grounds for dismissal by the transferor or the transferee and a dismissal, the grounds for which are such a transfer, . . . is hereby prohibited". For employees covered by the Unfair Dismissals Acts 1977-93, what this means is that a dismissal, either by the transferor or the transferee, on account of the transfer, is deemed to be automatically unfair. An employee dismissed on those grounds is entitled either to reinstatement, re-engagement or compensation, under the 1977-93 Acts, as the case may be. Where he was dismissed shortly before the transfer occurred, depending on the circumstances, his dismissal may be regarded as on account of the transfer and prima facie deemed to be unlawful.[63] Similarly, where the employee was dismissed very shortly after the transfer was concluded. If there is a reasonably extended period between the transfer and the dismissal, then the Directive's principal relevance is to carry over the continuity with the previous employer.

An unsatisfactory feature of the 1980 Regulations is that they do not expressly give the Employment Appeals Tribunal jurisdiction to deal with complaints of dismissal in contravention of their requirements. In the *Mythen* case,[64] however, it was held that the absence of an express jurisdiction does not disentitle that Tribunal to hear claims of this nature. The claim in essence is one of unfair dismissal, which is entirely within the Tribunal's competence.

For employees who are excluded from the scope of the 1977-93 Acts,[65] however, it would seem that they may have a right of action for damages for breach of statutory duty, that is breach of the Regulations, where they are dismissed because of the transfer. For the Regulations do not confine the prohibition to employees who are covered by those Acts. However, it was held by the Court of Appeal in England that the comparable Regulations there that give effect to the Directive do not confer a free standing right not to be unfairly dismissed by reason of the transfer of an undertaking.[66]

It also was held by the House of Lords[67] that where an employee was dismissed in breach of those Regulations just before or at the time of the transfer, the dismissal was effective in law and not a nullity. Consequently, those employees' contracts did not transfer over automatically to the successor; instead, their employment relationship ended, subject to such rights as the ex-employees may

---

62. This would seem to follow from Reg. 3 of the Regulations, as interpreted in the *Martin* case, *supra*, n.53.
63. *e.g. Litster* case [1990] 1 A.C. 546 and *Clarke & Takeley Ltd. v. Oakes* [1999] I.C.R. 276.
64. [1989] I.L.R.M. 844.
65. *e.g.* who do not have one year's continuous employment, who are above the normal retiring age, categories of trainers and apprentices, etc.; see *ante*, pp. 198-201.
66. *M.R.S. Environmental Services Ltd. v. Marsh* [1997] I.C.R. 995.
67. *Wilson v. St. Helens B.C.* [1999] 2 A.C. 52.

have to bring an unfair dismissal claim against the transferee. What happened there was that shortly following their dismissal, the employees accepted employment with the successor but, when subsequently it became clear that their new terms and conditions were not as favourable as previously, they contended that those better terms had been carried over by virtue of the Directive. But, it was held, they had been dismissed, which was effective in law, and they consequently had no entitlements under the Directive other than to claim for unlawful dismissal against the successor. The real problem there was that the requisite time for making an unfair dismissal claim had by then expired.

What exactly is meant by the phrase, the transfer being the "grounds for dismissal", will require elaboration by the courts. For instance, must the transfer be the only ground for the dismissal, or must it be the principal ground or does it suffice if one of the reasons for the dismissal is the transfer? A dismissal for these purposes includes constructive dismissal, that is where a substantial change for the worse in the employee's terms or conditions virtually forces him to resign.[68]

The prohibition against dismissals due to the business transfer does not apply where the employee was discharged "for economic, technical or organisational reasons entailing changes in the workforce".[69] Surprisingly, the exact meaning of this phrase has not yet been clarified by the European Court. The English Court of Appeal would not put the matter much further than to hold that the reason must be connected with the further conduct of the business as a going concern, as contrasted with making the transfer more attractive for the transferor.[70] The phrase in the Directive was "a very broad description of the whole range of circumstances that might … give rise to a justification for dismissal" and it would not be "helpful to try to circumscribe precisely all the varied circumstances which can amount to economic organisational reasons".[71] Those reasons have affinity with the concept of "redundancy" under the Redundancy Payments Acts.[72] Of course, under the Unfair Dismissals Acts 1977-93, while redundancy is a permitted ground for dismissal, dismissal for that reason may nevertheless be unfair because of some improper way the employer went about the matter.

Informing and consulting employees' representatives

As has been explained elsewhere,[73] both the transferor and the transferee are obliged to inform representatives of employees affected about aspects of the proposed transfer and to consult with them on those matters.

---

[68]   reg. 5(2).
[69]   reg. 5(1).
[70]   *Whitehouse v. Charles Blatchford & Sons Ltd.* [2000] I.C.R. 542.
[71]   *ibid.* at pp. 550 and 562.
[72]   See *ante*, p. 216.
[73]   *Industrial Relations Law* pp.82-83.

CHAPTER 10

EMPLOYER'S INSOLVENCY

Occasionally, an employer may become insolvent — he may be an individual who is adjudicated a bankrupt or who enters into an arrangement with all his creditors, or the employer is a company which is wound up because it cannot pay its debts, or it is placed in receivership or in court-supervised examination. For many years, the only special protection for employees in these circumstances was the preferential debts which they are entitled to be paid before the general creditors can get a penny. As a result of an E.C. initiative, an insolvency fund was established to meet various debts to employees whom an insolvent employer is unable to pay. The extent to which the Transfer of Undertakings Regulations apply to disposals made in the context of insolvency proceedings has not been fully clarified.

IMPACT ON THE EMPLOYMENT CONTRACT

An important preliminary question is the effect, under the general principles of contract law, of the insolvency in question on the workers' contracts of employment.[1] Does the insolvency operate to frustrate these contracts or otherwise terminate them, or do the contractual rights and obligations survive the onset of insolvency? There may be express or implied terms in a contract which provide answers to these questions. In the absence of such terms, the matter turns on the nature of the insolvency proceedings involved.

Bankruptcy

On a person being adjudicated a bankrupt, his property, subject to certain exceptions, immediately vests in the Official Assignee.[2] Since rights under an employment contract are not proprietary for these purposes, they will not vest in the Assignee once an employer is made bankrupt.[3] Whether the contract is thereupon lawfully terminated or is frustrated, or whether the bankruptcy operates to break the contract, depends on the bankrupt's own circumstances and the terms of the contract.

Liquidation

Where an insolvent company is put into liquidation, that may be an out-of-court creditors' voluntary liquidation or an official liquidation (or compulsory winding

---

[1.] See, generally, M. Freedland, *The Contract of Employment* (1976), Chap. 9.
[2.] See, generally, M. Forde, *Bankruptcy Law in Ireland* (1990), pp. 71-83.
[3.] *Re Collins* [1925] Ch. 556.

up) by order of the High Court.[4] Where the winding up is by order of the Court, publication of the winding up order is deemed to be notice to the entire world, including the company's employees, that they are dismissed.[5] Under the Companies Acts, that order operates retrospectively to when the petition was presented,[6] so that the deemed notice of dismissal would also operate retrospectively in this manner. If, under their contracts, the employees were entitled to advance notice of termination, they would be entitled to damages for breach of that provision. This rule applies regardless of the employee's status within the company and regardless of whether the job is subject to a specified notice period or is for a fixed term or indeed for life.[7] Strictly, publication of the winding up order does not terminate the contract because, in principle, the employee can refuse to accept the unlawful repudiation of the contract; but for all practical purposes the contract is brought to an end at that time.

However, the liquidator may want to carry on the business for the time being and to continue all or some of the employees in their jobs. He therefore is entitled to waive the deemed notices of dismissal and to continue employing the relevant employees under their existing contracts.[8] Unless there has been an unequivocal waiver, the company's employees will be treated as having been dismissed, although they may be re-employed by the liquidator on new terms for the purpose of the winding up.

Occasionally, a provisional liquidator is appointed by the court prior to ordering a winding up, whose task is to safeguard the company's assets. If that provisional liquidator is authorised to carry on the company's business for the time being, his appointment does not operate to discharge the employment contracts of the workforce.[9]

A creditor's voluntary liquidation commences when the members of the company pass a resolution that it be wound up because it cannot pay its debts. It has been held that the passing or indeed the publication of such resolution does not invariably operate as a notice of dismissal.[10] In particular circumstances, depending on the terms of the contract, the resolution to wind up may constitute notice of termination. The test is whether in all the circumstances the employee is justified in regarding the winding up as indicating an intention by the company to repudiate its obligations under the contract.[11] If employees are retained by the liquidator or are re-hired shortly after the resolution was passed, they are deemed to be still employed by the company.[12]

---

4. See, generally, M. Forde, *The Law of Company Insolvency* (1993), Part III, and Graham, "The Effect of Liquidation on Contracts of Service", 15 Mod. L. Rev. 48 (1952).
5. *Re General Rolling Stock Co.* (1866) 1 L.R. Eq. 346.
6. Companies Act 1963, s.220(2).
7. *Fowler v. Commercial Timber Co.* [1930] 2 K.B. 1; *cf. Re R. S. Newman Ltd.* [1916] 3 Ch. 309 and *Re T.N. Farrer Ltd.* [1937] Ch. 352.
8. *Re English Joint Stock Bank* (1867) 3 Eq. 341.
9. *Donnelly v. Gleeson* (Hamilton J., July 11, 1978); *cf. Re McEvanenhenry Ltd.* (Murphy J., May 15, 1986).
10. *Midland Counties Bank v. Attwood* [1905] 1 Ch. 357.
11. *Reigate v. Union Mf'g Co.* [1918] 1 K.B. 592.
12. *Collman v. Construction Industry Training Board* (1966) 1 T.L.R. 52.

Receivership

The appointment of a receiver over some or all of the employer's assets does not always mean that it is insolvent, although that usually is the case. A receiver's task is to take control of and to sell off the relevant assets and, from the proceeds of the sale, to pay the appointing creditor what he is owed. Occasionally, a receiver is appointed by order of the court but the usual form of receivership is where the appointment is made by a secured creditor under the terms of a debenture.[13] Frequently the receiver is authorised to continue managing the business until a buyer can be found who will purchase it as a going concern, and usually the receiver will be designated an agent of the company.

The effect on the employment relationship of the appointment of a receiver was analysed in *Griffiths v. Secretary of State*,[14] where the plaintiff was a managing director of a company when a debenture-holder appointed a receiver and manager over its entire assets. The position was explained by Lawson J. as follows:

> "The appointment by debenture-holders of a receiver and manager as agent of the company (the commonest case) . . . does not of itself automatically terminate contracts of employment previously made and subsisting between the relevant company and all its employees. There are three situations in which this may be qualified.
>
> The first situation is where . . . the appointment is accompanied by a sale of business; that will operate to terminate contracts of employment . . . because . . . there is no longer any business for which the employees can work.[15]
>
> The second situation is where . . . a receiver and manager enters into a new agreement with a particular employee that may be inconsistent with the continuation of his old service contract. . . .[16]
>
> The third situation . . . is where . . . the continuation of the employment of a particular employee is inconsistent with the role and functions of a receiver and manager. The mere fact that he is labelled 'managing director' does not . . . indicate that because he is so labelled his employment in that capacity or office is inconsistent with the position, role and functions of a receiver and manager. . . ."[17]

Where it is the Court which appoints the receiver and manager, "the result of such an appointment is to discharge the servants from their service to their original employer and that [may be] a wrongful dismissal for which an action would lie".[18] The reason for this rule perhaps is that this receiver is the agent of the Court.

---

13. See, generally, M. Forde, *supra*, n.4, Part I, and Davies & Freeland "The Effects of Receivership on Employees of Companies", (1980) 9 Ind. L. J. 95.
14. [1974] 1 Q.B. 468.
15. *e.g. Re Foster & Clarke Ltd.'s Indenture Trusts* [1966] 1 W.L.R. 125.
16. *e.g. Re Mack Trucks (Britain) Ltd.* [1967] 1 W.L.R. 780.
17. [1974] 1 Q.B. at 485-486.
18. *Reid v. Explosives Co.* (1887) 19 Q.B.D. 264 at 267.

If the receiver simply decides to retain an employee's services, the receiver is not personally responsible for the remuneration and for other incidents of the employment relationship. It would be otherwise if the employee was discharged and was then hired by the receiver under a new contract. In *Nicholl v. Cutts*,[19] the managing director of a company, of which he was a minority shareholder as well, sued a receiver who had been appointed over the company's assets, for remuneration. The receiver was appointed in March and dismissed the plaintiff in May, just before selling the company as a going concern. Because the receiver never entered into an employment contract with the plaintiff, he was not liable for the unpaid remuneration. It was also held that the plaintiff's unpaid salary for those three months could not be regarded as costs and expense, of the receivership.[20]

Court-supervised examination

There is no reason in principle why the appointment of an examiner into a company's affairs, under the Companies (Amendment) Act 1990 should bring an end to the employment contracts of the company's workforce. Even where the Court directs the examiner to take over the function of the company's directors, that should not affect the employees' contracts.

TRANSFER OF UNDERTAKINGS REGULATIONS

The strict contract law position of employees of insolvent businesses may be significantly modified by the European Communities (Safeguarding of Employees' Rights on Transfer of Undertakings) Regulations 1980,[21] as described in the previous chapter, although the precise application of these Regulations in insolvency situations requires further elaboration by the courts. The Regulations only apply to persons employed by the business in question at the date of the transfer. Therefore, if the insolvency operated as a dismissal before any transfer took place, the Regulations would not apply. This, of course, is not the case where the employee was dismissed in order to facilitate the transfer, other than for the specified "economic", etc., reasons.[22] It furthermore would seem that if the transfer took place before the expiry of the employee's notice period, the employment relationship continued in existence after the dismissal took place provided the employee did not accept the repudiation of his contract. In such a case, the Regulations would apply to any transfer of all or part of the business.

It was contended that the E.C. Directive, which gave rise to these Regulations,[23] does not apply where the transfer is being made in the context of insolvency administration. That view received some support from the European Commission and from Advocate General Slynn in the *Abels* case,[24] which

---

19. [1985] B.C.L.C. 322.
20. *cf. Powdrill v. Watson* [1995] 2 A.C. 394.
21. S.I. No. 306 of 1980. See, generally, C. Barnard, *E.C. Employment Law* (2nd ed., 2000), pp. 469-475.
22. Reg. 5(1).
23. Directive 77/187, O.J. No. L 61/26 (1977).
24. *Abels v. Administrative Board* (Case 135/83) [1985] E.C.R. 469.

concerned a transfer made by a Dutch company that was in *surseance van betaling,* a status resembling a stay on proceedings imposed by section 201 of the Companies Act 1963. It was argued that, insolvency being a very technical field, which would be the subject of E.C. approximating measures at some stage, the Directive should not be regarded as applying in those circumstances unless it explicitly provided otherwise, which it does not. Should they so choose, Member States remain free, under the Directive, to apply its provisions to insolvent businesses. There was also the practical consideration that the Directive's actual objects would be frustrated rather than advanced if it applied to insolvency disposals. It was said that:

> "A potential purchaser may be deterred from buying up businesses which are insolvent, but which might be capable of rescue, if they are obliged to take on all the employees. The only way to save the business may be to reduce the number of staff. It is in the interests of the labour force as a whole that such rescue attempts should be made, even if some staff have to go. In fact, rather than in theory, more jobs may be lost if purchasers are deterred by a rule that they must take on the employees and satisfy all obligations to them".[25]

But the E.C.J. declined to be guided by this analysis in its entirety. Some insolvency disposals fall within the Directive, for instance the disposal in the instant case. The fact that a court has authorised an employer to suspend payments to his creditors does not take him outside the Directive, because the undertaking continues as an active business entity; it could be different if the business had ceased entirely and all that remained were physical assets. Similarly in the *d'Urso* case,[26] which concerned the Italian special administration procedure for large undertakings in difficulty, where the business was continued with a view to it being reconstructed so that it could trade in the future, the Directive was held to apply. And in the *Jules Dethier* case,[27] which concerned the Belgian equivalent of a members' voluntary liquidation, the Directive too was held to apply.

What matters is the purpose of the insolvency procedure in question, not its form. Ordinarily, an insolvent liquidation is beyond the Directive because the realisation of assets and ensuing settlement of debts are exclusively for the benefit of the creditors; any continuation of the business is aimed solely at that objective. And in *d'Urso* the Court held that the Directive did not apply to the Italian creditors' arrangement procedure in the law on compulsory administrative liquidation, because its effects were comparable to those in bankruptcy proceedings, which are designed predominantly for the benefit of creditors.

In *Mythen v. Employment Appeals Tribunal,*[28] Barrington J. held that a sale of part of the business by a receiver, appointed under a debenture, came within the Directive. If receivers' disposals fell outside the Directive, its requirements could easily be avoided, because the most common form of receivership is an "entirely extra-judicial process . . . which might be employed much more easily than a liq-

---

25. Argument of E.C. Commission, *ibid.* at p. 474.
26. *Urso v. Ercole Marelli Electromeccanica Generale SpA* (Case C 362/89) [1991] E.C.R. 4105.
27. *Jules Dethier Equipment S.A. v. Dassy* (Case C 319/94) [1998] E.C.R. 1061.
28. [1989] I.L.R.M. 844.

uidation . . . to defeat the purposes of the Directive".[29] The *Litster* case[30] in Britain, where the Directive was held to apply, also involved a sale by a receiver. Because a creditor's voluntary liquidation could relatively easily be used to avoid the Regulations' requirements, it would seem that a disposal in that situation also falls within the Regulations. Of course, the Regulations will not apply where all that is transferred is the bare assets and not the going concern or the goodwill of all or part of the business.

PREFERENTIAL DEBTS

Where an individual is bankrupt or a company is insolvent, there are certain creditors who are entitled to be paid out of the insolvent estate before any payments can be made to the general creditors. The traditional justification for preferring employees of the insolvent in this manner is that they are very much in an unequal position when dealing with an employer who is in financial difficulties. Preferential treatment was first accorded to them in an era when there was no welfare state and trade unions hardly existed. Under the Preferential Payments in Bankruptcy (Ireland) Act 1889, arrears of salary owed to the bankrupt's employees, up to a specified amount, were made a preferential debt. The position is now covered by section 81 of the Bankruptcy Act 1988 and by section 285(2) of the Companies Act 1963, as amended in 1982. Under the companies and the bankruptcy legislation, the State is also a preferred creditor in respect of certain unpaid taxes. Employers are affected by these provisions in that unpaid tax deducted from the employee's remuneration and unpaid P.R.S.I. are preferred debts.[31]

Debts to employees

Only employees who work under a contract of employment benefit from these preferential debts provisions. Thus in *In re Sunday Tribune Ltd.*,[32] where several journalists with a Sunday newspaper claimed to be preferential creditors, some of those claims were rejected on the grounds that those journalists were independent contractors. In *Stakelum v. Canning*,[33] it was held that executive directors of companies, other than managing directors, can be employees for the purposes of this preference. Company liquidators and also company receivers are obliged to pay employees in accordance with the following preferences.[34]

Wages and salary

First and foremost are unpaid wages and salary owing for services rendered to the employer. This preference is subject to a financial ceiling: sums which are owing

---

[29.]   *ibid.* at 853. Similarly with the "hive down" in *Re Maxwell Fleet and Facilities M'gt Ltd.* [2000] I.C.R. 717. Compare *Mann v. Secretary of State for Employment* [1999] I.C.R. 898, concerning the Insolvency Fund Directive, *infra*, p. 251.

[30.]   *Litster v. Forth Dry Dock & Engineering Co.* [1990] 1 A.C. 546.

[31.]   See, generally, M. Forde, *Company Law* (3rd ed., 1999), pp. 747-748.

[32.]   [1984] I.R. 505.

[33.]   [1976] I.R. 314.

[34.]   Companies Act 1963, ss.285 and 98.

in excess of £2,500 are not preferred. In 1982 the ceiling for companies as employers was increased from £300;[35] this £2,500 sum may be varied by the Minister.[36]

There is no general definition of what is a "wage" or a "salary" for these purposes but it must mean remuneration for work done; it includes remuneration for periods of absence from work for "good cause" and on holidays.[37] In *In re M*[38] it was held that amounts deducted from earnings and credited to a holiday stamp scheme in the construction industry were wages, even though the employees were only entitled to have the sums deducted paid into what was described as a suspense account. The services in question must have been rendered during the four months immediately preceding the adjudication. Where the arrangement with a "farm labourer" is to pay him a lump sum at the end of the hiring or at the end of the year, the Court is empowered to determine how much of what is owing should be preferred.[39] All arrears of statutory minimum wages under the 2000 Act are preferred.[40]

Holiday pay

Accrued holiday remuneration at the date of the adjudication is preferred.[41]

Sick pay

Outstanding amounts due under an arrangement for sick pay are preferred.[42]

Pension contributions

Outstanding pension contributions under any scheme or arrangement made for superannuation are preferred whether they are employer's contributions or those deducted from the employee's remuneration.[43]

Compensation for dismissal

Three major statutory schemes exist for compensating employees who have been dismissed from their jobs in specified circumstances, *viz.* where they were not given the requisite statutory minimum notice, where they were made redundant, and where their dismissal was held to be unfair. Compensation which is awarded to a dismissed employee under any of these schemes is a priority debt.[44] Where the employer is unable to pay that compensation, the Protection of Employees

---

[35.] Companies (Amendment) Act 1982, s.10(b).
[36.] Companies Act 1963, s.285 (inserted by 1982 Act, s.10(e)); for individuals, see Bankruptcy Act 1988, s.81(1)(b)-(f).
[37.] *ibid.* s.285(11); *cf. Re A Company* [2000] I.C.R. 263.
[38.] [1955] N.I. 182.
[39.] Companies Act 1963, s.285(4).
[40.] National Minimum Wage Act 2000, s.40.
[41.] Companies Act 1963, s.285(2)(d).
[42.] *ibid.* s.285(2)(h) (inserted by 1982 Act, s.10(a)).
[43.] *ibid.* s.285(2)(i) (inserted by 1982 Act, s.10(a)).
[44.] Minimum Notice and Terms of Employment Act 1973, s.13, Redundancy Payments Act 1979, s.42, as amended, Unfair Dismissals Act 1977, s.12.

(Insolvency) Act 1984 requires those amounts to be paid by the Minister for Labour. In that event, the Minister is subrogated for the employees in respect of the amounts paid.

Compensation for accidents

In the case of insolvent companies, if the employee was injured in the course of his employment and has been awarded or stands to be awarded damages and costs in respect of that injury, the amount of those damages and the costs are a preferred debt.[45] However, this preference does not exist where the company is effectively indemnified by insurers against that liability. In such a case, the injured employee is in effect subrogated for the company and is entitled to be paid the full amount forthcoming on the insurance policy.[46]

Other compensation

All compensation payable under the Employment Equality Act 1998,[47] and under the legislation on maternity, adoptive, parental and carer's leave, is given priority.[48]

Sums advanced to pay employees

In the case of insolvent companies, where persons advanced money to the company for the purpose of paying employees' wages or salary, holiday remuneration or pension benefits, the lender is preferred to the extent that those employees would have been preferred if they had not been paid what was owing to them.[49] Thus, if a bank lends £20,000 to meet the payroll at the end of the week or the end of the month, it is a preferred creditor for that amount. Any form of "advance" to the employer comes within this preference; it need not strictly be a loan if those wages would have been a preferred debt if unpaid.[50] But the fact that a bank debits wages cheques to a separate wages account does not always entitle it to the preference.

THE INSOLVENCY FUND

At times an employer may be so heavily insolvent that there is not enough in his entire estate to satisfy even the preferential debts. Whatever assets he possessed may have been captured by a prior charge or be subject to leasing, hire purchase or retention of title arrangements. Even if there are enough assets to cover the preferential debts, the employees may have to wait years for the liquidator or Official Assignee to make a distribution. It was to deal with these eventualities

---

[45]   Companies Act 1963, s.285(2)(g).
[46]   Civil Liability Act 1961, s.62.
[47]   s.103.
[48]   Maternity Protection Act 1994, s.36, Adoptive Leave Act 1995, s.38, and Parental Leave Act 1998, s.24, and Carer's Leave Act 2001, s.25.
[49]   Companies Act 1963 (as supplemented by 1982 Act, s.10(c)).
[50]   *Waikato Savings Bank v. Andrews Furniture Ltd.* [1982] 2 N.Z.L.R. 520.

that the Protection of Employees (Employers' Insolvency) Act 1984 was passed. This Act sets up a fund administered by the Minister from which the equivalent of certain debts to employees can be paid; the Minister is then subrogated for those employees. This Act is based on the E.C. Directive 80/987 on the protection of employees in the event of the insolvency of their employer.[51] The Fund was known as the Redundancy and Employers' Insolvency Fund but in 1991 was amalgamated with the general Social Insurance Fund. No express provision is made for the extraterritorial application of this Act.[52]

Employees covered

Like the redundancy payments legislation, the 1984 Act applies only to employees who are insurable for all benefits under the Social Welfare Acts.[53] But the Minister, by order, can extend or restrict the personal scope of the Act. In 1988 employees over 66 years of age who otherwise would be insured for all benefits were brought within the Act.[54]

Debts payable

Those debts which eligible employees may recover from the fund are listed in section 6(2) of the 1984 Act as amended. These are as follows:

- Arrears of "normal weekly remuneration"[55] not exceeding £400 per week[56] and for a duration of no more than eight weeks.

- Arrears under a sick pay scheme, subject to the same £400 per week and eight-weeks ceiling; but also subject to a ceiling measured by reference to the injury or disability benefit and pay related benefit payable under the Social Welfare Acts.[57]

- Arrears of holiday pay, subject to the same £400 per week and eight-weeks ceiling.[58]

- Money in lieu of the minimum notice periods for dismissal prescribed by the Minimum Notice and Terms of Employment Act 1973, again subject to the same ceilings.

---

[51]. O.J. No. L 283/23 (1980). See, generally, C. Barnard, *E.C. Employment Law, op. cit.*, pp.498-506; and C. Quigley, *European Community Contract Law* (1998) pp.237-241. *cf. Francovitch v. Italy* (Case 9/90) [1991] E.C.R. 5357 and *Francovitch v. Italy (No. 2)* (Case 479/93) [1995] E.C.R. 3843.

[52]. *Cf. Everson v. Secretary of State* (Case 198/98) [2000] I.R.L.R. 202 on which country's insolvency fund is liable.

[53]. s. 3. *cf. Kenny v. Minister for Trade and Employment* [1999] E.L.R. 163.

[54]. S.I. No 48 of 1988.

[55]. As defined in s.6(9).

[56]. s.6(4)(a) and Protection of Employees (Employers' Insolvency) (Variation of Limit) Regulations, 2001, S.I. No 42.

[57]. s.6(4)(b) and S.I. No. 92 of 2001.

[58]. s.6(4)(a) and S.I. No. 42 of 2001.

- Damages, compensation, awards and fines payable under the Unfair Dismissals Acts 1977-93, the Redundancy Payments Acts 1967-79, the Employment Equality Act 1998,[59] and also under the Acts on maternity, adoptive, parental, and carer's leave.[60]

- Remuneration payable under Part VI of the Industrial Relations Act 1946.[61]

- Remuneration and compensation payable under the National Minimum Wage Act 2000.[62]

- Damages awarded for wrongful dismissal.[63]

- Unpaid employers' and employees' contributions to a pension scheme, to a maximum of 12 months' arrears.[64]

Where the amount payable under any of these heads is calculated on the basis of normal remuneration, the Fund will not pay out any on more than what represents £250 a week. The amount payable under some of these heads is subject to several other qualifications.

Where there are liabilities to the employee before the reference period commences and, during that period, some payments are made to him on those liabilities, those payments must first be set off against the pre-reference period liabilities and in priority to the claim in respect of that period. Thus, in *Regeling*,[65] in the eight months prior to his dismissal, the employee had been paid sporadically. On being dismissed, he claimed against the Fund to be paid for the entire three months, which was the reference period in the Netherlands, notwithstanding that occasional payments had been made during that time. His claim was upheld; those sums were deemed to discharge the employer's indebtedness prior to three months.

It was held by the House of Lords in the *Westwood* case[66] that payments made from a similar fund in Britain are subject to the collateral benefits principle. There the amount of unemployment benefit an employee drew immediately following his dismissal was deducted from the amount due to him in principle under the insolvency fund legislation and only the net sum was payable to him. This was because the mode of redress for not giving the minimum notice of dismissal required by statute is deemed to be an action for breach of contract. That being so, the successful plaintiff has a duty to mitigate his damages and it was previously held that, under the duty to mitigate, unemployment benefit received during the relevant period must be deducted from the overall sum due.[67] The legislative

---

[59.] s.103(3)-(6).

[60.] *supra*, n.48, ss.41, 40, 26, and 30 respectively.

[61.] s. 6(2)(vii) and S.I. No. 42 of 2001.

[62.] s.47.

[63.] s. 6(3).

[64.] S.I. No. 42 of 2001.

[65.] *Regeling v. Bestuur van de Bedrijfsvereniging voor de Metaalnijverheid* (Case C125/97) [1998] E.C.R. 4493.

[66.] *Westwood v. Secretary of State for Employment* [1985] A.C. 20.

[67.] *Parson v. B.N.M. Laboratories Ltd.* [1964] 1 Q.B. 95.

mechanism for recovery under the Minimum Notice and Terms of Employment Act 1973 is different from that in Britain but section 12(1) of that Act speaks of "recovering compensation for any loss sustained". In *Irish Leathers Ltd. v. Minister for Labour*[68] Barrington J. declined to follow *Westwood* because it was unsafe to follow the English precedents where there are differences of detail in the legislation. It was held that the fund should pay the full amount of the outstanding salary, without deducting any unemployment benefit the employee had received. Under the 1973 Act, he has a right to be paid a specified sum of money and whether at the same time he received unemployment benefit is outside that Act's concerns; it is entirely a matter between the employee and the social welfare authorities.

More recently it was held in Britain that the amount payable from the insolvency fund is the net amount after deducting income tax,[69] and, further, any sums an employee owes his employer may be set off against the sum due from the insolvency fund.[70]

Claims

Payment from the Fund is obtained principally by making an application by or on behalf of the employee to the Minister.[71] If the Minister is satisfied that the employee falls within the Act, that his employer is insolvent, and that all or part of any debt, described above, is owed to the employee, the Minister shall make the payment. What constitutes insolvency for these purposes is defined as an individual executing a deed of arrangement or being adjudicated bankrupt, and a company being put into receivership or being wound up, or possession being taken of company assets under a floating charge.[72] The Minister is empowered to require information regarding the debt in order to ascertain if the claim is well founded.[73] If there was some agreement between the employer and the applicant that an application should be made to the Fund in respect of a debt but the employer then had the means to pay that sum, the Minister can refuse to make a payment.[74]

In the case of an application for arrears of remuneration, sick pay or holiday pay, if the sum has been awarded by a court to the employee, then the obligation to make a payment from the Fund is immediate.[75] Where there has not been a court award under either of these heads, if an application for payment from the Fund is refused by the Minister the matter can be appealed to the Employment Appeals Tribunal.[76] Moreover, if the Minister, is in doubt whether any particular claim should be paid, he may refer the matter to the Tribunal for its determination.[77]

---

68. [1986] I.R. 177.

69. *Secretary of State for Employment v. Cooper* [1987] I.C.R. 766.

70. *Secretary of State for Employment v. Wilson* [1997] I.C.R. 408; *cf. Mann v. Secretary of State for Employment* [1999] I.C.R. 898.

71. s.6(1) and S.I. No. 349 of 1991; *cf. Minister for Labour v. Grace* [1993] 2 I.R. 53.

72. s.1(3); *cf.* s.4.

73. s.8.

74. s.6(8).

75. s.6(3).

76. s.9(1) and (4); *cf. Re Solus Teo.* [1990] I.L.R.M. 180.

CHAPTER 11

TRANSNATIONAL EMPLOYMENT

By transnational employment is meant situations where an employee does not work exclusively in one country but his job involves spending some or all of his time abroad. Merchant seamen and aircraft personnel are engaged in uniquely transnational work; so too are non-local diplomatic personnel. Modern developments in transport and the opening up of foreign markets, especially within the European Community, have resulted in an increasing number of personnel working for significant periods of time away from their employer's headquarters. Employments of this nature give rise to their own special legal problems, such as what law governs the employment relationship, what courts are competent to hear disputes arising from these relationships and to what extent do the labour laws of one State affect the legal position of employees who are working in another State. Many of the questions which arise in this particular context require consideration of the principles of the conflict of laws — otherwise known as private international law.[1] As has already been explained, aliens (other than nationals of E.C. Member States) need administrative authority to become employed in Ireland, and, within the European Community, discrimination against nationals of E.C. States and their dependants is prohibited.[2] In 1996 the E.C. Council adopted a Directive to deal with the position of workers who are posted by their employers to a different country.[3] There is a rigorous licensing regime for aircraft personnel and seafaring is the subject of extensive regulation.

APPLICABLE LAW

Where an employee works exclusively within Ireland, then his rights and obligations are determined exclusively by Irish law. If he works in some other State, his legal position is subject to the laws of that State. But where his work takes him to two or more States, the question then arises of which State's laws determine his entitlements and duties.

Contract

Often this question is resolved beforehand by the parties stipulating in the employment contract that it shall be governed by Irish law or by English law or

---

[1.] See, generally, W. Binchy, *Irish Conflict of Law* (1988) (hereinafter referred to as *Binchy*).

[2.] See *ante*, p. 153 *et seq.*

[3.] Directive 96/71, O.J. No. L 18/1 (1996). See, generally, C. Barnard, *E.C. Labour Law* (2nd ed., 2000), pp. 172-175, and Davies, "Posted Workers: Single Market or Protection of National Labour Law Systems?" 34 Comm. Mkt. L.R. 571 (1997). E.C. law also can affect income tax: *Finanzamt Koln-Alstadt v. Schumaker (Case 279/93)* [1995] E.C.R. 225.

by some other law, as the case may be. Generally, the parties' express choice of law will be accepted and given effect by the courts. Where the parties did not actually select a governing law, when a dispute arises the courts attempt to ascertain from all the circumstances which law they chose by implication.[4] Certain features of how the contract was concluded, its terms and the performance of the work may indicate that the parties had in mind one particular national law. For instance, if the contract was concluded in Connemara, was in the Irish language, and contained references to Irish legislation and Irish industrial relations procedures, this would suggest very strongly that the parties had intended that their relationship would be governed by the law of Ireland, even though much of the work under the contract was to be done abroad.

In the absence of an express or an implied choice of law, then the applicable law is that of the State with which the contract is most closely connected.[5] Sometimes there may be no difficulty in ascertaining what State this is; the overwhelming preponderance of features may relate to one particular State. For instance, if the contract was made in Ireland, both parties are Irish nationals and residents, the employer's headquarters are in Ireland, and a substantial amount of the employee's work must be performed here, then the relationship almost certainly is subject to Irish law. At times, however, the relationship's connections with two or more States may be approximately even. There is a tendency, where the connections with the State where a dispute is being heard are not less than those with another State, for the court to apply its State's laws. This is not entirely legal chauvinism; those laws have as strong a claim to apply as any other laws and those are the laws which the court understands best.

That judges can easily reach contrary conclusions on the question of which law should apply is illustrated by one of the principal modern cases dealing with this issue. In *Sayers v. International Drilling Co. N.V.,*[6] the plaintiff was injured when working on an oil rig off the coast of Nigeria. His employers were a Dutch company, which operated drilling rigs in many parts of the world. He was English, his contract was made in England and was in the English language, he was to be paid in pounds sterling and the contract was administered from London. A majority of the English Court of Appeal overcame the temptation to apply their own law in cases like this and held that the contract was governed by Dutch law. This was because the contract was in a standard form drawn up by a Dutch company to cater for workers of diverse nationalities who might be hired in different countries. Also, it contained an exclusion clause which would not be valid under English law.[7] The several English aspects of the contract were attributed by the Court more to administrative convenience than to any inferred intention as to which law shall apply.

The Rome Convention on the Law Applicable to Contractual Relations of 1980 was brought into force in Ireland by the Contractual Obligations (Applicable Law) Act 1991.[8] This is a treaty which purports to lay down a comprehensive

---

4. See, generally, *Binchy*, pp. 518 et seq.
5. *ibid.*
6. [1971] 1 W.L.R. 1176.
7. Law Reform (Personal Injuries) Act 1948, s.1(3).
8. See, generally, *Binchy* pp. 552 *et seq.*

set of rules for determining which particular law shall govern nearly all types of contracts containing a transnational element. Article 6 of the Convention deals with employment contracts and provides as follows:

> "1. Notwithstanding [the principle of the parties' freedom to choose the applicable law], in a contract of employment a choice of law made by the parties shall not have the result of depriving the employee of the protection afforded to him by the mandatory rules of the law which would be applicable . . . in the absence of choice.
>
> 2. [A] contract of employment shall, in the absence of choice . . . be governed:
>
> (a) by the law of the country in which the employee habitually carries out his work in performance of the contract, even if he is temporarily employed in another country; or
>
> (b) if the employee does not habitually carry out his work in any one country, by the law of the country in which the place of business through which he was engaged is situated
>
> unless it appears from the circumstances as a whole that the contract is more closely connected with another country, in which case the contract shall be governed by the law of that country."

In other words, in the absence of choice by the parties, an employment contract is governed by the law of the country in which the employee habitually carries out his work in performance of the contract, even if he is temporarily employed in another country. This concept of "habitually works" also exists in the E.C.-sponsored Convention regarding which courts have jurisdiction to hear disputes regarding transnational employment relationships.[9] It has been summed up as meaning the place where the employee had established the effective centre of his working activities and where or from which he performed the essential part of his duties.[10] If the employee does not habitually carry out his work in any one country, the contract is governed by the law of the country in which the place of business through which he was engaged is situated. Nevertheless, in each of these cases, if it appears from the circumstances as a whole that the contract is more closely connected with another country, then the contract is governed by the law of that country.

Even where the parties may have chosen an applicable law, in a contract of employment that choice of law will not have the result of depriving the employee of the protection afforded to him by the "mandatory rules" of the law which would have applied in the absence of choice. That is to say, regardless of what law the parties may have chosen, the peremptory requirements of whatever law would be applicable under 2(a) (habitually works) or 2(b) (where hired) will apply. The requirements of the Unfair Dismissals Acts are mandatory for this purpose.[11]

---

9. See *infra*, p. 261.
10. *Rutten v. Cross Medical Ltd.* (C 383/95) [1997] E.C.R. 57.
11. *Zimmerman v. Der Deutsche Schuliverein Ltd.* [1999] E.L.R. 211.

Tort

If the dispute is framed in tort rather than in contract, the outcome is determined by the "proper law" of the tort, which means the law with which the several features of the alleged wrong is most closely connected.[12] In deciding what law that is, account is taken of similar considerations as affect the proper law of the contract. Often the law governing the contract and the proper law of the tort will be the same. For instance in the *Sayers* case, the tort action as well as the employment contract were held to be subject to Dutch law. Where the law of the contract and of the tort are different, complications can arise, such as when the contract contains a clause which purports to exclude liability in tort.[13]

Statutory rights and duties

Whenever an employee is required to work outside the State for at least a month, his employer must furnish him with the following particulars prior to his departure, *viz*. the duration of his employment abroad, the currency in which he will be paid during that period, any benefit he will obtain for working abroad, and, where appropriate, the terms and conditions on which he is to return to the State.

When the question arises whether a particular piece of legislation grants rights to or imposes duties on the parties to an employment contract, the answer does not always turn on which State's law governs their contract in general terms. A feature of several of the modern employment protection Acts is that they expressly provide for the transnational situations in which they apply or do not apply. Thus, section 2(3) of the Unfair Dismissals Act 1977 excludes from the Act's scope employees who, under their contracts, "ordinarily worked" outside of Ireland, subject to some exceptions. And in 2000 regulations were adopted to remove difficulties caused by pension schemes that have members in the State and also in the United Kingdom. But there are some Acts which do not address themselves directly to this question.

Territoriality

One of the general principles of international law is the territoriality of regulatory legislation. This principle has two aspects. Generally, regulatory legislation will be applied to all relevant circumstances occurring within the legislating State. Thus, the Irish Road Traffic Acts apply to all situations involving road traffic in Ireland; the fact that the car in question was manufactured abroad or is owned or is being driven by a foreigner, or some other extra-territorial feature exists, does not prevent the Irish legislation from applying. Similarly, all consumer credit transactions occurring in Scotland are subject to the Scottish Consumer Credit Rules, regardless of whether some aspects of the transaction are not Scottish.[14]

In the employment law context, the territoriality principle is illustrated by two cases on the since-repealed Workmens' Compensation Acts. In *Scanlon v. Hartlepool S.S. Co.*,[15] the plaintiff was employed by an English shipping com-

---

[12.] See, generally, *Binchy*, Chap. 32.
[13.] *e.g.* the *Sayers* case [1971] 1 W.L.R. 1176. Compare *Coupland v. Arabian Gulf Petroleum Co.* [1983] 3 All E.R. 226.
[14.] *English v. Donnelly* (1958) S.C. 494.
[15.] [1929] I.R. 96.

pany which did not have any registered office in Ireland. He was injured while unloading cargo from one of the company's ships, which presumably was registered in England. However, that accident occurred in Ireland and the plaintiff claimed compensation under the Workmens' Compensation Act 1906. The contention that the extraterritorial features of the employment relationship prevented this Act from applying to the case was rejected. According to Sullivan P., "[a] person entering into a contract in the State is subject to all the conditions attached by our law to his contract, including, in the present case, liability to pay [workmen's] compensation and to have the question of such liability determined in the courts of this State".[16] The circumstances in *Santry v. Coast Line Ltd*[17] were similar. The plaintiff, who was employed by a British company on a British registered ship under articles entered into in London, was injured while the ship was proceeding down the River Lee in Cork. It was held that he was entitled to bring his workmen's compensation claim in this country.

The second part of the territoriality principle is that, generally, a State's regulatory legislation does not apply to events occurring outside the jurisdiction even though the events in question may have some connection with that State.[18] Of course, this is not the case where the Act by its very terms asserts an extra-territorial reach. Criminal laws are presumed not to be extra-territorial unless the legislation in question stipulates otherwise. Relying on the territoriality principle, the English courts declined to apply the Workmen's Compensation Act to events occurring abroad, despite their close connection with England, such as a fatal accident occurring in Malta to an English worker employed there by an English company for a temporary duration.[19] But in *Keegan v. Dawson*[20] the Supreme Court refused to follow these decisions on the grounds that they carried territoriality to an unjustifiable extreme. There the plaintiff, who was employed in Ireland by a Kildare horse trainer, was injured during the course of his work at Aintree racecourse in England. Fitzgibbon J. remarked that "[i]t has been said that hard cases make bad law, but it is often the laying down of bad law that makes the hard case, and . . . it would be a misinterpretation of the Workmen's Compensation Act to hold that a groom or a drover in charge of a wagon load of horses or cattle from, say, Sligo or Bundoran to Greenore for shipment to England, lost and recovered his right to compensation under the Act half a dozen times in the course of his journey according to the particular side of the [Northern Ireland] border upon which the railway track chanced for the moment to be".[21] Accordingly, it would be wrong to say that regulatory laws will never be given any extra-territorial effect. The nature of the rights and duties imposed by the law in question may dictate that it should apply to certain special circumstances occurring outside of the State but which are almost overwhelmingly connected with this State.

Some modern employment protection laws do not state the circumstances when they may have some extra-territorial application, notably the Minimum

---

[16]. *ibid.* at 97.

[17]. [1964] I.R. 439.

[18]. *Equal Employment Opportunities Comm. v. Arabian American Oil Co.*, 499 U.S. 244 (1991).

[19]. *Tomalin v. Pearson & Son Ltd.* [1909] 2 K.B. 61.

[20]. [1934] I.R. 232.

[21]. *ibid.* at 250.

Notice and Terms of Employment Act 1973, the Employment Equality Act 1998, the Transfer of Undertakings Regulations 1980,[22] and the legislation on the insolvency fund.[23] Accordingly, account should be taken of the kind of considerations referred to in the *Keegan* case in determining when sanctions provided for in these Acts would not apply to such events. Where the Act in question contains criminal or penal sanctions, it will be given no or very little extraterritorial effect unless it states otherwise. There is an implied territorial restriction in the legislation on the insolvency fund because being in insured employment is a prerequisite for obtaining a payment under it. Once an employee works outside the State for more than 52 weeks, he ceases to be so employed.[24]

Terms of contract

Where an employee is required to work outside the State for more than one month, his employer is required to inform him in writing of the following particulars, *viz*.[25] the period of his employment abroad, the currency in which he will be paid, any benefits in cash or kind arising from working abroad, and, where appropriate, the terms and conditions governing his repatriation.

Equality

Where the equality legislation is applicable in general terms, the prohibitions against discrimination do not apply where the job is likely to involve performing duties abroad but, by virtue of the laws or customs there, the job could not reasonably be performed by a person of the employee's sex, religion or race, as the case may be.[26]

Unfair dismissals

The question of the transnational impact of the Unfair Dismissals Acts 1977-93, is dealt with in section 2(3) of the 1997 Act: subject to some exceptions, the Act "shall not apply in relation to the dismissal of an employee who, under the relevant contract of employment, ordinarily worked outside the State. . . ." Accordingly, subject to the exception described below, if the employee worked predominantly abroad, he cannot claim the protection of these Acts; otherwise, provided the job has some connection with Ireland, they apply. Their application is not contingent on the employment contract being governed by Irish law.[27]

What exactly is meant by "ordinarily worked" abroad? Does it mean more than 50 per cent of the time, more than 60 per cent or whatever? Probably the nature of the particular job will affect how this question is answered. In the com-

---

[22.] *cf. Addison v. Denholm Ship Management (U.K.) Ltd.* [1997] I.C.R. 770, concerning employees working in "flotels" on the continental shelf.

[23.] *cf. Danmarks Aktive Handelsrejsende (for Mosbaek) v. Lonmodtagernes Garantifond* (Case 117/96) [1997] E.C.R. 5017 and *Everson v. Secretary of State* (Case 198/98) I.R.L.R. 202, on which country's insolvency fund bears liability.

[24.] *Kenny v. Minister for Trade and Employment* [2000] 1 I.R. 249.

[25.] Terms of Employment (Information) Act 1994, s.4.

[26.] Employment Equality Act 1998, ss.25(3) and 37(4).

[27.] *cf. McIlwraith v. Seitz Filtratian (G.B.) Ltd.* [1998] E.L.R. 105.

parable U.K. legislation, the phrase used is "ordinarily works" as contrasted with "worked". In *Wilson v. Maynard Shipbuilding Consultants A.B.*,[28] several propositions were laid down with reference to a similar provision in the U.K. legislation. Firstly, a person can ordinarily work in one place only; he cannot simultaneously ordinarily work abroad and in the State. Secondly, what matters is not the actual time worked abroad prior to the dismissal; the court should ascertain where, for the entire period envisaged by the contract, the employee was intended to be employed. Of course, the places where he worked prior to being dismissed may throw light on this question. Where the nature of the job involves considerable foreign travel, then the ordinary workplace may be the employer's base, even though the employee spends less than half of his working time there; for instance, in the case of airline pilots and stewards.[29] In difficult cases account can be taken of matters like where, under the contract, his travels are to begin and end, where his home is expected to be, what currency he is to be paid in and in what country is he covered by social security. Where an employee actually worked all his time in one place, the fact that under his contract he could have been posted to some other country does not mean that he did not ordinarily work where he had actually been employed.[30]

A person who ordinarily worked abroad, as contemplated by section 2(3) of the 1977 Act, is not excluded from the protection if either of the following conditions obtained. One is where, during the entire term of the contract, he was ordinarily resident in Ireland. The other condition is where, for that period, the employee was domiciled in Ireland and his employer was ordinarily resident here or, if a company, its principal place of business was in Ireland during the contract period.

Redundancy payments

Leaving aside entirely the question of working abroad, in order to fall within the Redundancy Payments Acts 1967-79, the employee must be significantly connected with the State because he must be insured for all benefits under the Social Welfare Acts. The social welfare legislation and regulations under it contain provisions regarding when persons are deemed to be insured even though their work has some extraterritorial features;[31] within the E.C., this issue is dealt with in Regulation 1408 of 1971.[32] Extra-territorial application of the redundancy law is dealt with in section 25 of the 1967 Act, which uses the same general criterion as the Unfair Dismissals Acts, being whether "under his contract of employment he ordinarily worked" in the State or abroad.

An employee who ordinarily worked outside the State is denied the lump sum compensation if, at the time he was dismissed, "he is outside the State". Thus, being abroad on the very day the dismissal occurred is fatal for these purposes.

---

28. [1978] 1 Q.B. 665.
29. *e.g. Maulik v. Air India* [1974] I.C.R. 528, *Todd v. British Midland Airways Ltd.* [1978] I.C.R. 959 and *Carver v. Saudi Arabian Airlines* [1999] I.C.R. 991.
30. *e.g. Janata Bank v. Ahmed* [1981] I.C.R. 791 and *Somali Bank v. Rahman* [1989] I.C.R. 314.
31. *cf. Kenny v. Minister for Trade and Employment* [2000] 1 I.R. 249.
32. O.J. No. L 149/2 (1971). See, generally C. Barnard, *EC Employment Law* (2nd ed., 2000), pp. 299-328.

Even if the employee ordinarily working abroad is in the State at that time, he is denied compensation unless he establishes the following: that immediately before he commenced working abroad he was (1) domiciled in Ireland, (2) employed by his present employer, and (3) in the State at the time of his dismissal in accordance with his employer's instructions or, alternatively, was not given a "reasonable opportunity" by his employer to be in the State at that time. What is meant by being denied a reasonable opportunity to be in Ireland at the date of dismissal will require clarification; does it mean that the employer should have offered him a reasonable opportunity to return, that is a positive obligation, or merely that the employer must not have unreasonably prevented him from returning?

Section 25 of the 1967 Act adds two riders, for which there is no equivalent in the Unfair Dismissals Act. Periods of service abroad are deemed to be service within the State for the purpose of calculating continuity of employment. Whether a similar provision is necessary to achieve this purpose for unfair dismissal is debatable. The other is that the employer may deduct from redundancy compensation payable any redundancy payment to which the employee may be entitled under some foreign statutory scheme where he is working.

ADJUDICATIVE JURISDICTION

A vital point in transnational employment situations can be which court or courts have jurisdiction to hear the case if a dispute arises. Even where the applicable law, say, is French law, an Irish court or tribunal may still be able to hear the dispute and decide it in accordance with the law of France, expert testimony being given of that law. Or the applicable law may be that of Ireland but a French court can still decide the dispute, applying Irish law. Where several countries' courts are competent to hear the case, then practical considerations govern the decision regarding which of them a plaintiff should proceed in, such as convenience in presenting the evidence, suitable procedural rules, availability of legal aid, and ease of enforcing any judgment obtained. The criteria governing adjudicative jurisdiction vary from state to state; in some countries the nationality of one of the parties is a vital matter, in other states it is important that the defendant, either personally or through an agent, is present in the country. Within the European Community there are now uniform rules concerning adjudicative jurisdiction in civil and commercial disputes, including employment.

E.C. and E.F.T.A.-based defendants

Where the defendant is an E.C.-based individual, company or other kind of body, this question is regulated by the Brussels Convention on Jurisdiction and the Enforcement of Judgments of 1968, as amended, which is in force in all the E.C. Member States. This Convention was implemented in Ireland by the Jurisdiction of Courts and Enforcement of Judgments (European Communities) Act 1998.[33] There is a similar treaty with the remaining E.F.T.A. States (Iceland, Norway and

---

[33.] See, generally, *Binchy*, pp.181 et seq.

Switzerland), the Lugano Convention of 1988, which became part of Irish law under that 1998 Act.

Regarding employment-related disputes,[34] the position is as follows: unlike in the Rome Convention on the Conflict of Laws,[35] there is no article specially devoted to employment cases. The key concept is a person's "domicile"; persons can be sued in the courts of the State where they are domiciled.[36] Thus, an Irish-registered company doing business in Ireland can be sued in this country and a French-registered company which is trading in France can be sued there. A person or body can be sued other than at their domicile in the following circumstances:

In an action arising out of a contract, the courts "for the place of performance of the obligation in question" also have jurisdiction.[37] For instance, if an Irish company hires a person to work for it in France, that person may sue the company for breach of contract in the French courts as well as in Ireland. The place of performance of the obligation in question is where the employee habitually carries out his work.[38] Where the contract of employment is performed in several Contracting States, the place of performance is the place where the employee has established the effective centre of his working activities and where, or from which, he in fact performs the essential part of his duties *vis-à-vis* the employer.[39] If the employee does not habitually carry out his work in any one country, the employer may also be sued in the courts for the place where the business which engaged the employee was or is now situated.[40]

Where the claim is being brought in tort or delict, the courts "for the place where the harmful event occurred" also have jurisdiction.[41] For instance, if the employee of an Irish company, who is based in France, is injured during a brief working visit to Italy, he may sue the company in tort in the Italian courts instead of in Ireland.

Where several defendants are being sued, proceedings can be brought against all of them in any court where any one of them is domiciled.[42] Thus, if a Belgian domiciliary had some involvement in the accident in Italy just referred to, he could be joined as a defendant in the Irish courts.

Occasionally, the parties may have agreed in advance that all disputes arising between them shall be heard in one designated court or country; these provisions are commonly referred to as "choice of forum" or "prorogation" clauses. A stipulation to that effect in an employment contract prevents the parties from proceeding against each other in any court other than the one or ones on which they had

---

[34.] *Soc. Sanicentral v. Collins* (Case 25/79) [1979] E.C.R. 3423.

[35.] *supra*, p. 254.

[36.] Art. 2. On what constitutes domicile, see *Binchy*, Chap. 6.

[37.] Art. 5(1).

[38.] *Ivenel v. Schwab* (Case 133/81) [1982] E.C.R. 1891, para. 20; *Six Constructions Ltd. v. Humbert* (Case 32/88) [1989] E.C.R. 341; *Mulox IBC Limited v. Geels* (Case 125/92) [1993] E.C.R. 4975.

[39.] *Rutten v. Cross Medical Ltd.* (Case 383/95) [1997] E.C.R. 57.

[40.] *Six Constructions Ltd. v. Humbert* (Case 32/88) [1989] E.C.R. 341; *Mulox IBC Limited v. Geels* (Case C 125/92) [1993] E.C.R. 4075; *Customs Made Commercials Ltd. v. Stawa Metallbau GmbH* (Case C 288/92) [1994] E.C.R. 2913.

[41.] Art. 5(3).

[42.] Art. 6(1); *cf. Turner v. Grovit* [2000] Q.B. 345.

agreed to confer exclusive jurisdiction.[43] Instead of a choice of forum clause, the parties may have previously agreed that disputes arising between them should be decided by way of arbitration. In that case, generally they must then resort to arbitration and any court proceedings commenced in connection with the employment contract will be stayed.[44]

Non E.C./E.F.T.A.-based defendants

Where the defendant is not present in Ireland and is not domiciled in any E.C. or E.F.T.A. State, the question of the jurisdiction of the Irish courts is governed by Order 11 of the Rules of the Superior Courts. These rules set out the circumstances in which a notice of proceedings can be served on defendants who are outside the State.[45] In employment-related cases, they can be sued in the Irish courts in the following situations.

Where the defendant is either domiciled or ordinarily resident in the State, he may be sued here regardless of what law governs the contract or where the breach of contract or tort occurred. In an action arising out of a contract, he can be sued here if either (a) the contract was made here, (b) the contract was made by an agent who was trading or residing here, or (c) the contract is governed by Irish law. In a tort action, he may be sued here if the tort was committed here.

Certain tort claims in the employment sphere can also be formulated as actions for breach of contract, such as claims against the employer for negligence.[46] Civil actions for breach of statutory duty are usually regarded as tort claims but not every right of action given by a statute will be characterised as a contract or a tort claim. The "division of all causes of action [at common law] into two classes, contract and tort" has been rejected by the Supreme Court.[47]

A "necessary and proper party" to an action being brought here may be joined as a defendant in the action.

What was said above about choice of forum clauses and arbitration agreements applies equally to claims being brought against non-E.C./E.F.T.A.-based defendants.

SEAFARING

Seafaring is perhaps the most highly regulated occupation of all. Legislation laying down the rights and duties of seafarers and the incidents of their employment can be traced back for centuries. Many of these measures were consolidated in the mammoth Merchant Shipping Act 1894, which remains in force. Space does not permit any thorough account of the 1894 Act's requirements, but the extent of their range can be gathered from the headings in sections 92-226 of that Act, under the general heading "Masters and Seamen":

[43.] Art. 17; *cf. Hough v. P. & O. Containers Ltd.* [1999] Q.B. 834.
[44.] Arbitration Act 1980, s.5.
[45.] See, generally, *Binchy*, pp. 123 *et seq.*
[46.] *e.g. Matthews v. Kuwait Bechtel Corp.* [1959] 2 Q.B. 57.
[47.] *Shipsey v. British & South American Steam Navigation Co.* [1936] I.R. 65 at 103.

Certificates of competency,[48]

Apprenticeship to the sea service,

Licences to supply seamen,

Engagement of seamen,

Agreements with lascars,

Rating of seamen,

Discharge of seamen,[49]

Payment of wages,

Advance and allotment of wages,

Seamen's money orders and savings banks,

Rights of seamen in respect of wages,[50]

Mode of recovering wages,

Power of courts to rescind contracts,

Property of deceased seamen,

Reimbursement of relief to seamen's families,

Destitute seamen,

Leaving seamen abroad,[51]

Distressed seamen,

Volunteering into the navy,

Provisions, health and accommodation,

Facilities for making complaint,

Protection of seamen from imposition,

Provisions as to discipline,

Official logs, local marine boards and mercantile marine officers,

Registration of and returns respecting seamen,

Sites for sailors' homes.

[48.] *cf.* Merchant Shipping (Certification of Seamen) Act 1979.
[49.] *cf. Merman v. Owners of S.S. Vica* [1942] I.R. 305.
[50.] *cf. Byrne v. Limerick S.S. Co.* [1946] I.R. 138, *The Royal Wells* [1985] Q.B. 86, *The Turridu* [2000] I.C.R. 354 and *The Ruta* [2000] 1 W.L.R. 2068.
[51.] *cf.* Merchant Shipping Act 1906, s.32.

These provisions apply to Irish-registered ships, their owners, masters and crew.[52] But they also apply in prescribed circumstances to foreign registered ships.[53] Special provision is made in the 1894 Act for employment on fishing boats.[54] All of the major employment laws of general application, for instance the Unfair Dismissals Acts 1977-93, and the Employment Equality Act 1978, also apply in principle to seafaring, provided the situation in question falls within their general transnational scope. These measures and the other laws of general application do not expressly lay down the special circumstances when they are applicable to seafaring.[55]

Because of its very nature, seafaring is one of the most international of activities. Prescribing standards for employment at sea has been a major concern of the International Labour Organisation, which has adopted over 50 conventions and recommendations on maritime work. These are sometimes described as the International Seafarers' Code and deal with matters such as minimum age and protection of young seafarers, vocational training, certificates of competency, articles of agreement, hours of work and paid holidays, safety and hygiene, inspection.

Section 12 of the Merchant Shipping Act 1947 gives the Minister for Enterprise and Employment very extensive authority, by regulation, to prescribe employment standards and rules for seafarers. Under this, he may "make such provisions as he thinks proper for promoting the welfare of seamen in Irish ships or at ports within the State or for maintaining in Irish ships suitable conditions of employment for seamen. . . ." The usual means by which international labour conventions for seamen are implemented is by statutory instrument under these powers. But the Minister's prescribing authority under section 12 is not confined to giving effect to the international standards.

FOREIGN EMBASSY AND CONSULAR EMPLOYEES

All of the senior staff in foreign embassies are civil servants of their employing government, and their rights and duties are governed by their appropriate civil service regulations. Frequently, local so-called "contract staff", such as typists and secretaries, drivers and gardeners are employed for comparatively menial tasks. There are no modern authorities regarding what law governs the employment contracts of these personnel — the *lex loci laboris* or the law of their employer-State? Although the Unfair Dismissals Acts 1977-93 and many other of the laws of general application do not apply to officers employed by or under the State or by local authorities, there is no express exclusion for those employed by foreign governments and foreign public agencies.

To the extent that these Acts may be applicable in principle to them, the statutory requirements may be unenforceable because of the "sovereign immunity" principle, which is now incorporated into the Diplomatic Relations and Immunities Act 1967. This Act gives effect to the Vienna Conventions on Diplomatic

---

[52] 1894 Act, s.260.
[53] *ibid.*, s.261.
[54] *ibid.*, ss.376-416.
[55] Compare to the position in Britain, where seafaring is directly addressed, e.g. *Wood v. Cunard Line Ltd.* [1991] I.C.R. 13 and *Haughton v. Olau Line (U.K.) Ltd.* [1986] 1 W.L.R. 503.

Relations of 1961 and on Consular Relations of 1963. For the purposes of the 1961 Convention, personnel are categorised as "diplomatic agents", "administrative and technical staff", "service staff" and "private servants";[56] the extent of the immunity enjoyed depends on the category the individual falls into.

However, this Act does not confer immunity on the foreign government as such, as contrasted with embassy officials. Most countries possess up to date legislation dealing with the immunities of foreign governments and agencies as such[57] but a measure along those lines has not so far been enacted in Ireland. The position, therefore, is governed by the "common law" for foreign sovereign immunity. It remains to be seen whether or to what extent traditional foreign State immunity will be held to be incompatible with the European Convention on Human Rights in, *inter alia*, the sphere of employment litigation.[58]

In *Government of Canada v. Employment Appeals Tribunal*,[59] a driver/ messenger employed in the Canadian embassy was sacked and commenced proceedings for unfair dismissal. The Canadian Government contended that the sovereign immunity principle deprived the courts and the E.A.T. of jurisdiction to hear the claim. It was held that the old doctrine of "absolute" immunity was no longer the law but immunity would still be afforded to actions which relate to the actual business or policy of a foreign government. Anything to do with the embassy prima facie concerns the foreign government. In particular, the "element of trust and confidentiality that is reposed in the driver of an embassy car creates a bond with his employers that has the effect of involving him in the employing government's public business organisation and interests".[60] The Canadian government were entitled to claim the immunity. In a similar English case[61] it was held that there was no jurisdiction to hear an unfair dismissal complaint by a clerk employed by the Indian High Commission in London. This was because his contractual duties involved exercising the Indian Government's public function and any hearing of the case most likely would involve an investigation into that public function. Accordingly, the very nature of the employee's job has a very significant bearing on whether the employer is entitled to claim immunity. Where the employer is not the State as such but a foreign public agency, the nature of its particular function also determines whether it would be entitled to immunity. Of course, the foreign government or agency may always choose to waive any immunity and contest the merits of the case. In neither the *Government of Canada* case nor the Indian case does it appear to have been contended that the immunity claim was a breach of the Constitution or of the European Convention, respectively.

---

56. Defined in Art. 1; *cf. Rivero v. Bundesanstalt fur Arbeit* (Case C 211/97).
57. See, generally, Fox, "Employment Contracts as an Exception to State Immunity: Is All Public Service Immune?", 66 B.Y.B.I.L. 97 (1995).
58. A ruling on this and related questions by the European Court of Human Rights is pending: *McElhinney v. Ireland, Aziz v. United Kingdom* and *Fogarty v. United Kingdom*. The *Fogarty* case involves a sex discrimination claim made against the United States but which could not be brought in the U.K. on account of the State Immunity Act 1978 (U.K.).
59. [1992] 2 I.R. 484.
60. *ibid.* at p.500, followed in *Geraghty v. Embassy of Mexico* [1998] E.L.R. 310.
61. *Sengupta v. Republic of India* [1983] I.C.R. 221; also *United Arab Emirates v. Abdelghafar* [1995] I.C.R. 65; *Ahmed v. Saudi Arabia* [1996] I.C.R. 25 and *Malaysian Industrial Development Authority v. Jevasingham* [1998] I.C.R. 307.

CHAPTER 12

EMPLOYEES AND COMPANY LAW

At one time the principal technique used to accommodate employee interests in companies was to grant workers and their representatives greater negotiating power in their dealings with employers. To this end, the Industrial Relations Act 1990 makes strikes and peaceful picketing in the context of a "trade dispute" lawful and confers extensive immunities from suit on trade unions. Over and above the employment legislation considered in the previous chapters, legislation dealing with companies as such rather than *qua* employers contain provisions specific to employees, although Irish law in this regard is far behind that of most other Western European countries.[1]

ENTITLEMENT TO ACCOMMODATE EMPLOYEES' INTERESTS

Formerly, unless there was authority in the memorandum and articles of association to do so, major decisions within companies could not be made with the primary object of furthering their employees' interests, at least where one or more of the shareholders objected. The law identified companies almost exclusively with their shareholders: directors must exercise their powers bona fide in what they consider is in the interests of the company;[2] special resolutions of shareholders or any class of shareholders are unlawful where they are not adopted bona fide for the benefit of the company as a whole.[3] And by "the company as a whole" was meant the shareholders in general or the hypothetical average shareholder. Ambiguous though these formulae may be, it was not permissible to place employees' interests squarely before those of the shareholders. The classic instance is *Parke v. Daily News Ltd.,*[4] where the directors of a newspaper company, that had sold off its assets, proposed to distribute most of the proceeds among its employees as *ex gratia* redundancy pay. One of the shareholders objected and that proposal was enjoined because such massive benevolence was not for the benefit of the company.

The position has been changed somewhat by section 52 of the Companies Act 1990, according to which "the matters to which directors of a company are to have regard in the performance of their functions shall include the interests of the company's employees in general, as well as the interests of its members".

This may not entirely reverse the position under the *Daily News* case. It deals only with the position of the directors and not alone allows them to take account

---

1. See, generally, M. Forde, *Company Law* (3rd ed., 1999) (hereinafter referred to as *Company Law*).
2. See *ibid.*, Chap.5.
3. See *ibid.*, Chap.10.
4. [1962] 1 Ch. 927.

of employees' interests but actually requires them to do so. However, section 52(2) adds that this obligation is owed only to the company and that the employees do not have a right of action to enforce compliance with its requirements. Where the benevolence towards employees would be *ultra vires* or unfairly discriminates against minority shareholders, it is not validated by section 52, in the sense that an objecting shareholder is entitled to have the proposed action blocked and, possibly, to recover extravagant payments that were made. Section 52 nevertheless is likely to have an indirect influence as indicating a general legislative policy in favour of upholding measures adopted by companies for the benefit of their employees.

Even in the past, devoting company resources to employees was permissible where that was incidental to and within the general scope of the company's business. As Bowen L.J. put it in *Hutton v. West Cork Rly. Co.*, where a debenture-holder-cum-shareholder objected to large gratuities the company's directors proposed to pay themselves before selling the entire undertaking,

> "most businesses require liberal dealings. The test . . . is . . . whether [the transaction is] done *bona fide* [and] is done within the ordinary scope of the company's business and whether it is reasonably incidental to the carrying on of the company's business for the company's benefit.
>
> Take this sort of instance: a railway company or the directors of the company, might send down all the porters at a railway station to have tea in the country at the expense of the company. Why should they not? It is for the directors to judge, provided it is a matter which is reasonably incidental to the carrying on of the business of the company, and a company which always treated its employees with Draconian severity, and never allowed them a single inch more than the strict letter of the bond, would soon find itself deserted — at all events unless labour was very much more easy to obtain in the market than it often is. The law does not say that there are to be no cakes and ale, but there are to be no cakes and ale except such as are required for the benefit of the company."[5]

Where all the shareholders agree with corporate benevolence to employees or otherwise, that does not render the company insolvent, there would seem to be no good reason for holding such generosity to be unlawful.

FINANCIAL PARTICIPATION BY EMPLOYEES

Some companies encourage and even help their employees to acquire shares in them. The view is that by having a financial stake in the firm and being entitled to participate in its distributed profits, employees will more readily identify with the company and indeed become participants in a form of economic democracy. On the other hand, there is a danger that workers who invest most of their savings in their employer's business will lose everything if it fails. It is for companies themselves to decide whether and on what terms shares should be offered to employ-

---

5.   (1883) 23 Ch. D. 645 at 672-673.

ees. There is no legal obligation on companies to allot shares to their employees as exists, for example, in France.[6] But a p.l.c. may not allot shares in exchange for any service contract.[7] One of the matters that the Pensions Board no doubt will regulate in due course is "self-investment" by occupational pension schemes, that is the fund investing heavily in the employing enterprise. The Taxes Consolidation Act 1997 provides a variety of tax incentives for schemes facilitating employees to purchase shares in their company.[8]

Financial assistance to acquire shares

Section 60 of the Companies Act 1963 not alone prohibits companies from giving financial assistance for or in connection with the purchase of their own shares but goes so far as to make this practice a criminal offence.[9] This prohibition is formulated in very extensive terms and also applies to assisting the acquisition of shares in the company's holding company, if it has one. However, it does not apply in two related circumstances as regards acquisitions of shares by a company's own employees.

One is where a private company loans money to any of its bona fide employees to enable them to acquire for themselves shares in it or in its holding company.[10] The other is where a private company provides money under a scheme whereby its shares are to be held by or on behalf of its employees or former employees, or employees of its subsidiaries.[11] Loans under the former cannot be made to directors who are also employees; but the scheme under the latter can include salaried directors. Furthermore, p.l.c.s can also give financial assistance for these two purposes, provided the funds come out of profits available for distribution or the company's net assets are not thereby reduced.[12]

Authority and pre-emption when allotting additional shares

Sections 20 and 23 of the Companies (Amendment) Act 1983 place certain restrictions on the freedom of companies to allot additional shares.[13] Under section 20, any share allotment must have received prior shareholder approval but there are several qualifications to this rule. Under section 23, the new shares must first be offered to the existing members on a pro rata basis before they can be offered to existing members otherwise or to persons who are not at present members of the company. This rule too is subject to several qualifications.

An exception is made to these authority and pre-emption requirements in respect of employee share schemes. They are defined as "any scheme for the time being in force, in accordance with which a company encourages or facilitates the holding of shares or debentures in the company or its holding company by or for the benefit of employees or former employees of the company or of any subsid-

---

6. Law No. 80-834 of October 24, 1980.
7. Companies (Amendment) Act 1983, s.26(2).
8. See, generally, K. Corrigan, *Revenue Law* (2000) Vol. 2 pp. 82 *et seq.*
9. See *Company Law*, pp. 303 *et seq.*
10. 1963 Act, s.60(13)(c).
11. *ibid.*, s.60(13)(b).
12. *ibid.*, s.60(15A)-(15C) (amended in 1983).
13. See *Company Law*, pp. 232 *et seq.*

iary",[14] including salaried directors. The requirement of shareholders' prior authority does not apply to shares being allotted in pursuance of such a scheme.[15] Shares being allotted in connection with these schemes need not be offered on a pre-emptive basis and employees offered shares under a scheme are not prevented by the 1983 Act from renouncing or assigning the offer, even to persons who are outside of the scheme.[16] P.l.c.s are not forbidden to allot shares under such schemes where less than one-quarter of their shares' nominal value has not been paid up.[17]

Share options as remuneration

Share option schemes have become a popular method of remuneration for executive employees and for directors of companies, and there is a notable trend towards extending these schemes to employees further down the company's hierarchy. These schemes encourage loyalty to the company and provide a distinct incentive to employees to work harder and more enthusiastically for it. The basic principle is very simple. The employees in question are given options to purchase a number of the company's shares at set prices and at set times; say the option is to buy 200 shares at, say, £1.20, £1.50 and £1.80 per share, respectively, during the next three years. If the company prospers during those years, the actual value of the shares when purchased will exceed the price at which the option may be exercised. For instance, say in year three here, the market value of the shares had risen to £2.50; accordingly, the employee stands to make a profit of 70 pence a share if he exercises his option then — assuming he immediately disposed of the shares. Formerly, the value of the option was measured for tax purposes at the time the employee became free to exercise it, regardless of whether or not he had exercised it.[18]

The option price and conditions

Obviously the most lucrative share options are those where the option price, that is the amount which must be paid for the shares, is much less than the actual share price at the time the option is exercised. As a matter of company law, ordinarily it is entirely a matter for the company's directors to determine what the option price shall be and when and under what conditions it may be exercised. There is no overriding duty on the directors or the company to allot shares for as high a premium as can be obtained in the market; nor is it wrong *per se* to allot shares at par even though other investors are prepared to pay a substantial premium for them. In *Hilder v. Dexter*[19] a company, in order to raise working capital, issued shares at par and gave its executives options to take further shares at par at some later stage. When the price of its shares rose in the market the holders of

---

[14.]   1983 Act, s.2(1).

[15.]   *ibid.*, s.20(10)(a).

[16.]   *ibid.*, s.20(13)(b).

[17.]   *ibid.*, s.28(4).

[18.]   *Abbott v. Philbin* [1961] A.C. 352. Today the relevant time is when the option is exercised or is otherwise realised.

[19.]   [1902] A.C. 474.

those options sought to exercise them. It was held that there is no "law" which obliges a company to issue its shares above par because they are saleable at a premium in the market.

The exercise of options will be made subject to certain terms and conditions, for instance, the times they may be exercised and in respect of how many shares, and when do the options lapse. Several conditions are very common in consequence of the tax legislation — notably those laid down in section 19 of the Finance Act 1976, and in the second schedule of that Act for obtaining Revenue approval for the scheme.[20]

That conditions in an option scheme will be strictly construed is illustrated by *Thompson v. ASDA-MFI Group p.l.c.*,[21] where an employee was perhaps unfairly deprived of the benefits of a scheme which applied to him. The plaintiff was employed by a department store company which was the defendant's wholly-owned subsidiary. By virtue of his employment, he could participate in a savings-related option scheme established by the defendant for the benefit of all of its employees and those employed by its subsidiaries. One of the conditions of the scheme, to obtain maximum advantage under the tax rules, was that options could only be exercised by persons presently employed by a company in the group.[22] If the plaintiff had been wrongfully or unfairly dismissed, presumably he would have been compensated for the loss of his options.

What happened here was that the defendant sold off to third parties its entire shareholding in the subsidiary which employed the plaintiff. The question to be decided was whether the plaintiff's options had thereby lapsed. He contended that they had not lapsed; either it was an implied term of his employment contract that the subsidiary would not be disposed of in such a way as might cause the options to lapse or, alternatively, the options survived the actual disposal. Those arguments were rejected. The court would not imply a term preventing the defendant from disposing of its subsidiary because any term of that nature lacked the requisite "business efficacy" for implying terms into contracts; such a term lacked all commercial reality. Moreover, in view of the U.K. Finance Act's condition that options must only be exercised by existing employees of the holding or group companies, it was not possible to imply a term that the option survived the disposal of the subsidiary, because the scheme was drawn up to secure maximum tax advantages.

Selling the shares

Many share option schemes place restrictions on the time and occasionally the circumstances in which those who have acquired shares under them may sell their shares. Under the 1986 rules for approved share option schemes, the shares cannot be made subject to any restrictions other than those applying to all of the shares in their class.[23] In addition to any restrictions on disposal which may exist under the scheme, the company's own articles of association may place restrictions on disposing of shares. Those restraints most likely apply to all categories

---

[20.] See, *supra*, n.8.
[21.] [1988] 1 Ch. 241.
[22.] Compare Finance Act 1986, Schedule 2, para. 5(2).
[23.] *ibid.*, para. 9(c).

of members, regardless of how they acquired their shares. The commonest of these in private companies is to give the directors an unfettered veto over whom shares may be transferred to.[24] This is often coupled with a pre-emption requirement, whereby the existing members or directors, as the case may be, are given a first option over shares being put up for sale, usually at a price to be determined by the company's auditors.

Termination of employment

Most share option schemes provide that the options shall cease once the individual ceases to be an employee of the company or of a company in the group, as the case may be. Sometimes they go so far as providing that shares acquired under the scheme shall revert to the company or one of its nominees. For instance, in *Walsh v. Cassidy & Co.*[25] the plaintiff acquired shares in the company under a provision in its articles whereby shares were to be allotted to all company employees. But another of these regulations authorised the directors to expropriate the shares of any member who is "employed in the company in any capacity [and who] ceases to be so employed by [it]". It is implicit in Kingsmill Moore J.'s judgment that such a power should be construed as narrowly as is reasonably possible. He suggested that the clause there might not authorise expelling a member who acquired shares for full value and who subsequently took up some employment in the company. But he emphasised that any expulsion falling four square within the clause's terms would not be set aside merely because it would result in considerable hardship. On the other hand, "fraudulent" exercises of the expulsion power would be restrained.

In *Micklefield v. S.A.C. Technology Ltd.,*[26] the employee shareholder was most unfortunate but it was not argued that he had been treated fraudulently. He was a company director and, under his contract, was entitled to six months' notice in writing of dismissal. He was entitled under a share option scheme to subscribe for shares at the end of a three-year period. When that period had almost expired, there was a very substantial difference between the option price and the price of the shares in the market, so that he stood to make a large profit. But he was peremptorily dismissed and given six months' salary in lieu of notice. He nonetheless sought to exercise his options a few days later, when they fell due, but the company refused to allot him the shares on the grounds that he was no longer its employee. It was held that, once he was dismissed with salary in lieu of notice, he had ceased to be an employee of the company; accordingly, he was ineligible under the very terms of the scheme to exercise the options. Although certain aspects of the employment contract may survive termination of that contract, the status or relationship of employer/employee comes to an end. The doctrine that a person would not be permitted to take advantage of his wrongs was held not applicable here because the dismissal was not unlawful.[27] Nor would the court

---

24. Companies Act 1963, Table A, part III, art. 3; *cf. Re Hafner* [1943] I.R. 426.
25. [1951] Ir. Jur. Rep. 47.
26. [1991] 1 All E.R. 275.
27. Compare *Levett v. Biotrace International p.l.c.* [1999] I.C.R. 818 (share option) and *Holt v. Faulks* [2000] 2 B.C.L.C. 816 (obligatory transfer of shares).

imply a term that no dismissal could take effect until notice of termination had expired in full.

Where an employee succeeds in a claim for unfair dismissal, he may be compensated for losing benefits under a share option scheme. Whether he will be so compensated when he claims for wrongful dismissal depends on the very terms of the option arrangements. Under the scheme which was considered in the *Micklefield* case, one of the terms was that, once any employee ceased to be employed for any reason, not alone did the options come to an end but he waived any entitlement to compensation for loss of any benefits under the option scheme.[28]

ASSOCIATED EMPLOYERS

Several of the Acts and regulations dealing with employment refer to an "associated employer". Frequently, these deem the length of a person's employment with the employer to include time spent working for an associate. For the purpose of drawing comparisons in order to determine whether there has been unlawful discrimination, it may be permissible to pick a comparator working for an associated employer. And where provision is made for persons to get back their jobs following a period of absence, it may be permissible to instead give them a similar job with an associated employer. Whether an employer is indeed associated for these purposes depends on the definition in the Act in question.

Thus, in the Employment Equality Act 1998, and also in the Acts that deal with maternity, adoptive and parental leave, the term is defined to mean "if one is a body corporate of which the other (whether directly or indirectly) has control or if both are bodies corporate of which a third person (whether directly or indirectly) has control".[29] Thus the test is *de jure* or even *de facto* control, there being no definition for the word "control". For the purpose of this test, it was held that although Teagasc is a State body and in very general terms is controlled by the State, that body and the Department of Agriculture could not be regarded as associated employers.[30]

Other legislation defines the term by reference to company law, for instance, section 16(4) of the Redundancy Payments Act 1967, whereby employers are deemed to be associated "if one is a subsidiary of the other, or both are subsidiaries of a third company"; "company" here is defined as "any body corporate" and "subsidiary" has the same meaning as in section 155 of the Companies Act 1963.

DIRECTORS' SERVICE AGREEMENTS

Not all directors have service contracts with their companies. But most full-time executive directors have those contracts, and the rights and duties of some non-executive directors may be set out in contracts with their company. The Employment Law aspects of these agreements must be viewed against the backdrop of

---

28. *cf. Leonard v. Strathclyde Buses Ltd.* [1998] S.C. 57.
29. s.2(2).
30. *Brides v. Minister for Agriculture* [1998] 4 I.R. 250.

Company Law, for the Companies Acts 1963-90, lay down special rules for directors' service contracts and their remuneration.

There is also the question of whether a director is an employee for the purpose of the employment and social welfare legislation. Salaried working directors, including managing directors, ordinarily would be regarded as employees.[31] That has been held to be the case even where the managing director also was the sole shareholder in the company.[32] All depends, however, on the facts of the particular case and, where the director is also the sole or a majority shareholder, much turns on whether there is a formal record of his employment terms and on whether he pays income tax and P.R.S.I. as an employee.[33]

Remuneration

The question of directors' remuneration[34] is a sensitive matter in many companies. In closely-held companies, tax considerations bear heavily on whether the directors are to be rewarded by emoluments that are subject to Schedule E or by generous expenses, both of which are deductible from the company's own tax bill; or else by way of dividends or, indeed, loans. At times, there may be concern that majority shareholders will occupy all the seats on the board, pay themselves handsome directors' fees and leave little or nothing for distribution by way of dividends. In large companies with many shareholders, the dilemma may be whether the directors are being adequately rewarded to ensure that they will give of their best in advancing the company's interests. "Golden handshakes" paid to retiring directors can give rise to concern among shareholders about for whose benefit the company is in fact being run: for the professional directors or for the shareholders.

The Companies Acts do not state who shall determine whether or how much the directors should be paid in fees and salaries, other than that no such payment may be made free of income tax.[35] The right given by section 50 of the 1990 Act to inspect directors' service contracts with a duration exceeding three years[36] now enables every shareholder to ascertain exactly how much those directors are being paid, in what manner, and for what services. Every set of annual accounts must contain or be accompanied by a statement showing the aggregate of, *inter alia*, directors' "emoluments".[37]

A pension is a form of deferred salary that an employer may be obliged by contract to pay or that may be paid as a gratuity. It depends on the circumstances whether a sum paid to a retiring or retired director is a pension or more in the nature of a "golden handshake"; although for the purpose of disclosure in the company's accounts, there are elaborate definitions of each of these terms. All that the Companies Acts require is that directors' pensions may not be paid free

---

[31] *Stakelum v. Canning* [1976] I.R. 314.

[32] *Lee v. Lee's Air Farming Ltd.* [1961] A.C. 12 and *Secretary of State v. Bottrill* [1999] I.C.R. 592.

[33] *ibid.* Compare *Parsons v. Albert J. Parsons & Sons Ltd.* [1979] I.C.R. 271, *Fleming v. Xanair Ltd.* [1998] S.C. 8 and *Connolly v. Sellers Arenascene Ltd.*, Times L.R. March 8 2001.

[34] See *Company Law*, pp.158 *et seq.*

[35] Companies Act 1963, s.185.

[36] See *infra*, p. 276.

[37] 1963 Act, s.191(1) and (2).

of income tax[38] and the aggregate amount of pensions must be shown in a company's annual accounts.[39] Companies in business have implied powers to agree to pay pensions to executive directors and, after those directors have died, may agree to pay pensions to their dependants.

"Golden handshakes" and "golden umbrellas"

The term "golden handshake" signifies sizeable payments made to company directors on their retirement other than by way of ordinary pensions. In sections 186-189 of the 1963 Act these are called "compensation for loss of office or as consideration for or in connection with retirement from office".[40] These payments usually used to be made in lump sums but tax considerations now compel companies to space them out over a number of years.[41] Golden handshakes may be either the estimated cost of removing a director from office prematurely or may be more in the nature of a gratuity. The Companies Acts require that these payments must not be made tax free[42] and the aggregate amount of them in any year must be disclosed in or along with the annual accounts.[43]

In order to be valid, the particulars, including the amount of any proposed payment connected with retirement, must be disclosed to the company's members, who must give their approval in general meeting.[44] Disclosure must be made while the payment is still only a proposal and it must be made to all the company's members, even to those who do not have full voting rights in general meeting,[45] like many preference shareholders. Parallel provisions exist for such payments intended to be made in the context of full or partial take-overs and purchases of sizeable assets from the company in question.[46] Any directors who are responsible for paying golden handshakes which have not been duly authorised by the members can be held liable for misapplication of the company's funds. And the recipients of unauthorised payments must repay the money.

A "golden umbrella" is a phrase often used to describe a service contract of a very long duration. The gilded element is that, if the employer wants to terminate the contract, he must pay the equivalent of the remuneration which would have been earned during the remainder of the contract. Thus, the longer the duration the higher the price to be paid in order to rid the company of the director. Section 28 of the Companies Act 1990 prohibits the conclusion of golden umbrellas with a duration of longer than five years, without the prior approval of an ordinary resolution of the company's members. That approval is required whether the contract is one of service or for services, that is whether under the contract the director is an employee or is to be treated as self-employed. Shareholder approval must be given to any service contract which the company is not completely free

---

38. *supra*, n.35.
39. 1963 Act, s.191(1) and (3).
40. *ibid.*, ss.186-189; see definition in s.189(3).
41. Finance Act 1967, s.114, as amended.
42. *supra*, n.35.
43. 1963 Act, s.191(1) and (4).
44. *ibid.*, s.186.
45. *Re Duomatic Ltd.* [1969] 2 Ch. D. 365.
46. 1963 Act, ss.187, 188 and 189(4).

to terminate lawfully within five years of the service commencing. In the case of a director of one or more companies within a group of companies, the approval must come from the members of the holding company. Before any approval can be given to these contracts, a written memorandum of the proposed terms must be available for inspection for at least 15 days prior to the general meeting taking place; that memorandum must also be available at the meeting. The terms of any service contract which contravenes these requirements are void and, on giving reasonable notice of dismissal, can be determined by the company at any time.

Inspecting service contracts

Another of the innovations introduced in 1990 is to entitle every shareholder to inspect a copy or a memorandum of the terms of many directors' service contracts, regardless of who is entitled to appoint directors or determine their remuneration. Section 50 of the 1990 Act requires that a copy or memorandum of the contract be kept at either the registered office, the principal place of business, or where the register of members is kept. This information must be open for inspection during business hours by any member, without charge. Similar information regarding directors of subsidiaries must be kept by the holding company. In the case of directors who work "wholly or mainly outside" the State, only the name of the director and the duration of the contract need be disclosed in this manner. Disclosure of a contract's terms is not required in this manner where it can be terminated by the company, without payment of compensation, by less than three years' notice.

Dismissing directors

Apart from their disqualifying provisions,[47] the Companies Acts do not set down grounds for removing directors from office. It used to be the case that, in the absence of express provision to the contrary in the company's regulations or in a service contract, shareholders did not possess the "inherent" power to remove directors of registered companies appointed for a definite period until that period had expired.[48] Article 99 of Table A provides that any or all of the directors can be removed by an ordinary resolution of the members. The regulations of some companies empower the directors themselves to remove any of their number from the board.

Right to dismiss

One of the most important rules in company law is section 182 of the 1963 Act, whereby shareholders, by passing an ordinary resolution, may remove any or all of the directors from the board before their periods of office expire.[49] That is to say, a simple majority of the members voting may immediately sack even the entire board. Consequently, the ultimate control over the running of companies lies with whoever owns or has influence over 50 per cent of the voting shares.

[47.] Companies Act 1990, ss.159-169.
[48.] *Imperial Hydropathic Hotel Co. v. Hampson* (1882) 23 Ch. D. 1.
[49.] See *Company Law*, pp. 151 *et seq.*

Persons seeking to take over a company may be satisfied with a 50 per cent stake, in that this brings them control of the management; although more often they may prefer at least a 75 per cent stake, so that they are in a position to alter the articles of association. In order to entrench the principle of simple majority rule on this matter, section 182 of the 1963 Act adds that the power to remove directors by ordinary resolution cannot be excluded by the articles of association or by a service contract; that power exists notwithstanding anything in the articles or in an agreement between the company and the director. But the section does not prohibit a contrary provision in the memorandum of association, nor separate voting agreements between shareholders, or between shareholders and directors, not to exercise their statutory power.[50]

A director of a private company who, under the articles of association, holds office for life is exempted from this rule.[51] Table A does not make any provision for life directors.

Damages

A director, especially an executive director, may hold office under a contract that runs for a set period or until terminated on expressly stated or impliedly provided for grounds. Section 182(7) of the 1963 Act and also article 99 of Table A stipulate that the statutory power to remove them by ordinary resolution shall not deprive the directors of any entitlement to damages or compensation they may possess. A director may lawfully be removed from office only in accordance with the service contract's provisions regarding notice and procedures, except where he has broken a major term of the contract, in which case he may be dismissed *instanter* once he has been given a fair opportunity to defend himself. The contractual terms may be express or implied. On account of section 182(7), it can be very expensive for the company to remove directors who have service contracts, especially where the members gave them golden umbrellas.

Whether a director was in fact removed from office depends on the circumstances of each case, the question being whether the company's conduct amounted to a repudiation of the service agreement. For instance in *Harold Holdsworth & Co. (Wakefield) Ltd. v. Caddies*,[52] the plaintiff was appointed director of a company for a five-year period, his function being defined as running the company and its associated companies in such manner as may from time to time be assigned to or vested in him by the board. Following differences that arose between them, the board resolved that the plaintiff should confine his attentions to just one company in the group. It was held that this was not a breach of the service agreement because, under its terms, the board reserved the power to limit his responsibilities as it saw fit. The mere appointment out of court by creditors of a receiver and manager to act for the company does not *ipso facto* amount to a repudiation of the service contract with a managing director.[53]

[50.] *Bushell v. Faith* [1970] A.C. 1099.
[51.] 1963 Act, s.182(1).
[52.] [1955] 1 All E.R. 725.
[53.] *Griffith v. Secretary of State* [1974] Q.B. 468.

In *Glover v. B.L.N. Ltd.*[54] the plaintiff's contract as managing director provided that he could be removed without compensation for serious misconduct, serious neglect of duties, wilful disobedience of reasonable orders and the like. One issue before the court was whether, when dismissing him, the defendant's board possessed sufficient evidence of serious misconduct and neglect on his part. It was held that only one of the many allegations made against him provided grounds for summary dismissal. At times, the required standard of performance must be implied from the surrounding circumstances. A director whose conduct repudiates the service agreement can be removed almost instantaneously. In *Carvill v. Irish Industrial Bank Ltd*[55] what was, to use a neutral term, unwise conduct on the part of a small bank's managing director was held by Kenny J. to warrant his immediate dismissal. But the Supreme Court concluded that, in the circumstances, his indiscretion was not sufficiently repudiatory for that purpose. Unless the contract provides for a fixed term of service or for dismissal only on stated grounds, a director may lawfully be removed for any reason whatsoever if given proper notice. Proper notice means the period stipulated in the contract or, where the contract is silent, a reasonable period. In *Carvill*, for example, it was found that 12 months was a reasonable period.

Requirements similar to natural justice must be complied with before the members can pass a resolution under section 182 of the Companies Act 1963 to remove a director. The proposed resolution must follow the section 142 extended notice procedure[56] and a copy of it must be forwarded by the company to the director in advance. Ordinarily, he is entitled to have written representations circulated to the shareholders and to speak at the general meeting on the resolution. It was held in the *Glover* case that it is an implied term of a director's service contract, especially one that lays down grounds for removal from the board, that the removal procedures be fair. If, for example, the grounds stated for dismissal are misconduct or neglect of duty, then the director must be "told of the charges against him [and be] allow[ed] to meet the charges . . . and afford[ed] an adequate opportunity of answering them. . . ."[57] It is of no relevance to this that the director is an employee and not an office-holder. Refusal to accord these procedural rights is a breach of contract regardless of how guilty the director may have been. The court in *Glover* did not consider whether or to what extent these rights could be excluded or waived by contract.

[54.] [1973] I.R. 388, discussed *ante*, pp. 169-170.
[55.] [1968] I.R. 325, discussed *ante*, p. 169.
[56.] *i.e.* 1963 Act, s.182.
[57.] [1973] I.R. at 425.

CHAPTER 13

THE PUBLIC SERVICE

The State is by far the largest employer in the country, if by the State is conceived central, regional and local government and all the other public sector agencies and bodies. Because of the *de facto* security of employment and statutorily-based generous pension schemes, jobs in the public service are often regarded as particularly attractive. Special conciliation and arbitration schemes have been established in order to cater for claims regarding remuneration and other employment grievances in much of the public sector.[1] From a legal point of view, public service employment is very different from that in the private sector because the position of many public employees is affected by detailed regulations which have no equivalent elsewhere. Moreover, the legal grievances of many public service employees are amenable to resolution through the procedure of judicial review.

AMBIT OF EMPLOYMENT LEGISLATION

Several of the employment laws considered so far in this book do not apply to certain parts of the public sector; the categories of public employees excluded from the legislation vary considerably from Act to Act. The reasons for these exclusions also differ. For instance, there may already exist adequate negotiating machinery within a category of employment in question that renders it unnecessary to have the statutory rules made applicable there. The public sector is very highly unionised, which significantly diminishes the need for employment protection there.

At one time it was a principle of statutory construction that an Act did not bind the State or restrict its rights unless an interpretation to that effect was clear and indispensable on the construction of the Act. But that is no longer the case.[2] Accordingly, it would seem that where the position under the Act in question is not clear, it should be deemed to apply to public service as much as to the private sector.

Some of the employment laws make it clear that they apply to the State and other public bodies as employers. Most of the major employment Acts passed in the 1990s, mainly to implement E.C. Directives, apply across the public sector, including civil servants and officers of local authorities and equivalent bodies, and even members of the Garda Síochána and the Defence Forces; for instance, the Payment of Wages Act 1991, the Terms of Employment (Information) Act 1994, the Maternity Protection Act 1994, the Adoptive Leave Act 1994 and the Protection of Young Persons (Employment) Act 1996. Although the Organisation

---

[1.] See, generally, *Industrial Relations Law*, Chap. 7.
[2.] *Howard v. C'mrs of Public Works* [1994] 1 I.R. 101.

of Working Time Act 1997 applies to most of the public sector, it does not yet cover members of the Garda Síochána and of the Defence Forces.[3] Members of the Garda Síochána and of the prison service are exempted from some of the sex equality provisions in the Employment Equality Act 1998,[4] and requirements regarding residence, citizenship and proficiency in the Irish language are not breaches of Part IV of that Act when applied to a broad range of public service employments.[5]

The E.C. Transfer of Undertakings Directive[6] has been held to apply to public service employment but not to transfers of administrative functions between public authorities. In *Henke v. Gemeinde Schierke*[7] several municipalities in Germany merged their administrative functions with a view to a more efficient management of them. A claim under the Directive by the secretary to the mayor of one of those towns was rejected by the European Court on the grounds that the "reorganisation of structures of the public administration or the transfer of administrative functions between public administrative authorities does not constitute a 'transfer of an undertaking' within the meaning of the Directive".[8] This is a wider exemption than what was urged by Advocate General Lenz, who recommended that only functions which relate purely to the exercise of public powers, for example those of the mayor, the police or prison staff, do not fall within the Directive. What the Court excluded were all "activities involving the exercise of public authority"; the focus is on the functions being transferred and not on the kind of work individuals may do in the discharge of an administrative function.

Many public sector workers are excluded from the Minimum Notice and Terms of Employment Act 1973, the Unfair Dismissals Act 1977, and the Protection of Employment Act 1977. Although the Transfer of Undertakings Regulations 1980 apply in the public as well as in the private sector, there are certain kinds of administrative reorganisations that fall outside its terms.[9] The most extensive exclusions are those in the Unfair Dismissals Acts which do not apply to, *inter alia*, the following categories:[10]

- A member of the Garda Síochána;

- A person in employment as a Member of the Defence Forces, the Judge Advocate-General, the Chairman of the Army Pensions Board or the ordinary member thereof who is not an Officer of the Medical Corps of the Defence Forces;

- A person employed by or under the State other than persons standing designated for the time being under section 17 of the Industrial Relations Act 1969;

---

3.   s.3(1).
4.   s.27.
5.   s.36.
6.   Directive 77/187; see *ante,* pp. 230 *et seq.*
7.   (Case 298/94) [1996] E.C.R. 4989.
8.   Para. 14.
9.   s.2(1)(d)-(j).
10. *supra,* n.7.

- Officers of a local authority for the purposes of the Local Government Act 1941;

- Officers of a health board (other than temporary officers), or a vocational education committee established by the Vocational Education Act 1930.[11]

The 1977-93 Acts and also the Protection of Employment Act 1977 stipulate that their requirements do not apply to "persons employed by or under the State", subject to certain qualifications. It can hardly be doubted that this category covers all civil servants and local government officers, as well as members of the Defence Forces and of the Garda Síochána. Since the Unfair Dismissals Acts expressly exclude the Gardaí and the Defence Forces and there is no similar provision in the other Act, an argument could be made that these groups do not come within the "employed by or under the State" category in those Acts. But that contention does not seem very convincing.

What of those who work for public agencies that receive their entire funding from the State but who are not civil servants in the strict legal sense, such as personnel in the Central Bank, solicitors who work for the Law Centres, primary and other teachers, and those employed in bodies like the Industrial Development Authority and Coras Trachtála? In *Central Bank v. Gildea*,[12] it was held that a security guard employed by the Central Bank did not come within this excluded category. There the Supreme Court confined the category to civil servants, whether in the service of the State or of the Government. Because the Central Bank was an entirely separate corporate body created by statute, which at any time can be repealed by the Oireachtas, the Court held that he was legally in no different a position from that of those working for the many "semi-state" bodies. Unlike the situation pertaining to civil servants, the terms and conditions of employment of the plaintiff there were not regulated by a comprehensive statutory code equivalent to the Civil Service Regulation Act 1956, but were simply governed by the contract he had with the Bank. Indeed, a clause in that contract expressly referred to the Unfair Dismissals Acts.

But certain groups who are employed by or under the State are covered by the above Acts. Persons designated under section 17(2) of the Industrial Relations Act 1969 come within the Unfair Dismissals Acts;[13] they are, principally, those who might be described as the non-"white collar" or the "industrial" civil service. Unestablished civil servants who were engaged on "subordinate duties" and also anybody engaged in "industrial work" came within the terms of the since-repealed 1973 Holidays Act.

The Unfair Dismissals Acts do not apply to "officers" of local authorities or of a health board (except temporary officers), or of a vocational education committee.[14] Local authority officers are excluded from the Protection of Employment Act 1977. But it is not each and every employee of these authorities and committees who are excluded. The question of who are "officers" as distinct from employees is dealt with earlier in this book.[15]

---

[11]. Amended by 1993 Act, s.3(a).
[12]. [1997] 1 I.R. 160.
[13]. s.2(1)(h).
[14]. s.2(1)(i) and (j), as amended by 1993 Act, s.3(a).
[15]. See *ante,* pp. 33-34 and *infra,* p 310.

Public sector workers are also protected by the European Convention on Human Rights and the State *qua* employer cannot, without adequate justification, impose conditions or restrictions on them which conflict with guaranteed rights.[16] But as regards access to civil service employment, the Strasbourg Court has consistently held that the Convention provides no protection. Regarding Article 6(1) of the Convention's guarantee of fair civil proceedings, formerly the attitude of the Strasbourg Court was that it had no application to disputes regarding civil servants' recruitment, careers and dismissal.[17] However, in the *Pellegrin* case[18] the Court held that this exclusion applied only to public sector workers "who occupy posts involving participation in the exercise of powers conferred by public law", meaning whose "duties typify the specific activities of the public service insofar as the latter is acting as the depository of public authority responsible for protecting the general interests of the State or other public authorities".[19] Mr Pellegrin, who was employed by the French Ministry of Co-operation and Development as one of its civilian cooperation staff in an African State, was held to come within this excluded category, in particular because he had a say in the Ministry's spending decisions. In determining which side of the line for this purpose public sector workers fall, the Strasbourg Court is guided by the criteria published by the European Commission for determining who are excluded from the E.C. Treaty's requirements on the free movement of workers.[20]

PUBLIC LAW RIGHTS AND REMEDIES

The term public law is a convenient label for constitutional law and administrative law. In Continental European countries, where there are special court structures for constitutional and administrative law cases (somewhat like the common law and the chancery courts structures in the past), the distinction between public and private law is of particular significance. A book on employment law is not the appropriate place to speculate on whether there exists in Ireland a body of public law in the Continental European sense. But the relevance of the distinction in the present context is that the State and public bodies and agencies, as employers, are subject to the general principles of constitutional and administrative law that are not generally applicable to private sector employments.[21] All employers in dealing with their employees are subject to legal constraints, notably, their obligations under the contract of employment and also the law of tort and general legislative provisions. The State and other public sector employers are subject to the same constraints; whatever element of sovereign immunity from tort liability

---

[16] *e.g. Vogt v. Germany* 21 E.H.R.R. 205 (1996) and *Willie v. Liechtenstein*, 8 B.H.R.C. 69 (1999). See, generally, Palmer, "Human Rights: Implications for Labour Law", (2000) 59 Cam L. Rev. 168.

[17] *e.g. Glasenapp v. Germany*, 9 E.H.R.R. 328 (1987), *Neigel v. France*, 30 E.H.R.R. 310 (1997), *Huber v. France*, 26 E.H.R.R. 457 (1998).

[18] Application 28541/95, Decision of December 8, 1999.

[19] Paras. 66 and 67.

[20] See *ante*, pp. 157-158 and C. Barnard, *E.C. Employment Law* (2nd ed., 2000) pp. 189-193.

[21] See, however, Beaton, "Public Law Influences in Contract Law", in J. Beatson & D. Friedman, *Good Faith and Fault in Contract Law* (1995) Chap.10.

as existed in 1922 has been declared unconstitutional[22] and there are no Continental European-style special principles and rules for contracts in the public sector, like the doctrine of *imprévision*.[23] Public sector employers must observe the rules of natural justice or constitutional justice (*i.e.* fair procedures), must respect substantive constitutional rights, and must not abuse their discretionary powers. There is also a vitally important procedural distinction in the public sector, *viz.* redress by way of judicial review.

Judicial review

Disputes with public authorities can be brought to court through what is known as the judicial review procedure, which is provided for in Order 84V of the Rules of the Superior Courts.[24] Thus, where a public service office-holder or his trade union or professional association believe that his employer has acted, or proposes to act, unlawfully, that question can be litigated through this procedure. As well as awarding damages or granting an injunction or making a declaration, the High Court when exercising judicial review can make orders of prohibition and mandamus, and quash decisions through orders of certiorari. Where redress by way of judicial review is not available, before he can succeed an aggrieved party must be able to point to a breach of contract, a tort, a breach of fiduciary duty or of some statutory duty. If his claim is based on a breach of statutory duty, it must be a duty which in the circumstances is owed to him and not just an obligation owed to the public at large. But a more extensive range of legal defects can be raised when proceeding by way of judicial review. Where the plaintiff does not have an employment contract, as is the position with civil servants and with many other public service office-holders, his normal mode of legal redress would then be by way of judicial review.

There are certain disadvantages in bringing a claim by way of judicial review. Proceedings can only be brought in the High Court. Before such proceedings will even be considered by the Court, the applicant must have *locus standi*. Proceedings should be brought within six months of the alleged illegality occurring, although the Court has a discretion to extend the time in an appropriate case.[25] Even if the applicant's legal argument is upheld, he will not invariably be given the remedy he seeks; for the Court has a discretion to refuse to grant a declaration, an injunction, certiorari, prohibition or mandamus in an appropriate case. Relief will be refused where the applicant did not show absolute good faith and did not make full disclosure of his circumstances. Relief will be withheld because of the applicant's general conduct and the reason for the application. And relief will be denied where the applicant did not act promptly, even within the six months, period. For instance, in *State (Cussen) v. Brennan*,[26] the unsuccessful applicant for an office in the Southern Health Board challenged the appointment

22. *Byrne v. Ireland* [1972] I.R. 241.
23. See, generally, D. Harris & D. Tallon eds., *Contract Law Today, Anglo-French Comparisons* (1989), pp. 228-232.
24. See, generally, C. Bradley, *Judicial Review* (2000) and G. Hogan & D. Morgan, *Administrative Law in Ireland* (3rd ed., 1998), Chap. 14.
25. *Cf. de Roiste v. Minister for Defence* [2001] E.L.R. 33.
26. [1981] I.R. 181.

which was made, on the grounds that a test of proficiency in Irish was unlawfully introduced into the selection criteria. As is explained below, the Supreme Court upheld his argument. But the Court declined to quash the irregular appointment because the applicant delayed for four months before bringing the proceedings and, in the meantime, the person appointed and the Health Board had entered into new commitments.

If the dispute is between private individuals or organisations, it is not amenable to judicial review. Even if the dispute is with the State or with some other public body or agency, if it concerns an essentially "private law" issue, it is not appropriate for judicial review. In the various Continental European countries, there is a vast and complex jurisprudence regarding what types of disputes are private law or public controversies; if they address public law questions, they must be heard by administrative tribunals as contrasted with the civil courts.

Two main questions arise. One is which employers are sufficiently a part of the public sector apparatus for at least some employment-related disputes with them to be amenable to judicial review. Undoubtedly, the State, local and regional authorities, health boards, vocational educational committees and the like fall within this zone. But what of State-owned public utilities and enterprises, such as Radio Telefís Éireann, Coras Trachtála, the Electricity Supply Board? The conventional wisdom is that employment disputes with these latter bodies and equivalent organisations fall outside judicial review, and instead must follow the same procedures as for private sector employments. It was held in Britain that the old National Coal Board was not a "public body" for the purpose of the Prevention of Corruption Acts.[27]

Secondly, regarding employers within the public zone, are all of their staff entitled to proceed, by way of judicial review, to assert their employment rights or is this procedure reserved for office-holders? Or, does the matter turn on the exact nature of the claim being made? For instance, if the office-holder also has an employment contract and the dispute relates to the contract, is it then a private law question and unsuitable for judicial review? If the applicant commenced private law proceedings but then decided instead to go by way of judicial review, is he estopped from taking that action? The conventional wisdom is that if the plaintiff works under an employment contract, ordinarily he cannot air his employment-related grievances by way of judicial review. Before 1990 a practical reason for excluding ordinary employees from judicial review was that, unlike many public service office-holders, they are protected by all the main employment protection legislation.

In *O'Neill v. Beaumont Hospital Board*,[28] where a consultant surgeon contested disciplinary decisions made against him by the management of the largest public hospital in the State, the Supreme Court expressed its doubt about "the basis of an application for judicial review concerning the decision by an employer provided for specifically in a contract of employment. . . ."[29] However, the respondents there conceded that the issue could be dealt with by way of judicial review. This question came before the Supreme Court again in *O'Neill v.*

[27.]   *R. v. Newbould* [1962] 2 Q.B. 102.
[28.]   [1990] I.L.R.M. 41.
[29.]   *ibid.* at 437.

Iarnród Éireann,[30] where the applicant sought to contest disciplinary measures taken against him by the State-owned railway undertaking. Those proceedings were the initial application for leave to seek judicial review, which is an *ex parte* process. For that reason, it was decided to allow the claim for relief to be instituted and the whole matter of the appropriateness of proceeding in that manner could then be fully argued at the *inter partes* hearing. Finlay C.J. and McCarthy J. reiterated the reservations about bringing what in essence are claims for breach of an employment contract in this manner. Hederman J. went further, concluding that the Order 84 procedure "lies only against public authorities in respect of duties conferred upon them by law" and that leave to proceed with the action should be refused there and then.

When, however, that Court had to bite the bullet on the question and come down on one side of the fence or the other, it opted for the more expansive view of the ambit of judicial review. That was in *Beirne v. Commissioner of An Garda Síochána*,[31] where it was held that a trainee garda was entitled to challenge her dismissal in this manner. She had not yet become a member of that force and her relationship with the Commissioner was based on contract. Notwithstanding and even though that contract contained a power to dismiss, Finlay C.J. held that the broad statutory power the Commissioner had to manage the force contained by implication a power of dismissal; it was this extra element that tipped the scales. It was subsequently followed in *Rafferty v. Bus Éireann*,[32] where two bus drivers along with their trade unions sought to contest their employer's proposed changes in rostering arrangements. Because section 18 of the Transport (Reorganisation of Córas Iompair Éireann) Act 1986 authorised Bus Éireann to employ persons and provided for the transfer over to that company of former employees of C.I.E. without their previous terms and conditions being worsened, Kelly J. held that there was a sufficient public element in the employment relationships that warranted proceeding by way of judicial review. Although "the contracts of employment [here] may originally have been private ones between employee and employer (albeit a public employer), they have been altered by statute and have been given an express statutory protection which is not the case in an ordinary private contract".[33] Accordingly, it would seem that nearly all public employment disputes can be processed in the High Court by way of judicial review.

Fair procedures

Many of the leading cases on the right to fair procedures, under the rubric of natural justice or constitutional justice, have concerned the treatment of public service office-holders and employees.[34] Where the relevant regulations lay down a procedure, then that procedure must be followed or, at least, only in very exceptional cases will departure from the prescribed procedure be permitted. Deviation from procedures so prescribed or from procedures required under general princi-

---

[30]. [1991] I.L.R.M. 129.
[31]. [1993] I.L.R.M. 1.
[32]. [1997] 2 I.R. 424.
[33]. *ibid.* at 440; *e.g. Eoghan v. University College Dublin* [1996] 1 I.R. 390.
[34]. See, generally, *Bradley, supra,* n.24, Chap. 14, and *Hogan and Morgan, supra,* n.24, Chaps 11 and 12.

ples of fairness generally will be upheld where the aggrieved party actually consented to or acquiesced in that departure. The extent of informed consent to constitute a waiver of procedural rights has not been explained by the courts and it would seem that extremely serious breaches of procedural propriety may be incapable of being waived.[35] Most of the reported cases on fair procedures concern dismissals, suspensions from employment, demotions and the like. Refusals to hire an applicant for a public service post can also be challenged on procedural grounds, although the procedure in question would need to be seriously flawed before such a contest could succeed.[36]

In *Keady v. Commissioner of An Garda Síochána,* [37] the plaintiff sought to radically extend the ambit of procedural protection in the public service, in particular in the Garda Síochána, by contending that allegations of very serious misconduct involving what may be criminal offences must be adjudicated upon in the courts and not simply by a tribunal of inquiry set up under the Garda Discipline Regulations. Just as much as disbarring professionals, such as solicitors and doctors and nurses, from practicing their profession is a matter over which the courts should have a direct say, it was argued that dismissing a member of the Garda in the above circumstances is similarly a "plenary" judicial function to be exercised by the courts and not by administrative tribunals within Article 37 of the Constitution. But the Supreme Court held that, when deciding on whether alleged serious misconduct had been established, the disciplinary tribunal does not exercise even "limited" judicial power. Further, unlike with professionals, disciplining members of the Garda has not historically been regarded as a judicial function and, moreover, Gardai hold office within the terms of the Garda Síochána Acts and regulations made under them, including those on disciplinary procedures.

Adequate hearing

One of the main tenets of administrative law is that a serious decision adverse to an individual should not be taken unless he is first given a fair hearing: the maxim *audi alteram partem.* In *State (Gleeson) v. Minister for Defence,*[38] the applicant, a three-star private in the army, was discharged on the grounds that his conduct was unsatisfactory. But he had never been informed of what allegations were being made against him and got no opportunity whatsoever to put his side of the story to the military authorities. It was held that his discharge was invalid because those authorities had not acted in accordance with natural or constitutional justice. According to Henchy J.:

> "We are not here concerned with discharges for creditable or neutral reasons. Where . . . as in this case, the discharge is for a reason that is discreditable, the fundamentals of justice require that the man shall have an opportunity of meeting the case for discharging him for that reason . . . .
> [W]here (as happened in this case) the reason for the discharge of a soldier

---

[35] *Corrigan v. Irish Land Comm.* [1977] I.R. 317 at 334.
[36] *O'Dwyer v. McDonagh* [1997] E.L.R. 91.
[37] [1992] 2 I.R. 197.
[38] [1976] I.R. 280.

is proposed to be established for the first time by the army authorities for the purpose of the discharge, with the result in that event that not only will his army career be abruptly terminated but that he will be cast out into civilian life with a permanent slur on him in the record of his military service — which may seriously damage his opportunities in life — and when he is to be marked down as a permanent reject for the purpose of enlistment again, it would be an affront to justice if the law were to hold that a decision with such drastic consequences for the man involved, and possibly for his dependants, could be made behind his back.

[T]he law applicable to a case such as this is clear and well established. The requirements of natural justice imposed an inescapable duty on the army authorities, before discharging the prosecutor from the army for the misconduct relied on, to give him due notice of the intention to discharge him, of the statutory reason for the proposed discharge, and of the essential facts and findings alleged to constitute that reason; and to give him a reasonable opportunity of presenting his response to that notice."[39]

Thirteen years later, the principle laid down here was extended to the dismissal of one of the most important office-holders in the State, the Commissioner of the Garda Síochána. In *Garvey v. Ireland*,[40] the plaintiff, the Garda Commissioner, was dismissed without any warning by the Government and was not given any reason for his discharge nor any opportunity to make representations against it. The Supreme Court held that his dismissal was void and ineffective. According to O'Higgins C.J., "even if the office of Commissioner . . . were stated to be an office from which the holder could be removed at [the Government's] pleasure, this would not relieve those who sought to exercise that power from the obligation and requirement to act in accordance with natural justice."[41] Before they could lawfully remove him, the Government was "bound to act fairly and must tell [him] of the reason or reasons for the proposed action and give him an opportunity of being heard."[42] In 1996 this principle was held to apply to even one of the most subordinate positions in the public service, a trainee Garda,[43] who is hardly a probationer and not even a member of that force. In 1997 this principle was held applicable to a decision to dismiss a postman for alleged serious misconduct.[44] In the following year it was held to apply to a decision to demote a prison officer for misconduct but, as the facts there were never in dispute and the officer never sought a hearing into the allegations against him, he had no good grounds for saying he did not get a fair hearing.[45]

Even where a dismissal does not involve or carry undertones of improper conduct or inefficiency by the official, he may be entitled to a hearing before being discharged. In *Maunsell v. Minister for Education*,[46] the plaintiff was an assistant

---

[39]. *ibid.* at 296.
[40]. [1981] I.R. 75.
[41]. *ibid.* at 97.
[42]. *ibid.*
[43]. *McAuley v. Commissioner of An Garda Síochána* [1996] 3 I.R. 208.
[44]. *Mooney v. An Post* [1998] 4 I.R. 288.
[45]. *Sheriff v. Corrigan* [2000] 1 I.L.R.M. 67.
[46]. [1940] I.R. 213.

national teacher employed in Ballyduff National School, Co. Kerry. Under a system then prevailing, described as "contrived to make a junior assistant teacher in a very real sense insurer of the average attendance of pupils at the school", if average school attendance over a certain period fell by a specified average, the assistant's salary was no longer payable; in effect, he would be dismissed. On the basis of the returns made by the headmaster to the Department of Education, the plaintiff's salary was withdrawn — having taught at that school for the previous 20 years. No advance warning of this decision was given to him and he got no opportunity to present his case. Gavan Duffy J. declared the decision invalid. The plaintiff had not received "fair notice that an inquiry was to be held to determine his fate, fair notice of the case against him and a fair opportunity to meet it".[47] But this case is something of an exception; ordinarily there must be some significant connotation of misconduct or impropriety before a right to a hearing can arise. In a later instance, *Maunsell* was explained as "turn[ing] upon the individual provisions of the regulation concerning assistant teachers" and as not being authority for the proposition that office-holders must be given some hearing before being made redundant in accordance with established redundancy procedures.[48]

Authority is sparse on the question of exactly what procedures should be followed at the hearing. While the ordinary rules of evidence need not apply,[49] the nature of certain allegations may be such as entitles the employee to cross-examine his accusers,[50] and, when Health Boards are investigating allegations against general practitioners, doctors should be furnished with copies of documentation relevant to the complaints which are in the Board's possession.[51] Where a customs and excise officer with 20 years' service was in jeopardy of being dismissed because he was allegedly dishonest in the discharge of his duties, the Supreme Court held that he was entitled to confront and cross-examine witnesses on key aspects of the case being made out against him.[52] There an official was accused of manipulating the declared values of cars that were imported and those transactions were subsequently the subject of a third-party valuation and a report. Because his request to cross-examine those valuers was refused on the grounds of administrative inconvenience in securing their attendance (they were in England), the decision to dismiss him was declared invalid as he had been denied fair procedures.[53] Similarly too, where a postmaster had been dismissed for alleged irregularities, the decision-maker had acted on an internal report, which had never been shown to the plaintiff and, subsequent to the hearing, the decision-maker made further enquiries about the plaintiff which influenced the decision about the latter's credibility. On account of these clear breaches of natural justice, the dismissal was quashed.[54]

---

47. *ibid.* at 234. Similarly, *Malloch v. Aberdeen Corp.* [1971] 1 W.L.R. 1578.
48. *Hickey v. Eastern Health Board* [1991] I.R. 208 at 212.
49. *Dietman v. Brent L.B.C.* [1987] I.C.R. 737.
50. *A Worker v. A Hospital* [1997] E.L.R. 214.
51. *O'Flynn v. Mid Western Health Board* [1989] E.L.R. 214.
52. *Gallagher v. Revenue Cm'rs* [1995] 1 I.R. 55.
53. Adopting *inter alia, R. v. Bord Visitors of Hull Prision, ex p. St. Germain* [1979] 1 W.L.R. 1401.
54. *Tierney v. An Post* [1999] E.L.R. 65 and 293.

In contrast, where a postman was in jeopardy of being dismissed for alleged dishonesty but, notwithstanding written requests to do so, declined to provide any account of the events in question, it was held that he could not then insist on a full oral hearing with cross-examination of his accusers.[55] There, one of the accusers gave evidence at the judicial review proceedings, but was not cross-examined, while the plaintiff declined to give any evidence there. That he had previously been acquitted of criminal charges relating to the alleged dishonesty was held not to be a bar to subsequent disciplinary action.

Among the questions still to be answered are how precise must the charges against the person be and how detailed an outline should he be given in advance of the evidence it is proposed to use against him. Where a probationer Garda was dismissed without being informed of the seriousness of the allegations against him or being shown copies of statements made by witnesses against him, it was held that the Commissioner had acted unlawfully.[56] Where grave charges are being made against the individual and where the consequences of an adverse finding could be serious for him, generally he is entitled to have legal representation at any oral hearing of the complaint.[57]

In a case involving disciplinary sanctions imposed on a naval officer, Lavan J. adopted the following statement of general principle:

> "Where a tribunal is required to act judicially, the procedures to be adopted by it must be reasonable having regard to this requirement and to the consequences for the person concerned in the event of an adverse decision. Accordingly, procedures which might afford a sufficient protection to the person concerned in one case and be acceptable might not be acceptable in a more serious case. In the present case, the principles of natural justice involved relate to the requirement that the person involved should be made aware of the complaint against them and should have an opportunity both to prepare and to present their defence. Matters to be considered are the form in which the complaint should be made, the time to be allowed to the person concerned to prepare a defence, and the nature of the hearing at which that defence may be presented. In addition depending upon the gravity of the matter, the person concerned may be entitled to be represented and may also be entitled to be informed of their rights. Clearly, matters of a criminal nature must be treated more seriously than matters of a civil nature, but ultimately the criterion must be the consequences for the person concerned of an adverse verdict."[58]

Absence of bias

Another of the central tenets of administrative law is that no one should act as a judge in his own cause: the maxim *nemo iudex in sua causa*. The test applied by

---

55. *Mooney v. An Post* [1998] 4 I.R. 288.
56. *Duffy v. Commissioner of An Garda Síochána* [1999] 2 I.R. 81. Compare *Deegan v. Minister for Finance* [2000] E.L.R. 190, where it was held that sufficient information given to the plaintiffs before it was decided to suspend them without full pay.
57. *Gallagher v. Revenue Commissioners* [1991] 2 I.R. 320.
58. *McDonough v. Minister for Defence* [1991] I.L.R.M. 115 at 121, adopting *Flanagan v. University College Dublin* [1989] I.L.R.M. 469 at 475.

the courts for this purpose, "in determining whether a tribunal . . . is impartial is that a member is not impartial if his own interest might be affected by the verdict, or he is so connected with the complainant that a reasonable man would think that he would come to the case with prior knowledge of the facts or that he might not be impartial".[59] Whether there is a real possibility of bias in any particular instance depends on the entire circumstances of the case. For instance, in *Heneghan v. Western Regional Fisheries Board*,[60] the plaintiff, an office-holder with the Board, had a dispute with his regional manager, which the Board arranged to investigate under its procedures. That investigation was carried out by the very same regional manager, who recommended the plaintiff's dismissal. His dismissal was held to be void because of the flagrant contravention of the *nemo iudex* principle. In *O'Neill v. Beaumont Hospital Board*,[61] the plaintiff was a consultant surgeon at the Hospital who was on a one-year probationary contract. At the end of that period, the Hospital's chief executive certified that the plaintiff's service had been unsatisfactory and the plaintiff then launched court proceedings challenging that certificate. In the meantime, the Hospital established an inquiry to investigate the plaintiff's service. Among the members of that committee of inquiry were the chief executive of the Hospital and two others who had expressed views adverse to the plaintiff. The Supreme Court granted an injunction against them participating in the inquiry because "a person in the position of the plaintiff who is a reasonable man and not either over-sensitive or careless of his own position, would have good grounds for fearing that he would not get, in respect of the issues involved . . . an independent hearing".[62]

In another and related Beaumont Hospital case, *Georgopoulos*,[63] the employer conducted a hearing into allegations of misconduct made against a registrar neurosurgeon, who had been dismissed from his one year's service contract. The tribunal set up engaged the services of a legal assessor who gave it certain advices but the nature of that advice was not disclosed to the plaintiff. The Supreme Court held that the *nemo iudex* principle had not been thereby breached. Similarly in *McAuley v. Keating*,[64] a trainee Garda challenged a decision to dismiss him for misconduct, on the grounds that the decision had been pre-judged by the respondent having notified him that a breach of discipline had occurred and that there would be a full enquiry into the matter. The Supreme Court rejected the allegation of bias.

The same conclusion was reached in *O'Dwyer v. McDonagh*,[65] where what happened in the course of interviewing for a promotional post in Limerick Regional Technical College was contested. The four-person panel had two internal members, including the director of the College, and two external assessors. When the interviews had concluded, the internal members expressed their preference for a candidate other than the applicant and prevailed on the two externals to

59. *O'Donoghue v. Veterinary Council* [1975] I.R. 398 at 405.
60. [1986] I.L.R.M. 225.
61. [1990] I.L.R.M. 419.
62. *ibid.* at 439.
63. *Georgopoulus v. Beaumont Hospital* [1998] 3 I.R. 132.
64. [1994] 4 I.R. 138.
65. [1997] E.L.R. 91.

so agree. Barr J. found that there had been no infringement of the *nemo iudex* principle. It had been argued that the two internal members had adopted an entrenched position of opposition to the applicant in connection with the post and that they had decided before the interview that she should not be appointed, but it was conceded that there was no *mala fides* on their part.

Expeditious hearing

Where there is an inordinate delay between the time the alleged wrong-doing took place and the disciplinary hearing into charges arising out of them, the court will enjoin the conduct of that hearing on the grounds that the lapse of time was unjust and oppressive. Where the disciplinary rules do not expressly require the matter to be dealt with quickly, the overriding criteria are in the general principles regarding undue delay in criminal and civil proceedings. Whether in any particular instance delay is so excessive as to be unlawful depends on a wide variety of factors; there is no simple test.[66] The rules govering discipline in the Garda Síochána emphasise expedition, using terms such as "as soon as practicable", "as soon as may be", and "without avoidable delay".

Reasons

Whether or to what extent the person or body making the disciplinary decision must furnish reasons for it remains to be clarified. However, since private sector employers are required by the Unfair Dismissals Acts to give reasons, it is difficult to see how the State *qua* employer is not subject to a similar obligation where a decision is taken to dismiss or to impose some other sanction.

Consultation

Several statutory provisions exist that require employers to consult with employees and also with their trade unions.[67] Where no such provision exists, there is very little judicial guidance as to when individual employees should be consulted before a decision is taken which adversely affects them to a significant degree, other than regarding disciplinary charges or dismissal.[68] Where an employer's action adversely affects a group of persons, the circumstances may require some prior consultation with their trade union or other representative association. Thus, in Britain an obligation to consult was held to exist when the G.C.H.Q. "spy" agency unilaterally amended employment conditions to prohibit employees from being trade union members.[69] It was also held there that a health authority should have consulted representatives of general practitioners before temporarily shutting down a hospital.[70]

---

[66]. *McNeill v. Commissioner An Garda Síochána* [1997] 1 I.R. 469.
[67]. *e.g.* Organisation of Working Time Act 1997, s.20.
[68]. An exception in *Maunsell v. Minister for Education* [1940] I.R. 213, *supra*, p. 287.
[69]. *Council of the Civil Service Unions v. Minister for the Civil Service* [1985] A.C. 374.
[70]. *R. v. Hillingdon Health Authority, ex p. Goodwin* [1984] I.C.R. 800; contrast *R. v. National Coal Board, ex p. National Union of Mineworkers* [1986] I.C.R. 791.

Suspension

Most, if not all, of the legislation on public service employment authorises the suspension of office-holders or employees in certain circumstances, frequently on reduced pay or on no pay. Any suspension other than within the strict terms of the relevant provision is not permissible.[71] Where the suspension is on full pay, so that certain enquiries may be carried out, it remains to be decided whether or not some form of prior hearing must be afforded. It was held by the Supreme Court in *Deegan v. Minister for Finance*,[72] where the plaintiffs, civil servants, were suspended on part pay, pending enquiries being conducted into alleged irregularities on their behalf, that they were entitled to be informed of the reasons, so that they could make representations to have their suspension terminated. It was further held there that they had been given sufficient information for that purpose.

Where a person has been suspended without pay and perhaps on part pay, that suspension should not be unduly prolonged. In *Flynn v. An Post*,[73] the plaintiff was suspended, in accordance with the suspension procedures for civil servants, in order to investigate allegations that he had stolen postal packages from his employer. At the same time, criminal charges were being brought against him in connection with the same circumstances, and the employer decided to prolong his suspension pending the outcome of the trial. The Supreme Court held that ordinarily a suspension of this nature should not continue indefinitely pending the outcome of the criminal case. Considerations of fair play for the individual demand that the administrative investigation into the allegation against him should proceed promptly; the contractual power is not one of virtual indefinite suspension. However, the individual may acquiesce in the prolongation of his suspension or there may be other exceptional circumstance which warrant its extension.

Double jeopardy

Where a person has been tried by a court and fully acquitted of charges, that is not a bar to him undergoing disciplinary proceedings which in effect amount to a re-trial of those charges; in general, there is no principle against double jeopardy in that sense. A contention for such a principle was rejected by the Supreme Court in *Mooney v. An Post*,[74] where a postman had been tried and acquitted of stealing postal packets but subsequently was dismissed for that reason. He was given every opportunity by his employer to adequately explain how those packets in his possession had disappeared but declined to furnish any explanation. The double jeopardy argument was held not to be based on authority and, further, "it would be absurd if a party who had failed to establish a proposition beyond all reasonable doubt should, by that fact alone, be debarred from attempting to establish the same proposition on the balance of probabilities".[75]

---

71. *Carr v. Minister for Education and Science* [2000] E.L.R. 78; *cf. Gogay v. Hertfordshire C.C.* [2000] I.R.L.R. 703.
72. [2000] E.L.R. 190.
73. [1987] I.R. 68. See *McGrath v. Minister for Justice* [2001] E.L.R. 15.
74. [1998] 4 I.R. 288.
75. *ibid.* at 297.

The Court there distinguished its earlier decision in *McGrath v. Commissioner of An Garda Síochána*,[76] in which the plaintiff had been acquitted of embezzlement charges. Disciplinary proceedings were then brought against him for corruptly and dishonestly taking money, in circumstances identical to those in the charges which failed. Lynch J. held that, while the exact circumstances about taking the money might be the subject of disciplinary proceedings, it was "not now open to the inquiry to investigate these matters on the basis that there was any element of corruption or dishonesty on the part of the applicant in relation to them".[77] Nor could the plaintiff be disciplined simply for having being charged with a criminal offence. In this case, the garda was acquitted by the jury because of insufficiency of evidence establishing fraud. His trial and the disciplinary proceedings would have focused on that very same issue — whether he had acted dishonestly. If the disciplinary tribunal found against him, that would in effect set at nought the outcome of the jury trial. Moreover, the normal practice in Garda discipline was not to seek to have matters re-tried in this manner and, indeed, under the present garda regulations, a re-trial of this nature is no longer possible. Upholding the judgment, the Supreme Court found that there was an element of issue estoppel between the two proceedings. But Finlay J. emphasised that "there cannot . . . be any general principle that an acquittal on a criminal charge in respect of an offence, irrespective of the reasons for such acquittal or the basis on which it was achieved, could be inevitably an estoppel preventing a disciplinary investigation arising out of the same set of facts".[78] In another Garda discipline case, *McCarthy*,[79] it was held by Flood J. that it was unfair and unlawful for the Garda authorities to seek to discipline the plaintiff for alleged wrong-doing, in respect of which he had undergone a criminal trial and had been acquitted. In the light of what was decided in *Mooney*, however, it would seem that *McCarthy* no longer represents the law.

Legitimate expectation

It has been recognised in recent years that public officers have certain "legitimate expectations" which do not amount to fully enforceable rights but which nevertheless obtain a degree of legal protection.[80] This doctrine closely resembles the "acquired rights" principle in the civil service laws of Continental European countries whereby, even though as a matter of strict law the State is empowered unilaterally to change employment terms and conditions in whatever way it sees fit, there are certain kinds of drastic changes it will not be allowed to make, or only make on certain conditions being satisfied.[81] That condition may be entirely procedural; in other words, some form of prior consultation or hearing is required before the change could be made, as in the British *G.C.H.Q.* case.[82] That condi-

---

[76.] [1991] 1 I.R. 69.

[77.] [1989] I.R. at 246.

[78.] [1991] 1 I.R. at 71.

[79.] *McCarthy v. Commissioner of An Garda Síochána* [1993] 1 I.R. 490.

[80.] See, generally, *Bradley, supra*, n.24, Chap. 15, and *Hogan and Moran, supra*, n.24, Chap. 16.

[81.] See, generally, Baade, "Acquired Rights of International Public Servants", 15 Amr. J. Comp. L. 251 (1967).

[82.] *supra*, n.69.

tion may be substantive; for instance, the proposed change may be permitted provided the persons affected are adequately compensated in some way. Or, the change may be one which can be implemented only when those affected have adequate opportunity to rearrange their affairs.

The principle of legitimate expectation in public law has been recognised by the Supreme Court. In the *Derrynaflan Chalice* case, Finlay C.J. stated that:

> "It would appear that the doctrine of 'legitimate expectation', sometimes described as 'reasonable expectation', has not in those terms been the subject matter of any decision of our courts. However, the doctrine connoted by such expressions is but an aspect of the well recognised equitable concept of promissory estoppel (which has been frequently applied in our courts), whereby a promise or representation as to intention may in certain circumstances be held binding on the representor or promisor. The nature and extent of that doctrine in circumstances such as those of this case has been expressed as follows.
>
> When the parties to a transaction proceed on the basis of an underlying assumption — either of fact or of law — whether due to misrepresentation or mistake makes no difference — on which they have conducted the dealing between them — neither of them will be allowed to go back on that assumption when it would be unfair or unjust to allow him to do so. If one of them does seek to go back on it, the courts will give the other such remedy as the equity of the case demands."[83]

An excellent example of the application of this principle to public officials is *Duggan v. An Taoiseach*,[84] which concerned civil servants affected by the discontinuance of the farm tax in early 1988. The plaintiffs were assigned to the farm tax division and were placed in grades, in an acting capacity, which were higher than the actual grades they held in the service. But they were never actually "established" in those higher grades. The farm tax was instituted in 1985 and three years later, for policy reasons, the Government discontinued collecting that tax before bringing in repealing legislation. In consequence, the plaintiffs were to be moved elsewhere in the civil service, probably at their established grades. They sought various reliefs against this occurring, such as orders that the tax shall continue to be collected until the Act was repealed and that they should thenceforth remain in the grades they were temporarily occupying. There was a general civil service practice that when a person was put into a higher grade on an acting basis, he was never actually taken out of that grade.

Hamilton P. refused to order that the tax should continue to be collected. He then pointed out that, whatever the general practice in the civil service was, it was made perfectly clear to the plaintiffs that they would be occupying higher grades in an acting capacity only and they accepted their appointments in writing on that basis. Accordingly, he could "find no basis for an expectation, reasonable or otherwise, on the[ir] part . . . that they would be continued in th[ose] posts or positions . . . in an established or permanent capacity"; the circumstances could not

---

83. *Webb v. Ireland* [1988] I.R. 353 at 384.
84. [1989] I.L.R.M. 710.

"give rise to a reasonable expectation by them that on the termination of the work of the Farm Tax Office, they would continue in the grades to which they had been appointed".[85] However, they all had a reasonable and legitimate expectation that their positions would be continued until the work of that office had been completed or been terminated lawfully. But that work was not completed. Nor was collecting the tax terminated lawfully; that required repealing legislation. Accordingly, their legitimate expectations had been terminated unlawfully. It was held that the Minister was entitled, under the Civil Service Acts, at any time to reassign them to their established grades, and an order would not be made requiring that they be continued in their acting grades for a temporary period. However, Hamilton P. found that "[t]he equity of their case . . . demands that they be compensated in damages for the frustration or breach of the[ir] legitimate expectations. . . ."[86] He therefore ordered that, for a specified period, they should continue to be paid the salary and they should benefit from the other terms and conditions attaching to their acting grades.

At first sight, this decision may seem unorthodox, in that it endorsed the principle of a substantive (as contrasted with an exclusively procedural) legitimate expectation and then did the virtually unprecedented, *viz.* award compensation to the frustrated expectees. However, it is entirely in line with the "acquired rights" doctrine in Continental European and international civil service law. That the Government acted unlawfully in ceasing to collect farm tax does not seem to have been the decisive factor, although that illegality certainly exacerbated the circumstances and virtually estopped the Government from contending that there were special circumstances that warranted disappointing the plaintiffs.

A substantive legitimate expectation was also held to have existed in *O'Leary v. Minister for Finance*,[87] where the plaintiff, an established civil servant in the office of the Director of Public Prosecutions (D.P.P.), was appointed a member of the Law Reform Commission. At the time of his appointment, an agreement was reached between the parties concerning the basis for calculating the applicant's remuneration, being slightly below that paid to secretaries of Departments, and the circumstances in which that rate might be upgraded. Two years later he sought an upgrade, which was refused. Subsequently, when he returned to the office of the D.P.P., he sought to be paid at a rate appropriate to being upgraded. It was held by Quirke J. that, in all the circumstances, he had a legitimate expectation to be so remunerated.

On two more recent occasions, however, expectees did not fare as well. In *Dohohue v. Revenue Commissioners*,[88] a claim by a dog-handler that he held that position for life and could never be re-assigned to a different post was rejected by Blaney J. There was no express promise nor even a fixed practice on which he could rely; that his appointment had been described as "permanent" was insufficient. And in *Eoghan v. University College Dublin*,[89] a claim by a professor at U.C.D. that he should be kept on in office after the stipulated age for retirement

---

85. *ibid.* at 727.
86. *ibid.* at 731.
87. [1988] 2 I.L.R.M. 321.
88. [1993] 1 I.R. 172.
89. [1996] 1 I.R. 390.

was rejected. Although in the past there had been a practice of retiring professors staying on for a period after their retirement date, in 1987 proposals were made by U.C.D. to end that practice, they had been commented on by the applicant, and, further, in the circumstances there were adequate grounds for the college discontinuing the practice. Shanley J. held that the legitimate expectation that arose there was purely procedural, *i.e.* to comment on proposals to end the concession to retiring professors, and adequate opportunity to make representations on the question had been afforded.

Grounds for discipline and dismissal

Usually the relevant statute, regulation or document will state the grounds on which office-holders can be disciplined and dismissed. The grounds on which workers with employment contracts only can be dismissed are dealt with in Chapter 7. It is a matter of interpretation of the relevant instrument or document whether the grounds stipulated are the exclusive grounds on which office-holders may be disciplined or dismissed.[90] The same general approach as was applied in the *Grehan* case[91] and in the *McClelland* case[92] would apply. Generally, the stated grounds for dismissal are the exclusive grounds unless the relevant instrument indicates the contrary. This is especially the case where it is within the employer's powers unilaterally to change the rules of appointment. As was stated in an English case concerning the dismissal of a probationary police officer, "[i]t is plain from the wording of the regulation that the power . . . to dispense with the services of a person accepted as a probationer constable is to be exercised, and exercised only, after due consideration of the specified [grounds]. It is not a discretion that may be exercised arbitrarily and without accountability".[93]

A person cannot be disciplined or dismissed on grounds which would be unconstitutional.[94] In the past sex discrimination was endemic in the public service, with married women being the target of uniquely discriminatory treatment; but that "marriage bar" was lifted in 1973.[95] Although there is a constitutional right, of uncertain degree, to privacy, it would seem that persons can be dismissed for how they conducted their own private lives where that behaviour significantly affects their work or work environment.[96] The freedom of senior civil servants to engage in politics is greatly circumscribed.[97] Formerly, all civil servants, including postmen and post office sorters, were banned from political activity, a rule which hardly would have withstood constitutional challenge.[98]

---

90. *e.g. Maunsell v. Minister for Education* [1940] I.R. 213.
91. *Grehan v. North Eastern Health Board* [1989] I.R. 422; see *ante*, p. 167.
92. *McClelland v. Northern Ireland General Health Services Board* [1957] 1 W.L.R. 594; see *ante*, p. 167.
93. *Chief Constable v. Evans* [1982] 1 W.L.R. 1155 at 1171.
94. See, generally, "Developments in the Law – Public Employment", 97 Harv. L. Rev. 1611 (1984), pp. 1738 *et seq.*
95. Civil Service (Employment of Married Women) Act 1973; *cf.* Garda Síochána Act 1958 and Defence (Amendment) Act 1979.
96. *Stroker v. Doherty* [1991] 1 I.R. 23 and *Flynn v. Power* [1985] I.R. 648.
97. Circular 21/32; see *post*, pp. 305-306.
98. *United States Civil Service Comm. v. National Ass'n of Letter Carriers*, 413 U.S. 548 (1973) and *Ahmed v. United Kingdom* 29 E.H.R.R. 1 (1998).

In *Garvey v. Ireland*,[99] which concerned the Garda Commissioner who was peremptorily dismissed without any reason being given, it was held that unless an office is defined as being "at the Government's pleasure" it is not tenable at pleasure. The plaintiff was dismissed under section 6(2) of the Police Forces Amalgamation Act 1925, which stipulates that the Garda Commissioner "may at any time be removed by" the Government. This, it was held, did not empower removal at the Government's whim without any reason whatsoever being assigned and affording the incumbent no opportunity to challenge the reason. In such cases, provided that fair procedures were followed and the grounds of dismissal were not unconstitutional, the Government "has the widest possible discretion as to the reasons or grounds upon which it may decide to act".[100] The tenure of civil servants is defined as being "at the will and pleasure of the Government".[101]

Where the grounds for dismissal are stipulated, the employing authority must satisfy itself, through the prescribed procedures, that those grounds exist in the circumstances. If the official seeks to challenge his dismissal in the courts, the question to be determined is not so much whether he should have been dismissed as whether sufficient grounds were established as would warrant a reasonable employer to dismiss him. For instance, in *State (McGarritty) v. Deputy Commissioner of An Garda Síochána*,[102] the applicant contested the decision to dismiss him from the Garda Síochána during his probationary period. His challenge to that decision on the merits was rejected by McWilliam J. because "[t]he Regulations vest the opinion-forming function exclusively in the Commissioner. . . . I cannot reject his opinion because I may have reached a contrary opinion. I am confined to deciding whether the opinion he did form is supported by the documentary material he had before him when he made his order".[103] This approach was endorsed by the Supreme Court in *Hynes v. Garvey*,[104] another Garda probationer case, and in *Stroker v. Doherty*,[105] a case concerning a permanent Garda officer, which emphasised the Court's reluctance to second-guess the disciplinary tribunal's assessment of the substantive merits of the case. Where, in the light of the evidence, the decision taken lacked factual basis or where it was not bona fide or it was unreasonable, the court may declare the decision void. In this way the Court can become involved to a degree in the actual merits of the decision, while still deferring to the employing authority's opinion. If in all the circumstances there was an unreasonable decision, it will not be let stand. Unreasonableness here means not that the Court might have taken a different view of the evidence, but that the decision "plainly and unambiguously flies in the face of fundamental reason and common sense".[106]

---

[99] [1981] I.R. 75.

[100] *ibid.* at 97; see too *ibid.* at 109.

[101] Civil Service Regulation Act 1950, s.5; see *infra*, p. 308; *cf. R. (McMorrow) v. Fitzgerald* [1918] 2 I.R. 103.

[102] 112 I.L.T.R. 25 (1978).

[103] *ibid.* at 30.

[104] [1978] I.R. 174.

[105] [1991] 1 I.R. 23.

[106] *ibid.* at 29.

In *State (Daly) v. Minister for Agriculture*,[107] a probationer civil servant, who was employed "at the will and pleasure of the Government", was dismissed. No reasons were given and when the decision was challenged in court the Minister still refrained from offering a reason. It was held by Barron J. that the Minister's decision, even under such a discretionary power, was subject to judicial review. The Minister's view "must be seen to be bona fide held, to be factually sustainable and not unreasonable".[108] Because the Minister persisted in not giving a reason, the Court could not then properly exercise its review functions. Accordingly, it was concluded, the Court must presume that there was no proper basis for the applicant's dismissal and that decision was held to be void.

THE CIVIL SERVICE

There is no statutory definition of who a civil servant is, although the term "established civil servant" is defined as a civil servant "whose service is in a capacity in respect of which a superannuation allowance may be granted".[109] The derivation of the term civil servant was explained by Kingsmill-Moore J. as follows:

> "The words 'civil service' and 'civil servant', though in frequent use on the lips of politicians and members of the general public, are not terms of legal art. The British Royal Commission on the Civil Service which reported in 1931 stated that 'there is nowhere any authoritative or exhaustive definition of the civil service.' The phrase seems to have been first used to describe the non-combatant service of the East India Company, and was well established in English political language by the middle of the nineteenth century.

> Though it may be difficult to frame an exact definition, it does not seem in any way impossible to reach an approximation to the meaning of the words sufficient to meet the requirements of the present case. In Britain civil servants were servants of the Crown, that is to say servants of the King in his political capacity, but not all servants of the Crown were civil servants. Those who used the strong arm — military, naval and police forces — were excluded from the conception, for the service was civil, not combatant; and so also, by tradition, were judges and holders of political offices. Civil servants were paid out of monies voted by Parliament and, if permanent, had the benefit of the Superannuation Acts. In theory, as servants of the King, they held their positions at pleasure but in practice they were treated as holding during good behaviour. . . .

> The bulk of British civil servants working in Ireland were taken into the service of Saorstát Éireann and the phrase, with the ideas attached to it, was assimilated into Irish political life. Soon it made its appearance in the Irish statute book, and, after the passing of our present constitution, in statutes of

---

[107] [1987] I.R. 165.
[108] *ibid.* at 172.
[109] Civil Service Regulation Act 1956, s.1(1).

the Republic. Borderline cases have been dealt with by special legislation. Persons have been deemed to be civil servants for one purpose and deemed not to be civil servants for another. But, if we substitute 'State' for 'King' the summary which I have already given corresponds to the present conception of civil servant in Ireland."[110]

The principal incidents of civil servants' positions are governed by the Civil Service Regulation Act 1956; the machinery for appointing them is governed by the Civil Service Commissioners Act 1956, and their pensions are governed by the Superannuation Acts 1834-1963. These Acts draw a distinction between civil servants of the Government and of the State. Again, as Kingsmill-Moore J. pointed out, this is something of a contradiction:

"The expression, 'civil service of the Government', unless given a restricted interpretation is a contradiction in terms. The status of a civil servant is that of a servant of the State. He may indeed be assigned to serve in any civil department of the State, or in the service of any organ of the State, including the Government, and the power of so assigning him may be conferred by law on the Government; but he is still a servant of the State. If, however, his service happens to be in one of the Departments of the Government he may conveniently be described as being also a servant of the Government."[111]

Since, under the Constitution, the Attorney General's office is separate from the Executive, persons working in that office are civil servants of the State as opposed to of the Government. The Courts Service Act 1998 deems staff of that service to be civil servants of the State. An ordinary member of the Labour Court was found to be a civil servant of the State[112] although, since he was appointed by and was under the control of the Minister for Labour, he would also seem to be a civil servant of the Government. One can be an office-holder working for the State and yet be neither a civil servant nor an employee, as was held to be the case with a rights commissioner at the Labour Court and, accordingly, he was not in insurable employment.[113]

Another distinction is that between the holders of designated offices and civil servants generally. A host of particular offices exist under legislation, for instance the Master of the High Court, the Taxing Master, the Director of Public Prosecutions, the Chief State Solicitor, the Governor of the Central Bank, the Information Commissioner, the Chairman of An Bord Pleanála, the Director General of Consumer Affairs and Fair Trade, the Data Protection Commissioner, and the President of the Human Rights Commission. The incidents of many of these distinct officeholders are regulated, in whole or in part, by legislation particular to the function being carried on. Except for the case involving the Garda Commissioner, there is no modern case law dealing with the incidents of these high offices.

While most civil servants work in the various Government Departments, under the control of the relevant Minister, they also can be assigned to the many statu-

---

[110.] *McLaughlin v. Minister for Social Welfare* [1958] I.R. 1 at 14-15.
[111.] *ibid.* at 16.
[112.] *Murphy v. Minister for Social Welfare* [1987] I.R. 295.
[113.] *Walker v. Dept. of Social, Community and Family Affairs* [1999] E.L.R. 260.

tory corporations that are involved in the public administration, for instance, the National Authority for Occupational Health and Safety, and the Employment Equality Agency, which since 1998 has been known as the Equality Authority. Express provision is often made for civil servants being assigned to bodies such as these, for instance section 24 of the Courts Service Act 1998 and section 22 of the Irish Sports Council Act 1999.

Appointment

Generally, civil servants are appointed only after taking part in a competition organised by the Civil Service Commissioners and being selected for appointment by the Commissioners. The objective of this procedure is to place civil service appointments outside of political control, thereby ensuring that applicants for posts who support the Government of the day are not given undue preference. The general qualifications for appointment laid down by section 17 of the Civil Service Commissioners Act 1956 are that the candidate:

"(a) ... possesses the requisite knowledge and ability to enter on the discharge of the duties of that position,

(b) he is within the age limits (if any) prescribed . . .,

(c) he is in good health and free from any physical defect or disease which would be likely to interfere with the proper discharge of his duties in that position and possesses the physical characteristics (if any) prescribed for the position . . .,

(d) he is suitable on grounds of character, and,

(e) he is suitable in all other relevant respects for appointment to that position."

Among the appointments to which this Act does not apply are some positions which can be filled by the Government,[114] certain "excluded positions" as defined in that Act,[115] and "scheduled occupations",[116] being what may be termed industrial civil servants, those hired on a part-time basis and persons employed by the Department of Foreign Affairs abroad in a clerical or ancillary capacity.

The only across-the-board legislative disqualification from appointment was section 34(3) of the Offences Against the State Act 1939. Any person who was convicted of a scheduled offence under that Act by the Special Criminal Court was disqualified, for the next seven years, from holding any office or employment which was remunerated out of the Central Fund or from money provided by the Oireachtas; a person holding such a job forfeited it and any pension rights on being convicted as described here. But the Government had an "absolute discretion" to remit the disqualification or forfeiture in whole or in part. In 1990 this section was held to be unconstitutional[117] because of its entirely indiscriminate

---

[114.] s.6(2)(a)(i).
[115.] ss.5 and 6.
[116.] s.4.
[117.] *Cox v. Ireland* [1992] 2 I.R. 503.

impact. It would seem that the State did not argue that, by virtue of the doctrine of the presumption of constitutionality, the complete discretion given to the Government to waive application of the rule in any individual case saved the section from invalidity.

The E.C. rules regarding the free movement of workers and banning discrimination against nationals of E.C. Member States to that end do not apply to "employment in the public service".[118] However, the ambit of this exclusion has been considerably narrowed by the European Court of Justice.[119]

Status

Are civil servants employed under a contract of employment or are they office-holders without any contract? If they are appointed by the Government for a specified period or task, they may very well have employment contracts as well as being office-holders. The exact status of civil servants generally was not clarified until 1995, principally because the various labour enactments and the social welfare laws usually make it clear whether or not their provisions apply to the civil service. In Britain it was confirmed in 1987 that civil servants there are not employed under an employment contract on the grounds that, when they are appointed, there is no intention by the Crown to create a contractual relationship with them.[120]

In *Gilheaney v. Revenue Commissioners*,[121] Costello P. came to the same conclusion. The status of civil servants in the Irish Free State was that they were "holders of an office and not employees", having been "appointed to their office by virtue of statutory powers, and in the absence of a clear contractual arrangement, held that office under terms and conditions established by the exercise of statutory powers and not by virtue of any agreement between the parties".[122] Their position had been described earlier by Gavan Duffy J. as follows:

> "There is no contract as to salary between the Minister and any one of [them], but each of them, with a tenure at will, enjoys an appointment under the State, carrying such remuneration as the Minister may from time to time determine, and the Minister has wide [statutory] powers for controlling and varying remuneration. . . . The Minister could not, even if he would, divest himself of the powers thus entrusted to him for the public weal and any circulars issued and communicated to candidates for appointment would seem to me quite irrelevant. . . ."[123]

That remained the position for civil servants appointed under the 1956 Act, a view fortified by section 17(2) of that Act which empowers the Minister "as he thinks fit [to] cancel or vary" any arrangements made for civil servants' terms and

---

[118] EC Treaty Article 39(4).

[119] See *ante*, pp. 157-158.

[120] *R. v. Civil Service Appeal Board, ex p. Bruce* [1988] 3 All E.R. 686.

[121] [1998] 4 I.R. 150.

[122] *ibid.* at p. 161.

[123] *Cogan v. Minister for Finance* [1941] I.R. 389 at 401; *cf.* Blair, "The Civil Servant – A States Relationship", 21 Mod. L. Rev. 265 (1958), *R v. Lord Chancellor's Department, ex parte Nangle* [1991] I.C.R. 743 and *Wells v. Newfoundland*, 177 D.L.R. (3d) 73 (1999).

conditions of employment. Such a sweeping discretion is incompatible with the Minister entering into legally binding obligations under a contract of employment.

Incidents of the office

The rights and duties of civil servants and their position generally are regulated by the Minister for Finance. Under section 17 of the Civil Service Regulation Act 1956, he may "make such arrangements as he thinks fit" in connection with the following matters:

"(a) the regulation and control of the Civil Service,

(b) the classification, re-classification, numbers and remuneration of civil servants,

(c) the fixing of —

(i)   the terms and conditions of service of civil servants, and

(ii) the conditions governing the promotion of civil servants."

Their remuneration and other terms and conditions of service are usually set out in circulars which the Minister issues from time to time. Section 16(1) of the 1956 Act endorses the aphorism "no work, no pay", by stipulating that a civil servant "shall not be paid remuneration in respect of any period of unauthorised absence from duty".

Altering the incidents

Section 17(2) of the 1956 Act says that the Minister "may cancel or vary these arrangements" referred to above. According to Gavan Duffy J. in the *Cogan* case,[124] the circulars issued by the Minister do not give rise to contractual entitlements and their contents may be altered by the Minister whenever he deems appropriate. More recently, that view was endorsed in the *Gilheaney* case,[125] which also held that those circulars could not even be the basis for a "legitimate expectation" because such an outcome would fall foul of section 17(2) of the 1956 Act. However, that conclusion by Costello P. seems to extend the administrative law principle against "fettering discretions" far beyond what is recognised in the case law on that topic. Even if section 17(2) constitutes a defence to being compelled to do what a circular said the Minister would do, it does not follow that the Minister may not have some legal obligation to compensate persons who altered their position in the light of what the circular in question stated.

This view was accepted by Quirke J. in the *O'Leary v. Minister for Finance*,[126] which concerned the terms on which a senior official in the office of the D.P.P. was seconded to the Law Reform Commission. In the circumstances, it was held that the plaintiff and the Minister of Finance had entered into a contract regarding those terms. Although section 17(2) of the 1956 Act permits the variation of any

---

124. *ibid.*
125. [1998] 4 I.R. 150.
126. [1998] 2 I.L.R.M. 321; see *supra*, p. 295.

such agreed terms, that discretion was subject to the doctrine of legitimate expectation where there is no "public interest" in that expectation being denied. Consequently, it was held, it was not demonstrated that a sufficient public interest existed that warranted the Minister reneging on the arrangements to which he had previously agreed. Indeed, much earlier, in *Duggan v. An Taoiseach*,[127] Hamilton P. applied this principle when civil servants were assigned to work in the Farm Tax Office, holding grades on an acting basis higher than their actual grades. Because the Government had not acted properly in ceasing to collect the farm tax, without repealing the relevant legislation, the plaintiffs' legitimate expectations to occupy higher grades were unlawfully interfered with. That loss, therefore, had to be compensated by their continuing to be paid at the higher grade levels for a period. Section 17(2) of the 1956 Act was not relied on in this case.

Common law and equitable rights and obligations

It would seem that what may be termed entitlements under the various Ministerial circulars may not be enforced against the Government as if they were binding contracts. There then is no way in which civil servants can compel compliance with those circulars, unless they resort to industrial action. Since 1982, industrial action by civil servants can be a "trade dispute", thereby qualifying those taking part in disputes to the immunities from liability for the economic torts contained in sections 10-12 of the Industrial Relations Act 1990, if they are members of licensed trade unions.[128] Whether the Minister can enforce his circulars by way of court action is a matter that seems never to have been considered, but, since they are neither contracts nor statutory instruments, it would appear that they are not directly enforceable. Of course they can be enforced indirectly by the Minister imposing disciplinary sanctions, up to even dismissal, where their requirements are being flouted.

A question which does not appear to have been considered by the Irish courts in modern times is whether civil servants have rights and obligations under the common law and under general equitable principles. The legal position, as expounded by the courts mainly in the last century, is that "public officers", including civil servants, are regarded as the repositories of the public's trust and confidence, and, on grounds of public policy, the common law and equity ensure that this trust is not abused.[129] Abuse of public office is a criminal offence at common law.[130] The classic formulation is that of Lord Mansfield in *R. v. Bembridge*, that:

> "if a man accepts an office of trust and confidence, concerning the public . . . he is answerable to the King for his execution of that office; and he can only answer to the King in a criminal prosecution. . . . [W]here there is a breach of trust, a fraud, or an imposition on a subject concerning the public, which

---

127. [1989] I.L.R.M. 710; see *supra*, pp. 294-295.
128. See *Industrial Relations Law*, pp. 15-16 and 210-211.
129. *cf. City of Boston v. Dolan*, 10 N.E. 2d 275 (1937).
130. See, generally, Finn, "Public Officers: Save Personal Liabilities", 51 Australian L.J. 313 (1977), J. Gabbett, *A Treatise on the Criminal Law* (1842), Vol. 1, Chap. 41, and J. Turner ed., *Russell on Crime* (12th ed., 1964), Chaps. 24-27.

as between subject and subject, would only be actionable by a civil action, yet as that concerns the King and the public (I use them as synonymous terms), it is indictable".[131]

Since there have been no prosecutions brought under this broad common law offence in recent times and as many forms of abuse of public office constitute statutory offences, it is possible that the common law offence has become obsolete. But prosecutions of this nature are occasionally brought in Britain.[132] The Prevention of Corruption Acts 1889-1916 have been made applicable to all persons who are remunerated from the Central Fund, which includes civil servants.[133]

The State, or whichever public authority employs the official in question, has certain civil remedies against him. The procedure used in the past for those claims was the information for equitable relief on the Revenue side of the Exchequer.[134] An official who makes an improper gain from his office will be held liable for it.[135] An officer who derives any personal profit from his misuse of public funds must account for that profit to the authority from whom he holds the office. For instance, in *Attorney General v. Edmunds*,[136] a civil servant was held liable to the Crown for having used public funds to buy quantities of stamps at a discount, which he then sold at full value. A public official is subject to the equitable duty to maintain the secrecy of information acquired by virtue of his office, at least in cases where the public interest or the interests of his employing authority so require. In *Attorney General v. Jonathan Cape Ltd.,* Widgery C.J. could "not see why the courts should be powerless to restrain the publication of public secrets, whilst enjoying the Argyll powers in regard to domestic secrets".[137] There, publication by the former Cabinet Minister Richard Crossman of what happened at numerous British Cabinet meetings was enjoined.[138] But the confidences of civil servants of foreign governments are not so readily enforceable.[139]

There is a tort of malicious abuse of public authority, or misfeasance in public office, where a public official who abuses his powers can be held liable in damages to persons who are the victims of that abuse.[140] What must be established to found a right of action was summarised in *Newell v. Starkie* as follows:

1. some legal right vested in the plaintiff;

2. the infraction or violation of that right;

3. the violation or the procuring of such violation knowingly and intentionally and without lawful justification.[141]

[131.] (1783) 3 Doug K.B. 327 at 332.

[132.] *e.g. R. v. Bowden* [1996] 1 W.L.R. 98.

[133.] *e.g. R. v. Llellwyn-Jones* [1968] 1 Q.B. 429.

[134.] *Attorney General v. Cochrane* (1810) Wright 10.

[135.] *Reading v. Attorney General* [1951] A.C. 507 and *Attorney General v. Blake* [2000] 3 W.L.R. 625.

[136.] (1868) L.R. 6 Eq. 381.

[137.] [1976] Q.B. 752 at 769.

[138.] See, too, the *Attorney General v. Guardian Newspapers Ltd. (No. 2)* [1990] A.C. 109 and *Lord Advocate v. Scotsman Publications Ltd.* [1990] A.C. 812.

[139.] *Attorney General for England and Wales v. Brandon Book Publishers Ltd.* [1987] I.L.R.M. 135.

[140.] *Three Rivers District Council v. Bank of England (No. 3)* [2000] 2 W.L.R. 1220.

[141.] [1917] 2 I.R. 73 at 80.

In that case a school inspector sued two of his superiors for unlawfully causing him to be reprimanded several times, then be suspended and finally be compelled to resign on a diminishing allowance. However, his claim failed because it was not brought within the then prescribed limitation period.[142] Where this tort is established, the official's employer can also be held vicariously liable in damages and the circumstances may well warrant the award of exemplary damages or punitive damages.

Statutory rights and duties

Some of the legislation giving employees rights does not apply to civil servants, although most of the Acts passed in the 1990s apply to them. Civil servants and other public officials fall within Article 141 (formerly 119) of the Rome Treaty, which gives a right to equal pay for equal work.[143] A question which has yet to be answered is whether civil servants' employment situation can be affected by directives of the E.C. under its approximation of laws powers. Although they are excluded from application of the free movement of labour principle,[144] there is no such exclusion in the Rome Treaty from the approximation of laws powers.

There are some Acts which apply with particular force to the duties of civil servants and other public officers. One is the Official Secrets Act 1963, which renders it a criminal offence for any person to disclose official secrets as defined in that Act or retain in his possession any official document or other information. What constitutes official information is defined very extensively as:

"any secret official code word or password, and any sketch, plan, model, article, note, document or information which is secret or confidential or is expressed to be either and which is or has been in the possession, custody or control of a holder of a public office, or to which he has or had access, by virtue of his office, and includes information recorded by film or magnetic tape or by any other recording medium."[145]

Secret information may be retained or disclosed where the person is duly authorised to do so or doing so is in accordance with the duties of his office.[146] Secret information also may be disclosed where doing so is in the person's "duty in the interest of the State to communicate it".[147] The mere certificate by the Minister that certain information is secret or confidential for these purposes is deemed to be "conclusive evidence" of that fact.[148]

Political activities

Many public officials are subject to restrictions regarding active involvement in politics. In 1932 the Minister for Finance set out in the form of a circular the

---

[142] Public Authorities Protection Act 1893 (repealed in 1954).
[143] *Johnston v. Chief Constable of the R.U.C.* (Case 222/84) [1986] E.C.R. 1651.
[144] See *ante,* pp. 157-158.
[145] s.2(1).
[146] s.4(1).
[147] *ibid.*
[148] s.2(3). This may be unconstitutional: *Maher v. Attorney General* [1973] I.R. 140.

kinds of political activities which civil servants are not allowed to undertake; in particular officials should not:

"(i) be a member of an association or serve on a committee having for its object the promotion of the interests of a political party or the promotion or the prevention of the return of a particular candidate to the Dáil,

(ii) support or oppose any particular candidate or party either by public statement or writing,

(iii) make any verbal statements in public (or which are liable to be published) [or] contribute to newspapers or other publications any letters or articles, conveying information, comment or criticism on any matter of current political interest, or which concerns the political action or position of the Government or of any member or group of members of the Oireachtas."[149]

But industrial civil servants are allowed to take part in any of these activities and to stand for election to local authorities.[150] Within the civil service conciliation and arbitration scheme, any staff association which is "affiliated to, or associated in any way with, any political organisation", will not be recognised by the Minister or, if recognised, will lose its recognition for that reason.

The statutes that establish many of the specialised corporations in the public sector stipulate that members of either House of the Oireachtas or of the European Parliament may not take up employment with them.[151] Further, if any employee is elected to any of those bodies, he stands seconded from the job for so long as he remains a member of that body.

Probation

Civil service appointments are usually subject to a period of probation. Where the individual fails to fulfil the conditions of probation, section 7 of the 1956 Act enables his appointment to be terminated. He can challenge that decision in court on the grounds that unfair procedures were followed. That decision can also be challenged on the grounds that it is not bona fide held, is not factually sustainable, or is wholly unreasonable.[152]

Discipline and dismissal

Section 15 of the Civil Service Regulation Act 1956 lays down the framework for disciplinary measures, other than suspension from duty. These apply where, in the opinion of the appropriate supervisory authority, the civil servant has "in relation to his official duties, been guilty of misconduct, irregularity, neglect or unsatisfactory behaviour. . . ." What procedures should be followed in these cases is not stated in the 1956 Act other than that the civil service regulations may prescribe for the matter to be referred to the Minister. There are few reported cases

---

[149.] Circular 21/32.
[150.] Circular 22/74.
[151.] *e.g.* Irish Sports Council Act 1999, s.24.
[152.] *State (Daly) v. Minister for Agriculture* [1987] I.R. 165 and *Whellan v. Minister for Justice* [1991] 1 I.R. 462.

on what procedures must be followed in order to comply with natural justice or constitutional justice in these cases, *i.e.* principally the maxims *audi alteram partem* and *nemo iudex in sua causa*, which were considered above.

Those disciplinary sanctions which can be imposed are a reduction in remuneration or a reduction in grade or rank; both of these can be applied together where a loss of public money or public funds resulted from the individual's action.

Section 9 of the 1956 Act sets out the procedures for discharge on medical grounds, where an established civil servant becomes "by reason of infirmity of mind or body, incapable of discharging the duties of his position and such infirmity is likely to be permanent".[153] If, after examining him, the medical officer concludes that he is so disabled, he can be required to tender his resignation. If he does not do so he will be deemed to have resigned.

Section 8 of the 1956 Act, which fixes the retiring age at 65 years, adds that any civil servant who attains the age of 60 years can be asked to retire and, if so requested, must retire. In *O'Reilly v. Minister for Industry and Commerce*,[154] in the course of reorganising a Department, where the applicant was regarded as no longer suitable for the tasks to be performed, he was asked to consider retiring and was told that he could be compelled to retire under section 8(2) of this Act. He retired but then took proceedings to have his retirement declared void because his decision was not voluntary but had been made under virtual duress. He succeeded; Carroll J. held that there was an overriding obligation to treat a person in his position with consideration and good faith, that he had been misled into believing that retirement would be forced on him under section 8(2), and that, accordingly, there was no effective resignation and he should be paid his remuneration for the intervening period.

Section 13 of the 1956 Act sets out when a civil servant can be suspended from duty without pay. This can happen where:

"(a) it appears to the suspending authority that the civil servant has been guilty of grave misconduct or grave irregularity warranting disciplinary action, or

(b) it appears to the suspending authority that the public interest may be prejudiced by allowing the civil servant to remain on duty, or

(c) a charge of grave misconduct or grave irregularity is made against the civil servant and it appears to the suspending authority that the charge warrants investigation."

If the individual is acquitted of the disciplinary charges, he must be paid his "ordinary remuneration" for the period of his suspension; in other cases, a direction may be made to pay all or some of that remuneration where "considerations of equity so require". Generally, before persons are suspended under this provision, they must be informed of the reason for such treatment, so that they can apply to have the decision revoked.[155] A suspension should not be unduly pro-

---

[153.] *cf. Ahern v. Minister for Industry and Commerce* [1991] 1 I.R. 462.
[154.] [1997] E.L.R. 48.
[155.] *Deegan v. Minister for Finance* [2000] E.L.R. 190.

longed, for instance, to await the outcome of criminal proceedings being brought against the individual.[156]

Section 5 of the 1956 Act which states that "[e]very established civil servant shall hold office at the will and pleasure of the Government", gives the Government a very extensive power to dismiss civil servants.

In the light of what was held in the *Garvey* case,[157] the Government has extremely wide discretion regarding why a civil servant should be dismissed, provided the grounds are not unconstitutional. It would seem that the individual must be furnished with reasons and given an opportunity to rebut them.[158] In 1971, in a case concerning the dismissal of a Scottish school teacher in circumstances which would not have adversely reflected on her, the House of Lords held that an office held at pleasure means that the person being dismissed need not be given the exact reasons but still must be afforded a hearing. According to Lord Wilberforce, "the very possibility of dismissal without reasons being given — action which may vitally affect a man's career or his pension — makes it all the more important for him, in suitable circumstances, to be able to state his case. [B]ut the courts will necessarily respect the right, for good reasons of public policy, to dismiss without assigned reasons. . . ."[159] Nevertheless, if judicial review is sought of the merits of the decision to dismiss, the Government must provide the court with some basis for accepting that the decision was bona fide held, sustainable and not unreasonable. In *State (Daly) v. Minister for Agriculture*,[160] it was held by Barron J. that, where the Minister will not even disclose to the court the grounds for his decision to dismiss a probationer, it must then be presumed that no good reason existed. Therefore, the decision was declared invalid.

LOCAL AND REGIONAL AUTHORITIES

The principal local and regional authorities are the urban corporations, county councils, regional health authorities, county committees of agriculture, vocational educational committees,[161] fisheries boards and harbour boards. Legislation regarding these bodies contain detailed provisions on the appointment, remuneration, terms and conditions of employment, discipline and dismissal of officers; notably, Part II of the Local Government Act 1941, as amended, Part II of the Health Act 1970, Part II of the Agriculture Act 1931, and sections 25-33 of the Fisheries Act 1980. Appointments to most of the offices under these Acts must be made with the approval of the Local Appointments Commission, which was established in 1926 in order to reduce political influence in local government staffing.[162] Elaborate pension arrangements exist principally under the Local Government (Superannuation) Act 1956.

[156.] *Flynn v. An Post* [1987] I.R. 68.
[157.] *Garvey v. Ireland* [1981] I.R. 75, see supra, p. 287.
[158.] *Deegan v. Minister for Finance* [2000] E.L.R. 190.
[159.] *Malloch v. Aberdeen Corp.* [1971] 1 WLR 1578 at 1597.
[160.] [1987] I.R. 165.
[161.] The position of V.E.C. employees is considered *infra*, p. 316.
[162.] Local Authorities (Officers and Employees) Act 1926.

A pronounced feature of all this legislation is the detailed control the Minister for Local Government or other relevant Ministers exercise over all personnel matters. Thus, under sections 19-23 of the Local Government Act 1941 the Minister is empowered to make regulations regarding the following matters: procedure for appointments, remuneration, travelling expenses, hours of duty, attendance records, sick and other leave, security for the due performance of functions, continuance in and cesser of office, age limits; regarding specified offices, the duties of the holders and the places or limits within which those duties should be performed; also, qualifications regarding character, age, health, physical characteristics, education, training, experience, residence. A qualification regarding sex may be prescribed only where "the duties of such office so require".[163] Local government is highly unionised and special conciliation and arbitration schemes exist for that sector.[164] Indeed, under section 14(5)(b) of the Health Act 1970, it is provided that when a health board chief executive officer is determining the remuneration and other terms of conditions of his staff, he must follow the Minister's directions. In doing so he "shall have regard to any arrangements in operation for conciliation and arbitration for persons affected by the determination". The precise legal consequences of this requirement do not appear to have been considered by the courts.

Appointment

Although the appointing authority usually is the relevant local government unit for which the person will work, generally the officer must first have been selected by the Local Appointments Commission.[165] No qualifications for the various local offices are prescribed by the legislation but the Minister has extensive powers to stipulate what qualifications shall be required.[166] Persons convicted by the Special Criminal Court of scheduled offences under the Offences Against the State Act 1939 were disqualified for the following seven years from holding any local government office or employment, but in 1990 that prohibition was declared unconstitutional.[167]

In *State (Cussen) v. Brennan*,[168] the plaintiff was an unsuccessful applicant for a position as paediatrician to the Southern Health Board. Qualifications for that job had been set by the Minister, but the Local Appointments Commission decided to give extra credit to applicants who had a good knowledge of the Irish language. The plaintiff attended the interview but did not submit himself for the Irish test. The Supreme Court held that the Commissioners had exceeded their powers by adopting the language test; their function was to select the best candidate with reference to the qualifications laid down by the Minister and they could not "add a new dimension" to those qualifications. As Henchy J. pointed out, the

---

[163.] Local Government Act 1941, s.21(2).
[164.] See *Industrial Relations Law*, pp. 205-206.
[165.] *cf. State (Minister for Local Government) v. Cork Mental Hospital* [1932] I.R. 207 and *State (Minister for Local Government) v. Ennis Mental Hospital* [1939] I.R. 258 and *Southern Health Board v. A Worker* [1999] E.L.R. 322.
[166.] Local Government Act 1941, s.19.
[167.] *Cox v. Ireland* [1992] 2 I.R. 503.
[168.] [1981] I.R. 181.

Commission could not award extra credit to a candidate because of his "knowledge of Sanskrit, his skill at chess, his talent as a musician, his proficiency at hurling or, for that matter, because of any abilities, achievements or qualities which were unrelated to the performance of the duties of the office".[169] At the very outset the Minister might have included proficiency in Irish as one of the qualifications, because "a law may provide that proficiency in Irish be a qualification for an office when [that] is relevant to the discharge of the duties of the office".[170] But the Commission went beyond the terms of reference in adopting that test. In the *Groener* case,[171] it was held that requiring applicants for vacancies as art teachers in a V.E.C. school, to demonstrate a working knowledge of, did not contravene the free movement of workers under the Rome Treaty.

Status

The various Acts dealing with local government service distinguish between employees and office-holders. But they do not define which groups of workers fall into each of these categories. It often is left to the court to decide in particular instances whether a local government worker is an officer or an employee. The context in which this question is posed varies. Many of the old cases concerned whether the person was an employed contributor for the purpose of the Social Welfare Acts. For instance, officials of a poor law union and the crier of the Belfast Recorders' Court were held not to be employees,[172] whereas a school attendance inspector fell into that category.[173] The standing solicitor to the Carrickmacross Rural District Council was held to be an officer in order to claim compensation for loss of office;[174] the Dublin City rate collector was held not to be a "clerk or servant" of the Dublin Corporation for the purpose of section 17 of the Larceny Act 1916;[175] a messenger and assistant keeper at the Cork Court House was held to be an officer for the purpose of qualifying for a pension;[176] a registered psychiatric nurse employed as a staff nurse at St. Mary's hospital was held to be an officer and thereby excluded from the Unfair Dismissals Act 1977;[177] whereas a messenger-labourer with the Dublin Corporation was merely an employee.[178] Section 11(1) of the Local Government Act 1955 empowers the Minister to determine whether a person is an officer for the purpose of the Local Government Acts and adds that his decision on this question shall be final.[179]

---

[169] *ibid.* at 192.

[170] *ibid.* at 194; *cf.* Local Authorities (Officers and Employees) Act 1983, s.2, and Agricultural Credit Act 1978, s.18.

[171] *Groener v. Minister for Education* (Case 379/87) [1989] E.C.R. 3967.

[172] *Re National Insurance Act 1911 – Officers of South Dublin Union* [1913] 1 I.R. 244 and *Irish Insurance C'mrs v. Craig* [1916] 2 I.R. 59.

[173] *O'Callaghan v. Irish Insurance C'mrs* [1915] 2 I.R. 262.

[174] *Phelan v. Minister for Local Government* [1930] I.R. 542.

[175] *People v. Warren* [1945] I.R. 24.

[176] *Flaherty v. Minister for Local Government* [1941] I.R. 587.

[177] *Western Health Board v. Quigley* [1982] I.L.R.M. 390.

[178] *R. (Dillon) v. Minister for Local Government* [1927] I.R. 474. Similarly, *Hanly v. Mayo V.E.C.* [1999] E.L.R. 10.

[179] *cf. State (Raftis) v. Leonard* [1960] I.R. 381.

Perhaps the context in which the question arises most often these days is to determine whether the Unfair Dismissals Acts 1977-93, apply; excluded from the scope of these Acts are, *inter alia*, "officers" of local authorities, of health boards (other than temporary officers), and of vocational education committees.[180]

Incidents of the Office

Local and regional government officers' remuneration and terms and conditions of employment are usually fixed by the Minister or by reference to his directions.[181] It would seem that, as a matter of law, these incidents of the job may be unilaterally altered to the office holder's detriment by the Minister or the authority empowered to determine these matters. *Thistle v. Monaghan County Council*[182] was one of a series of cases in the late 1920s when the remuneration of many local government workers was cut as an economic measure. The plaintiffs were attendants at the Monaghan and Cavan District Mental Hospital whose remuneration had been so reduced. The argument for upholding this wage cut was that, under the relevant Act, the Council could appoint such officers as it considered necessary and those officers "shall perform such duties and be paid such remuneration as the council may [decide]".[183] Under the Interpretation Act 1889, where an Act grants a power or imposes a duty, it "may be exercised or performed from time to time as occasion requires" unless the contrary intention appears. Accordingly, it was held, the power to determine remuneration may be exercised from time to time, by either increasing it or by reducing it.[184] Emphasis was placed on the fact that the plaintiffs were officers and not employees with contracts. Whether this construction would be followed today is debatable. If a power of unilateral reduction still exists, not alone must the prescribed procedure for doing so be scrupulously followed but "legitimate expectations" must be respected and constitutional justice and fair play must be observed.[185] In addition, the local government trade unions must be reckoned with.

What has been said above with regard to civil servants' common law and equitable rights and obligations also applies generally to local government officials. The Prevention of Corruption Acts 1889-1916 apply to them.[186] It has been held that only local government employees, and not officers, can be convicted of embezzlement under the Larceny Act.[187] Whether the Official Secrets Act 1963 applies to confidential information held by local government bodies could be debated.

[180.] 1977 Act, s.2(1)(j), amended by 1993 Act, s.3(a).
[181.] Local Government Act 1941, ss.19-21, as amended by Local Government Act 1955, ss.14-16, Vocational Education Act 1930, s.23(2), and Agriculture Act 1931.
[182.] [1931] I.R. 381.
[183.] Local Government (Ireland) Act 1898, s.84(1)(b).
[184.] Approving *Chambers v. Mayo Mental Hospital* [1930] I.R. 154; *cf. Woods v. Dublin Corp.* [1931] I.R. 396.
[185.] See *ante*, pp..
[186.] S.R. & O. No. 37 of 1928.
[187.] *People v. Warren* [1945] I.R. 24.

Discipline and dismissal

The grounds and procedures for disciplining and dismissing the various categories of local government officials is laid down in the relevant Acts in different degrees of detail. Officers of vocational educational committees and of committees of agriculture can be removed from office where the Minister considers that they are "unfit or incompetent to perform [their] duties."[188] Before deciding to remove them, the Minister must hold a "local inquiry" and consider the report made by the person who conducted that inquiry.[189] The power to suspend without pay officers of vocational education committees has been the subject of considerable litigation in recent years.

Permanent officers of health boards may be removed "because of misconduct or unfitness".[190] If the ground of dismissal is being absent from his duties without reasonable cause, he may be removed on the Minister's direction.[191] Where misconduct or unfitness are alleged, the matter must first be considered by a committee comprising a chairman, chosen by the Minister, persons chosen by him from a panel of names supplied by the chief executive officer of the health board concerned, and an equal number of persons selected by the Minister from a panel of names supplied by a trade union or trade union representatives of the officer's own class or grade.[192] Provision is also made for suspending health board officers without pay while allegations against them of misconduct or unfitness are being investigated.[193]

The suspension and removal of the officers of a local government body are regulated by sections 24-27 of the Local Government Act 1941. An officer can be required to resign where he never possessed the requisite qualifications for the job; also where, due to changes in the conditions of service or the nature or extent of the duties attached to the job, it is in the public interest that he resigns.[194] Where an officer refuses to resign, as requested in these circumstances, he can be removed from office. An officer can be suspended without pay where either the Minister or the relevant authority has reason to believe that he has "failed to perform satisfactorily the duties" of the office, that he "misconducted himself" in relation to the office, or that he was "otherwise unfit" to hold that office.[195] What amounts to being otherwise unfit for the office has not so far been clarified by the courts. Where the suspension ends, the Minister has a discretion to pay all or part of the remuneration which the officer would have earned during that period.[196]

A local government officer may be removed from office for the following reasons:

"(a) unfitness of such holder for such office;

---

188. Vocational Education Act 1930, s.27, and Agriculture Act 1931, s.23.
189. *ibid*; *cf. State (Curtin) v. Minister for Health* [1953] I.R. 93.
190. Health Act 1970, s.23(2).
191. *ibid.* s.23(3).
192. *ibid.* s.24.
193. *ibid.* s.22; *cf. Cox v. Electricity Supply Board (No. 3)* [1944] I.R. 81.
194. Local Government Act 1941, s.24.
195. *ibid.* s.27.
196. *ibid.* s.27(4).

(b) the fact that such holder has refused to obey or carry into effect any order lawfully given to him as the holder of such office or has otherwise misconducted himself in such office."[197]

The normal procedure for removal from office is to conduct a "local inquiry" into allegations in order to determine if any of these grounds can be established.[198] But where the Minister otherwise comes to the view that these grounds exist, he can notify the officer in question in writing of his intention to dismiss.[199] That officer then has seven days to make representations to the Minister, who can then order that the individual be removed from office. The Minister may empower local authorities to remove officers and may lay down the procedures to be followed in such cases.[200]

TEACHERS

There are five principal categories of teachers, namely national, secondary, vocational, regional technical college and university teachers.[201] The legal rights and duties of secondary teachers and of university teachers have rarely been the subject of litigation.

National schools

An extensive body of case law exists regarding the status, rights and duties of national teachers.[202] For many years a matter of particular concern to them was the absence of any statutory framework for the sector; that deficiency was resolved by the Education Act 1998, which broadly endorsed the system that obtained prior to then.

A minority of national teachers are employed directly by the State, most notably those who teach in the model schools. The great majority of national teachers are employed under the management system whereby, even though their salary is paid by the State, the hiring and directions regarding their work is done by or under local management boards. As described by Murnaghan J., the managerial system:

> "was adopted to obviate difficulties connected chiefly with religious belief. In most cases schools were not the property of the [State] but they were recognised by it as national schools. A manager, *e.g.* the parish priest or rector of the Church of Ireland, was nominated by an outside authority and the nomination was sanctioned by the [State] — when sanctioned the duties and

---

[197.] *ibid.* s.25(1).

[198.] *ibid.* s.25(2); *cf. State (Curtin) v. Minister for Health* [1953] I.R. 93.

[199.] *ibid.* s.25(3).

[200.] *ibid.* s.26; *cf. Cox v. Electricity Supply Board* [1943] I.R. 94, where the previous dismissals procedure is outlined in detail.

[201.] See generally, D. Glendenning, *Education and the Law* (1999) Chap. 11.

[202.] See, generally, Osborough, "Irish Law and the Rights of the National Schoolteacher", 14 Ir. Jur. 36 and 304 (1979).

functions of the manager were minutely provided for in Rules and Regulations made by the [State].

The selection of the teacher, who should, however, have the prescribed qualifications, was left to the manager, but the salary of the teacher was in general provided by the [State]. The teacher had, under the Rules . . . , to be appointed under an agreement in writing on one of the approved forms and the agreement so approved of contained a clause stating that the duties of teachers should be such as were prescribed in the Rules. . . ."[203]

There was a view that the national teacher's employer was the school manager and not the Department of Education, but that was rejected by the Supreme Court in 1940. In *McEneaney v. Minister for Education*[204] a school manager who "did not own the school and was not carrying it on for his personal benefit" was described as being "in the position of a trustee of an educational trust".[205] Two of the principal reported cases, *Leyden v. Attorney General*[206] and *McEneaney*, concerned unilateral alterations to the plaintiffs' employment contracts; in both cases the plaintiffs were backed by their trade union, the Irish National Teachers Organisation. In both cases, the teachers were appointed under regulations which contained "rule 108(c)", whereby the State "reserve[d] the right to alter the rates of grade salary and of continued good service salary. . . ." In *Leyden*, as an economy measure in 1923, the State cut teachers' salaries by 10 per cent. Although those salaries had been determined some years earlier by an arbitration award, it was held that rule 108(c) would permit reductions of that nature. The legal effects of the arbitration award were described there as follows: "if the award is put forward as an alteration of a legal contract between manager and teacher, no evidence of authority to make such alteration on the part of the teacher has been shown. In reality what took place was negotiation through collective bargaining, without any intention to alter legal contracts between managers and teachers, although such alteration would naturally follow subsequently."[207] Later, in *McEneaney* the Supreme Court "recognise[d] a power in the Department to make general reduction of pay as the necessities of the time may require".[208] However, the Court would not permit the unilateral imposition of new qualifications for existing teachers — in that case, a certificate of competency to give bilingual instruction. A change of terms of that nature was not contemplated by rule 108(c). In 1955, the Supreme Court held that the Department could introduce a higher salary scale for married teachers[209] — an arrangement which now of course would contravene the EEC Treaty and, apart from that, probably would be unconstitutional.

Under section 24 of the Education Act 1998, where teachers and other staff of a school are paid from money allocated by the Oireachtas, their terms and condi-

---

203. *McEneaney v. Minister for Education* [1941] I.R. 430 at 439.
204. *ibid.*
205. *ibid.* at 440.
206. [1926] I.R. 334.
207. *ibid.* at 360-361.
208. [1941] I.R. at 444.
209. *O'Callaghan v. Minister for Education* (Sup. Ct., November 30, 1955).

tions of employment may be determined by the Minister for Education, with the concurrence of the Minister for Finance. Regulations may be prescribed by the Minister on, *inter alia*, the appointment and qualifications of teachers.[210]

National teachers may fall into the category of persons who are employed "by or under the State" and are thereby excluded from the Unfair Dismissals Acts. If that is so, then their rights regarding dismissal are principally to have the terms of their contracts adhered to; they can be lawfully dismissed for the reasons and in accordance with the procedures laid down in their contracts. One of the earliest cases on the right of public officials to fair procedures if they are to be dismissed was *Maunsell v. Minister for Education*,[211] where the Minister ceased to pay a teacher's salary on the grounds that enrolments at his school fell below a specified level. The reason for the fall in numbers had been investigated by the Department without any reference to that teacher. Gavan Duffy J. found guidance in the lines of Seneca:

> *"Quicunque aliquid statuerit, parte inaudita altera,*
>
> *Aequum licet statuerit, haud aequus fuerit."*

Accordingly, it was held that:

> "[the] plaintiff was entitled to express notice of such an inquisition as that [carried out by the Department]. The principle is long and firmly established; it is elementary justice; it applies even where the person affected has no merits; it applies though the enactment does not seem to have contemplated notice; and it applies to every body having authority to adjudicate upon matters involving civil consequences to individuals."[212]

Secondary schools

Like national school teachers prior to 1998, there is no comprehensive Act that regulates the legal position of secondary teachers, who are hired by the various schools but whose salaries are paid by the Minister for Education. However, under the Intermediate Education (Ireland) Act 1914, a centralised register has been established for secondary school teachers and provision is made for paying capitation grants to secondary schools based on the number of pupils attending. Rules have been promulgated, without any immediate statutory basis, determining the manner in which incremental salaries are paid; in 1996 an attempt to have part of those rules declared invalid, on the grounds of unreasonableness and disproportionality, was rejected.[213]

Unlike national teachers, the question of who is the employer of secondary school teachers has not been ruled on in the superior courts. But in 1997, in a dispute concerning alleged deductions from salary not authorised by the Payment of Wages Act 1991, a division of the Employment Appeals Tribunal held that, at least for the purposes of that Act, they were employees of the State and not of the

---

[210.] s.33(c).
[211.] [1940] I.R. 213.
[212.] *ibid.* at 234. Distinguished unconvincingly in *Hickey v. Eastern Health Board* [1991] 1 I.R. 208.
[213.] *McCann v. Minister for Education* [1997] 1 I.L.R.M. 1.

schools where they taught.[214] It is debatable whether for the purposes of the Unfair Dismissals Act they are employed "by or under the State".

Vocational schools

The position of vocational teachers is regulated by the Vocational Education Acts 1930-99; their status, rights and duties are very similar to those of officers of local authorities, discussed above. The appointment, qualifications and remuneration of vocational teachers is regulated by the Minister for Education.[215] Provision is made for the suspension without pay of any V.E.C. office-holder where there is reason to believe he failed to perform his duties satisfactorily or he otherwise misconducted himself or was otherwise unfit for the office.[216] The statutory grounds for removal are unfitness to hold the office, refusal to obey or carry out a lawful order, or other misconduct.[217] On several occasions the proper procedures for suspending and for dismissing vocational teachers were considered by the courts.[218]

Third level

There are four major categories of third level colleges, *viz.* regional technical colleges, institutes of technology, universities, and private third level colleges; employment in the latter of these is not the subject of any statutory regulation.

Sections 11 and 12 of the Regional Technical Colleges Act 1992 contain general provisions regarding the staff of those colleges. While the college in question determines the terms and conditions of employment, including remuneration, they must be approved by the Minister.[219] An officer of the college cannot be removed without the consent of the Minister. Suspension and removal from office is subject to the same regime as for vocational teachers, described above. In 1996 an attempt to have the selection of a candidate for promotion declared invalid, on the grounds of alleged bias, failed.[220]

Sections 12 and 13 of the Dublin Institute of Technology Act 1992 contain general provisions regarding the staff of that body, which are broadly similar to those for regional training colleges, as just described. In 1997 an attempt to have elections of staff representatives to the governing body declared invalid, on the grounds of a gender-based system that was adopted, failed.[221] The Regional Technical Colleges (Amendment) Act 1999 is concerned primarily with establishing the Institute of Technology, Blanchardstown.

[214.] *Sullivan v. Dept. of Education* [1998] E.L.R. 217.

[215.] Vocational Education Act 1930, s.23(2).

[216.] Vocational Education (Amendment) Act 1944, s.7.

[217.] *ibid.*, s.8(1).

[218.] *e.g. Carr v. City of Limerick V.E.C.* [2000] E.L.R. 57, *Carr v. Minister for Education Science* [2000] E.L.R. 78, *Gunn v. Bord An Cholaiste Naisiunta Ealaine is Deartha* [1990] 2 I.R. 168, *State (Donegal V.E.C.) v. Minister for Education* [1985] I.R. 56, *Collins v. Co. Cork V.E.C.* (Sup. Ct., March 18, 1983), *Ni Bhedain v. Dublin V.E.C.* (Carroll J. January 28, 1983), *O'Callaghan v. Meath V.E.C.* (Costello J., November 20, 1990).

[219.] *cf. Minister for Education v. Letterkenny R.T.C.* [1997] 1 I.R. 433.

[220.] *O'Dwyer v. McDonagh* [1997] E.L.R. 91.

[221.] *Grennan v. Minister for Education* [1997] 3 I.R. 415.

In 1997, universities in the State became subject to comprehensive statutory regulation, the Universities Act 1997, section 24 of which deals with questions relating to staff. Appointments are made by each of the individual universities, each of which may determine its own terms and conditions of service, but such remuneration, allowances and expenses as may be paid must have Ministerial approval. Those financial constraints may be departed from when so agreed by the Higher Education Authority. Power to suspend and to dismiss university officers and employees is subject to "procedures ... and ... conditions specified in a statute made following consultation through normal industrial relations structures operating in the university with recognised staff associations or trade unions . . .".[222] In 1996 a challenge to the timing of when university professors in U.C.D. shall retire, on the grounds that the regime introduced there contravened legitimate expectations, failed.[223]

A feature of universities in many countries is what is known as the visitor, meaning a prominent individual who is appointed to investigate and determine internal disputes, such as between the institution in question and members of its staff. Universities and colleges which are constituted by charter usually have a visitation regime provided for in the charter.[224] Under section 19 of the Universities Act 1997, the Government is authorised to appoint visitors to institutions where there is no such provision. Usually visitors are serving or retired High Court or Supreme Court judges; at times, one or more other persons may combine with them as visitors. There is no set procedure for conducting visitations but they tend to function broadly like court or tribunal hearings.

In *Thomas v. University of Bradford*[225] the jurisdiction of a visitor to deal with employment-related disputes was considered by the House of Lords, which held that a visitor has an extensive exclusive jurisdiction, which can extend to disputes about the dismissal of lecturers and professors. But the question of visitors' exclusive or parallel jurisdiction does not appear to have been considered by the Irish courts. Decisions of visitors can be challenged by way judicial review.[226]

THE GARDA SÍOCHÁNA

The legal position of members of the Garda Síochána is governed principally by the Garda Síochána Act 1924, as amended, and regulations made under them.[227] Some of the modern labour legislation applies to the Gardaí but they are not covered by the Unfair Dismissals Acts 1977-94, and they are exempted from the Organisation of Working Time Act 1997,[228] and in some respects from requirements in the Employment Equality Act 1998.[229] Although they may not join trade unions, members of the Garda Síochána have their own representative associa-

---

[222] s.25(6).

[223] *Eoghan v. University College Dublin* [1996] 1 I.R. 390.

[224] *e.g.* Charter of the University of Dublin/Trinity College, Chap. III.

[225] [1987] A.C. 795; see, too, *Hines v. Birkbeck College* [1986] 1 Ch. 524.

[226] *e.g. Re Perry's Application* [1997] N.I. 282, *Re Wilson's Application* [1984] N.I. 63 and *R. v. Hull University Visitor, ex p. Page* [1993] A.C. 683.

[227] See, generally, D. Walsh, *The Irish Police* (1998).

[228] s.3(1) and (4).

tions for putting their case regarding remuneration and employment conditions.[230] A conciliation and arbitration scheme, similar to that for civil servants, exists for the Gardaí.[231] In contrast with civil servants and military personnel, the employment rights and obligations of policemen and women have been the subject of a considerable amount of litigation in recent years. Several of the leading cases on fair procedures for disciplining and dismissing public officials have involved members of the Garda, including the *Garvey* case,[232] where the head of the force was dismissed peremptorily and without being offered any reason for that action or any opportunity to rebut allegations that might be made against him.

In *Attorney General v. Dublin United Tramways Co. Ltd.,*[233] it was held that members of the Garda are employed under contracts of employment. Maguire P.'s reasoning was that "members of the Garda Síochána are . . . servants of the public in the employment of the Government. . . . [W]hile he remains a member of the Garda Síochána, [the Guard] is bound to render services to the public".[234] Accordingly, this was sufficient to create the relationship of master and servant.

Appointments of Gardaí, their promotion and disciplining and retirement are now regulated by statutory instruments issued in 1987, 1988, 1989 and 1990.[235] What is said above regarding civil servants' common law, fiduciary and statutory rights and duties applies as well to members of the Garda Síochána.

A special statutory scheme to compensate them or their dependants for malicious injuries and death occasioned in the performance of their duties was established by the Garda Síochána (Compensation) Act 1941, as amended. In order to obtain compensation under this scheme, the applicant must show that, when the Garda in question was injured, he either was on duty and performing his duties or, if not on duty, was acting in his general capacity as a policeman; or the applicant may show that the injury resulted from something the Garda had done as a member of the force or merely because of such membership.[236] The injuries in question must have been maliciously inflicted. In the *Harrington* case[237] in 1945 involving two Gardaí stationed at Nenagh, who were both found shot dead in the station storeroom, it seemed that one Garda shot the other and then committed suicide; there was evidence of private and personal differences between them. A claim by one of their dependants for compensation under the scheme was rejected because there was no evidence that the injuries were inflicted in relation to the deceased's duties as a Garda or his membership of the force.

---

229. ss.27, 36 and 37(6); *cf. Johnson v. Chief Constable of the R.U.C.* (Case 222/84) [1986] E.C.R. 1651.
230. See *Industrial Relations Law* at p. 195.
231. *ibid.* at p. 206.
232. *Garvey v. Ireland* [1981] I.R. 75.
233. [1939] I.R. 590.
234. *ibid.* at 597.
235. S.I. No. 164 of 1988 (Admissions and Appointments); No. 39 of 1987 (Promotions); No. 94 of the 1989 (Discipline); No. 318 of 1990 (Retirement); these have been amended from time to time.
236. 1941 Act, s.2. There is a considerable body of case law on these provisions.
237. *Harrington v. Minister for Finance* [1946] I.R. 320.

On a number of occasions decisions to transfer a member of the Garda from one location and set of duties to another have been contested in the courts, but so far it would seem that no challenge has succeeded.[238]

Members of the Garda can be disciplined and dismissed for the reasons and in accordance with the procedures laid down in the 1989 Disciplinary Regulations.[239] Provided the requisite procedures were followed, the courts are loath to second-guess the findings of a disciplinary tribunal regarding whether the Garda in question deserved to be punished or dismissed, once it is shown that a reasonable tribunal could have come to that conclusion on one view of the evidence.[240] Its determination will not be upset unless it took account of wholly irrelevant matters or it did not have regard to very relevant considerations, or the determination "plainly and unambiguously flies in the face of fundamental reason and common sense".[241] In *Stroker v. Doherty*,[242] where a Garda stationed in a small country town was dismissed for having used obscene language in connection with his wife in a public house and, on another occasion, for not assisting his wife to leave the public house when she was asked by the barman to go, McCarthy J. was "not prepared to hold that the conclusion . . . involved a rejection of, or disregard for fundamental reason or common sense". The judge observed that "in a small country community, members of the gardaí should be setting an example of decent conduct".[243] The Supreme Court there emphasised the general undesirability of the courts interfering with the merits of decisions taken by a body which is particularly well equipped for dealing with such questions.

On several occasions, however, disciplinary decisions have been successfully challenged on procedural grounds although the attempt to have the above procedures struck down, on the grounds that Garda discipline is a substantial judicial function that can only be done through the courts, was rejected by the Supreme Court.[244] In *O'Neill v. Commissioner of An Garda Síochána*,[245] the applicant was questioned in 1989 about alleged misconduct on his part. The matter was then handed over to the Director of Public Prosecutions, who preferred charges but subsequently withdrew them, in the belief that statements taken from the applicant would not be admitted in evidence against him because he had not been cautioned. In 1992 the applicant was served with a notice of summary dismissal under Regulation 40 of the 1989 Garda Regulations but it too was withdrawn and the more usual form of disciplinary proceedings were commenced against him. In the following year he was given notice of the charges and a hearing into them was fixed to commence at the beginning of 1994. It was held by the Supreme Court that disciplinary issues of this nature are expressly required by the Garda regulations to be conducted with reasonable expedition, which had not been done

---

238. *e.g. Doran v. Commissioner An Garda Síochána* [1994] 1 I.L.R.M. 303 and *Fitzpatrick v. Commissioner of An Garda Síochána* [1996] E.L.R. 244.
239. Garda Síochána Discipline Regulations, S.I. No. 94 of 1989, and see Walsh, *supra*, n. 29, Chaps 6 (offences) and 7 (procedure).
240. *cf. McHugh v. Commissioner of An Garda Síochána* [1986] I.R. 228.
241. *Stoker v. Doherty* [1991] 1 I.R. 23 at 29.
242. *ibid.*
243. *ibid.* at 29.
244. *Keady v. Commissioner of An Garda Síochána* [1992] 2 I.R. 197.
245. [1997] 1 I.R. 469.

in this instance. Referring the question to the D.P.P. and then opting for a while to deal with it under Regulation 40 did not relieve the Commissioner from his obligation to investigate and deal with the issue quickly.

In *McAuley*,[246] which concerned a trainee Garda, who did not come within the terms of the above regulations, it was held that the enquiry that resulted in his dismissal did not comply with the *audi alteram partem* principle and, in consequence, the decision to dismiss him was unlawful. An award of damages was upheld but it was held that there was no reason in principle why fresh disciplinary proceedings could not be instituted. In another case concerning a trainee Garda, *Duffy*,[247] the applicant was informed by the Commissioner that his services were being dispensed with on the grounds that he was unlikely to become a "well conducted and efficient member" of the force. But prior to then, disciplinary proceedings had been commenced against him. McGuinness J. held that, although his services could be dispensed with for reasons that would not warrant disciplinary sanctions and it was open to the Garda authorities to abandon the disciplinary proceedings, because the basis for the decision to dispense with his services was the allegation made in proceedings, he was entitled to a proper hearing on that allegation.

In *McCarthy*,[248] following the applicant's trial and acquittal by a jury on serious charges, similar charges were made against him within the disciplinary system, which were upheld there, and he was dismissed. That decision was declared invalid on the grounds that it was unfair and oppressive in the circumstances to subject him to double jeopardy. However, in the light of *Mooney v. An Post*,[249] this decision would seem no longer to represent the law.

In what may be described as very clear cases, Regulation 40 of the 1989 Regulations permits the Garda Commissioner to entirely by-pass normal disciplinary procedures and dismiss a member of the force whom he considers unfit to be in the force. But the member in question is entitled to an opportunity to demonstrate why in the circumstances he ought not be discharged and, where he requests them, must be given details of the alleged facts that constitute his wrong-doing.[250] Where the member in question has actually admitted to a serious breach of discipline, it was held that the Commissioner was entitled to dismiss him without entering into any enquiry.[251]

Following the enactment of the Garda Síochána (Complaints) Act 1996, a Complaint Board was established to investigate complaints made by members of the public against members of the force. Where a complaint discloses a breach of discipline, that Board can refer the case to a tribunal, which will adjudicate on the matter and can impose sanctions, ranging from a caution or reprimand to forced resignation and dismissal.

[246.] *McAuley v. Commissioner of An Garda Síochána* [1996] 3 I.R. 208.
[247.] *Duffy v. Commissioner An Garda Síochána* [1999] 2 I.R. 81.
[248.] *McCarthy v. Commissioner An Garda Síochána* [1997] 1 I.R. 469.
[249.] [1998] 4 I.R. 288.
[250.] *O'Shea v. Commissioner An Garda Síochána* [1944] 2 I.R. 408.
[251.] *State (Jordan) v. Commissioner Garda Síochána* [1987] I.L.R.M. 107.

THE DEFENCE FORCES

The legal position of members of the Defence Forces is governed principally by the Defence Act 1954, as amended. Although some of the modern labour legislation applies to them, they are not covered by the Unfair Dismissals Acts 1977-94, and they are exempted from the Organisation of Working Time Act 1997,[252] from some provisions of the Protection of Young Persons (Employment) Act 1996,[253] from the disputes-resolution procedures of the Acts on maternity, adoptive and parental leave,[254] and from certain provisions of the Employment Equality Act 1998.[255] Although they may not join trade unions, they have their own representative association through which grievances can be aired with the Minister for Defence.[256]

Unlike the position for instance in the United States, the rights and obligations of members of these forces (the Army, the Navy and the Air Force) have been the subject of very little litigation, except for the question of army pensions and, more recently, the controversial question of army deafness claims.[257] However, one of the leading authorities on the maxim *audi alteram partem* is *The State (Gleeson) v. Minister for Defence*,[258] which concerned the proper procedures for discharging members of the forces. More recently in *McDonagh v. Minister for Defence*,[259] Lavan J. castigated disciplinary action taken against a member of the naval service for having consulted the service's legal officer, as "unfair and capricious". The penalty imposed on the naval officer there was completely disproportionate to the alleged offence and, additionally, he was never given the opportunity to answer the charges made against him. Serious disciplinary charges in the armed forces are dealt with by way of court martial.[260]

Members of the forces do not hold their appointments under contracts of employment but have a status as defined by the Defence Acts. Unlike civil servants, however, it has been established that members of the forces have a legal right to be paid such remuneration as is owing to them under regulations made on foot of the Defence Acts. In a case in 1946[261] the Supreme Court gave a declaration that a captain in the Army Medical Service was entitled to the same rate of pay as for Commandants, as laid down in regulations in force at the time. What is said above regarding civil servants' common law, fiduciary and statutory rights and obligations applies as well to members of these forces.[262]

---

252. s.3(1) and (4).
253. s.6(5).
254. ss.30(2), 32(1) and 18(1) of the Acts of 1994, 1995 and 1998 respectively.
255. ss.36 and 37(6); *cf. Sirdar v. Secretary of State for Defence* (Case 273/97) [2000] I.C.R. 130 and *Kreil v. Germany* (Case C285/98) [2000] E.C.R.
256. Defence (Amendment) Act 1990.
257. Giving rise to the Civil Liability (Assessment of Hearing Injury) Act 1998.
258. [1976] I.R. 280.
259. [1991] I.L.R.M. 115.
260. *cf. Scariff v. Taylor* [1996] 1 I.R. 242.
261. *Fitzgerald v. Minister for Finance* [1946] I.R. 481.
262. *e.g. Reading v. Attorney General* [1951] A.C. 507.

CHAPTER 14

TAX AND P.R.S.I.

Income tax is a very significant feature of many employment relationships.[1] Under the Finance Act 2001, the rates of tax payable by a single person on taxable income were as follows: the first £20,000 at 20 per cent, and the remainder at 42 per cent. Married couples with one income must pay 20 per cent on the first £29,000 and, with two incomes 20 per cent on the first £40,000; thereafter, the rate is 42 per cent. The marginal rate of tax for most workers therefore is 42 per cent. On account of the comparatively high tax rates, employers and workers often seek ways to minimise their tax bills and, when evaluating various kinds of rewards for working, will be concerned more with the after-tax worth than the face value. In recent years profit-sharing and employee share schemes have become a feature of private sector employment in prosperous companies, and legislation has been enacted to remove several fiscal deterrents against participating in these schemes.

EMPLOYMENT OR OFFICE

The rules for taxing income differ somewhat depending on which schedule the income in question is being taxed under. Income earned by working for others can fall under Schedule D or Schedule E of the Taxes Consolidation Act 1997 ("the 1997 Act"). Schedule D is concerned with the income of self-employed persons; it is relatively favourable to them in that, *inter alia*, losses incurred in some years can be set off against gains made in other years, a wider range of earnings-related expenses are deductible from income and, before 1990, the actual amount of tax payable was calculated on a previous year basis. Schedule E deals with the income of employees and office-holders. Accordingly, the employee/self-employed distinction considered earlier in Chapter 2 is vital for income tax purposes and, indeed, one of the main incentives for employees seeking to become self-employed is to avail of the more favourable Schedule D tax regime.

Those who are taxable under Schedule E are the holders of:

"every public office or employment of profit, and in respect of every annuity, pension or stipend payable out of the public revenue of the State. . . . [and e]very person having or exercising an office or employment of profit . . . to whom any annuity, pension or stipend . . . is payable in respect of all salaries, fees, wages, perquisites or profits whatsoever therefrom.[2]

[1.] See, generally, K. Corrigan, *Revenue Law* (2000), Chap. 14 (thereinafter referred to as *Corrigan*), and J. Ward, *Judge Irish Income Tax* (1999-2000 ed.), Chaps 10 and 11.

[2.] Taxes Consolidation Act 1997, s.19(1)(2).

The same criteria and tests apply in determining if a person is an employee for tax purposes as apply for employment legislation and social security.[3] That the parties have described their relationship as one of self-employment is not conclusive on the issue.[4] What a tribunal and court will look for principally is the right to control in detail how the work is done and the absence of a significant entrepreneurial element.[5] Several of the leading cases on the distinction in this context concern persons claiming to be exercising their profession or vocation entirely or predominantly for one employer. For instance, in *Fall v. Hitchin*[6] the question was whether a professional dancer, who had a written contract with the Sadlers Wells Company, was an employee or self-employed. Under the contract, he was to be paid a weekly "fee" regardless of whether or not he was called on to dance in that week. During the tax year he had sought but was unsuccessful in securing other dancing engagements. But he did not intend to remain at Sadlers Wells and he regarded his engagement there as an interim one. It was held that he was an employee.[7] His position was contrasted with that in *Davies v. Braithwaite*,[8] where an actress argued that every one of her separate theatrical engagements were distinct contracts of employment for tax purposes. That contention was rejected and it was observed that "[w]here one finds a method of earning a livelihood which does not consist of the obtaining of a post and staying in it, but consists in a series of engagements and moving from one to the other . . . then each of those engagements cannot be considered an employment but is a mere engagement in the course of exercising a profession, and every profession and every trade does involve the making of successive engagements and successive contracts and, in one sense of the word, employments".[9]

Where the person in question can be classified as an "office-holder" then, regardless of his status under employment law, his earnings from the office are taxable under Schedule E. In *Edwards v. Clinch*,[10] which concerned whether an inspector who was specially appointed to hold a planning inquiry fell into this category, the term "office" was described as "a post which can be recognised as existing, whether it be occupied for the time being or vacant, and which, if occupied, does not owe its existence in any way to the identity of the incumbent or his appointment to the post. . . . [T]he office must owe its existence to some constituent instrument, whether it be a charter, statute, declaration of trust, contract (other than a contract of personal service) or instrument of some other kind. . . . [T]he office must have a sufficient degree of continuance to admit of its being held by successive incumbents; it need not be capable of permanent or prolonged or indefinite existence, but it cannot be limited to the tenure of one man. . . ."[11]

There is a list of offices in respect of which tax under Schedule E must be paid on their incomes,[12] namely:

---

3. *Fall v. Hitchen* [1973] 1 W.L.R. 286.
4. *Narich Pty. v. Commr's of Pay Roll Tax* [1984] I.C.R. 286.
5. e.g. *McDermott v. Loy* (Barron J. 29 July 1982).
6. [1973] 1 W.L.R. 286.
7. Similarly in the *Narich* case, *supra*, n.4.
8. [1931] 2 K.B. 628.
9. *ibid.* at 635-636.
10. [1981] 1 Ch.1.
11. *ibid.* at 6.
12. Taxes Consolidation Act 1997, s.19(2).

(a) offices belonging to either House of the Oireachtas;

(b) offices belonging to any court in the State;

(c) public offices under the State;

(d) offices of the Defence Forces;

(e) offices or employments of profit under any ecclesiastical body;

(f) offices or employments of profit under any company or society, whether corporate or not corporate;

(g) offices or employments of profit under any public institution, or on any public foundation of whatever nature, or for whatever purpose established;

(h) offices or employments of profit under any public corporation or local authority, or under any trustees or guardians of any public funds, tolls or duties;

(i) all other public offices or employments of profit of a public nature.

This list is not intended as a comprehensive statement of the office-holders who are taxable in this manner.

The taxpayer in *Edwards v. Clinch*[13] was one of a panel of 60 engineers who the Department of the Environment could call on to hold public enquiries. When so invited, there was no obligation to accept the nomination. A duly appointed inspector was responsible for the entire conduct of the enquiry and was remunerated exclusively by fees paid on a daily basis. Because each appointment was an ad hoc one and no question ordinarily arose of appointing an incumbent inspector's successor, it was held that the inspector there was not an office-holder. By contrast, a part-time consultant with a regional hospital board was held to be taxable under Schedule E,[14] as were non-executive directors of companies[15] and indeed a Scottish law firm which acted as the registrars of several companies.[16]

TAXABLE BENEFITS

What is taxable under Schedule E is described as "emoluments", which may be either cash payments or benefits in kind.[17] Occasionally, very substantial payments made to employees, which are not emoluments, may be taxable as gifts under the Capital Acquisitions Tax Act 1976. Emoluments are defined as "all salaries, fees, wages, perquisites or profits or gains whatsoever arising from an office or employment, or the amount of any annuity, pension or stipend, as the

---

[13.] [1981] 1 Ch.1.

[14.] *Mitchell and Eldon v. Ross* [1960] Ch. 145.

[15.] *McMillan v. Guest* [1942] A.C. 561.

[16.] *Inland Revenue v. Brander and Chuikshank* [1971] 1 W.L.R. 212; compare *McMenamin v. Diggles* [1991] 1 W.L.R. 1249.

[17.] See, generally, Kerridge, "The Taxation of Emoluments from Offices and Employments", 108 L.Q.R. 433 (1992).

case may be".[18] Thus, not alone money but anything representing money's worth can be emoluments and thereby taxable. In the case of benefits in kind, tax will only be charged to the extent that they can be converted into money.

Money payments

Not every payment made by an employer to his employee will be subject to income tax. The fact that the payment has some connection with the job does not always render it taxable; the payment must "arise from" the office or employment. This general principle was enunciated in the leading case of *Hochstrasser v. Meyes*[19] as follows:

> "it is a question to be answered in the light of the particular facts of every case whether or not a particular payment is or is not a profit arising from the employment. . . . [N]ot every payment made to an employee is necessarily made to him as a profit arising from his employment. Indeed . . . to be a profit arising from the employment the payment must be made in reference to the services the employee renders by virtue of his office, and it must be something in the nature of a reward for services, (past) present or future".[20]

Not alone must the payment be made to an employee but it must have been paid to him "in return for acting as or being an employee".[21] There are several categories of payment which do not "arise from" the employment and therefore are not taxable in principle, such as redundancy payments,[22] although special rules have been enacted to subject some of these payments to tax, such as "golden hand-shakes".[23]

The *Hochstrasser* case concerned a scheme whereby certain employees of Imperial Chemical Industries Ltd. were compensated by the company in respect of losses incurred by them on sales of their houses when they were moved from one location to another by the company. The company employed a very large workforce in a number of establishments in Britain. In their service contracts, these employees agreed to serve the company wherever they were posted. In order to facilitate transfers from one establishment to another, a scheme existed whereby married male employees could obtain interest free loans from the company to purchase houses. Additionally, if on being transferred they incurred a loss on the sale of their house, the company would make up that loss. When the tax-payer was transferred to a factory in Liverpool in 1950, he lost £350 on the sale of his house and he was then reimbursed that amount by the company. It was held that this money was not a taxable emolument because the circumstance which brought about the payment was not any service rendered by him but rather "his personal embarrassment in having sold his house for a smaller sum than he had given for it".[24] The payment was "no more taxable as a profit from his employ-

---

18. Taxes Consolidation Act 1997, s.112(1).
19. [1960] A.C. 376.
20. *ibid.* at 388. The word "past" in this passage may be open to question.
21. *ibid.* at 392.
22. *Mairs v. Haughey* [1994] 1 A.C. 303; *infra*, p. 327.
23. See *infra*, pp.340-341.
24. [1960] A.C. at 392.

ment than would a payment out of a provident or a distress fund set up by an employer for the benefit of employees whose personal circumstances might justify assistance".[25] The object of the payment was more to relieve the employee's distress than to reward him for his services to the company.

Similarly, redundancy payments, including payments made to compensate employees for waiving existing redundancy entitlements, are not taxable emoluments. In *Mairs v. Haughey*, [26] which arose out of the privatisation of Harland and Wolff in Belfast, the successor company (H. & W. 1989 Ltd.) agreed to take on existing employees, *inter alia*, on terms that they would waive their existing non-statutory enhanced redundancy entitlements for a cash payments. Lord Woolf, on appeal, pointed out the differences between remuneration and payment on redundancy. The latter, "whether statutory or non-statutory, involves an employee finding himself without a job through circumstances over which he has no control; [and] it does not give rise to a right to compensation unless the employee has been employed for a minimum period ...."[27] It is a "payment to compensate the employee for not being able to receive emoluments from his employment". It is "distinct from damages to which he would be entitled if his employment were terminated unlawfully". It further is "unlike a deferred payments of wages in that the entitlement to a redundancy payment is never more than a contingent entitlement, which no doubt both the employer and employee normally hope will never accrue". The distinction between the deferred payment of wages or salary and a redundancy payment "may be narrow but it is none the less real".

Gifts and other voluntary payments

That the payment is gratuitous, in the sense that it is not being made under a binding obligation, does not mean that it never falls within the tax net. The governing principle is that taxable income includes "all payments made to the holder of an office or employment as such, that is to say, by way of remuneration for services, even though such payments may be voluntary, but they do not include a mere gift or present (such as a testimonial) which is made to him on personal grounds and not by way of payment for his services".[28] Of course, if the gift is not remuneration but it exceeds £2,000, it falls subject to capital acquisitions tax.

There is a strong tendency to treat gratuitous payments by employers as taxable remuneration, especially when similar gifts are made to other employees. For instance, in *Laidler v. Perry*,[29] a group of companies gave each of its employees who had worked for it for longer than one year, a voucher for £10 as a Christmas present, which could be exchanged for goods in the shop of the employee's own choice. These were held to be taxable emoluments. It did not matter that the gifts were made to "help to maintain a feeling of happiness among the staff and to foster a spirit of personal relationship between management and staff".[30] This objective was described "[i]n less roundabout language" as simply "in order to

---

[25]   *ibid.*
[26]   [1994] 1 A.C. 303.
[27]   *ibid.* at 319 and 320.
[28]   *Reed v. Seymour* [1927] A.C. 554 at 559.
[29]   [1966] A.C. 16.
[30]   *ibid.* at 31.

maintain the quality of service given by the staff", meaning for "each recipient to go on working well".[31] Consequently, the vouchers arose from the employment itself.

Even a payment to a single employee which is given and is received as a gift may in the circumstances be remuneration for services rendered. That was held to be the case in *Wing v. O'Connell*,[32] where the owner of the horse that won the Irish Derby in 1921 subsequently sent the jockey a cheque for £400. The letter described the payment as "a present", congratulated the jockey for his "very fine riding" of the horse and expressed the hope that he "will soon ride him again to victory". According to Kennedy C.J., this payment was given for "professional work done and vocational services rendered in successfully steering the horse . . . to victory, in other words, for successfully accomplishing the object of his professional engagement, and that it was in the nature of a bonus or voluntary addition to the prescribed fee under the regulations".[33] The payment therefore was taxable income.

A rare instance of a gratuitous payment by an employer not being taxed is *Ball v. Johnson*,[34] concerning a bank clerk whose terms of employment required him to sit the examinations of the Institute of Bankers "in order to better qualify himself for his duties in the service of the bank". He duly worked for those examinations in his spare time and, having passed them, was paid £130 by his employer, in accordance with the long established practice. The payment was held not to be a profit arising from his employment and, accordingly, escaped tax. Similarly, when in 1940 the Governing Body of University College Dublin voted its retiring President, Dr. Coffey, a sum of £1,000 to mark his retirement and to show the Governors' high estimation of his contribution to the College, the payment was held to be in the nature of a gift and not taxable.[35]

Depending on the circumstances, gifts made by persons other than the recipient's employer may be taxable income. Examples of such payments include tips received by a taxi driver in the ordinary course of his work,[36] the Easter offering made to a Church of England parson,[37] and the customary presents of cash given to a huntsman at Christmas by other members of the hunt who were also his personal friends.[38]

Special contractual payments

Where the payment is made on foot of a contractual stipulation, in return for something other than services rendered, then that money may not be a taxable emolument. The best example is the *Hochstrasser* case,[39] where the payments to cover losses incurred when the I.C.I. employees changed their houses were made

---

31. *ibid.* at 36.
32. [1927] I.R. 84.
33. *ibid.* at 108.
34. (1971) 47 T.C. 155.
35. *Mulvey v. Coffey* [1942] I.R. 277.
36. *Calvert v. Wainwright* [1947] K.B. 526.
37. *Blaikston v. Cooper* [1909] A.C. 104.
38. *Wright v. Boyce* (1958) 38 T.C. 138.
39. [1960] A.C. 376.

under the terms of an enforceable contract and were not pure gifts. According to Lord Radcliffe, "while it is not sufficient to render a payment assessable that an employee would not have received it unless he had been an employee, it is assessable if it has been paid to him in return for acting or as being an employee".[40] In reaching their decision that the payment there was not for acting as an employee, the Lords laid stress on the fact that the taxpayer's salary compared favourably with that of employees in comparable circumstances but whose employers did not operate this kind of scheme. Similarly, when an amateur rugby football player got a signing-on-fee for turning professional and playing for his new club, the payment was held to be a capital sum received to compensate for the loss of amateur status, not a taxable emolument.[41]

But an inducement or signing-on fee, where some special extra ingredient does not exist, would not escape the income tax net.[42] In *Vaughan-Neill v. Inland Revenue*,[43] where a successful barrister agreed to give up his practice and work full-time for a large civil engineering company, an inducement fee of £40,000 paid to him by the company was held to be taxable. This was because the taxpayer was not giving up something exceptional in order to do the new job; the payment in fact was "an inducement to [him] to accept the professional and social consequences which flowed from his taking the proffered employment".[44] A similar conclusion was reached in *Glantre Engineering Ltd. v. Goodhand*,[45] where a lump sum was paid to a chartered accountant, who worked with a major international accountancy firm, to leave the firm and take up the position as financial director of a rapidly expanding engineering company. The view that this payment was made to compensate for the loss of professional status as a chartered accountant in a very large firm, the loss of the prospects of becoming a partner in that firm and the loss of security in the future, was rejected.

Payments made in connection with a change in the terms of employment are almost invariably taxable. Thus in *Holland v. Geoghegan*,[46] a dustman received a lump sum for giving up the right he had enjoyed to a share in the proceeds from a sale of salvage. In the previous year, when his employer sought to remove his and his co-employees' right to share in the salvage, they went on strike. The lump sum was offered by way of a settlement of the strike and to induce him back to work, although he did not agree to remain in the job for any longer than one week's notice. Nevertheless, the payment was held to be taxable because its main purpose was to get him back to work and it was "a form of substituted remuneration for his former rights to share in the proceeds of sale of the salvage".[47] The same conclusion was reached in a case where an employee, whose remuneration was based on a salary and a commission, agreed to give up his right to any commission in return for a lump sum.[48]

---

[40]   *ibid.* at 391-392.
[41]   *Jarrold v. Boustead* [1964] 1 W.L.R. 1357.
[42]   *Riley v. Coglan* (1967) 44 T.C. 481.
[43]   [1979] 1 W.L.R. 1283.
[44]   *ibid.* at 1293. Curiously, the Revenue did not attempt to tax this as an ordinary emolument but under special statutory provisions.
[45]   [1983] 1 All E.R. 542.
[46]   [1972] 1 W.L.R. 1473.
[47]   *ibid.* at 1481.
[48]   *McGregor v. Randall* [1984] 1 All E.R. 1092.

In *Hamblett v. Godfrey,*[49] the taxpayer was a civil servant employed at "G.C.H.Q." in Cheltenham, a famous information-gathering and secret service establishment. On account of the Government's concern about trade unionism and possible industrial action there, many employees were persuaded to sign agreements that they would resign from trade union membership, would not join any trade union, and would not even discuss with the officials of any union their terms of employment. For that undertaking, they were paid £1,000 each. It was held that this sum was taxable because its very source was the civil servants' employment. The rights which had been surrendered "had been enjoyed within the employer/employee relationship, [t]he removal of the rights involved changes in the conditions of service [and t]he payment was in recognition of th[ose] changes . . . ."[50] The view that what was surrendered were special personal rights was rejected since, whatever they were, they were still directly connected with the taxpayers' employment. A case could be made that the position in Ireland is different because the rights to join a trade union and to take part in its activities enjoy constitutional protection.

In *Clayton v. Gothorp,*[51] the taxpayer's wife obtained a loan from her employer to follow a course leading to a certificate for health visitors. She was employed as an assistant health visitor and, when getting the loan, agreed to serve the employer for at least 18 months after she obtained that qualification, at the end of which time the money then would become irrecoverable. The loan was paid to her in monthly installments throughout the duration of the course. Having succeeded in obtaining the qualification, she remained with the employer for 18 months and three days. It was held that the loan was a reward for past services and thereby taxable. The consideration given for the loan was the promise to follow the course and then work for at least 18 months, and it was working for that period which turned the loan into an absolute payment.

A lump sum payment made in return for a restrictive covenant was held not to fall within Schedule E, whether the covenant applies during the currency of the employment or on its termination. However, special rules now exist for taxing restrictive covenants.[52] Compensation paid for having resigned a position or as an inducement to resign — so-called golden handshakes — also are the subject of special rules.[53]

Payments by third parties

Where the payment is made not by the employer but by a third party, it may still be a taxable emolument. For it is not essential that the payment was for services rendered or to be rendered; the tax net falls once the payment is "from employment". The former English goalkeeper, Peter Shilton, fell foul of this rule when he was transferred from Nottingham Forest to Southampton in 1982.[54] Southampton agreed to pay him a regular remuneration and also a £75,000 signing-on fee,

49. [1987] 1 W.L.R. 357.
50. *ibid.* at 1370.
51. [1971] 1 W.L.R. 999.
52. Taxes Consolidation Act 1997, s.127; see *Corrigan,* Vol. 2, pp.108-109.
53. See *infra,* pp. 340-341.
54. *Shilton v. Wilmhurst* [1991] 1 A.C. 684.

which manifestly was taxable. But Nottingham also agreed to pay him £80,000 for agreeing to transfer clubs. That too, it was held, was a taxable emolument. There was nothing in the statutory definition of that term to justify the inference that tax will only be imposed on "an emolument provided by a person who has an interest in the performance by the employee of the services which he becomes bound to perform when he enters into the contract of employment".[55]

Payments to third parties

A payment made directly to a third party may in the circumstances constitute a taxable emolument. This is where the employer discharges an obligation incurred by the employee. For instance, in *Glynn v. C.I.R.*[56] the taxpayer was employed as an executive director at a monthly remuneration but his contract provided that a stipulated sum would be paid by the employer towards the costs of his children's education. School fees were paid directly by the employer to the child's school. Those were held to be taxable because money paid at an employee's request is the equivalent of money paid directly to him.

In *Rendell v. Went*,[57] while driving a car on the company's business, the taxpayer struck and killed a pedestrian. He intended to obtain legal advice from the Automobile Association but, when his employers learned that he would be prosecuted for serious driving offences, they instructed their own solicitors to spare no expense in the employee's defence. Leading Counsel were hired for the purpose and secured the employee's acquittal. As in the Christmas presents case, it was not seriously contested that the payment made by the employers for the legal defence here was not a taxable benefit in kind. The main issue was how to value that benefit for tax purposes. It was argued that tax should be assessed only on the excess over the amount which the employee would have expended on his own defence; that the extra paid by the employers in the circumstances was primarily for their own benefit — to ensure that a valued employee would not be convicted and imprisoned. That contention was rejected because the entire amount was spent for the employee's advantage, to prevent his going to prison. Expenditure is "not the less advantageous to an [employee] because it suits or advantages the company to make it".[58] Payments by employers to a superannuation fund are ordinarily taxable income under this principle[59] but special tax rules have been adopted for pension schemes.[60]

Arrangements, however, can exist whereby members of an employee's family obtain some financial benefit from his employer but that benefit is not his taxable income. Thus in *Barclays Bank Ltd. v. Naylor*,[61] a company had a scheme for providing scholarships to some of its employees' children. Under the scheme, payments would be made to cover the educational expenses of the children of I.C.I. employees who were based abroad. It was not a term of the employees' contracts

---

55. *ibid.* at 693.
56. [1990] 2 A.C. 298.
57. [1964] 1 W.L.R. 650.
58. *ibid.* at 659.
59. *Bruce v. Hatton* (1921) 8 T.C. 180.
60. Taxes Consolidation Act 1997, ss.770-790; see *Corrigan*, Chap. 9.
61. [1961] 1 Ch. 7.

that those payments would be made, although the employees confidently anticipated that their children would obtain the scholarships. On account of the manner
in which the scholarships were paid, they were deemed not to be the employees'
taxable income. For instead of I.C.I. directly paying all or part of the school bills,
the scheme provided the children directly with income which would then be used
by them for that purpose. Although the employees benefited to an extent from
this arrangement, in order to be assessed for tax it must be shown that "the very
money which was paid into [the child's] account by the trustees become his
father's income when the account was debited with the payment of the school
bills for which his father had incurred a liability".[62] In this case, the money was
the child's and not the parent's income.[63]

Deductions from remuneration

It is not essential that the remuneration arising from the job be actually paid over
to the employee; the earnings are taxable even though he has directed that part or
all of them shall be retained by the employer. For instance, in *Mahon v.
McLoughlin*,[64] under his contract an attendant at an asylum was obliged to pay 50
pence a week out of his salary towards his board and lodgings. It was held that
the gross salary was taxable because that was the sum which accrued to him from
his employment. It did not matter that he could not have been taxed on the value
of board and lodgings, which would be provided free of charge. According to
Rowlatt J.: "If a person is paid a wage with some advantage thrown in, you cannot add the advantage to the wage for the purpose of taxation unless that advantage can be turned into money. But when you have a person paid a wage with a
necessity — the contractual necessity if you like — to expend that wage in a particular way, then he must pay tax upon the gross wage, and no question of alien-
ability or inalienability arises."[65]

Similarly in *Dolan v. "K"*,[66] a nun of the Order of St. Louis who was a qualified schoolteacher was employed in that capacity at a school run by her Order.
Although she was paid a salary, in accordance with the Order's rules she handed
it all over to the Order. It was held that her salary was still subject to income tax.
But an employee is not liable for tax if he voluntarily renounced the emoluments
before they were credited to him.

Payments for expenses

As is explained below,[67] only a very narrow category of expenses incurred in connection with a person's employment are deductible expenses for income tax purposes. Where the employee is reimbursed for a genuine expense incurred on his
employer's behalf in the course of his work, generally that payment is not taxable. But payments in respect of expenses which are personal to the employee

---

[62] *ibid.* at 21.
[63] Similarly, *O'Coindealbhain v. O'Carroll* [1989] I.R. 229.
[64] (1926) 11 T.C. 83.
[65] *ibid.* at 89. See too, *Heaton v. Bell* [1969] 2 W.L.R. 735.
[66] [1944] I.R. 470.
[67] *infra*, pp. 335-338.

will be taxed. Perhaps the best example is the cost of travelling to or from work. Normally, that cost is not a deductible expense. Accordingly, in *Owen v. Pook*,[68] it was held that payments to an employee reimbursing him for the expense of travelling from one workplace to another was a taxable emolument. All payments to an employee arising out of his work are perquisites other than refunding deductible expenses. Taxable remuneration cannot be placed outside the tax net by describing it as expenses.

Benefits in kind

Income tax under Schedule E is charged on non-cash benefits provided to employees as well as on cash payments made, provided the benefit is something that is capable of being converted into money.

Value of benefits

Tax is chargeable on the "full amount" of emoluments and the word amount "denotes that in order to be taxable a perquisite must be either a cash or money payment or must be money's worth or of money value in the sense that it can be turned to pecuniary account".[69] An example of the general principle is *Wilkins v. Rogerson*,[70] where the taxpayer's employer decided to make a Christmas present to all the male members of his staff of a new suit of clothes up to the value of £15. Arrangements were made with a well known firm of tailors to supply appropriate suits to all the employees who accepted this offer. The issue to be determined was not whether these suits were benefits in kind, for incontrovertibly they were. What was in dispute was the value of the benefits for tax purposes. It was held that their value was what they were worth to each employee, meaning the price an employee could fetch if he sold his new suit. The principle is that a benefit in kind "should be assessed to income tax at its money value in the taxpayer's hands, that is to say, what he could get for it if he sold it as soon as he received it".[71]

Some of the leading cases on share options, before special rules were adopted for them, concern their proper valuation for these purposes.[72] There are also special rules for what are called preferential loans,[73] that is loans made directly or indirectly to an employee or his spouse at below-market interest rates in order to purchase a dwelling house to be occupied by the borrower.

Benefits not capable of being converted into money

Merely because a benefit is of some value to the recipient does not always render it taxable under Schedule E, although there now are extensive statutory exceptions to this principle. This was decided in *Tennant v. Smith*,[74] where a bank man-

---

[68] [1970] A.C. 244.

[69] *Heaton v. Bell* [1969] 2 W.L.R. 735 at 754.

[70] [1961] 1 Ch. 133.

[71] *ibid.* at 147.

[72] *e.g. Abbott v. Philbim* [1961] A.C. 352. Special rules are now laid down in the Taxes Consolidation Act 1997, s.128, and see *Corrigan*, Vol 2, pp. 82 *et seq.*

[73] Taxes Consolidation Act 1997, ss.122 and 122A, and see *Corrigan*, Vol. 2, pp. 76 *et seq.*

[74] [1892] A.C. 150.

ager resided free of charge in a house provided for him by the bank. He was required by the terms of his employment to live there. On the grounds that whatever benefit he may have derived from that arrangement could not be converted by him into money, it was held that tax could not be assessed on it. The principle is that there is a "limitation on the taxability of benefits in kind which are of a personal nature; it is not enough to say that they have a value to which there can be assigned a monetary equivalent".[75] In any event, residing in the bank house was an obligation imposed on the employee there and might not even be regarded as a benefit to him, although the case was not decided on this point.[76] The free use of a car or of other property, which could not be assigned, would escape taxation on this basis, as would the provision of free meals and insurance cover. However, section 118 of the Taxes Consolidation Act 1997 brings within the tax net many benefits that, under the above principle, would have escaped taxation.

Section 118 applies whenever "a body corporate incurs expenses in or in connection with the provision . . . for any person employed by it . . . of living or other accommodation, of entertainment, of domestic or other services or of other benefits or facilities of whatsoever nature and, apart from this section, the expense would not be chargeable to income tax. . . ." In order to come within the tax net, the expense incurred by the employer does not have to derive from the employment as some form of remuneration for services. Once any expense as described here is incurred by the employer, liability to tax under sections 118 is triggered. Once the employer incurs expense in providing living or other accommodation, entertainment, etc., for an employee or a member of his family, that employee is treated as having received a benefit in kind, the value of which can be measured by criteria set out in section 119 of the 1997 Act. The tax net extended to benefits provided not only by the employer but by a "connected person", that is by some other person who is connected with the employer in the manner defined in section 118(8) of the 1997 Act.

An exception is made for meals provided in a canteen, once those meals are provided for the staff,[77] and also for bus and train passes.[78] An exception too is made for living accommodation where, traditionally, an employee of that particular type was required to reside on premises provided by his employer.[79]

How benefits within section 118 are to be valued is as follows.[80] The gross amount of expense incurred by the employer (or connected person) or deemed to have been incurred in providing the benefit is ascertained. If the employee reimbursed any part of that expenditure, that sum is deducted from the gross amount. The taxable benefit is the net expense after any deduction. There are special computation rules for where the benefit consists of a transfer of property or permitting an employee to make use of property, for instance living accommodation. Regarding accommodation, the Revenue generally follow a rule of thumb, which has no statutory basis; they assume that the premises' annual value is 8 per cent

---

[75] *Heaton v. Bell* [1969] 2 W.L.R. 735 at 754.
[76] Compare *Heaton v. Bell* [1969] 2 W.L.R. 735.
[77] Taxes Consolidation Act 1997, s.118(4).
[78] *ibid.*, s.118(5A).
[79] *ibid.*, s. 118(3).
[80] For a detailed account, see *Corrigan*, Vol. 2, pp. 64 *et seq* which deals with, *inter alia*, valuation generally, living accommodation, motor cars, loans and educational trusts.

of its actual market value at the beginning of the tax year. All expenses incurred in connection with accommodation, like insurance, repairs and improvements are treated as covered by the assumed market value rental of the premises. There also are special rules for where a motor car is made available for the employee's private use. Of course, if the benefit in question is one which is capable of being converted into money, sections 118 and 119 do not apply to the situation; the ordinary approach to valuation applies instead.

ALLOWABLE EXPENSES

The kinds of expenses which are allowable against Schedule E income are very limited; a considerably more extensive range of expenses can be deducted from Schedule D income. Those expenses incurred by employees in connection with their work which can be deducted from their remuneration in order to determine their income tax liability are defined in section 114 of the 1997 Act as follows:

> "where the holder of an office or employment of profit is necessarily obliged to incur and defray out of the emoluments [thereof] the expenses of travelling in the performance of the duties of the office or employment, or otherwise to expend money wholly, exclusively, and necessarily in the performance of those duties ...."

Accordingly, for an employee to be able to deduct a work-related expense from his tax bill, the expense must have been incurred "wholly, exclusively and necessarily" in the performance of his duties.

Necessarily and exclusively incurred

In order for an expense incurred to be deductible, it must have been impossible to hold the job in question without making that expenditure; in incurring those expenses there must have been nothing optional on the part of the employee. The leading case on employees' expenses is *Ricketts v. Colquhoun*,[81] which concerned a London-based barrister who also held the part-time office of Recorder of Portsmouth. He would travel regularly from London to Portsmouth in order to perform his duties there. He then sought to have deducted the travelling expenses from his remuneration. Had he travelled in the course of work as a barrister, those expenses would be allowable from his self-employed remuneration. But they were not allowable from his Schedule E earnings as a Recorder; they were incurred, not in performing the tasks of that office, but only in order to get to and from the workplace. Had the taxpayer chosen to live in Portsmouth, those expenses would never have arisen. It would be different if travelling there from London was an intrinsic requirement of the job, as with commercial travellers.

The classic exposition of the rule is Lord Blanesburgh's, that "[u]ndoubtedly its most striking characteristic is its jealously restricted phraseology, some of it repeated to heighten the effect. . . . [T]he language of the rule points to the expenses with which it is concerned being only those which each and every occu-

---

[81.] [1926] A.C. 1.

pant of the particular office is necessarily obliged to incur in the performance of its duties — to expenses imposed on each holder ex necessitate of his office and to such expenses only".[82] Very few of the reported cases have been decided in favour of employed tax payers on this point. The commonest kinds of allowable expenditure are for special clothing and tools which are needed to do the work in question. The Revenue have agreed to appropriate rates for many kinds of occupation which require such expenditure.

In *O'Broin v. McGiolla Merdhre*,[83] the taxpayer was the County Engineer for Clare County Council. He claimed deductions from his salary in respect of subscriptions to professional associations, renewals of books and journals and expenses of a telephone at his home. These expenses were disallowed because they were not absolutely necessary for him to do his job, nor were they incurred exclusively for that purpose.[84] In *Kelly v. Quinn*,[85] the taxpayer was an army officer who was transferred to Athlone, leaving his family home in Dublin. Under army custom, a "batman" was assigned to him, whose main duties were to maintain the officer's uniform, keep his quarters clean and tidy, and make sure that he would be fit for parade at all times. The batman was appointed and paid by the army but, by a long standing custom, the officer paid him £1 per week. It was held that this sum was not an allowable expense. According to Kenny J., "[T]he gratuities were not paid in the performance of his duties; they were . . . paid for the purpose of making it possible for him to perform his duties. . . . [I]n addition, . . . the gratuities were not monies expended necessarily in the performance of the taxpayer's duties because . . . he could have performed his duties without the assistance of a batman".[86]

Even if a particular kind of expenditure is required by the employment contract's very terms, that does not always render it an allowable expense. For it must have been incurred in the actual performance of the employee's duties. Thus, generally, living expenses are not deductible, even if the employee is required to live in a designated place, because he has to live somewhere. By concession the Revenue may allow the costs of living away from home provided the employee has a permanent residence. Other examples of what is not deductible include expenses incurred in obtaining a job or in becoming qualified for a job. In *Lupton v. Potts*,[87] a solicitor's clerk claimed an allowance for what he had to pay to sit and pass the Law Society's examination, as required by the terms of his articles. These were held not to be allowable expenses, for his duties as an articled clerk were quite capable of being performed without incurring that outlay. The test is "not whether the employer imposes the expense but whether the duties do, in the sense that, irrespective of what the employer may prescribe, the duties cannot be performed without the particular outlay".[88] Similarly, the expenses incurred by a bank manager in joining several social clubs, on his employer's instructions in

---

[82]   *ibid.* at 7.
[83]   [1959] I.R. 98.
[84]   Similarly, *Fitzpatrick v. Inland Revenue C'mrs* [1994] 1 W.L.R. 306, *Owen v. Burden* [1971] 1 All E.R. 356 and *Simpson v. Tate* [1925] 2 K.B. 214.
[85]   [1964] I.R. 488.
[86]   *ibid.* at 495.
[87]   [1969] 1 W.L.R. 1749.
[88]   *ibid.* at 1754.

order to foster business contacts, were held not to be allowable.[89] Membership of those clubs was not absolutely essential in order to perform his duties as a bank manager. Exceptional circumstances can arise, however, where passing a particular examination or membership of a particular club is indeed necessary to do a job properly.[90]

Travel expenses

As the Portsmouth Recorder's case[91] illustrates, ordinarily expenses incurred in going to and from work are not deductible expenses. Similarly, in *Phillips v. Keane*,[92] where a schoolteacher acquired a pony and trap to travel five miles to school because he could not find suitable accommodation where the school was located, it was held that none of those expenses were deductible.

But where actually doing the job for which the person is employed requires travel, then expenses necessarily incurred in travelling are deductible, because they are exclusively and also necessarily incurred in the performance of the duties.[93] An example is *Marsden v. I.R.C.*,[94] which concerned an investigator in the audit department of the Revenue, whose job involved travelling throughout Lancashire. It was accepted that costs necessarily incurred by him in the course of his travel were deductible. He used a car for travelling and the issue to be determined was whether the full costs of travelling by car were deductible. On the grounds that it was not a condition of employment that he should have a car and also because no evidence was given to show that he could not have used public transport, it was held that only a part of the car costs incurred were deductible. That part was in fact met by a car allowance paid by his employers.

Where an employee has two entirely separate workplaces, the cost of travel between them may in special circumstances be deductible. This principle is illustrated by *Owen v. Pook*,[95] which concerned a medical practitioner, whose practice was in one town where he lived but who also held part-time appointments in a hospital 15 miles from there. From the evidence, it was quite clear that his duties usually began once he was called from his practice and set out for the hospital. On receiving a call, he frequently would telephone ahead instructions to the hospital staff and advise treatment. If mobile phones existed at the time, presumably he would have continued obtaining information and giving instructions in the course of the journey. For those reasons it was held that his travelling costs were necessarily incurred in the performance of his duties. Those expenses arose from the nature of his job and not merely from the fact that he choose to live 15 miles from the hospital. As Lord Wilberforce explained:

"the hospital management committee required the services of doctors on a part-time basis for emergencies; [they] would have to appoint a doctor with

89. *Brown v. Bullock* [1961] 1 W.L.R. 1095.
90. *e.g. Elwood v. Utiz* [1960] N.I. 93.
91. *Ricketts v. Colquhoun* [1926] A.C. 1; see *supra* p. 353.
92. [1925] I.R. 48.
93. *e.g. Jardine v. Gillespie* (1906) 6 T.C. 263.
94. [1965] 1 W.L.R. 734.
95. [1970] A.C. 244.

a practice of his own and also with suitable . . . experience: he might live and practice within 15 miles or one mile or 100 yards from the hospital: the choice in the matter, if any exists, does not lie with the doctor, who is there in his practice, but with the committee which decides, however near or far he works, to appoint him and to require him to discharge a part of his duty at his practice premises."[96]

Where employees are paid a travelling allowance by their employer, that is often a taxable emolument, especially when the sum is intended to defray expenses in travelling to and from work. However, where travelling costs are a deductible expense, as explained above, the employer's allowance is simply a reimbursement of those expenses. For instance, in *Owen v. Pook*,[97] where the doctor was paid a mileage allowance for travelling to the hospital when called out, those sums were held to be reimbursements of expenses. The travel allowance may be very generous, in which case the excess over the actual costs of travelling will be taxed as an emolument. Thus, where the allowance paid to a county council rent officer included the cost of putting the car on the road and maintaining it for the owner's use, that part of it was held not to be deductible.[98]

TERMINATION PAYMENTS

At times when persons' jobs come to an end, special payments are made to them in addition to their ordinary remuneration. At the "blue collar" level, these payments would often be described as compensation for redundancy; at the executive level, they may be described as golden handshakes. The reason for making special payments in these circumstances can vary considerably; it may be to induce the employee to leave his job or as a special reward for the work he had done for the employer, or it may simply be to compensate him for his reduced earnings when he leaves the job. How the special payments are made also varies; they may be a single big sum or may comprise several payments. Occasionally, instead of the job ending entirely, its terms and conditions may have been altered radically and the special payment is made in respect of the change of terms. Where the payment can be characterised as an emolument, it is taxable in the ordinary way. Where it is not an emolument, it may still fall within the special rules in section 123 of the Taxes Consolidation Act 1997 for golden handshakes.

Where the making of a special termination payment is provided for in the employment contract, then that sum is taxable remuneration regardless of how it may have been described by the parties. For clearly the sum is part of the payment being made for the services rendered. Even where payment of the special sum is not provided for in the original contract, the circumstances may indicate that it is an emolument of the job. There is always a strong presumption that payments made by an employer to an employee in connection with his job is indeed a taxable emolument.

---

96. *ibid.* at 263. Similarly, *Taylor v. Provan* [1975] A.C. 194.
97. [1970] A.C. 244.
98. *Perrons v. Spackman* [1981] 1 W.L.R. 1411.

Personal gifts

Exceptionally, the payment may be a pure gift to the employee in recognition of his past services rather than in payment for them. Where the payment is made to a number of employees, the burden of demonstrating that it is in the nature of a gift is particularly difficult. In *Mulvey v. Coffey*,[99] where a lump sum was paid to the President of University College Dublin on his retirement from that office, it was held that the payment was not taxable. The taxpayer had held that office for more than 30 years and, when he was retiring, the Governing Body of the College resolved to pay him £1,000 "on account of a great number of services unrewarded, as expressed in a labour of lengthened overtime work" during many years. It was held that there was evidence on which the Special Commissioners could have concluded that this sum was not an emolument.

Compensation for loss of rights

Exceptionally, the payment may be by way of compensation for the loss of some rights occurring when the job came to an end or its nature was drastically changed. It is often very difficult to determine the character of a payment to a holder of an office when his tenure of the office is determined or the terms on which he holds it were altered. In each case the question is whether, on the facts of the case, the lump sum paid is in the nature of remuneration or profits in respect of the office or is in the nature of a sum paid in consideration of the surrender by the recipient of his rights in respect of the office. Thus, damages paid for wrongful dismissal were held in *Glover v. B.L.N. Ltd. (No. 2)*[100] not to be emoluments. According to Kenny J., in such an action, "the damages are not an award of the remuneration which would have been earned: they are intended to compensate the plaintiff because he has not been allowed to earn it".[101] In *Henley v. Murray*,[102] the managing director of a company was asked to resign and was then paid a sum described as "compensation for loss of office." This was held not to be a taxable emolument because it was not a payment to him under his contract but instead compensation for abrogating that contract. Here the "contract itself goes altogether and some sum becomes payable for the consideration of the total abandonment of all the contractual rights which the other party had under the contract".[103] A feature of this case is that the lump sum paid was the equivalent of what he would have earned had he worked out his normal notice period, but that was immaterial to the outcome.

For the same reason, a payment made in settlement of a dispute about the lawfulness of a dismissal is not an emolument.[104] A payment made by an employer to his employee in the course of his employment in commutation of his pension rights is not an emolument.[105] Statutory redundancy payments are designated as

---

99. [1942] I.R. 277.
100. [1973] I.R. 432.
101. *ibid.* at 438.
102. [1950] 1 All E.R. 908.
103. *ibid.* at 909.
104. *Du Cross v. Ryall* (1935) 19 T.C. 444.
105. *Tilley v. Wales* [1943] A.C. 386.

tax free.[106] And in *Mairs v. Haughey*[107] it was held that payments made to employees, in return for them waiving non-statutory enhanced redundancy pay entitlements, were not emoluments; rather, those entitlements were payments to compensate the employees for not being able to receive emoluments from their employment.

A case which has caused some difficulty is *Hunter v. Dewhurst*,[108] involving the chairman of a company, the articles of association of which provided that its directors should be paid "compensation for loss of office" on their retiring after serving for at least five years. If the taxpayer simply retired and was then paid the compensation, that would have been taxable.[109] Instead, he had intended retiring but was persuaded to stay on. Again, if he was only paid an inducement to remain on with the company, that sum would have been taxable.[110] But the arrangement made here was that his work load would be lightened and his fees correspondingly reduced; he would also forego all claims to "compensation" under the terms of the articles of association, in return for which he was paid a substantial lump sum. By a bare majority, it was held that this sum was not an emolument. It was not received under the employment contract itself but was paid to obtain a release from a contingent liability under that contract.

Golden handshakes

The expression "golden handshake" commonly refers to many types of payments made when a person's job has come to an end; such payments are often made to company directors. As was demonstrated in *Mulvey v. Coffey*,[111] occasionally these payments are not taxable as emoluments of the office. However, the tax net was extended by section 123 of the Taxes Consolidation Act 1997 to catch most kinds of termination payments; at the same time, the actual tax liabilities can be reduced by spreading out those payments over a period of years. These rules do not apply to the following kinds of payments. One is where the office or employment came to an end by virtue of the holder's death, injury or disability.[112] Another is payments where the job involved a proportion of foreign service.[113] Special provisions exist for payments made for restrictive covenants.[114]

Subject to these exceptions, the payments which are rendered taxable by section 123 are as follows:

> "any payment (not otherwise chargeable to income tax) which is made, whether in pursuance of any legal obligation or not, either directly or indirectly in consideration or in consequence of, or otherwise in connection with, the termination of the holding of the office or employment or any change in its functions or emoluments, including any payment in commuta-

---

[106.] Taxes Consolidation Act 1997, s.203.
[107.] [1994] 1 A.C. 303.
[108.] (1932) 16 T.C. 605.
[109.] *Henry v. Foster* (1931) 16 T.C. 605.
[110.] *Cameron v. Prendergast* [1940] A.C. 549.
[111.] [1942] I.R. 277.
[112.] Taxes Consolidation Act 1997, s. 201(2)(a) and *O'Shea v. Mulqueen* [1995] 1 I.R. 514.
[113.] *ibid.* s. 201(4).
[114.] *ibid.* s. 127.

tion of annual or periodic payments (whether chargeable to tax or not) which would otherwise have been made as aforesaid."[115]

The kind of payments which are caught by this section include personal gifts or testimonials received when leaving a job; compensation paid when being dismissed from a job or where the job was otherwise terminated; salary in lieu of notice and damages for breach of the employment contract; redundancy payments (in excess of the statutory ceiling); a lump sum commuting pension rights. It does not matter if the payment is voluntary or is by legal obligation, or was made directly or indirectly; that it was paid to, or to the order of, the employee's spouse, relative or dependent;[116] that the consideration was in kind and not in cash. The reference to a payment connected with a "change of functions or emoluments" covers situations like in *Hunter v. Dewhurst*,[117] where there was not a complete termination of the employment. But it is doubtful if payments like those made in *Hochstrasser v. Mayes*,[118] to cover losses on the disposal of a house when changing job location, is really in connection with a change of function. It would seem that inducement payments which are not emoluments, like the payment to the amateur rugby footballer for becoming a professional,[119] are not connected with a change of function. There are no reported authorities so far on the meaning of this expression.

The amount of tax which is payable in respect of payments that fall within section 123 is significantly less than what would be paid if they were emoluments. Although they are deemed to be emoluments, the first £8,000 (sometimes less or more) is tax free and what is called "top slicing relief" enables the payments to be spread over several years and in effect taxed at the average rate of tax paid over that period.[120] There are two related kinds of relief to this end, contained in the Third Schedule to the Income Tax Act, as amended in 1980 and again in 1990. Paragraph 6 of that Schedule provides a relief by way of reduction of the sums chargeable and paragraph 8 a relief by way of reduction of tax.

P.A.Y.E.

For over 40 years, employees and pensioners have had a system of withholding income tax at source. What is known as "pay as you earn", or P.A.Y.E. for short, was first introduced in the Finance Act 1959, and detailed rules regarding its operation were prescribed in the Income Tax (Employments) Regulations 1960.[121] At present the basis for P.A.Y.E. is sections 983-997 of the Taxes Consolidation Act 1997. The basic rule is laid down in section 985 that "On the making of any payment of any emoluments . . . income tax shall . . . be deducted

---

[115] s.123(1).

[116] s.123(3).

[117] (1932) 16 T.C. 605.

[118] [1960] A.C. 376.

[119] *Jarrold v. Boustead* [1964] 1 W.L.R. 1357.

[120] Taxes Consolidation Act 1997, s. 123. For a full account of these reliefs, see *Corrigan*, Vol 2, pp. 48 *et seq*.

[121] S.I. No. 28 of 1960, as amended.

or repaid by the person making the payment". And "emoluments", which are made subject to P.A.Y.E., are defined in section 983 as "anything assessable to income tax under Schedule E and references to payments of emoluments include references to payments on account of emoluments". The remaining sections on this question deal principally with making regulations in order to implement section 985 and related administrative matters, such as interest due, payment by way of stamps, recovery of sums deducted and priority in bankruptcy. How the system is administered is still governed mainly by the Regulations of 1960, which have been amended on several occasions.

P.A.Y.E. was adopted in order to relieve employees of the difficulty of having to pay all of their income tax at once at the end of the tax year. Unless they saved up to make this payment or could borrow for that purpose, it often was extremely difficult to raise the necessary money. What P.A.Y.E. does is to spread the tax payment across the entire year, so that all or almost all tax due will have been paid over by the time the fiscal year comes to an end. Every time an employee is paid remuneration in cash, a sum is deducted on account in respect of his prospective income tax liability. A commentator has described the system as "combin[ing] the expedient with the objectionable. It is a rough and ready system which garnishes taxpayers' incomes, sometimes for debts they do not owe but subject in this event to refund. . . . It is surprising that this withholding system, to which so strong objections may be raised on grounds of principle, has aroused so little comment. It has probably done more to increase the tax collecting power of central government than any other one tax measure in any time in history".[122]

The rules for collection are designed to ensure, so far as is reasonably possible, that the aggregate of deductions made during the year will approximate to the tax payable on the employee's Schedule E income. This is done through a method of tax free allowances, which spreads each employee's personal allowances and other deductions evenly through the year and by a set of P.A.Y.E. tax tables under which tax is deducted from the net taxable pay at a rate or rates estimated according to the employee's expected income for the year.

Income subject to P.A.Y.E.

Anything which is assessable to income tax under Schedule E is an emolument for these purposes, including payments on account. Foreign-source income which does not come within schedule E falls outside P.A.Y.E., although Irish residents in receipt of foreign earnings may choose to have their income tax dealt with under the P.A.Y.E. system. Benefits in kind often are taxable emoluments, but P.A.Y.E. is not directly deducted in respect of those benefits because they are not payments.

Impracticable to apply P.A.Y.E.

Where an employer or employee can convince the Revenue that the deduction of income tax in their case under P.A.Y.E. is "impracticable", they can be exonerated from the system. But this exemption only applies where the Revenue have notified the employer of the exemption. Exemptions of this kind are rarely given;

[122.] McGregor, 4 *Canadian Tax Journal* (1956) at 173.

one situation where an employer could be exempted is where he is a foreign resident and is paying remuneration outside the State.

Operating the system

How the P.A.Y.E. system operates can be summarised as follows.[123]

Every employer who makes any payments of emoluments to any employee is required to register as an employer. He is thereafter required to implement the P.A.Y.E. procedure in respect of all emoluments paid by him and to account monthly to the Collector General for all tax deducted from employees. An employer who fails to deduct any tax which should have been deducted from any payments of emoluments may be held directly liable for that tax, but there are some relieving provisions in certain cases. The employer is also required to make returns of employees and tax deducted at the end of each tax year.

Every employee should obtain a certificate of the tax free allowances which are deducted throughout each tax year from the emoluments paid to him to arrive at his net taxable pay for each pay period on which the income tax deductible (or repayable) by his employer is calculated. The certificate of tax free allowances also specifies which P.A.Y.E. tax table is to be applied. The total tax free allowances for any year are estimated as the total personal allowances and other reliefs due to the employee, but may be reduced by any of these allowances applicable to other employments or required to offset benefits in kind (see below) and sometimes other income.

These are tax tables designed to spread each employee's tax payable each year as equally as possible over the year and to collect the tax on his emoluments at the rate expected to be payable by him as estimated by reference to his probable taxable income from all sources. The tax table selected, as considered appropriate to the individual's circumstances, applies one main rate for the year on the emoluments paid up to the expected net taxable pay for the year, but with provision for the application of higher rates if the cumulative net taxable earnings should exceed the estimated amount used at the beginning of the year in determining the relevant tax table. The main tax rate is linked to the individual's expected highest rate for the year. A separate tax table allowance is included in the tax free allowances to adjust for the non-application of tax rate bands below the main tax rate used.

The employer deducts income tax computed at the appropriate P.A.Y.E. tax table rate as applied to each employee's cumulative taxable pay at the time of each payment of emoluments. "Taxable pay" is "gross pay" less the employee's contributions (if any) to an exempt approved pension scheme or to a statutory scheme and his tax free allowances. "Gross pay" is, in effect, all payments of emoluments subject to P.A.Y.E. before any deductions for P.R.S.I. contributions, pensions scheme contributions, etc.

Section 985 of the 1997 Act and the Regulations provide for the deduction of P.A.Y.E. on the "payment" of emoluments. A benefit in kind (including the amount taxable in respect of an employer's provided car or an employer-preferential loan) is not regarded as a payment for this purpose. Consequently, the

---

[123.] For a fuller account, see J. Ward, *Judge Irish Income Tax* (1999-2000 ed.) Chap. 11.1.

amount taxable in respect of any such benefit is not included in "gross pay" or "taxable pay" and tax is not, therefore, deducted directly on such benefits in kind. However, the inspector of taxes seeks where possible to bring such benefits indirectly within the P.A.Y.E. system by deducting them from the individual's tax free allowances. If he does not deal with them in this way, he is able to make direct assessments under Schedule E on the benefits in kind.

By contrast, if payments in respect of expenses taxable under section 117 of the 1997 Act are made in the form of a round sum allowance, that is a payment of emoluments to the employee and should be included in gross and taxable pay. Payments by the employer to the employee as a direct reimbursement of actual expenses incurred wholly, exclusively and necessarily by the employee in performing the duties of his employment are not, in practice, normally included in taxable pay subject to P.A.Y.E.

The employer normally uses a tax deduction card supplied by the inspector for each employee for calculating the P.A.Y.E. deduction (or repayment) for each pay period throughout the year. This card provides for the calculation of cumulative taxable pay (cumulative pay less cumulative tax free allowances) for each period. The application of the relevant tax table rate to the cumulative taxable pay produces the cumulative tax payable at the end of the period. The tax actually deductible by the employer for a given pay period (*e.g.* month ending August 5) is the excess of the cumulative tax payable at the end of that period over the corresponding figure of cumulative tax payable at the end of the previous period (*e.g.* month ending July 5). If the cumulative tax payable at the end of the previous period should exceed the cumulative tax payable at the end of the current period, the employer should repay the excess to the employee on paying his emoluments for the current period.

After the end of each tax year, the employee's position should be reviewed by reference to his total earnings (and any other income) as chargeable to tax for the year and, of course, he should be given full allowance for his final personal allowances and reliefs. If the total income tax deducted (less any repayments) under the P.A.Y.E. system during the year results in an excess of total income tax payable (and paid) by him over his final income tax liability for the year, the employee is entitled to be repaid the excess by the Collector General. If the total income tax paid under P.A.Y.E. (and in any other way) is less than the final income tax payable, the inspector may assess the tax underpaid directly on the employee. Alternatively, the inspector may recover any underpayment by reducing the employee's tax free allowances for one or more of the following tax years.

There is provision for the employer to deduct income tax through the emergency card procedure in any case where he has not received from the employee the necessary certificate of tax free allowances or, alternatively, an employment cessation certificate on form P45 from a previous employer. In that this emergency card procedure only gives the employee minimum tax free allowances for the first four weeks of a new employment (and no allowances thereafter until the necessary certificate is received), it is very important for all employees to ensure that they comply with the necessary formalities so that they can obtain their proper allowances as soon as possible. When the proper certificate is obtained, the employee is entitled to be repaid any excess tax suffered through the emergency procedure.

P.R.S.I. CONTRIBUTIONS AND LEVIES

The State social security system provides a variety of benefits for persons who are suffering financial distress in several ways, for instance, occupational injury benefit for those who were injured at work, disablement benefit for those who otherwise suffer from a disability, unemployment benefit, maternity allowance, pensions. The main benefits are contributory, in the sense that claimants for those benefits must have paid a specified number of contributions into the Social Welfare Fund. Other benefits are non-contributory. Most modern social security systems are based on a contribution principle, which renders them a form of social insurance. In return for making a certain number of contributions to a fund, employees are insured against several kinds of social risk, like injury at work, disability, unemployment, etc. Additionally, being a contributory to the social welfare system is one of the conditions of obtaining the lump sum redundancy payment[124] and the payments made by the Minister for Labour when a person's employer becomes insolvent.[125]

Many social welfare benefits are financed partly by contributions made by the employees affected, partly by their employers' contributions and any deficit in the fund is subvented by the State. Rebates paid to employers who have made redundancy payments are also financed in this way, as are the payments made to those whose employer became insolvent. Prior to 1990 there were four separate funds which financed payments to employees or their dependants — the Redundancy Fund, the Employers' Insolvency Fund, the Occupational Injuries Fund and the Social Insurance Fund. These have now been amalgamated into a single Social Insurance Fund. On top of the social insurance contributions, employees must also pay a 2 per cent health contribution to the Fund. The 1 per cent employment levy was abolished in 1999.[126]

Insured employees' earnings

Employers' and employees' social insurance contributions are based on each employee's earnings. The employee in question must be in insured employment, be over 16 years of age and under 66 years of age.[127] Subject to conditions, persons outside this category may make voluntary contributions to the Fund.[128] Those persons who are in insured employment are set out in Part I of the first Schedule to the Social Welfare (Consolidation) Act 1993, being principally all persons employed in the State under a contract of employment, out-workers, midwives, certain ministers of religion, managers of an employment office, share fishermen and practically everyone working in the public service. However, the Minister is empowered by regulation to exclude most of these groups from the insured employment category.[129] Workers who are not deemed to be in insured employment for these purposes are listed in Part II of that Schedule. In order to

---

[124.] Redundancy Payments Act 1967, s.4, as amended.
[125.] Protection of Employees (Employer's Insolvency) Act 1984, s.3.
[126.] Social Welfare Act 1999, s. 34.
[127.] Social Welfare (Consolidation) Act 1993, s.9.
[128.] *Ibid*, ss.21-24.
[129.] *ibid.*, ss.21-24.

encourage employment, an employer who takes on an additional full-time employee does not have to pay employer's P.R.S.I. for him during his first two years of employment, provided the net increase in the workforce is maintained throughout that period.[130] To qualify for this exception, that employee, if over 23 years of age, must have been on the unemployment register for over 13 weeks; alternatively, is under 23 and taking up employment for the first time, or is getting a one-parent family allowance, or is registered with the Natural Rehabilitation Board, or was on a training course for over 13 weeks with F.A.S., C.E.R.T. or Teagasc.

Social insurance contributions are calculated by reference to what are called "reckonable earnings". Those are taxable earnings derived from insurable employment; accordingly, the basis for the exactions are the earnings which are subject to P.A.Y.E. The full definition of the term is as follows: "emoluments derived from insurable employment or insurable (occupational injuries) employment to which [the Social Welfare (Consolidation) Act 1993 applies] (other than non-pecuniary emoluments) reduced by so much of the allowable contribution referred to in regulations 59 and 60 of the Income Tax (Employment) Regulations 1960 . . . as is deducted on payment of those emoluments".[131]

Reckonable earnings, as here defined, are also the main basis for health contributions but that impost also applies to what are called "reckonable emoluments". Reckonable emoluments effectively are all non-pecuniary Schedule E emoluments which are not reckonable earnings.

Operating the system

How P.R.S.I. contributions and the employment levy operate can be summarised as follows.[132] The main legislative provisions are sections 9-16 of the Social Welfare (Consolidation) Act 1993 (social welfare contributions) and sections 4-11 of the Health Contributions Act 1979 (health contributions). The principal regulations are the Social Welfare (Collection of Employment Contributions by the Collector General) Regulations 1979[133] and the Health Contributions Regulations 1979.[134]

Every employer who makes payments which are charged to tax under Schedule E is required to pay over P.R.S.I. contributions when he is remitting to the Collector General tax deducted under P.A.Y.E. Employers' contributions and employees' contributions must be paid over at that time. Failure to make these payments is an offence and the amount due may be recovered in civil proceedings brought by the Minister for Social Welfare. There are similar provisions for the health contributions.

Contributions are levied on all employees who have reckonable earnings. Ordinarily those are deducted from the remuneration and paid over by the employer at the prescribed intervals. In April 2001 the amount of this contribu-

---

[130.] *ibid.*, s.9(3).
[131.] Social Welfare (Collection of Employment Contributions by the Collector General) Regulations 1979, reg.4.
[132.] For a fuller account, see J. Ward, *Judge Irish Income Tax* (1999-2000 ed.) Chap. 11.2.
[133.] S.I. No. 77 of 1979.
[134.] S.I. No. 107 of 1979.

tion was 4 per cent of the reckonable earnings, up to a maximum of £28,250 per annum. In addition, the employee must pay a 2 per cent health contribution without any upper limit.

Employers with employees in insurable employment must pay employers' contributions in respect of each of those employees. Those must be paid from the employer's own resources; it is an offence to deduct the sum from his employees' earnings.[135] In April 2001 the amount payable was 8.5 per cent of reckonable earnings under £280 per week or 12 per cent if earnings exceed that sum.

Originally fixed at 1 per cent, since 1987 the health contribution payable in respect of employees is 2 per cent of their reckonable income, regardless of how much they are earning. For the purpose of their collection and recovery, the sum due is deemed to be an employment contribution to be deducted from earnings.

[135.] Social Welfare Consolidation Act 1993, s. 10(5).

CHAPTER 15

OCCUPATIONAL PENSIONS

Many full time jobs today are pensionable in the sense that provision is made by employers to pay their employees a pension on their retirement from work.[1] In the past it was primarily public sector employments which were pensionable and one of the main attractions of working in the public service was the security of statutory pension arrangements.[2] More recently, however, occupational pensions have spread into the private sector. As well as private pensions arrangements, retired workers may also be entitled to pensions under the Social Welfare Acts.[3]

Although Part II of the Pensions 1990 Act established the Pensions Board to monitor pension schemes and to publish codes of practice regarding their administration, and lays down rules regarding funding, preservation of benefits, disclosure of information and equal treatment, the exact nature and terms of any particular pension scheme is left largely to be determined by the employers and employees affected. Different industries and different types of company and workforces may require somewhat distinctive pension arrangements. Questions to be decided when a company is adopting a pension scheme include, for example, which employees can be members of the scheme, what conditions must be met to become a member of a scheme and is membership to be entirely voluntary; shall the employer pay all the contributions or must the employees also pay contributions, and should provision be made for additional voluntary contributions; what benefits are to be paid under the scheme and how are the amounts of pensions to be determined; and what is to happen where members leave the scheme before they reach the prescribed retirement age.

Occupational pension schemes are usually based on a trust deed, whereby the employer undertakes to pay specified contributions towards a pension fund. When the fund's assets are held in trust, they are insulated from the employer's creditors in the event that he becomes insolvent. A trust deed will provide for the appointment of trustees of the fund and set out their obligations with regard to it, like the investment policy or criteria. The trustees then either manage the fund or appoint a committee of management for that purpose. Almost invariably one or more representatives of the employer will be appointed as fund trustees; there may also be trustees chosen by or on behalf of the employees and indeed by members who are in receipt of pensions. Usually, the provisions and rules of these schemes are summarised in booklets that are given to all scheme members. Insofar as such documents do not impose binding obligations on employers, ordi-

---

[1.] See generally, R. Nobles, *Pensions, Employment and the Law* (1993) and K. Finucane & B. Buggy, *Irish Pensions Law and Practice* (1996).

[2.] See generally, Finucane & Buggy, *supra*, Chap.8.

[3.] Social Welfare Consolidation Act 1993, Part II, Chaps. 12-16 (social insurance) and Part III Chaps. 4-6 (social assistance).

narily employers will be estopped from taking action contrary to what a booklet of this nature indicates that the employer will take.

Since 1921 approved pension schemes have enjoyed certain tax reliefs, on the basis that those schemes represented employees' savings, the majority of whom would at that time not pay tax. Prior to 1990, the conditions for obtaining Revenue approval for such schemes was practically the only way that pensions were subject to State regulation. These fiscal advantages are now provided for in sections 770-780 of the Taxes Consolidation Act 1997. Employers' and employees' contributions are deductible expenses against income tax[4] and neither income tax nor capital gains tax are charged on the income or gains accruing to the fund. But the benefits paid by the scheme become taxable emoluments.

Among the principal conditions for obtaining Revenue approval are:[5] that the employer must contribute to the fund; the beneficiaries are confined to his employees, along with their widows, widowers, children, dependants and personal representatives; employees' contributions cannot be repaid; the retirement age to qualify for a pension shall not be under 60 or over 70 years of age; the maximum benefit being 1/60th of final remuneration for each year of service, not to exceed 40 years. Unlike the position that obtained in Britain for some years,[6] there is no requirement that any surplus on a winding up be repaid to the employer. In an appropriate case the Revenue will give approval to a scheme which does not meet all the prescribed requirements; they have a discretion to sanction schemes which they consider acceptable albeit not satisfying all of these conditions. For this purpose they have published guidelines.

FUNDING

Funding pension schemes is concerned with how ultimate payment of the benefits in question is to be financed. A method which became common in France after the Second World War is the *répartition* or "unfunded" system; subject to the accumulation of very modest sums to cover demographic factors, the whole of any one year's contributions is paid out in benefit in that year to retired members. Existing employed members finance the pensions presently being paid, in the anticipation that, when they in turn become pensioners, their successors will continue contributing to the scheme. But schemes like this are risky when they do not cover a substantial number of employees. Most public sector systems in the State are financed in this "pay as you go" manner.

In the private sector in this country and in Britain the more common form of funding is to make advance provision, spread over the working life of a member, for benefits which it is intended to pay him on retirement. An infinite variety of ways exist for arranging the incidence of contributions during a working life. A scheme may be "non-contributory", meaning that it is funded entirely by payments from the employer; or it may be "contributory", meaning that it is partly funded by contributions deducted from the members' remuneration. Provision

---

4. Overruling *Bruce v. Hatton* [1922] 2 K.B. 206.
5. s.772.
6. Finance Act 1970 (UK).

may be made for members making voluntary contributions in addition to such contributions as they may be obliged to make. The minimum requirement should be that, at any given time, sufficient assets exist in the fund to ensure that, if the fund were terminated there and then, pensions could be provided for the remainder of the lives of those who are already retired, together with deferred pensions for existing members based on the duration of their service and their earnings up to that date.

The other side of the funding coin is the liabilities being incurred and the basis for determining the amount of benefits payable to pensioners. Schemes where the benefits are calculated by reference to the amount of contributions paid by or on behalf of an employee are known as "defined contribution" or "money purchase" schemes. In these, the accumulated contributions, plus the return on investments, are used to purchase an annuity. Alternatively, benefits in schemes are based by reference to the employees' salary, either final salary or average salary, or some other permutation. These are called "defined benefit" schemes. At present the dominant form of occupational pension scheme is "final salary" schemes, where benefits are calculated by reference to the salary the member had when or shortly before he took retirement; usually 1/60th of that sum for each year up to 40 years of service, which is the maximum that the Revenue will permit.

Funded pension schemes operate on the assumption that the contributions collected will accumulate to such extent that it will be possible to pay all of the promised benefits when they fall due. Subject to retaining an appropriate sum in order to ensure liquidity, contributions are used to purchase investments that, in the course of time, will yield income and capital gains. Accumulation of funds will depend on the success of the fund's investment policy; badly-advised investments will result in deficits, sound investments may very well give rise to a surplus in the fund. And the more successful the investments are, the less the employer will have to contribute in order to finance the "balance of cost" of the pensions. In the majority of schemes, investment simply consists in paying the contributions over to an insurance company; the test of that investment is measuring the performance of that company relative to other insurers.

Under the terms of pension trust deeds, investment is almost invariably the responsibility of the trustees, is usually expressed in quite wide terms and generally authorises delegating investment decisions to professional fund managers. On several occasions, decisions about where to invest fund assets have been the subject of litigation, the most controversial questions being those of "social investment" and "self-investment".

Usually, it is the fund's actuary who determines the overall shape of funding. He decides the employer's contribution rate, i.e. the percentage of overall remuneration that must be paid into the scheme. In "defined contribution" schemes, no particular expertise is required to determine how much should be paid to the fund, as it will be a fixed percentage of the members' salaries. Schemes usually entitle employers to cease making contributions on giving specified notice to that effect, frequently six months' notice. Thus all employers' contributions in these schemes are voluntary payments where, six months previously, they decided to continue with the scheme. Consequently, if an employer in such a scheme is not prepared to make higher contributions, as recommended by the actuary, he can give notice and thereby terminate his liability to the trustees.

Funding a "final salary" scheme raises two principal considerations that the actuary must address. Because the future benefits of current members are fixed by reference to salaries, which ordinarily increase over time and with inflation, a critical issue is the rate of return on investments relative to inflation, often referred to as the "real rate of return". Secondly, the cost of securing a pension raises steadily during the employee's period of service, because contributions made early in his career can be invested for much longer than those made near the end of his career. Thus, the cost of funding the current workforce's benefits will increase steadily during their working lifetime and, unless substantial numbers of new members join the scheme, contributions to it will need to be increased.

Where a pension fund is in substantial surplus, questions arise about what should be done about the surplus: for instance, whether or to what extent should benefits be increased or, alternatively, should there be a "contribution holiday" or, indeed, whether some of the surplus should be paid back to the employer.[7] Another source of controversy is how should the fund be divided where one or more of the companies that participate in the scheme has been sold.[8]

One of the objectives of the Pensions Act 1990, is to ensure that occupational pension schemes, which are not based on defined contributions, are properly funded. Section 43 of the 1990 Act sets out a "funding standard" for such schemes: the scheme's resources must be sufficient that, if it were wound up, its liabilities and the expenses of the dissolution would be covered. Determining whether a scheme meets the standard is a matter for investigation and assessment by an actuary.

Every three and a half years, the scheme's trustees are required to submit to the Pensions Board an actuarial funding certificate.[9] This is to be based on the findings of the scheme's actuary and will state whether or not the funding standard is being met. In the event of that standard not being satisfied, the trustees are required to draw up a funding proposal, to be submitted to the Board, which is designed to ensure that the scheme is fully funded before the next certification period comes about. Unless an adequate proposal has been submitted to them, the Board are empowered to direct the trustees to reduce the benefits which would be payable under the scheme, in such manner that the funding standard would be satisfied. By this means, it is expected that any deficiencies which may occur in the scheme will be overcome. But the 1990 Act does not contain provisions regarding how any surplus which may arise in the fund should or should not be disposed of.

EMPLOYERS

Employers play a vital role in these schemes; it is their contributions which fund them and, in contributory schemes, they pay the wages from which employees' contributions are deducted. A key role is also played by employers in establishing schemes; especially in non-unionised jobs, the employer is virtually free to dic-

7.   *e.g. Edge* v. *Pensions Ombudsman* [2000] Chap. 602.
8.   *e.g. Stanard* v. *Fisons Pension Trust* [1990] P.L.R. 179.
9.   ss.42 and 43.

tate all the terms and conditions of the scheme. Frequently, employers are empowered to appoint and to remove all or any of the trustees.[10] Often employers are empowered to determine how the surplus or part of it shall be allocated. Usually employers are entitled to terminate their liability to make contributions to the scheme by giving specified notice to the trustees to that effect. Some major decisions regarding these schemes must be taken jointly by employers and the trustees.

Employees' rights or entitlements vis-à-vis pension schemes do not ordinarily arise under contract; instead, they derive from being beneficiaries of a trust[11] and any rights that they indirectly have against their employer are enforced by the scheme's trustees. One of the requirements for Revenue approval of such schemes is that all employees are given written particulars of their scheme's essential features[12] and among the written particulars that must be given to employees, within the Terms of Employment (Information) Act 1994, are any terms and conditions of employment relating to pensions and pension schemes.[13] The annual accounts of registered companies must contain specified details of their occupational pension schemes.[14]

Under the Pensions Act 1990, it is the trustees and not the employer who are obliged to furnish details of the scheme to members and to other interested parties.[15] And in *Outram v. Academy Plastics Ltd.*[16] it was held that an employer who also was a trustee of its pension scheme was not legally obliged *qua* employer to advise its employees regarding that scheme; such a duty was not inherent in the employment contract and, it was held, did not arise in the law of tort. There the plaintiff was a widow of a former scheme member, who ceased membership after ten years when he resigned but did not re-join when he was re-employed. Had he rejoined, he would have been entitled to an enhanced pension when later he resigned due to ill health. Similarly, in *University of Nottingham* v. *Eyett*,[17] the plaintiff sought clarification from his employer about what his pension would be if he took early retirement on reaching 60 years of age in 1994; he was given the correct information but was not told that his pension would be increased if he retired on the earliest date after July 31, 1994. It was held that his employer was under no positive obligation to advise him on how best to exercise valuable rights under his contract, such as a benefit from deferring the date he retires. Exceptional circumstances can arise, however, where it will be an implied term of an employment contract that the employer is obliged to inform employees of changes in the pension scheme, where possession of that information is highly material to decisions the employees may make. Thus where a scheme was amended to permit members, for a 12 month period, to purchase additional vol-

---

10. But many schemes now must have some trustees chosen by the members: Pensions Act 1990, s.62 and Occupational Pension Schemes (Member Participation in the Selection of Persons for Appointment as Trustees) (No.2) Regs.1993, S.I. No. 399 of 1993.
11. *Bradstock Trustee Services Ltd. v. Nabarro Nathanson* [1995] 1 W.L.R. 1405.
12. Taxes Consolidation Act 1997, s.772(2)(b).
13. s.3(1)(k)(ii).
14. Companies (Amendment) Act 1986, schedule - provisions for liabilities and charges, 1.
15. s.28(1).
16. [2001] I.C.R. 367.
17. [1999] I.C.R. 721.

untary contributions but several of those members were never appraised of that change, it was held that their employer had contravened the implied term that he would take reasonable steps to notify them of such change.[18]

Except on the question of appointing trustees (where such power was conferred on the employer), it used to be thought that employers were entirely free to canvass their own interests when making decisions in the context of pension schemes. That no longer is the case; they now are required to act in good faith in this regard and, in exceptional circumstances (*e.g.* appointing trustees), they will be subject to the same fiduciary standards as apply to scheme trustees. Where the employer is the sole trustee or is one of the trustees, the usual fiduciary standards apply to its decisions and actions in that capacity.

It was held in *Imperial Group Pension Trust Ltd. v. Imperial Tobacco Ltd*[19] that powers of decision exerciseable by employers under pension schemes cannot be used for an improper purpose and must be referable to the financial and administrative interests of the scheme. In other words, employers cannot decide on one particular course of action just because it suits them. The reason for this is the hybrid nature of pension schemes; as Browne-Wilkinson VC explained:

> "Pension scheme trusts are of quite a different nature to traditional trusts
> .... Pension benefits are part of the consideration which an employee
> receives in return for the rendering of his services. In many cases . . . mem-
> bership of the pension scheme is a requirement of employment. In contribu-
> tory schemes . . . the employee is himself bound to pay his or her
> contributions. Beneficiaries of the scheme, the members, far from being vol-
> unteers have given valuable consideration. The company employer is not
> conferring a bounty."[20]

Accordingly, the "good faith" obligation, which underlies the employment relationship,[21] is carried over to pension schemes, and employers must act in good faith when they exercise any powers they possess under these schemes. Those powers are "subject to the implied limitation that the[y] shall not be exercised so as to destroy or seriously damage the relationship of confidence and trust between the company and its employees and former employees."[22]

That case concerned the role of an employer in the amendment of a scheme; often the power to amend is exerciseable jointly by the employer and the trustees. When a company is taken over, often the new owners attempt to acquire the surplus in the company's pension fund in order to help finance the acquisition. For that reason, pension fund rules regarding the surplus are often changed when a take-over bid is made, in order to close any further access to the surplus and thereby deter the bidder; this is one of the so-called "poison pills". In the *Imperial Tobacco* case, an amendment of that nature had been made but it failed to defeat the take-over. A new pension scheme was then established by the new owners for the company's new employees and proposals were made by the com-

---

[18.] *Scally v. Southern Health & Social Services Board* [1992] 1 A.C. 294.
[19.] [1991] 1 W.L.R. 589.
[20.] *ibid.* at p. 597.
[21.] see *ante* pp. 48-49.
[22.] [1991] 1 W.L.R. at p. 598.

pany to merge that scheme with the old one. One of the incentives being offered was that the new scheme provided for higher benefits. Although the old scheme was in a financial position to fund equally higher benefits, the employer indicated that it would never consent to make the amendments to the scheme which were necessary to permit payment of those higher benefits from the large surplus. However, it was held that the employer was exercising this veto unlawfully. The employer's power under the scheme, to give or withhold consent to amendments, was not untrammelled and could not be used for a clearly improper purpose, such as to put pressure on members to abandon their existing rights and to transfer to a scheme which provided for higher benefits but which, if wound up, vested the entire surplus in the employer. Under the old scheme, the members got the entire surplus on a dissolution.

An example of where a discretion conferred on the employer in that capacity was held to be a fiduciary power is *Mettoy Pension Trusts* v. *Evans*,[23] which concerned the division of a very substantial surplus in a scheme that was being wound up on the employer going into liquidation. One of the scheme's rules, adopted ten years earlier, gave the employer a general discretion to increase benefits to members; previously that discretion had vested in the trustees. Unless that power were characterised as fiduciary, it would be no more than a "pointless assertion" because all it would mean is that the employer "is free to make gifts to those beneficiaries out of property of which it is the absolute beneficial owner".[24] From the scheme members' point of view, a discretion in such terms would be entirely illusory. For instance, if the employer were taken over, the new owners would be free to appropriate the entire surplus for themselves, thereby partly funding their acquisition. Consequently, this power must be regarded as fiduciary and, since the company was being wound up, it could not be exercised by the receiver of the company's assets or its liquidator, on account of the conflict of interests that would confront him.

TRUSTEES

Overall responsibility for the pension fund and its administration will be conferred on trustees. Their principal function has been described as "to maintain a balance between assets and liabilities valued on that actuarial basis; so that, so far as the future can be foreseen, they will be in a position to provide pensions and other benefits in accordance with the rules throughout the life of the scheme. That task is to be performed by setting appropriate levels for employers' and members' contributions. If that task could be performed with perfect foresight there would be no surpluses and no deficits. But, because the task has to be performed in the real world, surpluses and deficits are bound to arise from time to time and prudent trustees will aim to ensure that the likelihood of surplus outweighs the risk of deficit."[25] Their rights and duties are based on the terms of the

---

[23.] [1990] 1 W.L.R. 1587.

[24.] *ibid.* at p.1615.

[25.] *Edge v. Pensions Ombudsman* [2000] Ch. 602 at p.623.

trust deed, the general principles of the law regarding trustees[26] and Part VI of the Pensions Act 1990.

The contention that the general law of trusts does not apply to pension fund trustees was rejected in *Cowan* v. *Scargill*,[27] a case which concerned what investment policy the National Union of Mineworkers' pension fund should follow. Megarry V.C., could:

> "see no reason for holding that different principles apply to pension fund trusts from those which apply to other trusts. Of course, there are many provisions in pension schemes which are not to be found in private trusts, and to these the general law of trusts will be subordinated. But subject to that, I think that the trusts of pension funds are subject to the same rules as other trusts. The large size of pension funds emphasises the need for diversification, rather than lessening it, and the fact that much of the fund has been contributed by members of the scheme seems to me to make it even more important that the trustees should exercise their powers in the best interests of the beneficiaries. In a private trust, most, if not all, of the beneficiaries are the recipients of the bounty of the settlor, whereas under the trusts of a pension fund many (though not all) of the beneficiaries are those who, as members, contributed to the funds so that in due time they would receive pensions. It is thus all the more important that the interests of the beneficiaries should be paramount, so that they may receive the benefits which in part they have paid for."[28]

This, however, may be overstating the true legal position somewhat. A strong argument could be made that, as a general principle, pension schemes are different in vital respects from family trusts and wills. The latter are funded by the original settlor by way of gift, whereas pension schemes are a form of deferred remuneration which have been established in trust form, often in order to secure tax advantages for approved schemes. Moreover, in many of these schemes, the beneficiaries (employees who ultimately will become pensioners) contribute directly to fund their benefits. Unlike the usual private trust, the rules of pension schemes are often incorporated, wholly or in part, into their beneficiaries' employment contracts; the members have enforceable contractual rights to participate in the fund in various ways. Given the very large sums that may be tied up in pension funds and the large number of potential beneficiaries, the limited scope of private trust law and that pension trust arrangements have a substantial contractual element, it may perhaps be a mistake to apply rigidly traditional trust law rules. In the *Scargill* case, the fund's trustees there sacked their lawyers and the case was argued by the N.U.M.'s president, who was not a lawyer, on mainly ideological grounds. If the arguments had focused more on legal principles and rules, it is possible that Megarry J. might have modified the analysis stated above.

[26.] See, generally, H. Delany, *Equity and the Law of Trusts in Ireland* (2 ed. 1999).

[27.] [1985] Chap. 270.

[28.] *ibid.* at p.290.

Appointment and removal

Usually, the trustees are individuals who are appointed and removable in accordance with the terms of the trust deed. Occasionally instead, the trustees may be either an outside trust corporation, which specialises in acting as a trustee in various contexts, or an "in-house" trust company which is specially incorporated for this purpose. The in-house company enables greater flexibility in managing the fund, its directors being in effect the trustees. Except where the trust deed provides to the contrary, the surviving trustees or trustee, or their personal representatives, possess a power under s.10 of the Trustee Act 1893, to appoint new trustees. Sections 23 and 25 of that Act empower the High Court to replace a trustee and to appoint additional trustees. The Court also has an inherent jurisdiction to remove a trustee where that is necessary for the proper execution of the trust.

These powers are now supplemented by powers under the Pensions Act 1990, which apply regardless of any contrary stipulation in the trust deed. Where there are no trustees or where the trustees cannot be found, the Pensions Board can intervene and appoint a new trustee or new trustees.[29] Where one or more trustees failed to carry out their legal duties, whether under the terms of the trust deed or under the general principles of law or the 1990 Act, or where they are acting in such a way as jeopardises the rights or interests of the members in the scheme, the High Court is empowered to remove those trustees and to appoint replacements.[30] Provision also is made for suspending one or more trustees pending investigation by the Board or the outcome of litigation.[31]

Powers and duties

Section 59 of the 1990 Act sets out the obligations of pension scheme trustees in general terms:

"Without prejudice to the duties of trustees generally and in addition to complying with the other requirements of this Act, the duties of trustees of [pension] schemes shall include the following:

(a) to ensure, in so far as is reasonable, that the contributions payable by the employer and the members of the scheme, where appropriate, are received;

(b) to provide for the proper investment of the resources of the scheme in accordance with the rules of the scheme;

(c) where appropriate, to make arrangements for the payment of the benefits as provided for under the rules of the scheme as they become due;

(d) to ensure that the proper membership and financial records are kept."

---

29. s.64.
30. s.63.
31. s.63A.

Among the other main duties imposed on trustees by the 1990 Act is ensuring that the pension scheme is registered with the Pensions Board.[32] The trustees must supply information on the following matters to the members of the fund and to some others: the scheme's constitution and its administration and finances, the rights and obligations that arise or may arise under the scheme, and such other relevant matters as were prescribed in regulations adopted in 1991.[33] As well as disclosure to members and prospective members, that information must be provided to those persons' spouses, to persons who are within the scope of the scheme and who qualify or prospectively qualify for its benefits, and to any licensed trade union which represents members of the scheme.[34]

The trustees must arrange to have the fund's accounts audited periodically[35] and also to have the scheme's assets and liabilities valued by an actuary.[36] They must prepare an annual report on the scheme in the form prescribed by the Minister.[37] They have certain duties with regard to the funding standard and the preservation of benefits,[38] as indicated below. Several powers and duties will be laid down in the trust deed, which most likely will follow a standard format.

Although trustees generally are not obliged to furnish beneficiaries with reasons for their decisions (except of course where the trust deed stipulates otherwise), that may not be the case with occupational pension fund trustees.

Being fiduciary agents, pension fund trustees are subject to the exacting fiduciary duties imposed by the principles of equity.[39] Except where provision to do so is made, they are not entitled to any remuneration for their services; they are not allowed to deal in or to purchase property belonging to the trust; they must not permit themselves to get into a situation where a substantial conflict exists or could very well exist between their own personal interests and the interests of the beneficiaries.[40] Trust powers should not be used for any personal advantage. And as it was put in the *Scargill* case, they must: "exercise their powers in the best interests of the present and future beneficiaries of the trust, holding the scales impartially between different classes of beneficiaries. . . . They must of course obey the law; but subject to that they must put the interests of their beneficiaries first. When the purpose of the trust is to provide financial benefits for the beneficiaries, as is usually the case, the best interests of the beneficiaries are normally their best financial interests."[41]

Judicial Review

In 1998-99 Scott V.C. and the English Court of Appeal endorsed the principle that fund trustees are entitled to a considerable amount of leeway in the manner

[32.] s.60.
[33.] s.54(1) and Occupational Pensions (Disclosure of Information) Regs. 1991, S.I. No. 215.
[34.] *ibid.*
[35.] s.56.
[36.] *ibid.*
[37.] s.55.
[38.] Parts III and IV.
[39.] See, generally, *Delany, supra* n.26, pp.387 *et seq.*
[40.] *Re Drexel Burnham Lambert U.K. Pension Plan* [1995] 1 W.L.R. 32.
[41.] *Cowan v. Scargill* [1985] Ch. 270 pp.286-287.

in which they exercise their discretionary powers; that the courts should not ordinarily intervene in such decisions simply because, if the decision had been one for the court to take, it would have decided differently; that on account of the composition of fund trustees, representing the employer and existing employees, some conflict of interests often is inevitable and has to be tolerated. The appropriate standard of review of the merits of any such decision was held to resemble the well-known *Wednesbury* principle in administrative law concerning judicial review of decisions of public bodies; what is referred to in Ireland as the "Stardust" principle.

In *Edge v. Pensions Ombudsman*,[42] the court considered what should be done with a large surplus in the fund that, if not reduced considerably, put the scheme in jeopardy of losing its tax exempt status. The appeal judges considered endorsed the following approach to reviewing these and similar questions:

> "(a) trustees must ask themselves the correct questions; (b) they must direct themselves correctly in law, in particular they must adopt a correct construction of the pension fund rules; and (c) they must not arrive at a perverse decision, i.e., a decision at which no reasonable body of trustees could arrive, and they must take into account all relevant but no irrelevant factors. The judge held that, if the trustees arrived at their decision acting within those limits, their decision could not be overturned by the courts."[43]

There, the trustees had decided to deal with the surplus by reducing both the employers' and the members' contributions, and also to increase benefits for members in service, but not to grant any additional benefits to ex-members who were drawing their pensions. It was contended that, by not giving those former members any share of the surplus, the trustees had contravened their obligation to act impartiality. On the general question of that duty, Scott V.C. asked:

> "What is 'undue partiality'? The trustees are entitled to be partial. They are entitled to exclude some beneficiaries from particular benefits and to prefer others. If what is meant by 'undue partiality' is that the trustees have taken into account irrelevant or improper or irrational factors, their exercise of discretion may well be flawed. But it is not flawed simply because someone else, whether or not a judge, regards their partiality as 'undue'. It is the trustees' discretion that is to be exercised. Except in a case in which the discretion has been surrendered to the court, it is not for a judge to exercise the discretion. The judge may disagree with the manner in which trustees have exercised their discretion but, unless they can be seen to have taken into account irrelevant, improper or irrational factors, or unless their decision can be said to be one that no reasonable body of trustees properly directing themselves could have reached the judge cannot interfere. In particular, he cannot interfere simply on the ground that the particularly showed to the preferred beneficiaries was in his opinion undue ....
>
> Neither a duty to act impartially nor a duty to act in the best interest of all the beneficiaries describes, in my judgment, the nature of the duty on the

---

42. [2000] Ch. 602.
43. *ibid.* p.628.

trustees when considering what steps to take to deal with the surplus. They had a discretionary power to make amendments to the rules in order to provide additional benefits to members, whether pensioners or still in service. It was within their discretion to provide benefits to members in service to the exclusion of members no longer in service. They certainly had a duty to exercise their discretionary power honestly and for the purposes for which the power was given and not so as to accomplish any ulterior purposes. But they were the judges of whether or not their exercise of the power was fair as between the benefited beneficiaries and other beneficiaries. Their exercise of the discretionary power cannot be set aside simply because a judge, whether the Pensions Ombudsman or any other species judge, thinks it was not fair."[44]

Another of the contentions there was that, because 18 of the 20 trustees were appointees of the employer and of the existing members, the decision to deal with the surplus in the manner adopted, that excluded the non-members, contravened the rule against trustees' conflicts of interests, i.e. that trustees should avoid any conflict between their own personal interests and the interests of their beneficiaries. But that argument ignored the fact that, under the very terms of the scheme there, the employer appointed some of the trustees, the employees selected another nine, there were two "closed fund" trustees and no provision had been made in the trust deed for the pensioners to appoint any trustees. In those circumstances, the traditional "self-dealing" rule could not be applied so hard and fast as to in effect require the trustees to invariably forfeit what may otherwise be a benefit to the constituency they represent or at least, if that constituency is to so benefit, comparable benefits should be afforded to the constituency which does not have representation in the trustees. As explained by the appeal judges:

> "it must have been obvious, at the time when the scheme was established, that the trustees would need, from time to time, to take decisions which required them to arrive at a balance between the interests of the employers (as contributors), the members in service (as contributors and as potential beneficiaries) and the pensioners. It is inevitable that such decisions will be perceived by some to favour one interest at the expense of another. But it could not have been intended that, if and when the validity of any particular decision reached by the trustees as a body was under challenge, the question 'on whom does the onus of proving that the decision was reached on a proper basis fall' would depend on whether the decision was said to favour the employers, the members in service or the pensioners."[45]

Investment

The power of investment is also governed by the Trustee (Authorised Investments) Act 1958, which lays down the types of securities in which trust funds may be invested. But the trust deed may confer an even more extensive investment power. In *Cowan v. Scargill*,[46] regarding the investment policy of the

---

44. *ibid.* at pp.618-619.
45. *ibid.* at p.632.
46. [1985] Ch. 270.

National Union of Miners' pension fund, it was held that some of the trustees had acted improperly by insisting that there should be no investment in industries which competed with coal and that investment outside of the United Kingdom should be substantially curtailed. That may have been the Union's own policy but it was held not to be in the best interests of the members of the fund, because it could have resulted in lower returns on investments. The power to invest, it was said, "must be executed so as to yield the best return for the beneficiaries, judged in relation to the risks of the investments in question; and the prospects of the yield of income and capital appreciation both have to be considered in judging the return from the investment. . . . In considering what investments to make trustees must put on one side their own personal interests and views."[47] However, the rules of any particular scheme may expressly or perhaps by implication permit what is termed "social investment" by the trustees. Indeed, what at first sight may seem to be social investment may on closer scrutiny be in the members' best financial interests as well.[48]

A question, which is often the source of considerable controversy, is the extent to which the fund may invest in the employer's own shares or business. This is not dealt with in the 1990 Act, but may very well be the subject of codes of conduct issued by the Pensions Board. Conventional wisdom has it that too many eggs should not be placed in the one basket and there is always a danger that employers, facing financial difficulties, may raid the fund, thereby putting at risk the very solvency of the fund. The rules of many funds permit what is termed "self-investment". In an unreported English case,[49] concerning the London Co-Operative Society pension fund, the rules permitted the fund to make loans to the Society. When loans were made to the Society at below the going market interest rate, their propriety was challenged by one of the beneficiaries. The issue to be determined was whether, in all the circumstances, that arrangement was in the interests of the beneficiaries as a whole than was lending money to third parties at the market rate of interest. The Society there was short of working capital and could not have paid market rates. With some reluctance, it was held that the loans there were permissible, provided they were not for indefinite periods; to rule otherwise would have required the trustees to allow the Society to become insolvent, to the detriment of the scheme's members. If a substantial proportion of those members were pensioners rather than present employees of the Society, the outcome might have been different. In the United States in 1978 the New York Teachers' Pension Fund was allowed to make loans to New York City at a time the City was facing bankruptcy[50] — nearly all of the teachers being City employees.

Closely related to self-investment is the question of the role of the fund when a take-over bid is made for the company. Where part of the fund's assets are shares in the company, in what circumstances should the general interests of the company, perhaps as seen by its directors and majority trustees, be placed before the immediate financial gain for the beneficiaries?

---

47. *ibid.* at p.287.
48. *e.g. Withers v. Teachers Retirement System of New York*, (1978) 447 F. Supp. 1248.
49. *Evans v. London Cooperative Soc. Ltd.* (*The Times* 6 July 1976).
50. *supra* n.48.

Amendment

A power which will be very carefully scrutinised by the courts is that of amending the scheme. It is common practice to provide in the deed for changes to be made to the scheme to meet new legislation or new circumstances of the employer's business, or to enlarge or restrict benefits, or for other unforeseen circumstances. The procedures laid down for making an amendment must be scrupulously followed. Where the reason for amendment is the merger of two or more schemes or to facilitate the wholesale transfer of membership, particular attention will be given to ensuring that the changes stay within the scheme's general objects and purposes. In *Re Courage Group's Pension Schemes*,[51] Millett J. indicated that a power of amendment will not be unduly constricted, observing that:

> "there are no special rules of construction applicable to a pension scheme; nevertheless, its provisions should wherever possible be construed to give reasonable and practical effect to the scheme, bearing in mind that it has to be operated against a constantly changing commercial background. It is important to avoid unduly fettering the power to amend the provisions of the scheme, thereby preventing the parties from making those changes which may be required by the exigencies of commercial life. This is particularly the case where the scheme is intended to be for the benefit not of the employees of a single company but of a group of companies. The composition of the group may constantly change as companies are disposed of and new companies are acquired; and such changes may need to be reflected by modifications to the scheme.[52]

To what extent the exercise of the power of amendment will be reviewed by the courts depends on how it is formulated and who is entitled to exercise it. Where that power is given to the trustees, it is of a fiduciary nature. Accordingly, they must take due account of all the relevant considerations and must not exercise it for a self-serving purpose or other improper purpose. Frequently, the power to amend is exerciseable jointly by the trustees and the employer.

THE SURPLUS

A matter of considerable controversy is, where there is a surplus of the fund's assets over its liabilities (i.e. over the amount needed to secure the promised benefits), who is entitled to that surplus. In particular, does the surplus belong to the members? This question can arise in a variety of contexts, for instance, whether the employer can take a "contributions holiday" or can reduce his contributions, in the circumstances; whether instead benefits should be increased; whether the rules can be amended so that the surplus can be extracted; how much must be paid out when a group of members transfer from one scheme to another? Many of these questions can arise when the scheme is on-going as well as when it is being

---

[51.] [1987] 1 W.L.R. 495.
[52.] *ibid.* at p.505.

wound up. Indeed, with an on-going scheme, the surplus does not represent any particular assets but is merely the actuary's view that the scheme is better funded than is necessary to meet liabilities.

Ideally all of these problems should have been expressly provided for in the rules but that is not always done. And while many rules provide that, on the scheme being wound up, the surplus assets shall be returned to the employer, this is not always enough to answer the question being posed. To an extent, the answer depends on how the employer's contributions to the fund are characterised. If pensions represent deferred remuneration for services rendered to the employer, then it should follow that the employer cannot simply recapture the unanticipated fruits of that remuneration. But the employer's contributions may be regarded as conditional; as entitling the members to the agreed benefits but any excess over what would fund those benefits is in essence a gift from the employer, thereby entitling him, as resulting trustee, to claim any surplus over the sum which must be paid under the fund's rules. The question has been touched on in several English decisions, without any conclusive answer being reached.

In one of them, where a successful take-over bidder sought to get at the surplus, the general position was described by Millet J. as follows:

> "In the case of most pension schemes ...[e]mployees are obliged to contribute a fixed proportion of their salaries or such lesser sum as the employer may from time to time determine. They cannot be required to pay more, even if the fund is in deficit; and they cannot demand a reduction or suspension of their own contributions if it is in surplus. The employer, by way of contrast, is obliged only to make such contributions if any as may be required to meet the liabilities of the scheme. If the fund is in deficit, the employer is bound to make it good; if it is in surplus, the employer has no obligation to pay anything. Employees have no right to complain if, while the fund is in surplus, the employer should require them to continue their contributions while itself contributing nothing. If the employer chooses to reduce or suspend their contributions, it does so ex gratia and in the interests of maintaining good industrial relations.

> From this, two consequences follow. First, employees have no legal right to 'a contribution holiday'. Secondly, any surplus arises from past overfunding, not by the employer and the employees pro rate to their respective contributions, but by the employer alone to the full extent of its past contributions and only subject thereto by the employees.

> It will, however, only be in rate cases that the employer will have any legal right to repayment of any part of the surplus .... Where the employer seeks repayment, the trustees or committee can be expected to press for generous treatment of employees and pensions, and the employer to be influenced by the desire to maintain good industrial relations with its workforce.

> [Where employees] have no legal right to participate in [scheme] surpluses, they are entitled to have them dealt with by consultation and negotiation between their employers with a continuing responsibility towards them and the committee of management with a discretion to exercise on their behalf, and not to be irrevocably parted from these surpluses by the unilateral deci-

sion of a take-over raider with only a transitory interest in the share capital of the companies which employ them."[53]

Considerations that arise when exercising any discretion regarding the surplus include how it came about; in particular, did it results from substantial over funding by the employer or from successful investment policy. What brought the issue to a head in *Edge v. Pensions Ombudsman*[54] was that the scheme had been so successful that it risked loosing Revenue approval unless the surplus was substantially reduced. The employer and the employees had equal representation in the trustees, who decided to reduce both employers' and employees' contributions and also to provide for increased benefits for members in service. Not surprisingly, the ex members then in receipt of benefit were unhappy, since they would not get any share of the surplus, and they complained to the Pensions Ombudsman. His decision, that the trustees had acted unlawfully, was rejected by Scott V.C. and on appeal. As was summarised above, the contention that there was an onus on the trustees to demonstrate that they had not acted with undue partiality was not accepted, nor was it accepted that there was an impermissible conflict of interests. Emphasis was placed in the central role of the employers in the fund, who were obliged to pay contributions to keep the scheme solvent and to employ workers who were willing to join the scheme and pay contributions. Accordingly, it was not improper for the trustees to take account of the employers' continued viability in deciding to lower their contributions.

Occasionally, it is the employer who under the scheme is given the decisive say in allocating any surplus that may arise. Where he has such say by virtue of being the sole trustee of the scheme, then he is bound to approach the question as any other trustee would, as outlined above. Where instead he has that power *qua* employer, he is bound by the less onerous duty to act in good faith. In the *British Coal Staff Scheme* case,[55] the employer purported to amend the scheme so that his liability to bear the cost of enhanced redundancy benefits could be set-off against the surplus. It was held that he could not extinguish his existing liability to the scheme, in the form of outstanding instalments, in this manner. But this was overruled in *National Grid Co. v. Mayes*[56] which concerned whether, on account of the substantial surplus, the employer should be absolved from his liability to pay contributions that were then due and payable. That called for careful analysis of terms in the scheme which had a complex history, was unusual in several respects and gave the employers a somewhat greater say than most modern schemes do. It was contended that scheme members have a legitimate expectation that discretions regarding the surplus will be exercised in their favour.[57] Because the scheme there gave the employers extensive unilateral discretionary powers, albeit but not an express power to waive such liabilities, an ambiguous stipulation was construed so as to permit them to treat their accrued liabilities to the fund as discharged out of its surplus and not as a prohibited payment from the fund to the employees.

---

[53]   *ibid.* at p.514.
[54]   [2000] Ch. 602.
[55]   *British Coal Corp. v. British Coal Staff Superannuation Scheme Trustees Ltd.* [1994] I.C.R. 537.
[56]   [2001] 1 WLR 865.
[57]   And so held by the Court of Appeal, [2000] I.C.R. 174.

Where the deed gives the employer an "absolute discretion" in this regard, it would appear that generally he has an entirely free hand as to how the surplus should be disposed of. Circumstances can arise, however, where the court will circumscribe even so broad a discretion, as occurred in *Mettoy Pension Trustees Ltd. v. Evans*,[58] where the employer had been forced into liquidation. The deed stated that any surplus remaining "may at the absolute discretion of the employer" be applied to secure further benefits, within prescribed limits; any further balance is payable to the employer. Because company directors become functus officio on a winding up, the company's discretion vested in the liquidator. What he would have liked to have done was decide not to apportion any of the surplus towards increasing pension benefits; his primary responsibility was to safeguard the creditors' interests and, obviously, if he decided not to allocate the surplus in that way, it could be used to pay the creditors. However, it was argued on behalf of the employees that the discretion given here was not absolute but was a fiduciary power, which required the liquidator to give due consideration to the interests of the employees in increased benefits. Discretions conferred in deeds fall into several categories and it was contended that several features of the scheme here rendered this discretion a fiduciary one, including the fact that the beneficiaries were not volunteers obtaining a gift; rather, "their rights have contractual and commercial origins, they are derived from the contracts of employment of the members, the benefits provided under the scheme have been earned by the service of the members under those contracts and, where the scheme is contributory, pro tanto by their contributions".[59] In construing the rules of a "balance of cost" pension scheme, it was said that "[o]ne cannot . . . start from an assumption that any surplus belongs morally to the employer."[60] The beneficiaries also are entitled to be considered for discretionary benefits. And where (as there) the employer (or liquidator) was prevented by a conflict of interests from exercising that discretion, the court would do so.

Where the scheme is being wound up, the continued viability of the employer is of far less significance to the members. The scheme may contain a formula for allocating the surplus at that stage, for instance that it be paid to the employer, that instead it shall be paid out in increased benefits or, alternatively, that it shall be divided among the employer, existing members and pensioners in some manner. Insofar as the trustees have a discretion as to how the surplus or part of it shall be distributed, the fiduciary principle applies. Where the scheme permits the trustees to increase benefits if there is a surplus on a winding up, then this power ranks ahead of any provision that the surplus shall be repaid to the employer.[61] If instead the employer has a discretion on the question, that must be exercised in good faith, which would require bona fide discussion with members' representatives.

If the scheme expressly or impliedly does not stipulate what is to happen to the surplus, then generally it must be repaid to those who made the contributions under the principle that, whenever a person establishes a trust and puts assets into

---

[58.] [1990] 1 W.L.R. 1587.
[59.] *ibid.* at p.1610.
[60.] *ibid.* at p.1619.
[61.] *Thrells Ltd. v. Lomas* [1993] 1 W.L.R. 456.

it, he is entitled to recover those assets in the event of it becoming impossible to carry out the terms of the trust; this is called a 'resulting trust'. In the context of pensions, the trust is to pay the defined benefits and, where there is a surplus on a winding up, those funds are not needed in order to finance the benefits. Accordingly, in the absence of any provision in the trust deed to the contrary, those assets must be returned to the contributors. This is the case even if it can be shown that, when the trust was being established, the provider of the assets did not want to retain any beneficial interest in them in the event of the trust failing, entirely or in part. As one judge put it, "a man does not cease to own property simply by saying "I don't want it". If he "tries to give it away, the question must always be, has he succeeded in doing so or not?"

Where there were employees' contributions, it may be difficult to give effect to the resulting trust principle in respect of those contributions because some of them may have died, others may be pensioners and others may have left the scheme for years. Thus in *Davis v. Richards & Wallingham Industries Ltd.*,[62] the scheme there had quite a complicated history, being amended on numerous occasions, including absorbing other pension schemes. Under the rules, employees' contributions were fixed at 5 per cent of salary and they would become entitled to specified pensions and other benefits. Because the trust deed did not indicate what should happen to any surplus on a winding up, it was held that the part of it representing employers' contributions should be repaid to the employer. But in the circumstances, it was not possible to do the same with the employees' contributions. The value of their benefits would be different for each employee, depending on how long he had served, how old he was when he joined and how old he was when he left. Two employees might have paid identical sums in contributions but have become entitled to benefits of a very different value. The point is particularly striking of the employees who exercised their option to a refund of contributions. How could a resulting trust work as between the various employees *inter se*? Furthermore, the scheme was established to take advantage of the legislation relevant to an exempt approved scheme and a contracted-out of scheme. Those very requirements, it was held, prevent imputing to the employees an intention that any surplus deriving from their contributions should be returned to them under a resulting trust. On the other hand, because the employer did not provide those funds, there could be no resulting trust in his favour. Accordingly, it vested in the Crown as *bona vacantia*.[63]

In contrast, in *Air Jamaica Ltd. v. Charlton*,[64] the resulting trust was held to exist for the benefit of the employee contributors as well as the employer. That was because a provision in the scheme was that the trustees should pay them additional benefits if the scheme were discontinued and it therefore was not possible to say that, on the winding up, they had got all that they had bargained for. Unlike in *Davis*, the surplus did not arise from over-funding but because the trust failed for other reasons. Additionally, the Privy Council was able to devise a method of distributing the employees' share of the surplus, being pro rata among the members and the estates of deceased members, in proportion to the contribu-

---

[62.] [1990] 1 W.L.R. 1511.
[63.] See State Property Act 1954, ss.27 and 29.
[64.] [1993] 1 W.L.R. 1399.

tions made by each of them, without regard to any benefits they may have received or to the dates on which they made their contributions.

TRANSFER OF UNDERTAKING

Most pension schemes contain a power to make transfer payments to a new scheme which the former employer's members wish to join on account of a business transfer, often referred to as "bulk transfer payments". These ensure that members transferring from one scheme have security for their benefits in the new scheme. Most pension schemes as well contain a power to grant accrued benefits to new employees joining the scheme in exchange for transfer payments. Where provision along these lines does not exist, often the scheme will be amended prior to the transfer in order that such arrangements can be made. Many schemes also provide for the substitution of the new employer for members' existing employer. Reaching agreement on transfer payments can be quite difficult on account of different rules and standards for scheme solvency.[65]

Another cause of difficulty where a business is being transferred is the surplus in the transferor's scheme, where the rules are not clear about what is to happen with that excess of assets over estimated liabilities. Insofar as the trustees have a discretion about the disposal of a surplus, it was held in the *Courage Group* case[66] that it should not be used to enable the new employer to finance that take-over. There, Millet J. refused to sanction the transfer of members from a scheme that was in substantial surplus to a new scheme, set up by their new employer, which had a very small surplus. Similarly, in the *Imperial Group* case,[67] Browne Wilkinson V.C. refused to sanction an amendment to a scheme, following a take over, which would enable the surplus to be paid out to the new employer.

Where all or part of the business is being transferred to another employer, the 1980 Transfer of Undertakings Regulations[68] require the transferee to retain in employment those who worked in the part being transferred, subject to certain exceptions. Further, all rights and liabilities vis-à-vis the transferor are transferred over or to the transferee. Of course employees who do not want to transfer are not obliged to do so and they may instead opt for redundancy. An exception, however, is made in respect of employees' rights to old-age, invalidity or survivors' benefit under supplementary company or inter-company pension schemes outside the Social Welfare Acts. Consequently, the transferee does not automatically assume the transferor's obligations to pay contributions to an equivalent pension scheme;[69] that liability remains with the transferor, which constitutes a significant gap in employment protection. That, however, may be filled by making appropriate provision in the transfer arrangements or in the pension scheme itself.

---

[65]. *e.g. Imperial Foods Ltd. Pension Scheme* [1986] 1 W.L.R. 717.
[66]. [1987] 1 W.L.R. 495.
[67]. [1991] 1 W.L.R. 589.
[68]. S.I. No. 306 of 1980; see *ante* p. 230 *et seq.*
[69]. *Eidesund v. Stavanger Catering A/S* (Case E2/95) [1996] I.R.L.R. 684 and *Adams v. Lancashire County Council* [1997] I.C.R. 834.

This exception in the 1980 Regulations is qualified by the proviso that "the transferee shall ensure that the interests of employees and of persons no longer employed in the transferor's business at the time of the transfer in respect of rights conferring on them immediate or prospective entitlement to old age benefits, including survivors' benefits, under such supplementary company pension schemes are protected." What exactly is required by this remains to be clarified.

EMPLOYER'S INSOLVENCY

Where the employer becomes insolvent, that may result in the pension scheme being wound up; this usually happens when the company is put into liquidation and often happens when a receiver has been appointed over its assets. If the scheme was properly funded, the trustees will be able to meet all its obligations to the members. If the scheme is in surplus, the question will then arise as to how that surplus should be distributed. Where under the trust deed the employer has a discretion regarding the surplus, the courts will not allow liquidators (who otherwise would obtain that discretion) to exercise it because of the plain conflict of interests that would arise, since liquidators' principal responsibility is to look after the interests of the general creditors.[70]

If, on the other hand, the scheme itself is insolvent, then questions arise about whether the trustees exercised their investment powers with all due care. Where an employer's contributions are owing to the fund, those sums are preferential debts in a winding up; this is also the case with employees' contributions to be deducted from their remuneration and payable by the employer.[71] It is only funds for the provision of "superannuation benefits" to which this preference applies. Provision is made by section 7 of the Protection of Employees (Employers' Insolvency) Act 1984 for the payment by the Minister of those outstanding contributions from the assets of the insolvency fund.[72] On making such a payment, the Minister becomes subrogated for whatever rights and remedies the fund's trustees may have against the employer. Ceilings are placed on the amounts of an employer's and employees' contributions which may be recovered in this manner from the Minister.

EARLY LEAVERS

A criticism levelled against many occupational pension schemes was that they penalised the early leaver, that is the person who left the pensionable employment before his due retirement age, often to work in some other job. Whether he could recover all or any of the contributions he had made to the scheme and/or the contributions made by the employer on his behalf depended on the rules of the par-

---

[70.] *Mettoy Pension Trustees Ltd. v. Evans* [1990] 1 W.L.R. 1587 and *Trells Ltd. v. Lomas* [1993] 1 W.L.R. 456.

[71.] Companies Act 1963, s.285(2)(i).

[72.] See *ante* p. 248 and the Protection of Employees (Employers' Insolvency) (Occupational Pension Scheme) (Forms and Procedure) Regs 1990, S.I. No. 121.

ticular scheme. Perhaps the most commonly adopted solution in those cases was to refund him his own contributions, together with a portion of the value accumulated on them. Especially for employees working for one employer for a long time before leaving, the loss of their employer's contributions was a heavy financial penalty they suffered on taking up another job. Those outcomes were a distinct obstacle to personal freedom and to the mobility of labour.

One of the most significant innovations in the 1990 Act Part III (sections 27-39) is to protect the early leaver by providing for portable pensions. Once an employee has served more than five years of reckonable service, the trustees are obliged to preserve his benefit. This can be done by him choosing to transfer to another pension scheme, which he is joining, an amount of money from the fund which is equal to the amount of his preserved benefit. Alternatively, that money can be used to purchase insurance annuities, which will yield him a pension; in defined circumstances the trustees may choose to preserve his benefit in this manner. These provisions, that do not apply retrospectively prior to January 1991, are amplified in regulations made in 1992 and in 1993 for the preservation of benefits.[73] A member who is entitled to have his pension preserved in accordance with the 1990 Act is not permitted to opt for a repayment of contributions made to the fund by him or on his behalf. These entitlements under Part III of the 1990 Act would appear to apply regardless of the reason why the employee left early, in particular, even if he was dismissed. It is unlikely that the provisions of a scheme that sought to exclude employees who were dismissed for misconduct and to forfeit contributions made by them and/or on their behalf would be upheld.

Where employees are compelled to leave a scheme early on account of ill health or the like,[74] they often qualify for benefit payments there and then, to continue until the prescribed retiring age, at which stage they may become entitled to a full pension.

DISCRIMINATION ON GROUNDS OF SEX AND MARITAL STATUS

Most Irish pension schemes treat men and women equally and the State social welfare pensions no longer discriminate between men and women.[75] However, there are private schemes which contain one form or another of sex discrimination that to a considerable extent are based on the assumption that men are the primary earners in families. Direct discrimination includes not permitting women or married women to join pension schemes and not paying benefits to widowers of female scheme members. Indirect discrimination can include, depending on the circumstances, not allowing part-time workers, or those who earn less than a particular threshold, or with several breaks in their employment record, from joining a scheme or obtaining certain benefits under a scheme.

---

73. Occupational Pension Schemes (Preservation of Benefits) Regs. 1992 (S.I. No. 445) and 1993 (S.I. No. 217).

74. *cf. Harris v. Lord Shuttleworth* [1994] I.C.R. 991 and *Derby Daily Telegraph Ltd. v. Pensions Ombudsman* [1999] I.C.R 1057.

75. Following *Cotter v. Minister for Social Welfare* (Case 377/89) [1991] E.C.R. 1155.

For many years there was a belief that qualification rules for occupational pension schemes were not caught by former Article 119 (now Art. 141) of the E.E.C. Treaty, a view which obtained some support from decisions of the European Court of Justice. However, in the *Bilka-Kaufhaus* case,[76] which concerned rules that excluded part-time workers from a German supplementary pensions scheme, it was held that the ordinary private pension is a form of "pay". Accordingly, rules which discriminated, directly or indirectly, on the basis of sex regarding eligibility for such pensions contravened Community law. Since far more women than men were engaged in part-time work in Germany, the eligibility rule in question was held to be unlawful. If, however, it could be demonstrated convincingly that there was a sound reason other than sex for excluding part-time workers from a scheme, there would not be a breach of Article 119. Later in the *Barber* case,[77] where a male insurance employee challenged differential retirement rules in a British "contracted out" pension scheme, it was held that Article 119 required that the actual amounts of the pension paid to men and women with equal seniority must always be the same. There, the Court condemned a rule whereby women qualified for a pension at the age of 57 and men at 62, and women qualified for an early pension at 50 years of age whereas men had to wait until they reached 55.

The full implications of these cases remain to be worked out;[78] they deal with a very complex set of problems, where the Community legislators had refrained from imposing across-the-board rules of equality. In between the times they were decided, Directive 86/378 on equal treatment in occupational social security schemes[79] was enacted. When the Pensions Bill was first published in 1989, it contained provisions on equal treatment in this field. But the *Barber* case, decided in May 1990, forced the draftsman back to the drawing board, to eventually produce Part VII of the Pensions Act 1990, which was enacted two months later. Questions about the extent to which the *Bilka-Kaufhaus* and the *Barber* rulings applied retrospectively are dealt with in several amendments made to that Act in 1996,[80] which were the subject of Protocol No. 2 to the Maastricht Treaty of 1992.

Equality between men and women is provided in sections 66, 67 and 70 of the 1990 Act, as amended. Subject to limited exceptions:

> "every occupational benefit scheme shall comply with the principle of equal treatment, [meaning] there shall be no discrimination on the basis of sex in respect of any matter relating to an occupational benefit scheme [and in particular] in relation to the manner in which [an employer] affords his employees access to [such] scheme".

---

[76] *Bilka Kaufhaus v. Weber von Hartz* (Case 170/84) [1984] E.C.R. 1607.

[77] *Barber v. Guardian Royal Exchange* (Case 262/88) [1990] E.C.R. 1889.

[78] See, generally, C. Barnard, *E.C. Employment Law* (2 ed. 2000) pp.329 et seq. and M. Bolger & C. Kimber, *Sex Discrimination Law* (2000) Chap. 6.

[79] O.J. L 225/4D (1986).

[80] Pensions Amendments Act 1996, ss.31-33, amending ss.71 and 74 of the 1990 Act and adding s.74A.

Sex discrimination here includes discrimination on the basis of family status and applies to members' dependants as well. It applies to indirect as well as to direct discrimination, and also to victimisation for making or supporting an anti-discrimination claim. In the case of indirect discrimination, those who seek to assert that it is justified have the onus of providing such justification.[81] Female employees may not be prejudiced in their pension entitlements due to their absence from work on paid maternity leave; similarly, where any employee is absent on paid family leave.[82]

Some exceptions to the equality principle are permitted by the 1990 Act as amended in 1997[83] in the light of several E.C.J. decisions on Article 141, especially the *Neath*[84] and the *Coloroll*[85] cases. In the former, it was held that the actuarial difference between men's and women's life expectancies could be taken into account in determining the size of employers' contributions to defined benefit schemes. In the latter case, this principle was extended to where a reversionary pension is payable to a dependant in return for a payment of part of the annual pension and where a reduced pension is paid when the employee takes early retirement. It was also held in the latter that employees' additional voluntary contributions are not pay for the purpose of Article 141. The present exceptions are as follows:

(a) Differences in employers' contributions to defined benefit schemes, based on actuarial factors reflecting disparate male/female mortality, designed to limit or remove differences between the amount of benefit that men and women members receive;

(b) Similarly based differences in employers' contributions in order to ensure that defined benefit schemes are adequately funded;

(c) Similarly based differences in the amount of benefits provided in defined contribution schemes;

(d) Similarly based elements of benefits provided in defined benefit schemes, such as transfer of pension rights, capitalising part of a periodic pension, a reduced pension on early retirement and a reversionary pension paid to a dependant when part of the pension has been surrendered;

(e) Special treatment for women in connection with pregnancy or childbirth, as provided for in section 72 of the 1990 Act: notably, those on maternity, paternity or family leave shall continue to accrue their pension entitlements;

(f) Different treatment with regard to additional benefits that are open to members on their election.

---

[81] s.68.

[82] ss.72 and 73.

[83] s.69, amended by the European Communities (Occupational Benefit Schemes) Regs. 1997, S.I. No. 286.

[84] *Neath v. Steeper* (Case 152/91) [1993] E.C.R. 6935.

[85] *Coloroll Pension Trustees Ltd v. Russell* (Case 200/91) [1994] E.C.R. 1389.

APPENDIX

STANDARD TERMS AND CONDITIONS OF EMPLOYMENT

1 Name

_____

2 Commencement of employment

2.1 Your employment began on _____

[2.2 Your employment with any previous employer does not count as part of your period of continuous employment.]

[2.2 Your employment with _____ from _____ continuous with your employment by the Company.]

[2.2 Your employment with:

(1) from _____ to _____, and

(2) from _____ to _____, and

(3) from _____ to _____, and

will be treated as continuous with your employment by the Company.]

3 Job title

3.1 Your job title is _____ .

[3.2 Your normal duties are as detailed in the job description [attached] [to be provided to you by the Personnel Department].]

3.3 In addition to your normal duties, you may be required to undertake other duties from time to time.

3.4 Until otherwise notified by the Company you are required to report to _____ .

4 Probationary period

4.1 The first _____ weeks of your employment will be probationary.

4.2 Your employment may be terminated on one week's notice given in writing by the Company at any time during or at the end of this period.

4.3 Your continued employment will be reviewed at the end of your probationary period [and if your continued employment is confirmed your [salary] [wages] may be increased from that date].

5 Salary/wages

5.1 Your [basic] [salary] [wages] at the commencement of your employment will be _____ per [annum] [week] [hour].

5.2 Your [salary] [wages] will be paid [monthly] [weekly] [in arrears] [_____ week[s] in advance and _____ week[s] in arrears] [by credit transfer] [unless an alternative method of payment has been agreed] [by cheque] [by cash] on the _____ day of each [month] [week] [four week payment period].

5.3 Your [salary] [wages] will be reviewed [annually] [with effect from, in each year.]

5.4 You will be notified in writing of any change to your [salary] [wages].

6 Bonus payments

[6.1 You will participate in the [_____] bonus scheme, full details of which are available on request from the Personnel Department. The Company reserves the right in its absolute discretion to terminate or amend [any] [the] bonus scheme without notice at any time or to exclude you from participation in [any] [the] bonus scheme without giving any reason.]

[6. I [Profit-sharing] [Personal Performance Related] bonus payments may be made from time to time at the Company's absolute discretion.]

6.2 Bonus payments will normally be paid in _____ in each year.

7 Commission

7.1 You [may] [will] be entitled to commission [according to] [calculated by reference to] _____

7.2 Commission payments will be paid by [credit transfer] [cheque] (cash) [on the _____ day of each [month] [day] [in each _____ year] in respect of the period _____

7.3 The Company reserves the right in its absolute discretion to terminate or amend the commission arrangements applicable to you without notice at any time or to exclude you from participation in any commission arrangements without giving any reason.

[8 Deductions

8.1 The Company has the right to deduct from your pay, any sums which you may owe the Company, including, without limitation, any overpayments or loans made to you by the Company, or losses suffered by the Company as a result of your negligence or breach of Company rules.

[9 Normal hours of work

9.1 You are normally required to work _____ hours per week, but the Company has the right to require you to remain away from work on full pay for such period and on such conditions as the Company may specify.

9.2 Your normal hours of work are _____ am to _____ pm [Monday to Friday] with a break of _____ for lunch [which must be taken between _____ [am] [pm] and _____ pm] and breaks of _____ for tea which must be taken between _____ am and _____ am and _____ pm and _____ pm respectively.

[9.3 You are also required to work such additional hours as may be necessary for the proper performance of your duties. There will be no additional payment for hours worked in excess of your normal hours of work [but you may, with the prior written consent of [the Company] [your Manager] be permitted to take time off in lieu of such excess hours worked provided you comply with such conditions as [may be imposed by the Company] [he may impose]].]

[9 Flexitime scheme

9.1 The Company currently operates a flexitime scheme ('the Scheme') which will apply to you until further notice.

9.2 The rules of the Scheme are as follows:

9.2.1 Your normal days of work are [Monday to Friday] inclusive.

9.2.2 You are required to work a minimum of _____ hours in any one flexitime period (as defined in clause 9.2.3 below) unless you are a part-time employee, in which case you will be notified separately of the hours applicable to you. All hours worked in excess of your minimum hours of work in any one flexitime period will be credited to you as 'excess hours worked'.

9.2.3 A flexitime period is a period of _____ weeks. The date of commencement of each flexitime period will be notified to you by the Company, either individually or by way of a general notice.

9.2.4 On the commencement of your employment you are required to work a minimum of seven hours in respect of each day remaining in the then current flexitime period. You will be credited with seven hours for each day before the commencement of your employment in the then current flexitime period. Thereafter you will be required to work the hours specified in clause 9.2.2 above.

9.2.5 On the days on which you are required to attend for work, you must be present at work during the Company's flexitime core time. The Company's flexitime core time is from _____ am to _____ .

9.2.6 You may commence work at any time between _____ am to _____ am and may finish work at any time between _____ pm and _____ pm subject always to the needs of the business. You will not be credited for hours worked before _____ am and after _____ pm except with the prior written consent of [your Manager] [the Company].

9.2.7 Lunch must be taken between _____ and _____ pm and these hours may not be varied except with the prior written consent of [your Manager] [the Company].

9.2.8 Provided that you are credited with a total of not less than _____ hours in respect of any one flexitime period (or such other minimum number of hours as may have been notified to you if you are a part-time employee) you may [with the prior consent of [your Manager] [the Company] take up to a maximum of two half days or one whole day off work in any one flexitime period (subject always to the needs of the business) provided that you have sufficient excess hours already credited to you to cover such absence.

9.2.9 The maximum credited time which may be carried forward to the following flexitime period is _____ hours.

9.2.10 You will be credited with _____ hours for each day of your basic Company holiday entitlement, each public holiday and each day of certified sickness absence.

9.3 The procedure for recording flexitime is that when you start or finish work you are required to clock in or out in accordance with the procedure in clause 10 below.

9.4 The Company reserves the right in its absolute discretion to terminate or amend the Scheme or to terminate your participation in it at any time.]

10 Clocking procedure

10. I You are required to clock in on [entering the Company's premises] [attending your place of work] and to clock out on leaving [the Company's premises] [your place of work] for any reason.

10.2 You must only use the clock [card] [key] assigned to you for this purpose and must not interfere in any way with it or the clocking equipment.

10.3 You must not clock in or clock out any other employee or permit someone to clock in or out for you or interfere with the clock card of any other employee for any reason.

11 Shift working

11.1 You may be required to undertake shift working from time to time [if so instructed by [the Company] [your Manager]].

11.2 Reasonable notice of such shift working will be given.

11.3 When you are required to work shifts the following hours of work will apply: _____ .

11.4 When payable shift working rates will be as follows: _____ .

12 Overtime

12.1 You [are] [may be] required to work overtime from time to time [if so instructed by [the Company] [your Manager]].

12.2 Reasonable notice of such overtime will be given.

12.3 All overtime must be authorised by [the Company] [your Manager].

12.4 No payment for overtime will be made unless it has been previously authorised by [the Company] [your Manager].

12.5 Overtime rates will only apply to hours worked in excess of _____ hours per week.

12.6 When payable overtime rates will be as follows

12.7 Payment for overtime will be made on your normal pay day for the pay period in which the overtime was worked.

13 Reductions in normal hours of work

13.1 The Company reserves the right to lay you off without pay or to make temporary reductions to your normal hours of work and to reduce your pay proportionately if in the view of the Company this should become necessary.

13.2 You will be given as much notice of lay-off or reduction in normal hours as the Company reasonably can give.

14 Basic company holiday entitlement

14.1 The Company's holiday year runs from _____ to _____ .

14.2 In each holiday year your basic Company holiday entitlement will be as follows:

Number of completed years of service before *Number of working days paid holiday*
in each year

Nil to _____ years   _____ days

_____ to _____ years   _____ days

Over _____ years   _____ days

14.3 You must give at least _____ weeks' notice, of proposed holiday dates and these must then be agreed with the Company. [You may not take more than _____ weeks holiday in any _____ month period.]

[14.4 You are required to retain a sufficient number of days from your basic Company holiday entitlement to cover the Company's [annual] [summer] [Christmas] shut down period. You will be notified by the Company either individually or by way of a general notice to staff no later than _____ in each year of the number of days holiday you are required to retain for this purpose.]

[14.5 If you are absent from work due to sickness for a continuous period of [four weeks or more] or for a total period of [eight weeks] in any one Company holiday year the Company reserves the right in its absolute discretion to reduce your basic Company holiday entitlement in respect of the Company holiday year in question as follows:

Total length of absence/absences in the company holiday year in question	*Number of days reduction in basic company holiday entitlement in the company holiday year in question*
4 weeks	_____ days
5 weeks	_____ days
6 weeks	_____ days
7 weeks	_____ days
8 weeks	_____ days
3 months	_____ days
4 months	_____ days
5 months	_____ days
6 months	_____ days
7 months	_____ days
8 months	_____ days
9 months	_____ days
10 months	_____ days
11 months	_____ days
12 months	_____ days

14.6 You may not carry any unused basic Company holiday entitlement forward to a subsequent holiday year. You will not be entitled to receive pay in lieu of holiday which is not taken except in accordance with clause 13.7 below.

[14.7 If you start or leave your employment during a holiday year your basic Company holiday entitlement in respect of the Company holiday year in question will be calculated at the rate of _____ days for each complete month of service in that holiday year.]

[14.7 If you start or leave your employment during a holiday year your basic Company holiday entitlement will be calculated as follows:

Number of complete months of service before the end of the holiday	*Number of working days paid holiday year in question*
1	_____ days
2	_____ days
3	_____ days
4	_____ days
5	_____ days
6	_____ days
7	_____ days
8	_____ days
9	_____ days
10	_____ days
11	_____ days

14.8 Upon termination of your employment you will be entitled to pay in lieu of any unused basic Company holiday entitlement [unless your employment is terminated by the Company for gross misconduct] or be required to repay to the Company pay received for holidays taken in excess of entitlement under clause 14.7. Any sums so due may be deducted from any money owing to you. The Company reserves the right to require you to take any unused holiday entitlement during your notice period, even if booked to be taken after the end of the notice period.

[14.9 For the purpose of calculating any pay due to you or owed by you to the Company in accordance with clause 14.7 above one day's pay shall be [1/365] [1/261] [1/253] 1/7] [1/5] of your [basic] [annual] [weekly] [salary] [wages].]

[14.9 Any pay due to you or owed by you to the Company in accordance with clause 14.7 above will be calculated by reference to your [basic] [annual] [weekly] [salary] [wages] and will be as follows

Number of complete months of service before the end of the holiday year in question	Number of working days paid holiday accrued
1	_____ days
2	_____ days
3	_____ days
4	_____ days
5	_____ days
6	_____ days
7	_____ days
8	_____ days
9	_____ days
10	_____ days
11	_____ days

For this purpose one day's pay shall be [1/36s] [1/261] [1/253] [1/7] [1/5] of your [basic] [annual] [weekly] [salary] [wages].]

15 Public holidays

15.1 You are entitled to all public holidays applicable to the country in which your normal place of work is situated in addition to your basic Company holiday entitlement and will be paid for each public holiday.

15.2 If a public holiday falls within the dates of your basic Company holiday entitlement you will be entitled to an additional day's paid holiday for each public holiday.

15.3 The Company reserves the right to require you to work on a public holiday, in return for which you shall be entitled to extra holiday, equal to the period worked, to be taken as agreed with [your manager] [the Company].

16 Notification of sickness or other absence

16.1 If you are absent from work for any reason and your absence has not previously been authorised by [the Company] [your Manager] you must inform [the Company] [your Manager] by _____ am on your first day of absence.

16.2 Any unauthorised absence must be properly explained and you must keep the Company informed daily until you have provided the Company with a medical certificate.

16.3 If you are absent from work due to sickness or injury which continues for more than seven days (including weekends) you must provide the Company with a medical certificate by the eighth day of sickness or injury. Thereafter medical certificates must be provided to the Company to cover any continued absence.

16.4 Immediately following your return to work after a period of absence which has not previously been authorised by [the Company] [your Manager] you are required to complete a Self-Certification form in the terms annexed stating the dates of and the reason for your absence, including details of sickness on non-working days as this information is required by the Company for calculating Statutory Sick Pay entitlement. Self-Certification forms will be retained in the Company's records.

17 Sick pay

17.1 If you are absent from work due to sickness or injury and comply with the requirements in this clause and clause 15 above regarding notification of absence, you will be paid Company Sick Pay in accordance with the terms of the Company's Sick Pay Scheme.

17.2 Under the provisions of the Company's Sick Pay Scheme you [will] [may] be entitled to Company Sick Pay [if you have completed months continuous service] [at the Company's absolute discretion].

17.3 Company Sick Pay [will] [may] be paid for up to a maximum of _____ [weeks] [months] in any _____ month period and when payable will be as follows:

For the first _____ (week) (month) period or periods in any such absences

(1) Full salary less any Social Welfare Benefits recoverable by you (whether or not recovered); or

(2) Full salary in which case you must refund to the Company on demand an amount equal to any Social Welfare Benefits recoverable by you (whether or not recovered).

For the second _____ (week) (month) period or periods of any such absences

(1) Half salary less any Social Welfare Benefits recoverable by you (whether or not recovered); or

(2) Half salary in which case you must refund to the Company on demand an amount equal to any Social Welfare Benefits recoverable by you (whether or not recovered).

17.4 The Company reserves the right to require you to be examined at any time by an independent doctor at its expense and to cease payment of Company Sick Pay if it is advised by the doctor that you are fit to return to work.

17.5 If you are absent from your duties due to sickness or injury for a period or periods in excess of your maximum Company Sick Pay entitlement the Company will not be obliged to make any further payments to you. However if the Company does decide, in its absolute discretion, to make any further payments to you (in whatever amount the Company may decide), any such further payments may be varied or discontinued at any time.

17.6 If you are absent from work for any reason (excluding annual and public holidays) for a period or periods in excess of _____ working days in any period of 12 months the Company will be entitled to terminate your employment at any time by written notice on the date specified in the notice.

18 Pension

[18.1 You are entitled to join the Company's (contributory) [non-contributory] pension scheme [when you first become eligible for membership]. [Full details of the Company's Pension Scheme may be obtained from _____ .] [A copy of the current explanatory booklet giving details of the Pension Scheme is attached].]

[18.2 There is no pension scheme applicable to your employment.]

[18.3 The Company shall be entitled at any time to terminate the scheme or your membership of it [subject to providing you with the benefit of an equivalent pension scheme ('the New Scheme') each and every benefit of which shall be not less favourable than the benefits provided to you under the existing scheme and to ensuring that you are fully credited in the New Scheme for your pensionable service in the existing scheme as if those years had been under the New Scheme].]

19 Notice

19.1 If your employment is confirmed at the end of your probationary period the period of notice to be given in writing by the Company or by you to terminate your employment is:

19.1.1   one week's notice if you have been continuously employed for less than two years; and then

19.1.2   one week's notice for each completed year of continuous service up to a maximum of 12 weeks' notice after 12 years continuous service.

19.2 The Company reserves the right to pay [salary] [wages] in lieu of notice.

19.3 Nothing in terms and conditions of employment shall prevent the Company from terminating your employment without notice or [salary] (wages) in lieu of notice in appropriate circumstances.

20 Grievance procedure

20.1 If you have any grievance relating to your employment you should raise the matter initially with _____ . You may be required to put any such grievance in writing.

20.2 Having enquired into your grievance the _____ will discuss it with you and will then notify you of his decision.

20.3 If the decision of the _____ is not acceptable you may then refer the matter in writing to _____ whose decision will be final and binding.

[20.4 When stating grievances you may be accompanied by fellow employee of your choice [or by a representative of [a] [any recognised] Trade Union of which you are a member.]]

21 Disciplinary procedures

21.1 The purpose of the disciplinary procedures is to ensure that the standards established by the Company's rules are maintained and that any alleged failure to observe the Company's rules is fairly dealt with. [The procedure will only apply to employees who have [successfully completed their probationary periods/completed 6 months/one two year[s] continuous employment.]]

21.2 All cases of disciplinary action under these procedures will be recorded and placed in the Company's records. A copy of the Company's relevant records will be supplied at your request.

21.3 Offences under the Company's disciplinary procedures fall into 3 categories namely: misconduct

gross misconduct

incapability

21.4 The following steps will be taken, as appropriate, in all cases of disciplinary action:

21.4.1 *Investigations:* No action will be taken before a proper investigation has been undertaken by the Company relating to the circumstances of the matter complained of. If appropriate, the Company may by written notice suspend you for a specified period during which time such an investigation will be undertaken. If you are so suspended your contract of employment will be deemed to continue together with all your rights under your contract including the payment of [salary] [wages], but during the period of suspension you will not be entitled to access to any of the Company's premises except at the prior request or with the prior consent of the Company and subject to such conditions as the Company may impose. The decision to suspend you will be notified to you by the [Personnel Manager] and confirmed in writing.

21.4.2 *Disciplinary hearings:* If the Company decides to hold a disciplinary hearing relating to the matter complained of, you will be given details of the complaint against you [at least [three] working days] before any such disciplinary hearing. At any disciplinary hearing you will be given an opportunity to state your case. You may also be accompanied by a fellow employee of your choice [or by a representative of [a] [any recognised] Trade Union of which you are a member]. No disciplinary penalty will be imposed without a disciplinary hearing.

21.4.3 *Appeals:* You have a right of appeal at any stage of the disciplinary procedures to the [Personnel Manager] or if he was involved at an earlier stage to the [Managing Director}. You should inform the [Personnel Manager] in writing of your wish to appeal within [five working days] of the date of the decision which forms the subject of your appeal.

The [Personnel Manager] or [Managing Director], as appropriate, will conduct an appeal hearing as soon as possible thereafter at which you will be given an opportunity to state your case and will be entitled to be accompanied by a fellow employee of your choice [or by a representative of [a] [any recognised] Trade Union of which you are a member].

The decision of the [Personnel Manager] or [Managing Director], as appropriate, will be notified to you in writing and will be final and binding.

21.5 Misconduct

21.5.1 The following offences are examples of misconduct:

— Bad time-keeping

— Unauthorised absence

— Minor damage to Company property

— Minor breach of Company rules

— Failure to observe Company procedures

— Abusive behaviour

— Sexual or racial harassment

These offences are not exclusive or exhaustive and offences of a similar nature will be dealt with under this procedure.

21.5.2 The following procedure will apply in cases of alleged misconduct:

First warning: This will be given by [your Manager] and may be oral or written according to the circumstances. In either event you will be advised that the warning constitutes the first formal stage of this procedure. If the warning is verbal a note that such a warning has been given will be placed in the Company's records.

Final warning: This will be given by the [Personnel Manager] and confirmed to you in writing. This warning will state that if you commit a further offence of misconduct during the period specified in it your employment will be terminated.

Dismissal: The decision to dismiss you will not be taken without reference to the [Personnel Manager] [Managing Director]. Dismissal will be notified to you in writing.

21.6 Gross misconduct

21.6.1   The following offences are examples of gross misconduct:
— Theft or unauthorised possession of any property or facilities belonging to the Company or any employee
— Unauthorised acceptance of gifts in contravention of clause 24 below - Serious damage to Company property
— Falsification of reports, accounts, expense claims or self-certification forms - [Clocking in or out offences]
— Refusal to carry out duties or reasonable instructions - Intoxication by reason of drink or drugs
— Having alcoholic drink or illegal drugs at your place of work, in your locker on your person or otherwise in your possession, custody or control on the Company's premises
— Serious breach of Company rules
— Dangerous or intimidatory conduct
— [Abuse of the Company's flexitime scheme]
These examples are not exhaustive or exclusive and offences of a similar nature will be dealt with under this procedure.

21.6.2   Gross misconduct will result in immediate dismissal without notice or pay in lieu of notice. The decision to dismiss will not be taken without reference to the [Personnel Manager] [Managing Director]. Dismissal will be notified to you in writing.

21.7 Incapability

21.7.1   The following are examples of incapability:
— Poor performance
— Incompetence
— Unsuitability
— Lack of application
These examples are not exhaustive or exclusive and instances of a similar nature will be dealt with under this procedure.

21.7.2   The following procedure will apply in cases of incapability:
First warning: This will be given by your Manager and will be confirmed to you in writing. This warning will specify the improvement required and will state that your work will be reviewed at the end of a period of _____ month[s] after the date of the warning.
Final warning: This will be given by the [Personnel Manager] and confirmed to you in writing. This warning will state that unless your work improves within a period of 1/3 month[s] after the date of the warning your employment will be terminated.
Dismissal: The decision to dismiss you will not be taken without reference to the [Personnel Manager] [Managing Director]. Dismissal will be notified to you in writing.

21.8 Subject to satisfactory performance and conduct any warning under these procedures will be removed from the Company's records after [two] years.

21.9 The Company reserves the right in its absolute discretion to waive any of the penalties referred to in clauses 21.5.2, 21.6.2 and 21.7.2 above and substitute any one or more of the following penalties namely:

21.9.1   *Demotion:* The Company may demote you by notice in writing giving details of any consequential changes to your terms and conditions of employment. In particular the notice will give details of any reduction to your [salary] [waged and/or any loss of benefits and/or privileges consequent upon such demotion. Demotion will be limited to a reduction of [ ] grades.

21.9.2   *Suspension:* The Company may suspend you from work with or without pay by notice in writing to this effect. Such notice will specify the dates of your suspension and the conditions applicable to your suspension. Suspension will be limited to not more than [ ] working days.

21.9.3   *[Bonus Scheme]:* The Company may exclude you from participating in [any] [the] bonus scheme referred to in clause [6] above by notice in writing to this effect. Such notice will specify the period of your exclusion from participation in [any] [the] bonus scheme.

22 Cars

22.1 You may only use your own car on Company business with the prior approval of _____ and you are responsible for ensuring that the vehicle is adequately insured.

22.2 A Company car [will] [may] be provided for your use for the better performance of your duties in accordance with and subject to the Company's Car Policy as amended from time to time. The Company reserves the right in its absolute discretion to withdraw the use of the car from you at any time without giving any reason [without compensation].

22.3 It is a condition in your employment that you have and keep a current driving licence. If you are disqualified from driving for any period the Company reserves the right to dismiss you. You must promptly notify the Company of any accidents while driving on Company business, any charges of driving offences brought against you by the police and of any endorsements imposed.

23 Expenses

[23.1 The Company will reimburse to you all expenses properly incurred by you in the proper performance of your duties, provided that on request you provide the Company with such vouchers or other evidence of actual payment of such expenses as the Company may reasonably require.]

24 Acceptance of gifts

24.1 You may not without prior written consent of [the Company] [your Manager] accept any gift and/or favour of whatever kind from any customer, client or supplier of the Company or any prospective customer, client or supplier of the Company.

25 Normal retirement age

You shall retire on reaching _____ years of age.

26 Other employment

26.1 You must devote the whole of your time, attention and abilities during your hours of work for the Company to your duties for the Company. You may not, under any circumstances, whether directly or indirectly, undertake any other duties, of whatever kind, during your hours of work for the Company.

26.2 You may not without the prior written consent of [the Company] [your Manager] (which will not be unreasonably withheld) engage, whether directly or indirectly, in any business or employment [which is similar to or in any way connected or competitive with the business of the Company in which you work] outside your hours of work for the Company.

27 Place of work

27.1 Your normal place of work will be _____ but the Company reserves the right to change this to any. place within _____ . You will be given at least one month's notice of any such change. However, the Company will, where appropriate, under its Relocation Policy from time to time provide you with financial or other relocation assistance.

27.2 You may be required to work at any of the Company's premises or at the premises of its customers, clients, suppliers or associates within Ireland [or overseas] from time to time. You will be reimbursed for any expenses properly incurred in connection with such duties in accordance with the Company's Expenses Policy as amended from time to time.

28 Confidentiality

28.1 You may not disclose any trade secrets or other information of a confidential nature relating to the Company or any of its associated companies or their business or in respect of which the Company owes an obligation of confidence to any third party during or after your employment except in the proper course of your employment or as required by law.

28.2 You must not remove any documents or computer disks or tapes containing any confidential information from the Company's premises at any time without proper advance authorisation. All such documents, disks or tapes and any copies are the Company's property.

29 Inventions

29.1 If you make any invention whether patentable or not which relates to or is capable of being used in any business of the Company with which you are (at the time of making the invention or have been (within the two years before that time) concerned to a material degree you must disclose it to the Company immediately.

29.2 As between you and the Company, the ownership of all inventions made by you will be determined in accordance with s. 53 of the Patents Act 1964.

30 Accommodation

30.1 For the better performance of your duties for the Company you are required to live in [details of property] which you will occupy upon the terms of the annexed licence agreement.

31 Health and Safety at work

31.1 The Company will take all reasonably practicable steps to ensure your health safety and social welfare while at work. You must familiarise yourself with the Company's Health and Safety Policy and its Safety and Fire rules. It is also your legal duty to take care for your own health and safety and that of your colleagues.

32 Changes to your terms of employment

32.1 The Company reserves the right to make reasonable changes to any of your terms and conditions of employment.

32.2 You will be notified of minor changes of detail by way of a notice to all employees and any such changes take effect from the date of the notice.

32.3 You will be given not less than one month's written notice of any significant changes which may be given by way of an individual notice or a general notice to all employees. Such changes will be deemed to be accepted unless you notify the Company of any objection in writing before the expiry of the notice period.

[*Name of Company*]

SELF CERTIFICATION FORM

TO BE COMPLETED BY EMPLOYEE IN THE PRESENCE OF HIS/HER
HEAD OF DEPARTMENT (in Block Capitals)

Name:

Department:

Period of incapacity: From:

                                                   To:

                                                   (Non-working days should be included)

Nature of incapacity: (State any illness, symptoms or describe injury)
Have you visited a doctor or hospital?
(If yes, state doctor or hospital, name and address and treatment or prescription received)

Signed:

TO BE COMPLETED BY YOUR HEAD OF DEPARTMENT

I am satisfied/I am not satisfied that the information above is correct.

Signed: Date

Position:

LICENCE AGREEMENT

From: [*Name of Company*]

To: [*Name of Company*]

Dated:

IN CONSIDERATION of and as a term of your employment by the Company and for the better performance of your duties as [*job title*] you are required to occupy the [*details of property*] upon the following terms and conditions:

(1) No rent will be payable in respect of such occupation.

(2) The Company will pay periodic outgoings payable in respect of the premises [other than telephone, water, gas and electricity charges].

(3) You will at all times keep the interior of the premises in a good state of decorative repair and not damage or injure the exterior of the premises.

(4) If at any time, for any reason, your employment by the Company in the above mentioned capacity shall cease, you will forthwith vacate the premises and your occupation shall cease immediately. If at any time, for any reason your place of work changes to a different location or you take up a new job with the Company and in either case the Company is not willing to continue providing you with accommodation you must vacate the premises within one calendar month.

(5) It is acknowledged by both parties that it is mutually intended that you will occupy the premises as service occupant and that nothing herein contained shall be construed to create the relationship of landlord and tenant.

SIGNED for and on behalf of _____
by _____
DIRECTOR

I agree that I occupy the said premises upon the terms above stated.
_____ [*Employee*]

Executive Employment Agreement

EMPLOYMENT AGREEMENT

Date: 19

Parties:
1 'The Company': _____ [Limited] [PLC] (registered no _____) whose registered office is at _____ .
2 'The Appointee': _____ of _____
Operative provisions:

1 Interpretation

1.1 The headings and marginal headings to the clauses are for convenience only and have no legal effect.

1.2 Any reference in this Agreement to any Act or delegated legislation includes any statutory modification or re-enactment of it or the provision referred to.

1.3 In this Agreement:

'ASSOCIATED COMPANY' means any company which for the time being is a company having an equity share capital (as defined in s. 155(5) of the Companies Act, 1963) of which not less than [25] per cent is controlled directly or indirectly by the Company [or its holding company] applying the provisions of s. 102 of the Corporation Tax Act, 1976, in the determination of control

'THE BOARD' means the Board of Directors of the Company and includes any committee of the Board duly appointed by it

'COMPANY INVENTION' means any improvement, invention or discovery made by the Appointee which is the property of the Company

'MANAGING DIRECTOR' means any person or persons jointly holding such office of the Company from time to time and includes any persons) exercising substantially the functions of a managing director or chief executive officer of the Company

'PENSION SCHEME' means the _____

'RECOGNISED STOCK EXCHANGE' means any body of persons which is for the time being a Recognised Investment Exchange for the purposes of the Companies Act 1990.

2 Appointment and duration

2.1 The Company appoints the Appointee and the Appointee agrees to act as [Managing Director] [Production Manager] [Assistant Director-Public Relations] [an Executive Director] of the Company [or in such other appointment as may from time to time be agreed] [or in such other appointment as the [Board] [Managing Director] [Company] may from time to time direct (such other appointment not to be of lower status than the Appointee's original appointment under this Agreement)]. [The Appointee accepts that the Company may [in emergencies] [at its discretion] require him to perform other duties or tasks not within the scope of his normal duties and the Appointee agrees to perform those duties or undertake those tasks as if they were specifically required under this Agreement].

2.2 The appointment shall [be deemed to have] commence[d] on _____20 _____ and shall continue (subject to earlier termination as provided in this Agreement) *either* [for a fixed period of [months] [years] from then until _____ 20 _____ [(or if renewed such later date as may be agreed by the parties and endorsed under their signatures in Part A of Schedule 1)] *or* (for a fixed period of _____ [months] [years] from then until _____ 20 _____ provided that on each anniversary of the commencement the then unexpired period shall automatically be renewed for a further _____ [months] _____ [years] (in place of the unexpired term) unless either party shall prior to any such renewal date give notice to the other party that the period will not be renewed whereupon the Agreement will instead terminate at the end of the then current fixed period.] *or* [for a period of _____ [months] [years] from then [or until such later date as may be agreed by the parties and endorsed under the signatures in Part A of Schedule 1] and afterwards until terminated by either party giving to the other not less than _____ [days] [calendar months] [years] prior notice expiring on or at any time after the end of the specified period.] *or* [until terminated by either party giving to the other not less than _____ [days] [calendar months] [years] prior notice [if given on or before _____ 20 and after then not less than _____ [days] [calendar months] [years] prior notice.] *or* [until terminated by the Company giving to the Appointee not less than _____ [days] [calendar months] [years] prior notice or by the Appointee giving to the Company not less than _____ [days] [calendar months] [years] prior notice.]

2.3 [With the prior consent of the Appointee] The Company may from time to time appoint any other person or persons to act jointly with the Appointee in his appointment.

2.4 The Appointee warrants that by virtue of entering into this Agreement [or the other agreements or arrangements made or to be made between the Company or any Associated Company and him] he will not be in breach of any express or implied terms of any contract with or of any other obligation to any third party binding upon him.

3 Duties of appointee

3.1 The Appointee shall:

3.1.1   devote [substantially] [the whole of his time, attention and ability] [so much of his time, attention and ability as is reasonably required] [so much of his time, attention and ability as the Board consider necessary] to the duties of his appointment;

3.1.2   faithfully and diligently perform those duties and exercise such powers consistent with them which are from time to time assigned to or vested in him;

3.1.3   obey all lawful and reasonable directions of the Board;

3.1.4   use his best endeavours to promote the. interests of the Company and its Associated Companies.

3.2 The Appointee shall (without further remuneration) if and for so long as the Company requires:

3.2.1   carry out [duties] [the duties of his appointment] on behalf of any Associated Company;

3.2.2   act as an officer of any Associated Company or hold any other appointment or office as nominee or representative of the Company or any Associated Company;

3.2.3   carry out such dudes and the duties attendant on any such appointment as if they were duties to be performed by him on behalf of the Company.

4 Reporting

4.1 The Appointee shall at all times keep the [Board] [person designated as his immediate superior] promptly and fully informed (in writing if so requested) of his conduct of the business or affairs of the Company and its Associated Companies and provide such explanations as [the Board] [his immediate superior] may require.

5 Secondment

5.1 The Company may without the Appointee's consent second him to be employed by any Associated Company without prejudice to his rights under this Agreement.

6 Place of work

6.1 The Appointee shall perform his duties at [the head office] of the Company and/or such other place of business of the Company or of any Associated Company as the Company requires [whether inside or outside Ireland but the Company shall not without his prior consent require him to go to or reside anywhere outside Ireland except for occasional visits in the ordinary course of his duties. In this clause, the term 'Ireland' includes Northern Ireland.]

6.2 The Appointee shall at all times reside within a radius of _____ miles from [the head office of the Company] [his place of work] from time to time. [If the Company shall [relocate its head office] [change his place of work] such that the Appointee has to relocate his residence to remain within that radius, the Company shall reimburse him his removal and other incidental expenses in accordance with its then current policy for relocation of executives.]

[7 Service occupancy

7.1 During the continuance of his appointment and for the better performance of the duties of his appointment, the Appointee shall occupy as a licensee only [that part of] the premises [called] [comprising _____ at] _____ or such other premises as the Company may from time to time specify on the terms set out in Schedule 5.]

8 Inventions

8.1 If at any time during his appointment the Appointee (whether alone or with any other person or persons) makes any invention, whether relating directly or indirectly to the business of the Company, the Appointee shall promptly disclose to the Company full details, including drawings and models, of such invention to enable the Company to determine whether it is a Company Invention. If the invention is not a Company Invention the Company shall treat all information disclosed to it by the Appointee as confidential information the property of the Appointee.

8.2 If the invention is a Company Invention the Appointee shall hold it in trust for the Company, and at the request and expense of the Company do all things necessary or desirable to enable the Company, or its nominee, to obtain the benefit of the Company Invention and to secure patent or other appropriate forms of protection for it throughout the World.

8.3 Decisions as to the patenting and exploitation of any Company Invention shall be in the sole discretion of the Company.

[8.4 The Appointee irrevocably appoints the Company to be his Attorney in his name and on his behalf to execute, sign and do all such instruments or things and generally to use the Appointee's name for the purpose of giving to the Company or its nominee the full benefit of the provisions of clause 8.2 and a certificate in writing signed by any Director or the Secretary of the Company, that any instrument or act falls within the authority hereby conferred, shall be conclusive evidence that such is the case so far as any third party is concerned].

9 Copyright

9.1 The Appointee shall promptly disclose to the Company all copyright works or designs originated conceived written or made by him alone or with others (except only those works originated conceived written or made by him wholly outside his normal working hours and wholly unconnected with his appointment) and shall until such rights shall be fully and absolutely vested in the Company hold them in trust for the Company.

9.2 The Appointee hereby assigns to the Company by way of future assignment all copyright design right and other proprietary rights if any for the full terms thereof throughout the World in respect of all copyright works and designs originated, conceived, written or made by the Appointee (except only those works or designs originated conceived written or made by the Appointee wholly outside his normal working hours and wholly unconnected with his appointment) during the period of his employment hereunder.

9.3 The Appointee hereby irrevocably and unconditionally waives in favour of the Company any and all moral rights conferred on him by law for any work in which copyright or design right is vested in the Company whether by Clause 9 or otherwise.

9.4 The Appointee will at the request and expense of the Company do all things necessary or desirable to substantiate the rights of the Company under clause 9.2 and 9.3.

10 Conflict of interest

10.1 During this Agreement the Appointee shall not (except as a representative or nominee of the Company or any Associated Company or otherwise with the prior consent in writing of the [Board] [Managing Director]) be directly or indirectly engaged concerned or interested in any other business which:

10.1.1   is wholly or partly in competition with [the] [any] business carried on by the [Company][the Company or any Associated Companies] or any of the foregoing by itself or themselves or in partnership, common ownership or as a joint venture with any third party; or

10.1.2   as regards any goods or services is a supplier to or customer of [the Company] [any such company];

Provided that the Appointee may hold (directly or through nominees) any units of any authorised unit trust and up to [five] per cent of the issued shares debentures or other securities of any class of any company whose shares are listed on a Recognised Stock Exchange or in respect of which dealing takes place in The International Stock Exchange of the United Kingdom and Republic of Ireland or the Unlisted Securities Market or the Third Market. The prior written consent of [the Board] [Managing Director] shall be required before the Appointee shall hold in excess of [five] per cent of the issued shares debentures or other securities of any class of any one such company.

10.2 Subject to any regulations from time to time issued by the Company which may apply to him, the Appointee shall not receive or obtain directly or indirectly any discount rebate commission or other inducement in respect of any sale or purchase of any goods or services effected or other business transacted (whether or not by him) by or on behalf of the Company or any Associated Company and if he (or any firm or company in which he is directly or indirectly engaged, concerned or interested) shall obtain any such discount rebate commission or inducement he shall immediately account to the Company for the amount received by him or the amount received by such firm or company. For the purpose of this clause the Appointee shall be deemed not to be engaged. concerned or interested in such a company as is referred to in the proviso to clause 10.1 [and the requirement in that proviso for prior consent shall be ignored].

11 [Share dealings

11.1 The Appointee shall comply where relevant with every rule of law, every regulation of The International Stock Exchange of the United Kingdom and Republic of Ireland and every regulation of the Company from time to time in force in relation to dealings in shares, debentures or other securities of the Company or any Associated Company and unpublished price sensitive information affecting the shares, debentures or other securities of any other company. Provided always that in relation to overseas dealings the Appointee shall also comply with all laws of the State and all regulations of the stock exchange market or dealing system in which such dealings take place.

11.2 The Appointee shall not (and shall procure so far as he is able that his spouse and children shall not) deal or become or cease to be interested (within the meaning of Part IV of the Companies Act 1990) in any securities of the company except in accordance with the Company's 'Rules for Securities Transactions by Directors' from time to time.]

12 Confidentiality

12.1 The Appointee shall not either during his appointment or at any time for one year after its termination:

12.1.1   disclose to any person or persons (except to those authorised by the Company to know or as otherwise required by law);

12.1.2   use for his own purposes or for any purposes other than those of the Company; or

12.1.3   through any failure to exercise all due care and diligence cause any unauthorised disclosure of

any confidential information of the Company (including in particular lists or details of customers of the Company or information relating to the working of any process or invention carried on or used by the Company or any Company Invention) or in respect of which the Company is bound by an obligation of confidence to a third party. These restrictions shall cease to apply to information or knowledge which may (otherwise than through the default of the Appointee) become available to the public generally [without requiring a significant expenditure of labour, skill or money].

12.2 The provisions of clause 12.1 shall apply mutatis mutandis in relation to the confidential or secret information of each Associated Company which the Appointee may have received or obtained during his appointment and the Appointee shall upon request enter into an enforceable agreement with any such company to the like effect.

12.3 All notes, memoranda, records and writing made by the Appointee relating to the business of the Company or its Associated Companies shall be and remain the property of the Company or Associated Company to whose business they relate and shall be delivered by him to the company to which they belong forthwith upon request.

[12.4 It is agreed that the information disclosed by the Appointee in Schedule 6A is prior knowledge of the Appointee and is expressly excluded from the ambit of this clause.]

13 Statements

13.1 The Appointee shall not at any time make any untrue or misleading statement in relation to the Company or any Associated Company.

14 Medical examination

14.1 The Appointee shall at the expense of the Company submit annually to a medical examination by a registered medical practitioner nominated by the Company and shall authorise such medical practitioner to disclose to and discuss with the Company's medical adviser the results of the examination and the matters which arise from it so that the Company's medical adviser can notify the Company of any matters he considers might impair the Appointee from properly discharging his duties.

15 Pay

15.1 During his appointment the Company shall pay to the Appointee:

[15.1.1]   a [basic] salary at the rate of IR£ _____ per year which shall accrue day-to-day and be payable by equal [monthly] [four weekly] instalments. The salary shall be deemed to include any fees receivable by the Appointee as a Director of the Company or any Associated Company, or of any other company or unincorporated body in which he holds office as nominee or representative of the Company or any Associated Company; [and

15.1.2   a commission calculated in accordance with the provisions of Schedule 2 payable in respect of each financial period of the Company (subject to any payment on account) within 21 days after the adoption of the accounts for that financial period at the Annual General Meeting.]

[15.2 The Appointee's [basic] salary shall be reviewed by the [Board] [Managing Director] [from time to time] [as at _____ each year] and the rate of [basic] salary may be increased by the Company with effect from that date by such amount if any as it shall think fit;]

[15.2 The Appointee's [basic] salary shall be reviewed and increased with effect from from _____ each year in accordance with the provisions of Schedule [3].)

[15.3 Notwithstanding the provisions of sub-clause 15.2 the Company shall not be required to increase the Appointee's salary if and to the extent only that the increased payment would be unlawful under the provisions of any legislation then in force during his appointment, or if the increased payment would not be an allowable cost for the purpose of increasing prices under the provisions of any legislation controlling prices or price increases.]

16 Pension

16.1 The Appointee shall be entitled to be and remain a member of the _____ Pension Scheme subject to the terms of its Deeds and Rules from time to time [details of which are available from _____]. [The Company shall be entitled at any time to terminate the Scheme or the Appointee's membership of it] [subject to providing him with the benefit of an equivalent pension scheme ('the New Scheme') each and every benefit of which shall be not less favourable than the benefits provided to the Appointee under the existing scheme and to ensuring that the Appointee is fully credited in the New Scheme for his pensionable service in the existing scheme as if such pensionable service had been under the New Scheme].

17 Insurances

17.1 The Appointee shall be entitled to participate at the Company's expense in the Company's permanent health insurance scheme and [for himself, his spouse [and dependant children]] in the Company's private medical expenses insurance scheme, subject always to the rules of such schemes [which are available from _____].

18 Car

18.1 [Subject to the Appointee holding a current full driving licence] the Company shall provide the Appointee with:

18.1.1   Option 1: a [e.g. Jaguar XJ6 Sovereign 3.6 litre] car or other car of equivalent price and status;

18.1.2   Option 2: a car of a make, model and specification [manufactured by a [EEC member state] company] of his choice provided that its manufacturer's list price (including Car Tax, Value Added Tax, extras, delivery and other similar charges) shall not be more than £ _____ (such limit to be reviewed by the Company from time to time and increased commensurately with increases in new car prices) and subject to the [Managing Director] [Board) approving such choice as commensurate with both the status of the Appointee and the image of the Company (which approval shall not be withheld unreasonably);

18.1.3   Option 3: a car of a make, model and specification selected by the Company (which in the reasonable opinion of the [Managing Director][Board] is commensurate with the status of the Appointee and the image of the Company);

18.1.4   Option 4: a car of a make, model and specification determined by reference to the Company's car [scheme] [policy] in effect from time to time for his sole business use and private use by him [and his spouse].

18.2 The Company shall:

18.2.1   Option 1: bear all standing and running expenses of the car [except for fuel consumed during [private use of the car] [use of the car by the Appointee for holiday purposes]] and any additional insurance costs incurred to permit the Appointee to use the car outside Ireland for private purposes;

18.2.2   Option 2: reimburse the Appointee for his business use of the car at [eg a rate per mile to be determined annually by the Company by reference to the then current estimate of standing and running costs for cars of the same engine capacity as the Appointee's company car prepared by the Automobile Association];

and shall replace such car [with the same or equivalent model]

18.2.3   Option A: when it has travelled [eg 45,000] miles or (if sooner) on the [eg third] anniversary of its purchase by the Company;

18.2.4   Option B: as provided in the Company's car [scheme] [policy] in effect from time to time;

18.3 The Appointee shall always comply with all regulations laid down by the Company from time to time with respect to company cars, and on the termination of his appointment for whatever reason and whether lawfully or unlawfully the Appointee shall forthwith return his company car to the Company [at its head office].

19 Expenses

19.1 The Company shall reimburse to the Appointee on a monthly basis all travelling, hotel, entertainment and other expenses reasonably incurred by him in the proper performance of his dudes subject to [the Appointee complying with such guidelines or regulations issued by the Company from time to time in this respect and to] the production to the Company of such vouchers or other evidence of actual payment of the expenses as the Company may reasonably require.

19.2 Where the Company issues a company sponsored credit or charge card to the Appointee he shall use such card only for expenses reimbursable under clause 19.1 above, and shall return it to the Company forthwith on the termination of his employment.

20 Holiday

20.1 In addition to public holidays the Appointee is entitled to [20] working days paid holiday in each [holiday] year [from _____ to _____] to be taken at such time or times as are agreed with the [Board] [Managing Director]. The Appointee shall not without the consent of the [Board] [Managing Director] carry forward any unused part of his holiday entitlement to a subsequent year.

20.2 For the [holiday] year during which his appointment commences or terminates, the Appointee is entitled to [1½] working days holiday for each [calendar month] completed in the employment of the Company for that year. On the termination of his appointment for whatever reason the Appointee shall [not] [as appropriate either] be entitled to pay in lieu of outstanding holiday entitlement [and shall] [or] be required to repay to the Company any salary received for holiday taken in excess of his actual entitlement. The basis for payment shall be [1⁄453] x annual [basic] salary for each day.

21 Incapacity

21.1 If the Appointee shall be prevented by illness (including mental disorder) injury or other incapacity from properly performing his duties hereunder he shall report this fact forthwith to the Company Secretary's office and if the Appointee is so prevented for seven or more consecutive days he shall provide a medical practitioner's statement on the eighth day and weekly thereafter so that the whole period of absence is certified by such statements. Immediately following his return to work after a period of absence the Appointee shall complete a Self-Certification form available from the Company Secretary's office detailing the reason for his absence.

21.2 If the Appointee shall be absent from his duties hereunder due to illness (including mental disorder) accident or other incapacity duly certified in accordance with the provisions of sub-clause 21.1 hereof he shall be paid his full remuneration hereunder [(including bonus and commission)] for up to _____ working days absence in any period of 12 months and thereafter such remuneration if any as the Board shall in its discretion from time to time allow provided that such remuneration shall be inclusive of any social welfare sickness benefit to which the Appointee is entitled under the provisions of the Social Welfare Acts and any such sickness or other benefits recoverable by the Appointee (whether or not recovered) may be deducted therefrom.

22 Termination of agreement

22.1 Automatic termination

This Agreement shall automatically terminate:

22.1.1   on the Appointee reaching [retirement age as defined in the Rules of the Pension Scheme] [his 65th birthday]; or

22.1.2   if the Appointee becomes prohibited by law from being a director; or

22.1.3   if he resigns his office; [or

22.1.4   if the office of director of the Company held by the Appointee is vacated pursuant to the Company's Articles of Association save if the vacation shall be caused by illness (including mental disorder) or injury.]

22.2 Suspension

In order to investigate a complaint against the Appointee of misconduct the Company is entitled to suspend the Appointee on full pay for so long as may be necessary to carry out a proper investigation and hold a disciplinary hearing.

22.3 Immediate dismissal

The Company may by notice terminate this Agreement with immediate effect if the Appointee:

22.3.1   commits any act of gross misconduct or repeats or continues (after written warning) any other [material] [serious] breach of his obligations under this Agreement; or.

22.3.2   is guilty of any conduct which in the [reasonable] opinion of the Board brings him, the Company or any Associated Company into [serious] disrepute; or

22.3.3   is convicted of any criminal offence punishable with 6 months or more imprisonment (excluding an offence under road traffic legislation in Ireland or elsewhere for which he is not sentenced to any term of imprisonment whether immediate or suspended); or

22.3.4   commits any act of dishonesty [whether] relating to the Company, any Associated Company, any of its or their employees or otherwise; or

22.3.5   becomes bankrupt or makes any arrangement or composition with his creditors generally; or

22.3.6   is in the [reasonable] opinion of the Board incompetent in the performance of his duties.

22.4 Dismissal on short notice

The Company may terminate this Agreement as follows:

22.4.1   notwithstanding clause 21.2 by not less than [3] months' prior notice given at any time while the Appointee is incapacitated by ill-health or accident from performing his duties under this Agreement and he has been so incapacitated for a period or periods aggregating _____ [days] [calendar months] in the preceding 12 months. [Provided that the Company shall withdraw any such notice if during the currency of the notice the Appointee returns to full time duties and provides a medical practitioner's certificate satisfactory to the Board to the effect that he has fully recovered his health and that no recurrence of his illness or incapacity can reasonably be anticipated.]

22.4.2   By not less than [one] month's prior notice if the Appointee has been offered but has refused to agree to the transfer of this Agreement by way of novation to a person firm or company which has acquired or agreed to acquire the whole or substantially the whole of the undertaking (as defined in the E.C. Safeguarding of Employees' Rights on Transfer of Undertaking) Regulations 1980 in which he is employed.

22.5 Pay in lieu

On serving notice for any reason to terminate this Agreement or at any time thereafter during the currency of such notice the Company shall be entitled to pay to the Appointee his [basic] salary (at the rate then current) for the unexpired portion of the duration of his appointment or entitlement to notice as may be the case.

22.6 Miscellaneous

On the termination of this Agreement for whatever reason, the Appointee shall:

22.6.1   at the request of the Company:

         (a) resign from office as a Director of the Company and from all offices held by him in any Associated Company and from all other appointments or offices which he holds as nominee or representative of the Company or any Associated Company; and

         (b) transfer without payment to the Company or as the Company may direct any qualifying shares provided by it to him;

         and if he should fail to do so within seven days the Company is hereby irrevocably authorised to appoint some person in his name and on his behalf to sign any documents or do any things necessary or requisite to give effect to these. Such resignations) shall be without prejudice to any claims which the Appointee may have against any company arising out of this Agreement or the termination thereof.

22.6.2   Immediately deliver to the Company or to its order all books, documents, papers, (including copies) materials, credit cards, keys and other property of or relating to the business of the Company or its Associated Companies then in his possession or which are or were last under his power or control.

23 Post termination obligations of the appointee

23.1 Non-competition

The Appointee shall not within the Prohibited Area for a period of _____ [months] [years] after the termination of his employment hereunder (however that comes about and whether lawful or not):

23.1.1   be directly or indirectly engaged concerned or interested [in any capacity] [whether as Director Principal Agent Partner Consultant Employee or otherwise] in any other business [of whatever kind] which is wholly or partly in competition with any business carried on by the [Company] [Company or any of its subsidiaries];

23.1.2   accept employment in any [executive] [technical] [sales] capacity with any business concern which is wholly or partly in competition with any business carried on by the [Company] [Company or any of its subsidiaries];

23.1.3   [provide [technical] [commercial] [or professional] advice to any business concern which is wholly or partly in competition with any business carried on by the [Company] [Company or any of its subsidiaries]J;

23.1.4   be directly or indirectly engaged concerned or interested [in any capacity] [whether as Director Principal Agent Partner Consultant Employee or otherwise] in any business concern which has at any time during the last _____ [months] [years] of the Appointee's employment hereunder supplied any goods materials or services to or been a customer of the [Company] [Company or any of its subsidiaries].

The provisions of sub-clauses 23.1.1, 23.1.2, 23.1.3 and 23.1.4 shall not restrain the Appointee from engaging in or accepting employment with any business concern where the Appointee's duties or work shall relate [either solely or exclusively to part or parts of the world outside the Prohibited Area or] to services goods or materials of a kind or nature with which the Appointee was not concerned to a material extent during the period of _____ [months] [years] prior to the termination of his employment hereunder.

23.2 Non-solicitation

The Appointee shall not within the Prohibited Area for a period of _____ [months] [years] after the termination of his employment hereunder (howsoever that comes about and whether lawfully or not) directly or indirectly and whether on his own behalf or on behalf of any other business concern person partnership firm company or other body which is wholly or partly in competition with [the] [any] business carried on by the Company:

23.2.1   Canvass solicit or approach or cause to be canvassed or solicited or approached for orders in respect of any services provided or any goods dealt in by the [Company] [Company and/or its subsidiaries] in respect of the provision or sale of which the Appointee was engaged during the last _____ [months] [years] of his employment with the Company any person or persons who at the date of the termination of the Appointee's appointment was negotiating with the Company for the supply of services or goods or within _____ [months] [years] prior to such date is or was a client or customer of the Company [or of its subsidiaries] or was in the habit of dealing with the Company [or its subsidiaries] and with whom the Appointee shall have dealt. [Provided that this restriction shall not apply to those clients or customers named in Schedule 6B which are agreed to be those introduced to the Company by the Appointee on the commencement of his Appointment.]

23.2.2   Interfere or seek to interfere or take such steps as may interfere with the continuance of supplies to the Company [and/or its subsidiaries] (or the terms relating to such supplies) from any suppliers who have been supplying components materials or services to the Company and/or its subsidiaries at any time during the last _____ [months] [years] of his employment hereunder.

23.2.3   Solicit or entice or endeavour to solicit or entice away from the Company [or its subsidiaries] or offer or cause to be offered any employment to any person employed by the Company [or its subsidiaries] in an [executive] [technical] [sales] capacity at the date of such termination for whom the Appointee is responsible.

23.2.4   Deal with any person or persons who or which at any time during the period of _____ [months] [years] prior to termination of the Appointee's employment hereunder have been in the habit of dealing under contract with the Company [or its subsidiaries].

23.3 For the purposes of clause 23 'Prohibited Area' means _____

23.4 The parties agree that each of the covenants set out in clauses 23.1 and 23.2 above is separate and severable and enforceable accordingly [and that if any of the restrictions shall be adjudged to be void or ineffective for whatever reason but would be adjudged to be valid and effective if part of the wording thereof were deleted, they shall apply with such modifications as may be necessary to make them valid and effective].

24 [Change in control (unquoted or private company)

24.1 If there is a change in control of the Company or of its holding company (as defined in s.155 of the Companies Act 1963), the Appointee shall be entitled to a severance payment in the event his appointment is terminated by dismissal or constructive dismissal (other than pursuant to clause 22.3) in connection with or within six months after the change in control. The amount of this payment shall [not be less than equivalent to _____ per cent of the Appointee's then salary for each full year of employment with the Company up to a maximum payment of _____ per cent of his then salary] [_____ months/years salary at the rate then payable] 'Control' means the holding of 50 per cent or more of the issued voting share capital of the Company or its holding company.

[24.2 The Appointee shall be entitled to terminate his employment by 30 days prior notice given at any time within six months of a change in control as defined in clause 24.1 [if that change in control was at any time opposed by the Company's or Holding Company's Board] and upon such voluntary termination the Appointee shall be entitled to a severance payment calculated in accordance with clause 24.1.]]

25 General

25.1 Other terms

The provisions of the Company's standard terms and conditions of employment (as amended from time to time) shall be terms of the Appointee's employment except so far as inconsistent with this Agreement.

25.2 Statutory particulars

The further particulars of terms of employment not contained in the body of this Agreement which must be given to the Appointee in compliance with s. 9 of the Minimum Notice and Terms of Employment Act, 1973, are given in Schedule 4.

25.3 Prior agreements

This Agreement [sets out the entire agreement and understanding of the parties and] is in substitution for any previous contracts of employment or for services between the Company or any of its Associated Companies and the Appointee (which shall be deemed to have been terminated by mutual consent).

25.4 Accrued rights

The expiration or termination of this Agreement however arising shall not operate to affect such of the provisions of this Agreement as are expressed to operate or have effect after then and shall be without prejudice to any accrued rights or remedies of the parties.

25.5 Proper law

The validity construction and performance of this Agreement shall be governed by the law of the Republic of Ireland.

25.6 Acceptance of juristiction

All disputes claims or proceedings between the parties relating to the validity construction or performance of this Agreement shall be subject to the non-exclusive jurisdiction of the High Court of Ireland ('the High Court') to which the parties irrevocably submit. [Each party irrevocably consents to the award or grant of any relief in any such proceedings before the High Court and either party shall be entitled to take proceedings in any other jurisdiction to enforce a judgment or order of the High Court.]

25.7 Notices

Any notice to be given by a party under this Agreement must be in writing [in the English language] and must be given by delivery at or sending [first class] post or other faster postal service, or telex, facsimile transmission or other means of telecommunication in permanent written form (provided the addressee has [his or its own] facilities for receiving such transmissions) to the last known postal address or relevant telecommunications number of the other party. Where notice is given by sending in a prescribed manner it shall be deemed to have been received when in the ordinary course of the means of transmission it would be received by the addressee. To prove the giving of a notice it shall be sufficient to show it was despatched. A notice shall have effect from the sooner of its actual or deemed receipt by the addressee.

SCHEDULE 1
Variations

Part 1
Extension of duration

By their respective signatures in Columns 3 and 4 opposite the relevant entry in Column I on the date stated in Column 2, the parties agree that the Appointee's employment is extended to the latest date stated in Column 1.

1	2	3	4
New Expiry Date	Date of this Entry	Signed on behalf of Company	Signed by the Appointee

Part 2
Increase in salary

By their respective signatures in Columns 4 and 5 set opposite the relevant entry in Column 1 on the date stated in Column 3 the parties agree that the Appointee's [basic] salary payable under clause 15.1.1 is increased to the annual rate stated in Column 1 with effect from the date stated in Column 2.

1	2	3	4	5
Revised Annual Rate of Salary	Effective Date of increase	Date of this Entry	Signed on behalf of the Company	Signed by the Appointee

SCHEDULE 2
Commission entitlement

1. Subject to the following provisions the Appointee's entitlement to commission under clause 15.1.2 for each complete financial period of the Company during the currency of this Agreement is _____ per cent of the [amount by which the] net profits of the Company and its subsidiaries] [and its Associated Companies] [exceed IRE _____] such net profits being ascertained as provided in paragraph 6 below.

[2. The Appointee's entitlement to commission is limited to a maximum of [IRE _____] [[eg half] his basic salary] in respect of any financial period.]

[3. If during the currency of this Agreement any financial period of the Company shall have a duration other than 365 days (or 366 days in the case of a leap year) the figure of IR£ _____ in clause 15.1.2 shall be adjusted in the same proportion as the number of complete days of the financial period bears to 365.]

4. If the Agreement commences or terminates during the currency of any financial year paragraph[s] [1] [and 2] shall be read and construed as if the references to the net profits of the Company [and its subsidiaries] [and its Associated Companies] for the relevant financial period [and to the figure of IRE _____] [and in paragraph 2 to the figure of IR£ _____] were references to such proportion of such figures of IR £ _____] and to such proportion of such figure of IR£ _____ as the number of days served by the Appointee under this Agreement during such financial period bears to the total number of days in that financial period.

5. The certificate of the auditors of the Company as to the amount of commission payable shall in the absence of manifest error be final and binding upon the parties and in so certifying the auditors shall be deemed to be acting as experts and not liable in negligence to any person in respect thereof.

6. The net profits of the Company [and its subsidiaries] [and its Associated Companies] means the [consolidated] net revenue profits for such financial period as shown by the audited [consolidated] Profit and Loss Account of the Company [and its subsidiaries] [and its Associated Companies] subject to the following adjustments (if not already taken into account in the Profit and Loss Accounts):

6.1 Before deducting:
6.1.1   (subject to 6.2 below) taxation shown by the audited [consolidated] Profit and Loss Account of the [Company];
6.1.2   the commission payable to the Appointee and any other remuneration calculated on or variable with profits payable to any other director, officer or employee of the Company [and its subsidiaries] [and its Associated Companies];
[6.1.3   inter-company charges debited for the financial period.]
6.2 After deducting:
6.2.1   overseas taxation (other than that for which credit or relief against Irish taxation has been or will be allowed);
[6.2.2   income from fixed assets and trade investments].
6.3 Before adding or deducting profits or losses on the revaluation of any assets or any adjustment arising on the translation into pounds IR of assets and liabilities denominated in foreign currencies.

6.4 Before adjustment for extraordinary items not deriving from the ordinary activities of the Company and [its subsidiaries] [and its Associated Companies] as required by the Statement of Standard Accounting Practice No 6 (SSAP 6).

6.5 Excluding profits or losses of a capital nature.

6.6 [If the Company issues shares for consideration and the Board is of the opinion that the income arising from that consideration will result in the material enlargement of net profits then such adjustment shall be made in the calculation of net profits or the Appointee's rate of commission (or partly one and partly the other) as the Company and the Appointee may agree or failing agreement as the auditors in their absolute discretion determine to be fair and reasonable for the purpose of counter-acting an enlargement of commission otherwise resulting from the acquisition of additional profits (directly or indirectly) through such increase of issued shared capital.] In so determining, the auditors shall be deemed to be acting as experts and not liable in negligence to any person in respect thereof.

7. The Company (acting by unanimous decision of the Board) may in its discretion pay to the Appointee from time to time during a financial period an interim payment or payments on account of commission. If the payments in any financial period exceed the commission ultimately payable for such year the Board will at its option either carry forward the balance on account of any remuneration due for the next financial period or require that it be repaid by the Appointee within 21 days after the adoption of the accounts for that financial period at the Annual General Meeting.

SCHEDULE 3
Cost of living increase

(1. For the purposes of this Schedule the Appointee's Notional Salary shall, at the date of this Agreement be IR£ _____].

2. If, at any review of the Appointee's salary under clause 15.1.3, the latest figure available of the index of retail prices maintained by the _____ ('the Index') is greater than the figure of the Index taken for the purpose of the last review (or in the case of the first review only, the latest figure of the Index published immediately before the date of this Agreement) then the Company shall with effect from the review date [increase the Appointee's salary by the same percentage as the percentage increase in the Index since the previous review] [increase the Appointee's Salary (as previously increased) by the money amount of the increase in Notional Salary caused by increasing it by the same percentage as the percentage increase in the Index since the last previous review].

3. If prior to the date of any such review the basis of computation of the said Index shall have changed from that subsisting at the date of this Agreement or at the date taken for the purpose of the last previous review as the case may be any official reconciliation between the two bases of computation published shall be binding upon the parties.

4. In the absence of such official reconciliation such adjustments shall be made to the figure of the said Index at the date of any such review to make it correspond as nearly as possible to the previous method of computation and such adjusted figure shall be considered for the purpose of this Schedule to the exclusion of the actual published figure and any dispute regarding such adjustment shall be referred to the auditors for the time being of the Company whose decision shall be final and binding on the parties. In so deciding, the auditors shall be deemed to be acting as experts and not liable in negligence to any person in respect thereof.

SCHEDULE 4
Minimum Notice and Terms of Employment Act, 1973, section 9

The following information is given to supplement the information given in the body of the Agreement in order to comply with the requirements of the Act above.

1. The Appointee's employment by the Company commenced on _____ [No employment of the Appointee with a previous employer] (The Appointee's employment with _____] counts as part of the Appointee's continuous employment with the Company [and his continuous employment began on _____].

2. The Appointee's hours of work are the normal hours of the Company from am to _____ pm Monday to Friday each week together with such additional hours as may be necessary so as properly to fulfil his duties.

3. The Appointee is subject to the Company's Disciplinary Rules and Disciplinary Procedures copies of which have been given to the Appointee.

4. If the Appointee has any grievance relating to his employment (other than one relating to a disciplinary decision) he should refer such grievance to the [Managing Director] [Chairman of the Board] [and if the grievance is not resolved by discussion with him it will be referred to the Board for resolution.]

SCHEDULES

Service occupancy
See the form suggested ante p.

SCHEDULE 6

A   List of prior knowledge

B   List of clients/customers

INDEX